Networking

ALL-IN-ONE

FOR

DUMMIES®

5TH EDITION

by Doug Lowe

WILEY

John Wiley & Sons, Inc.

Networking All-in-One For Dummies®, 5th Edition

Published by
John Wiley & Sons, Inc.
111 River Street
Hoboken, NJ 07030-5774

www.wiley.com

For general information on our other products and services, please contact our Customer Care Department within the U.S. at 877-762-2974, outside the U.S. at 317-572-3993, or fax 317-572-4002.

For technical support, please visit www.wiley.com/techsupport.

Wiley publishes in a variety of print and electronic formats and by print-on-demand. Some material included with standard print versions of this book may not be included in e-books or in print-on-demand. If this book refers to media such as a CD or DVD that is not included in the version you purchased, you may download this material at http://booksupport.wiley.com. For more information about Wiley products, visit www.wiley.com.

Library of Congress Control Number: 2012950499

ISBN: 978-1-118-38098-7 (pbk); ISBN 978-1-118-38099-4 (ebk); ISBN 978-1-118-38100-7 (ebk); ISBN 978-1-118-38101-4 (ebk) Manufactured in the United States of America

10 9 8 7 6 5 4 3 2 1

WILEY

About the Author

Doug Lowe has written a whole bunch of computer books, including more than 50 *For Dummies* books, among them *Networking For Dummies*, 9th Edition; *Java All-in-One For Dummies*, 4th Edition, and *PowerPoint 2012 For Dummies*. He lives in sunny Fresno, California, where the motto is "Fres-YES." He is the Information Technology Director at Blair, Church & Flynn

Consulting Engineers in nearby Clovis, CA, where the motto is "Fres-NO."

Dedication

This one is for Kristen.

Author's Acknowledgments

I'd like to thank everyone who was involved with the fifth edition of this book, especially the most excellent project editor Chris Morris, who once again has championed this book through all of the editorial details needed to put a book of this scope together on time. Thanks also to Dan DiNicolo, who once again gave the manuscript a thorough review to ensure the technical accuracy of every sentence and in the process offered many excellent suggestions for improvements, and to copy editors Teresa Artman and Kathy Simpson, who whipped my prose into shape, crossing all the i's and dotting all the t's, or something like that. And as always, thanks to all the behind-the-scenes people who chipped in with help I'm not even aware of.

Publisher's Acknowledgments

We're proud of this book; please send us your comments at `http://dummies.custhelp.com`. For other comments, please contact our Customer Care Department within the U.S. at 877-762-2974, outside the U.S. at 317-572-3993, or fax 317-572-4002.

Some of the people who helped bring this book to market include the following:

Acquisitions and Editorial

Senior Project Editor: Christopher Morris

Acquisitions Editor: Amy Fandrei

Copy Editors: Teresa Artman and Kathy Simpson

Technical Editor: Dan DiNicolo

Editorial Manager: Kevin Kirschner

Editorial Assistant: Leslie Saxman

Sr. Editorial Assistant: Cherie Case

Cover Photo: © Baris Simsek / iStockphoto

Cartoons: Rich Tennant (`www.the5thwave.com`)

Composition Services

Project Coordinator: Katie Crocker

Layout and Graphics: Joyce Haughey, Corrie Niehaus, Amy Hassos

Proofreaders: Jessica Kramer, Evelyn C. Wellborn

Indexer: BIM Indexing & Proofreading Services

Publishing and Editorial for Technology Dummies

Richard Swadley, Vice President and Executive Group Publisher

Andy Cummings, Vice President and Publisher

Mary Bednarek, Executive Acquisitions Director

Mary C. Corder, Editorial Director

Publishing for Consumer Dummies

Kathleen Nebenhaus, Vice President and Executive Publisher

Composition Services

Debbie Stailey, Director of Composition Services

Contents at a Glance

Table of Contents

Introduction

*W*elcome to the fifth edition of *Networking All-in-One For Dummies,* the one networking book that's designed to replace an entire shelf full of the dull and tedious networking books you'd otherwise have to buy. This book contains all the basic and not-so-basic information you need to know to get a network up and running and to stay on top of the network as it grows, develops problems, and encounters trouble.

If you're just getting started as a network administrator, this book is ideal. As a network administrator, you have to know about a lot of different topics: installing and configuring network hardware, installing and configuring network operating systems, planning a network, working with TCP/IP, securing your network, working with mobile devices, backing up your data, and many others.

You can, and probably eventually will, buy separate books on each of these topics. It won't take long before your bookshelf is bulging with 10,000 or more pages of detailed information about every imaginable nuance of networking. But before you're ready to tackle each of those topics in depth, you need to get a bird's-eye picture. This book is the ideal way to do that.

And if you already own 10,000 pages or more of network information, you may be overwhelmed by the amount of detail and wonder, "Do I really need to read 1,000 pages about Bind to set up a simple DNS server?" or "Do I really need a six-pound book to show me how to install Linux?" Truth is, most 1,000-page networking books have about 100 or so pages of really useful information — the kind you use every day — and about 900 pages of excruciating details that apply mostly to networks at places like NASA and the CIA.

The basic idea of this book is that I've tried to wring out the 100 or so most useful pages of information on nine different networking topics: network basics, building a network, network administration and security, troubleshooting and disaster planning, working with TCP/IP, home networking, wireless networking, Windows server operating systems, and Linux.

So whether you've just been put in charge of your first network or you're a seasoned pro, you've found the right book.

About This Book

Networking All-in-One For Dummies, 5th Edition, is intended to be a reference for all the great things (and maybe a few not-so-great things) that you may need to know when you're setting up and managing a network. You can, of course, buy a huge 1,000-page book on each of the networking topics covered in this book. But then, who would you get to carry them home from the bookstore for you? And where would you find the shelf space to store them? In this book, you get the information you need all conveniently packaged for you in between one set of covers.

This book doesn't pretend to be a comprehensive reference for every detail of these topics. Instead, this book shows you how to get up and running fast so that you have more time to do the things you really want to do. Designed using the easy-to-follow *For Dummies* format, this book helps you get the information you need without laboring to find it.

Networking All-in-One For Dummies, 5th Edition, is a big book made up of several smaller books — minibooks, if you will. Each of these minibooks covers the basics of one key element of network management, such as setting up network hardware, installing a network operating system, or troubleshooting network problems. Whenever one big thing is made up of several smaller things, confusion is always a possibility. That's why *Networking All-in-One For Dummies,* 5th Edition, is designed to have multiple access points (I hear an acronym coming on — MAP!) to help you find what you want. At the beginning of the book is a detailed table of contents that covers the entire book. Then each minibook begins with a minitable of contents that shows you at a glance what chapters are included in that minibook. Useful running heads appear at the top of each page to point out the topic discussed on that page. And handy thumb tabs run down the side of the pages to help you find each minibook quickly. Finally, a comprehensive index lets you find information anywhere in the entire book.

This isn't the kind of book you pick up and read from start to finish, as though it were a cheap novel. (If I ever see you reading it at the beach, I'll kick sand in your face.) This book is more like a reference — the kind of book you can pick up, turn to just about any page, and start reading. You don't have to memorize anything in this book. It's a need-to-know book: You pick it up when you need to know something. Need to know how to set up a DHCP server in Windows? Pick up the book. Need to know how to create a user account in Linux? Pick up the book. Otherwise, put it down, and get on with your life.

How to Use This Book

This book works like a reference. Start with the topic you want to find out about. Look for it in the table of contents or in the index to get going. The table of contents is detailed enough that you should be able to find most of the topics you're looking for. If not, turn to the index, where you can find even more detail.

The book is loaded with information, of course, so if you want to take a brief excursion into your topic, you're more than welcome. If you want to know the big security picture, read the whole chapter on security. If you just want to know how to make a decent password, read just the section on passwords. You get the idea.

Whenever I describe a message or information that you see on the screen, I present it as follows:

```
A message from your friendly network
```

If you need to type something, you see the text you need to type like this: **Type this stuff**. In this example, you type **Type this stuff** at the keyboard and press Enter. An explanation usually follows, just in case you're scratching your head and grunting, "Huh?"

How This Book Is Organized

Each of the nine minibooks contained in *Networking All-in-One For Dummies,* 5th Edition, can stand by itself. The first minibook covers the networking basics that you should know to help you understand the rest of the stuff in this book. If you've been managing a network for a while already, you probably know all this stuff, of course, so you can probably skip Book I or just skim it for laughs. The remaining minibooks cover a variety of networking topics that you would normally find covered in separate books. Here's a brief description of what you find in each minibook.

Book 1: Networking Basics

This minibook covers the networking basics that you need to understand to get going. You find out what a network is, how networking standards work, what hardware components are required to make up a network, and what network operating systems do. You discover the difference between peer-to-peer networking and client-server networking. And you get a comparison of the most popular network operating systems, including the current incarnations of Windows Server and Linux.

Book II: Building a Network

In this minibook, you find the ins and outs of building a network. First, you see how to create a plan for your network. After all, planning is the first step of any great endeavor. Then you discover how to install network hardware, such as network interface cards, and how to work with various types of networking cable. You receive some general pointers about installing a network server operating system. You gain insight into how to configure various versions of Windows to access a network and an overview of how virtualization technologies like VMware can help you manage your servers. Finally, you get an overview of cloud computing and a description of how it can affect your networking environment.

Book III: Network Administration and Security

In this minibook, you discover what it means to be a network administrator, with an emphasis on how to secure your network so that it's safe from intruders but at the same time allow your network's users access to everything they need. In the real world, this responsibility isn't as easy as it sounds. This minibook begins with an overview of what network administrators do. Then it describes some of the basic practices of good network security, such as using strong passwords and providing physical security for your servers. It includes detailed information about setting up and managing network user accounts, using virus scanners, setting up firewalls, backing up network data, keeping network software up to date, working with virtual private networks (VPNs), and troubleshooting common network problems.

Book IV: TCP/IP and the Internet

This minibook is devoted to the most popular network technology on the planet: TCP/IP. (Actually, it may be the most popular protocol in the universe. The aliens in *Independence Day* had a TCP/IP network on their spaceship, enabling Will Smith and Jeff Goldblum to hack their way in. The aliens should have read the section on firewalls in Book III.)

Book V: Wireless Networking

In this minibook, you discover the ins and outs of setting up and securing a wireless network.

Book VI: Mobile Networking

This minibook is devoted to the special requirements for managing mobile users who want to connect to your network. Here, you'll find chapters on working with the most popular types of smartphones, including BlackBerry, iPhone, and Android devices, as well as information about incorporating netbooks into your network.

Book VII: Windows Server 2012 Reference

This minibook describes the basics of setting up and administering a server using the latest version of Windows Server 2012. You also find helpful information about its predecessors, Windows Server 2008 and Windows Server 2003. You find chapters on installing a Windows server, managing user accounts, setting up a file server, and securing a Windows server. Also, you find a handy reference to the many Windows networking commands that you can use from a command prompt.

Book VIII: Using Other Windows Servers

This minibook shows you the basics of setting up other popular Windows server products, including the IIS Web server, Exchange Server 2010 for managing e-mail, SQL Server 2012 for databases, and SharePoint 2010 for creating intranet sites.

Book IX: Managing Linux Systems

Linux has fast become an inexpensive alternative to Windows and NetWare. In this minibook, you discover the basics of installing and managing Linux. You find out how to install Fedora; work with Linux commands and GNOME (a popular graphical interface for Linux); configure Linux for networking; set up a Windows-compatible file server by using Samba; and run popular Internet servers such as DHCP, Bind, and Sendmail. Also, you get a concise Linux command reference that will turn you into a Linux command-line junkie in no time.

Icons Used in This Book

Like any *For Dummies* book, this book is chock-full of helpful icons that draw your attention to items of particular importance. You find the following icons throughout this book:

Hold it — technical stuff is just around the corner. Read on only if you have your pocket protector.

Pay special attention to this icon; it lets you know that some particularly useful tidbit is at hand.

Did I tell you about the memory course I took?

Danger, Will Robinson! This icon highlights information that may help you avert disaster.

Where to Go from Here

Yes, you can get there from here. With this book in hand, you're ready to plow right through the rugged networking terrain. Browse the table of contents, and decide where you want to start. Be bold! Be courageous! Be adventurous! And above all, have fun!

Occasionally, we update our technology books. If this book has technical updates, they'll be posted at www.dummies.com/go/networkingaio fd5eupdates.

Book I

Networking Basics

The 5th Wave   By Rich Tennant

"It worked, honey! I'm connected to the network!"

Contents at a Glance

Chapter 1: Understanding Networks

In This Chapter

✔ Introducing computer networks

✔ Finding out all about clients, servers, and peers

✔ Understanding the various types of networks

✔ Figuring out the disadvantages of networking

The first computer network was invented when ancient mathematicians connected their abacuses (or is it *abaci?*) with kite string so they could instantly share their abacus answers with each other. Over the years, computer networks have become more and more sophisticated. Now, instead of string, networks use electrical cables, fiber optic cables, or wireless radio signals to connect computers to each other. The purpose, however, has remained the same: sharing information and getting work done faster.

This chapter describes the basics of what computer networking is and how it works.

Defining a Network

A *network* is simply two or more computers, connected, so that they can exchange information (such as e-mail messages or documents) or share resources (say, disk storage or printers). In most cases, this connection is made via electrical cables that carry the information in the form of electrical signals. Other types of connections are used, too. For example, computers can communicate via fiber optic cables at extremely high speeds by using impulses of light. And in a wireless network, computers communicate by using radio signals. Look, Ma! No hands!

In addition to the hardware that supports a network, you also need special software to enable communications. In the early days of networking, you had to add this software to each computer on the network. Nowadays, network support is built in to all major operating systems, including all current versions of Windows, Macintosh operating systems, and Linux.

Network building blocks

All networks, large or small, require specialized network hardware to make them work. For a small network, this hardware may consist of nothing more than computers equipped with network ports, a cable for each computer, and a network switch that all the computers plug in to via the cable. Larger networks probably have additional components, such as routers or repeaters.

Small or large, though, all networks are built from the following basic building blocks:

✦ **Client computers:** These computers are what end users use to access the resources of the network. Client computers are typically computers located on users' desks. They usually run a desktop version of Windows. In addition, the client computers usually run some type of application software, such as Microsoft Office. Client computers are sometimes referred to as *workstations*.

✦ **Server computers:** These computers provide shared resources, such as disk storage and printers, as well as network services, such as e-mail and Internet access. Server computers typically run a specialized network OS, such as Windows Server, NetWare, or Linux, along with special software to provide network services. For example, a server may run Microsoft Exchange to provide e-mail services for the network, or it may run Apache Web Server so that the computer can serve web pages.

✦ **Network interface:** This interface — sometimes called a *network port* — is installed on a computer to enable the computer to communicate over a network. Almost all network interfaces implement a networking standard called *Ethernet*.

A network interface is sometimes called a "NIC," which is techie for *network interface card.* In the early days of networking, you actually had to install a separate circuit card on the computer to provide a network interface. Nowadays, nearly all computers come with network interfaces built in as an integral part of the computer's motherboard. Although separate network cards are rarely required these days, the term "NIC" is still frequently used to refer to the network interface.

You well might still have to install separate network interface cards to provide more than one network interface on a single computer, or to replace a built-in network interface that has malfunctioned without having to replace the entire motherboard.

✦ **Cable:** Computers in a network are usually physically connected to each other using cable. Although several types of cable have been popular over the years, most networks today use a twisted-pair cable, which is also known by its official designation, 10BaseT. Twisted-pair cable is also sometimes referred to as Cat-5 or Cat-6 cable. These terms refer to the standards that determine the maximum speed with which the cable can carry data: Cat-6 is rated for more speed than Cat-5.

Twisted-pair cable can also be referred to simply as "copper" to distinguish it from fiber optic cable, which is used for the highest-speed network connections. Fiber optic cable uses strands of glass to transmit light signals at very high speeds.

In many cases, connecting cables are run through the walls and converge on a central room (a wiring closet). For smaller networks, though, the cables are often just strung along the floor, hidden behind desks and other furniture whenever possible.

✦ **Switches:** You don't typically use network cable to connect computers directly to each other. Instead, each computer is connected by cable to a central switch, which connects to the rest of the network. Each switch contains a certain number of ports, typically 8 or 16. (Do the math: You use an eight-port switch to connect up to eight computers.)

Switches can be connected to each other to build larger networks. For more information about switches, see the "Network Topology" section later in this chapter.

✦ **Wireless networks:** In a wireless network, most cables and switches are moot. Radio transmitters and receivers take the place of cables. Of course, the main advantage of wireless networking is its flexibility: no cables to run through walls or ceilings, and client computers located anywhere within range of the network broadcast. The trade-off (you knew there was a catch, right?) of wireless networks is that they are inherently less secure than a cabled network.

✦ **Network software:** What really makes a network work is software, which has to be set up just right to get a network working. Server computers typically use a special network operating system (NOS) to function efficiently, and client computers need to have their network settings configured properly to access the network.

One of the most important networking choices to make is which NOS to use on the network's servers. Much of the task of building a new network and managing an existing one is setting up and maintaining the NOS on the servers.

Seeing the benefits of networking

Truth time: Computer networks are a pain to set up. Having said that, the benefits of using a network make the pain worthwhile. And, you don't have to be a Ph.D. to understand the benefits of networking. In fact, you learned everything in kindergarten applies to the benefits of networking. In a nutshell, networks are all about sharing: information, resources, and applications.

✦ **Sharing information:** Networks allow users to share information in several different ways. The most common way is sharing individual files. For example, two or more people can work together on a single spreadsheet file or word processing document. In most networks, a large hard drive on a central server computer is set up as a common storage area where users can store files to be shared with other users.

Networks allow users to communicate with each other in other ways. For example, with messaging applications, network users exchange messages using an e-mail app, such as Microsoft Outlook. Users can also hold online meetings over a network. In fact, with inexpensive video cameras and the right software, users can hold videoconferences over the network.

✦ **Sharing resources:** Network users can share certain computer resources, such as printers or hard drives, resulting in significant cost savings. For example, instead of buying separate printers for each user in the group, go for a single high-speed printer with advanced features (collating, stapling, and duplex printing) that an entire workgroup can share.

Hard drives can also be shared resources. In fact, providing users with access to a shared hard drive is the most common method of sharing files on a network. A computer whose main purpose in life is to host shared hard drives is a *file server*.

In actual practice, entire hard drives aren't usually shared. Instead, individual folders on a networked hard drive are shared. This way, the network administrator can allow different network users to have access to different shared folders. For example, a company may set up shared folders for its sales department and accounting department. Then, sales personnel can access the sales department's folder, and accounting personnel can access the accounting department's folder. And, for security reasons, the sales department can be locked out of the accounting department's folder, and vice versa.

You can share other resources on a network, too: for example, an Internet connection. In the early days of the Internet, each user accessing the Internet typically had a personal modem connection. Nowadays, networks typically provide a shared, high-speed Internet connection that everyone on the network can access.

✦ **Sharing applications:** One of the most common reasons for networking in many businesses is so that several users can work together on a single business application. For example, an accounting department may have special software that can be used from several computers at the same time. Or a sales-processing department may have an order-entry application that runs on several computers to handle a large volume of orders.

Comparing Clients and Servers

A network computer that manages the hard drives, printers, and other resources shared with other network computers is a *server.* This term will comes up repeatedly throughout this book, so burn it into your brain. Write it on the back of your left hand.

Any network computer that's not a server is a *client.* You have to remember this term, too. Write it on the back of your right hand.

Only two kinds of computers are on a network: servers and clients. Look at your left hand and then look at your right hand. Do not wash your hands until you have these terms memorized.

The distinction between servers and clients in a network would be some-what fun to study in a sociology class. Think of the haves and the have-nots in society:

+ **Have:** Usually, the most powerful and expensive computers in a network are the servers. This fact makes sense because every user on the net-work shares the server's resources.

+ **Have not:** The cheaper and less-powerful computers in a network are the clients. Clients are the computers used by individual users for every-day work. Because clients' resources don't have to be shared, they don't have to be as fancy.

Most networks have more clients than servers. For example, a network with ten clients can probably get by with 1 server.

+ **Have or have-not:** In some networks, a clear line of class exists between servers and clients. In other words, a computer is either a server or a client, and not both. A server can't become a client, nor can a client become a server.

Other networks are more progressive, allowing any computer in the network to be a server and allowing any computer to be both server and client at the same time. The network illustrated in Figure 1-1, later in this chapter, is this type of network.

Understanding Dedicated Servers and Peers

In some networks, a server computer is a server computer and nothing else, dedicated solely to the task of providing shared resources, such as hard drives and printers, that network client computers access. Such a server is a "dedicated" server because it can perform no other tasks than network services. A network that relies on dedicated servers is sometimes called a *client/server network.*

Other networks take an alternative approach, enabling any computer on the network to function as both a client and a server. Thus, any computer can share its printers and hard drives with other computers on the network. And while a computer is working as a server, you can still use that same computer for other functions such as word processing. This type of network is a *peer-to-peer network* — all the computers are thought of as peers, or equals.

While you're walking the dog tomorrow morning, ponder these points concerning the difference between dedicated server networks and peer-to-peer networks:

✦ Peer-to-peer networking has been built in to all versions of Windows since Windows 95. Thus, you don't have to buy any additional software to turn your computer into a server. All you have to do is enable the Windows server features.

✦ The network server features built in to desktop versions of Windows (including Windows 8, 7, Vista, and XP) aren't very efficient because these versions of Windows weren't designed primarily to be network servers. If you're going to dedicate a computer to the task of being a full-time server, use a full-fledged NOS, such as Windows Server 2012 or 2008.

Seeing Networks Big and Small

Networks come in all sizes and shapes. In fact, networks are commonly based on the geographical size they cover, as described in the following list:

✦ **Local area networks (LAN):** In this type of network, computers are relatively close together, such as within the same office or building.

Don't let the descriptor "local" fool you. A LAN doesn't imply that a network is small. A LAN can contain hundreds or even thousands of computers. What makes a network a LAN is that all its connected computers are located within close proximity. ("Local." Hmm. Go figga.) Usually a LAN is contained within a single building, but a LAN can extend to several buildings on a campus (like a campus area network; CAN), provided that the buildings are close to each other (typically within 300 feet of each other although greater distances are possible with special equipment).

✦ **Wide area networks (WAN):** These networks span a large geographic territory, such as an entire city or a region or even a country. WANs are typically used to connect two or more LANs that are relatively far apart. For example, a WAN may connect an office in San Francisco with an office in New York.

The geographic distance, not the number of computers involved, makes a network a WAN. If an office in San Francisco and an office in New York each have only one computer, the WAN will have a grand sum of two computers — but will span more than 3,000 miles.

✦ **Metropolitan area networks (MAN):** This kid of network is smaller than a typical WAN but larger than a LAN. Typically, a MAN connects two or more LANs within the same city but that are far enough apart that the networks can't be connected via a simple cable or wireless connection.

Understanding Network Topology

Network topology refers to the shape of how the computers and other network components are connected to each other. Each type of network topology (bus, star, expanding star, ring, and mesh) offers advantages and disadvantages.

In the following discussion of network topologies, I use two important terms:

✦ **Node:** A device connected to the network. For your purposes here, a node is the same as a computer. Network topology deals with how the nodes of a network are connected.

✦ **Packet:** A message sent over the network from one node to another node. Each packet includes

  • The address of the node that sent the packet

  • The address of the node to which the packet is being sent

  • Data

Bus topology

In a bus topology, nodes are strung together in a line, as shown in Figure 1-1. Think of the entire network as a single cable, with each node "tapping" into the cable so it can listen in on the packets being sent over that cable. If you're old enough to remember party telephone lines, you get the idea.

In a bus topology, every node on the network can see every packet sent on the cable. Each node looks at each packet to determine whether the packet is intended for it. If so, the node claims the packet. If not, the node ignores the packet. This way, each computer can respond to data sent to it but ignore data sent to other computers on the network.

Figure 1-1:
Bus
topology.

If the cable in a bus network breaks, the entire network is effectively disabled. Obviously, nodes on opposite sides of the break can't continue to communicate because data can't span the gap created by the break. However, even those nodes on the same side of the break are unable to communicate with each other because the open end of the cable left by the break disrupts the proper transmission of electrical signals.

In the early days of Ethernet networking, bus topology was commonplace. Bus topology has given way to star topology (see the next section), but even for most networks today, many networks today still have elements that rely on bus topology.

Star topology

In a star topology, each network node is connected to a central device — a hub or a switch — as shown in Figure 1-2. Star topologies are commonly used with LANs.

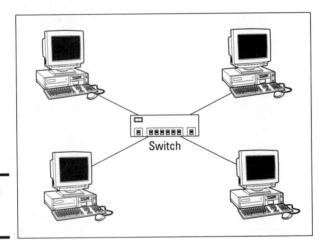

Figure 1-2:
Star
topology.

If a cable in a star network breaks, only the node connected to that cable is isolated from the network. The other nodes can continue to operate without interruption — unless, of course, the node that's isolated because of the break happens to be the file server.

CAL STUFF

About hubs and switches

In the prehistoric days of networking (that is, the 1990's), it was common to use devices known as *hubs* rather than switches. Externally, a hub looks a lot like a switch. But internally, hubs are very different from switches.

Simply put, a hub doesn't know anything about the computers that are connected to each of its ports. So when a computer connected to a hub sends a packet to a computer that's connected to another port, the hub sends a duplicate copy of the packet to all its ports.

In contrast, a switch has knowledge about the computers that are connected to its ports. As a result, when a switch receives a packet intended for a particular computer, it sends the packet only to the port that the recipient is connected to.

Strictly speaking, only networks that use switches have a true star topology. If the network uses a hub, the network topology has the physical appearance of a star, but is actually a bus. That's because when a hub is used, each computer on the network sees all the packets sent over the network, just like in a bus topology. In a true star topology, as when a switch is used, each computer sees only those packets that were sent specifically to it, as well as packets that were specifically sent to all computers on the network; those types of packets are *broadcast packets*.

Expanding stars

Physicists say that the universe is expanding, and network administrators know they're right. A simple bus or star topology is suitable only for small networks — say, with a dozen or so computers. For larger networks, it's common to create more complicated topologies that combine stars and buses.

For example, you can use a bus to connect several stars. In this case, two or more hubs or switches are connected to each other, using a bus. Each hub or switch is then the center of a star that connects two or more computers to the network. This type of arrangement is commonly used in buildings with two or more distinct workgroups. The bus that connects the switches is sometimes called a *backbone*.

Another way to expand a star topology is to use *daisy-chaining*. A switch is connected to another switch as if it were one of the nodes on the star. Then, this second switch serves as the center of a second star. For more information, refer to Chapter 3 of this minibook.

Ring topology

In a ring topology (see Figure 1-3), packets are sent around the circle from computer to computer. Each computer looks at each packet to decide whether the packet was intended for it. If not, the packet is passed on to the next computer in the ring.

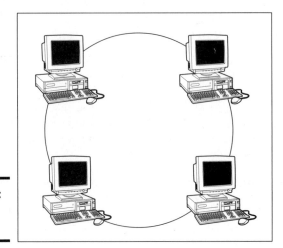

Figure 1-3:
Ring
topology.

Years ago, ring topologies were common in LANs because two popular networking technologies used rings: ARCNET and token ring. ARCNET is still used for certain applications (such as factory automation) but is rarely used in business networks. Token ring is still a popular network technology for IBM midrange computers. Although plenty of token ring networks are still in existence, not many new networks use token ring any more.

Ring topology was also used by FDDI, which was one of the first types of fiber optic network connections. FDDI has given way to more efficient fiber optic techniques, however. Ring networks have all but vanished from business networks.

Mesh topology

A *mesh topology* has multiple connections between each node on the network, as shown in Figure 1-4. The advantage of using a mesh topology is that if one cable breaks, the network can use an alternative route to deliver its packets.

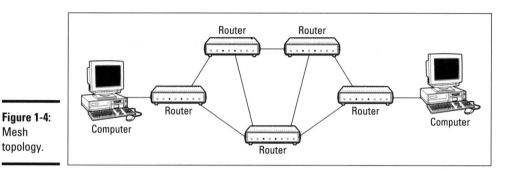

Figure 1-4:
Mesh
topology.

Mesh networks aren't very practical in a LAN setting. For example, to network eight computers in a mesh topology, each computer would have to have 7 network interface cards, and 28 cables would be required to connect each computer to the 7 other computers in the network. Obviously, this scheme isn't very scalable.

However, mesh networks are common for MANs and WANs. These networks use *routers,* which (um) route packets from network to network. For reliability and performance reasons, routers are usually arranged in a way that provides multiple paths between any two nodes on the network in a mesh-like arrangement.

Chapter 2: Understanding Network Protocols and Standards

In This Chapter

✓ Discovering protocols

✓ Deciphering the layers of the OSI reference model

✓ Understanding an Ethernet

✓ Getting the inside scoop on TCP/IP and IPX/SPX

✓ Finding out about other important protocols

*P*rotocols and standards make networks work together. Protocols make it possible for the various components of a network to communicate with each other, and standards make it possible for different manufacturers' network components to work together. This chapter introduces you to the protocols and standards that you're most likely to encounter when building and maintaining a network.

Understanding Protocols

A *protocol* is simply a set of rules that enable effective communications to occur. You encounter protocols every day and probably don't even realize it. When you pay for groceries with a debit card, the clerk tells you how much the groceries cost, and then you swipe your debit card in the card reader, punch in your security code, indicate whether you want cash back, enter the amount of the cash back if you so indicated, and verify the total amount. You then cross your fingers behind your back and say a quiet prayer while the machine authorizes the purchase. Assuming the amount is authorized, the machine prints out your receipt.

Here's another example of an everyday protocol: making a phone call. You probably take most of the details of the phone-calling protocol for granted, but it's pretty complicated if you think about it:

✦ When you pick up a phone, you listen for a dial tone before dialing the number (unless you're using a cell phone). If you don't hear a dial tone, you know that someone else in your family is talking on the phone, or something is wrong with your phone.

✦ When you hear the dial tone, you dial the number of the party you want to reach. If the person you want to call is in the same area code, you simply dial that person's seven-digit phone number. If the person is in a different area code, you dial 1, the three-digit area code, and the person's seven-digit phone number.

✦ If you hear a series of long ringing tones, you wait until the other person answers the phone. If the phone rings a certain number of times with no answer, you hang up and try again later. If you hear a voice say, "Hello," you begin a conversation with the other party. If the person on the other end of the phone has never heard of you, you say, "Sorry, wrong number," hang up, and try again.

✦ If you hear a voice that rambles on about how they're not home but they want to return your call, you wait for a beep and leave a message.

✦ If you hear a series of short tones, you know the other person is talking to someone else on the phone. So you hang up and try again later.

✦ If you hear a sequence of three tones that increase in pitch, followed by a recorded voice that says "We're sorry . . ." you know that the number you dialed is invalid. Either you dialed the number incorrectly, or the number has been disconnected.

You get the point. Exchanges — using a debit card or making a phone call — follow the same rules every time they happen.

Computer networks depend upon many different types of protocols. These protocols are very rigidly defined, and for good reason. Network cards must know how to talk to other network cards to exchange information, operating systems must know how to talk to network cards to send and receive data on the network, and application programs must know how to talk to operating systems to know how to retrieve a file from a network server.

Protocols come in many different types. At the lowest level, protocols define exactly what type of electrical signal represents a 1 and what type of signal represents a 0. At the highest level, protocols allow (say) a computer user in the United States to send an e-mail to another computer user in New Zealand — and in between are many other levels of protocols. You find out more about these levels of protocols (often called "layers") in the upcoming section, "The Seven Layers of the OSI Reference Model."

Protocols tend to be used together in matched sets called *protocol suites.* The two most popular protocol suites for networking are TCP/IP and Ethernet. TCP/IP, originally developed for Unix networks, is the protocol of the Internet and most local area networks (LANs). Ethernet is a low-level protocol that spells out the electrical characteristics of the network hardware used by most LANs. A third important protocol is IPX/SPX, which is an alternative to TCP/IP, and originally developed for NetWare networks. In the early days of networking, IPX/SPX was widely used in LANs, but TCP/IP is now the preferred protocol.

Understanding Standards

As I mention earlier, a *standard* is an agreed-upon definition of a protocol. In the early days of computer networking, each computer manufacturer developed its own networking protocols. As a result, you couldn't easily mix equipment from different manufacturers on a single network.

Then along came standards to save the day. Hurrah! Because standards are industry-wide protocol definitions not tied to a particular manufacturer, you can mix and match equipment from different vendors. As long as the equipment implements the standard protocols, it should be able to coexist on the same network.

Many organizations are involved in setting standards for networking. The five most important organizations are

✦ **American National Standards Institute (ANSI):** www.ansi.org The official standards organization in the United States. ANSI is pronounced *AN-see.*

✦ **Institute of Electrical and Electronics Engineers (IEEE):** www.ieee.org An international organization that publishes several key networking standards — in particular, the official standard for the Ethernet networking system (known officially as IEEE 802.3). IEEE is pronounced *eye-triple-E.*

✦ **International Organization for Standardization (ISO):** www.iso.org A federation of more than 100 standards organizations throughout the world. If I had studied French in high school, I'd probably understand why the acronym for International Organization for Standardization is ISO, and not IOS.

✦ **Internet Engineering Task Force (IETF):** www.ietf.org The organization responsible for the protocols that drive the Internet.

✦ **World Wide Web Consortium (W3C):** www.w3.org An international organization that handles the development of standards for the World Wide Web.

Seeing the Seven Layers of the OSI Reference Model

"OSI" sounds like the name of a top-secret government agency you hear about only in Tom Clancy novels. What it really stands for in the networking world is Open Systems Interconnection, as in the Open Systems Interconnection Reference Model, affectionately known as the *OSI model.*

The OSI model breaks the various aspects of a computer network into seven distinct layers. These layers are kind of like the layers of an onion: Each successive layer envelops the layer beneath it, hiding its details from the levels above. The OSI model is also like an onion in that if you start to peel it apart to have a look inside, you're bound to shed a few tears.

The OSI model is not a networking standard in the same sense that Ethernet and TCP/IP are networking standards. Rather, the OSI model is a framework into which the various networking standards can fit. The OSI model specifies what aspects of a network's operation can be addressed by various network standards. So, in a sense, the OSI model is sort of a standard of standards.

Table 2-1 summarizes the seven layers of the OSI model.

Table 2-1		The Seven Layers of the OSI Model
Layer	*Name*	*Description*
1	Physical	Governs the layout of cables and devices, such as repeaters and hubs.
2	Data Link	Provides MAC* addresses to uniquely identify network nodes and a means for data to be sent over the Physical layer in the form of packets. Bridges and switches are Layer 2 devices.
3	Network	Handles routing of data across network segments.
4	Transport	Provides for reliable delivery of packets.
5	Session	Establishes sessions between network applications.
6	Presentation	Converts data so that systems that use different data formats can exchange information.
7	Application	Allows applications to request network services.

* MAC = Media Access Control. Read more about MAC and bridges and switches in "The Data Link layer."

The first three layers are sometimes called the *lower layers.* They deal with the mechanics of how information is sent from one computer to another over a network. Layers 4–7 are sometimes called the *upper layers.* They deal with how application software can relate to the network through application programming interfaces.

The following sections describe each of these layers in greater detail.

The seven layers of the OSI model are a somewhat idealized view of how networking protocols should work. In the real world, actual networking protocols don't follow the OSI model to the letter. The real world is always messier. Still, the OSI model provides a convenient — if not completely accurate — conceptual picture of how networking works.

The Physical layer

The bottom layer of the OSI model is the *Physical layer.* It addresses the physical characteristics of the network, such as the types of cables used to connect devices, the types of connectors used, how long the cables can be, and so on. For example, the Ethernet standard for 10BaseT cable specifies the electrical characteristics of the twisted-pair cables, the size and shape of the connectors, the maximum length of the cables, and so on. The star, bus, ring, and mesh network topologies described in Chapter 1 of this minibook apply to the Physical layer.

Another aspect of the Physical layer is the electrical characteristics of the signals used to transmit data over the cables from one network node to another. The Physical layer doesn't define any meaning to those signals other than the basic binary values of 1 and 0. The higher levels of the OSI model must assign meanings to the bits that are transmitted at the Physical layer.

One type of Physical layer device commonly used in networks is a *repeater,* which is used to regenerate the signal whenever you need to exceed the cable length allowed by the Physical layer standard. 10BaseT hubs are also Physical layer devices. (I talk a bit about hubs in Chapters 1 and 3 of this minibook.) Technically, they're known as *multiport repeaters* because the purpose of a hub is to regenerate every packet received on any port on all the hub's other ports. Repeaters and hubs don't examine the contents of the packets that they regenerate, though. If they did, they would be working at the Data Link layer, and not at the Physical layer.

The *network adapter* (also called a network interface card; NIC) installed in each computer on the network is a Physical layer device. You can display information about the network adapter (or adapters) installed in a Windows computer by displaying the adapter's Properties dialog box, as shown in Figure 2-1. To access this dialog box in Windows, open the Control Panel, choose Network and Sharing Center, and then choose Change Adapter Settings. Then right-click the Local Area Connection icon and choose Properties from the menu that appears.

The Data Link layer

The *Data Link layer* is the lowest layer at which meaning is assigned to the bits that are transmitted over the network. Data link protocols address things, such as the size of each packet of data to be sent, a means of addressing each packet so that it's delivered to the intended recipient, and a way to ensure that two or more nodes don't try to transmit data on the network at the same time.

The Data Link layer also provides basic error detection and correction to ensure that the data sent is the same as the data received. If an uncorrectable error occurs, the data link standard must specify how the node is to be informed of the error so that it can retransmit the data.

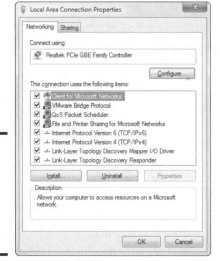

Figure 2-1:
The
Properties
dialog
box for a
network
adapter.

At the Data Link layer, each device on the network has an address: the Media Access Control (MAC). This address is hard-wired into every network device by the manufacturer. MAC addresses are unique; no two network devices made by any manufacturer anywhere in the world can have the same MAC address.

You can see the MAC address for a computer's network adapter by opening a command window and running the `ipconfig /all` command, as shown in Figure 2-2. In this example, the MAC address of the network card is 00-40-F4-CD-A9-50. (The `ipconfig` command refers to the MAC address as the *physical address*.)

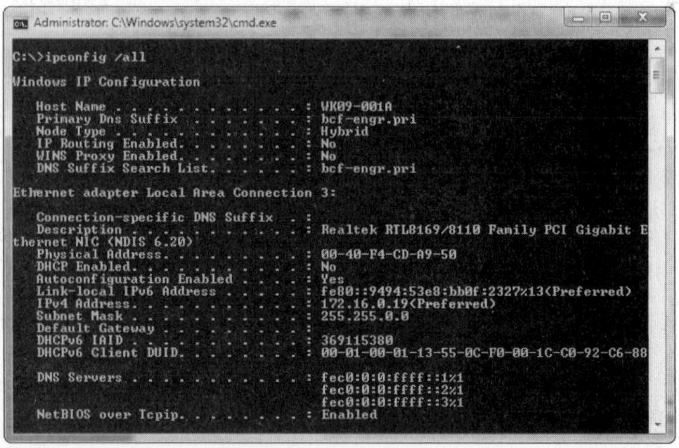

Figure 2-2:
Display
the MAC
address of
a network
adapter.

CSMA/CD is a mouthful!

An important function of the Data Link layer is to make sure that two computers don't try to send packets over the network at the same time. If they do, the signals will collide with each other, and the transmission will be garbled. Ethernet accomplishes this feat by using CSMA/CD. This phrase is a mouthful, but if you take it apart piece by piece, you'll get an idea of how it works.

✓ *Carrier Sense* means that whenever a device wants to send a packet over the network media, it first listens to the network media to see whether anyone else is already sending a packet. If it doesn't hear any other signals on the media, the computer assumes that the network is free, so it sends the packet.

✓ *Multiple Access* means that nothing prevents two or more devices from trying to send a message at the same time. Sure, each device listens before sending. However, suppose that two devices listen, hear nothing, and then proceed to send their packets at the same time? Picture what happens when you and someone else arrive at a four-way stop sign at the same time. You wave the other driver on, he or she waves you on, you wave, he or she waves, you both wave, and then you both go at the same time.

✓ *Collision Detection* means that after a device sends a packet, it listens carefully to see whether the packet crashes into another packet. This is kind of like listening for the screeching of brakes at the four-way stop. If the device hears the screeching of brakes, it waits a random period of time and then tries to send the packet again. Because the delay is random, two packets that collide are sent again after different delay periods, so a second collision is unlikely.

CSMA/CD works pretty well for smaller networks. After a network hits about 30 computers, however, packets start to collide like crazy, and the network slows to a crawl. When that happens, the network should be divided into two or more separate sections that are sometimes called *collision domains*.

One of the most import functions of the Data Link layer is to provide a way for packets to be sent safely over the physical media without interference from other nodes attempting to send packets at the same time. The two most popular ways to do this are CSMA/CD and token passing. (Take a deep breath. CSMA/CD stands for Carrier Sense Multiple Access/Collision Detection.) Ethernet networks use CSMA/CD, and token ring networks use token passing. (Read more about token rings in Chapter 1 of this minibook.)

Two types of Data Link layer devices are commonly used on networks:

✦ **Bridge:** An intelligent repeater that's aware of the MAC addresses of the nodes on either side of the bridge and can forward packets accordingly.

✦ **Switch:** An intelligent hub that examines the MAC address of arriving packets to determine which port to forward the packet to.

The Network layer

The *Network layer* handles the task of routing network messages from one computer to another. The two most popular Layer 3 protocols are IP (which is usually paired with TCP) and IPX (typically paired with SPX for use with Novell and Windows networks).

Network layer protocols provide two important functions: logical addressing and routing. The following sections describe these functions.

Logical addressing

As I mention earlier, every network device has a physical address — a MAC address — assigned to the device at the factory. When you buy a network interface card to install into a computer, the MAC address of that card is fixed and can't be changed. So what happens if you want to use some other addressing scheme to refer to the computers and other devices on your network? This is where the concept of logical addressing comes in; with a logical address, you can access a network device by using an address that you assign.

Logical addresses are created and used by Network layer protocols, such as IP or IPX. The Network layer protocol translates logical addresses to MAC addresses. For example, if you use IP as the Network layer protocol, devices on the network are assigned IP addresses, such as 207.120.67.30. Because the IP protocol must use a Data Link layer protocol to send packets to devices, IP must know how to translate the IP address of a device to the device's MAC address.

You can use the `ipconfig` command (shown earlier in Figure 2-2) to see the IP address of your computer. The IP address shown in that figure is 172.16.0.19. Another way to display this information is to use the System Information command, found on the Start menu under Start➪All Programs➪Accessories➪System Tools➪System Information. The IP address is highlighted in Figure 2-3. Notice that the System Information program displays a lot of other useful information about the network besides the IP address. For example, you can also see the MAC address and what protocols are being used.

Although the exact format of logical addresses varies depending on the protocol being used, most protocols divide the logical address into two parts:

✦ **Network address:** Identifies which network the device resides on

✦ **Device address:** Identifies the device on that network

In a typical IP address — say, 192.168.1.102 — the network address is 192.168.1, and the device address (called a *host address* in IP) is 102.

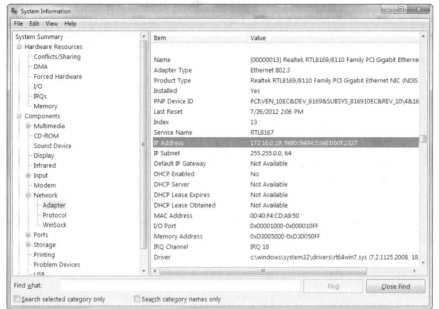

Figure 2-3:
Find
network
information
from System
Information.

Similarly, IPX addresses consist of two parts: a network address and a node address. In an IPX address, the node address is the same as the MAC address. As a result, IPX doesn't have to translate between Layer 2 and Layer 3 addresses.

Routing

Routing comes into play when a computer on one network needs to send a packet to a computer on another network. In this case, a router is used to forward the packet to the destination network. In some cases, a packet may have to travel through several intermediate networks in order to reach its final destination network. You can find out more about routers in Chapter 3 of this minibook.

An important feature of routers is that you can use them to connect networks that use different Layer 2 protocols. For example, a router can be used to send a packet from an Ethernet to a token ring network. As long as both networks support the same Layer 3 protocol, it doesn't matter whether their Layer 1 and Layer 2 protocols are different.

A protocol is considered routable if it uses addresses that include a network part and a host part. Any protocol that uses physical addresses isn't routable because physical addresses don't indicate to which network a device belongs.

The Transport layer

The *Transport layer* is where you find two of the most well-known networking protocols: TCP (typically paired with IP) and SPX (typically paired with IPX). As its name implies, the Transport layer is concerned with the transportation of information from one computer to another.

The main purpose of the Transport layer is to ensure that packets are transported reliably and without errors. The Transport layer does this task by establishing connections between network devices, acknowledging the receipt of packets, and resending packets that aren't received or are corrupted when they arrive.

In many cases, the Transport layer protocol divides large messages into smaller packets that can be sent over the network efficiently. The Transport layer protocol reassembles the message on the receiving end, making sure that all the packets that make up a single transmission are received so that no data is lost.

For some applications, speed and efficiency are more important than reliability. In such cases, a connectionless protocol can be used. As you can likely guess, a connectionless protocol doesn't go to the trouble of establishing a connection before sending a packet: It simply sends the packet. TCP is a connection-oriented Transport layer protocol. The connectionless protocol that works alongside TCP is User Datagram Protocol (UDP).

You can view information about the status of TCP and UDP connections by running the Netstat command from a command window, as Figure 2-4 shows. In the figure, you can see that several TCP connections are established.

Figure 2-4:
See TCP and UDP connections.

In fact, you can use the command Netstat /N to see the numeric network addresses instead of the names. With the /N switch, the output in Figure 2-4 would look like this:

```
Active Connections

   Proto  Local Address        Foreign Address       State
   TCP    127.0.0.1:2869       127.0.0.1:54170       ESTABLISHED
   TCP    127.0.0.1:5357       127.0.0.1:54172       TIME_WAIT
   TCP    127.0.0.1:27015      127.0.0.1:49301       ESTABLISHED
   TCP    127.0.0.1:49301      127.0.0.1:27015       ESTABLISHED
   TCP    127.0.0.1:54170      127.0.0.1:2869        ESTABLISHED
   TCP    192.168.1.100:49300  192.168.1.101:445     ESTABLISHED
```

TCP is a connection-oriented Transport layer protocol. *UDP* is a connection-less Transport layer protocol.

The Session layer

The *Session layer* establishes *conversations* — sessions — between net-worked devices. A *session* is an exchange of connection-oriented transmissions between two network devices. Each transmission is handled by the Transport layer protocol. The session itself is managed by the Session layer protocol.

A single session can include many exchanges of data between the two computers involved in the session. After a session between two computers has been established, it's maintained until the computers agree to terminate the session.

The Session layer allows three types of transmission modes:

✦ **Simplex:** Data flows in only one direction.

✦ **Half-duplex:** Data flows in both directions, but only in one direction at a time.

✦ **Full-duplex:** Data flows in both directions at the same time.

In actual practice, the distinctions in the Session, Presentation, and Application layers are often blurred, and some commonly used protocols actually span all three layers. For example, SMB — the protocol that is the basis of file sharing in Windows networks — functions at all three layers.

The Presentation layer

The *Presentation layer* is responsible for how data is represented to applications. Most computers — including Windows, Unix, and Macintosh computers — use ASCII to represent data. However, some computers (such as IBM mainframe computers) use a different code (Extended Binary Coded Decimal Interchange Code; EBCDIC).

ASCII and EBCDIC aren't compatible. To exchange information between a mainframe computer and a Windows computer, the Presentation layer must convert the data from ASCII to EBCDIC, and vice versa.

Besides simply converting data from one code to another, the Presentation layer can also apply sophisticated compression techniques so that fewer bytes of data are required to represent the information when it's sent over the network. At the other end of the transmission, the Presentation layer then uncompresses the data.

The Presentation layer can also scramble the data before it's transmitted and then unscramble it at the other end by using a sophisticated encryption technique that even Sherlock Holmes would have trouble breaking.

The Application layer

The highest layer of the OSI model, the Application layer deals with the techniques that application programs use to communicate with the network. The name of this layer is a little confusing. Application programs (such as Microsoft Office or QuickBooks) aren't a part of the Application layer. Rather, the Application layer represents the programming interfaces that application programs use to request network services.

Some of the better-known Application layer protocols are

+ **Domain Name System (DNS):** For resolving Internet domain names
+ **File Transfer Protocol (FTP):** For file transfers
+ **Simple Mail Transfer Protocol (SMTP):** For e-mail
+ **Server Message Block (SMB):** For file sharing in Windows networks
+ **Network File System (NFS):** For file sharing in Unix networks
+ **Telnet:** For terminal emulation

Following a Packet through the Layers

Figure 2-5 shows how a packet of information flows through the seven layers as it travels from one computer to another on the network. The data begins its journey when an end-user application sends data to another network computer. The data enters the network through an Application layer inter-face, such as SMB. The data then works its way down through the protocol stack. Along the way, the protocol at each layer manipulates the data by adding header information, converting the data into different formats, com-bining packets to form larger packets, and so on. When the data reaches the Physical layer protocol, it's placed on the network media (in other words, the cable) and sent to the receiving computer.

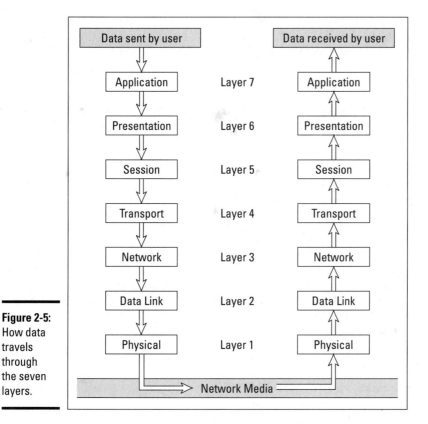

Figure 2-5:
How data
travels
through
the seven
layers.

When the receiving computer receives the data, the data works its way up through the protocol stack. Then, the protocol at each layer reverses the processing that was done by the corresponding layer on the sending computer. Headers are removed, data is converted back to its original format, packets that were split into smaller packets are recombined into larger messages, and so on. When the packet reaches the Application layer protocol, it's delivered to an application that can process the data.

The Ethernet Protocol

As I mention earlier, the first two layers of the OSI model deal with the physical structure of the network and the means by which network devices can send information from one device on a network to another. By far, Ethernet is the most popular set of protocols for the Physical and Data Link layers.

Ethernet has been around in various forms since the early 1970s. (For a brief history of Ethernet, see the sidebar, "Ethernet folklore and mythology.") The current incarnation of Ethernet is defined by the 802.3 IEEE standard.

Various flavors of Ethernet operate at different speeds and use different types of media. However, all the versions of Ethernet are compatible with each other, so you can mix and match them on the same network by using devices such as bridges, hubs, and switches to link network segments that use different types of media.

The actual transmission speed of Ethernet is measured in millions of bits per second, or Mbps. Ethernet comes in three different speed versions:

✦ **Standard Ethernet:** 10 Mbps

✦ **Fast Ethernet:** 100 Mbps

✦ **Gigabit Ethernet:** 1,000 Mbps

Network transmission speed refers to the maximum speed that can be achieved over the network under ideal conditions. In reality, the actual throughput of an Ethernet network rarely reaches this maximum speed.

Ethernet operates at the first two layers of the OSI model — the Physical and the Data Link layers. However, Ethernet divides the Data Link layer into two separate layers: the Logical Link Control (LLC) layer and the Medium Access Control (MAC) layer. Figure 2-6 shows how the various elements of Ethernet match up to the OSI model.

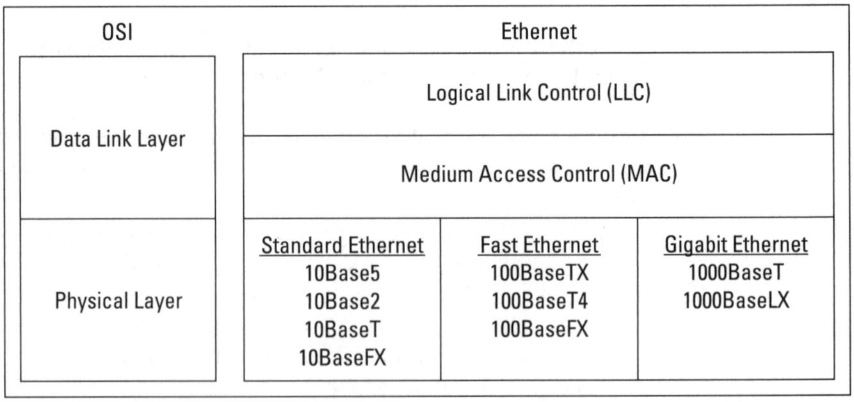

OSI	Ethernet		
Data Link Layer	Logical Link Control (LLC)		
	Medium Access Control (MAC)		
Physical Layer	Standard Ethernet 10Base5 10Base2 10BaseT 10BaseFX	Fast Ethernet 100BaseTX 100BaseT4 100BaseFX	Gigabit Ethernet 1000BaseT 1000BaseLX

Figure 2-6: Ethernet and the OSI model.

The following sections describe Standard Ethernet, Fast Ethernet, and Gigabit Ethernet in more detail.

Standard Ethernet

Standard Ethernet is the original Ethernet. It runs at 10 Mbps, which was considered fast in the 1970s but is pretty slow by today's standards. Although plenty of existing Standard Ethernet is still in use, it's considered obsolete and should be replaced by Gigabit Ethernet as soon as possible.

Ethernet folklore and mythology

Here's how Ethernet came to be so popular. The original idea for the Ethernet was hatched in the mind of Robert Metcalfe, a graduate computer science student at Harvard University. Looking for a thesis idea in 1970, he refined a networking technique used in Hawaii — the AlohaNet (actually a wireless network) — and developed a technique that would enable a network to efficiently use as much as 90 percent of its capacity. By 1973, he had his first Ethernet network up and running at the famous Xerox Palo Alto Research Center (PARC). Bob dubbed his network "Ethernet" in honor of the thick network cable, which he called "the ether." (Xerox PARC was busy in 1973. In addition to Ethernet, PARC developed the first personal computer that used a graphical user interface (GUI) complete with icons, windows, and menus, and the world's first laser printer.)

In 1979, Xerox began working with Intel and DEC (a once-popular computer company) to make Ethernet an industry standard networking product. Along the way, they enlisted the help of the IEEE, which formed committee number 802.3 and began the process of standardizing Ethernet in 1981. The 802.3 committee released the first official Ethernet standard in 1983.

Meanwhile, Bob Metcalfe left Xerox, turned down a job offer from Steve Jobs to work at Apple computers, and started a company called the Computer, Communication, and Compatibility Corporation — now known as 3Com. 3Com has since become one of the largest manufacturers of Ethernet equipment in the world.

Standard Ethernet comes in four incarnations, depending on the type of cable used to string the network together:

✦ **10Base5:** This original Ethernet cable was thick (about as thick as your thumb), heavy, and difficult to work with. It's seen today only in museum exhibits.

✦ **10Base2:** This thinner type of coaxial cable (it resembles television cable) became popular in the 1980s and lingered into the early 1990s. Plenty of 10Base2 cable is still in use, but it's rarely installed in new networks. 10Base2 (like 10Base5) uses a bus topology, so wiring a 10Base2 network involves running cable from one computer to the next until all the computers are connected in a segment.

✦ **10BaseT:** Unshielded twisted-pair (UTP) cable became popular in the 1990s because it's easier to install, lighter, and more reliable, and also it offers more flexibility in how networks are designed. 10BaseT networks use a star topology with hubs at the center of each star. Although the maximum length of 10BaseT cable is only 100 meters, hubs can be chained to extend networks well beyond the 100-meter limit.

10BaseT cable has four pairs of wires twisted together throughout the entire span of the cable. However, 10BaseT uses only two of these wire pairs, so the unused pairs are spares.

✦ **10BaseFL:** Fiber optic cables were originally supported at 10 Mbps by the 10BaseFL standard. However, because faster fiber optic versions of Ethernet now exist, 10BaseFL is rarely used.

Fast Ethernet

Fast Ethernet refers to Ethernet that runs at 100 Mbps, which is 10 times the speed of Standard Ethernet. Here are the three varieties of Fast Ethernet:

✦ **100BaseT4:** The 100BaseT4 protocol allows transmission speeds of 100 Mbps over the same UTP cable as 10BaseT networks. To do this, it uses all four pairs of wire in the cable. 100BaseT4 simplifies the task of upgrading an existing 10BaseT network to 100 Mbps.

✦ **100BaseTX:** The most commonly used standard for office networks today is 100BaseTX, which transmits at 100 Mbps over just two pairs of a higher grade of UTP cable than the cable used by 10BaseT. The higher-grade cable is Category 5. Most new networks are wired with Cat5 or better cable.

✦ **100BaseFX:** The fiber optic version of Ethernet running at 100 Mbps is 100BaseFX. Because fiber optic cable is expensive and tricky to install, it isn't used much for individual computers in a network. However, it's commonly used as a network backbone. For example, a fiber backbone is often used to connect individual workgroup hubs to routers and servers.

Gigabit Ethernet

Gigabit Ethernet is Ethernet running at a whopping 1,000 Mbps, which is 100 times faster than the original 10 Mbps Ethernet. Gigabit Ethernet was once considerably more expensive than Fast Ethernet, so it was used only when the improved performance justified the extra cost. However, today Gigabit Ethernet is the standard for nearly all desktop and laptop PCs.

Gigabit Ethernet comes in two flavors:

✦ **1000BaseT:** Gigabit Ethernet can run on Cat5 UTP cable, but higher grades such as Cat5e or Cat6 are preferred because they're more reliable.

✦ **1000BaseLX:** Several varieties of fiber cable are used with Gigabit Ethernet, but the most popular is 1000BaseLX.

The TCP/IP Protocol Suite

TCP/IP, the protocol on which the Internet is built, is not a single protocol but rather an entire suite of related protocols. TCP is even older than Ethernet. It was first conceived in 1969 by the Department of Defense. For more on the history of TCP/IP, see the sidebar, "The fascinating story of TCP/IP," later in this chapter. Currently, the Internet Engineering Task Force (IETF) manages the TCP/IP protocol suite.

The TCP/IP suite is based on a four-layer model of networking similar to the seven-layer OSI model. Figure 2-7 shows how the TCP/IP model matches up with the OSI model and where some of the key TCP/IP protocols fit into the model. As you can see, the lowest layer of the model, the Network Interface layer, corresponds to the OSI model's Physical and Data Link layers. TCP/IP can run over a wide variety of Network Interface layer protocols, including Ethernet, as well as other protocols, such as token ring and FDDI (an older standard for fiber optic networks).

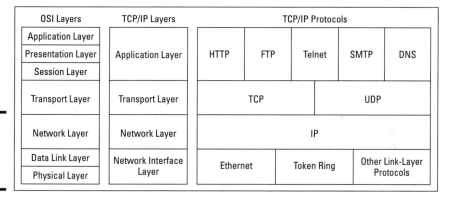

Figure 2-7:
TCP/IP and
the OSI
model.

The Application layer of the TCP/IP model corresponds to the upper three layers of the OSI model — the Session, Presentation, and Application layers. Many protocols can be used at this level. A few of the most popular are HTTP, FTP, Telnet, SMTP, DNS, and SNMP.

You can find out about many of the details of these and other TCP/IP protocols in Book IV. In the following sections, I just want to point out a few more details of the three most important protocols in the TCP/IP suite: IP, TCP, and UDP.

IP

Internet Protocol (IP) is a Network layer protocol responsible for delivering packets to network devices. The IP protocol uses logical IP addresses to refer to individual devices rather than physical (MAC) addresses. Address Resolution Protocol (ARP) handles the task of converting IP addresses to MAC addresses.

TECHNICAL STUFF

10Base what?

The names of Ethernet cable standards resemble the audible signals a quarterback might shout at the line of scrimmage. In reality, the cable designations consist of three parts:

✔ The first number is the speed of the network in Mbps. So, 10BaseT is for 10 Mbps networks (Standard Ethernet), 100BaseTX is for 100 Mbps networks (Fast Ethernet), and 1000BaseT is for 1,000 Mbps networks (Gigabit Ethernet).

✔ "Base" (short for "baseband") indicates the type of network transmission that the cable uses. Baseband transmissions carry one signal at a time and are relatively simple to implement. The alternative to baseband is *broadband,* which can carry more than one signal at a time but is more difficult to implement. At one time, broadband incarnations of the 802.*x* networking standards existed, but they have all but fizzled due to lack of use.

✔ The tail end of the designation indicates the cable type. For coaxial cables, a number is used that roughly indicates the maximum length of the cable in hundreds of meters. 10Base5 cables can run up to 500 meters. 10Base2 cables can run up to 185 meters. (The IEEE rounded 185 up to 200 to come up with the name 10Base2.) If the designation ends with a T, twisted-pair cable is used. Other letters are used for other types of cables.

Because IP addresses consist of a network part and a host part, IP is a routable protocol. As a result, IP can forward a packet to another network if the host isn't on the current network. After all, the capability to route packets across networks is where IP gets its name. An *internet* is a just a series of two or more connected TCP/IP networks that can be reached by routing.

TCP

Transmission Control Protocol (TCP) is a connection-oriented Transport layer protocol. TCP lets a device reliably send a packet to another device on the same network or on a different network. TCP ensures that each packet is delivered, if at all possible, by establishing a connection with the receiving device and then sending the packets. If a packet doesn't arrive, TCP resends the packet. The connection is closed only after the packet has been successfully delivered or an unrecoverable error condition has occurred.

One key aspect of TCP is that it's always used for one-to-one communications. In other words, TCP allows a single network device to exchange data with another single network device. TCP isn't used to broadcast messages to multiple network recipients. Instead, UDP is used for that purpose.

Many well-known Application layer protocols rely on TCP. For example, when a user running a web browser requests a page, the browser uses HTTP (HyperText Transfer Protocol) to send a request via TCP to a web server. When that web server receives the request, it uses HTTP to send the requested web page back to the browser, again via TCP. Other Application layer protocols that use TCP include Telnet (for terminal emulation), FTP (for file exchange), and SMTP (for e-mail).

UDP

User Datagram Protocol (UDP) is a connectionless Transport layer protocol used when the overhead of a connection isn't required. After UDP has placed a packet on the network (via the IP protocol), it forgets about it. UDP doesn't guarantee that the packet arrives at its destination. Most applications that use UDP simply wait for any replies expected as a result of packets sent via UDP. If a reply doesn't arrive within a certain period of time, the application either sends the packet again or gives up.

Probably the best-known Application layer protocol that uses UDP is the Domain Name System (DNS). When an application needs to access a domain name (such as www.wiley.com), DNS sends a UDP packet to a DNS server to look up the domain. When the server finds the domain, it returns the domain's IP address in another UDP packet. (Actually, the process is much more complicated than that. For a more detailed explanation, see Book IV, Chapter 4.)

Other Protocols Worth Knowing About

Although the vast majority of networks now use Ethernet andTCP/IP, a few other networking protocols are still in use and are therefore worth knowing about. In particular:

✦ **Network Basic Input/Output System (NetBIOS):** The basic application programming interface for network services on Windows computers. It's installed automatically when you install TCP/IP, but doesn't show up as a separate protocol when you view the network connection properties. (Refer to Figure 2-1.) NetBIOS is a Session layer protocol that can work with Transport layer protocols, such as TCP, SPX, or NetBEUI.

✦ **Network BIOS Extended User Interface (NetBEUI):** A Transport layer protocol designed for early IBM and Microsoft networks. NetBEUI is now considered obsolete.

✦ **IPX/SPX:** A protocol suite made popular in the 1980s by Novell for use with its NetWare servers. TCP/IP has become so dominant that IPX/SPX is rarely used now.

✦ **AppleTalk:** Apple's suite of network protocols. The AppleTalk suite includes a Physical and Data Link layer protocol called LocalTalk, but can also work with standard lower-level protocols, including Ethernet and token ring.

✦ **Systems Network Architecture (SNA):** An IBM networking architecture dating back to the 1970s, when mainframe computers roamed the earth and PCs had barely emerged from the primordial computer soup. SNA was designed primarily to support huge terminals such as airline reservations and banking systems, with tens of thousands of terminals attached to central host computers. Now that IBM mainframes support TCP/IP and terminal systems have all but vanished, SNA is beginning to fade away. Still, many networks that incorporate mainframe computers have to contend with SNA.

The fascinating story of TCP/IP

Some people are fascinated by history. They subscribe to cable TV just to get the History Channel. If you're one of those history buffs, you may be interested in the following chronicle of TCP/IP's humble origins. (For maximum effect, play some melancholy violin music in the background as you read the rest of this sidebar.)

In the summer of 1969, the four mop-topped singers from Liverpool were breaking up. The war in Vietnam was escalating. Astronauts Neil Armstrong and Buzz Aldrin walked on the moon. And the Department of Defense built a computer network called ARPANET to link its defense installations with several major universities throughout the United States.

By the early 1970s, ARPANET was becoming difficult to manage. So it was split into two networks: one for military use, called MILNET; and the other for nonmilitary use. The nonmilitary network retained the name ARPANET. To link MILNET with ARPANET, a new method of connecting networks — Internet Protocol (IP) — was invented.

The whole purpose of IP was to enable these two networks to communicate with each other.

Fortunately, the designers of IP realized that it wouldn't be too long before other networks wanted to join in the fun, so they designed IP to allow for more than two networks. In fact, their ingenious design allowed for tens of thousands of networks to communicate via IP.

The decision was a fortuitous one, as the Internet quickly began to grow. By the mid-1980s, the original ARPANET reached its limits. Just in time, the National Science Foundation (NSF) decided to get into the game. NSF had built a network called NSFNET to link its huge supercomputers. NSFNET replaced ARPANET as the new background for the Internet. Around that time, such magazines as *Time* and *Newsweek* began writing articles about this new phenomenon called the Internet, and the *Net* (as it became nicknamed) began to grow like wildfire. Soon NSFNET couldn't keep up with the growth, so several private commercial networks took over management of the Internet backbone. The Internet has grown at a dizzying rate ever since, and nobody knows how long this frenetic growth rate will continue. One thing is sure: TCP/IP is now the most popular networking protocol in the world.

Chapter 3: Understanding Network Hardware

In This Chapter

✔ Introducing servers

✔ Working with network interface cards

✔ Becoming familiar with network cable, network hubs, and switches

✔ Comparing repeaters, bridges, and routers

✔ Figuring out network storage

The building blocks of networks are network hardware devices, such as servers, adapter cards, cables, hubs, switches, routers, and so on. This chapter provides an overview of these building blocks.

Servers

Server computers are the lifeblood of any network. Servers provide the shared resources that network users crave, such as file storage, databases, e-mail, web services, and so on. Choosing the equipment you use for your network's servers is one of the key decisions you'll make when you set up a network. In the following sections, I describe some of the various ways you can equip your network's servers.

Right off the bat, I want to make one thing clear: Only the smallest networks can do without at least one dedicated server computer. For a home network or a small office network with only a few computers, you can get away with true peer-to-peer networking (where each client computer shares its resources such as file storage or printers, and a dedicated server computer isn't needed). For a detailed explanation of why this isn't a good idea for larger networks, see Chapter 3 of this minibook, as well as Book II, Chapter 1.

What's important in a server

Here are some general things to keep in mind when picking a server computer for your network:

✦ **Scalability:** The ability to increase the size and capacity of the server computer without unreasonable hassle. Purchasing a server computer that just meets your current needs is a major mistake because (rest assured) your needs will double within a year. If at all possible, equip your servers with far more disk space, RAM, and processor power than you currently need.

✦ **Reliability:** The old adage "you get what you pay for" applies especially well to server computers. Why spend $10,000 on a server computer when you can buy one with seemingly similar specifications at a discount electronics store for a mere $2,000? Well, reliability! When a client computer fails, only the person who uses that computer is affected. When a server fails, however, everyone on the network is affected. The less-expensive computer is probably made of inferior components that are more likely to fail.

✦ **Availability:** This concept is closely related to reliability. When a server computer fails, how long does it take to correct the problem and get the server up and running again? Server computers are designed so their components can be easily diagnosed and replaced, which minimizes the downtime that results when a component fails. In some servers, components are *hot swappable* (certain components can be replaced without shutting down the server). Some servers are fault-tolerant so that they can continue to operate even if a major component fails.

✦ **Service and support:** Service and support are often overlooked factors when picking computers. If a component in a server computer fails, do you have someone on site qualified to repair the broken computer? If not, you should get an on-site maintenance contract for the computer.

Don't settle for a maintenance contract that requires you to take the computer in to a repair shop or, worse, mail it to a repair facility. You can't afford to be without your server that long.

Components of a server computer

The hardware components that make up a typical server computer are similar to the components used in less-expensive client computers. However, server computers are usually built from higher-grade components than client computers for the reasons given in the preceding section. The following paragraphs describe the typical components of a server computer:

✦ **Motherboard:** A motherboard is the computer's main electronic circuit board to which all the other components of your computer are connected. More than any other component, the motherboard *is* the computer. All other components attach to the motherboard.

The major components on the motherboard include the processor (CPU), supporting circuitry (the chipset), memory, expansion slots, a standard IDE hard drive controller, and I/O ports for devices such as keyboards, mice, and printers. Some motherboards also include additional built-in features such as a graphic adapter, SCSI disk controller, or network interface.

✦ **Processor:** The CPU is the brain of the computer. Although the processor isn't the only component that affects overall system performance, it's the one that most people think of first when deciding what type of server to purchase. At the time of this writing, Intel had two processor models specifically designed for use in server computers:

- *Itanium 9300:* Quad (4) core, 1.60–1.73GHz

- *Xeon:* Dual–octo core (2–8), 1.8–3.3GHz

Each motherboard is designed to support a particular type of processor. CPUs come in two basic mounting styles: slot or socket. However, you can choose from several types of slots and sockets, so you have to make sure that the motherboard supports the specific slot or socket style used by the CPU. Some server motherboards have two or more slots or sockets to hold two or more CPUs.

Clock speed refers to how fast the basic clock that drives the processor's operation ticks. In theory, the faster the clock speed, the faster the processor. However, clock speed alone is reliable only for comparing processors within the same family. In fact, Intel Itanium processors are faster than Xeon processors at the same clock speed. (Itanium processor models contain more advanced circuitry than the older model, so they can accomplish more work with each tick of the clock.)

The number of processor cores also has a dramatic effect on performance. Each processor core acts as if it's a separate processor. Most server computers use dual-core (two processor cores) or quad-core (four cores) chips.

✦ **Memory:** Don't scrimp on memory. People rarely complain about servers having too much memory. Many different types of memory are available, so you have to pick the right type of memory to match the memory supported by your motherboard. The total memory capacity of the server depends on the motherboard. It isn't unusual to see servers configured with anywhere from 32GB–512GB RAM.

✦ **Hard drives:** Most desktop computers use inexpensive SATA hard drives, which are adequate for individual users. (Because of its low cost, SATA drives are often used in inexpensive servers.) Because performance is more important for servers, though, SCSI drives are typically used instead. For the best performance, use the SCSI drives along with a high-performance SCSI controller card.

✦ **Network connection:** The network connection is one of the most important parts of any server. Many servers have network adapters built into the motherboard. If your server isn't equipped as such, you'll need to add a separate network adapter card. See the section, "Network Interface Cards," later in this chapter, for more information.

✦ **Video:** Fancy graphics aren't that important for a server computer. You can equip your servers with inexpensive generic video cards and monitors without affecting network performance. (This is one of the few areas where it's acceptable to cut costs on a server.)

✦ **Power supply:** Because a server usually has more devices than a typical desktop computer, it requires a larger power supply (typically 600 watts). If the server houses a large number of hard drives, it may require an even larger power supply.

Server form factors

Form factor refers to the size, shape, and packaging of a hardware device. Server computers typically come in one of three form factors:

✦ **Tower case:** Most servers are housed in a traditional tower case, similar to the tower cases used for desktop computers. A typical server tower case is 18" high, 20" deep, and 9" wide with room inside for a motherboard, five or more hard drives, and other components. Tower cases also come with built-in power supplies.

Some server cases include advanced features specially designed for servers, such as redundant power supplies (so both servers can continue operating if one of the power supplies fails), hot-swappable fans, and hot-swappable disk drive bays. (*Hot-swappable* components can be replaced without powering down the server.)

✦ **Rack mount:** If you need only a few servers, tower cases are fine. You can just place the servers next to each other on a table or in a cabinet that's specially designed to hold servers. If you need more than a few servers, though, space can quickly become an issue. For example, what if your departmental network requires a bank of ten file servers? You'd need a pretty long table.

Rack-mount servers are designed to save space when you need more than a few servers in a confined area. A rack-mount server is housed in a small chassis that's designed to fit into a standard 19" equipment rack. The rack allows you to vertically stack servers to save space.

✦ **Blade servers:** Blade servers are designed to save even more space than rack-mount servers. A *blade server* is a server on a single card that can be mounted alongside other blade servers in a blade chassis, which itself fits into a standard 19" equipment rack. A typical blade chassis holds six or more servers, depending on the manufacturer.

Saving space with a KVM switch

If you have more than two or three servers in one location, consider getting a KVM switch to save space by connecting several server computers to a single keyboard, monitor, and mouse. Then, you can control any of the servers from a single keyboard, monitor, and mouse by turning a dial or by pressing a button on the KVM switch.

Simple KVM switches are mechanical affairs that let you choose from 2–16 (or more) computers.

More elaborate KVM switches can control more computers, using a pop-up menu or a special keyboard combination to switch among computers. Some advanced KVMs can even control a mix of PCs and Macintosh computers from a single keyboard, monitor, and mouse.

To find more information about KVM switches, search online for **"KVM"**.

One of the key benefits of using blade servers is that you don't need a separate power supply for each server. Instead, the blade enclosure provides power for all its blade servers. Some blade server systems provide rack-mounted power supplies that can serve several blade enclosures mounted in a single rack.

In addition, the blade enclosure provides keyboard, video, and mouse (KVM) switching so that you don't have to use a separate KVM switch. You can control any of the servers in a blade server network from a single keyboard, monitor, and mouse. (For more information, see the sidebar, "Saving space with a KVM switch.")

Another big benefit of using blade servers is that they drastically cut down the amount of cable clutter. With rack-mount servers, each server requires its own power, keyboard, video, mouse, and network cables. With blade servers, a single set of cables can service all the servers in a blade enclosure.

Network Interface Cards

Every computer on a network, both clients and servers, requires a network interface card (NIC) to access the network. A NIC is usually a separate adapter card that slides into one of the server's motherboard expansion slots. However, most newer computers have a NIC built into the motherboard, so a separate card isn't needed.

For client computers, you can usually get away with using the inexpensive built-in NIC because client computers are used to connect only one user to the network. However, the NIC in a server computer connects many network users to the server. As a result, it makes sense to spend more money on a higher-quality NIC for a heavily used server. Most network administrators prefer to use name-brand cards from manufacturers such as Intel, SMC, or 3Com.

Most NICs made today support 1 Gbps networking and will also support slower 100 Mbps and even ancient 10 Mbps networks. These cards automatically adjust their speed to match the speed of the network. So, you can use a gigabit card on a network that has older 100 Mbps cards without trouble. You can find inexpensive gigabit cards for as little as $5 each, but a typical name-brand card (such as Linksys or Intel) will cost around $30.

Here are a few other points to ponder concerning NICs:

✦ A NIC is a Physical layer and a Data Link layer device. Because a NIC establishes a network node, it must have a physical (MAC) network address. (Read about MAC addresses in Chapter 2 of this minibook.) The MAC address is burned into the NIC at the factory, so you can't change it. Every NIC ever manufactured has a unique MAC address.

✦ For server computers, it makes sense to use more than one NIC. That way, the server can handle more network traffic. Some server NICs have two or more network interfaces built into a single card.

✦ Fiber optic networks also require NICs. Fiber optic NICs are still too expensive for desktop use in most networks. Instead, they're used for high-speed backbones. If a server connects to a high-speed fiber backbone, it will need a fiber optic NIC that matches the fiber optic cable being used.

Network Cable

Nearly all modern networks are constructed using twisted-pair cable, which looks a little like phone cable but is subtly different. (Read about this cable type in Chapter 2 of this minibook.)

You may encounter other types of cable in an existing network: coax cable that resembles TV cable, thick yellow cable that used to be the only type of cable used for Ethernet, fiber optic cables that span long distances at high speeds, or thick twisted-pair bundles that carry multiple sets of twisted-pair cable between wiring closets in a large building. But as I mention, twisted-pair cable works for nearly all new networks.

 A choice that's becoming more popular every day is to forego network cable and instead build your network using wireless network components. Because Book V is devoted exclusively to wireless networking, I don't describe wireless network components in this chapter.

Coaxial cable

A type of cable that was once popular for Ethernet networks is coaxial cable, sometimes called *thinnet* or *BNC cable* because of the type of connectors used on each end of the cable. Thinnet cable operates only at 10 Mbps and is rarely used for new networks. However, you'll find plenty of existing thinnet networks still being used. Figure 3-1 shows a typical coaxial cable.

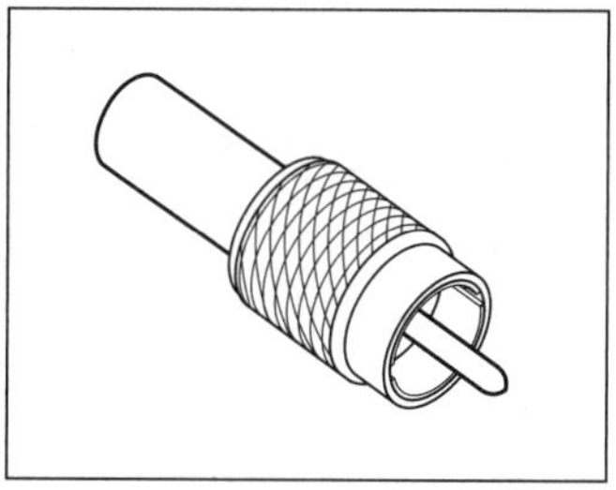

Figure 3-1:
Coax cable.

Here are some salient points about coaxial cable:

✦ You attach thinnet to the network interface card by using a goofy twist-on BNC connector. You can purchase preassembled cables with BNC connectors already attached in lengths of 25' or 50', or you can buy bulk cable on a big spool and attach the connectors yourself with a special tool. (I suggest buying preassembled cables, though. Attaching connectors to bulk cable can be tricky.)

✦ With coaxial cables, you connect your computers point-to-point in a bus topology. (Read about topologies in Chapter 1 of this minibook.) At each computer, a T connector is used to connect two cables to the network interface card.

✦ A special terminator plug is required at each end of a series of thinnet cables. The terminator prevents data from spilling out the end of the cable and staining the carpet.

✦ The cables strung end-to-end from one terminator to the other are collectively called a *segment.* The maximum length of a thinnet segment is about 200 meters (m; actually, 185m). You can connect as many as 30 computers on one segment. To span a distance greater than 185m or to connect more than 30 computers, you must use two or more segments with a repeater to connect each segment.

✦ Although Ethernet coaxial cable resembles TV coaxial cable, the two types of cable aren't interchangeable. Don't try to cut costs by wiring your network with cheap TV cable.

Twisted-pair cable

The most popular type of cable today is twisted-pair cable (UTP). (The U stands for "unshielded," but no one says "unshielded twisted pair." Just "twisted pair.") UTP cable is even cheaper than thin coaxial cable. Best of all, many modern buildings are already wired with twisted-pair cable because this type of wiring is often used with modern phone systems. Figure 3-2 shows a twisted-pair cable.

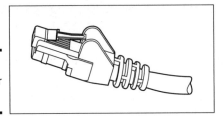

Figure 3-2:
Twisted-pair
cable.

When you use UTP cable to construct an Ethernet network, you connect the computers in a star arrangement. (Read about topologies in Chapter 1 of this minibook.) In the center of the star is a hub. Depending on the model, Ethernet switches enable you to connect from 4 to 48 computers using UTP.

An advantage of UTP's star arrangement is that if one cable goes bad, only the computer attached to that cable is affected; the rest of the network continues to chug along. With coaxial cable, a bad cable affects the entire network, and not just the computer to which the bad cable is connected.

Here are a few other details that you should know about twisted-pair cabling:

✦ UTP cable consists of pairs of thin wire twisted around each other; several such pairs are gathered up inside an outer insulating jacket. Ethernet uses two pairs of wires, or four wires altogether. The number of pairs in a UTP cable varies, but it's often more than two.

✦ UTP cable comes in various grades: categories. Don't use anything less than Cat5e cable for your network. Although cheaper, UTP may not be able to support faster networks.

Although higher-category cables are more expensive than lower-category cables, the real cost of installing Ethernet cabling is the labor required to actually pull the cables through the walls. As a result, I recommend that you always spend the extra money to buy Cat5e cable.

If you want to sound like you know what you're talking about, say "Cat5e" instead of "Category 5e." More nerd-speak: The *e* stands for "enhanced."

✦ Many existing networks are cabled with Cat5 cable, which is fine for 100Mbps networks but isn't rated for Gigabit networks. Cat5e cable and Cat6 cable support 1,000 Mbps networks.

✦ UTP cable connectors look like modular phone connectors but are a bit larger. UTP connectors are officially called "RJ-45 connectors."

✦ Like thinnet cable, UTP cable is also sold in prefabricated lengths. However, RJ-45 connectors are much easier to attach to bulk UTP cable than BNC cables are to attach to bulk coaxial cable. As a result, I suggest that you buy bulk cable and connectors unless your network consists of just two or three computers. A basic crimp tool to attach the RJ-45 connectors costs about $50.

✦ The maximum allowable cable length between the hub and the computer is 100m (about 328′).

Switches

The biggest difference between using coaxial cable and twisted-pair cable is that when you use twisted-pair cable, you also must use a switch. Years ago, switches were expensive devices — expensive enough that most do-it-yourself networkers who were building small networks opted for thinnet cable in order to avoid the expense and hassle of using hubs.

Nowadays, the cost of switches has dropped so much that the advantages of twisted-pair cabling outweigh the hassle and cost of using switches. With twisted-pair cabling, you can more easily add new computers to the network, move computers, find and correct cable problems, and service the computers that you need to remove from the network temporarily.

In some older networks, you may see a hub used instead of a switch. Hubs were popular because they were less expensive than switches. However, the cost of switches has come down dramatically, pushing hubs into relic status. If you have an older network that uses hubs and seems to run slowly, you can probably improve the network's speed by replacing the older hubs with newer switches. For more information, see the sidebar, "Hubs and switches demystified."

If you use twisted-pair cabling, you need to know some of the ins and outs of using hubs:

✦ Because you must run a cable from each computer to the switch, find a central location for the switch to which you can easily route the cables.

✦ The switch requires electrical power, so make sure that an electrical outlet is handy.

✦ Purchase a switch with at least twice as many connections as you need. Don't buy a four-port switch if you want to network four computers because when (not *if*) you add the fifth computer, you have to buy another switch.

✦ You can connect — daisy-chain — switches to one another, as shown in Figure 3-3. You connect one end of a cable to a port on one switch and the other end to a port on the other switch. On some switches, you must use a special designated port for daisy-chaining, so be sure to read your instructions to make sure that you daisy-chain it properly.

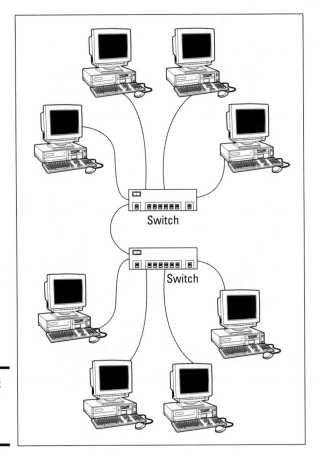

Figure 3-3:
Daisy-
chaining
switches.

✦ You can't daisy-chain more than three switches, so if you have a large number of computers, carefully design your network so that no more than three switches are daisy-chained. Fortunately, you can get stackable switches that have high-speed direct connections that enable two or more switches to be counted as a single switch.

✦ Expensive network hubs have network-management features that support Simple Network Management Protocol (SNMP). Such hubs are *managed hubs.* Unless your network is very large and you know what SNMP is, don't bother with the more expensive managed hubs. You'd be paying for a feature that you may never use.

✦ For large networks, you may want to consider using a *managed switch,* which allows you to monitor and control various aspects of the switch's operation from a remote computer. The switch can alert you when something goes wrong with the network, and it can keep performance statistics so that you can determine which parts of the network are heavily used and which aren't. A managed switch costs two or three times as much as an unmanaged switch, but for larger networks, the benefits of managed switches are well worth the additional cost.

Hubs and switches demystified

Both hubs and switches let you connect multiple computers to a twisted-pair network. Switches are more efficient than hubs, but not just because they're faster. If you really want to know, here's the actual difference between a hub and a switch:

✔ **Hub:** Every packet that arrives at the hub on any of its ports is automatically sent out on every other port. The hub has to do this because it's a Physical layer device, so it has no way to keep track of which computer is connected to each port. For example, suppose that John's computer is connected to port 1 on an 8-port hub, and Andrea's computer is connected to port 5. If John's computer sends a packet of information to Andrea's computer, the hub receives the packet on port 1 and then

sends it out on ports 2–8. All the computers connected to the hub get to see the packet so that they can determine whether the packet was intended for them.

✔ **Switch:** This Data Link layer device can look into the packets that pass through it to examine a critical piece of Data Link layer information: the MAC address. With this information in hand, a switch can keep track of which computer is connected to each of its ports. So if John's computer on port 1 sends a packet to Andrea's computer on port 5, the switch receives the packet on port 1 and then sends the packet out on port 5 only. This process is not only faster, but also improves the security of the system because other computers don't see packets that aren't meant for them.

Repeaters

A *repeater* (sometimes called an *extender*) is a gizmo that gives your network signals a boost so that the signals can travel farther. It's kind of like a Gatorade station in a marathon. As the signals travel past the repeater, they pick up a cup of Gatorade, take a sip, splash the rest of it on their heads, toss the cup, and hop in a cab when they're sure that no one is looking.

You need a repeater when the total length of a single span of network cable exceeds 100m (328'). The 100m length limit applies to the cable that connects a computer to the switch or the cable that connects switches to each other when switches are daisy-chained. In other words, you can connect each computer to the switch with no more than 100m of cable, and you can connect switches to each other with no more than 100m of cable.

Figure 3-4 shows how you can use a repeater to connect two groups of computers that are too far apart to be strung on a single segment. When you use a repeater like this, the repeater divides the cable into two segments. The cable length limit still applies to the cable on each side of the repeater.

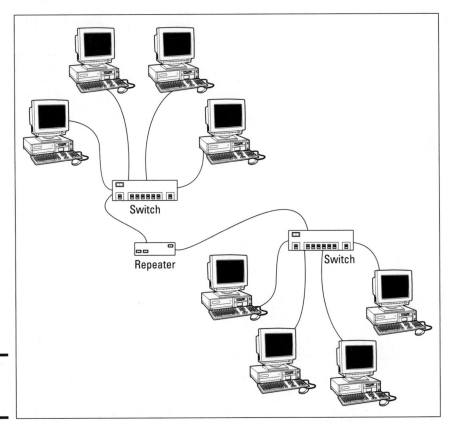

Figure 3-4:
Using a
repeater.

Here are some points to ponder when you lie awake tonight wondering about repeaters:

✦ Repeaters are not typically used with twisted-pair networks.

Well, technically, that's not true because the switches themselves function as repeaters. So what I really meant is that you typically see repeaters as stand-alone devices only when a single cable segment would be more than 100m.

✦ A basic rule of Ethernet life is that a signal can't pass through more than three repeaters on its way from one node to another. That doesn't mean you can't have more than three repeaters or switches, but if you do, you have to carefully plan the network cabling so that the three-repeater rule isn't violated.

✦ Repeaters are legitimate components of a by-the-book Ethernet network. They don't extend the maximum length of a single segment; they just enable you to tie two segments together. Beware of the little black boxes that claim to extend the segment limit beyond the standard 100-meter limit for 10/100BaseT cable. These products usually work, but playing by the rules is better.

Bridges

A *bridge* connects two networks so that they act as if they're one network. Bridges are used to partition one large network into two smaller networks for performance reasons. You can think of a bridge as a kind of smart repeater.

Repeaters listen to signals coming down one network cable, amplify them, and send them down the other cable. They do this blindly, paying no attention to the content of the messages that they repeat.

In contrast, a bridge is a little smarter about the messages that come down the pike. For starters, most bridges have the capability to listen to the network and automatically figure out the address of each computer on both sides of the bridge. Then the bridge can inspect each message that comes from one side of the bridge and broadcast it on the other side of the bridge, but only if the message is intended for a computer that's on the other side.

This key feature enables bridges to partition a large network into two smaller, more efficient networks. Bridges work best in networks that are highly segregated. For example (humor me here — I'm a Dr. Seuss fan), suppose that the Sneetches networked all their computers and discovered that although the Star-Bellied Sneetches' computers talked to each other frequently and the Plain-Bellied Sneetches' computers also talked to each other frequently, rarely did a Star-Bellied Sneetch's computer talk to a Plain-Bellied Sneetch's computer.

A bridge can partition the Sneetchnet into two networks: the Star-Bellied network and the Plain-Bellied network. The bridge automatically learns which computers are on the Star-Bellied network and which are on the Plain-Bellied network. The bridge forwards messages from the Star-Bellied side to the Plain-Bellied side (and vice versa) only when necessary. The overall performance of both networks improves, although the performance of any network operation that has to travel over the bridge slows down a bit.

Here are a few additional things to consider about bridges:

✦ Some bridges also have the capability to translate the messages from one format to another. For example, if the Star-Bellied Sneetches build their network with Ethernet and the Plain-Bellied Sneetches use token ring, a bridge can tie the two together.

✦ You can purchase a basic bridge to partition two Ethernet networks for about $500. More sophisticated bridges can cost as much as $5,000 or more.

✦ For simple bridge applications, you don't need an expensive specialized bridge device; instead, you can just use a switch. After all, a switch is effectively a multiport bridge.

✦ If you've never read Dr. Seuss' classic story of the Sneetches, you should.

Routers

A router is like a bridge, but with a key difference. Bridges are Data Link layer devices, so they can tell the MAC address of the network node to which each message is sent, and can also forward the message to the appropriate segment. However, they can't peek into the message itself to see what type of information is being sent. In contrast, a router is a Network layer device, so it can work with the network packets at a higher level. In particular, a router can examine the IP address of the packets that pass through it. And because IP addresses have both a network and a host address, a router can determine what network a message is coming from and going to. Bridges are ignorant of this information.

One key difference between a bridge and a router is that a bridge is essentially transparent to the network. In contrast, a router is itself a node on the network, with its own MAC and IP addresses. This means that messages can be directed to a router, which can then examine the contents of the message to determine how it should handle the message.

You can configure a network with several routers that can work cooperatively together. For example, some routers are able to monitor the network to determine the most efficient path for sending a message to its ultimate destination. If a part of the network is extremely busy, a router can automatically route messages along a less-busy route. In this respect, the router is kind of like a traffic reporter up in a helicopter. The router knows that the 101 is bumper-to-bumper all the way through Sunnyvale, so it sends the message on 280 instead.

Here's some additional information about routers:

✦ The functional distinctions between bridges and routers — and switches and hubs, for that matter — get blurrier all the time. As bridges, hubs, and switches become more sophisticated, they're able to take on some of the chores that used to require a router, thus putting many routers out of work.

✦ Some routers are nothing more than computers with several network interface cards and special software to perform the router functions.

✦ Routers can also connect networks that are geographically distant from each other via a phone line (using modems) or Integrated Services Digital Network (ISDN).

✦ You can also use a router to join your LAN to the Internet. Figure 3-5 shows a router used for this purpose.

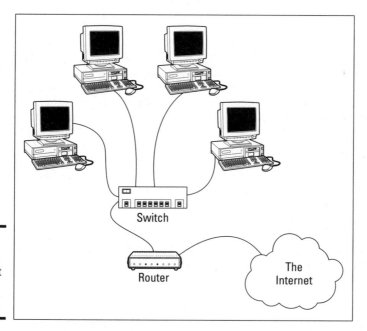

Figure 3-5:
Connect to
the Internet
with a
router.

Network Attached Storage

Many network servers exist solely to make disk space available to network users. As networks grow to support more users, and users require more disk space, network administrators are constantly finding ways to add more storage to their networks. One way to do that is to add more file servers.

However, a simpler and less-expensive way is to use network attached storage (NAS).

A *NAS* device is a self-contained file server that's preconfigured and ready to run. All you have to do to set it up is take it out of the box, plug it in, and turn it on. NAS devices are easy to set up and configure, easy to maintain, and less expensive than traditional file servers.

Don't confuse NAS with a related technology, a storage area network (SAN). SAN is a much more complicated and expensive technology that provides huge quantities of data storage for large networks. For more information on SAN, see the sidebar, "SAN is NAS spelled backward."

A typical entry-level NAS device is the Dell PowerVault NX300. This self-contained file server, built into a small rack-mount chassis, supports up to four hard drives with a total capacity up to 12TB. The NX300 uses a Xeon processor and two built-in gigabit network ports.

The Dell NX300 runs a special version of Windows Server 2008 (Windows Storage Server 2008), and this version of Windows is designed specifically for NAS devices. It allows you to configure the network storage from any computer on the network by using a web browser.

Some NAS devices use customized versions of Linux rather than Windows Storage Server. Also, in some systems, the OS resides on a separate hard drive isolated from the shared disks. This prevents the user from inadvertently damaging the OS.

Network Printers

Although you can share a printer on a network by attaching the printer to a server computer, many printers have network interfaces built in. This lets you connect the printer directly to the network. Then, network users can connect to the printer and use it without going through a server.

Even if you connect a printer directly to the network, I recommend having the printer managed by a server computer running a network operating system (NOS), such as Windows Server 2003 or 2007. That way, the server can store print jobs sent to the printer by multiple users and print the jobs in the order in which they were received. Read more about NOSes in the next chapter.

SAN is NAS spelled backward

Don't confuse storage area network (SAN) and network attached storage (NAS). Both refer to relatively new network technologies that help you manage network disk storage. However, NAS is a much simpler and less-expensive technology. A NAS device is nothing more than an inexpensive self-contained file server. Using NAS devices actually simplifies the task of adding storage to a network because the NAS eliminates the chore of configuring a network operating system for routine file-sharing tasks.

A SAN is designed for managing very large amounts of network storage — sometimes downright huge amounts. A SAN consists of three components: storage devices (perhaps hundreds of them), a separate high-speed network (usually fiber optic) that directly connects the storage devices to each other, and one or more SAN servers that connect the SAN to the local area network (LAN). The SAN server manages the storage devices attached to the SAN and allows users of the LAN to access the storage.

Setting up and managing a storage area network is a job for a SAN expert. For more information about storage area networks, see the home page of the Storage Networking Industry Association at www.snia.org.

Chapter 4: Understanding Network Operating Systems

In This Chapter

✔ Understanding what network operating systems do

✔ Figuring out the advantages of Windows Server 8

✔ Taking a look at other Windows Server versions

✔ Delving into peer-to-peer networking

✔ Exploring other network operating systems

*O*ne of the basic choices that you must make is which network operating system (NOS) to use as the foundation for your network. This chapter begins with a description of several important features found in all NOSes. Then it provides an overview of the advantages and disadvantages of the most popular NOSes.

Network Operating System Features

All NOSes, from the simplest to the most complex, must provide certain core functions: connect to other computers on the network, share files and other resources, provide for security, and so on. In the following sections, I describe some of these core NOS features in general terms.

Network support

An NOS must support a wide variety of networking protocols to meet the needs of its users because a large network typically consists of a mixture of various versions of Windows, as well as a few scattered Macintosh (mostly in the art department) and possibly some Linux computers. The computers often have distinct protocols.

Many servers have more than one network interface card (NIC) installed. In that case, an NOS must be able to support multiple network connections. Ideally, the NOS should have the ability to balance the network load among its network interfaces. In addition, in the event that one of the connections fails, an NOS should be able to seamlessly switch to another connection.

Finally, most NOSes include a built-in ability to function as a router that connects two networks. The NOS router functions should also include firewall features to keep unauthorized packets from entering the local network.

File-sharing services

One of the most important functions of an NOS is its ability to share resources with other network users. The most common shared resource is the server's file system. A network server must be able to share some or all of its disk space with other users so that those users can treat the server's disk space as an extension of their own computers' disk spaces.

The NOS allows the system administrator to determine which portions of the server's file system to share. Although an entire hard drive can be shared, this isn't common. Instead, individual directories or folders are shared. The administrator can control which users are allowed to access each shared folder.

Because file sharing is the reason why many network servers exist, NOSes have more sophisticated disk management features than are found in desktop OSes. For example, most NOSes can manage two or more hard drives as if they were a single drive. In addition, most can create *mirrors,* which automatically keep backup copies of drives on a second drive.

Multitasking

Only one user at a time uses a desktop computer; however, multiple users simultaneously use server computers. As a result, an NOS must provide support for multiple users who access the server remotely via the network.

At the heart of multiuser support is *multitasking,* which is the capability of an OS to execute more than one program (a task or a process) at a time. Multitasking OSes are like the guy who used to spin plates balanced on sticks on the old *Ed Sullivan Show.* He'd run from plate to plate, trying to keep them all spinning so they wouldn't fall off the sticks — and just for grins, he was blindfolded or rode on a unicycle.

Although multitasking creates the appearance that two or more programs are executing on the computer at one time, in reality, a computer with a single processor can execute only one program at a time. The OS switches the CPU from one program to another to create the appearance that several programs are executing simultaneously, but at any given moment, only one of the programs is actually executing. The others are patiently waiting for their turns. (However, if the computer has more than one CPU, the CPUs *can* execute programs simultaneously, which is multiprocessing.)

To see multitasking in operation on a Windows computer, press Ctrl+Alt+Delete to bring up the Windows Task Manager and then click the Processes tab. All the tasks currently active on the computer appear.

For multitasking to work reliably, the NOS must completely isolate the executing programs from each other. Otherwise, one program may perform an operation that adversely affects another program. Multitasking operating systems do this by providing each task with its own unique address space that makes it almost impossible for one task to affect memory that belongs to another task.

In most cases, each program executes as a single task or process within the memory address space allocated to the task. However, a single program can also be split into several tasks. This technique is usually called *multithreading,* and the program's tasks are *threads.*

The two approaches to multitasking are

✦ **Preemptive:** The OS decides how long each task gets to execute before it should step aside so that another task can execute. When a task's time is up, the OS task manager interrupts the task and switches to the next task in line. All NOSes in widespread use today use preemptive multitasking.

✦ **Nonpreemptive:** Each task that gets control of the CPU is allowed to run until it voluntarily gives up control so that another task can run. Nonpreemptive multitasking requires less OS overhead because the OS doesn't have to keep track of how long each task has run. However, programs have to be carefully written so they don't hog the computer all to themselves.

Directory services

Directories are everywhere. When you need to make a phone call, you look up the number in a phone directory. When you need to find the address of a client, you look up the name in your Rolodex. And when you need to find the Sam Goody store at a shopping mall, you look for the mall directory.

Networks have directories, too. Network directories provide information about the resources that are available on the network, such as users, computers, printers, shared folders, and files. Directories are an essential part of any NOS.

In early NOSes, such as Windows NT 3.1 and NetWare 3.*x,* each server computer maintained its own directory database of resources that were available on just that server. The problem with that approach was that network administrators had to maintain each directory database separately. That wasn't too bad for networks with just a few servers, but maintaining the directory on a network with dozens or even hundreds of servers was next to impossible.

In addition, early directory services were application specific. For example, a server would have one directory database for user logins, another for file sharing, and yet another for e-mail addresses. Each directory had its own tools for adding, updating, and deleting directory entries.

Most modern networks — particularly those based on Windows servers — use the Active Directory (AD) directory service. AD is essentially a database that organizes information about a network and allows users and computers to gain permission to access network resources. AD is simple enough to use for small networks with just a few dozen computers and users, but powerful enough to work with large networks containing tens of thousands of computers.

Security services

All NOSes must provide some measure of security to protect the network from unauthorized access. Hacking seems to be the national pastime these days. With most computer networks connected to the Internet, anyone anywhere in the world can and probably will try to break into your network.

The most basic type of security is handled through *user accounts,* which grant individual users the right to access the network resources and also govern what resources each user can access. User accounts are secured by passwords, so, good password policy is a cornerstone of any security system. Most NOSes let you establish password policies, such as requiring that passwords have a minimum length and include a mix of letters and numerals. In addition, passwords can be set to expire after a certain number of days, so users can be forced to frequently change their passwords.

Most NOSes also provide for *data encryption,* which scrambles data before it is sent over the network or saved on disk, and *digital certificates,* which are used to ensure that users are who they say they are and files are what they claim to be.

Microsoft Server Operating Systems

Over the years, Microsoft has released several versions of its Windows-based server OS: Windows NT Server 4, Windows 2000 Server, Windows Server 2003, Windows Server 2008, and now Windows Server 2012. Because Windows Server 2012 is so new, most organizations are still using Windows Server 2008 or 2003. In fact, plenty of organizations are using Windows 2000 Server, and a few (mostly on deserted islands cut off from civilization) still run Windows NT Server 4.

NTFS drives

All server versions of Windows use a special type of formatting for hard drives, different from the standard FAT system used by MS-DOS since the early 1980s. (FAT stands for File Allocation Table, in case you're interested.) The file system — NTFS (NT File System) — offers many advantages over FAT drives:

✔ Improved efficiency using hard drive space. NTFS can cram more data onto a given hard drive than FAT.

✔ Better security features than FAT drives. NTFS stores security information on disk for each file and directory. In contrast, FAT has only rudimentary security features.

✔ More reliable drives. NTFS keeps duplicate copies of important information, such as the location of each file on the hard drive. If a problem develops on an NTFS drive, Windows NT Server can probably correct the problem without losing any data. FAT drives are prone to losing information.

Each new version builds on the previous version by introducing new and improved features. However, keep in mind as you read the following sections that Windows NT Server 4, Windows 2000 Server, and Windows Server 2003 are considered obsolete.

Windows NT Server 4

Windows NT Server was the last in a long series of Windows servers dubbed *NT,* which stood for New Technology. The "new technology" that got everyone so excited about Windows NT in the first place was 32-bit processing, which was a huge step up from the 16-bit processing of earlier versions of Windows. Windows NT was the first Microsoft OS that was reliable enough to work as a network server on large networks. Pushing 20 years old, though, Windows NT 4 is hopelessly obsolete, but NT 4 is still important because of its legacy. Many OS features first introduced as part of Windows NT 4 are still in use.

Probably the most important feature of Windows NT is its directory model, which is based on the concept of domains: a group of computers managed by a single directory database. To access shared resources within a domain, you must have a valid user account within the domain and also be granted rights to access the resources in which you're interested. The domain system uses 15-character NetBIOS names to access individual computers within a domain and to name the domain itself.

Windows 2000 Server

Windows 2000 Server built on the strengths of Windows NT Server 4 by adding new features that made Windows 2000 Server faster, easier to manage, more reliable, and easier to use for large and small networks alike.

The most significant new feature offered by Windows 2000 Server was Active Directory (AD), which provided a single directory of all network resources and enabled program developers to incorporate the directory into their programs. AD dropped the 15-character domain and computer names in favor of Internet-style DNS names, such as Marketing.MyCompany.com or Sales. YourCompany.com. (However, it still supports the old-style names for older clients that don't deal well with DNS names.)

Windows 2000 Server came in three versions:

+ **Windows 2000 Server:** A basic server, designed for small- to medium-sized networks. It included all the basic server features, including file and printer sharing, and acted as a web and e-mail server.

+ **Windows 2000 Advanced Server:** The next step up, designed for larger networks. Advanced Server could support server computers with up to 8GB of memory (not hard drive — RAM!) and four integrated processors instead of the single processor that desktop computers and most server computers had.

+ **Windows 2000 Datacenter Server:** Supported servers that have as many as 32 processors with up to 64GB of RAM and was specially designed for large database applications.

For small networks (50 or fewer computers), Microsoft offered a Small Business Server bundle, which included the following components for one low, low price:

+ **Windows Server 2003:** The OS for your network server

+ **Exchange Server 2003:** For e-mail and instant messaging

+ **SQL Server 2000:** A database server

+ **FrontPage 2000:** For building websites

+ **Outlook 2000:** For reading e-mail

Windows Server 2003

The next server version of Windows — Windows Server 2003 — built on Windows 2000 Server, with the following added features:

✦ An improved version of AD with tighter security, an easier-to-use interface, and better performance.

✦ A better and easier-to-use system management interface (Manage My Server). For those who prefer using a command line interface (CLI), Windows Server 2003 included a more comprehensive set of CLI tools. And the familiar Microsoft Management Console tools from Windows 2000 Server were still viable.

✦ A major change in the application programming interface (API) for Windows programs: the .NET Framework.

✦ Support for ever-larger clusters of computers. (A *cluster* is a set of computers that work as if they were a single server.) Windows 2000 Server Datacenter Edition and previous versions supported clusters of four servers; Windows Server 2003 Enterprise and Datacenter Editions supported clusters of eight servers. (Obviously, this is a benefit only for very large networks. The rest of us should just grin and say, "Cool!")

✦ An enhanced distributed file system that lets you combine drives on several servers to create one shared volume.

✦ Support for storage area networks (SANs).

✦ A built-in Internet firewall to secure your Internet connection.

✦ A new version of Microsoft's web server, Internet Information Services (IIS) 6.0.

Like its predecessor, Windows Server 2003 shipped in several versions:

✦ **Standard Edition:** If you're using Windows Server 2003 as a file server or to provide other basic network services, you'll use this basic version. Standard Edition can support servers with up to four processors and 4GB of RAM.

✦ **Web Edition:** A version of Windows 2003 optimized for use as a web server.

✦ **Enterprise Edition:** Designed for larger networks, this version can support servers with up to eight processors, 32GB of RAM, server clusters, and advanced features designed for high performance and reliability.

✦ **Datacenter Edition:** The most powerful version of Windows 2003, with support for servers with 64 processors, 64GB of RAM, and server clusters, as well as advanced fault-tolerance features designed to keep the server running for mission-critical applications.

Windows Server 2008

In February of 2008, Microsoft released Windows Server 2008, which added many new features:

✦ Even more enhancements to AD, including the ability to manage digital certificates, a new type of domain controller called a *read-only domain controller,* and the ability to stop and restart AD services without shutting down the entire server.

✦ A new graphical user interface (GUI) based on Windows Vista, including the new Server Manager all-in-one management tool.

✦ A new version of the OS — Server Core — which has no GUI. Server Core is run entirely from the command line or by a remote computer that connects to the server via Microsoft Management Console. Server Core was designed to provide efficient file servers, domain controllers, or DNS and DHCP servers.

✦ Remote connection enhancements that enable computers to establish web-based connections to the server using the HTTPS protocol without having to establish a virtual private network (VPN) connection.

✦ Yet another new version of the Internet Information Services (IIS) Web server (7.0).

Windows Server 2008 R2

In the fall of 2009, Microsoft issued an update to Windows Server 2008, officially called Windows Server 2008 R2. Network administrators the world over rejoiced, in part because most of them are also *Star Wars* fans and they can now refer to their favorite operating system as "R2."

R2 built upon Windows Server 2008 with a variety of new features, including virtualization features that let you run more than one instance of the OS on a single server computer, a new version of IIS (7.5), and support for up to 256 processors.

Also, R2 officially dropped support for 32-bit processors. In other words, R2 only runs on server-class 64-bit processors, such as Itanium and Xeon.

Windows Server 2012

The newest version of Windows Server, officially known as Windows Server 2012, offers many significant improvements over Windows Server 2008, the most notable being the new Metro UI, which is designed for use with touch-sensitive displays.

Other new features of Windows Server 2012 include

✦ A new file system — ReFS — that replaces NTFS, providing better performance and reliability.

✦ A redesigned task manager designed to highlight which system tasks are drawing more of the server's CPU, memory, and disk and network I/O capacity.

✦ IP Address Management, which is a feature designed to automatically discover what IP addresses are being used by computers and other devices on the network.

✦ The ability to support servers with as many as 640 processors and 4TB of RAM.

Other Server Operating Systems

Although Windows Server is the most popular choice for an NOS, it isn't the only game in town. The following sections briefly describe three other server choices: Linux, Macintosh OS X Server, and Novell NetWare.

Linux

Perhaps the most interesting OS available today is Linux, which is a free OS based on Unix, which is a powerful network OS often used on large networks. Linux was started by Linus Torvalds, who thought it would be fun to write a version of Unix in his free time — as a hobby. He enlisted help from hundreds of programmers throughout the world, who volunteered their time and efforts via the Internet. Today, Linux is a full-featured version of Unix; its users consider it to be as good as or better than Windows.

Linux offers the same networking benefits as Unix and can be an excellent choice as a server OS.

Apple Mac OS X Server

All the other server OSes I describe in this chapter run on Intel-based PCs with Pentium or Pentium-compatible processors. But what about Macintosh computers? After all, Macintosh users need networks, too. For Macintosh networks, Apple offers Mac OS X Server, which has all the features you'd expect in a server OS: file and printer sharing, Internet features, e-mail, and so on.

Novell NetWare

NetWare was once the king of NOSes. Today, NetWare networks are rare. NetWare has always had an excellent reputation for reliability. In fact, some network administrators swear that they have NetWare servers on their networks that have been running continuously, without a single reboot, since Ronald Reagan was president. (Unfortunately, there hasn't been a major upgrade to NetWare since George W. Bush's first term.)

Novell released the first version of NetWare in 1983, two years before the first version of Windows and four years before Microsoft's first network OS, the now-defunct LAN Manager. Over the years, NetWare has gone through many versions. The most important versions were

✦ NetWare version 3.*x,* the version that made NetWare famous. NetWare 3.*x* used a now-outdated directory scheme called the *bindery.* Each NetWare 3.*x* server has a bindery file that contains information about the resources on that particular server. With the bindery, you had to log on separately to each server that contained resources you wanted to use.

✦ NetWare 4.*x,* in which NetWare Directory Service (NDS) replaced the bindery. NDS is similar to AD. It provides a single directory for the entire network rather than separate directories for each server.

✦ NetWare 5.*x* was the next step. It introduced a new user interface based on Java for easier administration, improved support for Internet protocols, multiprocessing with up to 32 processors, and many other features.

✦ NetWare 6.0 introduced a variety of new features, including the new Novell Storage Services disk management system; web-based access to network folders and printers; and built-in support for Windows, Linux, Unix, and Macintosh file systems.

✦ Novell released its last major version of NetWare (6.5) in summer, 2003. It included improvements to its browser-based management tools and was bundled with open source servers, such as Apache and MySQL.

Beginning in 2005, NetWare has transformed itself into a Linux-based system called Open Enterprise System (OES). In OES, the core of the operating system is Linux, with added applications that run the traditional NetWare services such as directory services. (For more information, see "Linux," earlier in this chapter.)

Peer-to-Peer Networking with Windows

If you're not up to the complexity of dedicated network OSes, you may want to opt for a simple peer-to-peer network based on a desktop version of Windows.

Advantages of peer-to-peer networks

The main advantage of using a peer-to-peer network is the ease of set up and use. Peer-to-peer networks rely on the limited network server features that are built into Windows, such as the ability to share files and printers. Recent versions of Windows, including Windows 8, 7, Vista, and Windows XP, include wizards that automatically configure a basic network for you so that you don't have to manually configure any network settings. Another advantage of using a peer-to-peer network is reduced cost:

✦ You don't need a dedicated server computer because any computer on the network can function as both a network server and a workstation. (You can configure a computer as a dedicated server for better performance, but that also negates the cost benefit of not having a dedicated server computer.

✦ Because peer-to-peer networks are easier to set up and use, you spend less time figuring out how to make the network work and keep it working. And, as Einstein proved, time is money (hence his famous equation, $E = M\$^2$).

✦ Consider the cost of the server OS itself. Windows Server can cost as much as \$200 per user, so the total cost increases as your network grows, although the cost per user drops. For a peer-to-peer Windows server, you pay for Windows once. You don't pay any additional charges based on the number of users on your network.

Drawbacks of peer-to-peer networks

Yes, peer-to-peer networks are easier to install and manage than domain-based networks, but they do have their drawbacks:

✦ Because peer-to-peer networks are based on computers running client versions of Windows, they're subject to the inherent limitations of those Windows versions. Client versions of Windows are designed primarily to be an OS for a single-user desktop computer rather than function as part of a network. These versions can't manage a file or printer server as efficiently as a real NOS.

✦ If you don't set up a dedicated network server, someone (hopefully, not you) may have to live with the inconvenience of sharing his computer with the network. With Windows Server, the server computers are dedicated to network use, so no one has to put up with this inconvenience.

✦ Although a peer-to-peer network may have a lower cost per computer for smaller networks, the cost difference between peer-to-peer networks and Windows Server is less significant in larger networks (say, ten or more clients).

✦ Peer-to-peer networks don't work well when your network starts to grow. Peer-to-peer servers just don't have the security or performance features required for a growing network.

Windows 8

The current version of Windows — Windows 8 — sports a new Metro UI, in which applications are represented as tiles rather than icons. The Metro UI is designed to use with touch-sensitive screens and resembles interfaces found on touch-screen smartphones and tablet computers.

Windows 8 provides the following networking features:

✦ Built-in file and printer sharing allows you to share files and printers with other network users.

✦ A Network Setup Wizard automatically sets the most common configuration options. The wizard eliminates the need to work through multiple Properties dialog boxes to configure network settings.

✦ An Internet Connection Sharing (ICS) feature allows a Windows computer to share an Internet connection with other users. The ICS feature includes firewall features that protect your network from unauthorized access via the Internet connection.

✦ A built-in firewall protects the computer when connected to the Internet.

✦ Simple user account management lets you create multiple users and assign passwords.

✦ Built-in support for wireless networking makes connecting to a wireless network a breeze.

✦ Advanced network diagnostics and troubleshooting tools help you find and correct networking problems.

Windows 8 comes in three editions:

✦ **Windows 8,** the basic edition, targeted at home users.

✦ **Windows 8 Pro,** an advanced version targeted at businesses. For business networks, Windows 8 Pro will be the preferred edition.

✦ **Windows 8 RT**, a version designed for use with smart phones and tablet computers.

Workgroups versus domains

In a Windows network, a *domain* is a group of server computers that share a common user account database. A user at a client computer can log in to a domain to access shared resources for any server in the domain. Each domain must have at least one server computer designated as the *domain controller,* which is ultimately in charge of the domain. Most domain networks share this work among at least two domain controllers, so that if one of the controllers stops working, the network can still function.

A peer-to-peer network can't have a domain because it doesn't have a dedicated server computer to act as a domain controller. Instead, computers in a peer-to-peer network are grouped in *workgroups,* which are simply groups of computers that can share resources with each other. Each computer in a workgroup keeps track of its own user accounts and security settings, so no single computer is in charge of the workgroup.

To create a domain, you have to designate a server computer as the domain controller and configure user accounts. Workgroups are much easier to administer. In fact, you don't have to do anything to create a workgroup except decide on the name you want to use. Although you can have as many workgroups as you want on a peer-to-peer network, most networks have just one workgroup. That way, any computers on the network can share resources with any other computer on the network.

One of the most common mistakes when setting up a peer-to-peer network is misspelling the workgroup name on one of the computers. For example, suppose you decide that all the computers should belong to a workgroup named MYGROUP. If you accidentally spell the workgroup name MYGRUOP for one of the computers, that computer will be isolated in its own workgroup. If you can't locate a computer on your network, the workgroup name is one of the first things to check.

Windows 7

Windows 7, the predecessor to Windows 8, is similar to Windows 8 (but without the Metro interface). Windows 7 comes in six editions:

✦ **Starter:** A simplified version available only pre-installed on computer systems from manufacturers (such as Dell).

✦ **Home Basic:** A special version available only in certain geographic markets (such as China, India, and Pakistan) but not available in Europe or the United States.

✦ **Home Premium:** The standard edition for home use. You can use the Home Premium edition to build a simple peer-to-peer network, but not as part of a domain-based network.

✦ **Professional:** Designed for business users with domain networks.

✦ **Enterprise:** The complete version of Windows 7, which includes all the features of Windows 7 Professional and a few extra bells and whistles. This edition is available only to large businesses that have volume licenses with Microsoft.

✦ **Ultimate:** The retail version of the Enterprise Edition. This version includes all of the features of Windows 7 Enterprise but can be purchased individually by home or small business users.

Older Windows versions

Previous versions of Windows also offer peer-to-peer networking features. The following list summarizes the networking features of the major Windows releases prior to Windows Vista:

✦ **Windows Vista:** Windows Vista, the long-awaited replacement for Windows XP, offered an improved UI over Windows XP. However, Vista was a sluggish performer and not very well regarded.

✦ **Windows XP:** This is still a popular version of Windows even though it was replaced by Windows Vista in 2005.

✦ **Windows Millennium (Me):** This release was aimed at home users. It provided a Home Networking Wizard to simplify the task of configuring a network. It was the last version of Windows that was based on the old 16-bit MS-DOS code.

✦ **Windows 2000 Professional:** This desktop version of Windows 2000 Server has powerful peer-to-peer networking features similar to those found in Windows XP although they are a bit more difficult to set up. It was the first desktop version of Windows that integrated well with AD.

✦ **Windows 98 and Windows 98 Second Edition (SE):** These were popular upgrades to Windows 95 that enhanced its basic networking features.

✦ **Windows 95:** This was the first 32-bit version of Windows. However, it still relied internally on 16-bit MS-DOS code, so it wasn't a true 32-bit operating system. It provided basic peer-to-peer network features, with built-in drivers for common network adapters and basic file- and printer-sharing features.

✦ **Windows for Workgroups:** This was the first version of Windows to support networking without requiring an add-on product. It simplified the task of creating NetBIOS-based networks for file and printer sharing. However, it had only weak support for TCP/IP.

Book II

Building a Network

Contents at a Glance

Chapter 1: Planning a Network

In This Chapter

✔ Making a network plan

✔ Taking stock of your computer stock

✔ Making sure that you know why you need a network

✔ Making the three basic network decisions that you can't avoid

✔ Using a starter kit

✔ Looking at a sample network

Okay, so you're convinced that you need to network your computers. What now? Do you stop by Computers-R-Us on the way to work, install the network before drinking your morning coffee, and expect the network to be fully operational by noon?

I don't think so.

Networking your computers is just like any other worthwhile endeavor: Doing it right requires a bit of planning. This chapter helps you to think through your network before you start spending money. It shows you how to come up with a networking plan that's every bit as good as the plan that a network consultant would charge thousands of dollars for. See? This book is already saving you money!

Making a Network Plan

Before you begin any networking project, whether a new network installation or an upgrade of an existing network, make a detailed plan *first*. If you make technical decisions too quickly, before studying all the issues that affect the project, you'll regret it. You'll discover too late that a key application won't run over the network, the network has unacceptably slow performance, or key components of the network don't work together.

Here are some general thoughts to keep in mind while you create your network plan:

✦ **Don't rush the plan.** The most costly networking mistakes are the ones that you make before you install the network. Think things through and consider alternatives.

✦ **Write down the network plan.** The plan doesn't have to be a fancy, 500-page document. If you want to make it look good, pick up a 1/2" three-ring binder, which is big enough to hold your network plan with room to spare.

✦ **Ask someone else to read your network plan before you buy anything.** Preferably, ask someone who knows more about computers than you do.

✦ **Keep the plan up to date.** If you add to the network, dig up the plan, dust it off, and update it.

"The best laid schemes of mice and men gang aft agley, and leave us naught but grief and pain for promised joy." Robert Burns lived a few hundred years before computer networks, but his famous words ring true. A network plan isn't chiseled in stone. If you discover that something doesn't work the way you thought it would, that's okay. Just change your plan.

Being Purposeful

One of the first steps in planning your network is making sure that you understand why you want the network in the first place. Here are some of the more common reasons for needing a network, all of them quite valid:

✦ *My co-worker and I exchange files using CDs or flash drives just about every day.* With a network, trading files is easier.

✦ *I don't want to buy everyone a color laser printer when I know the one we have now just sits there taking up space most of the day.* So wouldn't buying a network be better than buying a color laser printer for every computer?

✦ *I want everyone to be able to access the Internet.* Many networks, especially smaller ones, exist solely for sharing an Internet connection.

✦ *Business is so good that one person typing in orders eight hours each day can't keep up.* With a network, more than one person can enter orders, which expedites orders and possibly saves on overtime expenses.

✦ *My brother-in-law just put in a network at his office.* No one wants to be behind the times.

✦ *I already have a network, but it's so old that it may as well be made of kite string and tin cans.* An improved network speeds up access to shared files, provides better security, and is easier to manage.

After you identify all the reasons why you think you need a network, write them down. Don't worry about winning the Pulitzer Prize for your stunning prose. Just make sure that you write down what you expect a network to do for you. If you were making a 500-page networking proposal, you'd place the description of why a network is needed in a tabbed section labeled Justification. In your 1/2" network binder, file the description under Purpose.

As you consider the reasons why you need a network, you may conclude that you don't need a network after all. That's okay. You can always use the binder for your stamp collection.

Taking Stock

One of the most challenging parts of planning a network is figuring out how to work with the computers that you already have. In other words, how do you get from here to there? Before you can plan how to get "there," you have to know where "here" is. In other words, you have to take a thorough inventory of your current computers.

What you need to know

You need to know the following information about each of your computers:

✦ **The processor type and, if possible, its clock speed:** It would be nice if each of your computers had a shiny new i7 6-Core processor. In most cases, though, you find a mixture of computers: some new, some old, some borrowed, some blue. You may even find a few archaic Pentium computers.

You can't usually tell what kind of processor that a computer has just by looking at the computer's case. But you can easily find out by right-clicking Computer on the Start menu and choosing Properties.

✦ **The size of the hard drive and the arrangement of its partitions:** To find the size of your computer's hard drive in Windows 8, 7, or Vista, open the Computer window, right-click the drive icon, and choose the Properties command from the shortcut menu that appears. Figure 1-1 shows the Properties dialog box for a 922GB hard drive that has about 867GB of free space.

If your computer has more than one hard drive, Windows lists an icon for each drive in the Computer window. Jot down the size and amount of free space available on each drive.

✦ **The amount of memory:** To find this information in Windows, right-click Computer from the Start menu and choose the Properties command. The amount of memory on your computer is shown in the dialog box that appears. For example, Figure 1-2 shows the System Properties dialog box for a computer with 8GB of RAM.

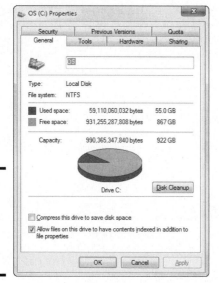

Figure 1-1:
The
Properties
dialog box
for a disk
drive.

Figure 1-2:
The
Properties
page for a
computer
with 8GB of
RAM.

✦ **The operating system version:** This you can also deduce from the
System Properties dialog box. For example, the Properties page shown
in Figure 1-2 indicates that the computer is running Windows 7 Ultimate.

✦ **What type of network card, if any, is installed in the computer:** The easiest way to get this information is to right-click Computer from the Start menu, choose Manage, click Device Manager, right-click the network adapter, and choose Properties. For example, Figure 1-3 shows the Properties dialog box for the network adapter that's built into the motherboard on my computer.

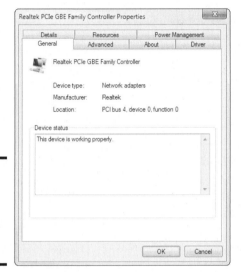

**Book II
Chapter 1**

Planning a Network

Figure 1-3:
The Properties page for a network adapter.

Device Manager is also useful for tracking down other hardware devices attached to the computer.

✦ **What network protocols are in use:** To determine this in Windows Vista, open Control Panel, open Network and Sharing Center, click Manage Network Connections, and then right-click the Local Area connection and choose Properties. In Windows 7 or 8, open Control Panel, click View Network Status and Tasks, click Change Adapter Settings, then right-click the Local Area Connection and choose Properties. The dialog box shown in Figure 1-4 appears.

✦ **What kind of printer, if any, is attached to the computer:** Usually, you can tell just by looking at the printer. You can also tell by double-clicking the Printers icon in Control Panel.

✦ **Any other devices connected to the computer:** A DVD or Blu-ray drive? Scanner? External disk or tape drive? Video camera? Battle droid? Hot tub?

✦ **Which driver and installation disks are available:** Hopefully, you'll be able to locate the disks or CDs required by hardware devices such as the network card, printers, scanners, and so on. If not, you may be able to locate the drivers on the Internet.

✦ **What software is used on the computer:** Microsoft Office? AutoCAD? QuickBooks? Make a complete list and include version numbers.

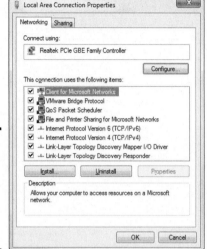

Figure 1-4:
The Properties page for a local area network connection.

Programs that gather information for you

Gathering information about your computers is a lot of work if you have more than a few computers to network. Fortunately, several software programs are available that can automatically gather the information for you. These programs inspect various aspects of a computer, such as the CPU type and speed, amount of RAM, and the size of the computer's hard drives. Then they show the information on the screen and give you the option of saving the information to a hard drive file or printing it.

Windows comes with just such a program: Microsoft System Information. Choose Start⇨All Programs⇨Accessories⇨System Tools⇨System Information.

When you fire up Microsoft System Information, you see a window similar to the one shown in Figure 1-5. Initially, Microsoft System Information displays basic information about your computer, such as your version of Microsoft Windows, the processor type, the amount of memory on the computer, and so on. You can obtain more detailed information by clicking Hardware Resources, Components, or other categories in the left side of the window.

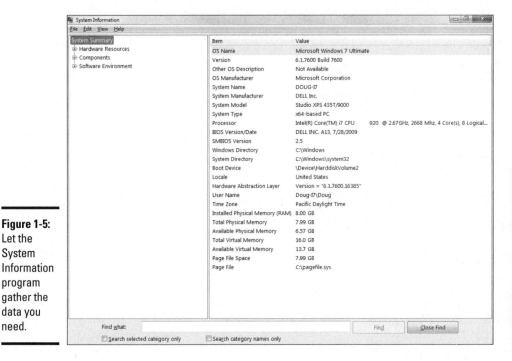

Figure 1-5:
Let the
System
Information
program
gather the
data you
need.

To Dedicate or Not to Dedicate: That Is the Question

One of the most basic questions that a network plan must answer is whether
the network will have one or more dedicated servers, or rely completely on
peer-to-peer networking.

A *peer-to-peer* network doesn't have a dedicated server computer. Read
more about this type of network, as well as dedicated servers, in Chapter 1
of Book I.

If the only reason for purchasing your network is to share a printer and
exchange an occasional file, you may not need a dedicated server computer.
In that case, you can create a peer-to-peer network by using the computers
that you already have. However, all but the smallest networks will benefit
from having a separate, dedicated server computer — and here's why:

✦ **Using a dedicated server computer makes the network faster, easier
to work with, and more reliable.** Consider what happens when the user
of a server computer (doubling as a workstation) decides to turn off
the computer, not realizing that someone else is accessing files on that
hard drive.

✦ **You don't necessarily have to use your biggest and fastest computer as your server computer.** I've seen networks where the slowest computer on the network is the server. This advice is especially true when the server is mostly used to share a printer or to store a small number of shared files. So if you need to buy a computer for your network, consider promoting one of your older computers to be the server and using the new computer as a client.

Types of Servers

Assuming that your network will require one or more dedicated servers, you should next consider what types of servers the network will need. In some cases, a single server computer can fill one or more of these roles. Whenever possible, limit each server computer to a single server function.

File servers

File servers provide centralized disk storage conveniently shared by client computers on the network. The most common file server task is storing shared files and programs. For example, members of a small workgroup can use a file server to store common Microsoft Office documents.

You set file servers to ensure that two users don't try to update the same file at the same time. The file servers do this by *locking* a file while a user updates the file so that other users can't access the file until the first user finishes. For document files (for example, word processing or spreadsheet files), the whole file is locked. For database files, the lock can be applied just to the portion of the file that contains the record or records being updated.

Print servers

Sharing printers is another main reason why many small networks exist. Although it isn't necessary, a server computer can be dedicated for use as a *print server,* whose sole purpose is to collect information being sent to a shared printer by client computers and print it in an orderly fashion.

✦ A single computer may double as both a file server and a print server, but performance is better if you use separate print and file server computers.

✦ With inexpensive inkjet printers running about $100, just giving each user a dedicated printer is tempting. However, you get what you pay for. Instead of buying $100 printers for 15 users, you may be better off buying one $1,500 laser printer and sharing it. The $1,500 laser printer will be much faster, will probably produce better-looking output, and will be less expensive to operate.

Web servers

A *web server* runs software that enables the computer to host a World Wide Web (via the Internet) website or a website on a private intranet. The two most popular web server programs are Microsoft IIS (Internet Information Services), which runs on Windows systems and Apache, an open source web server that runs on Linux systems.

Mail servers

A *mail server* handles the network's e-mail needs. It is configured with e-mail server software, such as Microsoft Exchange Server. Exchange Server is designed to work with Microsoft Outlook, the e-mail client software that comes with Microsoft Office.

Most mail servers actually do much more than just send and receive electronic mail. For example, here are some of the features that Exchange Server offers beyond simple e-mail:

✦ Collaboration features that simplify managing collaborative projects

✦ Audio and video conferencing

✦ Chat rooms and instant messaging (IM) services

✦ Microsoft Exchange Forms Designer, which lets you develop customized forms for applications, such as vacation requests or purchase orders

Database servers

A *database server* is a server computer that runs database software, such as Microsoft SQL Server 2008. Database servers are usually used along with customized business applications, such as accounting or marketing systems.

Choosing a Server Operating System

If you determine that your network will require one or more dedicated servers, the next step is to determine what network operating system (NOS) those servers should use. If possible, all the servers should use the same NOS so that you don't find yourself supporting different OSes.

Although you can choose from many NOSes, from a practical point of view, your choices are limited to the following:

✦ Windows Server 2012 or 2008

✦ Linux or another version of Unix

For more information, read Book I, Chapter 4.

Planning the Infrastructure

You also need to plan how to connect the computers in the network: determining which network topology the network will use, what type of cable will be used, where the cable will be routed, and what other devices (such as repeaters, bridges, hubs, switches, and routers) will be needed. (Read about all these components in Book I.)

Although you have many cabling options to choose from, you'll probably use Cat 5e (or better) UTP for most — if not all — of the desktop client computers on the network. However, you have many decisions to make beyond this basic choice:

✦ Where will you place workgroup hubs or switches? On a desktop somewhere within the group or in a central wiring closet?

✦ How many client computers will you place on each hub or switch, and how many hubs or switches will you need?

✦ If you need more than one hub or switch, what type of cabling will you use to connect the hubs and switches to one another?

For more information about network cabling, see Book II, Chapter 2, and Book I, Chapter 3.

If you're installing new network cable, don't scrimp on the cable itself. Because installing network cable is a labor-intensive task, the cost of the cable itself is a small part of the total cable installation cost. And if you spend a little extra to install higher-grade cable now, you won't have to replace the cable in a few years when it's time to upgrade the network.

Drawing Diagrams

One of the most helpful techniques for creating a network plan is to draw a picture of it. The diagram can be a detailed floor plan, showing the actual location of each network component: a *physical map.* If you prefer, the diagram can be a *logical map,* which is more abstract and Picasso-like. Any time you change the network layout, update the diagram. Also include a detailed description of the change, the date that the change was made, and the reason for the change.

You can diagram very small networks on the back of a napkin, but if the network has more than a few computers, you'll want to use a drawing program to help you create the diagram. One of the best programs for this purpose is Microsoft Visio, shown in Figure 1-6.

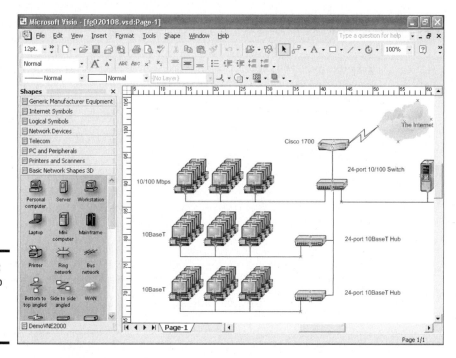

Book II
Chapter 1

Planning a Network

Figure 1-6:
Using Visio
to draw a
network
diagram.

Here's a rundown of some of the features that make Visio so useful:

✦ Smart shapes and connectors maintain the connections drawn between
network components, even if you rearrange the layout of the components on the page.

✦ Stencils provide dozens of useful shapes for common network components — not just for client and server computers, but for routers, hubs,
switches, and just about anything else you can imagine. If you're really
picky about the diagrams, you can even purchase stencil sets that have
accurate drawings of specific devices, such as Cisco routers or IBM
mainframe computers.

✦ You can add information to each computer or device in the diagram,
such as the serial number or physical location. Then, you can quickly
print an inventory that lists this information for each device in the
diagram.

✦ You can easily create large diagrams that span multiple pages.

Sample Network Plans

Here are some network plans from real-life situations. These examples illustrate many of the network design issues I've covered so far in this chapter. The stories you're about to read are true. The names have been changed to protect the innocent.

Building a small network: California Sport Surface, Inc.

California Sport Surface, Inc. (CSS) is a small company specializing in the installation of outdoor sports surfaces, such as tennis courts, running tracks, and football fields. CSS has an administrative staff of just four employees who work out of a residential office. The company currently has three computers:

✦ A brand-new Dell desktop computer running Windows 8, shared by the president (Mark) and vice president (Julie) to prepare proposals and marketing brochures, handle correspondence, and manage other miscellaneous chores. This computer has a built-in Gigabit Ethernet network port.

✦ An older Gateway computer running Windows XP Home Edition, used by the bookkeeper (Erin), who uses QuickBooks to handle the company's accounting needs. This computer has a built-in 10/100 Mbps Ethernet port.

✦ A notebook that runs Windows 7, used by the company's chief engineer (Daniel), who often takes it to job sites to help with engineering needs. This computer has a built-in 10/100 Mbps Ethernet port.

The company owns just one printer, a moderately priced inkjet printer connected to Erin's computer. The computers aren't networked, so whenever Mark, Julie, or Daniel needs to print something, the file must be copied to a flash drive and given to Erin, who then prints the document. The computer shared by Mark and Julie is connected to the Internet via a residential DSL connection.

The company wants to install a network to support these three computers. Here are the primary goals of the network:

✦ Provide shared access to the printer so that users don't have to exchange data on flash drives to print their documents.

✦ Provide shared access to the Internet connection so that users can access the Internet from any of the computers.

✦ Allow for the addition of another desktop computer, which the company expects to purchase within the next six months, and potentially another notebook computer. (If business is good, the company hopes to hire another engineer.)

✦ The network should be intuitive to the users and shouldn't require extensive upkeep.

CSS's networking needs can be met with the simple peer-to-peer network diagrammed in Figure 1-7.

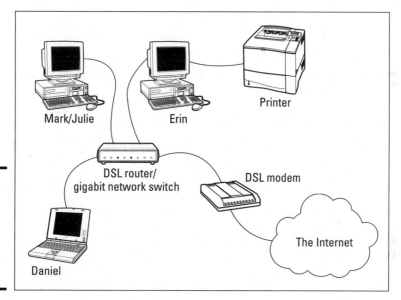

Figure 1-7:
California
Sport
Surface's
new peer-
to-peer
network.

Here's what the network requires:

✦ A local-area network (LAN) that will connect the three computers using a combination DSL router and network switch. The router should have at least six network ports. The company initially needs just four network ports, but will need six when it adds additional computers.

✦ The firewall features of the DSL router will need to be enabled to protect the network from Internet hackers.

✦ Erin's computer will need to be configured to enable File and printer sharing, and the printer will need to be shared.

Connecting two networks: Creative Course Development, Inc.

Creative Course Development, Inc. (CCD) is a small educational publisher located in central California that specializes in integrated math and science curriculum for primary and secondary grades. It publishes a variety of course materials, including textbooks, puzzle books, and CD-ROM software.

CCD leases two adjacent office buildings, separated by a small courtyard. The creative staff, which consists of a dozen writers and educators, works in Building A. The sales, marketing, and administrative staff (six employees) works in Building B.

The Building A staff has a dozen relatively new personal computers, all running Windows Vista Business Edition, and a server computer running Windows 2003 Server. These computers are networked via a single 24-port gigabit network switch. A T1 line connected to the network through a small Cisco router provides Internet access.

The Building B staff has a hodgepodge of computers: some running Windows 8 but most running Windows 7. They have a small Windows 2008 server that meets their needs. The older computers have 10/100BaseT network interfaces; the newer ones have Gigabit interfaces. However, the computers are all connected to a 10/100 Mbps Ethernet switch with 12 ports. Internet access is provided by an ISDN connection.

Both groups are happy with their computers and networks. The problem is that the networks can't communicate with each other. For example, the creative team in Building A prepares weekly product-development status reports to share with the Administrative staff in Building B, and they frequently go to the other building to look into important sales trends.

Although several solutions to this problem exist, the easiest is to create a wide-area network (WAN) by bridging the networks with a pair of wireless switches. To do this, CCD should purchase two wireless access points: one plugged into the gigabit switch in Building A, and the other plugged into the switch in Building B. After the access points are configured, the two networks will function as a single network. Figure 1-8 shows a logical diagram for the completed network.

Although the wireless solution to this problem sounds simple, a number of complications still need to be dealt with. Specifically:

+ Depending on the environment and the construct of the buildings themselves (concrete is an impedance), the wireless access points may have trouble establishing a link between the buildings. It may be necessary to locate the devices on the roof. In that case, CCD will have to spend a little extra money for weatherproof enclosures.

+ Before the networks were connected, each network had its own DHCP server to assign IP addresses to users as needed. Unfortunately, both DHCP servers have the same local IP address (192.168.0.1). When the networks are combined, one of these DHCP servers will have to be disabled.

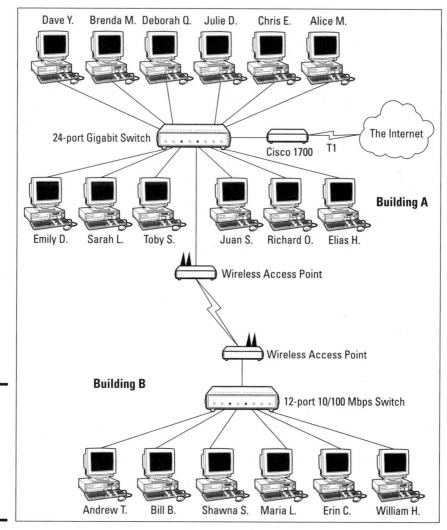

Figure 1-8:
Creative
Course
Development's
wireless
network
solution.

- ✦ Both networks had their own Internet connections. With the networks
  bridged, CCD can eliminate the ISDN connection altogether. Users in both
  buildings can get their Internet access via the shared T1 connection.

- ✦ The network administrator will also have to determine how to handle
  directory services for the network. Previously, each network had its own
  domain. With the networks bridged, CCD may opt to keep these domains
  separate, or it may decide to merge them into a single domain. (Doing so
  will require considerable work, so the company will probably leave the
  domains separate.)

Improving network performance: DCH Accounting

DCH Accounting is an accounting firm that has grown in two years from 15 employees to 35, all located in one building. Here's the lowdown on the existing network:

✦ The network comprises 35 client computers and three servers running Windows 2008 Server.

✦ The 35 client computers run a variety of Windows operating systems. About one-third (11) run Windows Vista Professional. The rest run Windows XP Professional. None of the computers run Windows 7 or 8.

✦ The Windows Vista computers all have Gigabit Ethernet cards. The older computers have 10/100 Mbps cards.

✦ The server computers are somewhat older computers that have 10/100 Mbps network interfaces.

✦ All the offices in the building are wired with Category 5e wiring to a central wiring closet, where a small equipment rack holds two 24-port 10/100 switches.

✦ Internet access is provided through a T1 connection with a Cisco 1700 router.

Lately, network performance has been noticeably slow, particularly Internet access and large file transfers between client computers and the servers. Users have started to complain that sometimes the network seems to crawl.

The problem is most likely that the network has outgrown the old 10/100BaseT switches. All network traffic must flow through them, and they're limited to the speed of 100 Mbps. As a result, the new computers with the Gigabit Ethernet cards are connecting to the network at 100 Mbps.

The performance of this network can be dramatically improved in two steps. The first step is to replace the 10/100 Mbps network interface cards in the three servers with gigabit cards (or, better yet, replace the servers with newer models). Second, add a 24-port gigabit switch to the equipment rack. The equipment rack can be rewired, as shown in Figure 1-9.

1. **Connect the servers, the Cisco router, and the gigabit clients to the new gigabit switch. This will use 15 of the 24 ports.**

2. **Connect the two 10/100 switches to the new gigabit switch. This will use 2 more ports, leaving 7 ports for future growth.**

3. **Divide the remaining clients between the two 10/100 switches. Each switch will have 12 computers connected.**

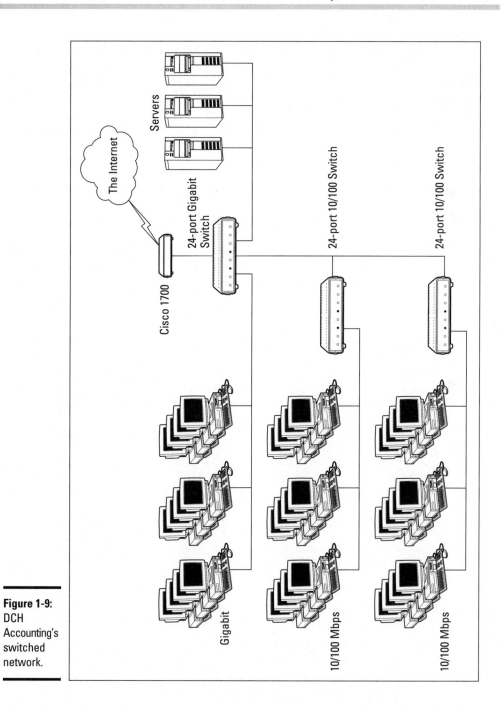

Figure 1-9:
DCH
Accounting's
switched
network.

This arrangement connects all the gigabit clients to gigabit switch ports and 100 Mbps clients to 100 Mbps switch ports.

For even better performance, DCH can simply replace both switches with 24-port gigabit switches.

Chapter 2: Installing Network Hardware

In This Chapter

✓ Installing network interface cards

✓ Installing network cable

✓ Attaching cable connectors

✓ Figuring out pinouts for twisted-pair cabling

✓ Building a crossover cable

✓ Installing switches

*A*fter you plan your network, then comes the fun of actually putting everything together. In this chapter, I describe some of the important details for installing network hardware, including cables, switches, network interface cards, and professional touches, such as patch panels.

Installing a Network Interface Card

To connect a computer to your network, the computer must have a network interface. Virtually all computers sold in the last ten years or so have a network interface built-in on the motherboard. However, you may still encounter the occasional older computer that doesn't have a built-in network interface. In that case, you must install a network interface card (NIC) to enable the computer for your network. Installing a network interface card is a manageable task, but you have to be willing to roll up your sleeves.

If you've installed one adapter card, you've installed them all. In other words, installing a network interface card is just like installing a modem, a new video controller card, a sound card, or any other type of card. If you've ever installed one of these cards, you can probably install a network interface card blindfolded.

(Installing a network adapter in an older laptop can be trickier than installing one in an older desktop computer. The instructions in this chapter apply only to desktop computers.)

Here's a step-by-step procedure for installing a NIC:

1. **Gather the network card and the driver disks. While you're at it, get your Windows installation CD, just in case.**

2. **Shut down Windows and then turn off the computer and unplug it.**

Never work in your computer's insides with the power on or the power cord plugged in!

3. **Touch some metal.**

Touch your desk or a metal pipe or the refrigerator, for example. The idea is to discharge any static electricity that might have built up in your body.

4. **Remove the cover from your computer.**

Figure 2-1 shows the screws that you must typically remove in order to open the cover. Put the screws someplace where they won't wander off.

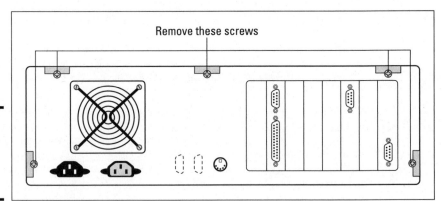

Remove these screws

Figure 2-1:
Remove your computer's cover.

For a name-brand computer (say, Dell or Compaq), opening the cover may be trickier than just removing a few screws. You may need to consult the unit's manual to find out how to open the case.

5. **Find an unused expansion slot inside the computer.**

The expansion slots are lined up in a neat row near the back of the computer; you can't miss 'em. Any computer less than five years old should have at least two or three slots known as *PCI slots.*

6. **When you find a slot that doesn't have a card in it, remove the metal slot protector from the back of the computer's chassis.**

If a small retaining screw holds the slot protector in place, remove the screw and keep it in a safe place. Then pull the slot protector out and put the slot protector in a box with all your other old slot protectors.

(After a while, you'll collect a whole bunch of slot protectors. Keep them as souvenirs or Christmas tree ornaments.)

7. Insert the NIC into the slot.

Line up the connectors on the bottom of the card with the connectors in the expansion slot and then press the card straight down. Sometimes you have to press uncomfortably hard to get the card to slide into the slot.

8. Secure the NIC with the screw that you removed in Step 5.

9. Put the computer case back together.

Watch out for the loose cables inside the computer; you don't want to pinch them with the case as you slide it back on. Secure the case with the screws that you removed in Step 3.

10. Plug in the computer and turn it back on.

If you're using a Plug and Play card with Windows, the card is automatically configured after you start the computer again. If you're working with an older computer or an older NIC, you may need to run an additional software installation program. See the installation instructions that come with the NIC card for details.

Installing Twisted-Pair Cable

Most Ethernet networks are built using twisted-pair cable, which resembles phone cable but isn't the same. Twisted-pair cable is sometimes called "UTP." For more information about the general characteristics of twisted-pair cable, see Book I, Chapter 3.

In the following sections, you find out what you need to know to select and install twisted-pair cable.

Cat got your tongue?

Twisted-pair cable grades are categories specified by the ANSI/EIA standard 568. ANSI stands for American National Standards Institute; EIA stands for Electronic Industries Association. The higher the number, the faster the data transfer rate, so Cat5 is faster than Cat2. If you want to sound like you know what you're talking about, say "Cat 5" instead of "Category 5." Twisted pair is often referred to as UTP (unshielded twisted pair). Now you're hip.

Cable categories

Twisted-pair cable comes in various grades, or *Categories*.

Higher-Category cables are more expensive than lower-Category cables, but the real cost of installing Ethernet cabling is the labor required to actually pull the cables through the walls. You should never install anything less than Category 5 cable. And if at all possible, invest in Category 5e (the *e* stands for enhanced) or even Category 6 cable to allow for upgrades to your network.

Table 2-1 lists the various categories of twisted-pair cable.

Table 2-1	Twisted-Pair Cable Categories	
Category	*Maximum Data Rate*	*Intended Use*
1	1 Mbps	Voice only
2	4 Mbps	4 Mbps token ring
3	16 Mbps	10BaseT Ethernet
4	20 Mbps	16 Mbps token ring
5	100 Mbps (2 pair)	100BaseT Ethernet
	1,000 Mbps (4 pair)	Gigabit Ethernet
5e	1,000 Mbps (2 pair)	Gigabit Ethernet
6	1,000 Mbps (2 pair)	Gigabit Ethernet
6a	10,000 Mbps	10 gigabit (experimental)
7	10,000 Mbps	10 gigabit (experimental)

What's with the pairs?

Most twisted-pair cable has four pairs of wires, for a total of eight wires. Standard Ethernet actually uses only two of the pairs, so the other two pairs are unused. You may be tempted to save money by purchasing cable with just two pairs of wires, but that's a bad idea. If a network cable develops a problem, you can sometimes fix it by switching over to one of the extra pairs. If you try to carry a separate connection over the extra pairs, though, electrical interference will prevent the signals from getting through.

Don't give in to temptation to use the extra pairs for some other purpose, such as for a voice line. The electrical noise generated by voice signals in the extra wires can interfere with your network.

Plenum space

Plenum space is a compartment in the building's air distribution system — typically, the space above a suspended ceiling or under a raised floor.

The area above a suspended ceiling is *not* a plenum space if both the delivery and return lines of the air conditioning and heating system are ducted. Plenum cable is required only if the air conditioning and heating system are not ducted. When in doubt, have the local inspector look at your facility before you install cable.

To shield or not to shield

Unshielded twisted-pair cable (UTP) is designed for normal office environments. When you use UTP cable, you must be careful not to route cable close to fluorescent light fixtures, air conditioners, or electric motors (such as automatic door motors or elevator motors). UTP is the least expensive type of cable.

In environments with a lot of electrical interference, such as factories, you may want to use shielded twisted-pair cable (STP). STP can cost up to three times more than regular UTP, so you won't want to use STP unless you have to. With a little care, UTP can withstand the amount of electrical interference found in a normal office environment.

Most STP cable is shielded by a layer of aluminum foil. For buildings with unusually high amounts of electrical interference, you can use more expensive, braided copper shielding for even more protection.

When to use plenum cable

The outer sheath of both shielded and unshielded twisted-pair cable comes in two varieties:

✦ **PVC:** The most common and least expensive type.

✦ **Plenum:** A special type of fire-retardant cable designed for use in the plenum space of a building (typically, in the hollows below a floor or above a ceiling)

Plenum cable has a special Teflon coating that not only resists heat, but also gives off fewer toxic fumes if it does burn. Unfortunately, plenum cable costs more than twice as much as ordinary PVC cable.

Most local building codes require that you use plenum cable whenever the wiring is installed within the plenum space of the building.

Sometimes solid, sometimes stranded

The actual copper wire that composes the cable comes in two varieties: solid and stranded. Your network will have some of each.

✦ **Stranded cable:** Each conductor is made from a bunch of very small wires twisted together. Stranded cable is more flexible than solid cable, so it doesn't break as easily. However, stranded cable is more expensive than solid cable and isn't very good at transmitting signals over long distances. Stranded cable is best used for patch cables, such as the cable used to connect a computer to a wall jack or the cable used to connect patch panels to hubs and switches.

Strictly speaking, the cable that connects your computer to the wall jack is a *station cable* — not a patch cable. Patch cables are used in the wiring closet, usually to connect patch panels to switches.

✦ **Solid cable:** Each conductor is a single solid strand of wire. Solid cable is less expensive than stranded cable and carries signals farther, but it isn't very flexible. If you bend it too many times, it will break. Solid cable is usually used for permanent wiring within the walls and ceilings of a building.

Installation guidelines

The hardest part about installing network cable is the physical task of pulling the cable through ceilings, walls, and floors. This job is just tricky enough that I recommend that you don't attempt it yourself except for small offices. For large jobs, hire a professional cable installer. You may even want to hire a professional for small jobs if the ceiling and wall spaces are difficult to access.

Here are some general pointers to keep in mind if you decide to install cable yourself:

✦ You can purchase twisted-pair cable in prefabricated lengths, such as 50', 75', or 100'. You can also special-order prefabricated cables in any length you need. However, attaching connectors to bulk cable isn't that difficult. I recommend that you use prefabricated cables only for very small networks and only when you don't need to route the cable through walls or ceilings.

✦ Always use a bit more cable than you need, especially if you're running cable through walls. For example, when you run a cable up a wall, leave a few feet of slack in the ceiling above the wall. That way, you'll have plenty of cable if you need to make a repair later on.

✦ When running cable, avoid sources of interference, such as fluorescent lights, big motors, x-ray machines, and so on. The most common source of interference for cables that are run behind dropped ceiling panels are fluorescent lights; be sure to give light fixtures a wide berth as you run your cable. Three feet should do it.

✦ The maximum allowable cable length between a hub and the computer is 100 meters (m; about 328').

✦ If you must run cable across the floor where people walk, cover the cable so that no one trips over it. Inexpensive cable protectors are available at most hardware stores.

✦ When running cables through walls, label each cable at both ends. Most electrical supply stores carry pads of cable labels that are perfect for the job. These pads contain 50 sheets or so of precut labels with letters and numbers. They look much more professional than wrapping a loop of masking tape around the cable and writing on the tape with a marker.

If nothing else, use a permanent marker to write directly on the cable.

✦ When several cables come together, tie them with plastic cable ties. Avoid using masking tape if you can; the tape doesn't last, but the sticky glue stuff does. It's a mess a year later. Cable ties are available at electrical supply stores.

✦ Cable ties have all sorts of useful purposes. Once on a backpacking trip, I used a pair of cable ties to attach an unsuspecting buddy's hat to a high tree limb. He wasn't impressed with my innovative use of the cable ties, but my other hiking companions were.

✦ When you run cable above suspended ceiling panels, use cable ties, hooks, or clamps to secure the cable to the actual ceiling or to the metal frame that supports the ceiling tiles. Don't just lay the cable on top of the tiles.

Getting the tools that you need

Of course, to do a job right, you must have the right tools.

Start with a basic set of computer tools, which you can get for about $15 from any computer store or large office-supply store. These kits include the right screwdrivers and socket wrenches to open up your computers and insert adapter cards. (If you don't have a computer toolkit, make sure that you have several flat-head and Phillips screwdrivers of various sizes.)

If all your computers are in the same room and you're going to run the cables along the floor and you're using prefabricated cables, the computer tool kit should contain everything that you need.

If you're using bulk cable and plan on attaching your own connectors, you need the following tools in addition to the tools that come with the basic computer tool kit:

✦ **Wire cutters:** You need big ones for thinnet cable; smaller ones are okay for 10BaseT cable. If you're using yellow cable, you need the Jaws of Life.

✦ **Crimp tool:** Use this tool to attach the connectors to the cable. Don't use a cheap $10 crimp tool. A good one will cost $100 but will save you many headaches in the long run. Remember this adage: When you crimp, you mustn't scrimp.

✦ **Wire stripper:** You need this only if the crimp tool doesn't include a wire stripper.

If you plan on running cables through walls, you need these additional tools:

✦ **A hammer**

✦ **A bell**

✦ **A song to sing:** Just kidding about these last two.

✦ **A keyhole saw:** This is useful if you plan on cutting holes through walls to route your cable.

✦ **A flashlight**

✦ **A ladder**

✦ **Someone to hold the ladder**

✦ **Possibly a fish tape:** A *fish tape* is a coiled-up length of stiff metal tape. To use it, you feed the tape into one wall opening and fish it toward the other opening, where a partner is ready to grab it when the tape arrives. Next, your partner attaches the cable to the fish tape and yells something like, "Let 'er rip!" or "Bombs away!" Then you reel in the fish tape and the cable along with it. (You can find fish tape in the electrical section of most well-stocked hardware stores.)

If you plan on routing cable through a concrete subfloor, you need to rent a jackhammer and a backhoe and hire someone to hold a yellow flag while you work.

Pinouts for twisted-pair cables

Each pair of wires in a twisted-pair cable is one of four colors: orange, green, blue, or brown. The two wires that make up each pair are complementary: One is a solid color, and the other is white with a stripe of the corresponding color. For example, the orange pair has an orange wire and then a white wire with an orange stripe. Likewise, the blue pair has a blue wire and a white wire with a blue stripe.

When you attach a twisted-pair cable to a modular connector or jack, you must match up the right wires to the right pins. You can use several different standards to wire the connectors. To confuse matters, you can use one of the two popular standard ways of hooking up the wires. One is known as EIA/TIA 568A; the other is EIA/TIA 568B, also known as AT&T 258A. Table 2-2 shows both wiring schemes.

It doesn't matter which of these wiring schemes you use, but pick one and stick with it. If you use one wiring standard on one end of a cable and the other standard on the other end, the cable won't work.

Table 2-2	Pin Connections for Twisted-Pair Cable		
Pin Number	*Function*	*EIA/TIA 568A*	*EIA/TIA 568B AT&T 258A*
Pin 1	Transmit +	White/green	White/orange
Pin 2	Transmit −	Green	Orange
Pin 3	Receive +	White/orange	White/green
Pin 4	Unused	Blue	Blue
Pin 5	Unused	White/blue	White/blue
Pin 6	Receive −	Orange	Green
Pin 7	Unused	White/brown	White/brown
Pin 8	Unused	Brown	Brown

Book II
Chapter 2

Installing Network
Hardware

10BaseT and 100BaseT actually use only two of the four pairs, connected to pins 1, 2, 3, and 6. One pair is used to transmit data, and the other is used to receive data. The only difference between the two wiring standards is which pair is used to transmit data and which pair is used to receive data. In the EIA/TIA 568A standard, the green pair is used to transmit and the orange pair is used to receive. In the EIA/TIA 568B and AT&T 258A standards, the orange pair is used to transmit and the green pair to receive.

If you want, you can get away with connecting only pins 1, 2, 3, and 6. However, I suggest that you connect all four pairs as indicated in Table 2-2.

Attaching RJ-45 connectors

RJ-45 connectors for twisted-pair cables aren't too difficult to attach if you have the right crimping tool. The trick is in both making sure that you attach each wire to the correct pin and pressing the tool hard enough to ensure a good connection.

Here's the procedure for attaching an RJ-45 connector:

1. **Cut the end of the cable to the desired length.**

   Make sure that you make a square cut — not a diagonal cut.

2. **Insert the cable into the stripper portion of the crimp tool so that the end of the cable is against the stop.**

   Squeeze the handles and slowly pull the cable out, keeping it square. This strips off the correct length of outer insulation without puncturing the insulation on the inner wires.

3. **Arrange the wires so that they lay flat and line up according to Table 2-2.**

   You'll have to play with the wires a little bit to get them to lay out in the right sequence.

4. **Slide the wires into the pinholes on the connector.**

   Double-check to make sure that all the wires slipped into the correct pinholes.

5. **Insert the plug and wire into the crimping portion of the tool and then squeeze the handles to crimp the plug.**

   Squeeze it tight!

6. **Remove the plug from the tool and double-check the connection.**

   You're done!

Here are a few other points to remember when dealing with RJ-45 connectors and twisted-pair cable:

✦ The pins on the RJ-45 connectors aren't numbered, but you can tell which is pin 1 by holding the connector so that the metal conductors are facing up, as shown in Figure 2-2. Pin 1 is on the left.

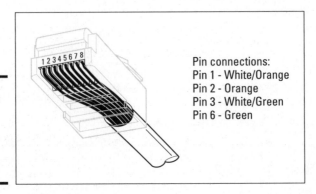

Figure 2-2:
Attaching
an RJ-45
connector
to twisted-
pair cable.

Pin connections:
Pin 1 - White/Orange
Pin 2 - Orange
Pin 3 - White/Green
Pin 6 - Green

✦ Some people wire 10BaseT cable differently — using the green and white pair for pins 1 and 2 and the orange and white pair for pins 3 and 6. This doesn't affect the operation of the network (the network is color-blind), *as long as the connectors on both ends of the cable are wired the same!*

✦ If you're installing cable for a Fast Ethernet system, you should be extra careful to follow the rules of Cat5 cabling. That means, among other things, making sure that you use Cat5 components throughout. The cable and all the connectors must be up to Cat5 specs. When you attach the connectors, don't untwist more than one-half inch of cable. And don't try to stretch the cable runs beyond the 100m maximum. When in doubt, have cable for a 100 Mbps Ethernet system professionally installed.

Crossover cables

You can use a *crossover cable* to connect two computers directly to each other (without a switch), but crossover cables are more often used to daisy-chain hubs and switches to each other.

To create your own crossover cable, to reverse the wires on one end of the cable, as shown in Table 2-3. This table shows how you should wire both ends of the cable to create a crossover cable. Connect one end according to the Connector A column and the other end according to the Connector B column.

You don't need to use a crossover cable if one of the switches or hubs that you want to connect has a crossover port, usually labeled *Uplink*. If the switch has an Uplink port, you can daisy-chain it by using a normal network cable. For more information about daisy-chaining hubs and switches, see the section, "Installing Switches," later in this chapter.

Table 2-3	Creating a Crossover Cable	
Pin	*Connector A*	*Connector B*
Pin 1	White/green	White/orange
Pin 2	Green	Orange
Pin 3	White/orange	White/green
Pin 4	Blue	Blue
Pin 5	White/blue	White/blue
Pin 6	Orange	Green
Pin 7	White/brown	White/brown
Pin 8	Brown	Brown

Wall jacks and patch panels

From the files of "Sure, You Could Do This, But Here's Why This Is a Bad Idea," you could run a single length of cable from a network switch in a wiring closet through a hole in the wall, up the wall to the space above the ceiling, through the ceiling space to the wall in an office, down the wall, through a hole, and all the way to a desktop computer. Here's the pitfall, though: Every time someone moves the computer or even cleans behind it, the cable will get moved a little bit. Eventually, the connection will fail, and the RJ-45 plug will have to be replaced. Then the cables in the wiring closet will quickly become a tangled mess.

The smarter path is to put a wall jack at the user's end of the cable and connect the other end of the cable to a patch panel. Then, the cable itself is completely contained within the walls and ceiling spaces. To connect a computer to the network, you plug one end of a patch cable (properly called a *station cable*) into the wall jack and plug the other end into the computer's network interface. In the wiring closet, you use a patch cable to connect the wall jack to the network switch. Figure 2-3 shows how this arrangement works.

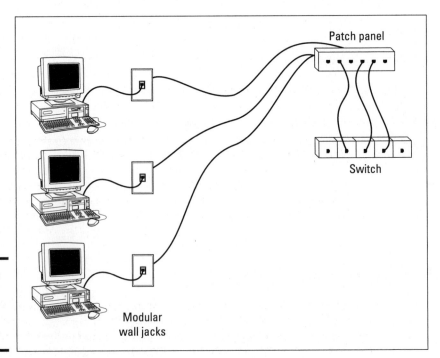

Figure 2-3:
Using wall jacks and patch panels.

Patch panel

Switch

Modular wall jacks

Connecting a twisted-pair cable to a wall jack or a patch panel is similar to connecting it to an RJ-45 plug. However, you don't usually need any special tools. Instead, the back of the jack has a set of slots that you lay each wire across. You then snap a removable cap over the top of the slots and press it down. This forces the wires into the slots, where little metal blades pierce the insulation and establish the electrical contact.

When you connect the wire to a jack or patch panel, be sure to untwist as little of the wire as possible. If you untwist too much of the wire, the signals that pass through the wire may become unreliable.

Installing Switches

Setting up a network switch is remarkably simple. In fact, you need to know only a few details:

✦ Installing a switch is usually very simple. Just plug in the power cord and then plug in patch cables to connect the network.

✦ Each port on the switch has an RJ-45 jack and a single LED indicator labeled *Link* that lights up when a connection has been established on the port. If you plug one end of a cable into the port and the other end into a computer or other network device, the Link light should come on. If it doesn't, something is wrong with the cable, the hub (or switch port), or the device on the other end of the cable.

✦ Each port may also have an LED indicator that flashes to indicate network activity. If you stare at a switch for awhile, you can find out who uses the network most by noting which activity indicators flash the most.

✦ The ports may also have a Collision indicator that flashes whenever a packet collision occurs on the port. It's perfectly acceptable for this light to flash now and then, but if it flashes a lot, you may have a problem with the network. Usually, this just means that the network is overloaded and should be segmented with a switch to improve performance. In some cases, though, a flashing Collision indicator may be caused by a faulty network node that clogs up the network with bad packets.

Daisy-Chaining Switches

If a single switch doesn't have enough ports for your entire network, you can connect switches together by *daisy-chaining* them. If one of the switches has an uplink port, you can use a normal patch cable to connect the uplink port to one of the regular ports on the other switch. If neither device has an uplink port, use a crossover cable to connect them. (For instructions on making a crossover cable, see the section, "Crossover cables," earlier in this chapter.)

On some hubs and switches, a button is used to switch one of the ports between a normal port and an uplink port. This button is often labeled MDI/ MDIX. To use the port as a normal port, switch the button to the MDI position. To use the port as an uplink port, switch the button to MDIX.

Some hubs and switches have a separate jack for the uplink port, but it turns out that the uplink port shares one of the normal ports internally. If that's the case, plugging a cable into the uplink port disables one of the normal ports. You shouldn't plug cables into both of these jacks. If you do, the switch won't work properly.

Note that the number of switches that you can chain together is limited. For 10BaseT networks, you shouldn't connect more than three switches to each other. For 100 Mbps or gigabit segments, you can chain only two switches together.

You can get around this rule by using *stackable switches.* Stackable switches have a special type of cable connector that connects two or more switches in a way that lets them function as if they were a single switch. Stackable switches are a must for large networks.

Chapter 3: Setting Up a Network Server

In This Chapter

✓ Thinking about the different ways to install a network operating system

✓ Getting ready for the installation

✓ Installing a network operating system

✓ Figuring out what to do after you install the network operating system

*A*fter you've installed the network cables and other devices, such as hubs and switches, the next step in building a network is usually setting up a server. After you physically connect the server computer to the network, you can install the network operating system (NOS) on the server. Then, you can configure it to provide the network services that you expect and need from the server.

The Many Ways to Install a Network Operating System

Regardless of which NOS you choose to use for your network servers, you can use any of several common ways to actually install the NOS software on the server computer. The following sections describe these alternatives.

Full install versus upgrade

One of the basic NOS installation choices is whether you want to perform a full installation or an upgrade installation. In some cases, you may be better off performing a full installation even if you're installing the NOS on a computer that already has an earlier version of the NOS installed.

✦ **Full:** If you're installing the NOS on a brand-new server, you'll be performing a *full installation* that installs the OS and configures it with default settings.

✦ **Upgrade:** If you're installing the NOS on a server computer that already has a server operating system installed, you can perform an *upgrade installation* that replaces the existing operating system with the new one but retains as many of the settings from the existing operating system as possible.

✦ **Multiboot:** You can also perform a full installation on a computer that already has an OS installed. In that case, you have the option of deleting the existing operating system or performing a *multiboot installation* that installs the new server OS alongside the existing OS. Then, when you restart the computer, you can choose which operating system you want to run.

Although multiboot installation may sound like a good idea, it's fraught with peril. I suggest that you avoid multiboot unless you have a specific reason to use it. For more information about multiboot setups, see the sidebar, "Giving multiboot the boot."

You can't upgrade a client version of Windows to a server version. Instead, you must perform a full installation, which deletes the existing Windows OS, or a multiboot installation, which leaves the existing client Windows intact. Either way, however, you can preserve existing data on the Windows computer when you install the server version.

Giving multiboot the boot

Multiboot installations enable you to have more than one OS on a single computer. Of course, only one OS can be running at any time. When you boot the computer, a menu appears with each installed OS listed. You can choose which OS to boot from this menu.

Multiboot is most useful for software developers or network managers who want to make sure that software is compatible with a wide variety of OSes. Rather than set up a bunch of separate computers with different OS versions, you can install several OSes on a single PC and use that one PC to test the software. For production network servers, however, you probably don't need to have more than one OS installed.

If you still insist on loading two or more OSes on a network server, be sure to install each

OS into its own disk partition. Although most NOSes let you install two (or more) OSes into a single partition, doing so is not a very good idea. To support two OSes in a single partition, both systems have to play a risky shell game with key system files — moving or renaming them each time you restart the computer. Unfortunately, things can go wrong. For example, if lightning strikes and the power goes out just as the NOS is switching the startup files around, you may find yourself with a server that can't boot to any of its installed OSes.

The best way to set up a multiboot system is to install each OS into its own partition. Then, you can use a boot manager program to choose the partition you want to boot from when you start the computer.

Installing over the network

Normally, you install the NOS directly from the CD-ROM distribution discs on the server's CD-ROM drive. However, you can also install the OS from a shared drive located on another computer, provided that the server computer already has access to the network. You can either use a shared CD-ROM drive or you can copy the entire contents of the distribution CD-ROM disc onto a shared hard drive.

Obviously, the server computer must have network access in order for this technique to work. If the server already has an OS installed, it probably already has access to the network. If not, you can boot the computer from a floppy that has basic network support.

If you're going to install the NOS onto more than one server, you can save time by first copying the distribution CD onto a shared hard drive. That's because even the fastest CD-ROM drives are slower than the network. Even with a basic 100 Mbps network, access to hard drive data over the network is much faster than access to a local CD-ROM drive.

Automated and remote installations

In case you find yourself in the unenviable position of installing an NOS onto several servers, you can use a few tricks to streamline the process:

✦ **Automated:** *Automated setup* lets you create a setup script that provides answers to all the questions asked by the installation program. After you create the script, you can start the automated setup, leave, and come back when the installation is finished. Creating the setup script is a bit of work, so automated setup makes sense only if you have more than a few servers to install.

✦ **RIS:** Microsoft has a feature called *Remote Installation Services* (RIS) that lets you install Windows server versions from a remote network location without even going to the server computer. This is tricky to set up, however, so it's really worth it only if you have a lot of servers on which to install OSes. (You can also use RIS to install client OSes.)

Gathering Your Stuff

Before you install an NOS, you should gather everything you need so you don't have to look for something in the middle of the setup. The following sections describe the items you're most likely to need.

A capable server computer

Obviously, you have to have a server computer on which to install the NOS. Each NOS has a list of the minimum hardware requirements supported by the OS. For example, Table 3-1 summarizes the minimum requirements for the Standard Edition of the current edition of Windows Server, known as Windows Server 2012.

My suggestion is that you take these minimums with a grain of salt. Windows Server 2012 will crawl like a snail with 512MB of RAM; I wouldn't bother with less than 4GB, and 16GB is a more appropriate minimum for most purposes.

Table 3-1	Minimum Hardware Requirements for Windows Server 2012
Item	*Windows Server 2012*
CPU	1.4 GHz
RAM	512MB
Free disk space	32GB

You should also check your server hardware against the list of compatible hardware published by the maker of your NOS. For example, Microsoft publishes a list of hardware that it has tested and certified as compatible with Windows servers. This list is the Hardware Compatibility List (HCL). You can check the HCL for your specific server by going to the Microsoft website at

```
www.microsoft.com/windows/compatibility/windows-7/
    en-us/default.aspx
```

You can also test your computer's compatibility by running the Check System Compatibility option from the Windows distribution CD-ROM.

You can find more specific details on server computer recommendations in Book I, Chapter 3.

The server OS

You also need a server OS to install. You'll need either the distribution CDs or DVDs or access to a copy of them over the network. In addition to the discs, you need the product key to successfully install the product. If you have the actual CDs or DVDs, the product key should be on a sticker attached to the case.

Other software

In most cases, the installation program should be able to automatically con-figure your server's hardware devices and install appropriate drivers. Just in case, though, you should dig out the driver disks that came with your devices, such as network interface cards (NICs), SCSI devices, DVD drives, printers, scanners, and so on.

A working Internet connection

This isn't an absolute requirement, but the installation will go much smoother if you have a working Internet connection before you start. The installation process may use this Internet connection for several things:

✦ **Downloading late-breaking updates or fixes to the operating system.**

This can eliminate the need to install a service pack after you finish installing the NOS.

✦ **Locating drivers for nonstandard devices**

This can be a big plus if you can't find the driver disk for your obscure SCSI card.

✦ **Activating the product after you complete the installation (for Microsoft OSes)**

A good book

You'll spend lots of time watching progress bars during installation, so you may as well have something to do while you wait. May I recommend *The Hitchhiker's Guide to the Galaxy?*

Making Informed Decisions

When you install an NOS, you have to make some decisions about how you want the OS and its servers configured. Most of these decisions aren't cast in stone, so don't worry if you're not 100 percent sure how you want every-thing configured. You can always go back and reconfigure things. However, you'll save yourself time if you make the right decisions up front rather than just guess when the setup program starts asking you questions.

The following list details most of the decisions that you'll need to make. (This list is for Windows Server 2012 installations. For other network operat-ing systems, the decisions may vary slightly.)

✦ **The existing OS:** If you want to retain the existing OS, the installation program can perform a multiboot setup, which allows you to choose which operating system to boot to each time you start the computer.

This is rarely a good idea for server computers, so I recommend that you elect to delete the existing OS.

✦ **Partition structure:** Most of the time, you'll want to treat the entire server disk as a single partition. However, if you want to divide the disk into two or more partitions, you should do so during setup. (Unlike most of the other setup decisions, this one is hard to change later.)

✦ **File system:** Windows Server 2012 provides two choices for the file system to format the server's disk: NT File System (NTFS) and Resilient File System (ReFS). The NTFS file system has been around since 1993. ReFS is a brand new file system which offers several important improvements over NTFS. However, because it is so new, most network administrators are going to be reluctant to use it — at least not right away. So NTFS will still be the file system of choice for the time being.

✦ **Computer name:** During the OS setup, you're asked to provide the computer name used to identify the server on the network. If your network has only a few servers, you can just pick a name such as Server01 or MyServer. If your network has more than a few servers, you'll want to follow an established guideline for creating server names.

✦ **Administrator password:** Okay, this one is tough. You don't want to pick something obvious, like Password, Administrator, or your last name. On the other hand, you don't want to type in something random that you'll later forget because you'll find yourself in a big pickle if you forget the administrator password. I suggest that you make up a complex password comprising a mix of uppercase and lowercase letters, some numerals, and a special symbol or two; then write it down and keep it in a secure location where you know it won't get lost.

✦ **Networking protocols:** You'll almost always need to install the TCP/IP protocol, the Microsoft network client protocol, and file and printer sharing. Depending on how the server will be used, you may want to install other protocols as well.

✦ **TCP/IP configuration:** You'll need to know what IP address to use for the server. Even if your network has a DHCP server to dynamically assign IP addresses to clients, most servers use static IP addresses.

✦ **Workgroup or domain:** You'll need to decide whether the server will join a domain or just be a member of a workgroup. In either case, you'll need to know the domain name or the workgroup name.

Final Preparations

Before you begin the actual installation, you should take a few more steps:

✦ Clean up the server's disk by uninstalling any software that you don't need and removing any old data that is no longer needed. This cleanup is especially important if you're converting a computer that's been in use as a client computer to a server. You probably don't need Microsoft Office or a bunch of games on the computer after it becomes a server.

✦ Do a complete backup of the computer. Operating system setup programs are almost flawless, so the chances of losing data during installation are minimal. But you still face the chance that something may go wrong.

✦ If the computer is connected to an uninterruptible power supply (UPS) that has a serial or USB connection to the computer, unplug the serial or USB connection. In some cases, this control connection can confuse the operating system's setup program when it tries to determine which devices are attached to the computer.

✦ If the computer has hard drives compressed with DriveSpace or DoubleSpace, uncompress the drives before you begin.

✦ Light some votive candles, take two Tylenol, and put on a pot of coffee.

Installing a Network Operating System

The following sections present an overview of a typical installation of Windows Server 2012. Although the details vary, the overall installation process for other network operating systems is similar.

In most cases, the best way to install Windows Server 2012 is to perform a new install directly from the DVD installation media. Although upgrade installs are possible, your server will be more stable if you perform a new install. (For this reason, most network administrators avoid upgrading to Windows Server 2012 until it's time to replace the server hardware.)

To begin the installation, insert the DVD distribution media in the server's DVD drive and then restart the server. This causes the server to boot directly from the distribution media, which initiates the setup program.

As the setup program proceeds, it leads you through two distinct installation phases: Collecting Information and Installing Windows. The following sections describe these installation phases in greater detail.

Phase 1: Collecting Information

In the first installation phase, the setup program asks for the preliminary information that it needs to begin the installation. A setup wizard prompts you for the information necessary to install Windows Server 2012. Specifically:

✦ **Language:** Select your language, time-zone, and keyboard type.

✦ **Product Key:** Enter the 25-character product key that came with the installation media. If setup says you entered an invalid product key, double-check it carefully. You probably just typed the key incorrectly.

✦ **Operating System Type:** The setup program lets you select Windows Server 2012 Standard Edition or Core. Choose Standard Edition to install the full server operating system; choose Core if you want to install the new text-only version.

✦ **License Agreement:** The official license agreement is displayed. You have to agree to its terms in order to proceed.

✦ **Install Type:** Choose an Upgrade or Clean Install type.

✦ **Disk Location:** Choose the partition in which you want to install Windows.

Phase 2: Installing Windows

In this phase, Windows setup begins the actual process of installing Windows. The following steps are performed in sequence:

1. **Copying Files:** Compressed versions of the installation files are copied to the server computer.

2. **Expanding Files:** The compressed installation files are expanded.

3. **Installing Features:** Windows server features are installed.

4. **Installing Updates:** The setup program checks Microsoft's Web site and downloads any critical updates to the operating system.

5. **Completing Installation:** When the updates are installed, the setup program reboots so it can complete the installation.

Configuring Your Server

After you've installed Windows Server 2012, the computer automatically reboots, and you're presented with the Server Manager program as shown in Figure 3-1.

From Server Manager, you can perform a number of tasks that are necessary to configure the server for production use. In particular, you'll need to:

✦ Configure network settings, especially if the server needs a static IP address.

✦ Set the computer name to something other than the default generated by the setup program.

✦ Join a domain.

✦ Add additional server roles, such as DHCP, DNS, IIS, and so on.

✦ Add more operating system features.

✦ Configure security features, such as the Windows Firewall.

For more information about completing the server configuration, refer to Chapter 1 of Book VII.

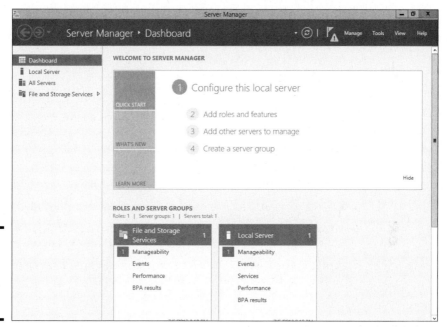

Book II
Chapter 3

Setting Up a
Network Server

Figure 3-1:
The
Windows
2012 Server
Manager.

Chapter 4: Configuring Windows Clients

In This Chapter

✓ Configuring network connections for Windows clients

✓ Setting the computer name, description, and workgroup

✓ Joining a domain

✓ Setting logon options

*B*efore your network setup is complete, you must configure the network's client computers. In particular, you have to configure each client's network interface card so that it works properly, and you have to install the right protocols so that the clients can communicate with other computers on the network.

Fortunately, the task of configuring client computers for the network is child's play in Windows. For starters, Windows automatically recognizes your network interface card when you start up your computer. All that remains is to make sure that Windows properly installed the network protocols and client software.

With each version of Windows, Microsoft has simplified the process of configuring client network support. In this chapter, I describe the steps for configuring networking for Windows XP, Windows Vista, Windows 7, and Windows 8.

Configuring Network Connections

Windows automatically detects the presence of a network adapter; normally, you don't have to install device drivers manually for the adapter. When Windows detects a network adapter, it automatically creates a network connection and configures it to support basic networking protocols. You may need to change the configuration of a network connection manually, however. The procedures for Windows XP and Vista are described in the following sections.

Configuring Windows XP network connections

The following steps show how to configure your network connection on a Windows XP system:

1. **Choose Start➪Control Panel to open the Control Panel.**

2. **Double-click the Network Connections icon.**

The Network Connections folder appears, as shown in Figure 4-1.

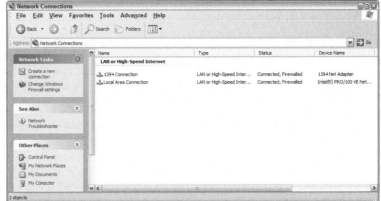

Figure 4-1:
The
Network
Connections
folder.

3. **Right-click the connection that you want to configure and then choose Properties from the contextual menu that appears.**

Either way, the Properties dialog box for the network connection appears, as shown in Figure 4-2.

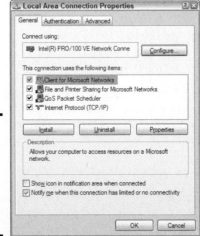

Figure 4-2:
The
Properties
dialog
box for a
network
connection.

4. To configure the network adapter card settings, click Configure.

This action summons the Properties dialog box for the network adapter, as shown in Figure 4-3. This dialog box has five tabs that let you configure the NIC:

- *General:* This tab shows basic information about the NIC, such as the device type and status. For example, the device shown in Figure 4-3 is an Intel Pro 100 network interface. (It's installed in slot 3 of the computer's PCI bus.)

If you're having trouble with the adapter, you can click the Troubleshoot button to open the Windows XP Hardware Troubleshooter. You can also disable the device if it's preventing other components of the computer from working properly.

- *Advanced:* This tab lets you set a variety of device-specific parameters that affect the operation of the NIC. Some cards allow you to set the speed parameter (typically, at 10 Mbps or 100 Mbps) or the number of buffers the card should use.

Consult the manual that came with the card before you play around with any of those settings.

- *Driver:* This tab displays information about the device driver that's bound to the NIC and lets you update the driver to a newer version, roll back the driver to a previously working version, or uninstall the driver.

- *Resources:* With this tab, you can use manual settings to limit the system resources used by the card — including the memory range, I/O range, IRQ, and DMA channels.

Figure 4-3:
The
Properties
dialog
box for a
network
adapter.

Intel(R) PRO/100 VE Network Connection Properties

General | Advanced | Driver | Resources | Power Management

Intel(R) PRO/100 VE Network Connection

Device type: Network adapters
Manufacturer: Intel
Location: PCI bus 3, device 8, function 0

Device status

This device is working properly.

If you are having problems with this device, click Troubleshoot to start the troubleshooter.

Troubleshoot...

Device usage:
Use this device (enable)

OK | Cancel

In the old days, before Plug and Play cards, you had to configure these settings whenever you installed a card, and it was easy to create resource conflicts. Windows configures these settings automatically so that you should rarely need to fiddle with them.

- *Power Management:* This tab lets you set power-management options. You can specify that the network card be shut down whenever the computer goes into sleep mode — and that the computer wake up periodically to refresh its network state.

When you click OK to dismiss the network adapter's Properties dialog box, the network connection's Properties dialog box closes. Select the Change Settings of This Connection option again to continue the procedure.

5. **Make sure that the network items your client requires are listed in the network connection Properties dialog box.**

   The following list describes the most important items you commonly see listed here:

   - *Client for Microsoft Networks:* This item is required if you want to access a Microsoft Windows network. It should always be present.

   - *File and Printer Sharing for Microsoft Networks:* This item allows your computer to share its files or printers with other computers on the network.

   This option is usually used with peer-to-peer networks, but you can use it even if your network has dedicated servers. If you don't plan to share files or printers on the client computer, however, you should disable this item.

   - *Internet Protocol (TCP/IP):* This item enables the client computer to communicate by using the TCP/IP protocol.

   If all servers on the network support TCP/IP, this protocol should be the only one installed on the client.

6. **If a protocol that you need isn't listed, click the Install button to add the needed protocol.**

   A dialog box appears, asking whether you want to add a network client, protocol, or service. Click Protocol and then click Add. A list of available protocols appears. Select the one you want to add; then click OK. (You may be asked to insert a disc or the Windows CD.)

7. **Make sure that the network client that you want to use appears in the list of network resources.**

   For a Windows-based network, make sure that Client for Microsoft Networks is listed. For a NetWare network, make sure that Client Service for NetWare appears. If your network uses both types of servers, you can choose both clients.

If you have NetWare servers, use the NetWare client software that comes with NetWare rather than the client supplied by Microsoft with Windows.

8. **If the client that you need isn't listed, click the Install button to add the client that you need, click Client, click Add; then choose the client that you want to add, and click OK.**

   The client you select is added to the network connection's Properties dialog box.

9. **To remove a network item that you don't need (such as File and Printer Sharing for Microsoft Networks), select the item, and click the Uninstall button.**

   For security reasons, you should make it a point to remove any clients, protocols, or services that you don't need.

10. **To configure TCP/IP settings, click Internet Protocol (TCP/IP); click Properties to display the TCP/IP Properties dialog box; adjust the settings; and then click OK.**

    The TCP/IP Properties dialog box, shown in Figure 4-4, lets you choose among these options:

    - *Obtain an IP Address Automatically:* Choose this option if your network has a DHCP server that assigns IP addresses automatically. Choosing this option dramatically simplifies administering TCP/IP on your network. (See Book IV, Chapter 3, for more information about DHCP.)

    - *Use the Following IP Address:* If your computer must have a specific IP address, choose this option and then type the computer's IP address, subnet mask, and default gateway address. (For more information about these settings, see Book IV, Chapter 2.)

    - *Obtain DNS Server Address Automatically:* The DHCP server can also provide the address of the Domain Name System (DNS) server that the computer should use. Choose this option if your network has a DHCP server. (See Book IV, Chapter 4, for more information about DNS.)

    - *Use the Following DNS Server Addresses:* Choose this option if a DNS server isn't available. Then type the IP addresses of the primary and secondary DNS servers.

Configuring Windows Vista network connections

The procedure for configuring a network connection on Windows Vista is similar to the procedure for Windows XP, except that Microsoft decided to bury the configuration dialog boxes a little deeper in the bowels of Windows.

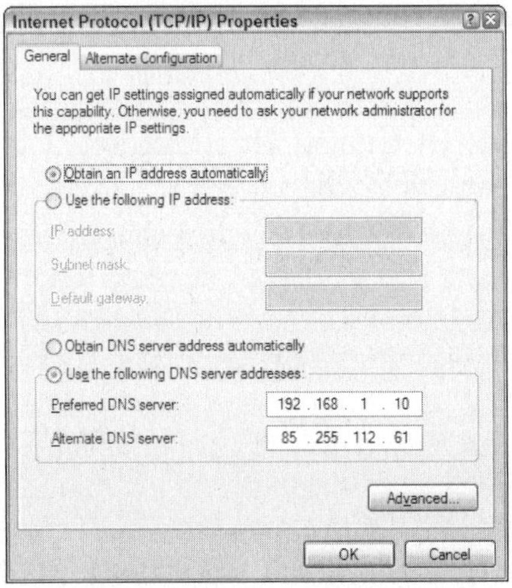

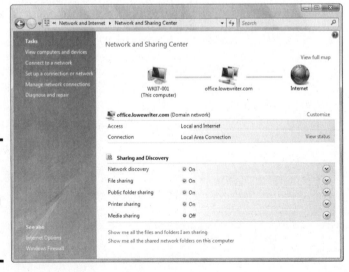

Figure 4-4:
Configuring
TCP/IP.

To find the settings you need, follow these steps:

1. **Choose Start⊳Control Panel to open the Control Panel.**

2. **Choose View Network Status and Tasks under the Network and Internet heading.**

This step opens the Network and Sharing Center, shown in Figure 4-5.

Figure 4-5:
The
Network
and Sharing
Center
(Windows
Vista).

3. Click Manage Network Connections.

The Network Connections folder appears, as shown in Figure 4-6.

Figure 4-6:
The
Network
Connections
folder
(Windows
Vista).

4. Right-click the connection that you want to configure and then choose Properties from the contextual menu that appears.

The Properties dialog box for the network connection appears, as shown in Figure 4-7. If you compare this dialog box with the dialog box that was shown earlier, in Figure 4-2, you see that they're similar.

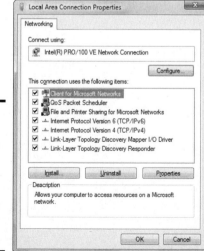

Figure 4-7:
The
Properties
dialog
box for a
network
connection
(Windows
Vista).

5. **Click Configure to configure the network connection.**

From this point, the steps for configuring the network connection are the same as they are for Windows XP. As a result, you can continue by beginning with Step 4 in the preceding section, "Configuring Windows XP network connections."

Configuring Windows 7 and Windows 8 network connections

The procedure for configuring a Windows 7 network connection is similar to the Windows Vista procedure, with just a few minor variations. Here are the steps:

1. **Open the Control Panel.**

In Windows 7, choose Start⇨Control Panel to open the Control Panel.

In Windows 8, right-click the bottom-left corner of the screen and then choose Control Panel from the contextual menu.

2. **Choose Network and Sharing Center.**

This step opens the Network and Sharing Center, shown in Figure 4-8.

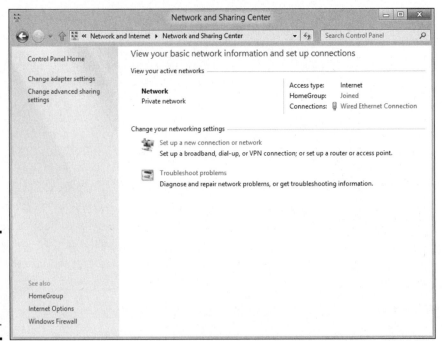

Figure 4-8:
The
Network
and Sharing
Center
(Windows 8).

3. **Click the Change Adapter Settings link on the left.**

   The Network Connections folder appears, as shown in Figure 4-9.

4. **Right-click the connection that you want to configure and then choose Properties from the contextual menu that appears.**

   The Properties dialog box for the network connection appears, as shown in Figure 4-10. If you compare this dialog box with the dialog box that was shown earlier, in Figure 4-2, you see that they're the same.

5. **Click Configure to configure the network connection.**

   From this point, the steps for configuring the network connection are the same as they are for Windows XP. As a result, you can continue by beginning with Step 4 in the earlier section "Configuring Windows XP network connections."

Figure 4-9:
The Network Connections folder (Windows 8).

**Book II
Chapter 4**

**Configuring
Windows Clients**

Figure 4-10:
The
Properties
dialog
box for a
network
connection
(Windows 8).

Configuring Client Computer Identification

Every client computer must identify itself to participate in the network. The computer identification consists of the computer's name, an optional description, and the name of either the workgroup or the domain to which the computer belongs.

The computer name must follow the rules for NetBIOS names; it may be 1 to 15 characters long and may contain letters, numbers, or hyphens but no spaces or periods. For small networks, it's common to make the computer name the same as the username. For larger networks, you may want to develop a naming scheme that identifies the computer's location. A name such as `C-305-1` may be assigned to the first computer in Room 305 of Building C, for example, or `MKTG010` may be a computer in the Marketing department.

If the computer will join a domain, you need to have access to an Administrator account on the domain unless the administrator has already created a computer account on the domain. Note that only the following versions of Windows have the capability to join a domain:

✦ Windows 8 Professional and Enterprise

✦ Windows 7 Professional, Enterprise, and Ultimate

✦ Windows Vista Business, Enterprise, and Ultimate

✦ Windows XP Professional

When you install Windows on the client system, the Setup program asks for the computer name and workstation or domain information. You can change this information later, if you want. The procedure varies depending on the Windows version you're using.

Configuring Windows XP computer identification

To change the computer identification in Windows XP, follow these steps:

1. **Open the Control Panel (Start➪Control Panel), and double-click the System icon to open the System Properties dialog box.**

2. **Click the Computer Name tab.**

The computer identification information is displayed.

3. **Click the Change button.**

This step displays the Computer Name Changes dialog box, as shown in Figure 4-11.

4. **Type the new computer name and then specify the workgroup or domain information.**

To join a domain, select the Domain radio button and type the domain name in the appropriate text box. To join a workgroup, select the Workgroup radio button and type the workgroup name in the corresponding text box.

5. **Click OK.**

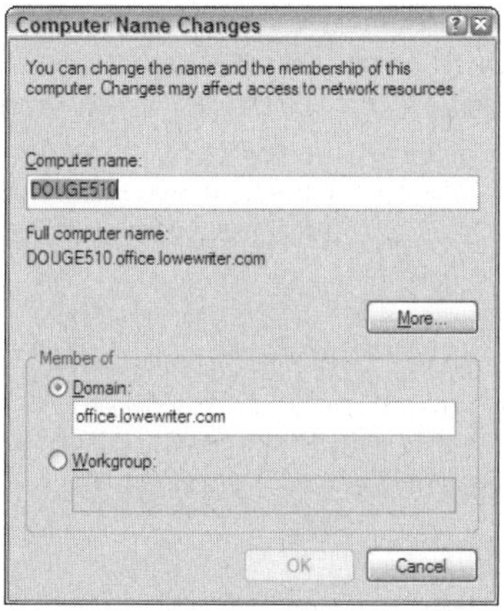

Book II
Chapter 4

Configuring Windows Clients

Figure 4-11:
The Computer Name Changes dialog box (Windows XP).

Computer Name Changes

You can change the name and the membership of this computer. Changes may affect access to network resources.

Computer name:
DOUGE510

Full computer name:
DOUGE510.office.lowewriter.com

More...

Member of

⦿ Domain:
office.lowewriter.com

◯ Workgroup:

OK   Cancel

6. **If you're prompted, enter the username and password for an Administrator account.**

You're asked to provide this information only if a computer account hasn't already been created for the client computer.

7. **When a dialog box appears, informing you that you need to restart the computer, click OK; then restart the computer.**

You're done!

Configuring computer identification on Windows Vista, Windows 7, or Windows 8

To change the computer identification in Windows Vista, Windows 7, or Windows 8, follow these steps:

1. **Open the Control Panel.**

   In Windows Vista or Windows 7, choose Start⇨Control Panel to open the Control Panel.

   In Windows 8, right-click the bottom-left corner of the screen and then choose Control Panel from the contextual menu.

2. **Double-click the System icon.**

   This step displays the System information window. Figure 4-12 shows the Windows 8 version, but the Windows Vista and Windows 7 versions are similar. Notice the section that lists computer name, domain, and workgroup settings.

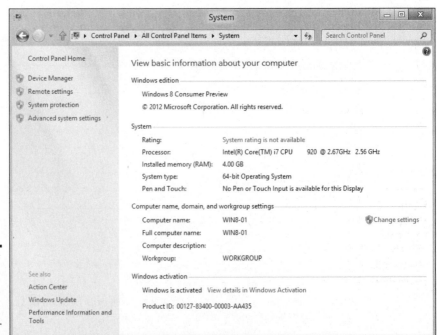

Figure 4-12:
The System information window (Windows 8).

3. **Click the Change Settings link in the bottom-right corner.**

   If a dialog box appears and asks for your permission to continue, click Continue. The System Properties dialog box appears, as shown in Figure 4-13.

4. **Click the Change button.**

   This step displays the Computer Name/Domain Changes dialog box, as shown in Figure 4-14.

5. **Enter the computer name and the workgroup or domain name.**

   If you want to join a domain, choose the Domain option button, and type the domain name. To join a workgroup, choose the Workgroup option button, and type the workgroup name.

6. **Click OK.**

7. **Enter the username and password for an Administrator account when prompted.**

   You're asked to provide this information only if a computer account hasn't already been created for the client computer.

8. **When a dialog box appears, informing you that you need to restart the computer, click OK; then restart the computer.**

   The computer is added to the domain or workgroup.

**Book II
Chapter 4**

Configuring
Windows Clients

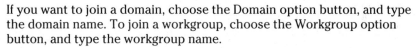

Figure 4-13:
The System
Properties
dialog box
(Windows 8).

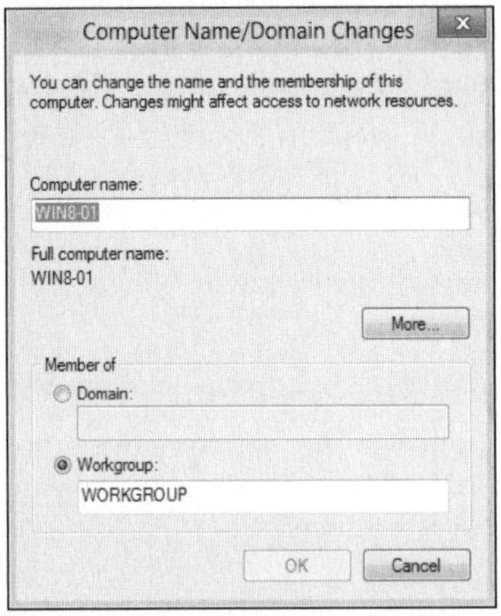

Figure 4-14:
The
Computer
Name/
Domain
Changes
dialog box
(Windows 7).

Computer Name/Domain Changes

You can change the name and the membership of this
computer. Changes might affect access to network resources.

Computer name:
WIN8-01

Full computer name:
WIN8-01

More...

Member of

○ Domain:

◉ Workgroup:
WORKGROUP

OK   Cancel

Configuring Network Logon

Every user who wants to access a domain-based network must log on to the
domain by using a valid user account. The user account is created on the
domain controller — not on the client computer.

Network logon isn't required to access workgroup resources. Instead, workgroup resources can be password-protected to restrict access.

When you start a Windows computer that's been configured to join
a domain, as described in the section "Configuring Client Computer
Identification," earlier in this chapter, the Log On to Windows dialog box is
displayed. The user can use this dialog box to log on to a domain by entering
a domain username and password and then selecting the domain that she
wants to log on to (from the Log On To drop-down list).

You can create local user accounts in Windows that allow users to access
resources on the local computer. To log on to the local computer, the user
selects This Computer from the Log On To drop-down list and enters the
username and password for a local user account. When a user logs on by
using a local account, he isn't connected to a network domain. To log on to a
domain, the user must select the domain from the Log On To drop-down list.

If the computer isn't part of a domain, Windows can display a friendly logon
screen that displays an icon for each of the computer's local users. The user
can log on simply by clicking the appropriate icon and entering a password.
(This feature isn't available for computers that have joined a domain.)

Note that if the user logs on by using a local computer account rather than a domain account, she can still access domain resources. A Connect To dialog box appears whenever the user attempts to access a domain resource. Then the user can enter a domain username and password to connect to the domain.

Configuring
Windows Clients

Chapter 5: Macintosh Networking

In This Chapter

✔ **Hooking up a Macintosh network**

✔ **Using a Macintosh network**

✔ **Mixing Macs and PCs**

*T*his book dwells on networking Windows-based computers, as though Microsoft were the only game in town. I'm sure plenty of people in Redmond, WA (where Microsoft is headquartered) wished that it were so. But alas, there is an entirely different breed of computer: the Apple Macintosh, more commonly referred to simply as *Mac*.

Every Macintosh ever built, even an original 1984 model, includes networking support. Newer Macintosh computers have better built-in networking features than older Macintosh computers, of course. The newest Macs include either built-in gigabit Ethernet connections or 802.11n wireless connections, or both. Support for these network connections is pretty much automatic, so all you have to do is plug your Mac into a network or connect to a wireless network, and you're ready to go.

This chapter presents what you need to know to network Mac computers. You'll learn how to control basic Mac network options such as TCP/IP and file sharing. And you'll learn how to join a Mac to a Windows domain network.

Basic Mac Network Settings

Most network settings on an OS X are automatic. If you wish, you can look at and change the default network settings by following these steps:

1. **Choose System Preferences, then choose Networking.**

The Network preferences page appears, as shown in Figure 5-1.

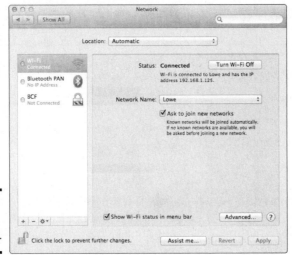

Figure 5-1:
Network
preferences.

2. Click Advanced.

The advanced network settings are displayed, as shown in Figure 5-2.

Figure 5-2:
Advanced
network
settings.

3. Click the TCP/IP tab to view or change the TCP/IP settings.

This brings up the TCP/IP settings, as shown in Figure 5-3. From this
page, you can view the IP currently assigned IP address for the computer. And, if you wish, you can assign a static IP address by changing
the Configure IPv4 drop down setting from Using DHCP to Manually.

Then, you can enter your own IP address, subnet mask, and router address.

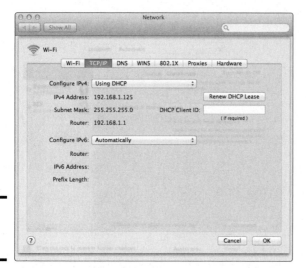

**Book II
Chapter 5**

**Macintosh
Networking**

Figure 5-3:
TCP/IP
settings.

4. **Click the DNS tab to view or change the DNS settings.**

   This brings up the DNS settings shown in Figure 5-4. Here, you can see the DNS servers currently being used, and you can add additional DNS servers if you wish.

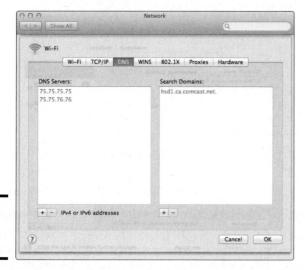

Figure 5-4:
DNS
settings.

5. **Click the Hardware tab to view hardware information.**

   This brings up the DNS settings shown in Figure 5-5. The most useful bit of information on this tab is the MAC address, which is sometimes needed to set up wireless network security. (For more information, refer to Chapter 2 of Book V.)

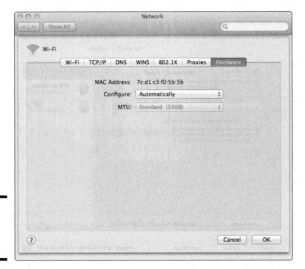

Figure 5-5:
Hardware
settings.

What About OS X Server?

At one time, Apple offered a dedicated network operating system known as Mac OS X Server (the *X* is pronounced *Ten,* not *Ex).* In 2011, Apple merged Mac OS X Server with its desktop operating system and made the server components of the operating system available as an inexpensive add-on you can purchase from the App Store. For the latest version of OS X (10.8, released in July of 2012), the Server App enhancement can be purchased for under $20.

The Server App download adds a variety of network server features to OS X, including:

✔ **Apache web server,** which also runs on Windows and Linux systems

✔ **MySQL,** which is also available in Windows and Linux versions

✔ **Wiki Server,** which lets you set up web-based wiki, blog, and calendaring sites

✔ **NetBoot,** a feature that simplifies the task of managing network client computers

✔ **Spotlight Server,** which lets you search for content on remote file servers

✔ **Podcast Producer,** which lets the create and distribute multimedia programs

Joining a Domain

If you are using a Mac in a Windows domain environment, you can join the Mac to the domain by following these steps:

1. Choose Settings, then choose Users & Groups.

This brings up the Users and Groups page, as shown in Figure 5-6.

Figure 5-6:
Users and
Groups.

2. Select the user account you want to join to the domain, then click Login Options.

The Login Options page appears, as shown in Figure 5-7.

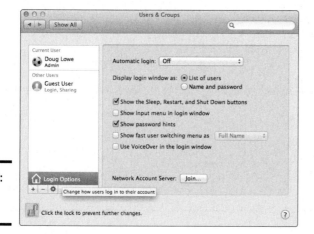

Figure 5-7:
Login
options.

3. **If the lock icon at the bottom left corner of the page is locked, click it and enter your password when prompted.**

   By default, the user login options are locked to prevent unauthorized changes. This step unlocks the settings so that you can join the domain.

4. **Click the Join button.**

   You are prompted to enter the name of the domain you want to join, as shown in Figure 5-8.

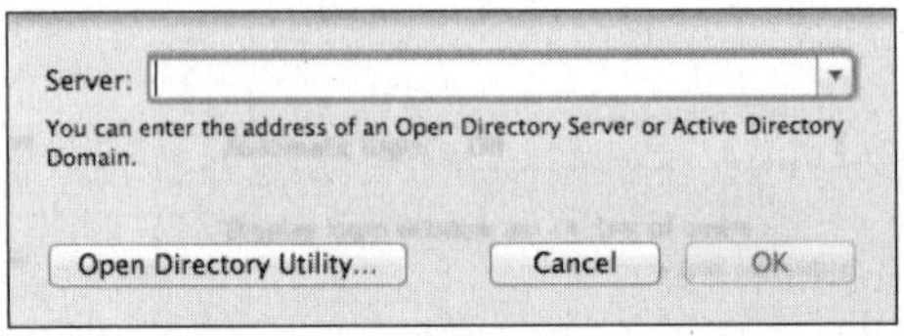

Figure 5-8:
Joining a
domain.

5. **Enter the name of the domain you want to join.**

   When you enter the domain name, the dialog box will expand to allow you to enter domain credentials to allow you to join the domain, as shown in Figure 5-9.

Figure 5-9:
Authenti-
cating with
the domain.

6. **Enter the name and password of a domain administrator account, then click OK.**

   You are returned to the Login Options page, which shows that you have successfully joined the domain as shown in Figure 5-10.

7. **Close the Users & Groups window.**

Figure 5-10:
Congratula-
tions! You
have now
joined the
domain.

Connecting to a Share

Once you have joined a domain, you can access its network shares via the
Finder. Just follow these steps:

1. **Click Finder.**

This opens the Finder, as shown in Figure 5-11.

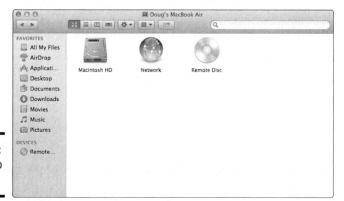

Figure 5-11:
Welcome to
the Finder.

2. **Choose Go⇨Connect to Server.**

The Connect to Server dialog box appears.

3. **Type the smb path that leads to the server share you want to connect to.**

   To type a smb path, follow this syntax:

   ```
   smb://server-name/share-name
   ```

   Replace the `server-name` with the name of the server that contains the share and `share-name` with the name of the share. For example, to connect to a share named `files` on a server named `lowe01`, type `smb://lowe01/files`.

4. **Click Connect.**

   You'll be prompted for login credentials.

5. **Enter a domain username and password, then click OK.**

   Precede the user name with the domain name, separated by a backslash. For example, if the domain name is `lowewriter.pri` and the user name is `Doug`, enter `lowewriter.pri\Doug` as the username.

   Once connected, the files in the share will be displayed in the Finder window. You can then open files directly from the share (provided you have the right software, such as Microsoft Office, to read the files). You can also drag and drop files between the Mac and the file shares.

Chapter 6: Configuring Other Network Features

In This Chapter

✔ Setting up network printers

✔ Configuring your client computer's Internet connections

✔ Mapping network drives

*A*fter you have your network servers and clients up and running, you still have many details to attend to before you can pronounce your network "finished." In this chapter, you discover a few more configuration chores that have to be done: configuring Internet access, setting up network printers, configuring e-mail, and configuring mapped network drives.

Configuring Network Printers

Before network users can print on the network, the network's printers must be properly configured. For the most part, this task is a simple one. All you have to do is configure each client that needs access to the printer.

 Before you configure a network printer to work with network clients, read the client configuration section of the manual that came with the printer. Many printers come with special software that provides more advanced printing and networking features than the standard features provided by Windows. If so, you may want to install the printer manufacturer's software on your client computers rather than use the standard Windows network printer support.

Adding a network printer

The exact procedure for adding a network printer varies a bit, depending on the Windows version that the client runs. The following steps describe the procedure for Windows 7 and Windows 8 (the procedure for Windows Vista is similar):

1. **Open the Control Panel; then choose Devices and Printers.**

2. **Click the Add a Printer button on the toolbar.**

This step starts the Add Printer Wizard, shown in Figure 6-1.

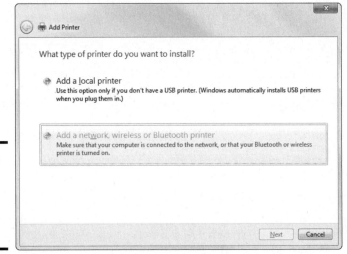

Figure 6-1:
The Add
Printer
Wizard
comes to
life.

3. **Select the Add a Network, Wireless or Bluetooth Printer option.**

   The wizard searches the network for available printers and displays a
   list of the printers it finds, as shown in Figure 6-2.

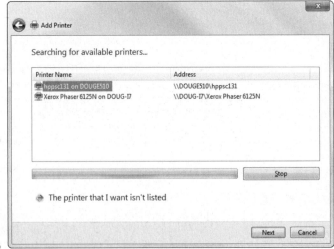

Figure 6-2:
The Add
Printer
Wizard asks
you to pick a
printer.

4. **Click the printer you want to use.**

   If you can't find the printer you want to use, click The Printer That I
   Want Isn't Listed and enter the UNC or IP address for the printer when
   prompted.

5. **Click Next to add the printer.**

The wizard copies to your computer the correct printer driver for the network printer. (You may be prompted to confirm that you want to add the driver. If so, click Install Driver to proceed.)

Next, the Add Printer Wizard displays a screen that shows the printer's name and asks whether you want to designate the printer as your default printer.

6. **If you want, designate the printer as your default printer.**

7. **Click Next to continue.**

A final confirmation dialog box is displayed.

8. **Click Finish.**

You're done!

Accessing a network printer using a web interface

Printers that have a direct network connection often include a built-in web server that lets you manage the printer from any browser on the network. Figure 6-3 shows the home page for a Xerox Phaser 6125 printer. This web interface lets you view status information about the printer and check the printer's configuration. You can even view error logs to find out how often the printer jams.

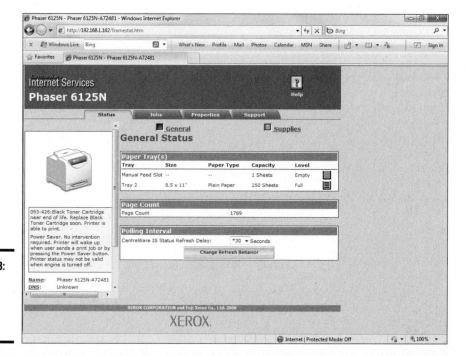

Figure 6-3:
Using a
printer's
web
interface.

To call up a printer's web interface, enter its IP address or host name in the address bar of any web browser.

In addition to simply displaying information about the printer, you can adjust the printer's configuration from a web browser. Figure 6-4 shows the Network Settings page for the Xerox printer. Here, you can change the network configuration details, such as the TCP/IP host name, IP address, subnet mask, domain name, and so on. Other configuration pages allow you to tell the printer to send an e-mail notification to an address that you specify whenever you encounter a problem with the printer.

As the network administrator, you may need to visit the printer's web page frequently. I suggest that you add it to your browser's Favorites menu so that you can get to it easily. If you have several printers, add them to a folder named Network Printers.

Figure 6-4:
Changing
network
settings via
a printer's
web
interface.

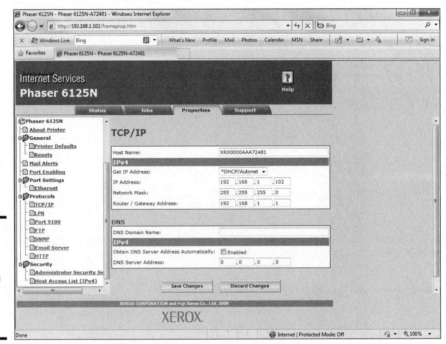

Configuring Internet Access

To enable the network users to access the Internet, you need to make sure that the TCP/IP configuration settings on each client computer are set correctly. If you have a high-speed Internet connection (such as T1, DSL, cable, or ISDN) connected to the Internet via a router, and your network uses DHCP for automatic TCP/IP configuration, you may not need to do anything special to get your clients connected to the Internet.

Configuring clients for DHCP

The easiest way to configure client computers to access the Internet via a shared high-speed connection is to use DHCP. DHCP automatically distributes the detailed TCP/IP configuration information to each client. Then, if your configuration changes, all you have to do is change the DHCP server's configuration. You don't have to change each client manually. Also, the DHCP server prevents common manual configuration errors, such as assigning the same IP address to two computers.

Book II
Chapter 6

Configuring Other
Network Features

Setting up the DHCP server

Before you configure the clients to use DHCP, you should set up the DHCP server. The DHCP server's configuration should include

+ A scope that specifies the range of IP addresses and the subnet mask to be distributed to client computers

+ The IP address of the router that should be used as the default gateway for client computers to reach the Internet

+ The IP addresses of the DNS servers that clients should use

Note that DHCP can be provided either by a server computer or by an intelligent router that has built-in DHCP. For more information about configuring DHCP, see Book IV, Chapter 3.

Setting up Windows clients

After the DHCP server is configured, setting up Windows clients to use it is a snap. Just follow these steps for Windows 7 or Windows 8:

1. **Open the Control Panel, and click View Network Status and Tasks.**

2. **Click Change Adapter Settings.**

3. **Right-click the LAN connection icon, and choose Properties from the contextual menu.**

   This brings up the Local Area Connection Properties dialog box, as shown in Figure 6-5.

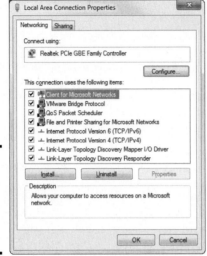

Figure 6-5:
The Local
Area
Connection
Properties
dialog box.

4. **Select Internet Protocol Version 4 (TCP/IPv4) from the list of items used by the connection and then click the Properties button.**

   This displays the Internet Protocol Version 4 (TCP/IP) Properties dialog box, as shown in Figure 6-6.

Figure 6-6:
The Internet
Protocol
Version 4
(TCP/IPv4)
Properties
dialog box.

5. **Make sure that both the Obtain an IP Address Automatically and Obtain DNS Server Address Automatically options are selected.**

   These options enable DHCP for the client.

6. **Click OK to return to the Local Area Connection Properties dialog box; then click OK again.**

That's all there is to it. The computer is configured to use DHCP. You should check to make sure that every computer on your network is configured for DHCP.

Configuring TCP/IP manually

If your network doesn't have a DHCP server, you'll have to configure the TCP/IP configuration manually for each computer. Start by deciding the IP address that you want to assign to each computer. Then follow the preceding procedure on every computer. When you get to Step 4, enter the computer's IP address as well as the IP address of the default gateway (your Internet router) and the IP addresses of your DNS servers.

Frankly, setting up a DHCP server is a lot easier than configuring each computer's TCP/IP information manually unless your network has only two or three computers. So unless your network is tiny, get a DHCP server.

Nearly all routers, both wired and wireless, include a DHCP feature that's enabled by default. So you don't have to go to great lengths to enable DHCP; just connect your computers to a DHCP-enabled router and you're done.

Book II
Chapter 6

Configuring Other Network Features

Mapping Network Drives

One of the main reasons that users want to use a network is to access shared disk storage located on network file servers. Although you can do this in several ways, the most common method is called *mapping*. Mapping assigns a drive letter to a shared folder on a network server. Then the user can use the drive letter to access the shared folder as though that folder were a local drive.

Before you map network drives for your network's client computers, you should devise a strategy for sharing folders and mapping them to drives. Here are just two possibilities:

+ **For private storage,** you can create a separate shared folder for each user on the file server and then map a drive letter on each user's computer to that user's shared folder. You can create shares named jBrannan, dHodgson, and mCaldwell, for example. Then you can map drive N: to jBrannan on jBrannan's computer, dHodgson on dHodgson's computer, and mCaldwell on mCaldwell's computer.

+ **For shared storage for an entire department,** you can create a share for the entire department and then map a drive to that share on each computer in the department. You may map drive M: to a share named Marketing for the entire Marketing department to use, for example.

After you've decided how to map the file server's shared folder, the next step is creating and sharing the folders on the server. For information about how to do that, refer to the appropriate chapters on specific network operating systems later in this book.

When you're ready to map drives on the client computers, follow these steps:

1. **Open Windows Explorer.**

   In Windows 7, choose Start⇨Computer.

   In Windows 8, right-click the bottom-left corner of the desktop, and choose Windows Explorer from the contextual menu.

2. **Click the Map Network Drive button.**

   The Map Network Drive dialog box appears, as shown in Figure 6-7.

3. **Select the drive letter that you want to map from the Drive drop-down list.**

4. **Type a valid path to the server and share what you want to map in the Folder text box.**

   To map a folder named pCaldwell on a server named MKTSERVER, for example, type **\\MKTSERVER\pCaldwell**.

   If you don't know the server or share name, click the Browse button, and browse your way to the folder that you want to map.

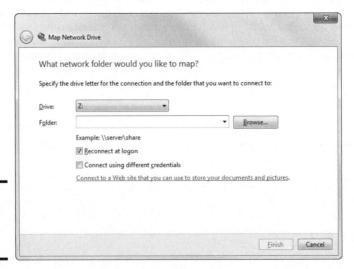

Figure 6-7:
Mapping
a network
drive.

5. **To cause the network drive to be automatically mapped each time the user logs on, select the Reconnect at Logon check box.**

   If you leave this check box deselected, the drive is mapped only until the next time you shut down Windows or log off.

6. **Click Finish.**

   That's it! You're done.

If you're the type who prefers to do things through the command line, you can map network drives quickly by using the NET USE command at a command prompt. Here's a NET USE command that maps drive Z: to \\MKTSERVER\pCaldwell:

```
net use z: \\MKTSERVER\pCaldwell /persistent:yes
```

Specifying /persistent:yes causes the drive to be remapped each time the user logs on. To remove a drive mapping via the command line, use a command like this:

```
net use z: /delete
```

Here, the mapping for drive Z: is removed.

Setting up drive mappings manually as described here works well enough for small networks, but not so well for large networks. If a server or share name changes, would you want to go to 200 computers to update drive mappings? How about 2,000 computers? For larger networks, you're more likely to use either logon scripts or group policies to configure network storage for end users. You can find more information about logon scripts and group policies in Book VII, Chapters 4 and 6.

**Book II
Chapter 6**

Configuring Other
Network Features

Chapter 7: Verifying Your Network Installation

In This Chapter

✔ Checking the network configuration settings

✔ Pinging yourself and others

✔ Making sure that you can log on

✔ Verifying mapped drives and checking network printers

You've installed all the network cards, plugged in all the cables, and configured all the software. One task remains, however, before you can declare your network finished: You must verify that the network works as expected.

Verifying a network isn't difficult. All you have to do is make sure that users can log on and access the network resources they need. If everything works the way it should, you can declare victory, give yourself a high five, and take the afternoon off. If not, you have to do some troubleshooting to determine the source of the problem.

In this short chapter, I describe some of the tests that you should perform to make sure that your network is functioning. Along the way, I suggest a few of the most common problems that may interrupt the network. The focus of this chapter, however, is on verifying that your network is functioning — not on troubleshooting it if it isn't. For information about network troubleshooting, refer to Book III, Chapters 6 and 7, as well as Book VII, Chapter 7.

Incidentally, most of the techniques described in this chapter work from a command prompt. You can open a command prompt in Windows Vista or Windows 7 by clicking the Start button, typing **cmd**, and pressing Enter. In Windows XP, choose Start➪Run, type **cmd**, and then click OK.

Is the Computer Connected to the Network?

This one is easy to check. Just check the Link light on the computer's network interface card and the light on the network hub or switch port that the computer is connected to. If both are lit, the computer is connected to the network. If one isn't lit, or both aren't lit, you have a connection problem. Several things may be wrong:

✦ The patch cable that connects the computer to the wall outlet or that connects to the hub or switch may be bad. Replace it with one that you know is good to verify this problem.

✦ The cable running between the wall outlet and the patch panel may be bad. The cable may be physically broken, or it may be routed right next to a 20,000-watt generator or an elevator motor.

✦ The computer's NIC may be bad or configured incorrectly. Check the configuration settings. If necessary, replace the card.

✦ The hub or switch may be bad.

Is the Network Configuration Working?

You can run three commands from a command window to verify the basic configuration of each computer. These commands are `net config workstation`, `net config server`, and `ipconfig`.

The `net config workstation` command displays basic information about the computer's network configuration. Here's a sample of the output it displays:

```
C:>net config workstation
Computer name                         \\WIN8_01
Full Computer name                    WIN8_01
User name                             doug@lowewriter.com
Workstation active on
      NetbiosSmb (000000000000)
      NetBT_Tcpip_{FC6D2F39-FDDD-448E-9B3C-0C12847F2B61} (0050BA843911)
Software version                      Windows 8
Workstation domain                    WORKGROUP

Logon domain                          MicrosoftAccount
COM Open Timeout (sec)                0
COM Send Count (byte)                 16
COM Send Timeout (msec)               250
The command completed successfully.
```

The most important information to check in the `net config workstation` command's output is the computer name and domain information.

If the computer is configured to enable file and print sharing, you can also run `net config server` to display basic information about the server configuration. Here's a sample of its output:

```
C:>net config server
Server Name                           \\WIN8_01
Server Comment
Software version                      Windows 8
Server is active on
      NetbiosSmb (000000000000)
      NetBT_Tcpip_{FB6D2F79-FDDF-418E-9B7C-0C82887F2A61} (0050ba843911)
```

```
Server hidden                        No
Maximum Logged On Users              20
Maximum open files per session       16384
Idle session time (min)              15
The command completed successfully.
```

The `ipconfig` command displays information about the computer's TCP/IP configuration. If you type **ipconfig** by itself, the computer's IP address, subnet mask, and default gateway are displayed. If you type **ipconfig /all**, you see more detailed information. Here's typical output from the `ipconfig /all` command:

```
C:>ipconfig /all
Windows IP Configuration
        Host Name . . . . . . . . . . . . : WIN8_02
        Primary Dns Suffix  . . . . . . . :
        Node Type . . . . . . . . . . . . : Hybrid
        IP Routing Enabled. . . . . . . . : No
        WINS Proxy Enabled. . . . . . . . : No
Ethernet adapter Local Area Connection:
        Connection-specific DNS Suffix  . : we1.client2.attbi.com
        Description . . . . . . . . . . . : D-Link DFE-530TX+ PCI Adapter
        Physical Address. . . . . . . . . : 00-50-BA-84-39-11
        Dhcp Enabled. . . . . . . . . . . : Yes
        Autoconfiguration Enabled . . . . : Yes
        IP Address. . . . . . . . . . . . : 192.168.1.100
        Subnet Mask . . . . . . . . . . . : 255.255.255.0
        Default Gateway . . . . . . . . . : 192.168.1.1
        DHCP Server . . . . . . . . . . . : 192.168.1.1
        DNS Servers . . . . . . . . . . . : 204.127.198.19
                                            63.240.76.19
        Lease Obtained. . . . . . . . . . : Wednesday, July 25, 2012 7:47:09 PM
        Lease Expires . . . . . . . . . . : THURSDAY, July 25, 2012 7:47:09 PM
```

The most important information to glean from this output is the computer's IP address. You should also verify that the default gateway matches the IP address of your Internet router and that the IP addresses for the DHCP and DNS servers are correct.

Can the Computers Ping Each Other?

A basic test that you can perform to ensure that your network is functioning is to use the `ping` command from a command prompt to make sure that the computers on the network can contact each other. The `ping` command simply sends a packet to another computer and requests that the second computer send a packet back in reply. If the reply packet is received, `ping` displays a message indicating how long it took to hear from the other computer. If the reply packet isn't received, `ping` displays an error message indicating that the computer couldn't be reached.

You should try several `ping` tests. First, you can make sure that TCP/IP is up and running by having the computer try to ping itself. Open a command prompt, and type **ping 127.0.0.1**. (127.0.0.1 is the standard loopback address that a computer can use to refer to itself.) If you prefer, you can type **ping localhost** instead.

Next, have the computer ping itself by using the IP address displayed by the \ `ipconfig` command. If `ipconfig` says the computer's IP address is 192.168.0.100, type **ping 192.168.0.100** at the command prompt.

Now try to ping your servers. You'll have to run `ipconfig` at each of the servers to determine their IP addresses. Or you can just ping the computer's name.

A final test is to make sure that you can ping the workstation from other computers on the network. You don't have to try to ping every computer from every other computer on the network unless you've determined that you have a connectivity problem that you need to pinpoint. You should try to ping each workstation from each of the servers, however, just to make sure that the servers can see the workstations. Make a list of the IP addresses of the workstations as you test them, and then take that list to the servers and ping each IP address on the list.

Can You Log On?

After you've established that the basic network connections are working, the next step is verifying that network logon works. This set is as simple as attempting to log on from each computer by using the correct user account for the computer. If you can't log on, several things may be causing the problem. Here are the most common:

✦ You may not have the right user account information. Double-check the username, password, and domain.

✦ Make sure that the domain name is correct.

✦ Passwords are case-sensitive. Make sure that you typed the password correctly and that the Caps Lock key isn't on.

✦ You may not have a computer account for the computer. Double-check the computer name, and make sure that you have a valid computer account on the server.

✦ Double-check the user account policies to make sure that they don't contain something that would prevent the user from logging on, such as a time-of-day restriction.

Are Network Drives Mapped Correctly?

After you know the user can log on, you should make sure that mapped network drives are available. To do so, type **net use** at a command prompt. You'll see a list of all the network mappings, such as this:

```
C:>net use
New connections will be remembered.
Status  Local  Remote              Network
-------------------------------------------------------------
OK      M:     \\Doug\Prod         Microsoft Windows Network
OK      X:     \\Doug\admin        Microsoft Windows Network
OK      Z:     \\Doug\Marketing    Microsoft Windows Network
The command completed successfully.
```

Here, you can see that three drives are mapped, and you can tell the server and share name for each mapped drive.

Next, try to display a directory list of each drive to make sure that you can actually reach it. You might type **dir m:**, for example. If everything is working, you see a directory of the shared folder you've mapped to drive M:.

**Book II
Chapter 7**

Verifying
Your Network
Installation

Do Network Printers Work?

The final test I describe in this chapter is making sure that your network printers work. The easiest way to do this is to print a short document to the network printer and make sure that the document prints. I suggest that you open Notepad (choose Start⇨Accessories⇨Notepad), type a few words (such as **Yo, Adrian!**), and then choose File⇨Print to bring up the Print dialog box. Select the network printer, and click OK.

If the network printer doesn't appear in the list of available printers, go to the Printers and Faxes window, and recheck the network printer. You may have configured the printer incorrectly. If the configuration looks okay, go to the printer itself, and make sure that it's turned on and ready to print.

Chapter 8: Going Virtual

In This Chapter

✓ Examining the basics of virtualization

✓ Weighing the benefits of virtualization

✓ Installing VMware Player

✓ Creating and using virtual machines

*V*irtualization is one of the hottest trends in networking today. According to some industry pundits, virtualization is the best thing to happen to computers since the invention of the transistor. If you haven't already begun to virtualize your network, you're standing on the platform watching as the train is pulling out.

This chapter is a brief introduction to virtualization, with an emphasis on using it to leverage your network server hardware to provide more servers using less hardware. In addition to the general concepts of virtualization, you find out how to experiment with virtualization by using VMware's free virtualization product, called VMware Player.

Mastering a virtualization environment calls for a book of its own. I recommend two titles, both from John Wiley & Sons: *Virtualization For Dummies,* by Bernard Golden, and *VMware Infrastructure 3 For Dummies,* by William Lowe (no relation, honest).

Understanding Virtualization

The basic idea behind virtualization is to use software to simulate the existence of hardware. This powerful idea enables you to run more than one independent computer system on a single physical computer system. Suppose that your organization requires a total of 12 servers to meet its needs. You could run each of these 12 servers on a separate computer, in which case you would have 12 computers in your server room, or you could use virtualization to run these 12 servers on just 2 computers. In effect, each of those computers would simulate six separate computer systems, each running one of your servers.

Each of the simulated computers is called a *virtual machine,* or *VM.* For all intents and purposes, each virtual machine appears to be a complete, self-contained computer system with its own processor (or, more likely, processors), memory, disk drives, CD-ROM/DVD drives, keyboard, mouse, monitor, network interfaces, USB ports, and so on.

The long trek of virtualization

Kids these days think they invented everything, including virtualization.

Little do they know.

Virtualization was developed for PC-based computers in the early 1990s, around the time Captain Picard was flying the Enterprise around in *Star Trek: The Next Generation*.

But the idea is much older than that.

The first virtualized server computers predate Captain Picard by about 20 years. In 1972, IBM released an operating system called simply VM, which had nearly all the basic features found in today's virtualization products.

VM allowed the administrators of IBM's System/370 mainframe computers to create multiple independent virtual machines, each of which was called (you guessed it) a virtual machine, or VM. This terminology is still in use today.

Each VM could run one of the various guest operating systems that were compatible with the System/370 and appeared to this guest operating system to be a complete, independent System/370 computer with its own processor cores, virtual memory, disk partitions, and input/output devices.

The core of the VM system itself was called the *hypervisor* — another term that persists to this day.

The VM product that IBM released in 1972 was actually based on an experimental product that IBM released on a limited basis in 1967.

So whenever someone tells you about this new technology called *virtualization,* you can tell them that it was invented when *Star Trek* was on TV. When they ask, "You mean the one with Picard?" you can say, "No, the one with Kirk."

Like a real computer, each virtual machine requires an operating system to do productive work. In a typical network server environment, each virtual machine runs its own copy of Windows Server 2008 (or an earlier version). The operating system has no idea that it's running on a virtual machine rather than on a real machine.

Here are a few terms you need to be familiar with if you expect to discuss virtualization intelligently:

✦ **Host:** The actual physical computer on which one or more virtual machines run.

✦ **Bare metal:** Another term for the host computer that runs one or more virtual machines.

✦ **Guest:** Another term for a virtual machine running on a host.

✦ **Guest operating system:** An operating system that runs within a virtual machine. By itself, a guest is just a machine; it requires an operating system to run. The guest operating system is what brings the guest to life.

As far as licensing is concerned, Microsoft treats each virtual machine as a separate computer. Thus, if you run six guests on a single host, and each guest runs Windows Server 2008, you need six licenses of Windows Server 2008.

✦ **Hypervisor:** The virtualization operating system that creates and runs virtual machines.

There are two basic types of hypervisors: Type 1 and Type 2. A *Type 1 hypervisor* is a hypervisor that itself runs directly on the bare metal. A *Type 2 hypervisor* is a hypervisor that runs within an operating system, which in turn runs on the bare metal.

For production use, you should always use Type 1 hypervisors because they're much more efficient than Type 2 hypervisors. Type 1 hypervisors are considerably more expensive than Type 2 hypervisors, however. As a result, many people use inexpensive or free Type 2 hypervisors to experiment with virtualization before making a commitment to purchase an expensive Type 1 hypervisor.

Looking at the Benefits of Virtualization

You might suspect that virtualization is inefficient because a real computer is inherently faster than a simulated computer. Although it's true that real computers are faster than simulated computers, virtualization technology has become so advanced that the performance penalty for running on a virtualized machine rather than a real machine is only a few percent.

The small amount of overhead imposed by virtualization is usually more than made up for by the simple fact that even the most heavily used servers spend most of their time twiddling their digital thumbs, waiting for something to do. In fact, many servers spend nearly *all* their time doing nothing. As computers get faster and faster, they spend even more of their time with nothing to do.

Virtualization is a great way to put all this unused processing power to good use.

Besides this basic efficiency benefit, virtualization has several compelling benefits:

✦ **Hardware cost:** You typically can save a lot of money by reducing hardware costs when you use virtualization. Suppose that you replace ten servers that cost $4,000 each with one host server. Granted, you'll probably spend more than $4,000 on that server, because it needs to be maxed out with memory, processor cores, network interfaces, and so on. So you'll probably end up spending $15,000 or $20,000 for the host server. Also, you'll end up spending something like $5,000 for the hypervisor software. But that's still a lot less than the $40,000 you would have spent on ten separate computers at $4,000 each.

+ **Energy costs:** Many organizations have found that going virtual has reduced their overall electricity consumption for server computers by 80 percent. This savings is a direct result of using less computer hardware to do more work. One host computer running ten virtual servers uses approximately one-tenth the energy that would be used if each of the ten servers ran on separate hardware.

+ **Recoverability:** One of the biggest benefits of virtualization isn't the cost savings, but the ability to recover quickly from hardware failures. Suppose that your organization has ten servers, each running on separate hardware. If any one of those servers goes down due to a hardware failure — say, a bad motherboard — that server will remain down until you can fix the computer. On the other hand, if those ten servers are running as virtual machines on two different hosts, and one of the hosts fails, the virtual machines that were running on the failed host can be brought up on the other host in a matter of minutes.

 Granted, the servers will run less efficiently on a single host than they would have on two hosts, but the point is that they'll all be running after only a short downtime.

 In fact, with the most advanced hypervisors available, the transfer from a failing host to another host can be done automatically and instantaneously, so downtime is all but eliminated.

+ **Disaster recovery:** Besides the benefit of recoverability when hardware failures occur, an even bigger benefit of virtualization comes into play in a true disaster-recovery situation. Suppose that your organization's server infrastructure consists of 20 separate servers. In the case of a devastating disaster, such as a fire in the server room that destroys all hardware, how long will it take you to get all 20 of those servers back up and running on new hardware? Quite possibly, the recovery time will be measured in weeks.

 By contrast, virtual machines are actually nothing more than files that can be backed up onto tape. As a result, in a disaster-recovery situation, all you have to do is rebuild a single host computer and reinstall the hypervisor software. Then you can restore the virtual-machine backups from tape, restart the virtual machines, and get back up and running in a matter of days instead of weeks.

Getting Started with Virtualization

Virtualization is a complex subject, and mastering the ins and outs of working with a full-fledged virtualization system like VMware Infrastructure is a topic that's beyond the scope of this book. You can dip your toes into the shallow end of the virtualization pond, however, by downloading and experimenting with VMware's free virtualization product, called VMware Player. You can download it from `www.vmware.com`.

Figure 8-1 shows VMware Player's main screen. From this screen, you can create a new virtual machine or run one of the virtual machines you've already created. As you can see in the figure, I've created several virtual machines, including a few that run various versions of Fedora (a popular Linux distribution) as well as two that run Windows Server 2008.

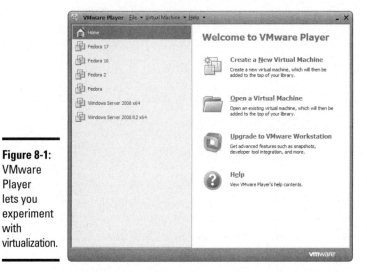

Figure 8-1:
VMware
Player
lets you
experiment
with
virtualization.

**Book II
Chapter 8**

Going Virtual

You can run an existing virtual machine by selecting the VM and clicking Play Virtual Machine. This launches the virtual machine, which opens in a new window, as shown in Figure 8-2. When you launch a virtual machine, the VM behaves exactly as a real computer would when you power it up: First, it initializes its virtual hardware devices; then it loads the guest operating system that has been installed in the VM. In Figure 8-2, Windows Server 2008 has booted up and is waiting for you to press Ctrl+Alt+Del to log on.

The prompt to press Ctrl+Alt+Del shown in Figure 8-2 illustrates one of the peculiar details of running a virtual machine within a host operating system (in this case, running Windows Server 2008 R2 within Windows 7 Ultimate). When you press Ctrl+Alt+Del, which operating system — the host or the guest — responds? The answer is that the host operating system responds to Ctrl+Alt+Del, so the guest operating system never sees it.

To get around this limitation, VMware uses the special keyboard short-cut Ctrl+Alt+End to send a Ctrl+Alt+Del to the guest operating system. Alternatively, you can use the VM pull-down menu that appears in the menu bar above the virtual-machine menu. This menu lists several actions that can be applied to the virtual machine, including Send Ctrl+Alt+Del.

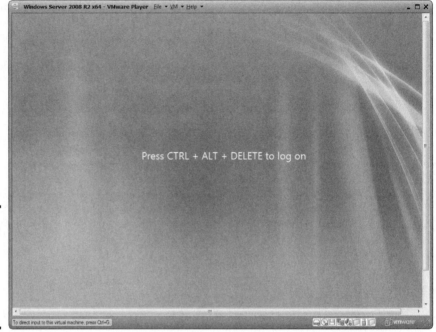

Figure 8-2:
A virtual machine running Windows Server 2008 R2.

Another detail you should know about when working with a VM is that when you click in the virtual machine's window, the VM captures your mouse and keyboard, so your input will be directed to the virtual machine rather than the host computer. If you want to break the bonds of the virtual machine and return to the host computer, press Ctrl and Alt simultaneously.

Creating a Virtual Machine

Creating a new virtual machine in VMware Player is relatively easy. In fact, the most challenging part is getting hold of the installation disc for the operating system you want to install on the VM. Remember that a virtual machine is useless without a guest operating system, so you need to have the installation disc available before you create the virtual machine.

If you just want to experiment with virtualization and don't have extra licenses of a Windows server operating system, you can always download an evaluation copy of Windows Server 2008 R2 from www.microsoft.com/windowsserver2008. The evaluation period is six months, so you'll have plenty of time to experiment.

The downloadable trial version of Windows Server 2008 R2 comes in the form of an `.iso` file, which is an image of a DVD file that you can mount within your virtual machine as though it were a real disk.

When you have your `.iso` file or installation disc ready to go, you can create a new virtual machine by following these steps:

1. **Click Create a New Virtual Machine on the VMware Player home screen (refer to Figure 8-1).**

This brings up the New Virtual Machine Wizard, as shown in Figure 8-3.

**Book II
Chapter 8**

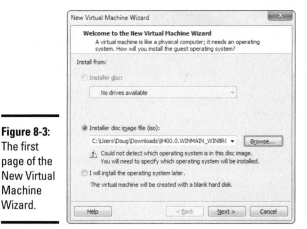

Figure 8-3:
The first
page of the
New Virtual
Machine
Wizard.

Going Virtual

2. **Choose the installation option you want to use.**

You have three choices:

- *Installer Disc:* Select this option and then choose from the drop-down list the drive you'll install from if you want to install from an actual CD or DVD.

- *Install Disc Image File (iso):* Select this option, click the Browse button, and browse to the `.iso` file that contains the installation image.

- *I Will Install the Operating System Later:* Select this option if you want to create the virtual machine now but install the operating system later.

Note that the remaining steps in this procedure assume that you select a Windows Server 2012 `.iso` file as the installation option.

3. **Click Next.**

   The screen shown in Figure 8-4 appears. You can enter the product key now or skip this step until later.

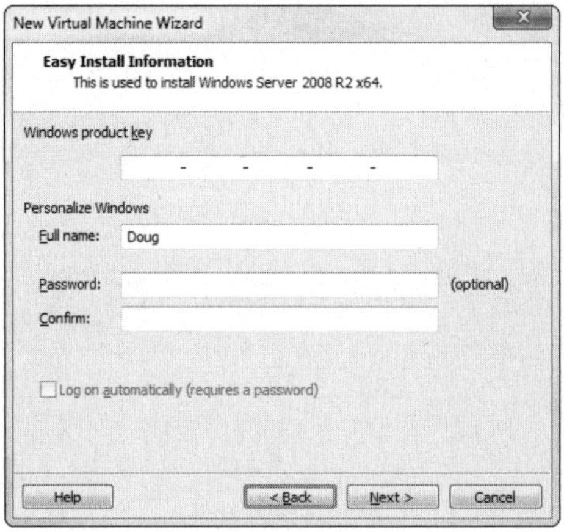

Figure 8-4: The New Virtual Machine Wizard asks for your product key.

4. **If you have the Windows product key, enter it, and click Next; otherwise, just click Next.**

   You can always enter the product key later if you don't have it handy now. Either way, the screen shown in Figure 8-5 appears next.

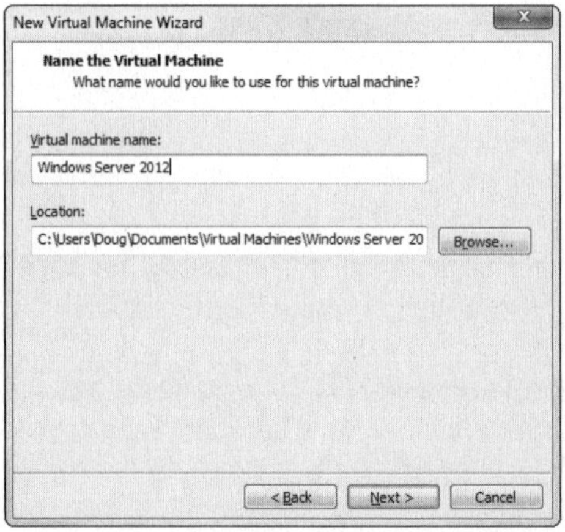

Figure 8-5: Creating a name and specifying the VM disk location.

5. **Enter a name for the virtual machine.**

6. **Enter the location of the virtual machine's disk file.**

If you want, you can click the Browse button and browse to the folder where you want to create the file.

7. Click Next.

The wizard asks for the size of the disk to create for the virtual machine, as shown in Figure 8-6.

Figure 8-6:
Specifying
the VM disk
size.

8. Set the size of the virtual machine's hard drive.

The default setting is 40GB, but you can change it depending on your needs. Note that you must have sufficient space available on the host computer's disk drive.

9. Click Next.

The wizard displays a final confirmation page, as shown in Figure 8-7.

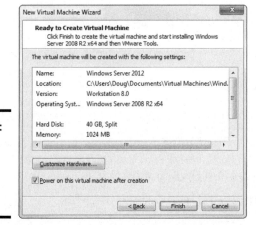

Figure 8-7:
VMware
is ready
to create
the virtual
machine.

10. **Click Finish.**

The wizard creates the virtual machine and then starts it. Because the machine doesn't have an operating system installed, it boots from the CD/DVD installation image you specified back in Step 2. In this case, I booted with the Windows Server 2008 R2 evaluation software disk image, so the new virtual machine displays the Install Windows screen, as shown in Figure 8-8.

11. **Follow the steps to install the operating system.**

Installing an operating system in a virtual machine is exactly the same as installing it on a physical computer, except that the installation screens appear within a virtual-machine window.

When the operating system is installed, you're done! Then you can proceed to use the virtual machine.

Figure 8-8:
Installing
Windows
Server
2008 R2 in
a virtual
machine.

You can adjust the hardware configuration of a virtual machine by choosing VM⇨Settings while the virtual machine is running. This command brings up the Virtual Machine Settings dialog box, as shown in Figure 8-9. From this dialog box, you can adjust the virtual machine's hardware configuration, including the amount of RAM available to the VM and the number of processor cores. You can also adjust the disk drive size; add CD, DVD, or floppy drives; and configure network adapters, USB connections, and sound and display settings.

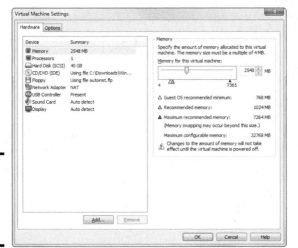

Figure 8-9:
Configuring
virtual-
machine
settings.

Chapter 9: Cloudy with a Chance of Gigabytes

In This Chapter

↙ Examining the basics of cloud computing

↙ Looking at three kinds of cloud computing services

↙ Understanding the pros and cons of cloud computing

↙ Perusing a few of the major cloud computing service providers

*I*n her classic children's book *Cloudy with a Chance of Meatballs*, Judi Barrett tells the story of the town of Chewandswallow, where food falls from the sky. Clouds rain down such essentials as juice and soup, and when it snows, the snow is made of ice cream.

Cloud computing is a bit like that. In a computer network, the essentials are not juice, soup, and ice cream, but CPU cycles, disk storage, and software. Traditionally, these essentials have been provided by local server computers, whether real or virtual. But in recent years, more and more companies have been obtaining these essential resources from the "cloud" — that is, from the Internet.

This chapter is a brief introduction to cloud computing. You discover what it is, the pros and cons of adopting it, and what services are provided by the major cloud computer providers.

Introducing Cloud Computing

The basic idea behind cloud computing is to outsource one or more of your networked computing resources to the Internet. The cloud represents a new way of handling common computer tasks. Following are a few examples of how the cloud way differs from the traditional way:

✦ **E-mail services**

  • The traditional way to provide e-mail services is to install Microsoft Exchange on a local server computer. Then your clients can connect use Microsoft Outlook to connect to the Exchange server to send and receive e-mail.

- The cloud computing way is to contract with an Internet-based e-mail provider such as Google Mail (Gmail). Cloud-based e-mail services typically charge a low monthly per-user fee, so the amount you pay for your e-mail service depends solely on the number of e-mail users you have.

✦ **Disk storage**

- The traditional way to provide disk storage for your network applications is to set up a local file server computer with a large amount of shared disk space.

- The cloud way is to sign up for an Internet file storage service and store your data on the Internet. Cloud-based file storage typically charges a small monthly per-gigabyte fee, so you pay only for the storage you use. The disk capacity of cloud-based storage is essentially unlimited.

✦ **Accounting services**

- The traditional way to handle accounting services for your company is to purchase expensive accounting software and install it on a local server computer.

- The cloud way is to sign up for a web-based accounting service. Then all your accounting data is saved and managed on the provider's servers, not on yours.

Looking at the Benefits of Cloud Computing

Cloud computing is a different way of doing networking, but it isn't different just for the sake of being different: Often, it's different because it's better. Following are a few of the main benefits of moving to cloud-based networking:

✦ **Cost effective:** Cloud-based computing typically is less expensive than traditional computing. Consider a typical file server application: To implement a file server, first you must purchase a file server computer with enough disk space to accommodate your users' needs, which amounts to 1TB of disk storage. You want the most reliable data storage possible, so you purchase a server-quality computer and fully redundant disk drives. For the sake of this discussion, figure that the total price of the server — including its disk drive, the operating-system license, and the labor cost of setting it up — is about $10,000. Assuming that the server will last for four years, that comes to about $2,500 per year.

If you instead acquire your disk storage from a cloud-based file sharing service, you can expect to pay about one fourth of that amount for an equivalent amount of storage.

The same economies apply to most other cloud-based solutions. For Cloud-based e-mail solutions, for example, typically cost around $5 per month per user — well under the cost of setting up and maintaining a Microsoft Exchange server.

✦ **Scalable:** So what happens if you guess wrong about the storage requirements of your file server, and your users end up needing 2TB instead of just 1TB? With a traditional file server, you must purchase additional disk drives to accommodate the extra space. Sooner than you want, you'll run out of capacity in the server's cabinet. Then you'll have to purchase an external storage cabinet. Eventually, you'll fill that up too.

Now suppose that after you've expanded your server capacity to 2TB, your users' needs contract to just 1TB. Unfortunately, you can't return disk drives for a refund.

With cloud computing, you pay only for the capacity you're actually using, and you can add capacity whenever you need it. In the file server example, you can write as much data as you need to the cloud storage. Each month, you're billed according to your actual usage. Thus, you don't have to purchase and install additional disk drives to add storage capacity.

✦ **Reliable:** Especially for smaller businesses, cloud services are much more reliable than in-house services. Just a week before I wrote this chapter, the tape drive that a friend uses to back up his company's data failed. As a result, he was unable to back up data for three days while the tape drive was repaired. Had he been using cloud-based backup, he could have restored his data immediately and wouldn't have been without backups for those three days.

The reason for the increased reliability of cloud services is simply a matter of scale. Most small businesses can't afford the redundancies needed to make their computer operations as reliable as possible. My friend's company can't afford to buy two tape drives so that an extra is available in case the main one fails.

By contrast, cloud services are usually provided by large companies such as Amazon, Google, Microsoft, and IBM. These companies have state-of-the-art data centers with multiple redundancies for their cloud services. Cloud storage may be kept on multiple servers so that if one server fails, others can take over the load. In some cases, these servers are in different data centers in different parts of the country. Thus, your data will still be available even in the event of a disaster that shuts down an entire data system.

✦ **Hassle-free:** Face it, IT can be a hassle. With cloud-based services, you basically outsource the job of complex system maintenance chores such as software upgrade, patches, hardware maintenance, backup, and so on. You get to consume the services while someone else takes care of making sure that the services run properly.

**Book II
Chapter 9**

**Cloudy with a
Chance of Gigabytes**

✦ **Globally accessible:** One of the best things about cloud services is that they're available anywhere you have an Internet connection. Suppose that you have offices in five cities. Using traditional computing, each office would require its own servers, and you'd have to carefully design systems that allowed users in each of the offices to access shared data.

With cloud computing, each office simply connects to the Internet to access the cloud applications. Cloud-based applications are also great if your users are mobile because they can access the applications anywhere they can find an Internet connection.

Detailing the Drawbacks of Cloud Computing

Although cloud computing has many advantages over traditional techniques, it isn't without its drawbacks. Here are some of the most significant roadblocks to adopting cloud computing:

✦ **Entrenched applications:** Your organization may depend on entrenched applications that don't lend themselves especially well to cloud computing — or that at least require significant conversion efforts to migrate to the cloud.

Fortunately, many cloud providers offer assistance with this migration. And in many cases, the same application that you run locally can be run in the cloud, so no conversion is necessary.

✦ **Internet connection speed:** Cloud computing shifts much of the burden of your network to your Internet connection. Your users used to access their data on local file servers over gigabit-speed connections; now they must access data over slower bandwidth Internet connections.

Although you can upgrade your connection to higher speeds, doing so will cost money — money that may offset the money you otherwise save from migrating to the cloud.

✦ **Internet connection reliability:** The cloud resources you access may feature all the redundancy in the world, but if your users access the cloud through a single Internet connection, that connection becomes a key point of vulnerability. Should it fail, any applications that depend on the cloud will be unavailable. If those applications are mission-critical, business will come to a halt until the connection is restored.

There are two ways to mitigate this risk:

• *Make sure that you're using an enterprise-class Internet connection,* not a consumer-class connection. Enterprise-class connections are more expensive but provide much better fault tolerance and repair service than consumer-class connections do.

• *Provide redundant connections if you can.* That way, if one connection fails, traffic can be rerouted through alternative connections.

✦ **Security threats:** You can bet your life that hackers throughout the world are continually probing for ways to break through the security perimeter of all the major cloud providers. When they do, your data may be exposed.

The best way to mitigate this threat is to ensure that strong password policies are enforced.

Examining Three Basic Kinds of Cloud Services

Three distinct kinds of services can be provided via the cloud: applications, platforms, and services. The following paragraphs describe these three types of cloud services in greater detail.

Applications

Most often referred to as *Software as a Service (SaaS)*, fully functional applications can be delivered via the cloud. One of the best-known examples is Google Apps, a suite of cloud-based office applications designed to compete directly with Microsoft's traditional office applications, including Word, Excel, PowerPoint, Access, and Outlook. Google Apps can also replace the back-end software often used to support Microsoft Office, including Exchange and SharePoint.

When you use a cloud-based application, you don't have to worry about any of the details that are commonly associated with running an application on your network, such as deploying the application and applying product upgrades and software patches. Cloud-based applications usually charge a small monthly fee based on the number of users running the software, so costs are low.

Also, as a cloud-based application user, you don't have to worry about providing the hardware or operating-system platform on which the application will run. The application provider takes care of that detail for you, so you can focus simply on developing the application to best serve your users' needs.

Platforms

Also referred to as *Platform as a Service (PaaS)*, this class of service refers to providers that give you access to a remote virtual operating platform on which you can build your own applications.

At the simplest level, a PaaS provider gives you a complete, functional remote virtual machine that's fully configured and ready for you to deploy your applications to. If you use a web provider to host your company's website, you're already using PaaS: Most web host providers give you a functioning Linux system, fully configured with all the necessary servers, such as

Apache or MySQL. All you have to do is build and deploy your web application on the provider's server.

More-complex PaaS solutions include specialized software that your custom applications can tap to provide services such as data storage, online order processing, and credit card payments. One of the best-known examples of this type of PaaS provider is Amazon.

 When you use PaaS, you take on the responsibility of developing your own custom applications to run on the remote platform. But the PaaS provider takes care of the details of maintaining the platform itself, including the base operating system and the hardware on which the platform runs.

Infrastructure

If you don't want to delegate the responsibility of maintaining operating systems and other elements of the platform, you can use *Infrastructure as a Service (IaaS)*. When you use IaaS, you're purchasing raw computing power that's accessible via the cloud. Typically, IaaS provides you access to a remote virtual machine. It's up to you to manage and configure the remote machine however you want.

Public Clouds vs. Private Clouds

The most common form of cloud computing uses what is known as a *public cloud* — that is, cloud services that are available to anyone in the world via the Internet. Google Apps for Business is an excellent example of a public cloud service. Anyone with access to the Internet can access the public cloud services of Google Apps for Business: Just point your browser to `http://apps.google.com`.

A public cloud is like a public utility, in that anyone can subscribe to it on a pay-as-you-go basis. One of the drawbacks of public cloud services is that they're inherently insecure. When you use a public cloud service, you're entrusting your valuable data to a third party that you cannot control. Sure, you can protect your access to your public cloud services by using strong passwords, but if your account names and passwords are compromised, your public cloud services can be hacked into, and your data can be stolen. Every so often, we all hear news stories about how this company's or that company's back-door security has been compromised.

Besides security, another drawback of public cloud computing is that it is dependent on high-speed, reliable Internet connections. Your cloud service provider may have all the redundancy in the world, but if your connection to the Internet goes down, you won't be able to access your cloud services. And if your connection is slow, your cloud services will be slow.

A *private cloud* is a system that mimics many of the features of cloud computing but is implemented on a private hardware within a local network, so it isn't accessible to the general public. Private clouds are inherently more secure because the general public cannot access them. Also, they're dependent only on private network connections, so they aren't subject to the limits of a public Internet connection.

As a rule, private clouds are implemented by large organizations that have the resources available to create and maintain their own cloud servers.

A relative newcomer to the cloud computing scene is the *hybrid cloud,* which combines the features of public and private clouds. Typically, a hybrid cloud system uses a small private cloud that provides local access to some of the applications and the public cloud for others. You might maintain your most frequently used data on a private cloud for fast access via the local network and use the public cloud to store archives and other less-frequently-used data, for which performance isn't as much of an issue.

Introducing Some of the Major Cloud Providers

Hundreds, if not thousands, of companies provide cloud services. Most of the cloud computing done today, however, is provided by just a few providers, which are described in the following sections.

Amazon

By far the largest provider of cloud services in the world is Amazon. Amazon launched its cloud platform, called *Amazon Web Services (AWS)*, in 2006. Since then, hundreds of thousands of customers have signed up. Some of the most notable users of AWS include Netflix, Pinterest, and Instagram.

AWS includes the following features:

✦ *Amazon CloudFront,* a PaaS content-delivery system designed to deliver web content to large numbers of users.

✦ *Amazon Elastic Compute Cloud* (also called *Amazon EC2)*, an IaaS system that provides access to raw computing power.

✦ *Amazon Simple Storage Service* (also called *Amazon S3)*, which provides web-based data storage for unlimited amounts of data.

✦ *Amazon Simple Queue Service* (also called *Amazon SQS)*, which provides a data transfer system that lets applications send messages to other applications. SQS enables you to build applications that work together.

✦ *Amazon Virtual Private Cloud* (also called *Amazon VPC)*, which uses virtual private network (VPN) connections to connect your local network to Amazon's cloud services.

Google

Google is also one of the largest providers of cloud services. Its offerings include the following:

✦ *Google Apps,* a replacement for Microsoft Office that provides basic e-mail, word processing, spreadsheet, and database functions via the cloud. Google Apps is free to the general public and can even be used free by small businesses (up to 50 users). For larger businesses, Google offers an advanced version called *Google Apps for Business.* For $5 per month per user, you get extra features such as 25GB of e-mail data per user, archiving, and advanced options for customizing your account policies.

✦ *Google Cloud Connect,* a cloud-based solution that lets you work with Google cloud data directly from within Microsoft Office applications.

✦ *Google App Engine,* a PaaS interface that lets you develop your own applications that work with Google's cloud services.

✦ *Google Cloud Print,* which lets you connect your printers to the cloud so that they can be accessed from anywhere.

✦ *Google Maps*, which is a Global Information System (GIS).

Microsoft

Microsoft has its own cloud strategy that is designed, in part, to protect its core business of operating systems and Office applications against competition from other cloud providers, such as Google Apps.

The following paragraphs summarize several of Microsoft's cloud offerings:

✦ *Microsoft Office 365,* a cloud-based version of Microsoft Office. According to Microsoft's website, Office 365 provides "anywhere access to cloud-based email, web conferencing, file sharing, and Office Web Apps at a low predictable monthly cost." For more information, check out `www.office365.com`.

✦ *Windows Azure,* a PaaS offering that lets you build websites, deploy virtual machines that run Windows Server or Linux, or access cloud versions of server applications such as SQL Server.

✦ *Microsoft Business Productivity Suite,* a SaaS product that provides cloud-based access to two of Microsoft's most popular productivity servers: Microsoft Exchange and Microsoft SharePoint. The suite lets you deploy these servers without having to create and maintain your own local servers.

Getting Into the Cloud

So now that you've seen how cool cloud computing can be, what should you do to take your network toward the cloud? Allow me to make a few recommendations:

+ **Don't depend on a poor Internet connection.** First and foremost, before you take any of your network operations to the cloud, make sure that you're *not* dependent on a consumer-grade Internet connection if you decide to adopt cloud computing. Consumer-grade Internet connections can be fast, but when an outage occurs, there's no telling how long you'll wait for the connection to be repaired. You definitely don't want to wait for hours or days while the cable company thinks about sending someone out to your site. Instead, spend the money for a high-speed enterprise-class connection that can scale as your dependence on it increases.

+ **Assess what applications you may already have running on the cloud.** If you use Gmail rather than Exchange for your e-mail, congratulations! You're already a cloud user. Other examples of cloud services that you may already be using include a remote web or FTP host, Dropbox or another file sharing service, Carbonite or another online backup service, a payroll service, and so on.

+ **Don't move to the cloud all at once.** Start by identifying a single application that lends itself to the cloud. If your engineering firm archives projects when they close and wants to get them off your primary file server but keep them readily available, look to the cloud for a file storage service.

+ **Go with a reputable company.** Google, Amazon, and Microsoft are all huge companies with proven track records in cloud computing. Many other large and established companies also offer cloud services. Don't stake your company's future on a company that didn't exist six months ago.

+ **Research, research, research.** Pour yourself into the web, and buy a few books. *Cloud Computing For Dummies,* by Judith Hurwitz, Robin Bloor, Marcia Kaufman, and Fern Halper (John Wiley & Sons, Inc.), is a good place to start.

Book III

Networking Administration and Security

"Well, whoever stole my passwords was sure clever. Especially since none of my reminders are missing."

Contents at a Glance

Chapter 1: Help Wanted: Job Description for a Network Administrator

In This Chapter

✔ Deciphering the many jobs of the network administrator

✔ Dusting, vacuuming, and mopping

✔ Managing the network users

✔ Choosing the right tools

✔ Getting certified

*H*elp wanted. Network administrator to help small business get control of a network run amok. Must have sound organizational and management skills. Only moderate computer experience required. Part-time only.

Does this ad sound like one that your company should run? Every network needs a network administrator, whether the network has 2 computers or 200. Of course, managing a 200-computer network is a full-time job, whereas managing a 2-computer network isn't. At least, it shouldn't be.

This chapter introduces you to the boring job of network administration. Oops . . . you're probably reading this chapter because you've been elected to be the network manager, so I'd better rephrase that: This chapter introduces you to the wonderful, exciting world of network management! Oh, boy! This is going to be fun!

Knowing What Network Administrators Do

Simply put, network administrators administer networks, which means that they take care of the tasks of installing, configuring, expanding, protecting, upgrading, tuning, and repairing the network. Network administrators take care of the network hardware, such as cables, hubs, switches, routers, servers, and clients, as well as network software, such as network operating systems, e-mail servers, backup software, database servers, and application software. Most importantly, network administrators take care of network users by answering their questions, listening to their troubles, and solving their problems.

On a big network, these responsibilities constitute a full-time job. Large networks tend to be volatile: Users come and go, equipment fails, cables break, and life in general seems to be one crisis after another.

Smaller networks are much more stable. After you get your network up and running, you probably won't have to spend much time managing its hardware and software. An occasional problem may pop up, but with only a few computers on the network, problems should be few and far between.

Regardless of the network's size, all network administrators must attend to several common chores:

✦ **Equipment upgrades:** The network administrator should be involved in every decision to purchase new computers, printers, or other equipment. In particular, the network administrator should be prepared to lobby for the most network-friendly equipment possible, such as network-ready printers, ample network disk storage, and an adequate backup system.

✦ **Configuration:** The network administrator must put on the pocket protector whenever a new computer is added to the network. The network administrator's job includes considering what changes to make to the cabling configuration, what computer name to assign to the new computer, how to integrate the new user into the security system, what rights to grant the user, and so on.

✦ **Software upgrades:** Every once in a while, your trusty OS vendor (likely, Microsoft) releases a new version of your network operating system (NOS). The network administrator must read about the new version and decide whether its new features are beneficial enough to warrant an upgrade. In most cases, the hardest part of upgrading to a new version of your network operating system is determining the *migration path* — that is, how to upgrade your entire network to the new version while disrupting the network or its users as little as possible. Upgrading to a new NOS version is a major chore, so you need to carefully consider the advantages that the new version can bring.

✦ **Patches:** Between upgrades, Microsoft releases patches and service packs that fix minor problems with its server OSes. For more information, see the section "Patching Up Your Operating System and Software" later in this chapter. (Other software vendors also regularly release patches and service packs, so it isn't only Microsoft software that must be kept up to date.)

✦ **Performance maintenance:** One of the easiest traps that you can get sucked into is the quest for network speed. The network is never fast enough, and users always blame the hapless network manager. So the administrator spends hours and hours tuning and tweaking the network to squeeze out that last two percent of performance. You don't want to get caught in this trap, but in case you do, Chapter 8 of this minibook can help. It clues you in to the basics of tuning your network for best performance.

✦ **Ho-hum chores:** Network administrators perform routine chores, such as backing up the servers, archiving old data, freeing up server hard drive space, and so on. Much of network administration is making sure that things keep working and finding and correcting problems before any users notice that something is wrong. In this sense, network administration can be a thankless job.

✦ **Software inventory:** Network administrators are also responsible for gathering, organizing, and tracking the entire network's software inventory. You never know when something is going to go haywire on Joe in Marketing's ancient Windows XP computer and you're going to have to reinstall that old copy of WordPerfect. Do you have any idea where the installation discs are?

Choosing the Part-Time Administrator

The larger the network, the more technical support it needs. Most small networks — with just a dozen or so computers — can get by with a part-time network administrator. Ideally, this person should be a closet computer geek: someone who has a secret interest in computers but doesn't like to admit it. Someone who will take books home with him or her and read them over the weekend. Someone who enjoys solving computer problems just for the sake of solving them.

The job of managing a network requires some computer skills, but it isn't entirely a technical job. Much of the work that the network administrator does is routine housework. Basically, the network administrator dusts, vacuums, and mops the network periodically to keep it from becoming a mess.

Here are some additional ideas on picking a part-time network administrator:

✦ The network administrator needs to be an organized person. Conduct a surprise office inspection and place the person with the neatest desk in charge of the network. (Don't warn them in advance, or everyone may mess up their desks intentionally the night before the inspection.)

✦ Allow enough time for network administration. For a small network (say, no more than 20 or so computers), an hour or two each week is enough. More time is needed upfront as the network administrator settles into the job and discovers the ins and outs of the network. After an initial settling-in period, though, network administration for a small office network doesn't take more than an hour or two per week. (Of course, larger networks take more time to manage.)

✦ Make sure that everyone knows who the network administrator is and that the network administrator has the authority to make decisions about the network, such as what access rights each user has, what files can and can't be stored on the server, how often backups are done, and so on.

✦ Pick someone who is assertive and willing to irritate people. A good network administrator should make sure that backups are working *before* a hard drive fails and make sure that antivirus protection is in place *before* a virus wipes out the entire network. This policing will irritate people, but it's for their own good.

✦ In most cases, the person who installs the network is also the network administrator. This is appropriate because no one understands the network better than the person who designs and installs it.

✦ The network administrator needs an understudy — someone who knows almost as much about the network, is eager to make a mark, and smiles when the worst network jobs are delegated.

✦ The network administrator has some sort of official title, such as Network Boss, Network Czar, Vice President in Charge of Network Operations, or Dr. Network. A badge, a personalized pocket protector, or a set of Spock ears helps, too.

Establishing Routine Chores

Much of the network administrator's job is routine stuff — the equivalent of vacuuming, dusting, and mopping. Or if you prefer, changing the oil and rotating the tires every 3,000 miles. Yes, it's boring, but it has to be done.

✦ **Backup:** The network administrator needs to make sure that the network is properly backed up. If something goes wrong and the network isn't backed up, guess who gets the blame? On the other hand, if disaster strikes, yet you're able to recover everything from yesterday's backup with only a small amount of work lost, guess who gets the pat on the back, the fat bonus, and the vacation in the Bahamas? Chapter 9 of this minibook describes the options for network backups. You'd better read it soon.

✦ **Protection:** Another major task for network administrators is sheltering your network from the evils of the outside world. These evils come in many forms, including hackers trying to break into your network and virus programs arriving through e-mail. Chapter 4 of this minibook describes this task in more detail.

✦ **Clean-up:** Users think that the network server is like the attic: They want to throw files up there and leave them forever. No matter how much storage your network has, your users will fill it up sooner than you think. So the network manager gets the fun job of cleaning up the attic once in a while. Oh, joy. The best advice I can offer is to constantly complain about how messy it is up there and warn your users that spring cleaning is coming up.

Managing Network Users

Managing network technology is the easiest part of network management. Computer technology can be confusing at first, but computers aren't nearly as confusing as people. The real challenge of managing a network is managing the network's users.

The difference between managing technology and managing users is obvious: You can figure out computers, but you can never really figure out people. The people who use the network are much less predictable than the network itself. Here are some tips for dealing with users:

+ **Training:** Training is a key part of the network manager's job. Make sure that everyone who uses the network understands it and knows how to use it. If the network users don't understand the network, they may unintentionally do all kinds of weird things to it.

+ **Respect:** Never treat your network users like they're idiots. If they don't understand the network, it isn't their fault. Explain it to them. Offer a class. Buy them each a copy of *Networking All-in-One For Dummies* and tell them to read it during their lunch hour. Hold their hands. But don't treat them like idiots.

+ **Aids:** Make up a network cheat sheet that contains everything that the users need to know about using the network on one page. Make sure that everyone gets a copy.

+ **Responsive:** Be as responsive as possible when a network user complains of a network problem. If you don't fix the problem soon, the user may try to fix it. You probably don't want that.

The better you understand the psychology of network users, the more prepared you'll be for the strangeness they often serve up. Toward that end, I recommend that you read the *Diagnostic and Statistical Manual of Mental Disorders* (also known as *DSM-IV*) cover to cover.

Book III
Chapter 1

Job Description
for a Network
Administrator

Patching Up Your Operating System and Software

One of the annoyances that every network manager faces is applying software patches to keep your OS and other software up to date. A software *patch* is a minor update that fixes small glitches that crop up from time to time, such as minor security or performance issues. These glitches aren't significant enough to merit a new version of the software, but they're important enough to require fixing. Most patches correct security flaws that computer hackers have uncovered in their relentless attempts to prove that they're smarter than security programmers.

Periodically, all the recently released patches are combined into a *service pack*. Although the most diligent network administrators apply all patches as they're released, many administrators just wait for the service packs.

For all versions of Windows, you can use Windows Update to apply patches to keep your operating system and other Microsoft software up to date. You can find Windows Update in the Start menu. Or, you can fire up Internet Explorer and browse to `http://update.microsoft.com`. Windows Update automatically scans your computer's software and creates a list of software patches and other components that you can download and install. You can also configure Windows Update to automatically notify you of updates so that you don't have to remember to check for new patches.

For larger networks, you can set up a server that runs Microsoft's Software Update Services (SUS) to automate software updates. SUS essentially lets you set up your own Windows Update site on your own network. Then, you have complete control over how software updates are delivered to the computers on your network. For more information, see

`www.microsoft.com/windowsserversystem/updateservices`

Discovering Software Tools for Network Administrators

Network administrators need certain tools to get their jobs done. Administrators of big, complicated, and expensive networks need big, complicated, and expensive tools. Administrators of small networks need small tools.

Some of the tools that the administrator needs are hardware tools, such as screwdrivers, cable crimpers, and hammers. The tools that I'm talking about here, however, are software tools. Here's a sampling of the tools you'll need:

✦ **A diagramming tool:** A diagramming tool lets you draw pictures of your network. Visio (from Microsoft) is great for drawing the types of diagrams you'll want to make as a network administrator.

✦ **A network discovery program:** For larger networks, you may want to invest in a network discovery program such as NetworkView (`www.networkview.com`) that can automatically document your network's structure for you. These programs scan the network carefully, looking for computers, printers, routers, and other devices. They then create a database of the network components, draw diagrams for you, and chug out helpful reports.

✦ **The network's built-in tools:** Many software tools that you need to manage a network come with the network itself. As the network administrator, read through the manuals that come with your network software to see what management tools are available. For example, Windows includes a `net diag` command that you can use to make sure that all the computers on a network can communicate with each other. (You can run `net diag` from an MS-DOS prompt.) For TCP/IP networks, you can use the TCP/IP diagnostic commands summarized in Table 1-1. For more information about these commands, check out Book IV, Chapter 6.

Table 1-1	TCP/IP Diagnostic Commands
Command	*What It Does*
arp	Displays address resolution information used by the Address Resolution Protocol (ARP)
hostname	Displays your computer's host name
ipconfig	Displays current TCP/IP settings
nbtstat	Displays the status of NetBIOS over TCP/IP connections
netstat	Displays statistics for TCP/IP
nslookup	Displays Domain Name System (DNS) information
ping	Verifies that a specified computer can be reached
route	Displays the PC's routing tables
tracert	Displays the route from your computer to a specified host

**Book III
Chapter 1**

**Job Description
for a Network
Administrator**

✦ **System Information:** This program that comes with Windows is a useful utility for network managers.

✦ **Hotfix Checker:** This handy tool from Microsoft scans your computers to see what patches need to be applied. You can download the free Hotfix Checker from Microsoft online (search for "**hfnetchk.exe**").

✦ **Microsoft Baseline Security Analyzer:** If you prefer GUI-based tools, check out Microsoft Baseline Security Analyzer. You can download it from Microsoft online for free of charge (search for "**Microsoft Baseline Security Analyzer**").

✦ **A utility program:** I suggest that you get one of those 100-in-1 utility programs, such as Symantec's Norton Utilities. Norton Utilities includes invaluable utilities for repairing damaged hard drives, rearranging the directory structure of your hard drive, gathering information about your computer and its equipment, and so on.

Never use a hard drive repair program that wasn't designed to work with the OS or version that your computer uses or the file system you've installed. Any time that you upgrade to a newer version of your operating system, you should also upgrade your hard drive repair programs to a version that supports the new operating system version.

✦ **A protocol analyzer:** A *protocol analyzer* monitors and logs the individual packets that travel along your network. (Protocol analyzers are also called *packet sniffers*.) You can configure the protocol analyzer to filter specific types of packets, watch for specific types of problems, and provide statistical analysis of the captured packets. Most network administrators agree that Sniffer, by NetScout (`www.netscout.com`), is the best protocol analyzer available. However, it's also one of the most expensive. If you prefer a free alternative, check out Ethereal, which you can download free from `www.ethereal.com`.

✦ **Network Monitor:** All current versions of Windows include Network Monitor, which provides basic protocol analysis and can often help solve pesky network problems.

Building a Library

One of Scotty's best lines in the original *Star Trek* series was when he refused to take shore leave so he could get caught up on his technical journals. "Don't you ever relax?" asked Kirk. "I am relaxing!" Scotty replied.

To be a good network administrator, you need to read computer books. Lots of them. And you need to enjoy doing it. If you're the type who takes computer books with you to the beach, you'll make a great network administrator.

You need books on a variety of topics. I'm not going to recommend specific titles, but I do recommend that you get a good, comprehensive book on each of the following topics:

✦ Network security and hacking

✦ Wireless networking

✦ Network cabling and hardware

✦ Ethernet

✦ Windows Server 2008 or 2012

✦ Windows 7 or 8

✦ Linux

✦ TCP/IP

✦ DNS

✦ Sendmail or Microsoft Exchange Server, depending on which e-mail server you use

In addition to books, you may also want to subscribe to some magazines to keep up with what's happening in the networking industry. Here are a few you should probably consider, along with their web addresses:

✦ *InformationWeek:* `www.informationweek.com`

✦ *InfoWorld:* `www.infoworld.com`

✦ *Network Computing:* `www.networkcomputing.com`

✦ *Network World:* `www.networkworld.com`

✦ *2600 The Hacker Quarterly* (a great magazine on computer hacking and security): `www.2600.com`

The Internet is one of the best sources of technical information for network administrators. You'll want to stock your browser's Favorites menu with plenty of websites that contain useful networking information. In addition, you may want to subscribe to one of the many online newsletters that deliver fresh information on a regular basis via e-mail.

Getting Certified

Remember the scene near the end of *The Wizard of Oz* when the Wizard grants the Scarecrow a diploma, the Cowardly Lion a medal, and the Tin Man a testimonial?

Network certifications are kind of like that. I can picture the scene now:

> *The Wizard:* "And as for you, my network-burdened friend, any geek with thick glasses can administer a network. Back where I come from, there are people who do nothing but configure Cisco routers all day long. And they don't have any more brains than you do. But they do have one thing you don't have: certification. And so, by the authority vested in me by the Universita Committeeatum E Pluribus Unum, I hereby confer upon you the coveted certification of CND."
>
> *You:* "CND?"
>
> *The Wizard:* "Yes, that's, uh, *Certified Network Dummy.*"
>
> *You:* "The Seven Layers of the OSI Reference Model are equal to the Sum of the Layers on the Opposite Side. Oh, joy, rapture! I feel like a network administrator already!"

My point is that certification in and of itself doesn't guarantee that you really know how to administer a network. That ability comes from real-world experience — not exam crams.

Nevertheless, certification is becoming increasingly important in today's competitive job market. So you may want to pursue certification, not just to improve your skills, but also to improve your résumé. Certification is an expensive proposition. Each test can cost several hundred dollars, and depending on your technical skills, you may need to buy books to study or enroll in training courses before you take the tests.

You can pursue two basic types of certification: vendor-specific certification and vendor-neutral certification. The major software vendors such as Microsoft and Cisco provide certification programs for their own equipment and software. CompTIA, a nonprofit industry trade association, provides the best-known vendor-neutral certification.

The following sections describe some of the certifications offered by CompTIA, Microsoft, Novell, and Cisco.

CompTIA

www.comptia.org

✦ **A+** is a basic certification for an entry-level computer technician. To attain A+ certification, you have to pass two exams: one on computer hardware, the other on operating systems.

✦ **Linux+ Powered by LPI** covers basic Linux skills such as installation, operations, and troubleshooting. This certification is vendor neutral, so it doesn't depend on any particular version of Linux.

✦ **Network+** is a popular vendor-neutral networking certification. It covers four major topic areas: Media and Topologies, Protocols and Standards, Network Implementation, and Network Support.

✦ **Server+** covers network server hardware. It includes details such as installing and upgrading server hardware, installing and configuring an NOS, and so on.

✦ **Security+** is for security specialists. The exam topics include general security concepts, communication security, infrastructure security, basics of cryptography, and operational/organizational security.

Microsoft

www.microsoft.com/learning/mcp

✦ **MCTS** (Microsoft Certified Technology Specialist) is a certification in a specific Microsoft technology or product.

✦ **MCITP** (Microsoft Certified IT Professional) is a certification in deploying and maintaining IT infrastructure.

✦ **MCSE** (Microsoft Certified Solutions Expert) is a prestigious certification for networking professionals who design and implement networks. To gain this certification, you have to pass several rigorous exams. Microsoft offers separate Windows Server 2008 and Windows Server 2012 certification tracks.

✦ **MCSA** (Microsoft Certified Solutions Associate) is for networking professionals who administer existing networks.

Cisco

`www.cisco.com/certification`

✦ **CCNA** (Cisco Certified Network Associate) is an entry-level apprentice certification. A CCNA should be able to install, configure, and operate Cisco equipment for small networks (under 100 nodes).

✦ **CCNP** (Cisco Certified Network Professional) is a professional-level certification for Cisco equipment. A CCNP should be able to install, configure, and troubleshoot Cisco networks of virtually any size.

✦ **CCDA** (Cisco Certified Design Associate) is an entry-level certification for network design.

✦ **CCDP** (Cisco Certified Design Professional) is for network design professionals. Both the CCDA and CCNA certifications are prerequisites for the CCDP.

✦ **CCIE** (Cisco Certified Internetwork Expert) is the top dog of Cisco certifications.

✦ **And much more!** There are many more Cisco certifications to choose from, including certification for security, voice technology, wireless networking, and more.

Gurus Need Gurus, Too

No matter how much you know about computers, plenty of people know more than you do. This rule seems to apply at every rung of the ladder of computer experience. I'm sure that a top rung exists somewhere, occupied by the world's best computer guru. However, I'm not sitting on that rung, and neither are you. (Not even Bill Gates is sitting on that rung. In fact, Bill Gates got to where he is today by hiring people on higher rungs.)

As the local computer guru, one of your most valuable assets can be a knowledgeable friend who's a notch or two above you on the geek scale. That way, when you run into a real stumper, you have a friend to call for advice. Here are some tips for handling your own guru:

✦ In dealing with your own guru, don't forget the Computer Geek's Golden Rule: "Do unto your guru as you would have your own users do unto you." Don't pester your guru with simple stuff that you just haven't spent the time to think through. If you have thought it through and can't come up with a solution, however, give your guru a call. Most computer experts welcome the opportunity to tackle an unusual computer problem. It's a genetic defect.

✦ If you don't already know someone who knows more about computers than you do, consider joining your local PC users' group. The group may even have a subgroup that specializes in your networking software or may be devoted entirely to local folks who use the same networking software that you use. Odds are good that you're sure to make a friend or two at a users' group meeting. Also, you can probably convince your boss to pay any fees required to join the group.

✦ If you can't find a real-life guru, try to find an online guru. Check out the various computing newsgroups on the Internet. Subscribe to online newsletters that are automatically delivered to you via e-mail.

Helpful Bluffs and Excuses

As network administrator, you just won't be able to solve a problem sometimes, at least not immediately. You can do two things in this situation. The first is to explain that the problem is particularly difficult and that you'll have a solution as soon as possible. The second solution is to look the user in the eyes and, with a straight face, try one of these phony explanations:

✦ Blame it on the version of whatever software you're using. "Oh, they fixed that with version 39."

✦ Blame it on cheap, imported memory chips.

✦ Blame it on Democrats. Or Republicans. Doesn't matter.

✦ Blame it on oil company executives.

✦ Blame it on global warming.

✦ Hope that the problem wasn't caused by stray static electricity. Those types of problems are very difficult to track down. Tell your users that not properly discharging themselves before using their computers can cause all kinds of problems.

✦ You need more memory.

✦ You need a bigger hard drive.

✦ You need a faster processor.

✦ Blame it on Jar-Jar Binks.

✦ You can't do that in Windows 8.

✦ You can only do that in Windows 8.

✦ Could be a virus.

✦ Or sunspots.

✦ No beer and no TV make Homer something something something. . . .

Chapter 2: Security 101

*1*f you're not on a network, computer security is easy. You simply lock your door when you leave work for the day rest easy, secure in the knowledge that the bad guys have to break down the door to get to your computer.

A network changes all that. Now, anyone with access to any computer on the network can break into the network and steal *your* files. Not only do you have to lock your door, but you also have to make sure that other people lock their doors, too.

Fortunately, network operating systems (NOSes) have built-in provisions for network security, making it difficult for someone to steal your files, even if they do break down the door. All modern NOSes have security features that are more than adequate for all but the most paranoid users.

And when I say *more* than adequate, I mean it. Most networks have security features that would make even Maxwell Smart happy. Using all these security features is kind of like Smart insisting that the Chief lower the "Cone of Silence" (which worked so well that Max and the Chief couldn't hear each other!).

Don't make your system so secure that even the good guys can't get their work done.

If any computer on your network is connected to the Internet, you have to contend with a whole new world of security issues. For more information about Internet security, see Chapter 4 of this minibook. Also, if your network supports wireless devices, you have to contend with wireless security issues. For more information about security for wireless networks, see Book V, Chapter 2.

Do You Need Security?

Most small networks are in small businesses or departments where everyone knows and trusts everyone else. Folks don't lock up their desks when they take a coffee break, and although everyone knows where the petty cash box is, money never disappears.

Network security isn't necessary in an idyllic setting like this one — or is it? You bet it is. Here's why any network should be set up with at least some minimal concern for security:

+ **Mitts off:** Even in the friendliest office environment, some information is and should be confidential. If this information is stored on the network, you want to store it in a directory that's available only to authorized users.

+ **Hmm:** Not all security breaches are malicious. A network user may be routinely scanning files and come across a filename that isn't familiar. The user may then call up the file, only to discover that it contains confidential personnel information, juicy office gossip, or your résumé. Curiosity, rather than malice, is often the source of security breaches.

+ **Trust:** Sure, everyone at the office is trustworthy now. However, what if someone becomes disgruntled, a screw pops loose, and he decides to trash the network files before jumping out the window? Or what if someone decides to print a few $1,000 checks before packing off to Tahiti?

+ **Temptation:** Sometimes the mere opportunity for fraud or theft can be too much for some people to resist. Give people free access to the payroll files, and they may decide to vote themselves a raise when no one is looking.

  If you think that your network contains no data worth stealing, think again. For example, your personnel records probably contain more than enough information for an identity thief: names, addresses, phone numbers, Social Security numbers, and so on. Also, your customer files may contain your customers' credit card numbers.

+ **Malice:** Hackers who break into your network may not be interested in stealing your data. Instead, they may be looking to plant a *Trojan horse* program on your server, which enables them to use your server for their own purposes. For example, someone may use your server to send thousands of unsolicited spam e-mail messages. The spam won't be traced back to the hackers; it will be traced back to you.

+ **Whoops:** Finally, bear in mind that not everyone on the network knows enough about how your operating system and the network work to be trusted with full access to your network's data and systems. One careless mouse click can wipe out an entire directory of network files. One of the best reasons for activating your network's security features is to protect the network from mistakes made by users who don't know what they're doing.

Considering Two Approaches to Security

When you're planning how to implement security on your network, you should first consider which of two basic approaches to security you will take:

✦ **Open-door:** You grant everyone access to everything by default and then place restrictions just on those resources to which you want to limit access.

✦ **Closed-door:** You begin by denying access to everything and then grant specific users access to the specific resources that they need.

In most cases, an open-door policy is easier to implement. Typically, only a small portion of the data on a network really needs security, such as confidential employee records or secrets such as the Coke recipe. The rest of the information on a network can be safely made available to everyone who can access the network.

A closed-door approach results in tighter security, but can lead to the Cone of Silence Syndrome: Like Max and the Chief who can't hear each other talk while they're under the Cone of Silence, your network users will constantly complain that they can't access the information that they need. As a result, you'll find yourself frequently adjusting users' access rights. Choose the closed-door approach only if your network contains a lot of very sensitive information — and only if you're willing to invest time administrating your network's security policy.

Think of an open-door approach as an *entitlement model,* in which the basic assumption is that users are entitled to network access. In contrast, a closed-door policy is a *permissions model,* in which the basic assumption is that users aren't entitled to anything but must get permission for every network resource that they access.

**Book III
Chapter 2**

Security 101

Physical Security: Locking Your Doors

The first level of security in any computer network is physical security. I'm amazed when I walk into the reception area of an accounting firm and see an unattended computer sitting on the receptionist's desk. As often as not, the receptionist has logged on to the system and then walked away from the desk, leaving the computer unattended.

Physical security is important for workstations but vital for servers. Any hacker worth his salt can quickly defeat all but the most paranoid security measures if he or she can gain physical access to a server. To protect the server, follow these guidelines:

- ✦ Lock the computer room.

- ✦ Give the keys only to people you trust.

- ✦ Keep track of who has the keys.

- ✦ Mount the servers on cases or racks with locks.

- ✦ Disable the floppy drive on the server. (A common hacking technique is to boot the server from a floppy, thus bypassing the carefully crafted security features of the network operating system.)

- ✦ Keep a trained guard dog in the computer room and feed it only enough to keep it hungry and mad. (Just kidding.)

There's a big difference between a locked door and a door with a lock. Locks are worthless if you don't use them.

Client computers should be physically secure as well. Instruct users to not leave their computers unattended while they're logged on. In high-traffic areas (such as the receptionist's desk), users should secure their computers with the keylock. Additionally, users should lock their office doors when they leave.

Here are some other potential threats to physical security that you may not have considered:

- ✦ **Off-hours personnel:** The nightly cleaning crew probably has complete access to your facility. How do you know that the person who vacuums your office every night doesn't really work for your chief competitor or doesn't consider computer hacking to be a sideline hobby? You don't, so you'd better consider the cleaning crew a threat.

- ✦ **Dumpster diving:** What about your trash? Paper shredders aren't just for Enron accountants. Your trash can contain all sorts of useful information: sales reports, security logs, printed copies of the company's security policy, even handwritten passwords. For the best security, every piece of paper that leaves your building via the trash bin should first go through a shredder.

- ✦ **Backups:** Where do you store your backup tapes? Don't just stack them up next to the server. Not only does that make them easy to steal, it also defeats one of the main purposes of backing up your data in the first place: securing your server from physical threats, such as fires. If a fire burns down your computer room and the backup tapes are sitting unprotected next to the server, your company may go out of business — and you'll certainly be out of a job. Store the backup tapes securely in a fire-resistant safe and keep a copy off-site, too.

- ✦ **Hubs and servers:** I've seen some networks in which the servers are in a locked computer room, but the hubs or switches are in an unsecured closet. Remember that every unused port on a hub or a switch represents an open door to your network. The hubs and switches should be secured just like the servers.

Securing User Accounts

Next to physical security, the careful use of user accounts is the most important type of security for your network. Properly configured user accounts can prevent unauthorized users from accessing the network, even if they gain physical access to the network. The following sections describe some of the steps that you can take to strengthen your network's use of user accounts.

Obfuscating your usernames

Huh? When it comes to security, *obfuscation* simply means picking obscure usernames. For example, most network administrators assign usernames based on some combination of the user's first and last names, such as BarnyM or baMiller. However, a hacker can easily guess such a user ID if she knows the name of at least one employee. After the hacker knows a username, she can focus on breaking the password.

You can slow down a hacker by using more obscure names — and here's how:

+ Add a random three-digit number to the end of the name. For example: BarnyM320 or baMiller977.

+ Throw a number or two into the middle of the name. For example: Bar6nyM or ba9Miller2.

+ Make sure that usernames are different from e-mail addresses. For example, if a user's e-mail address is `baMiller@Mydomain.com`, do *not* use baMiller as the user's account name. Use a more obscure name.

Do *not* rely on obfuscation to keep people out of your network! Security by obfuscation doesn't work. A resourceful hacker can discover even the most obscure names. The purpose of obfuscation is to slow down intruders — not to stop them. If you slow down an intruder, you're more likely to discover that she is trying to crack your network before she successfully gets in.

Using passwords wisely

One of the most important aspects of network security is using passwords. Usernames aren't usually considered secret. And even if you use obscure names, casual hackers will eventually figure them out.

Passwords, on the other hand, are indeed top secret. Your network password is the one thing that keeps an impostor from logging on to the network by using your username and therefore receiving the same access rights that you ordinarily have. *Guard your password with your life.*

Here are some tips for creating good passwords:

✦ Don't use obvious passwords, such as your last name, your kid's name, or your dog's name.

✦ Don't pick passwords based on your hobbies, either. A friend of mine is into boating, and his password is the name of his boat. Anyone who knows him can guess his password after a few tries. Five lashes for naming your password after your boat.

✦ Store your password in your head, not on paper. Especially bad: Writing down your password on a sticky note and sticking it on your computer's monitor. Ten lashes for that. (If you must write down your password, write it on digestible paper that you can swallow after you memorize the password.)

✦ Most NOSes enable you to set an expiration time for passwords. For example, you can specify that passwords expire after 30 days. When a user's password expires, the user must change it. Your users may consider this process a hassle, but it helps to limit the risk of someone swiping a password and then trying to break into your computer system later.

✦ You can also configure user accounts so that when they change passwords, they can't specify a password that they've used recently. For example, you can specify that the new password can't be identical to any of the user's past three passwords.

✦ You can also configure security policies so that passwords must include a mixture of uppercase letters, lowercase letters, numerals, and special symbols. Thus, passwords like DIMWIT or DUFUS are out. Passwords like 87dIM@wit or duF39&US are in.

✦ Use a biometric ID device, like a fingerprint reader, as a way to keep passwords. These devices store your passwords in a secret encoded file, then supply them automatically to whatever programs or websites require them — but only after the device has read your fingerprint. Fingerprint readers, which used to be exotic and expensive, are available for as little as $50.

A password-generator For Dummies

How do you come up with passwords that no one can guess but that you can remember? Most security experts say that the best passwords don't correspond to any words in the English language, but consist of a random sequence of letters, numbers, and special characters. Yet, how in the heck are you supposed to memorize a password like Dks4%DJ2, Especially when you have to change it three weeks later to something like 3pQ&X(d8?

Here's a compromise solution that enables you to create passwords that consist of two four-letter words back to back. Take your favorite book (if it's this one, you need to get a life) and turn to any page at random. Find the first four- or five-letter word on the page. Suppose that word is `When`. Then repeat the process to find another four- or five-letter word; say you pick the word `Most` the second time. Now combine the words to make your password: `WhenMost`. I think you agree that `WhenMost` is easier to remember than `3PQ&X(D8` and is probably just about as hard to guess. I probably wouldn't want the folks at the Los Alamos Nuclear Laboratory using this scheme, but it's good enough for most of us.

Here are some additional thoughts on concocting passwords from your favorite book:

+ If the words end up being the same, pick another word. And pick different words if the combination seems too commonplace, such as `WestWind` or `FootBall`.

+ For an interesting variation, insert the page numbers on which you found both words either before or after the words. For example: `135Into376Cat` or `87Tree288Wing`. The resulting password will be a little harder to remember, but you'll have a password worthy of a Dan Brown novel.

+ To further confuse your friends and enemies, use archaic language: for example, medieval words from Chaucer's *Canterbury Tales.* Chaucer is a great source for passwords because he lived before the days of word processors with spell-checkers. He wrote *seyd* instead of *said, gret* instead of *great,* and *litel* instead of *little.* And he used lots of seven-letter and eight-letter words suitable for passwords, such as *glotenye* (gluttony), *benygne* (benign), and *opynyoun* (opinion). And he got an A in English.

+ If you do decide to go with passwords such as `KdI22UR3xdkL`, you can find random password generators on the Internet. Just go to a search engine, such as Google (`www.google.com`), and search for *password generator.* You can find web pages that generate random passwords based on criteria that you specify, such as how long the password should be, whether it should include letters, numbers, punctuation, uppercase and lowercase letters, and so on.

If you use any of these password schemes and someone breaks into your network, don't blame me. You're the one who's too lazy to memorize `D#Sc$h4@bb3xaz5`.

Securing the Administrator account

At least one network user must have the authority to use the network without any of the restrictions imposed on other users. This user — the *administrator* — is responsible for setting up the network's security system. To do that, the administrator must be exempt from all security restrictions.

Many networks automatically create an administrator user account when you install the network software. The username and password for this initial administrator are published in the network's documentation and are the same for all networks that use the same NOS. One of the first things that you must do after getting your network up and running is to change the password for this standard administrator account. Otherwise, your elaborate security precautions will be a complete waste of time. Anyone who knows the default administrator username and password can access your system with full administrator rights and privileges, thus bypassing the security restrictions that you so carefully set up.

Don't forget the password for the administrator account! If a network user forgets his password, you can log on as the supervisor and change that user's password. If you forget the administrator's password, though, you're stuck.

Hardening Your Network

In addition to taking care of physical security and user account security, you should also take steps to protect your network from intruders by configuring the other security features of the network's servers and routers. The following sections describe the basics of hardening your network.

Using a firewall

A *firewall* is a security-conscious router that sits between your network and the outside world and prevents Internet users from wandering into your local area network (LAN) and messing around. Firewalls are the first line of defense for any network that's connected to the Internet.

You should *never* connect a network to the Internet without installing a carefully configured firewall. For more information about firewalls, read Chapter 4 of this minibook.

Disabling unnecessary services

A typical NOS can support dozens of different types of network services: file and printer sharing, web server, mail server, and many others. In many cases, these features are installed on servers that don't need or use them.

When a server runs a network service that it doesn't really need, the service not only robs CPU cycles from other services that are needed, but also poses an unnecessary security threat.

When you first install an NOS on a server, you should enable only those network services that you know the server will require. You can always enable services later if the needs of the server change.

Patching your servers

Hackers regularly find security holes in network operating systems. After those holes are discovered, the OS vendors figure out how to plug the hole and then release a software patch for the security fix. The trouble is that most network administrators don't stay up to date with these software patches. As a result, many networks are vulnerable because they have well-known holes in their security armor that should have been fixed but weren't.

Even though patches are a bit of a nuisance, they're well worth the effort for the protection that they afford. Fortunately, newer versions of the popular network operating systems have features that automatically check for updates and let you know when a patch should be applied.

Securing Your Users

Security techniques — physical security, user account security, server security, and locking down your servers — are child's play compared with the most difficult job of network security: securing your network's users. All the best-laid security plans are for naught if your users write down their passwords on sticky notes and post them on their computers.

The key to securing your network users is to create a written network security policy and stick to it. Have a meeting with everyone to go over the security policy to make sure that everyone understands the rules. Also, make sure to have consequences when violations occur.

Here are some suggestions for some basic security rules you can incorporate into your security policy:

✦ Never write down your password or give it to someone else.

✦ Accounts should not be shared. Never use someone else's account to access a resource that you can't access under your own account. If you need access to some network resource that isn't available to you, you should formally request access under your own account.

✦ Likewise, never give your account information to a co-worker so that he or she can access a needed resource. Your co-worker should instead formally request access under his or her own account.

✦ Don't install any software or hardware on your computer — especially wireless access devices or modems — without first obtaining permission.

✦ Don't enable file and printer sharing on workstations without first getting permission.

✦ Never attempt to disable or bypass the network's security features.

Chapter 3: Managing User Accounts

In This Chapter

✔ Understanding user accounts

✔ Looking at the built-in accounts

✔ Using rights and permissions

✔ Working with groups and policies

✔ Running login scripts

*U*ser accounts are the backbone of network security administration. You can determine who can access your network, as well as what network resources each user can and can't access. You can restrict access to the network to just specific computers or to certain hours of the day, and you can lock out users who no longer need to access your network.

The specific details for managing user accounts are unique to each network operating system (NOS) and are covered in separate chapters later in this book. This chapter simply introduces you to the concepts of user account management so you know what you can and can't do, regardless of which NOS you use.

Exploring What User Accounts Consist Of

User accounts allow the network administrator to determine who can access the network and what network resources each user can access. Every user who accesses a network must have a user account. In addition, user accounts can be customized to provide many convenience features for users, such as a personalized Start menu or a display of recently used documents.

Every user account is associated with a username (sometimes called a *user ID*), which the user must enter when logging on to the network. Each account also has other information associated with it:

✦ **The user's password:** This also includes the password policy, such as how often the user has to change his or her password, how complicated the password must be, and so on.

✦ **The user's contact information:** This includes full name, phone number, e-mail address, mailing address, and other related information.

✦ **Account restrictions:** This includes restrictions that allow the user to log on only during certain times of the day. This feature enables you to restrict your users to normal working hours so that they can't sneak in at 2 a.m. to do unauthorized work. This feature also discourages your users from working overtime because they can't access the network after hours, so use it judiciously. You can also specify that the user can log on only at certain computers.

✦ **Account status:** You can temporarily disable a user account so that the user can't log on.

✦ **Home directory:** This specifies a shared network folder where the user can store documents.

✦ **Dial-in permissions:** These authorize the user to access the network remotely.

✦ **Group memberships:** These grant the user certain rights based on groups to which they belong. For more information, see the section, "Assigning Permissions to Groups," later in this chapter.

Looking at Built-In Accounts

Most NOSes come preconfigured with two built-in accounts: Administrator and Guest. In addition, some server services, such as web or database servers, create their own user accounts under which to run. The following sections describe the characteristics of these accounts.

The Administrator account

The Administrator account is the King of the Network. This user account isn't subject to any of the account restrictions to which other, mere mortal accounts must succumb. If you log on as the administrator, you can do anything.

Because the Administrator account has unlimited access to your network, you should secure it *immediately* after you install the server. When the NOS Setup program asks for a password for the Administrator account, start off with a good random mix of uppercase and lowercase letters, numbers, and symbols. Don't pick some easy-to-remember password to get started, thinking you'll change it to something more cryptic later. You'll forget, and in the meantime, someone will break in and reformat the server's C: drive or steal your customers' credit card numbers.

Here are a few additional things worth knowing about the Administrator account:

✦ You can't delete it. The system must always have an administrator.

✦ You can grant administrator status to other user accounts. However, you should do so only for users who really need to be administrators.

✦ You should use it only when you really need to do tasks that require administrative authority. Many network administrators grant administrative authority to their own user accounts. That isn't a very good idea. If you're killing some time surfing the web or reading your e-mail while logged on as an administrator, you're just inviting viruses or malicious scripts to take advantage of your administrator access. Instead, you should set yourself up with two accounts: a normal account that you use for day-to-day work, and an Administrator account that you use only when you need it.

✦ The default name for the Administrator account is usually simply Administrator. You may want to consider changing this name. Better yet, change the name of the Administrator account to something more obscure and then create an ordinary user account that has few (if any) rights and give that account the name Administrator. That way, hackers who spend weeks trying to crack your Administrator account password will discover that they've been duped after they finally break the password. In the meantime, you'll have a chance to discover their attempts to breach your security and take appropriate action.

✦ Above all, don't forget the Administrator account password. Write it down in permanent ink and store it in Fort Knox, a safe deposit box, or some other secure location.

**Book III
Chapter 3**

**Managing User
Accounts**

The Guest account

Another commonly created default account is the Guest account, which is set up with a blank password and few (if any) access rights. A Guest account is designed to allow people to step up to a computer and log on, but after they do, it then prevents them from doing anything. Sounds like a waste of time to me. I suggest disabling the Guest account.

Service accounts

Some network users aren't actual people. I don't mean that some of your users are subhuman. Rather, some users are actually software processors that require access to secure resources and therefore require user accounts. These user accounts are usually created automatically for you when you install or configure server software.

For example, when you install the Microsoft web server (IIS), an Internet user account called IUSR is created. The complete name for this account is IUSR_<servername>. So if the server is named WEB1, the account is named IUSR_WEB1. IIS uses this account to allow anonymous Internet users to access the files of your website.

As a general rule, don't mess with these accounts unless you know what you're doing. For example, if you delete or rename the IUSR account, you must reconfigure IIS to use the changed account. If you don't, IIS will deny access to anyone trying to reach your site. (Assuming that you *do* know what you're doing, renaming these accounts can increase your network's security. However, don't start playing with these accounts until you research the ramifications.)

Assigning User Rights

User accounts and passwords are only the front line of defense in the game of network security. After a user gains access to the network by typing a valid user ID and password, the second line of security defense — rights — comes into play.

In the harsh realities of network life, all users are created equal, but some users are more equal than others. The Preamble to the Declaration of Network Independence contains the statement, "We hold these truths to be self-evident, that *some* users are endowed by the network administrator with certain inalienable rights. . . ."

Here's a partial list of the user rights that are possible with Windows servers:

✦ **Log on locally.** The user can log on to the server computer directly from the server's keyboard.

✦ **Change system time.** The user can change the time and date registered by the server.

✦ **Shut down the system.** The user can perform an orderly shutdown of the server.

✦ **Back up files and directories.** The user can perform a backup of files and directories on the server.

✦ **Restore files and directories.** The user can restore backed-up files.

✦ **Take ownership of files and other objects.** The user can take over files and other network resources that belong to other users.

Controlling User Access with Permissions (Who Gets What)

User rights control what a user can do on a network-wide basis. *Permissions* enable you to fine-tune your network security by controlling access to specific network resources, such as files or printers, for individual users or groups. For example, you can set up permissions to allow users in the accounting department to access files in the server's \ACCTG directory. Permissions can also enable some users to read certain files but not modify or delete them.

Each NOS manages permissions in a different way. Whatever the details, the effect is that you can give permission to each user to access certain files, folders, or drives in certain ways.

Any permissions that you specify for a folder apply automatically to any of that folder's subfolders, unless you explicitly specify a different set of permissions for the subfolder.

Windows refers to file system rights as *permissions.* Windows servers have six basic permissions, listed in Table 3-1. You can assign any combination of Windows permissions to a user or group for a given file or folder. To assign these permissions, simply right-click the file or folder you want to assign the permissions to, choose Properties, and then open the Permissions tab.

For more information about setting permissions in Windows Server, refer to Chapter 5 of Book VII.

Table 3-1	Windows Basic Permissions	
Permission	*Abbreviation*	*What the User Can Do*
Read	R	Open and read the file
Write	W	Open and write to the file
Execute	X	Run the file
Delete	D	Delete the file
Change	P	Change the permissions for the file
Take Ownership	O	Take ownership of the file

Note the last permission listed in Table 3-1. In Windows, the concept of file or folder ownership is important. Every file or folder on a Windows server system has an owner. The *owner* is usually the user who creates the file or folder. However, ownership can be transferred from one user to another. So why the Take Ownership permission? This permission prevents someone from creating a bogus file and giving ownership of it to you without your permission. Windows doesn't allow you to give ownership of a file to another user. Instead, you can give another user the right to take ownership of the file. That user must then explicitly take ownership of the file.

Assigning Permissions to Groups

A *group account* doesn't represent an individual user. Instead, it represents a group of users who use the network in a similar way. Instead of granting access rights to each user, grant the rights to the group and then assign individual users to the group. When you assign a user to a group, that user inherits the rights specified for the group.

For example, suppose you create an Accounting group and then give those group members access to the network's accounting files and applications. Then, instead of granting each Accounting user access to those files and applications, you simply make each accounting user a member of the Accounting group.

Here are a few additional details about groups:

✦ **Groups are key to network-management nirvana.** As much as possible, avoid managing network users individually. Instead, clump them into groups and manage the groups. When all 50 users in the accounting department need access to a new file share, would you rather update 50 user accounts — or just one group account?

✦ **A user can belong to more than one group.** As I mention earlier, a user in a group inherits the rights of that group — and belonging to more than one group can prove helpful. For example, suppose you have Accounting, Sales, Marketing, and Finance groups. A user who needs to access Accounting and Finance can be made a member of both groups.

✦ **You can grant or revoke specific rights to individual users to override the group settings.** For example, you may want to allow department managers only to modify files in a folder while all other users can read but not modify the files.

Understanding User Profiles

A *user profile* is a Windows feature that keeps track of an individual user's preferences for his Windows configuration. For a non-networked computer, profiles enable two or more users to use the same computer, each with their own desktop settings, such as wallpaper, colors, Start menu options, and so on.

The real benefit of user profiles becomes apparent when profiles are used on a network. A user's profile can be stored on a server computer and accessed whenever that user logs on to the network from any Windows computer on the network.

The following are some of the elements of Windows that are governed by settings in the user profile:

✦ Desktop settings from the Display Properties dialog box, including wallpaper, screen savers, and color schemes

✦ Start menu programs and Windows toolbar options

✦ Favorites, which provide easy access to the files and folders that the user accesses frequently

✦ Network settings, including drive mappings, network printers, and recently visited network locations

✦ Application settings, such as option settings for Microsoft Word

✦ The Documents/My Documents folder (OS-dependent)

Automating Tasks with Logon Scripts

A *logon script* is a batch file that runs automatically whenever a user logs on. Logon scripts can perform several important logon tasks for you, such as mapping network drives, starting applications, synchronizing the client computer's time-of-day clock, and so on. Logon scripts reside on the server, in a special folder named NETLOGON. Each user account can specify whether to use a logon script and which script to use.

Here's a sample logon script that maps a few network drives and synchronizes the time:

```
net use m: \\MYSERVER\Acct
net use n: \\MYSERVER\Admin
net use o: \\MYSERVER\Dev
net time \\MYSERVER /set /yes
```

Logon scripts are a little out of vogue because most of what a logon script does can be done via user profiles. Still, many administrators prefer the simplicity of logon scripts, so they're still used even on Windows Server 2008 and 2012 systems.

**Book III
Chapter 3**

Managing User Accounts

Chapter 4: Firewalls and Virus Protection

In This Chapter

☑ Understanding what firewalls do

☑ Examining the different types of firewalls

☑ Looking at virus protection

☑ Discovering Windows security

*I*f your network is connected to the Internet, a whole host of security issues bubble to the surface. You probably connected your network to the Internet so that your network's users could access the Internet. Unfortunately, however, your Internet connection is a two-way street. Not only does it enable your network's users to step outside the bounds of your network to access the Internet, but it also enables others to step in and access your network.

And step in they will. The world is filled with hackers looking for networks like yours to break into. They may do it just for fun, or they may do it to steal your customer's credit card numbers or to coerce your mail server into sending thousands of spam messages on their behalf. Whatever their motive, rest assured that your network will be broken into if you leave it unprotected.

This chapter presents an overview of two basic techniques for securing your network's Internet connection: firewalls and virus protection.

Firewalls

A *firewall* is a security-conscious router that sits between the Internet and your network with a single-minded task: preventing *them* from getting to *us*. The firewall acts as a security guard between the Internet and your local area network (LAN). All network traffic into and out of the LAN must pass through the firewall, which prevents unauthorized access to the network.

Some type of firewall is a must-have if your network has a connection to the Internet, whether that connection is broadband (cable modem or digital subscriber line; DSL), T1, or some other high-speed connection. Without it, sooner or later a hacker will discover your unprotected network and tell his friends about it. Within a few hours, your network will be toast.

You can set up a firewall two basic ways. The easiest way is to purchase a *firewall appliance,* which is basically a self-contained router with built-in firewall features. Most firewall appliances include a web-based interface that enables you to connect to the firewall from any computer on your network using a browser. You can then customize the firewall settings to suit your needs.

Alternatively, you can set up a server computer to function as a firewall computer. The server can run just about any network operating system (NOS), but most dedicated firewall systems run Linux.

Whether you use a firewall appliance or a firewall computer, the firewall must be located between your network and the Internet, as shown in Figure 4-1. Here, one end of the firewall is connected to a network hub, which is in turn connected to the other computers on the network. The other end of the firewall is connected to the Internet. As a result, all traffic from the LAN to the Internet and vice versa must travel through the firewall.

The term *perimeter* is sometimes used to describe the location of a firewall on your network. In short, a firewall is like a perimeter fence that completely surrounds your property and forces all visitors to enter through the front gate.

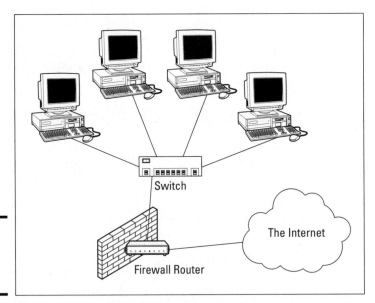

Figure 4-1:
Using a
firewall
appliance.

The Many Types of Firewalls

Firewalls employ four basic techniques to keep unwelcome visitors out of your network. The following sections describe these basic firewall techniques.

Packet filtering

A *packet-filtering* firewall examines each packet that crosses the firewall and tests the packet according to a set of rules that you set up. If the packet passes the test, it's allowed to pass. If the packet doesn't pass, it's rejected.

Packet filters are the least expensive type of firewall. As a result, packet-filtering firewalls are very common. However, packet filtering has a number of flaws that knowledgeable hackers can exploit. As a result, packet filtering by itself doesn't make for a fully effective firewall.

Packet filters work by inspecting the source and destination IP and port addresses contained in each Transmission Control Protocol/Internet Protocol (TCP/IP) packet. TCP/IP *ports* are numbers assigned to specific services that help to identify for which service each packet is intended. For example, the port number for the HTTP protocol is 80. As a result, any incoming packets headed for an HTTP server will specify port 80 as the destination port.

Port numbers are often specified with a colon following an IP address. For example, the HTTP service on a server whose IP address is 192.168.10.133 would be 192.168.10.133:80.

Literally thousands of established ports are in use. Table 4-1 lists a few of the most popular ports.

**Book III
Chapter 4**

Firewalls and Virus
Protection

Table 4-1	Some Well-Known TCP/IP Ports
Port	**Description**
20	File Transfer Protocol (FTP)
21	File Transfer Protocol (FTP)
22	Secure Shell Protocol (SSH)
23	Telnet
25	Simple Mail Transfer Protocol (SMTP)
53	Domain Name Server (DNS)
80	World Wide Web (HyperText Transport Protocol; HTTP)
110	Post Office Protocol (POP3)

(continued)

Table 4-1 *(continued)*

Port	Description
119	Network News Transfer Protocol (NNTP)
137	NetBIOS Name Service
138	NetBIOS Datagram Service
139	NetBIOS Session Service
143	Internet Message Access Protocol (IMAP)
161	Simple Network Management Protocol (SNMP)
194	Internet Relay Chat (IRC)
389	Lightweight Directory Access Protocol (LDAP)
396	NetWare over IP
443	HTTP over TLS/SSL (HTTPS)

The rules that you set up for the packet filter either permit or deny packets that specify certain IP addresses or ports. For example, you may permit packets that are intended for your mail server or your web server and deny all other packets. Or, you may set up a rule that specifically denies packets that are heading for the ports used by NetBIOS. This rule keeps Internet hackers from trying to access NetBIOS server resources, such as files or printers.

One of the biggest weaknesses of packet filtering is that it pretty much trusts that the packets themselves are telling the truth when they say who they're from and who they're going to. Hackers exploit this weakness by using a hacking technique called *IP spoofing,* in which they insert fake IP addresses in packets that they send to your network.

Another weakness of packet filtering is that it examines each packet in isolation without considering what packets have gone through the firewall before and what packets may follow. In other words, packet filtering is *stateless.* Rest assured that hackers have figured out how to exploit the stateless nature of packet filtering to get through firewalls.

In spite of these weaknesses, packet filter firewalls have several advantages that explain why they are commonly used:

✦ **Efficient:** They hold up each inbound and outbound packet for only a few milliseconds while they look inside the packet to determine the destination and source ports and addresses. After these addresses and ports are determined, the packet filter quickly applies its rules and either sends the packet along or rejects it. In contrast, other firewall techniques have a more noticeable performance overhead.

✦ **Almost completely transparent to users:** The only time a user will be aware that a packet filter firewall is being used is when the firewall rejects packets. Other firewall techniques require that clients and/or servers be specially configured to work with the firewall.

✦ **Inexpensive:** Even consumer-grade routers include built-in packet filtering.

Stateful packet inspection (SPI)

Stateful packet inspection (SPI) is a step up in intelligence from simple packet filtering. A firewall with stateful packet inspection looks at packets in groups rather than individually. It keeps track of which packets have passed through the firewall and can detect patterns that indicate unauthorized access. In some cases, the firewall may hold on to packets as they arrive until the firewall gathers enough information to make a decision about whether the packets should be authorized or rejected.

Stateful packet inspection was once found only on expensive, enterprise-level routers. Now, however, SPI firewalls are affordable enough for small- or medium-sized networks to use.

Circuit-level gateway

A *circuit-level gateway* manages connections between clients and servers based on TCP/IP addresses and port numbers. After the connection is established, the gateway doesn't interfere with packets flowing between the systems.

For example, you could use a Telnet circuit-level gateway to allow Telnet connections (port 23) to a particular server and prohibit other types of connections to that server. After the connection is established, the circuit-level gateway allows packets to flow freely over the connection. As a result, the circuit-level gateway can't prevent a Telnet user from running specific programs or using specific commands.

Application gateway

An *application gateway* is a firewall system that is more intelligent than a packet-filtering firewall, stateful packet inspection, or circuit-level gateway firewall. Packet filters treat all TCP/IP packets the same. In contrast, application gateways know the details about the applications that generate the packets that pass through the firewall. For example, a web application gateway is aware of the details of HTTP packets. As a result, it can examine more than just the source and destination addresses and ports to determine whether the packets should be allowed to pass through the firewall.

In addition, application gateways work as proxy servers. Simply put, a *proxy server* is a server that sits between a client computer and a real server. The proxy server intercepts packets that are intended for the real server and processes them. The proxy server can examine the packet and decide to pass it on to the real server, or it can reject the packet. Or, the proxy server may be able to respond to the packet itself without involving the real server at all.

For example, web proxies often store copies of commonly used web pages in a local cache. When a user requests a web page from a remote web server, the proxy server intercepts the request and checks whether it already has a copy of the page in its cache. If so, the web proxy returns the page directly to the user. If not, the proxy passes the request on to the real server.

Application gateways are aware of the details of how various types of TCP/IP servers handle sequences of TCP/IP packets to can make more intelligent decisions about whether an incoming packet is legitimate or is part of an attack. As a result, application gateways are more secure than simple packet-filtering firewalls, which can deal with only one packet at a time.

The improved security of application gateways, however, comes at a price. Application gateways are more expensive than packet filters, both in terms of their purchase price and in the cost of configuring and maintaining them. In addition, application gateways slow network performance because they do more detailed checking of packets before allowing them to pass.

The Built-In Windows Firewall

Windows comes with a built-in packet-filtering firewall. If you don't have a separate firewall router, you can use this built-in firewall to provide a basic level of protection. Note, however, that you should rely on the Windows firewall only as a last resort. If at all possible, use a separate firewall rather than the Windows firewall to protect your network.

Here are the steps to activate the firewall in Windows 7 or 8:

1. **Choose Start⇨Control Panel.**

2. **In the Control Panel, click System and Security.**

3. **On the System and Security page, click Windows Firewall.**

4. **On the Windows Firewall page, click Turn Windows Firewall On or Off.**

   The page shown in Figure 4-2 appears.

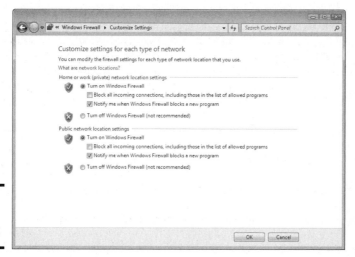

Figure 4-2:
Activating
the firewall.

5. **Select the Turn On Windows Firewall radio button.**

   Note that there are two such buttons: one for home and work (private) networks and one for public networks. If you have a separate router for your work or home network, you can leave the home and work (private) network firewall turned off. But always turn on the firewall for public networks.

6. **Click OK.**

   The firewall is enabled.

Do *not* enable Windows Firewall if you're using a separate firewall router to protect your network. Because the other computers on the network are connected directly to the router and not to your computer, Windows Firewall won't protect the rest of the network. Additionally, as an unwanted side effect, the rest of the network will lose the ability to access your computer.

Windows Firewall is turned on by default. If your computer is already behind a firewall, you should disable Windows Firewall. (In some cases, the network's group policy settings may prevent you from disabling Windows Firewall. In that case, you must change the group policy so that Windows Firewall can be disabled. For more information about group policy, see Book VII, Chapter 6.)

Virus Protection

Viruses are one of the most misunderstood computer phenomena around these days. What is a virus? How does it work? How does it spread from computer to computer? I'm glad you asked.

What is a virus?

Make no mistake — viruses are real. Now that most people are connected to the Internet, viruses have really taken off. Every computer user is susceptible to attacks by computer viruses, and using a network increases your vulnerability because it exposes all network users to the risk of being infected by a virus that lands on any one network user's computer.

Viruses don't just spontaneously appear out of nowhere. Viruses are computer programs that are created by malicious programmers who've lost a few screws and should be locked up.

What makes a virus a virus is its capability to make copies of itself that can be spread to other computers. These copies, in turn, make still more copies that spread to still more computers, and so on, ad nauseam.

Then, the virus patiently waits until something triggers it — perhaps when you type a particular command or press a certain key, when a certain date arrives, or when the virus creator sends the virus a message. What the virus does when it strikes also depends on what the virus creator wants the virus to do. Some viruses harmlessly display a "gotcha" message. Some send an e-mail to everyone it finds in your address book. Some wipe out all the data on your hard drive. Ouch.

Many years ago, in the prehistoric days of computers, viruses were passed from one computer to another by latching themselves onto floppy disks. Whenever you borrowed a floppy disk from a buddy, you ran the risk of infecting your own computer with a virus that may have stowed away on the disk.

Virus programmers have discovered that e-mail is a very efficient method to spread their viruses. Typically, a virus masquerades as a useful or interesting e-mail attachment, such as instructions on how to make $1,000,000 in your spare time, pictures of naked celebrities, or a Valentine's Day greeting from your long-lost sweetheart. When a curious but unsuspecting user opens the attachment, the virus springs to life, copying itself onto the user's computer — sometimes sending copies of itself to all the names in the user's address book.

After the virus works its way onto a networked computer, the virus can then figure out how to spread itself to other computers on the network. It can also spread itself by burrowing into a flash drive so that when the flash drive is inserted into another computer, that computer may become infected as well.

Here are some more tidbits about protecting your network from virus attacks:

✦ The term *virus* is often used to refer not only to true virus programs (which are able to replicate themselves) but also to any other type of program that's designed to harm your computer. These programs include so-called *Trojan horse* programs that usually look like games but are, in reality, hard drive formatters.

✦ A *worm* is similar to a virus, but it doesn't actually infect other files. Instead, it just copies itself onto other computers on a network. After a worm has copied itself onto your computer, there's no telling what it may do there. For example, a worm may scan your hard drive for interesting information, such as passwords or credit card numbers, and then e-mail them to the worm's author.

✦ Computer virus experts have identified several thousand "strains" of viruses. Many of them have colorful names, such as the I Love You virus, the Stoned virus, and the Michelangelo virus.

✦ Antivirus programs can recognize known viruses and remove them from your system, and they can spot the telltale signs of unknown viruses. Unfortunately, the idiots who write viruses aren't idiots (in the intellectual sense), so they're constantly developing new techniques to evade detection by antivirus programs. New viruses are frequently discovered, and antivirus programs are periodically updated to detect and remove them.

Antivirus programs

The best way to protect your network from virus infection is to use an antivirus program. These programs have a catalog of several thousand known viruses that they can detect and remove. In addition, they can spot the types of changes that viruses typically make to your computer's files, thus decreasing the likelihood that some previously unknown virus will go undetected.

It would be nice if Windows came with built-in antivirus software, but alas — it does not. Free options are available, such as Microsoft Security Essentials, but you're better off purchasing a high-quality antivirus program on your own. The two best-known antivirus programs for Windows are Norton AntiVirus by Symantec and VirusScan Enterprise by McAfee.

The people who make antivirus programs have their fingers on the pulse of the virus world and frequently release updates to their software to combat the latest viruses. Because virus writers are constantly developing new viruses, your antivirus software is next to worthless unless you keep it up to date by downloading the latest updates.

**Book III
Chapter 4**

Firewalls and Virus Protection

Here are several approaches to deploying antivirus protection on your network:

- ✦ **Install antivirus software on each network user's computer.** This technique would be the most effective if you could count on all your users to keep their antivirus software up to date. Because that's an unlikely proposition, you may want to adopt a more reliable approach to virus protection.

- ✦ **Managed antivirus services place antivirus client software on each client computer in your network.** Then, an antivirus server automatically updates the clients on a regular basis to make sure that they're kept up to date.

- ✦ **Server-based antivirus software protects your network servers from viruses.** For example, you can install antivirus software on your mail server to scan all incoming mail for viruses and remove them before your network users ever see them.

- ✦ **Some firewall appliances include antivirus enforcement checks that don't allow your users to access the Internet unless their antivirus software is up to date.** This type of firewall provides the best antivirus protection available.

Safe computing

Besides using an antivirus program, you can take a few additional precautions to ensure virus-free computing. If you haven't talked to your kids about these safe-computing practices, you had better do so soon.

- ✦ **Regularly back up your data.** If a virus hits you, and your antivirus software can't repair the damage, you may need the backup to recover your data. Make sure that you restore from a backup that was created before you were infected by the virus!

- ✦ **If you buy software from a store and discover that the seal has been broken on the disk package, take the software back.** Don't try to install it on your computer. You don't hear about tainted software as often as you hear about tainted beef, but if you buy software that's been opened, it may well be laced with a virus infection.

- ✦ **Use your antivirus software to scan your disk for virus infection after your computer has been to a repair shop or worked on by a consultant.** These guys don't intend harm, but they occasionally spread viruses accidentally, simply because they work on so many strange computers.

- ✦ **Don't open e-mail attachments from people you don't know or attachments you weren't expecting.**

- ✦ **Use your antivirus software to scan any floppy disk or CD that doesn't belong to you before you access any of its files.**

Using Windows Action Center

Windows Action Center, which comes with Windows, monitors the status of security-related issues on your computer. You can summon the Windows Action Center by opening the Control Panel, clicking System and Security, and then clicking Action Center; see Figure 4-3.

Figure 4-3:
The
Windows
Action
Center.

**Book III
Chapter 4**

**Firewalls and Virus
Protection**

The Windows Action Center alerts you to issues with your computer's security status as well as reminds you of maintenance that should be done, such as installing operating system updates.

Here are additional points to ponder concerning the Windows Action Center:

✦ A flag icon (shown in the margin) appears in the notification area on the right end of the Windows taskbar to alert you to items you should attend to in the Windows Action Center.

✦ Earlier versions of Windows included a similar feature called the Windows Security Center, which you can access from the Control Panel.

Chapter 5: Extending Your Network with VPN Access

In This Chapter

✔ Examining VPN uses

✔ Looking at how VPN works

✔ Considering VPN clients and servers

✔ Pondering VPN hardware and software

*T*oday's network users frequently need to access their networks from remote locations: home offices, hotel rooms, beach villas, and their kid's soccer fields. In the early days of computer networking, the only real option for remotely accessing a network was to set up dialup access with telephone lines and modems, which was slow and unreliable. Today, enabling remote access to a local area network (LAN) is easily done with a virtual private network. Simply put, a virtual private network (VPN) enables remote users to access a LAN via any Internet connection.

This chapter is a short introduction to VPNs. You find out the basics of what a VPN is, how to set one up, and how to access one remotely. Enjoy!

Understanding VPN

A *virtual private network* (VPN) is a type of network connection that creates the illusion that you're directly connected to a network when in fact, you're not. For example, suppose you set up a LAN at your office, but you also occasionally work from home. But how will you access the files on your work computer from home?

♦ You could simply copy whatever files you need from your work computer onto a flash drive and take them home with you, work on the files, copy the updated files back to the flash drive, and take them back to work with you the next day.

♦ You could e-mail the files to your personal e-mail account, work on them at home, and then e-mail the changed files back to your work e-mail account.

♦ You could get a laptop and use the Windows Offline Files feature to automatically synchronize files from your work network with files on the laptop.

Accessing your computer remotely

One of the most common reasons for setting up a VPN connection is to allow you to access your work computer from a remote computer, such as your home computer or a mobile computer. Once connected, the work computer's desktop appears in a window on the remote computer. The technology that enables this remote access is *Remote Desktop Connection*, or *RDC*.

Before you can use RDC to connect remotely, you must enable remote access on your work computer: Right-click Computer on the Start menu and choose Properties, and then click Advanced System Settings. Click the Remote tab, and then select Allow Connections Only

from Computers Running Remote Desktop with Network Level Authentication. This option lets you grant remote access only to specific users, whom you can designate by clicking the Select Users button.

After remote access has been granted, you can access the computer remotely by connecting to the network with a VPN. Then choose Start⇨All Programs⇨Remote Desktop Connection. Enter the name of the computer you want to connect to, and then click Connect. You're prompted for your Windows username and password. After it's all connected, you can access the remote computer's desktop in a window.

Or, you could set up a VPN that allows you to log on to your work network from home. The VPN uses a secured Internet connection to connect you directly to your work network, so you can access your network files as if you had a really long Ethernet cable that ran from your home computer all the way to the office and plugged directly into the work network.

There are at least three situations in which a VPN is the ideal solution:

✦ One or more workers need to occasionally work from home (as in the scenario just described). In this situation, a VPN connection establishes a connection between the home computer and the office network.

✦ Mobile users — who may not ever actually show up at the office — need to connect to the work network from mobile computers, often from locations like hotel rooms, clients' offices, airports, or coffee shops. This type of VPN configuration is similar to the home user's configuration, except that the exact location of the remote user's computer is not fixed.

✦ Your company has offices in two or more locations, each with its own LAN, and you want to connect the locations so that users on either network can access each other's network resources. In this situation, the VPN doesn't connect a single user with a remote network; instead, it connects two remote networks to each other.

Looking at VPN Security

The *V* in VPN stands for *virtual*, which means that a VPN creates the appearance of a local network connection when in fact the connection is made over a public network — the Internet. The term "tunnel" is sometimes used to describe a VPN because the VPN creates a tunnel between two locations, which can only be entered from either end. The data that travels through the tunnel from one end to the other is secure as long as it is within the tunnel — that is, within the protection provided by the VPN.

The *P* in VPN stands for *private*, which is the purpose of creating the tunnel. If the VPN didn't create effective security so that data can enter the tunnel only at one of the two ends, the VPN would be worthless; you may as well just open your network and your remote computer up to the Internet and let the hackers have their way.

Prior to VPN technology, the only way to provide private remote network connections was through actual private lines, which were (and still are) very expensive. For example, to set up a remote office you could lease a private T1 line from the phone company to connect the two offices. This private T1 line provided excellent security because it physically connected the two offices and could be accessed only from the two endpoints.

VPN provides the same point-to-point connection as a private leased line, but does it over the Internet instead of through expensive dedicated lines. To create the tunnel that guarantees privacy of the data as it travels from one end of the VPN to the other, the data is encrypted using special security protocols.

The most important of the VPN security protocols is *Internet Protocol Security* (IPSec), which is a collection of standards for encrypting and authenticating packets that travel on the Internet. In other words, it provides a way to encrypt the contents of a data packet so that only a person who knows the secret encryption keys can decode the data. And it provides a way to reliably identify the source of a packet so that the parties at either end of the VPN tunnel can trust that the packets are authentic.

 Referring to the OSI reference model (see Book 1, Chapter 2), the IPSec protocol operates at Layer 3 of the OSI model (the Network layer). What that means is that the IPSec protocol has no idea what kind of data is being carried by the packets it encrypts and authenticates. The IPSec protocol concerns itself only with the details of encrypting the contents of the packets (sometimes called the *payload*) and ensuring the identity of the sender.

Another commonly used VPN protocol is Layer 2 Tunneling Protocol (L2TP). This protocol doesn't provide data encryption. Instead, it's designed to create end-to-end connections — *tunnels* — through which data can travel.

Book III
Chapter 5

Extending Your
Network with
VPN Access

L2TP is actually a combination of two older protocols: Layer 2 Forwarding Protocol (L2FP, from Cisco), and Point-to-Point Tunneling Protocol (PPTP, from Microsoft).

Many VPNs today use a combination of L2TP and IPSec: L2TP Over IPSec. This type of VPN combines the best features of L2TP and IPSec to provide a high degree of security and reliability.

Understanding VPN Servers and Clients

A VPN connection requires a VPN server — the gatekeeper at one end of the tunnel — and a VPN client at the other end. The main difference between the server and the client is that the client initiates the connection with the server, and a VPN client can establish a connection with just one server at a time. However, a server can accept connections from many clients.

Typically, the VPN server is a separate hardware device, most often a security appliance such as a Cisco ASA security appliance. VPN servers can also be implemented in software. For example, Windows Server 2008 includes built-in VPN capabilities even though they're not easy to configure. And a VPN server can be implemented in Linux as well.

Figure 5-1 shows one of the many VPN configuration screens for a Cisco ASA appliance. This screen provides the configuration details for an IPSec VPN connection. The most important item of information on this screen is the Pre-Shared Key, which is used to encrypt the data sent over the VPN. The client will need to provide the identical key in order to participate in the VPN.

A VPN client is usually software that runs on a client computer that wants to connect to the remote network. The VPN client software must be configured with the IP address of the VPN server as well as authentication information such as a username and the Pre-Shared Key that will be used to encrypt the data. If the key used by the client doesn't match the key used by the server, the VPN server will reject the connection request from the client.

Figure 5-2 shows a typical VPN software client. When the client is configured with the correct connection information (which you can do by clicking the New button), you just click Connect. After a few moments, the VPN client will announce that the connection has been established and the VPN is connected.

A VPN client can also be a hardware device, like another security appliance. This is most common when the VPN is used to connect two networks at separate locations. For example, suppose your company has an office in Pixley and a second office in Hooterville. Each office has its own network with servers and client computers. The easiest way to connect these offices with a VPN would be to put an identical security appliance at each location. Then, you could configure the security appliances to communicate with each other over a VPN.

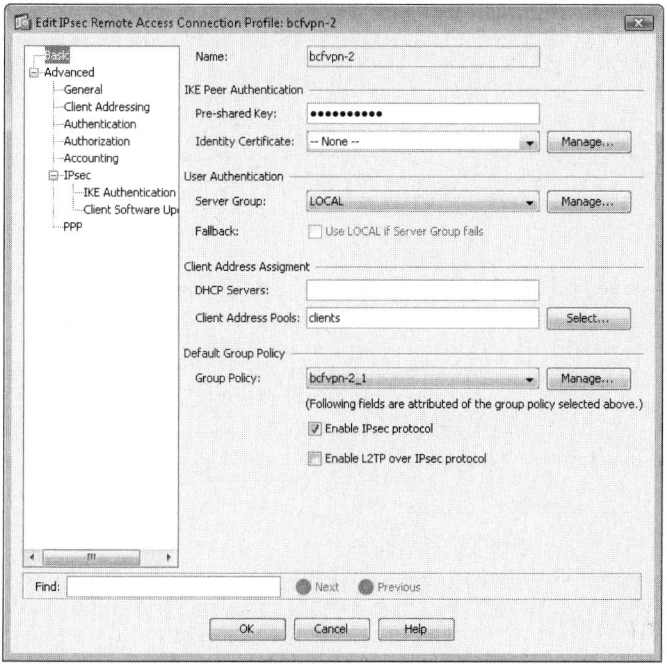

Figure 5-1:
An IPSec configuration page on a Cisco ASA security appliance.

Figure 5-2:
A VPN client.

Chapter 6: Managing Network Software

In This Chapter

✔ Understanding the types of software licenses

✔ Using license servers

✔ Exploring the deployment options

✔ Keeping up to date with patches and service packs

*A*n important task of any network administrator is managing the various bits and pieces of software that are used by your users throughout the network. Most, if not all, of your network users will have a version of Microsoft Office installed on their computers. Depending on the type of business, other software may be widely used. For example, accounting firms require accounting software; engineering firms require engineering software; and the list goes on.

Long gone are the days when you could purchase one copy of a computer program and freely install it on every computer on your network. Most software has built-in features — commonly called "copy protection" — designed to prevent such abuse. But even in the absence of copy protection, nearly all software is sold with a license agreement that dictates how many computers you can install and use the software on. As a result, managing software licenses is an important part of network management.

Some software programs have a license feature that uses a server computer to regulate the number of users who can run the software at the same time. As the network administrator, your job is to set up the license server and keep it running.

Another important aspect of managing software on the network is figuring out the most expedient way to install the software on multiple computers. The last thing you want to do is manually run the software's Setup program individually on each computer in your network. Instead, you'll want to use the network itself to aid in the deployment of the software.

Finally, you'll want to ensure that all the software programs installed throughout your network are kept up to date with the latest patches and updates from the software vendors.

This chapter elaborates on these aspects of network software management.

Understanding Software Licenses

Contrary to popular belief, you don't really buy software. Instead, you buy the right to use the software. When you purchase a computer program at a store, all you really own after you complete the purchase is the box the software comes in, the disks/discs the software is recorded on, and a license that grants you the right to use the software according to the terms offered by the software vendor. The software itself is still owned by the vendor.

That means that you're obligated to follow the terms of the license agreement that accompanies the software. Very few people actually read the complete text of a software agreement before they purchase and use software. If you do, you'll find that a typical agreement contains restrictions, such as the following:

+ **You're allowed to install the software on one and only one computer.** Some license agreements have specific exceptions to this, allowing you to install the software on a single computer at work and a single computer at home, or on a single desktop computer and a single notebook computer, provided that both computers are used by the same person. However, most software licenses stick to the one-computer rule.

+ **The license agreement probably allows you to make a backup copy of the disks/discs.** The number of backup copies you can make, though, is probably limited to one or two.

+ **You aren't allowed to reverse-engineer the software.** In other words, you can't use programming tools to dissect the software in an effort to learn the secrets of how it works.

+ **Some software restricts the kinds of applications it can be used for.** For example, you might purchase a student or home version of a program that prohibits commercial use. And some software — for example, Oracle's Java — prohibits its use for nuclear facilities.

+ **Some software has export restrictions that prevent you from taking it out of the country.**

+ **Nearly all software licenses limit the liability of the software vendor to replacing defective installation disks/discs.** In other words, the software vendor isn't responsible for any damage that might be caused by bugs in the software. In a few cases, these license restrictions have been set aside in court, and companies have been held liable for damage caused by defective software. For the most part, though, you use software at your own risk.

In many cases, software vendors give you a choice of several different types of licenses to choose from. When you purchase software for use on a network, you need to be aware of the differences between these license types so you can decide which type of license to get. The most common types are

✦ **Retail:** The software you buy directly from the software vendor, a local store, or an online store. A retail software license usually grants you the right for a single user to install and use the software. Depending on the agreement, the license may allow that user to install the software on two computers — one at work and one at home. The key point is that only one user may use the software. (However, it is usually acceptable to install the software on a computer that's shared by several users. In that case, more than one user can use the software, provided they use it one at a time.)

The main benefit of a retail license is that it stays with the user when the user upgrades his or her computer. In other words, if you get a new computer, you can remove the software from your old computer and install it on your new computer.

✦ **OEM:** For software that's installed by a computer manufacturer on a new computer. (OEM stands for *original equipment manufacturer.*) For example, if you purchase a computer from Dell and order Microsoft Office Professional along with the computer, you're getting an OEM license. The most important thing to know about an OEM license is that it applies only to the specific computer for which you purchased the software. You are never allowed to install the software on any computer other than the one for which you purchased the software.

Thus, if one day in a fit of rage you throw your computer out the fifth floor window of your office and the computer smashes into little pieces in the parking lot below, your OEM version of Office is essentially lost forever. When you buy a replacement computer, you'll have to buy a new OEM license of Office for the new computer. You can't install the old software on the new computer.

If this sounds like a severe limitation, it is. However, OEM licenses are usually substantially less expensive than retail licenses. For example, a retail license of Microsoft Office 2010 Professional sells for about $500. The OEM version is less than $400.

✦ **Volume:** Allows you to install and use the software on more than one computer. The simplest type of volume license simply specifies how many computers on which you can install the software. For example, you might purchase a 20-user version of a program that allows you to install the software on 20 computers. Usually, you're on the honor system to make sure that you don't exceed the quantity. You want to set up some type of system to keep track of this type of software license. For example, you could create an Excel spreadsheet in which you record the name of each person for whom you install the software.

Volume licenses can become considerably more complicated. For example, Microsoft offers several different types of volume license programs, each with different pricing and different features and benefits. Table 6-1 summarizes the features of the more popular license programs. For more information, refer to www.microsoft.com/licensing.

**Book III
Chapter 6**

**Managing Network
Software**

Table 6-1	Microsoft Volume License Plans
Plan	*Features*
Open License	Purchase as few as five end-user licenses.
Open Value	Purchase as few as five end-user licenses and receive free upgrades during the subscription term (three years).
Select License	This is a licensing program designed for companies with 250 or more employees.
Enterprise	This is an alternative to the Select License program that's designed to cost-effectively provide Windows Vista, Office, and certain other programs throughout an organization of at least 250 employees.

✦ **Subscription:** A *subscription* isn't really a separate type of license but rather an optional add-on to a volume license. The added subscription fee entitles you to technical support and free product upgrades during the term of the subscription, which is usually annual. For some types of products, the subscription also includes periodic downloads of new data. For example, antivirus software usually includes a subscription that regularly updates your virus signature data. Without the subscription, the antivirus software would quickly become ineffective.

Using a License Server

Some programs let you purchase network licenses that enable you to install the software on as many computers as you want, but regulate the number of people who can use the software at any given time. To control how many people use the software, a special license server is set up. Whenever a user starts the program, the program checks with the license server to see whether a license is available. If so, the program is allowed to start, and the number of available licenses on the license server is reduced by one. Later, when the user quits the program, the license is returned to the server.

One of the most commonly used license server software is FlexNet Publisher, by Flexera Software. (This program used to be named FlexLM, and many programs that depend on it still distribute it as FlexLM.) It's used by AutoCAD as well as by many other network software applications. FlexNet Publisher uses special license files issued by a software vendor to indicate how many licenses of a given product you purchased. Although the license file is a simple text file, its contents are cryptic and generated by a program that only the software vendor has access to. Here's an example of a typical license file for AutoCAD:

```
SERVER server1 000ecd0fe359
    USE_SERVER
    VENDOR adskflex port=2080
    INCREMENT 57000ARDES_2010_0F adskflex 1.000 permanent 6 \
        VENDOR_STRING=commercial:permanent BORROW=4320
SUPERSEDE \
        DUP_GROUP=UH ISSUED=07-May-2007 SN=339-71570316 SIGN="102D \
        85EC 1DFE D083 B85A 46BB AFB1 33AE 00BD 975C 8F5C 5ABC 4C2F \
        F88C 9120 0FB1 E122 BA97 BCAE CC90 899F 99BB 23C9 CAB5 613F \
        E7BB CA28 7DBF 8F51 3B21" SIGN2="033A 6451 5EEB 3CA4 98B8 F92C \
        184A D2BC BA97 BCAE CC90 899F 2EF6 0B45 A707 B897 11E3 096E 0288 \
        787C 997B 0E2E F88C 9120 0FB1 782C 00BD 975C 8F5C 74B9 8BC1"
```

(Don't get any wild ideas here. I changed the numbers in this license file so that it won't actually work. I'm not crazy enough to publish an actual valid AutoCAD license file!)

One drawback to opting for software that uses a license server is that you have to take special steps to run the software when the server isn't available. For example, what if you have AutoCAD installed on a notebook computer, but you want to use it while you're away from the office? In that case, you have two options:

✦ **Use virtual private network (VPN) software to connect to the network.** After you're connected with the VPN, the license server will be available so you can use the software. (Read about VPNs in the preceding chapter.)

✦ **Borrow a license.** When you borrow a license, you can use the software for a limited period of time while you're disconnected from the network. Of course, the borrowed license is subtracted from the number of available licenses on the server.

In most cases, the license server is a mission-critical application — as important as any other function on your network. If the license server goes down, all users who depend on it will be unable to work. Don't worry; they'll let you know. They'll be lining up outside your door demanding to know when you can get the license server up and running so they can get back to work.

Because the license server provides such an important function, treat it with special care. Make sure that the license server software runs on a stable, well-maintained server computer. Don't load up the license server computer with a bunch of other server functions.

And make sure that it's backed up. If possible, install the license server software on a second server computer as a backup. That way, if the main license server computer goes down and you can't get it back up and running, you can quickly switch over to the backup license server.

Options for Deploying Network Software

After you acquire the correct license for your software, the next task of the network administrator is to deploy the software: that is, installing the software on your users' computers and configuring the software so that it runs efficiently on your network. The following sections describe several approaches to deploying software to your network.

Deploying software manually

Most software is shipped on CD or DVD media along with a Setup program that you run to install the software. The Setup program usually asks you a series of questions, such as where you want the program installed, whether you want to install all of the program's features or just the most commonly used features, and so on. You may also be required to enter a serial number, registration number, license key, or other code that proves you purchased the software. When all these questions are answered, the Setup program then installs the program.

If only a few of your network users will be using a particular program, the Setup program may be the most convenient way to deploy the program. Just take the installation media with you to the computer you want to install the program on, insert the disc into the CD/DVD drive, and run the Setup program.

When you finish manually installing software from a CD or DVD, don't forget to remove the disc from the drive! It's easy to leave the disc in the drive, and if the user rarely or never uses the drive, it might be weeks or months before anyone discovers that the disc is missing. By that time, you'll be hard pressed to remember where it is.

Running Setup from a network share

If you plan on installing a program on more than two or three computers on your network, you'll find it much easier to run the Setup program from a network share rather than from the original CDs or DVDs. To do so, follow these steps:

1. **Create a network share and a folder within the share where you can store the Setup program and other files required to install the program.**

I usually set up a share named Software and then create a separate folder in this share for each program I want to make available from the network. You should enable Read access for all network users, but allow full access only for yourself and your fellow administrators. (Read more about setting permissions in Chapter 3 of this minibook.)

Read more about creating shares and setting permissions in Chapter 5 of Book VII.

2. **Copy the entire contents of the program's CD or DVD to the folder you create in Step 1.**

   To do so, insert the CD or DVD in your computer's CD/DVD drive. Then, use Windows Explorer to select the entire contents of the disc and drag it to the folder you create in Step 1.

   Alternatively, you can choose Start➪Run and enter **cmd** to open a command prompt. Then, enter a command, such as this:

   ```
   xcopy d:\*.* \\server1\software\someprogram\*.* /s
   ```

   In this example, `d:` is the drive letter of your CD/DVD drive, `server1` is the name of your file server, and `software` and `someprogram` are the names of the share and folder you created in Step 1.

3. **To install the program on a client computer, open a Windows Explorer window, navigate to the share and folder you create in Step 1, and double-click the `Setup.exe` file.**

   This launches the Setup program.

4. **Follow the instructions displayed by the Setup program.**

   When the Setup program is finished, the software is ready to use.

Copying the Setup program to a network share spares you the annoyance of carrying the installation discs to each computer you want to install the software on. It doesn't spare you the annoyance of purchasing a valid license for each computer, though! It's illegal to install the software on more computers than the license you acquired from the vendor allows.

Installing silently

Copying the contents of a program's installation media to a network share does spare you the annoyance of carrying the installation discs from computer to computer, but you still have to run the Setup program and answer all its annoying questions on every computer. Wouldn't it be great if there were a way to automate the Setup program so that after you run it, it runs without any further interaction from you? With many programs, you can.

In some cases, the Setup program itself has a command line switch that causes it to run silently. You can usually find out what command line switches are available by entering the following at a command prompt:

```
setup /?
```

With luck, you'll find that the Setup program itself has a switch, such as `/quiet` or `/silent`, that installs the program with no interaction, using the program's default settings.

If the Setup program doesn't offer any command line switches, don't despair. The following procedure describes a technique that often lets you silently install the software:

1. **Open an Explorer window and navigate to**

   - *Windows 8, Windows 7, and Vista:* `C:\Users\`*name*`\AppData\ Local\Temp`

   - *Windows XP:* `C:\Documents and Settings\`*name*`\Local Settings\Temp`

   Then, delete the entire contents of this folder.

   This is the Temporary folder where various programs deposit temporary files. Windows may not allow you to delete every file in this folder, but it's a good idea to begin this procedure by emptying the Temp folder as much as possible.

2. **Run the Setup program and follow the installation steps right up to the final step.**

   When you get to the confirmation screen that says the program is about ready to install the software, stop! *Do not* click the OK or Finish button.

3. **Return to the Temp folder you open in Step 1, and then poke around until you find the `.msi` file created by the Setup program you run in Step 2.**

   The `.msi` file is the actual Windows Installer program that Setup runs to install the program. It may have a cryptic name, such as `84993882.msi`.

4. **Copy the `.msi` file to the network share from which you want to install the program on your client computers.**

   For example, `\\`*server1*`\`*software*`\`*someprogram*.

5. **(Optional) Rename the `.msi` file to `setup.msi`.**

   This step is optional, but I prefer to run `setup.msi` rather than `84993882.msi`.

6. **Use Notepad to create a batch file to run the `.msi` file with the `/quiet` switch.**

   To create the batch file

   a. *Right-click in the folder where the `.msi` file is stored.*

   b. *Choose New➪Text Document.*

   c. *Change the name of the text document to `Setup.bat`.*

   d. *Right-click the `Setup.bat` file and choose Edit.*

   e. *Add the following line to the file:*

   ```
   setup.msi /quiet
   ```

7. **Save the file.**

    You can now install the software by navigating to the folder you created the `setup.bat` file in and double-clicking the `setup.bat` file.

Creating an administrative installation image

Some software, such as Microsoft Office and AutoCAD, comes with tools that let you create a fully configured silent setup program that you can then use to silently install the software. For Microsoft software, this silent setup program is called an "administrative installation image." (Note that the OEM versions of Microsoft Office don't include this feature. You need to purchase a volume license to create an administrative installation.)

To create an administrative image, you simply run the configuration tool supplied by the vendor. The configuration tool lets you choose the installation options you want to have applied when the software is installed. Then, it creates a network setup program on a network share that you specify. You can then install the software on a client computer by opening an Explorer window, navigating to the network share where you saved the network setup program, and running the network setup program.

Pushing out software with group policy

One final option you should consider for network software deployment is using Windows Group Policy to automatically install software to network users. Group Policy is a feature of recent versions of Windows Server (2003 and later) that lets you create policies that are assigned to users. You use the Windows Group Policy feature to specify that certain users should have certain software programs available to them.

Note that group policies aren't actually assigned to individual users, but to Organizational Units (OUs), which are used to categorize users in Active Directory. Thus, you might create a Group Policy to specify that everyone in the Accounting Department OU should have Microsoft Excel.

Then, whenever anyone in the Accounting department logs on to Windows, Windows checks to make sure that Excel is installed on the user's computer. If Excel is *not* installed, Windows advertises Excel on the computer. *Advertising* software on a computer means that a small portion of the software is downloaded to the computer — just enough to display an icon for the program on the Start menu and to associate Excel with the Excel file extensions (`.xls`, `.xlsx`).

If the user clicks the Start menu icon for the advertised application or attempts to open a document that's associated with the advertised application, the application is automatically installed on the user's computer. The user will have to wait a few minutes while the application is installed, but the installation is automatic.

Book III
Chapter 6

Managing Network Software

For more information about setting up group policy software installation, search Google or any other search engine for *Group Policy Software.*

Keeping Software Up to Date

One of the annoyances that every network manager faces is applying software patches to keep the operating system and other software up to date. A software *patch* is a minor update that fixes the small glitches that crop up from time to time, such as minor security or performance issues. These glitches aren't significant enough to merit a new version of the software, but they're important enough to require fixing. Most patches correct security flaws that computer hackers have uncovered in their relentless attempts to wreak havoc on the computer world.

Periodically, all the recently released patches are combined into a service pack. Although the most diligent network administrators apply all patches when they're released, many administrators just wait for the service packs.

Windows includes the Windows Update feature that automatically installs patches and service packs when they become available. These patches apply not just to Windows but to other Microsoft software as well. To use Windows Update, open the Control Panel, click System and Security, and then click Windows Update. A window appears, such as the one shown in Figure 6-1.

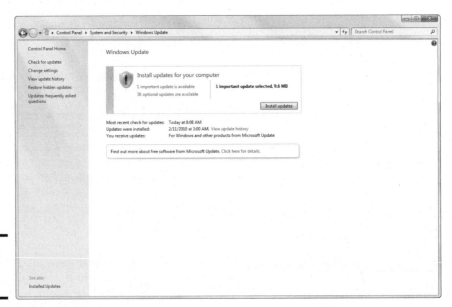

Figure 6-1:
Windows
Update.

From the Windows Update window, you can click the Install Updates button to download any updates that apply to your computer. You can also configure Windows Update so that it automatically checks for updates and installs them without asking. To set this option, click the Change Settings link. This displays the Windows Update Change Settings page, as shown in Figure 6-2.

The Important Updates drop-down list gives you several options for automatic operation:

✦ **Install Updates Automatically:** Checks for updates on a regular basis and installs them without asking. You can specify how often to check for updates and at what time.

✦ **Download Updates But Let Me Choose Whether to Install Them:** If you're a picky computer user, you should choose this option. It automatically downloads the updates but then gives you the option of whether or not to install them. This lets you opt out of updates you may not want.

✦ **Check for Updates But Let Me Choose Whether to Download and Install Them:** This option lets you determine which updates should be downloaded.

✦ **Never Check for Updates:** This option disables automatic updates altogether.

Book III
Chapter 6

Managing Network Software

Figure 6-2:
Changing the Windows Update settings.

Chapter 7: Solving Network Problems

In This Chapter

✓ Checking the obvious things

✓ Fixing computers that have expired

✓ Pinpointing the cause of trouble

✓ Restarting client and server computers

✓ Reviewing network event logs

✓ Keeping a record of network woes

*F*ace it: Networks are prone to breaking.

They have too many parts. Cables. Connectors. Cards. Switches. Routers. All these parts must be held together in a delicate balance, and the network equilibrium is all too easy to disturb. Even the best-designed computer networks sometimes act as if they're held together with baling wire, chewing gum, and duct tape.

To make matters worse, networks breed suspicion. After your computer is attached to a network, users begin to blame the network every time something goes wrong, regardless of whether the problem has anything to do with the network. You can't get columns to line up in a Word document? Must be the network. Your spreadsheet doesn't add up? The @@#$% network's acting up again. The stock market's down? Arghhh!!!!!!

The worst thing about network failures is that sometimes they can shut down an entire company. It's not so bad if just one user can't access a particular shared folder on a file server. If a critical server goes down, however, your network users may be locked out of their files, applications, e-mail, and everything else they need to conduct business as usual. When that happens, they'll be beating down your doors and won't stop until you get the network back up and running.

In this chapter, I review some of the most likely causes of network trouble and suggest some basic troubleshooting techniques that you can employ when your network goes on the fritz.

When Bad Things Happen to Good Computers

Here are some basic troubleshooting steps explaining what you should examine at the first sign of network trouble. In many (if not most) of the cases, one of the following steps can get your network back up and running:

1. **Make sure that your computer and everything attached to it is plugged in.**

   Computer geeks love it when a user calls for help, and they get to tell the user that the computer isn't plugged in or that its power strip is turned off. They write it down in their geek logs so that they can tell their geek friends about it later. They may even want to take your picture so that they can show it to their geek friends. (Most "accidents" involving computer geeks are a direct result of this kind of behavior. So try to be tactful when you ask a user whether he or she is sure the computer is actually turned on.)

2. **Make sure that your computer is properly connected to the network.**

3. **Note any error messages that appear on the screen.**

4. **Try restarting the computer.**

   An amazing number of computer problems are cleared up by a simple restart of the computer. Of course, in many cases, the problem recurs, so you'll have to eventually isolate the cause and fix the problem. Some problems are only intermittent, and a simple reboot is all that's needed.

5. **Try the built-in Windows network troubleshooter.**

   For more information, see the section, "Using the Windows Networking Troubleshooter," later in this chapter.

6. **Check the free disk space on your computer and on the server.**

   When a computer runs out of disk space or comes close to it, strange things can happen. Sometimes you get a clear error message indicating such a situation, but not always. Sometimes the computer just grinds to a halt; operations that used to take a few seconds now take a few minutes.

7. **Do a little experimenting to find out whether the problem is indeed a network problem or just a problem with the computer itself.**

   See the section, "Time to Experiment," later in this chapter, for some simple things that you can do to isolate a network problem.

8. **Try restarting the network server.**

   See the section, "Restarting a Network Server," later in this chapter.

Fixing Dead Computers

If a computer seems totally dead, here are some things to check:

✦ **Make sure that the computer is plugged in.**

✦ **If the computer is plugged into a surge protector or a power strip, make sure that the surge protector or power strip is plugged in and turned on.** If the surge protector or power strip has a light, it should be glowing. Also, the surge protector may have a reset button that needs to be pressed.

✦ **Make sure that the computer's On/Off switch is turned on.** This advice sounds too basic to even include here, but many computers have two power switches: an on/off switch on the back of the computer, and a push-button on the front that actually starts the computer. If you push the front button and nothing happens, check the switch on the back to make sure it's in the ON position.

To complicate matters, newer computers have a Sleep feature, in which they appear to be turned off but really they're just sleeping. All you have to do to wake such a computer is jiggle the mouse a little. (I used to have an uncle like that.) It's easy to assume that the computer is turned off, press the power button, wonder why nothing happened, and then press the power button and hold it down, hoping it will take. If you hold down the power button long enough, the computer will actually turn itself off. Then, when you turn the computer back on, you get a message saying the computer wasn't shut down properly. Arghhh! The moral of the story is to jiggle the mouse if the computer seems to have nodded off.

✦ **If you think the computer isn't plugged in but it looks like it is, listen for the fan.** If the fan is running, the computer is getting power, and the problem is more serious than an unplugged power cord. (If the fan isn't running but the computer is plugged in and the power is on, the fan may be out to lunch.)

✦ **If the computer is plugged in and turned on but still not running, plug a lamp into the outlet to make sure that power is getting to the outlet.** You may need to reset a tripped circuit breaker or replace a bad surge protector. Or you may need to call the power company. (If you live in California, don't bother calling the power company. It probably won't do any good.)

✦ **Check the surge protector.** Surge protectors have a limited life span. After a few years of use, many surge protectors continue to provide electrical power for your computer, but the components that protect your computer from power surges no longer work. If you're using a surge protector that is more than two or three years old, replace the old surge protector with a new one.

✦ **Make sure that the monitor is plugged in and turned on.** The monitor has a separate power cord and switch. (The monitor actually has two cables that must be plugged in. One runs from the back of the monitor to the back of the computer; the other is a power cord that comes from the back of the monitor and must be plugged into an electrical outlet.)

✦ **Make sure that all cables are plugged in securely.** Your keyboard, monitor, mouse, and printer are all connected to the back of your computer by cables.

Make sure that the other ends of the monitor and printer cables are plugged in properly, too.

✦ **If the computer is running but the display is dark, try adjusting the monitor's contrast and brightness.** Some monitors have knobs that you can use to adjust the contrast and brightness of the monitor's display. They may have been turned down all the way.

Ways to Check a Network Connection

The cables that connect client computers to the rest of the network are finicky beasts. They can break at a moment's notice, and by "break," I don't necessarily mean "to physically break in two." Although some broken cables look like someone got to the cable with pruning shears, most cable problems aren't visible to the naked eye.

✦ **Twisted-pair cable:** If your network uses twisted-pair cable, you can quickly tell whether the cable connection to the network is good by looking at the back of your computer. Look for a small light located near where the cable plugs in; if this light is glowing steadily, the cable is good. If the light is dark or it's flashing intermittently, you have a cable problem (or a problem with the network card or the hub or switch that the other end of the cable is plugged in to).

If the light isn't glowing steadily, try removing the cable from your computer and reinserting it. This action may cure the weak connection.

✦ **Patch cable:** Hopefully, your network is wired so that each computer is connected to the network with a short (six feet or so) patch cable. One end of the patch cable plugs into the computer, and the other end plugs into a cable connector mounted on the wall. Try quickly disconnecting and reconnecting the patch cable. If that doesn't do the trick, try to find a spare patch cable that you can use.

✦ **Switches:** Switches are prone to having cable problems, too — especially switches that are wired in a "professional manner," involving a rat's nest of patch cables. Be careful whenever you enter the lair of the rat's nest. If you need to replace a patch cable, be very careful when you disconnect the suspected bad cable and reconnect the good cable in its place.

A Bunch of Error Messages Just Flew By!

Error messages that display when your computer boots can provide invaluable clues to determine the source of the problem.

If you see error messages when you start up the computer, keep the following points in mind:

+ **Don't panic if you see a lot of error messages.** Sometimes, a simple problem that's easy to correct can cause a plethora of error messages when you start your computer. The messages may look as if your computer is falling to pieces, but the fix may be very simple.

+ **If the messages fly by so fast that you can't see them, press your computer's Pause key.** Your computer comes to a screeching halt, giving you a chance to catch up on your error-message reading. After you've read enough, press the Pause key again to get things moving. (On keyboards that don't have a Pause key, pressing Ctrl+Num Lock or Ctrl+S does the same thing.)

+ **If you miss the error messages the first time, restart the computer and watch them again.**

+ **Better yet, press F8 when you see the Starting Windows message.** This displays a menu that allows you to select from several startup options.

Double-Checking Your Network Settings

I swear that there are little green men who sneak into offices at night, turn on computers, and mess up TCP/IP configuration settings just for kicks. These little green men are affectionately known as *networchons*.

Remarkably, network configuration settings sometimes get inadvertently changed so that a computer, which enjoyed the network for months or even years, one day finds itself unable to access the network. So one of the first things you do, after making sure that the computers are actually on and that the cables aren't broken, is a basic review of the computer's network settings. Check the following:

+ **At a command prompt, run `ipconfig` to make sure that TCP/IP is up and running on the computer and that the IP addresses, subnet masks, and default gateway settings look right.**

+ **Call up the network connection's Properties dialog box and make sure that the necessary protocols are installed correctly.**

✦ **Open the System Properties dialog box (double-click System in Control Panel) and check the Computer Name tab.**

Make sure that the computer name is unique and also that the domain or workgroup name is spelled properly.

✦ **Double-check the user account to make sure that the user really has permission to access the resources he needs.**

For more information about network configuration settings, see Book II, Chapters 3 and 6.

Using the Windows Networking Troubleshooter

Windows comes with a built-in troubleshooter that can often help you to pin down the cause of a network problem. Figure 7-1 shows the Windows 8 version. Answer the questions asked by the troubleshooter and click Next to move from screen to screen. The Networking Troubleshooter can't solve all networking problems, but it does point out the causes of the most common problems.

Figure 7-1:
The
Windows 8
Networking
Trouble-
shooter.

The procedure for starting Networking Troubleshooter depends on which version of Windows you're using:

✦ **Windows 8 and Windows 7:** Open Control Panel, click View Network Status and Tasks, and then click Troubleshoot Problems. Then select the troubleshooter that seems most directly related to the problem you're experiencing. You'll find troubleshooters for wireless network problems, home networks, and local area network (LAN) and Internet connections.

✦ **Windows Vista:** Choose Start⟹Help and Support, click Troubleshooting, and then click the link for the network troubleshooter that seems most directly related to the problem you're experiencing. You'll find trouble-shooters for wireless network problems, home networks, and local area network (LAN) and Internet connections.

✦ **Windows XP:** Choose Start⟹Help and Support⟹Networking and the Web⟹Fixing Network or Web Problems. Then click Home and Small Office Networking Troubleshooter.

Time to Experiment

If you can't find some obvious explanation for your troubles — like the computer is unplugged — you need to do some experimenting to narrow down the possibilities. Design your experiments to answer one basic question: Is it a network problem or a local computer problem?

Here are some ways you can narrow down the cause of the problem:

✦ **Try performing the same operation on someone else's computer.** If no one on the network can access a network drive or printer, something is probably wrong with the network. On the other hand, if the error occurs on only one computer, the problem is likely with that computer. The wayward computer may not be reliably communicating with the network or configured properly for the network, or the problem may have nothing to do with the network at all.

✦ **If you're able to perform the operation on another computer without problems, try logging on to the network with another computer using your own username.** Then see whether you can perform the operation without error. If you can, the problem is probably on your computer. If you can't, the problem may be with the way your user account is configured.

✦ **If you can't log on at another computer, try waiting for a bit.** Your account may be temporarily locked out. This can happen for a variety of reasons — the most common of which is trying to log on with the wrong password several times in a row. If you're still locked out an hour later, call the network administrator and offer a doughnut.

**Book III
Chapter 7**

Solving Network
Problems

Who's on First?

When troubleshooting a networking problem, it's often useful to find out who is actually logged on to a network server. For example, if a user can't access a file on the server, you can check whether the user is logged on. If so, you know that the user's account is valid, but the user may not have permission to access the particular file or folder that he's attempting to access. On the other hand, if the user isn't logged on, the problem may lie with the account itself or how the user is attempting to connect to the server.

It's also useful to find out who's logged on in the event that you need to restart the server. For more information about restarting a server, see the section, "Restarting a Network Server," later in this chapter.

To find out who is currently logged on to a Windows server, right-click the Computer icon on the desktop and choose Manage from the menu that appears. This brings up the Computer Management window. Open System Tools in the tree list and then open Shared Folders and select Sessions. A list of users who are logged on appears.

You can immediately disconnect all users by right-clicking Sessions in the Computer Management window and choosing All Tasks➪Disconnect All. Be warned, however, that this can cause users to lose data.

Restarting a Client Computer

Sometimes, trouble gets a computer so tied up in knots that the only thing you can do is reboot. In some cases, the computer just starts acting weird. Strange characters appear on the screen, or Windows goes haywire and doesn't let you exit a program. Sometimes, the computer gets so confused that it can't even move. It just sits there, like a deer staring at oncoming headlights. It won't move, no matter how hard you press Esc or Enter. You can move the mouse all over your desktop, or you can even throw it across the room, but the mouse pointer on the screen stays perfectly still.

When a computer starts acting strange, you need to reboot. If you must reboot, you should do so as cleanly as possible. I know this procedure may seem elementary, but the technique for safely restarting a client computer is worth repeating, even if it is basic:

1. **Save your work if you can.**

Use the File➪Save command to save any documents or files that you were editing when things started to go haywire. If you can't use the menus, try clicking the Save button on the toolbar. If that doesn't work, try pressing Ctrl+S (the standard keyboard shortcut for the Save command).

2. **Close any running programs if you can.**

   Use the File⇨Exit command or click the Close button in the upper-right corner of the program window. Or press Alt+F4.

3. **Restart the computer.**

   - *Windows XP:* Choose Start⇨Turn Off Computer to summon the Shut Down Windows dialog box. Select the Restart option, and then click OK.

   - *Windows 7 and Vista:* Click the Start button, click the right arrow that appears at the bottom-right corner of the Start menu, and then click Restart.

   - *Windows 8:* Oddly enough, shutting down Windows 8 is a bit challenging. You can stare at the Windows 8 desktop all day and not find an intuitive way to shut down your computer. The secret lies in the Charms Bar, which you can find by hovering the mouse over the lower right corner of the screen. Next, click the Settings icon, and then click the Shut Down icon.

If restarting your computer doesn't seem to fix the problem, you may need to turn your computer off and then turn it on again. To do so, follow the previous procedure but choose Shut Down instead of Restart.

Here are a few things to try if you have trouble restarting your computer:

1. **If your computer refuses to respond to the Start⇨Shut Down command, try pressing Ctrl+Alt+Delete.**

   This is called the "three-finger salute." It's appropriate to say, "Queueue" while you do it.

   When you press Ctrl+Alt+Delete, Windows displays a dialog box that enables you to close any running programs or shut down your computer entirely.

2. **If pressing Ctrl+Alt+Delete doesn't do anything, you've reached the last resort. The only thing left to do is turn off the computer by pressing the power On/Off button and holding it down for a few seconds.**

   Turning off your computer by pressing the power button is a drastic action that you should take only after your computer becomes completely unresponsive. Any work you haven't yet saved to disk is lost. (Sniff.) (If your computer doesn't have a Reset button, turn off the computer, wait a few moments, and then turn the computer back on again.)

If at all possible, save your work before restarting your computer. Any work you haven't saved is lost. Unfortunately, if your computer is totally tied up in knots, you probably can't save your work. In that case, you have no choice but to push your computer off the digital cliff.

Booting in Safe Mode

Windows provides a special start-up mode called *Safe Mode* that's designed to help fix misbehaving computers. When you start your computer in Safe Mode, Windows loads only the most essential parts of itself into memory — the bare minimum required for Windows to work. Safe Mode is especially useful when your computer has developed a problem that prevents you from using the computer at all.

To boot your computer in Safe Mode, first restart the computer. Then, as soon as the computer begins to restart, start pressing the F8 key — just tap away at it until a menu titled Advanced Boot Options appears. One of the options on this menu is Safe Mode; use the up- or down-arrow keys to select that option and then press Enter to boot in Safe Mode.

Using System Restore

System Restore is a Windows feature that periodically saves important Windows configuration information and allows you to later return your system to a previously saved configuration. This can often fix problems by reverting your computer to a time when it was working.

By default, Windows saves restore points whenever you install new software on your computer or apply a system update. Restore points are also saved automatically every seven days.

Although System Restore is turned on by default, you should verify that System Restore is active and running to make sure that System Restore points are being created. To do that, right-click Computer in the Start menu, choose Properties, and then click the System Protection tab. The dialog box shown in Figure 7-2 is displayed. Verify that the Protection status for your computer's C: drive is On. If it isn't, select the C: drive and click the Configure button to configure System Restore for the drive.

If your computer develops a problem, you can restore it to a previously saved restore point by clicking System Restore on the System Protection tab. This brings up the System Restore Wizard, as shown in Figure 7-3. This wizard allows you to select the restore point you want to use.

Here are a few additional thoughts to remember about System Restore:

✦ System Restore *does not* delete data files from your system. Thus, files in your Documents folder won't be lost.

✦ System Restore *does* remove any applications or system updates you've installed since the time the restore point was made. Thus, you need to reinstall those applications or system updates — unless, of course, you determine that an application or system update was the cause of your problem in the first place.

✦ System Restore automatically restarts your computer. The restart may be slow because some of the changes made by System Restore happen after the restart.

✦ Do *not* turn off or cut power to your computer during System Restore. Doing so may leave your computer in an unrecoverable state.

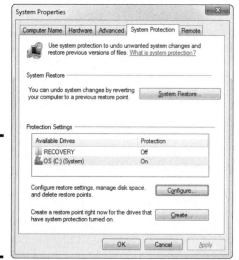

Figure 7-2:
The System Protection tab of the System Properties dialog box.

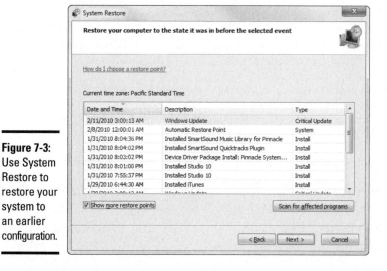

Figure 7-3:
Use System Restore to restore your system to an earlier configuration.

Restarting Network Services

Once in awhile, the OS service that supports the task that's causing you trouble inexplicably stops or gets stuck. If users can't access a server, it may be because one of the key network services has stopped or is stuck.

You can review the status of services by using the Services tool, as shown in Figure 7-4. To display it, right-click Computer on the Start menu and choose Manage; then, expand the Services and Applications node and click Services. Review this list to make sure that all key services are running. If an important service is paused or stopped, restart it.

Which services qualify as "important" depends on what roles you define for the server. Table 7-1 lists a few important services that are common to most Windows network operating systems (NOS). However, many servers require additional services besides these. In fact, a typical server will have many dozens of services running simultaneously.

Key services usually stop for a reason, so simply restarting a stopped service probably won't solve your network's problem — at least, not for long. You should review the System log to look for any error messages that may explain why the service stopped in the first place.

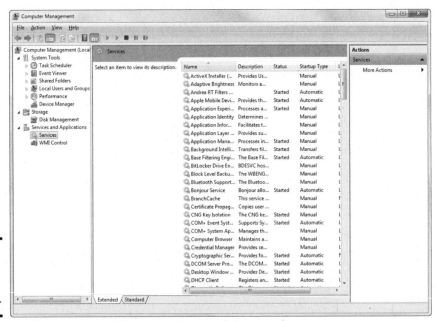

Figure 7-4:
Looking at
services
(Windows 8).

Table 7-1	**Key Windows Services**
Service	*Description*
Computer Browser	Maintains a list of computers on the network that can be accessed. If this service is disabled, the computer won't be able to use browsing services, such as My Network Places.
DHCP Client	Enables the computer to obtain its IP address from a Dynamic Host Configuration Protocol (DHCP) server. If this service is disabled, the computer's Internet Protocol (IP) address won't be configured properly.
DNS Client	Enables the computer to access a Domain Name Server (DNS) server to resolve DNS names. If this service is disabled, the computer won't be able to handle DNS names, including Internet addresses and Active Directory names.
Server	Provides basic file- and printer-sharing services for the server. If this service is stopped, clients won't be able to connect to the server to access files or printers.
Workstation	Enables the computer to establish client connections with other servers. If this service is disabled, the computer won't be able to connect to other servers.

Restarting a Network Server

Sometimes, the only way to flush out a network problem is to restart the network server that's experiencing trouble.

Restarting a network server is something you should do only as a last resort. Windows Server is designed to run for months or even years at a time without rebooting. Restarting a server invariably results in a temporary shutdown of the network. If you must restart a server, try to do it during off hours if possible.

Before you restart a server, check whether a specific service that's required has been paused or stopped. You may be able to just restart the individual service rather than the entire server. For more information, see the section, "Restarting Network Services," earlier in this chapter.

Here's the basic procedure for restarting a network server:

1. **Make sure that everyone is logged off the server.**

The easiest way to do that is to restart the server after normal business hours, when everyone has gone home for the day. Then, you can just shut down the server and let the shutdown process forcibly log off any remaining users.

To find out who's logged on, refer to the earlier section, "Who's on First?"

2. **After you're sure the users have logged off, shut down the network server.**

   You want to do this step behaving like a good citizen if possible — decently, and in order. Use the Start⇨Shut Down command to shut down the server. This summons a dialog box that requires you to indicate the reason for the shutdown. The information you supply here is entered into the server's System log, which you can review by using Event Viewer.

3. **Reboot the server computer or turn it off and then on again.**

   Watch the server start up to make sure that no error messages appear.

4. **Tell everyone to log back on and make sure that everyone can now access the network.**

Remember the following when you consider restarting the network server:

+ **Restarting the network server is more drastic than restarting a client computer.** Make sure that everyone saves his or her work and logs off the network before you do it! You can cause major problems if you blindly turn off the server computer while users are logged on.

+ **Obviously, restarting a network server is a major inconvenience to every network user.** Better offer treats.

Looking at Event Logs

One of the most useful troubleshooting techniques for diagnosing network problems is to review the network operating system's built-in event logs. These logs contain information about interesting and potentially troublesome events that occur during the daily operation of your network. Ordinarily, these logs run in the background, quietly gathering information about network events. When something goes wrong, you can check the logs to see whether the problem generated a noteworthy event. In many cases, the event logs contain an entry that pinpoints the exact cause of the problem and suggests a solution.

To display the event logs in a Windows server, use Event Viewer, which is available from the Administrative Tools menu. For example, Figure 7-5 shows an Event Viewer from a Windows Server 2012 system. The tree listing on the left side of Event Viewer lists five categories of events that are tracked: Application, Security, System, Directory Service, and File Replication Service. Select one of these options to see the log that you want to view. For details about a particular event, double-click the event to display a dialog box with detailed information about the event.

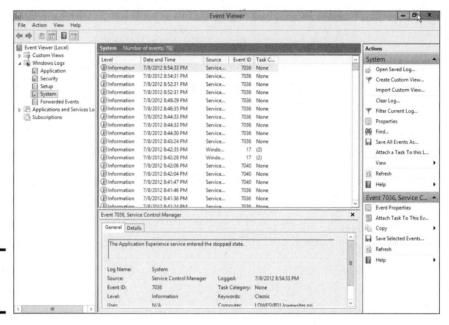

Figure 7-5:
Event
Viewer.

Documenting Your Trials and Tribulations

Book III
Chapter 7

Solving Network
Problems

For a large network, you probably want to invest in problem-management software that tracks each problem through the entire process of troubleshooting, from initial report to final resolution. For small- and medium-sized networks, it's probably sufficient to put together a three-ring binder with pre-printed forms. Or record your log in a Word document or an Excel spreadsheet.

Regardless of how you track your network problems, the tracking log should include the following information:

✦ **The real name and the network username of the person reporting the problem**

✦ **The date the problem was first reported**

✦ **An indication of the severity of the problem**

Is it merely an inconvenience, or is a user unable to complete his or her work because of the problem? Does a workaround exist?

✦ **The name of the person assigned to resolve the problem**

✦ **A description of the problem**

✦ **A list of the software involved, including versions**

✦ A description of the steps taken to solve the problem

✦ A description of any intermediate steps that were taken to try to solve the problem, along with an indication of whether those steps were "undone" when they didn't help solve the problem

✦ The date the problem was finally resolved

Chapter 8: Network Performance Anxiety

In This Chapter

✔ Understanding performance problems

✔ Looking at bottlenecks

✔ Developing a procedure for solving performance problems

✔ Monitoring performance

✔ Implementing other tips for speeding up your network

*N*etwork performance refers to how efficiently the network responds to users' needs. Any access to resources that involves a network will be slower than similar access that doesn't involve a network. For example, it takes longer to open a Word document that resides on a network file server than it takes to open a similar document that resides on a user's local hard drive. However, it shouldn't take *much* longer. If it does, you have a network performance problem.

This chapter is a general introduction to the practice of tuning your network so that it performs as well as possible. Keep in mind that many specific bits of network tuning advice are scattered throughout this book. In this chapter, you can find some specific techniques for analyzing your network's performance, taking corrective action when a performance problem develops, and charting your progress.

Why Administrators Hate Performance Problems

Network performance problems are among the most difficult network problems to track down and solve. If a user simply can't access the network, it usually doesn't take long to figure out why: A cable is broken, a network card or hub is malfunctioning, a user doesn't have permission to access the resource, and so on. After a little investigation, the problem usually reveals itself. You fix it and move on to the next problem.

Unfortunately, performance problems are messier. Here are just a few of the reasons that network administrators hate performance problems:

✦ **Performance problems are difficult to quantify.** Exactly how much slower is the network now than it was a week ago, a month ago, or even a year ago? Sometimes the network just feels slow, but you can't quite define exactly how slow it really is.

✦ **Performance problems usually develop gradually.** Sometimes, a network slows down suddenly and drastically. More often, though, the network gradually gets slower, a little bit at a time, until one day when the users notice that the network is slooow.

✦ **Performance problems often go unreported.** Users gripe about the problem to each other around the water cooler, but they don't formally contact you to let you know that their network seems 10 percent slower than usual. As long as they can still access the network, they just assume that the problem is temporary or just in their imaginations.

✦ **Many performance problems are intermittent.** Sometimes, a user calls you and complains that a certain network operation has become slower than molasses — and by the time you get to the user's desk, the operation performs like a snap. Sometimes, you can find a pattern to the intermittent behavior, such as it's slower in the morning than in the afternoon, or it's only slow while backups are running or while the printer is working. Other times, you can't find a pattern. Sometimes the operation is slow; sometimes it isn't.

✦ **Performance tuning is not an exact science.** Improving performance sometimes involves educated guesswork. Will upgrading all the users from 100 Mbps to Gigabit Ethernet improve performance? Probably. Will segmenting the network improve performance? Maybe. Will adding another 4GB of RAM to the server improve performance? Hopefully.

✦ **The solution to performance problems is sometimes a hard sell.** If a user can't access the network because of a malfunctioning component, there's usually not much question that the purchase of a replacement is justified. However, if the network is slow and you think you can fix it by upgrading the entire network to Gigabit Ethernet, you may have trouble selling management on the upgrade.

What Exactly Is a Bottleneck?

A *bottleneck* does not in any way refer to the physique of your typical computer geek. (Well, I guess it *could,* in some cases.) Rather, computer geeks coined the phrase when they discovered that the tapered shape of a bottle of Jolt Cola limited the rate at which they could consume the beverage. "Hey," a computer geek said one day, "the gently tapered narrowness of this bottle's neck imposes a distinct limiting effect upon the rate at which I can consume the tasty caffeine-laden beverage contained within. This draws to mind a hitherto undiscovered yet obvious analogy to the limiting effect that a single slow component of a computer system can have upon the performance of the system as a whole."

"Fascinating!" replied all the other computer geeks, who were fortunate enough to be present at that historic moment.

The term stuck and is used to this day to draw attention to the simple fact that a computer system is only as fast as its slowest component. It's the computer equivalent of the old truism that a chain is only as strong as its weakest link.

For a simple demonstration of this concept, consider what happens when you print a word processing document on a slow printer. Your word processing program reads the data from disk and sends it to the printer. Then you sit and wait while the printer prints the document.

Would buying a faster CPU or adding more memory make the document print faster? No. The CPU is already much faster than the printer, and your computer already has more than enough memory to print the document. The printer itself is the bottleneck, so the only way to print the document faster is to replace the slow printer with a faster one.

Here are some other random thoughts about bottlenecks:

✦ **A computer system always has a bottleneck.** For example, suppose that you decided that the bottleneck on your file server is a slow IDE hard drive, so you replace it with the fastest SCSI drive money can buy. Now, the hard drive is no longer the bottleneck: The drive can process information faster than the controller card to which the disk is connected. You haven't really eliminated the bottleneck: You just moved it from the hard drive to the disk controller. No matter what you do, the computer will always have some component that limits the overall performance of the system.

✦ **One way to limit the effect of a bottleneck is to avoid waiting for the bottleneck.** For example, print spooling lets you avoid waiting for a slow printer. Spooling doesn't speed up the printer, but it does free you to do other work while the printer chugs along. Similarly, disk caching lets you avoid waiting for a slow hard drive.

✦ **One of the reasons computer geeks are switching from Jolt Cola to Snapple is that Snapple bottles have wider necks.**

The Five Most Common Network Bottlenecks

Direct from the home office in sunny Fresno, California, here are the ten — oops, five — most common network bottlenecks, in no particular order.

The hardware inside your servers

Your servers should be powerful computers capable of handling all the work your network will throw at them. Don't cut corners by using a bottom-of-the-line computer that you bought at a discount computer store.

The following are the four most important components of your server hardware:

+ **Processor:** Your server should have a powerful processor. As a general rule, any processor that's available in a $500 computer from a store that sells TVs and washing machines as well as computers is not a processor that you want to see in your file server. In other words, avoid processors that are designed for consumer-grade home computers. For optimum performance, your servers should use server-class Itanium or Xeon processors.

+ **Memory:** You can't have too much memory. Memory is cheap, so don't skimp. Don't even think about running a server with less than 8GB of RAM.

+ **Disk:** Don't mess around with inexpensive SATA hard drives. To be respectable, you should have nothing but SCSI drives.

+ **Network interface:** A $9.95 network card might be fine for your home network, but don't use one in a file server that supports 50 users and then expect to be happy with the server's performance. Remember that the server computer uses the network a lot more than any of the clients, so equip your servers with good network cards.

The server's configuration options

All network operating systems (NOSes) have options that you can configure. Some of these options can make the difference between a pokey network and a zippy network. Unfortunately, no hard-and-fast rules exist for setting these options. Otherwise, you wouldn't have options.

The following are some of the more important tuning options available for most servers:

+ **Virtual memory options:** *Virtual memory* refers to disk paging files that the server uses when it doesn't have enough real memory to do its work. Few servers ever have enough real memory, so virtual memory is always an important server feature. You can specify the size and location of the virtual memory paging files. For best performance, you should provide at least 1.5 times the amount of real memory. For example, if you have 16GB of real memory, allocate at least 24GB of virtual memory. If necessary, you can increase this size later.

✦ **Network protocols:** Make sure that your network protocols are configured correctly; remove any protocols that aren't necessary.

✦ **Free disk space on the server:** Servers like to have plenty of breathing room on their disks. If the amount of free disk space on your server drops precipitously low, the server chokes up and slows to a crawl. Make sure that your server has plenty of space: A few dozen GBs of unused disk space provide a healthy buffer.

Servers that do too much

One common source of network performance problems is servers that are overloaded with too many duties. Just because modern network operating systems come equipped with dozens of different types of services doesn't mean that you should enable and use them all on a single server. If a single server is bogged down because of too much work, add a second server to relieve the first server of some of its chores. Remember the old saying: "Many hands make light work."

For example, if your network needs more disk space, consider adding a second file server rather than adding another drive to the server that already has four drives that are nearly full. Or better yet, purchase a file server appliance that is dedicated just to the task of serving files.

As a side benefit, your network will be easier to administer and more reliable if you place separate functions on separate servers. For example, if you have a single server that doubles as a file server and a mail server, you'll lose both services if you have to take down the server to perform an upgrade or repair a failed component. However, if you have separate file and mail server computers, only one of the services will be interrupted if you have to take down one of the servers.

The network infrastructure

A network *infrastructure* comprises the cables and any switches, hubs, routers, and other components that sit between your clients and your servers. The following network infrastructure items can slow down your network:

✦ **Switches:** Because switches are so inexpensive now, you can affordably solve a lot of performance problems by replacing outdated hubs with switches. Using switches instead of hubs reduces the overall load on your network. Also, make sure that your switches can handle the performance requirements of your network. For best performance, the switches should have gigabit ports. (Read about these ports in Book I.)

✦ **Segment sizes:** Keep the number of computers and other devices on each network segment to a reasonable number. About 20 devices is usually the right number. (Note that if you replace your old hubs with switches, you instantly cut the size of each segment because each port on a switch constitutes a separate segment.)

✦ **The network's speed:** If you have an older network, you'll probably discover that many — if not all — of your users are still working at 100 Mbps. Upgrading to gigabit speed will speed up the network dramatically.

✦ **The backbone speed:** If your network uses a backbone to connect segments, consider upgrading the backbone to 1 Gbps. (Read about backbones in Book I.)

The hardest part about improving the performance of a network is determining what the bottlenecks are. With sophisticated test equipment and years of experience, network gurus can make pretty good educated guesses. Without the equipment and experience, you can still make pretty good uneducated guesses.

Malfunctioning components

Sometimes a malfunctioning network card or other component slows down the network. For example, a switch may malfunction intermittently, occasionally letting packets through but dropping enough of them to slow down the network. After you identify the faulty component, replacing it will restore the network to its original speed.

Tuning Your Network the Compulsive Way

You have two ways to tune your network. The first is to think about it a bit, take a guess at what may improve performance, try it, and see whether the network seems to run faster. This approach is how most people go about tuning the network.

Then you have the compulsive way, which is suitable for people who organize their sock drawers by color and their food cupboards alphabetically by food groups. The compulsive approach to tuning a network goes something like this:

1. **Establish a method for objectively testing the performance of some aspect of the network.**

This method is *benchmarking,* and the result of your benchmark is a *baseline.*

2. **Change one variable of your network configuration and rerun the test.**

For example, suppose you think that increasing the size of the disk cache can improve performance. Change the cache size, restart the server, and run the benchmark test. Note whether the performance improves, stays the same, or becomes worse.

3. **Repeat Step 2 for each variable that you want to test.**

Here are some salient points to keep in mind if you decide to tune your network the compulsive way:

✦ **If possible, test each variable separately.** In other words, reverse the changes you made to other network variables before proceeding.

✦ **Write down the results of each test.** That way, you have an accurate record of the impact that each change made on your network's performance.

✦ **Be sure to change only one aspect of the network each time you run the benchmark.** If you make several changes, you won't know which one caused the change. One change may improve performance, but the other change may worsen performance so that the changes cancel each other out — kind of like offsetting penalties in a football game.

✦ **If possible, conduct the baseline test during normal working hours.** That way, the network is undergoing its normal workload.

✦ **To establish your baseline performance, run your benchmark test two or three times to make sure that the results are repeatable.**

Monitoring Network Performance

One way to monitor network performance is to use a stopwatch to see how long it actually takes to complete common network tasks, such as opening documents or printing reports. If you choose to monitor your network by using the stopwatch technique, you'll want to get a clipboard, baseball cap, and gray sweat suit to complete the ensemble.

A more high-tech approach to monitoring network performance is to use a monitor program that automatically gathers network statistics for you. After you set up the monitor, it plugs away, silently spying on your network and recording what it sees in performance logs. You can then review the performance logs to see how your network is doing.

For large networks, you can purchase sophisticated monitoring programs that run on their own dedicated servers. For small- and medium-sized networks, you can probably get by with the built-in monitoring facilities that come with the network operating system. For example, Figure 8-1 shows the Performance Monitor tool that comes with Windows Server 2012. Other operating systems come with similar tools.

Book III
Chapter 8

Network
Performance
Anxiety

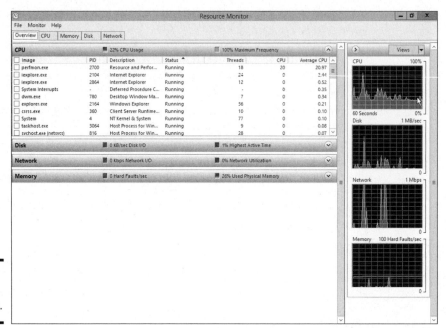

Figure 8-1:
Monitoring
performance.

Windows Performance Monitor lets you keep track of several different aspects of system performance at once. You track each performance aspect by setting up a counter. You can choose from dozens of different counters. Table 8-1 describes some of the most commonly used counters. Note that each counter refers to a server object, such as physical disk, memory, or processor.

Table 8-1		Commonly Used Performance Counters
Object	*Counter*	*Description*
Physical Disk	% Free Space	Percentage of free space on the server's physical disks. Should be at least 15%.
Physical Disk Length	Average Queue	Indicates how many disk operations are waiting while the disk is busy servicing other disk operations. Should be two or fewer.
Memory	Pages per second	Number of pages retrieved from the virtual memory page files per second (pps). A typical threshold is about 2,500 pps.
Processor	% Processor Time	Indicates the percentage of the processor's time that it's busy doing work rather than sitting idle. Should be 85% or less.

Here are a few more things to consider about performance monitoring:

✦ **Performance Monitor enables you to view real-time data or to view data that you can save in a log file.** Real-time data gives you an idea about what's happening with the network at a particular moment, but the more useful information comes from the logs.

✦ **You can schedule logging to occur at certain times of the day and for certain intervals.** For example, you may schedule the log to gather data every 15 seconds from 9:00 to 9:30 every morning and then again from 3:00 to 3:30 every afternoon.

✦ **Even if you don't have a performance problem now, you should set up performance logging and let it run for a few weeks to gather baseline data.** If you develop a problem, this baseline data will prove invaluable while you research the problem.

✦ **Don't leave performance logging turned on all the time.** Gathering performance data slows down your server. Use it only occasionally to gather baseline data or when you're experiencing a performance problem.

More Performance Tips

Here are a few last-minute performance tips that barely made it in:

✦ **You can often find the source of a slow network by staring at the network hubs or switches for a few minutes.** These devices have a colorful array of green and red lights. The green lights flash whenever data is transmitted; the red lights flash when a collision occurs. An occasional red flash is normal, but if one or more of the red lights is flashing repeatedly, the network interface card (NIC) connected to that port may be faulty.

✦ **Check for scheduled tasks, such as backups, batched database updates, or report jobs.** If at all possible, schedule these tasks to run after normal business hours, such as at night when no one is in the office. These jobs tend to slow down the network by hogging the server's hard drives.

✦ **Sometimes, faulty application programs can degrade performance.** For example, some programs develop a *memory leak:* They use memory but then forget to release the memory after they finish. Programs with memory leaks can slowly eat up all the memory on a server, until the server runs out and grinds to a halt. If you think a program has a memory leak, contact the manufacturer of the program to see whether a fix is available.

✦ **Spyware can slow a system to a crawl.** A common source of performance problems on client computers is *spyware,* those annoying programs that you almost can't help but pick up when you surf the Internet. Fortunately, you can remove spyware with a variety of free or inexpensive spyware removal tools. For more information, use Google or another search engine to search for spyware removal.

Chapter 9: Backing Up Your Data

In This Chapter

✔ **Understanding the need for backups**

✔ **Working with tape drives and other backup media**

✔ **Understanding the different types of backups**

✔ **Mastering tape rotation and other details**

*I*f you're the hapless network manager, the safety of the data on your network is your responsibility. In fact, it's your primary responsibility. You get paid to lie awake at night worrying about your data. Will it be there tomorrow? If it's not, can you get it back? And — most important — if you can't get it back, will you have a job tomorrow?

This chapter covers the ins and outs of being a good, responsible, trust-worthy network manager. No one gives out merit badges for this stuff, but someone should.

Backing Up Your Data

Having data backed up is the cornerstone of any disaster recovery plan. Without backups, a simple hard drive failure can set your company back days or even weeks while it tries to reconstruct lost data. In fact, without backups, your company's very existence is in jeopardy.

The main goal of a backup is simple: Keep a spare copy of your network's critical data so that no matter what happens, you never lose more than one day's work. The stock market may crash, hanging chads may factor into another presidential election, and George Lucas may decide to make a pre-prequel. When you stay on top of your backups, though, you'll never lose more than one day's work.

The way to do this, naturally, is to make sure that data is backed up on a daily basis. For many networks, you can back up all the network hard drives every night. And even if full nightly backups aren't possible, you can still use techniques that can ensure that every file on the network has a backup copy that's no more than one day old.

Where to Back Up Your Data

If you plan on backing up the data on your network server's hard drives, you obviously need some type of media on which to back up the data. You could copy the data onto CDs, but a 500GB hard drive would need more than 750 CDs for a full backup. That's a few more discs than most people want to keep in the closet. You could use DVDs, but you'll still need about a dozen of them, as well as an hour or so to fill each one. Sigh. That means devoting a Saturday to creating your backup.

Because of the limitations of CDs and DVDs, most network administrators back up network data to another type of storage device. The three most common options are described in this list:

✦ **Tape:** Magnetic tape is the oldest storage medium for backups and is still one of the most widely used. One big advantage of tape backups is that tape cartridges are small and can thus be easily transported to an offsite location.

✦ **Network Attached Storage (NAS):** A *Network Attached Storage* device connects directly to your network. NAS devices are often used as backup devices because they're inexpensive. In addition, because they're relatively small and easy to remove, like tape, they can be transported offsite.

✦ **Cloud backup:** An increasingly popular option is to use a third-party service to back up data to a remote location via the Internet. Cloud backup has the advantage of already being offsite.

Backing Up to Tape

One of the benefits of tape backup is that you can run it unattended. In fact, you can schedule a tape backup to run automatically during off hours when no one is using the network. For unattended backups to work, though, you must ensure that you have enough tape capacity to back up your entire network server's hard drive without having to manually switch tapes. If your network server has only 100GB of data, you can easily back it up onto a single tape. If you have 1,000GB of data, however, invest in a tape drive that features a magazine changer that can hold several tapes and automatically cycle them in and out of the drive. That way, you can run your backups unattended.

You can choose from several distinct types of tape backup systems:

✦ **Travan drives:** A popular style of tape backup for small servers is a Travan drive, which comes in a variety of models with tape capacities ranging from 20GB to 40GB. You can purchase a 20GB drive for less than $200.

✦ **DAT, DLT, and LTO units:** For larger networks, you can get tape backup units that offer higher capacity and faster backup speed than Travan drives — for more money, of course. Digital Audio Tape (DAT) units can back up as much as 80GB on a single tape, and DLT (Digital Linear Tape) drives can store up to 800GB on one tape. Linear Tape Open (LTO) drives can store 1.5TB on a single tape. DAT, DLT, and LTO drives can cost $1,000 or more, depending on the capacity.

✦ **Robotic units:** If you're really up the backup creek, with hundreds of gigabytes to back up, you can get robotic tape backup units that automatically fetch and load tape cartridges from a library. That way, you can do complete backups without having to load tapes manually. As you can likely guess, these units aren't inexpensive: Small ones, which have a library of about eight tapes and a total backup capacity of more than 5,000GB, start at about $4,000.

Backup Software

All versions of Windows come with a built-in backup program. In addition, most tape drives come with backup programs that are often faster or more flexible than the standard Windows backup.

You can also purchase sophisticated backup programs that are specially designed for networks that have multiple servers with data that must be backed up. For a basic Windows file server, you can use the backup program that comes with Windows Server. Server versions of Windows come with a decent backup program that can run scheduled, unattended tape backups.

Backup programs do more than just copy data from your hard drive to tape. Backup programs use special compression techniques to squeeze your data so that you can cram more data onto fewer tapes. Compression factors of 2:1 are common, so you can usually squeeze 100GB of data onto a tape that would hold only 50GB of data without compression. (Tape drive manufacturers tend to state the capacity of their drives by using compressed data, assuming a 2:1 compression ratio. Thus, a 200GB tape has an uncompressed capacity of 100GB.)

Whether you achieve a compression factor of 2:1 depends on the nature of the data you're backing up:

✦ **Documents:** If your network is used primarily for Microsoft Office applications and is filled with Word and Excel documents, you'll probably get better than 2:1 compression.

✦ **Graphics:** If your network data consists primarily of graphic image files, you probably won't get much compression. Most graphic image file formats are already compressed, so they can't be compressed much more by the backup software's compression methods.

Backup programs also help you keep track of which data has been backed up and which hasn't. They also offer options, such as incremental or differential backups that can streamline the backup process, as I describe in the next section.

If your network has more than one server, invest in good backup software. The most popular is Yosemite Backup, made by BarracudaWare (www. barracudaware.com). Besides being able to handle multiple servers, one of the main advantages of backup software (such as Yosemite Backup) is that it can properly back up Microsoft Exchange server data.

Types of Backups

You can perform five different types of backups. Many backup schemes rely on full daily backups, but for some networks, using a scheme that relies on two or more of these backup types is more practical.

The differences among the five types of backups involve a little technical detail known as the archive bit. The *archive bit* indicates whether a file has been modified since it was backed up. The archive bit is a little flag that's stored along with the filename, creation date, and other directory information. Any time a program modifies a file, the archive bit is set to the On position. That way, backup programs know that the file has been modified and needs to be backed up.

The differences among the various types of backups center on whether they use the archive bit to determine which files to back up, as well as whether they flip the archive bit to the Off position after they back up a file. Table 9-1 summarizes these differences, which I explain in the following sections.

Backup programs allow you to select any combination of drives and folders to back up. As a result, you can customize the file selection for a backup operation to suit your needs. For example, you can set up one backup plan that backs up all a server's shared folders and drives, plus its mail server stores, but then leaves out folders that rarely change, such as the operating system folders or installed program folders. You can then back up those folders on a less-regular basis. The drives and folders that you select for a backup operation are collectively called the *backup selection*.

The archive bit would have made a good Abbott and Costello routine. ("All right, I wanna know who modified the archive bit." "What." "Who?" "No, What." "Wait a minute . . . just tell me what's the name of the guy who modified the archive bit!" "Right.")

Table 9-1	How Backup Types Use the Archive Bit	
Backup Type	*Selects Files Based on Archive Bit?*	*Resets Archive Bits After Backing Up?*
Normal	No	Yes
Copy	No	No
Daily	No*	No
Incremental	Yes	Yes
Differential	Yes	No

*Selects files based on the Last Modified date.

Normal backups

A *normal backup* — also called a *full backup* — is the basic type of backup. In a normal backup, all files in the backup selection are backed up regardless of whether the archive bit has been set. In other words, the files are backed up even if they haven't been modified since the last time they were backed up. When each file is backed up, its archive bit is reset, so backups that select files based on the archive bit setting won't back up the files.

When a normal backup finishes, none of the files in the backup selection has its archive bit set. As a result, if you immediately follow a normal backup with an incremental backup or a differential backup, files won't be selected for backup by the incremental or differential backup because no file will have its archive bit set.

The easiest backup scheme is to simply schedule a normal backup every night. That way, all your data is backed up on a daily basis. Then, if the need arises, you can restore files from a single tape or set of tapes. Restoring files is more complicated when other types of backups are involved.

Do normal backups nightly if you have the tape capacity to do them unattended — that is, without having to swap tapes. If you can't do an unattended normal backup because the amount of data to be backed up is greater than the capacity of your tape drive(s), you have to use other types of backups in combination with normal backups.

If you can't get a normal backup on a single tape, and you can't afford a second tape drive or a tape changer, take a hard look at the data that's being included in the backup selection. I recently worked on a network that was difficult to back up onto a single tape. When I examined the data that was being backed up, I discovered a large amount of static data that was essentially an online archive of old projects. This data was necessary because network users needed it for research purposes, but the data was read-only. Even though the data never changed, it was being backed up to tape every night, and the backups required two tapes. After I removed this data from the cycle of nightly backups, the backups were able to squeeze onto a single tape again.

If you remove static data from the nightly backup, make sure that you have a secure backup of the static data on tape, CD-RW, or some other media.

Copy backups

A *copy backup* is similar to a normal backup except that the archive bit isn't reset when each file is copied. As a result, copy backups don't disrupt the cycle of normal and incremental or differential backups.

Copy backups usually aren't incorporated into regular, scheduled backups. Instead, you use a copy backup when you want to do an occasional one-shot backup. If you're about to perform an operating system upgrade, for example, you should back up the server before proceeding. If you do a full backup, the archive bits are reset, and your regular backups are disrupted. If you do a copy backup, however, the archive bits of any modified files remain unchanged. As a result, your regular normal and incremental or differential backups are unaffected.

If you don't incorporate incremental or differential backups into your backup routine, the difference between a copy backup and a normal backup is moot.

Daily backups

A *daily backup* backs up just those files that changed the same day when the backup was performed. A daily backup examines the modification date stored with each file's directory entry to determine whether a file should be backed up. Daily backups don't reset the archive bit.

I'm not a big fan of this option because of the small possibility that some files may slip through the cracks. Someone may be working late one night and modify a file after the evening's backups have completed — but before midnight — meaning that those files won't be included in the following night's backups. Incremental or differential backups, which rely on the archive bit rather than the modification date, are more reliable.

Incremental backups

An *incremental backup* backs up only those files that were modified since the last time you did a backup. Incremental backups are a lot faster than full backups because your network users probably modify only a small portion of the files on the server on any given day. As a result, if a full backup takes three tapes, you can probably fit an entire week's worth of incremental back-ups on a single tape.

When an incremental backup copies each file, it resets the file's archive bit. That way, the file will be backed up again before your next normal backup only when a user modifies the file again.

Here are some thoughts about using incremental backups:

✦ **The easiest way to use incremental backups is the following:**

- A *normal* backup every Monday

  If your full backup takes more than 12 hours, you may want to do it on Friday so that it can run over the weekend.

- An *incremental* backup on each remaining normal business day (for example, Tuesday, Wednesday, Thursday, and Friday)

✦ **When you use incremental backups, the complete backup consists of the full backup tapes and all the incremental backup tapes that you've made since you did the full backup.**

If the hard drive crashes, and you have to restore the data onto a new drive, you first restore Monday's normal backup and then restore each of the subsequent incremental backups.

✦ **Incremental backups complicate restoring individual files because the most recent copy of the file may be on the full backup tape or on any of the incremental backups.**

Backup programs keep track of the location of the most recent version of each file to simplify the process.

✦ **When you use incremental backups, you can choose whether you want to**

- Store each incremental backup on its own tape.

- Append each backup to the end of an existing tape.

Often, you can use a single tape for a week of incremental backups.

Differential backups

A *differential backup* is similar to an incremental backup except that it doesn't reset the archive bit when files are backed up. As a result, each differential backup represents the difference between the last normal backup and the current state of the hard drive.

To do a full restore from a differential backup, you first restore the last normal backup and then restore the most recent differential backup.

Suppose that you do a normal backup on Monday and differential backups on Tuesday, Wednesday, and Thursday, and your hard drive crashes Friday morning. On Friday afternoon, you install a new hard drive. To restore the data, you first restore the normal backup from Monday. Then you restore the differential backup from Thursday. The Tuesday and Wednesday differential backups aren't needed.

The main difference between incremental and differential backups is that

✦ *Incremental* backups result in smaller and faster backups.

✦ *Differential* backups are easier to restore.

If your users often ask you to restore individual files, consider using differential backups.

Local versus Network Backups

When you back up network data, you have two basic approaches to running the backup software:

✦ You can perform a *local backup,* in which the backup software runs on the file server itself and backs up data to a tape drive that's installed in the server.

✦ Or you can perform a *network backup,* in which you use one network computer to back up data from another network computer. In a network backup, the data has to travel over the network to get to the computer that's running the backup.

If you run the backups from the file server, you'll tie up the server while the backup is running, and users will complain that their server access has slowed to a snail's pace. On the other hand, if you run the backup over the network from a client computer or a dedicated backup server, you'll flood the network with gigabytes of data being backed up. Then your users will complain that the entire network has slowed to a snail's pace.

Network performance is one of the main reasons why you should try to run your backups during off hours, when other users aren't accessing the network. Another reason to run backups during off hours is so that you can perform a more thorough backup. If you run your backup while other users are accessing files, the backup program is likely to skip any files that are being accessed by users at the time the backup runs. As a result, your backup won't include those files. Ironically, the files most likely to get left out of the backup are often the files that need backing up the most, because they're the files that are being used and modified.

Here are some extra thoughts on client and server backups:

✦ **Backing up directly from the server isn't necessarily more efficient than backing up from a client because data doesn't have to travel over the network.** The network may well be faster than the tape drive. The network probably won't slow down backups unless you back up during the busiest time of the day, when hordes of network users are storming the network gates.

✦ **To improve network backup speed and to minimize the effect that network backups have on the rest of the network, consider using a 1,000 Mbps switch instead of a normal 100 Mbps switch to connect the servers and the backup client.** That way, network traffic between the server and the backup client won't bog down the rest of the network.

✦ **Any files that are open while the backups are running won't get backed up.** That's usually not a problem, because backups are run at off hours when people have gone home. If someone leaves his computer on with a Word document open, however, that Word document won't be backed up. One way to solve this problem is to set up the server so that it automatically logs everyone off the network before the backups begin.

✦ **Some backup programs have special features that enable them to back up open files.** The Windows Server 2003 and 2008 backup programs do this by creating a snapshot of the volume when it begins, thus making temporary copies of any files that are modified during the backup. The backup backs up the temporary copies rather than the versions being modified. When the backup finishes, the temporary copies are deleted.

Book III
Chapter 9

Backing Up
Your Data

How Many Sets of Backups Should You Keep?

Don't try to cut costs by purchasing one backup tape and reusing it every day. What happens if you accidentally delete an important file on Tuesday and don't discover your mistake until Thursday? Because the file didn't exist on Wednesday, it won't be on Wednesday's backup tape. If you have only one tape that's reused every day, you're outta luck.

The safest scheme is to use a new backup tape every day and keep all your old tapes in a vault. Pretty soon, though, your tape vault can start looking like the warehouse where they stored the Ark of the Covenant at the end of *Raiders of the Lost Ark*.

As a compromise between these two extremes, most users purchase several tapes and rotate them. That way, you always have several backup tapes to fall back on, just in case the file you need isn't on the most recent backup tape. This technique is *tape rotation,* and several variations are commonly used:

+ **The simplest approach is to purchase three tapes and label them A, B, and C.** You use the tapes on a daily basis in sequence: A the first day, B the second day, and C the third day; then A the fourth day, B the fifth day, C the sixth day, and so on. On any given day, you have three generations of backups: today's, yesterday's, and the day-before-yesterday's. Computer geeks like to call these the *grandfather, father,* and *son* tapes.

+ **Purchase five tapes and use one each day of the workweek.** This is another simple approach.

+ **A variation of the A, B, and C approach is to buy eight tapes.** Take four of them, and write *Tuesday* on one label, *Wednesday* on the second, *Thursday* on the third, and *Friday* on the fourth label. On the other four tapes, write *Monday 1, Monday 2, Monday 3,* and *Monday 4.* Now tack up a calendar on the wall near the computer, and number all the Mondays in the year: 1, 2, 3, 4, 1, 2, 3, 4, and so on.

On Tuesday through Friday, you use the appropriate daily backup tape. When you run a full backup on Monday, consult the calendar to decide which Monday tape to use. With this scheme, you always have four weeks' worth of Monday backup tapes, plus individual backup tapes for the rest of the week.

+ **If bookkeeping data lives on the network, make a backup copy of all your files (or at least all your accounting files) immediately before closing the books each month; then retain those backups for each month of the year.** This doesn't necessarily mean that you should purchase 12 additional tapes. If you back up just your accounting files, you can probably fit all 12 months on a single tape. Just make sure that you back up with the "append to tape" option rather than the "erase tape" option so that the previous contents of the tape aren't destroyed. Also, treat this accounting backup as completely separate from your normal daily backup routine.

Keep at least one recent full backup at another location. That way, if your office should fall victim to an errant Scud missile or a rogue asteroid, you can re-create your data from the backup copy that you stored offsite. Make sure that the person entrusted with the task of taking the backups to this offsite location is trustworthy.

A Word about Tape Reliability

From experience, I've found that although tape drives are very reliable, they do run amok once in a while. The problem is that they don't always tell you when they're not working. A tape drive (especially one of the less-expensive Travan drives; refer to "All about Tapes and Tape Drives," earlier in this chapter) can spin along for hours, pretending to back up your data — but in reality, your data isn't being written reliably to the tape. In other words, a tape drive can trick you into thinking that your backups are working just fine. Then, when disaster strikes and you need your backup tapes, you may just discover that the tapes are worthless.

Don't panic! Here's a simple way to assure yourself that your tape drive is working. Just activate the "compare after backup" feature of your backup software. As soon as your backup program finishes backing up your data, it rewinds the tape, reads each backed-up file, and compares it with the original version on the hard drive. If all files compare, you know that your backups are trustworthy.

Here are some additional thoughts about the reliability of tapes:

✦ The compare-after-backup feature doubles the time required to do a backup, but that doesn't matter if your entire backup fits on one tape. You can just run the backup after hours. Whether the backup and repair operation takes one hour or ten doesn't matter, as long as it's finished by the time the network users arrive at work the next morning.

✦ If your backups require more than one tape, you may not want to run the compare-after-backup feature every day. Be sure to run it periodically, however, to check that your tape drive is working.

✦ If your backup program reports errors, throw away the tape, and use a new tape.

✦ Actually, you should ignore that last comment about waiting for your backup program to report errors. You should discard tapes *before* your backup program reports errors. Most experts recommend that you should use a tape only about 20 times before discarding it. If you use the same tape every day, replace it monthly. If you have tapes for each day of the week, replace them twice yearly. If you have more tapes than that, figure out a cycle that replaces tapes after about 20 uses.

**Book III
Chapter 9**

**Backing Up
Your Data**

About Cleaning the Heads

An important aspect of backup reliability is proper maintenance of your tape drives. Every time you back up to tape, little bits and specks of the tape rub off onto the read and write heads inside the tape drive. Eventually, the heads become too dirty to read or write data reliably.

To counteract this problem, clean the tape heads regularly. The easiest way to clean them is to use a cleaning cartridge for the tape drive. The drive automatically recognizes when you insert a cleaning cartridge and then performs a routine that wipes the cleaning tape back and forth over the heads to clean them. When the cleaning routine is done, the tape is ejected. The whole process takes only about 30 seconds.

Because the maintenance requirements of drives differ, check each drive's user's manual to find out how and how often to clean the drive. As a general rule, clean drives once weekly.

The most annoying aspect of tape drive cleaning is that the cleaning cartridges have a limited life span, and unfortunately, if you insert a used-up cleaning cartridge, the drive accepts it and pretends to clean the drive. For this reason, keep track of how many times you use a cleaning cartridge and replace it as recommended by the manufacturer.

Backup Security

Backups create an often-overlooked security exposure for your network: No matter how carefully you set up user accounts and enforce password policies, if any user (including a guest) can perform a backup of the system, that user may make an unauthorized backup. In addition, your backup tapes themselves are vulnerable to theft. As a result, make sure that your backup policies and procedures are secure by taking the following measures:

+ **Set up a user account for the user who does backups.** Because this user account has backup permission for the entire server, guard its password carefully. Anyone who knows the username and password of the backup account can log on and bypass any security restrictions that you place on that user's normal user ID.

+ **Counter potential security problems by restricting the backup user ID to a certain client and a certain time of the day.** If you're really clever (and paranoid), you can probably set up the backup user's account so that the only program it can run is the backup program.

+ **Use encryption to protect the contents of your backup tapes.**

+ **Secure the backup tapes in a safe location, such as . . . um, a safe.**

Chapter 10: Disaster Recovery and Business Continuity Planning

In This Chapter

✔ Realizing the need for backups

✔ Making a plan

✔ Practicing disaster recovery

✔ Remembering tape rotation and other details

*O*n April Fools' Day about 20 years ago, my colleagues and I discovered that some loser had broken into the office the night before and pounded our computer equipment to death with a crowbar. (I'm not making this up.)

Sitting on a shelf right next to the mangled piles of what used to be a Wang minicomputer system was an undisturbed disk pack that contained the only complete backup of all the information that was on the destroyed computer. The vandal didn't realize that one more swing of the crowbar would have escalated this major inconvenience into a complete catastrophe. Sure, we were up a creek until we could get the computer replaced. And in those days, you couldn't just walk into your local Computer Depot and buy a new computer off the shelf — this was a Wang minicomputer system that had to be specially ordered. After we had the new computer, though, a simple restore from the backup disk brought us right back to where we were on March 31. Without that backup, getting back on track would have taken months.

I've been paranoid about disaster planning ever since. Before then, I thought that disaster planning meant doing good backups. That's a part of it, but I can never forget the day we came within one swing of the crowbar of losing everything. Vandals are probably much smarter now: They know to smash the backup disks as well as the computers themselves. Being prepared for disasters entails much more than just doing regular backups.

Nowadays, the trendy term for disaster planning is a business continuity plan (BCP). I suppose the term "disaster planning" sounded too negative, like we were planning for disasters to happen. The new term refocuses attention on the more positive aspect of preparing a plan that will enable a business to carry on with as little interruption as possible in the event of a disaster.

For more in-depth information about this topic, please refer to *IT Disaster Recovery Planning For Dummies* by Peter Gregory.

Assessing Different Types of Disasters

Disasters come in many shapes and sizes. Some types of disasters are more likely than others. For example, your building is more likely to be struck by lightning than to be hit by a comet. In some cases, the likelihood of a particular type of disaster depends on where you're located. For example, crippling snowstorms are more likely in New York than in Florida.

In addition, the impact of each type of disaster varies from company to company. What may be a disaster for one company may only be a mere inconvenience for another. For example, a law firm may tolerate a disruption in telephone service for a day or two. Loss of communication via phone would be a major inconvenience but not a disaster. To a telemarketing firm, however, a day or two with the phones down is a more severe problem because the company's revenue depends on the phones.

One of the first steps in developing a business continuity plan is to assess the risk of the various types of disasters that may affect your organization. Weigh the likelihood of a disaster happening with the severity of the impact that the disaster would have. For example, a meteor crashing into your building would probably be pretty severe, but the odds of that happening are miniscule. On the other hand, the odds of your building being destroyed by fire are much higher, and the consequences of a devastating fire would be about the same as those from a meteor impact.

The following sections describe the most common types of risks that most companies face. Notice throughout this discussion that although many of these risks are related to computers and network technology, some are not. The scope of business continuity planning is much larger than just computer technology.

Environmental disasters

Environmental disasters are what most people think of first when they think of disaster recovery. Some types of environmental disasters are regional. Others can happen pretty much anywhere.

+ **Fire:** Fire is probably the first disaster that most people think of when they consider disaster planning. Fires can be caused by unsafe conditions; carelessness, such as electrical wiring that isn't up to code; natural causes, such as lightning strikes; or arson.

+ **Earthquakes:** Not only can earthquakes cause structural damage to your building, but they can also disrupt the delivery of key services and utilities, such as water and power. Serious earthquakes are rare and unpredictable, but some areas experience them with more regularity than others. If your business is located in an area known for earthquakes, your BCP should consider how your company would deal with a devastating earthquake.

+ **Weather:** Weather disasters can cause major disruption to your business. Moderate weather may close transportation systems so that your employees can't get to work. Severe weather may damage your building or interrupt delivery of services, such as electricity and water.

+ **Water:** Flooding can wreak havoc with electrical equipment, such as computers. If floodwaters get into your computer room, chances are good that the computer equipment will be totally destroyed. Flooding can be caused not only by bad weather but also by burst pipes or malfunctioning sprinklers.

+ **Lightning:** Lightning storms can cause electrical damage to your computer and other electronic equipment from lightning strikes as well as surges in the local power supply.

Deliberate disasters

Some disasters are the result of deliberate actions by others. For example:

+ **Intentional damage:** Vandalism or arson may damage or destroy your facilities or your computer systems. The vandalism or arson may be targeted at you specifically, by a disgruntled employee or customer, or it may be random. Either way, the effect is the same.

  Don't neglect the possibility of sabotage. A disgruntled employee who gets hold of an administrator's account and password can do all sorts of nasty things to your network.

+ **Theft:** Theft is always a possibility. You may come to work someday to find that your servers or other computer equipment have been stolen.

+ **Terrorism:** Terrorism used to be something that most Americans weren't concerned about, but September 11, 2001, changed all that. No matter where you live in the world, the possibility of a terrorist attack is real.

Disruption of services

You may not realize just how much your business depends on the delivery of services and utilities. A BCP should take into consideration how you will deal with the loss of certain services:

✦ **No juice:** Electrical power is crucial for computers and other types of equipment. During a power failure once (I live in California, so I'm used to it), I discovered that I can't even work with pencil and paper because all my pencil sharpeners are electric. Electrical outages are not uncommon, but the technology to deal with them is readily available. Uninterruptible power supply (UPS) equipment is reliable and inexpensive.

✦ **No communications:** Communication connections can be disrupted by many causes. A few years ago, a railroad overpass was constructed across the street from my office. One day, a backhoe cut through the phone lines, completely cutting off our phone service — including our Internet connection — for a day and a half.

✦ **No water:** An interruption in the water supply may not shut down your computers, but it can disrupt your business by forcing you to close your facility until the water supply is reestablished.

Equipment failure

Modern companies depend on many different types of equipment for their daily operations. The failure of any of these key systems can disrupt business until the systems are repaired:

✦ **Computer equipment failure can obviously affect business operations.**

✦ **Air-conditioning systems are crucial to regulate temperatures, especially in computer rooms.** Computer equipment can be damaged if the temperature climbs too high.

✦ **Elevators, automatic doors, and other equipment may also be necessary for your business.**

Other disasters

You should assess many other potential disasters. Here are just a few:

✦ Labor disputes

✦ Loss of key staff because of resignation, injury, sickness, or death

✦ Workplace violence

✦ Public health issues, such as epidemics, mold infestations, and so on

✦ Loss of a key supplier

✦ Nearby disaster, such as a fire or police action across the street that results in your business being temporarily blocked off

Analyzing the Impact of a Disaster

With a good understanding of the types of disasters that can affect your business, you can turn your attention to the impact that these disasters can have on your business. The first step is to identify the key business processes that can be impacted by different types of disasters. These business processes are different for each company. For example, here are a few of the key business processes for a publishing company:

+ **Editorial,** such as managing projects through the process of technical editing, copyediting, and production

+ **Acquisition,** such as determining product development strategies, recruiting authors, and signing projects

+ **Human resource,** such as payroll, hiring, employee review, and recruiting

+ **Marketing,** including sales tracking, developing marketing materials, sponsoring sales conferences, and exhibiting at trade events

+ **Sales and billing,** such as filling customer orders, maintaining the company website, managing inventory, and handling payments

+ **Executive and financial,** such as managing cash flow, securing credit, raising capital, deciding when to go public, and deciding when to buy a smaller publisher or sell out to a bigger publisher

The impact of a disruption to each of these processes will vary. One common way to assess the impact of business process loss is to rate the impact of various degrees of loss for each process. For example, you may rate the loss of each process for the following time frames:

+ 0 to 2 hours

+ 2 to 24 hours

+ 1 to 2 days

+ 2 days to 1 week

+ More than 1 week

For some business processes, an interruption of two hours or even one day may be minor. For other processes, even the loss of a few hours may be very costly.

Developing a Business Continuity Plan

A BCP is simply a plan for how you will continue operation of your key business processes should the normal operation of the process fail. For example, if your primary office location is shut down for a week because of a major fire across the street, you won't have to suspend operations if you have a business continuity plan in place.

The key to a BCP is redundancy of each component that is essential to your business processes. These components include:

✦ **Facilities:** If your company already has multiple office locations, you may be able to temporarily squeeze into one of the other locations for the duration of the disaster. If not, you should secure arrangements in advance with a real estate broker so that you can quickly arrange an alternate location. By having an arrangement made in advance, you can move into an emergency location on a moment's notice.

✦ **Computer equipment:** It doesn't hurt to have a set of spare computers in storage somewhere so that you can dig them out to use in an emergency. Preferably, these computers would already have your critical software installed. The next best thing would be to have detailed plans available so that your IT staff can quickly install key software on new equipment to get your business up and running.

Always keep a current set of backup tapes at an alternate location.

✦ **Phones:** Discuss emergency phone services in advance with your phone company. If you're forced to move to another location on 24-hour notice, how quickly can you get your phones up and running? And can you arrange to have your incoming toll-free calls forwarded to the new location?

✦ **Staff:** Unless you work for a government agency, you probably don't have redundant employees. However, you can make arrangements in advance with a temp agency to provide clerical and administrative help on short notice.

✦ **Stationery:** This sounds like a small detail, but you should store a supply of all your key stationery products (letterhead, envelopes, invoices, statements, and so on) in a safe location. That way, if your main location is suddenly unavailable, you don't have to wait a week to get new letterhead or invoices printed.

✦ **Hard copy files:** Keep a backup copy of important printed material (customer billing files, sales records, and so on) at an alternate location.

Holding a Fire Drill

Remember in grade school when the fire alarm would go off and your teacher would tell you and the other kids to calmly put down your work and walk out to the designated safe zone in an orderly fashion? Drills are important so that if a real fire occurs, you don't run and scream and climb all over each other in order to be the first one to get out.

Any disaster recovery plan is incomplete unless you test it to see whether it works. Testing doesn't mean that you should burn your building down one day to see how long it takes you to get back up and running. You should, though, periodically simulate a disaster in order to prove to yourself and your staff that you can recover.

The most basic type of disaster recovery drill is a simple test of your network backup procedures. You should periodically attempt to restore key files from your backup tapes just to make sure that you can. You achieve several benefits by restoring files on a regular basis:

✦ **Tapes are unreliable.** The only way to be sure that your tapes are working is to periodically restore files from them.

✦ **Backup programs are confusing to configure.** I've seen people run backup jobs for years that don't include all the data they think they're backing up. Only when disaster strikes and they need to recover a key file do they discover that the file isn't included in the backup.

✦ **Restoring files can be a little confusing, especially when you use a combination of normal and incremental or differential backups.** Add to that the pressure of having the head of the company watching over your shoulder while you try to recover a lost file. If you regularly conduct file restore drills, you'll familiarize yourself with the restore features of your backup software in a low-pressure situation. Then, you can easily restore files for real when the pressure's on.

You can also conduct walkthroughs of more serious disaster scenarios. For example, you can set aside a day to walk through moving your entire staff to an alternate location. You can double-check that all the backup equipment, documents, and data are available as planned. If something is missing, it's better to find out now rather than while the fire department is still putting water on the last remaining hot spots in what used to be your office.

**Book III
Chapter 10**

**Disaster Recovery
and Business
Continuity Planning**

Book IV

TCP/IP and the Internet

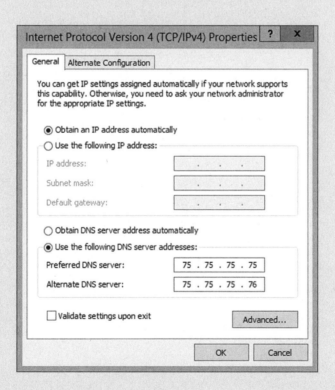

Contents at a Glance

Chapter 1: Introduction to TCP/IP and the Internet

In This Chapter

✓ Introducing the Internet

✓ Familiarizing yourself with TCP/IP standards

✓ Figuring out how TCP/IP lines up with the OSI reference model

✓ Discovering important TCP/IP applications

Many years ago, Transmission Control Protocol/Internet Protocol (TCP/IP) was known primarily as the protocol of the Internet. The biggest challenge of getting a local area network (LAN) connected to the Internet was figuring out how to mesh TCP/IP with the proprietary protocols that were the basis of the LANs — most notably Internetwork Packet Exchange/Sequenced Packet Exchange (IPX/SPX) and NetBIOS Extended User Interface (NetBEUI).

But then, some years ago, network administrators realized that they could save the trouble of combining TCP/IP with IPX/SPX and NetBEUI by eliminating IPX/SPX and NetBEUI from the equation altogether. As a result, TCP/IP is not just the protocol of the Internet now, but it's also the protocol on which most LANs are based.

This chapter is a gentle introduction to the Internet in general and the TCP/IP suite of protocols in particular. After I get the introductions out of the way, you'll be able to focus more in-depth on the detailed TCP/IP information given in the remaining chapters of Book IV.

What Is the Internet?

The Goliath of all computer networks, the Internet links hundreds of millions of computer users throughout the world. Strictly speaking, the Internet is a network of networks. It consists of hundreds of thousands of separate computer networks, all interlinked, so that a user on any of those networks can reach out and potentially touch a user on any of the other networks. This network of networks connects more than half a billion computers to each other. (That's right, *billion* with a *b*.)

TECHNICAL STUFF

Just how big is the Internet?

Because the Internet is not owned or controlled by any one organization, no one knows how big the Internet really is. Several organizations do attempt to periodically determine the size of the Internet, including the Internet Systems Consortium (ISC), which completed its last survey January, 2012 and found more than 888 million host computers are connected to the Internet. The same survey showed a mere 433 million hosts as of January, 2007, so the size of the Internet more than doubled in five years. The first year the ISC did the survey (1993), it found only 1.3 million host computers.

Unfortunately, no one knows how many actual users are on the Internet. Each host can support a single user — or in the case of domains, hundreds of thousands or perhaps even millions of users. No one really knows. Still, the indisputable point is that the Internet is big and growing every day.

If you're already on the 'Net and are interested, you can check the latest Internet statistics from ISC by visiting its website at www.isc.org.

One of the official documents (RFC 2026) of the Internet Engineering Task Force (IETF) defines the Internet as "a loosely organized international collaboration of autonomous, interconnected networks." Broken down piece by piece, this definition encompasses several key aspects of what the Internet is

✦ **Loosely organized:** No single organization has authority over the Internet. As a result, the Internet is not highly organized. Online services, such as America Online or MSN, are owned and operated by individual companies that control exactly what content appears on the service and what software can be used with the service. No one exercises that kind of control over the Internet. As a result, you can find just about any kind of material imaginable on the Internet. No one guarantees the accuracy of information that you find on the Internet, so you have to be careful as you work your way through the labyrinth.

✦ **International:** Nearly 200 countries are represented on the Internet, from Afghanistan to Zimbabwe.

✦ **Collaboration:** The Internet exists only because many different organizations cooperate to provide the services and support needed to sustain it. For example, much of the software that drives the Internet is open source software that's developed collaboratively by programmers throughout the world, who constantly work to improve the code.

✦ **Autonomous:** The Internet community respects that organizations that join the Internet are free to make their own decisions about how they configure and operate their networks. Although legal issues sometimes boil up, for the most part, each player on the Internet operates independently.

✦ **Interconnected:** The whole key to the Internet is the concept of *interconnection,* which uses standard protocols that enable networks to communicate with each other. Without the interconnection provided by the TCP/IP protocol, the Internet would not exist.

✦ **Networks:** The Internet would be completely unmanageable if it consisted of half a billion individual users, all interconnected. That's why the Internet is often described as a network of networks. Most individual users on the Internet don't access the Internet directly. Instead, they access the Internet indirectly through another network, which may be a LAN in a business or academic environment, or a dialup or broadband network provided by an Internet service provider (ISP). In each case, however, the users of the local network access the Internet via a gateway IP router.

The Internet is composed of several distinct types of networks: Government agencies, such as the Library of Congress and the White House; military sites (did you ever see *War Games* or any of the *Terminator* movies?); educational institutions, such as universities and colleges (and their libraries); businesses, such as Microsoft and IBM; ISPs, which allow individuals to access the Internet; and commercial online services, such as America Online and MSN.

A Little Internet History

The Internet has a fascinating history, if such things interest you. There's no particular reason why you should be interested in such things, of course, except that a superficial understanding of how the Internet got started may help you to understand and cope with the way this massive computer network exists today. So here goes.

The Internet traces its beginnings back to a small network called ARPANET, built by the Department of Defense in 1969 to link defense installations. ARPANET soon expanded to include not only defense installations but universities as well. In the 1970s, ARPANET was split into two networks: one for military use (renamed MILNET) and the original ARPANET (for nonmilitary use). The two networks were connected by a networking link called IP — the *Internet protocol* — so called because it allowed communication between two networks.

The good folks who designed IP had the foresight to realize that soon, more than two networks would want to be connected. In fact, they left room for tens of thousands of networks to join the game, which is a good thing because it wasn't long before the Internet began to take off.

By the mid-1980s, ARPANET was beginning to reach the limits of what it could do. Enter the National Science Foundation (NSF), which set up a nationwide network designed to provide access to huge *supercomputers,* those monolithic computers used to discover new prime numbers and calculate the orbits of distant galaxies. The supercomputers were never put to much use, but the network that was put together to support the supercomputers — NSFNET — was used. In fact, NSFNET replaced ARPANET as the new backbone for the Internet.

Then, out of the blue, it seemed as if the whole world became interested in the Internet. Stories about it appeared in *Time* and *Newsweek.* Any company that had "dot com" in its name practically doubled in value every month. Al Gore claimed he invented the Internet. The Net began to grow so fast that even NSFNET couldn't keep up, so private commercial networks got into the game. The size of the Internet nearly doubled every year for most of the 1990s. Then, in the first few years of the millennium, the growth rate slowed a bit. However, the Internet still seems to be growing at the phenomenal rate of about 30 to 50 percent per year, and who knows how long this dizzying rate of growth will continue.

TCP/IP Standards and RFCs

The TCP/IP protocol standards that define how the Internet works are managed by the IETF. However, the IETF doesn't impose standards. Instead, it simply oversees the process by which ideas are developed into agreed-upon standards.

An Internet standard is published in the Request for Comments (RFC) document. When a document is accepted for publication, it is assigned an RFC number by the IETF. The RFC is then published. After it's published, an RFC is never changed. If a standard is enhanced, the enhancement is covered in a separate RFC.

At the time of this writing, more than 3,500 RFCs were available from the IETF website (www.ietf.org). The oldest RFC is RFC 0001, published in April, 1969. It describes how the host computers communicated with each other in the original ARPANET. The most recent RFC (as of May, 2012) is RFC 6636, a proposed standard entitled "Tuning the Behavior of the Internet Group Management Protocol (IGMP) and Multicast Listener Discovery (MLD) for Routers in Mobile and Wireless Networks."

Not all RFCs represent Internet standards. The following paragraphs summarize the various types of RFC documents:

✦ **Internet Standards Track:** This type of RFC represents an Internet standard. Standards Track RFCs have one of three maturity levels, as described in Table 1-1. An RFC enters circulation with Proposed Standard status but may be elevated to Draft Standard status — and, ultimately, to Internet Standard status.

Table 1-1   Maturity Levels for Internet Standards Track RFCs

Maturity Level	Description
Proposed Standard	Generally stable, have resolved known design choices, are believed to be well understood, have received significant community review, and appear to enjoy enough community interest to be considered valuable.
Draft Standard	Well understood and known to be quite stable. At least two interoperable implementations must exist, developed independently from separate code bases. The specification is believed to be mature and useful.
Internet Standard	Have been fully accepted by the Internet community as highly mature and useful standards.

✦ **Experimental specifications:** These are a result of research or development efforts. They're not intended to be standards, but the information they contain may be of use to the Internet community.

✦ **Informational specifications:** These simply provide general information for the Internet community.

✦ **Historic specifications:** These RFCs have been superceded by a more recent RFC and are thus considered obsolete.

✦ **Best Current Practice (BCP):** RFCs are documents that summarize the consensus of the Internet community's opinion on the best way to perform an operation or procedure. BCPs are guidelines, not standards.

Table 1-2 summarizes the RFCs that apply to the key Internet standards described in this book.

Table 1-2   RFCs for Key Internet Standards

RFC	Date	Description
768	August, 1980	User Datagram Protocol (UDP)
791	September, 1981	Internet Protocol (IP)
792	September, 1981	Internet Control Message Protocol (ICMP)
793	September, 1981	Transmission Control Protocol (TCP)
826	November, 1982	Ethernet Address Resolution Protocol (ARP)
950	August, 1985	Internet Standard Subnetting Procedure
959	October, 1985	File Transfer Protocol (FTP)
1034	November, 1987	Domain Names — Concepts and Facilities (DNS)

(continued)

Table 1-2 *(continued)*

RFC	Date	Description
1035	November, 1987	Domain Names — Implementation and Specification (DNS)
1939	May, 1996	Post Office Protocol Version 3 (POP3)
2131	March, 1997	Dynamic Host Configuration Protocol (DHCP)
2236	November, 1997	Internet Group Management Protocol (IGMP) (Updates RFC 1112)
2616	June, 1999	Hypertext Transfer Protocol — HTTP/1.1
5321	October, 2008	Simple Mail Transfer Protocol (SMTP)

My favorite RFC is 1149, an experimental specification for the "Transmission of IP datagrams on avian carriers." The specification calls for IP datagrams to be written in hexadecimal on scrolls of paper and secured to "avian carriers" with duct tape. (Not surprisingly, it's dated 1 April, 1990. Similar RFCs are frequently submitted on April 1.)

The TCP/IP Protocol Framework

Like the seven-layer OSI reference model, TCP/IP protocols are based on a layered framework. TCP/IP has four layers, as shown in Figure 1-1. These layers are described in the following sections.

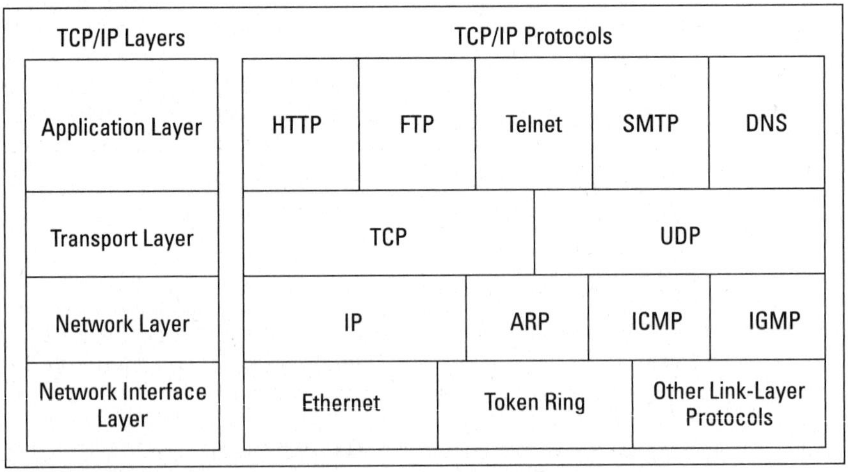

TCP/IP Layers	TCP/IP Protocols				
Application Layer	HTTP	FTP	Telnet	SMTP	DNS
Transport Layer	TCP			UDP	
Network Layer	IP		ARP	ICMP	IGMP
Network Interface Layer	Ethernet		Token Ring		Other Link-Layer Protocols

Figure 1-1:
The four layers of the TCP/IP framework.

Network Interface layer

The lowest level of the TCP/IP architecture is the Network Interface layer. It corresponds to the OSI Physical and Data Link layers. You can use many different TCP/IP protocols at the Network Interface layer, including Ethernet and token ring for LANs and protocols such as X.25, Frame Relay, and ATM for wide area networks (WANs).

The Network Interface layer is assumed to be unreliable.

Network layer

The Network layer is where data is addressed, packaged, and routed among networks. Several important Internet protocols operate at the Network layer:

✦ **Internet Protocol (IP):** A routable protocol that uses IP addresses to deliver packets to network devices. IP is an intentionally unreliable protocol, so it doesn't guarantee delivery of information.

✦ **Address Resolution Protocol (ARP):** Resolves IP addresses to hardware Media Access Control (MAC) addresses, which uniquely identify hardware devices.

✦ **Internet Control Message Protocol (ICMP):** Sends and receives diagnostic messages. ICMP is the basis of the ubiquitous `ping` command.

✦ **Internet Group Management Protocol (IGMP):** Used to multicast messages to multiple IP addresses at once.

Transport layer

The Transport layer is where sessions are established and data packets are exchanged between hosts. Two core protocols are found at this layer:

✦ **Transmission Control Protocol (TCP):** Provides reliable connection-oriented transmission between two hosts. TCP establishes a session between hosts, and then ensures delivery of packets between the hosts.

✦ **User Datagram Protocol (UDP):** Provides connectionless, unreliable, one-to-one or one-to-many delivery.

Application layer

The Application layer of the TCP/IP model corresponds to the Session, Presentation, and Application layers of the OSI reference model. A few of the most popular Application layer protocols are

✦ **HyperText Transfer Protocol (HTTP):** The core protocol of the World Wide Web.

✦ **File Transfer Protocol (FTP):** A protocol that enables a client to send and receive complete files from a server.

✦ **Telnet:** The protocol that lets you connect to another computer on the Internet in a terminal emulation mode.

✦ **Simple Mail Transfer Protocol (SMTP):** One of several key protocols that are used to provide e-mail services.

✦ **Domain Name System (DNS):** The protocol that allows you to refer to other host computers by using names rather than numbers.

Chapter 2: Understanding IP Addresses

In This Chapter

✔ Delving into the binary system

✔ Digging into IP addresses

✔ Finding out how subnetting works

✔ Looking at network address translation

*O*ne of the most basic components of TCP/IP is IP addressing. Every device on a TCP/IP network must have a unique IP address. In this chapter, I describe the ins and outs of these IP addresses. Enjoy!

Understanding Binary

Before you can understand the details of how IP addressing works, you need to understand how the binary numbering system works because binary is the basis of IP addressing. If you already understand binary, please skip to the section "Introducing IP Addresses." I don't want to bore you with stuff that's too basic.

Counting by ones

Binary is a counting system that uses only two numerals: 0 and 1. In the decimal system (with which most people are accustomed), you use 10 numerals: 0–9. In an ordinary decimal number — such as 3,482 — the rightmost digit represents ones; the next digit to the left, tens; the next, hundreds; the next, thousands; and so on. These digits represent powers of ten: first 10^0 (which is 1); next, 10^1 (10); then 10^2 (100); then 10^3 (1,000); and so on.

In binary, you have only two numerals rather than ten, which is why binary numbers look somewhat monotonous, as in 110011, 101111, and 100001.

The positions in a binary number (called *bits* rather than *digits*) represent powers of two rather than powers of ten: 1, 2, 4, 8, 16, 32, and so on. To figure the decimal value of a binary number, you multiply each bit by its corresponding power of two and then add the results. The decimal value of binary 10111, for example, is calculated as follows:

$$
\begin{array}{rcccc}
1 & \times 2^0 = 1 & \times 1 = & 1 \\
+ 1 & \times 2^1 = 1 & \times 2 = & 2 \\
+ 1 & \times 2^2 = 1 & \times 4 = & 4 \\
+ 0 & \times 2^3 = 0 & \times 8 = & 0 \\
+ 1 & \times 2^4 = 1 & \times 16 = & \underline{16} \\
& & & 23
\end{array}
$$

Fortunately, converting a number between binary and decimal is something a computer is good at — so good, in fact, that you're unlikely ever to need to do any conversions yourself. The point of learning binary is not to be able to look at a number such as 1110110110110 and say instantly, "Ah! Decimal 7,606!" (If you could do that, Piers Morgan would probably interview you, and they would even make a movie about you.)

Instead, the point is to have a basic understanding of how computers store information and — most important — to understand how the binary counting system works, which I describe in the following section.

Here are some of the more interesting characteristics of binary and how the system is similar to and differs from the decimal system:

✦ **In decimal, the number of decimal places allotted for a number determines how large the number can be.** If you allot six digits, for example, the largest number possible is 999,999. Because 0 is itself a number, however, a six-digit number can have any of 1 million different values.

Similarly, the number of bits allotted for a binary number determines how large that number can be. If you allot eight bits, the largest value that number can store is 11111111, which happens to be 255 in decimal.

✦ **To quickly figure how many different values you can store in a binary number of a given length, use the number of bits as an exponent of two.** An eight-bit binary number, for example, can hold 2^8 values. Because 2^8 is 256, an eight-bit number can have any of 256 different values. This is why a *byte* — eight bits — can have 256 different values.

✦ **This "powers of two" thing is why computers don't use nice, even, round numbers in measuring such values as memory or disk space.** A value of 1K, for example, is not an even 1,000 bytes: It's actually 1,024 bytes because 1,024 is 2^{10}. Similarly, 1MB is not an even 1,000,000 bytes but instead 1,048,576 bytes, which happens to be 2^{20}.

One basic test of computer nerddom is knowing your powers of two because they play such an important role in binary numbers. Just for the fun of it, but not because you really need to know, Table 2-1 lists the powers of two up to 32.

Table 2-1 also shows the common shorthand notation for various powers of two. The abbreviation *K* represents 2^{10} (1,024). The *M* in *MB* stands for 2^{20}, or 1,024K, and the *G* in *GB* represents 2^{30}, which is 1,024MB. These shorthand notations don't have anything to do with

TCP/IP, but they're commonly used for measuring computer disk and memory capacities, so I thought I'd throw them in at no charge because the table had extra room.

Table 2-1				Powers of Two		
Power	*Bytes*	*Kilobytes*	*Power*	*Bytes*	*K, MB, or GB*
2^1	2		2^{17}	131,072	128K
2^2	4		2^{18}	262,144	256K
2^3	8		2^{19}	524,288	512K
2^4	16		2^{20}	1,048,576	1MB
2^5	32		2^{21}	2,097,152	2MB
2^6	64		2^{22}	4,194,304	4MB
2^7	128		2^{23}	8,388,608	8MB
2^8	256		2^{24}	16,777,216	16MB
2^9	512		2^{25}	33,554,432	32MB
2^{10}	1,024	1K	2^{26}	67,108,864	64MB
2^{11}	2,048	2K	2^{27}	134,217,728	128MB
2^{12}	4,096	4K	2^{28}	268,435,456	256MB
2^{13}	8,192	8K	2^{29}	536,870,912	512MB
2^{14}	16,384	16K	2^{30}	1,073,741,824	1GB
2^{15}	32,768	32K	2^{31}	2,147,483,648	2GB
2^{16}	65,536	64K	2^{32}	4,294,967,296	4GB

Doing the logic thing

One of the great things about binary is that it's very efficient at handling special operations: namely, logical operations. Four basic logical operations exist although additional operations are derived from the basic four operations. Three of the operations — AND, OR, and XOR — compare two binary digits (bits). The fourth (NOT) works on just a single bit.

The following list summarizes the basic logical operations:

✦ **AND:** Compares two binary values. If both values are 1, the result of the AND operation is 1. If one or both of the values are 0, the result is 0.

✦ **OR:** Compares two binary values. If at least one value is 1, the result of the OR operation is 1. If both values are 0, the result is 0.

✦ **XOR:** Compares two binary values. If one of them is 1, the result is 1. If both values are 0 or if both values are 1, the result is 0.

✦ **NOT:** Doesn't compare two values but simply changes the value of a single binary value. If the original value is 1, NOT returns 0. If the original value is 0, NOT returns 1.

Table 2-2 summarizes how AND, OR, and XOR work.

Table 2-2		Logical Operations for Binary Values		
First Value	*Second Value*	*AND*	*OR*	*XOR*
0	0	0	0	0
0	1	0	1	1
1	0	0	1	1
1	1	1	1	0

Logical operations are applied to binary numbers that have more than one binary digit by applying the operation one bit at a time. The easiest way to do this manually is to line the two binary numbers on top of one another and then write the result of the operation beneath each binary digit. The following example shows how you would calculate 10010100 AND 11011101:

```
      10010100
AND   11011101
      10010100
```

As you can see, the result is 10010100.

Working with the binary Windows Calculator

The Calculator program that comes with all versions of Windows has a special Programmer mode that many users don't know about. When you flip the Calculator into this mode, you can do instant binary and decimal conversions, which can occasionally come in handy when you're working with IP addresses.

To use the Windows Calculator in Programmer mode, launch the Calculator by choosing Start➪All Programs➪Accessories➪Calculator. Then, choose the View➪Programmer command from the Calculator menu. The Calculator changes to a fancy programmer model in which all kinds of buttons appear, as shown in Figure 2-1.

Figure 2-1:
The free
Windows
Programmer
Calculator.

You can switch the number base by using the Hex, Dec, Oct, and Bin radio buttons to convert values between base 16 (hexadecimal), base 10 (decimal), base 8 (octal), and base 2 (binary). For example, to find the binary equivalent of decimal 155, enter **155** and then select the Bin radio button. The value in the display changes to 10011011.

Here are a few other things to note about the Programmer mode of the Calculator:

✦ Although you can convert decimal values to binary values with the programmer Calculator, the Calculator can't handle the dotted-decimal IP address format that's described later in this chapter. To convert a dotted-decimal address to binary, just convert each octet separately. For example, to convert 172.65.48.120 to binary, first convert 172; then convert 65; then convert 48; and finally, convert 120.

✦ The programmer Calculator has several features that are designed specifically for binary calculations, such as AND, OR, XOR, and so on.

✦ The Calculator program in Windows versions prior to Windows 7 does not have the programmer mode. However, those versions do offer a scientific mode that provides binary, hexadecimal, and decimal conversions.

**Book IV
Chapter 2**

**Understanding IP
Addresses**

Introducing IP Addresses

An *IP address* is a number that uniquely identifies every host on an IP network. IP addresses operate at the Network layer of the TCP/IP protocol stack, so they are independent of lower-level Data Link layer MAC addresses, such as Ethernet MAC addresses.

IP addresses are 32-bit binary numbers, which means that theoretically, a maximum of something in the neighborhood of 4 billion unique host addresses can exist throughout the Internet. You'd think that would be enough, but TCP/IP places certain restrictions on how IP addresses are allocated. These restrictions severely limit the total number of usable IP addresses. Many experts predict that we will run out of IP addresses as soon as next year. However, new techniques for working with IP addresses have helped to alleviate this problem, and a standard for 128-bit IP addresses has been adopted, though it still is not yet in widespread use.

Networks and hosts

IP stands for *Internet protocol,* and its primary purpose is to enable communications between networks. As a result, a 32-bit IP address actually consists of two parts:

+ **The network ID (or network address):** Identifies the network on which a host computer can be found

+ **The host ID (or host address):** Identifies a specific device on the network indicated by the network ID

Most of the complexity of working with IP addresses has to do with figuring out which part of the complete 32-bit IP address is the network ID and which part is the host ID, as described in the following sections.

As I describe the details of how host IDs are assigned, you may notice that two host addresses seem to be unaccounted for. For example, the Class C addressing scheme, which uses eight bits for the host ID, allows only 254 hosts — not the 256 hosts you'd expect. The host ID can't be 0 (the host ID is all zeros) because that address is always reserved to represent the network itself. And the host ID can't be 255 (the host ID is all ones) because that host ID is reserved for use as a broadcast request that's intended for all hosts on the network.

The dotted-decimal dance

IP addresses are usually represented in a format known as *dotted-decimal notation.* In dotted-decimal notation, each group of eight bits — an *octet* — is represented by its decimal equivalent. For example, consider the following binary IP address:

```
11000000101010001000100000011100
```

To convert this value to dotted-decimal notation, first divide it into four octets, as follows:

```
11000000 10101000 10001000 00011100
```

Then, convert each of the octets to its decimal equivalent:

```
11000000 10101000 10001000 00011100
192      168      136      28
```

Then, use periods to separate the four decimal numbers, like this:

```
192.168.136.28
```

This is the format in which you'll usually see IP addresses represented.

Figure 2-2 shows how the 32 bits of an IP address are broken down into four octets of eight bits each. As you can see, the four octets of an IP address are often referred to as *w, x, y,* and *z*.

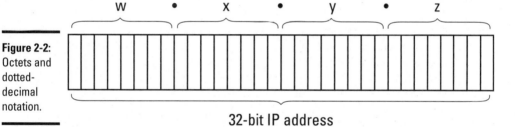

Figure 2-2:
Octets and dotted-decimal notation.

32-bit IP address

Classifying IP Addresses

When the original designers of the IP protocol created the IP addressing scheme, they could have assigned an arbitrary number of IP address bits for the network ID. The remaining bits would then be used for the host ID. For example, suppose that the designers decided that half of the address (16 bits) would be used for the network, and the remaining 16 bits would be used for the host ID. The result of that scheme would be that the Internet could have a total of 65,536 networks, and each of those networks could have 65,536 hosts.

In the early days of the Internet, this scheme probably seemed like several orders of magnitude more than would ever be needed. However, the IP designers realized from the start that few networks would actually have tens of thousands of hosts. Suppose that a network of 1,000 computers joins the Internet and is assigned one of these hypothetical network IDs. Because that network will use only 1,000 of its 65,536 host addresses, more than 64,000 IP addresses would be wasted.

What about IPv6?

Most of the current Internet is based on version 4 of the Internet Protocol, also known as IPv4. IPv4 has served the Internet well for more than 20 years. However, the growth of the Internet has put a lot of pressure on IPv4's limited 32-bit address space. This chapter describes how IPv4 has evolved to make the best possible use of 32-bit addresses. Eventually, though, all the addresses will be assigned, and the IPv4 address space will be filled to capacity. When that happens, the Internet will have to migrate to the next version of IP, known as IPv6.

IPv6 is also called *IP next generation,* or *IPng,* in honor of the favorite television show of most Internet gurus, *Star Trek: The Next Generation.*

IPv6 offers several advantages over IPv4, but the most important is that it uses 128 bits for Internet addresses instead of 32 bits. The number of host addresses possible with 128 bits is a number so large that it would have made Carl Sagan proud. It doesn't just double or triple the number of available addresses, or even a thousand-fold or even a million-fold. Just for the fun of it, here is the number of unique Internet addresses provided by IPv6:

340,282,366,920,938,463,463,374,607,431,768,211,456

This number is so large it defies understanding. If the Internet Assigned Numbers Authority (IANA) had been around at the creation of the universe and started handing out IPv6 addresses at a rate of one per millisecond — that is, 1,000 addresses every second — it would now, 15 billion years later, have not yet allocated even 1 percent of the available addresses.

The transition from IPv4 to IPv6 has been slow. IPv6 is available on all new computers and has been supported on Windows since Windows XP Service Pack 1 (released in 2002). However, most ISPs still base their service on IPv4. Thus, the Internet will continue to be driven by IPv4 for at least a few more years.

As a solution to this problem, the idea of IP address classes was introduced. The IP protocol defines five different address classes: A, B, C, D, and E. Each of the first three classes, A–C, uses a different size for the network ID and host ID portion of the address. Class D is for a special type of address called a *multicast address.* Class E is an experimental address class that isn't used.

The first four bits of the IP address are used to determine into which class a particular address fits, as follows:

✦ **Class A:** The first bit is zero.

✦ **Class B:** The first bit is one, and the second bit is zero.

✦ **Class C:** The first two bits are both one, and the third bit is zero.

✦ **Class D:** The first three bits are all one, and the fourth bit is zero.

✦ **Class E:** The first four bits are all one.

Because Class D and E addresses are reserved for special purposes, I focus the rest of the discussion here on Class A, B, and C addresses. Table 2-3 summarizes the details of each address class.

Table 2-3			IP Address Classes		
Class	Address Number Range	Starting Bits	Length of Network ID	Number of Networks	Hosts
A	1-126.x.y.z	0	8	126	16,777,214
B	128-191.x.y.z	10	16	16,384	65,534
C	192-223.x.y.z	110	24	2,097,152	254

Class A addresses

Class A addresses are designed for very large networks. In a Class A address, the first octet of the address is the network ID, and the remaining three octets are the host ID. Because only eight bits are allocated to the network ID and the first of these bits is used to indicate that the address is a Class A address, only 126 Class A networks can exist in the entire Internet. However, each Class A network can accommodate more than 16 million hosts.

Only about 40 Class A addresses are actually assigned to companies or organizations. The rest are either reserved for use by the Internet Assigned Numbers Authority (IANA) or are assigned to organizations that manage IP assignments for geographic regions such as Europe, Asia, and Latin America.

Just for fun, Table 2-4 lists some of the better-known Class A networks. You'll probably recognize many of them. In case you're interested, you can find a complete list of all the Class A address assignments at

```
www.iana.org/assignments/ipv4-address-space/
    ipv4-address-space.xml
```

You may have noticed in Table 2-3 that Class A addresses end with 126.x.y.z, and Class B addresses begin with 128.x.y.z. What happened to 127.x.y.z? This special range of addresses is reserved for loopback testing, so these addresses aren't assigned to public networks.

Book IV
Chapter 2

Understanding IP
Addresses

Table 2-4   Some Well-Known Class A Networks

Network	Description	Network	Description
3	General Electric Company	32	AT&T Global Network Services
4	Level 3 Communications.	33	DLA Systems Automation Center
6	Army Information Systems Center	35	MERIT Computer Network
8	Bolt Beranek and Newman Inc.	38	Performance Systems International
9	IBM	40	Eli Lilly and Company
11	DoD Intel Information Systems	43	APNIC
12	AT&T Bell Laboratories	44	Amateur Radio Digital Communications
13	Xerox Corporation	45	ARIN
15	Hewlett-Packard Company	46	RIPE NCC
16	Digital Equipment Corporation	47	Bell-Northern Research
17	Apple Computer Inc.	48	Prudential Securities Inc.
18	MIT	51	UK Government Department for Work and Pensions
19	Ford Motor Company	52	E.I. duPont de Nemours and Co., Inc.
20	Computer Sciences Corporation	53	Cap Debis CCS (Germany)
22	Defense Information Systems Agency	54	Merck and Co., Inc.
25	UK Ministry of Defense	55	DoD Network Information Center
26	Defense Information Systems Agency	56	U.S. Postal Service
28	Decision Sciences Institute (North)	57	SITA
29–30	Defense Information Systems Agency		

Class B addresses

In a Class B address, the first two octets of the IP address are used as the network ID, and the second two octets are used as the host ID. Thus, a Class B address comes close to my hypothetical scheme of splitting the address down the middle, using half for the network ID and half for the host ID. It isn't identical to this scheme, however, because the first two bits of the first octet are required to be 10, in order to indicate that the address is a Class B address. As a result, a total of 16,384 Class B networks can exist. All Class B addresses fall within the range 128.*x*.*y*.*z* to 191.*x*.*y*.*z*. Each Class B address can accommodate more than 65,000 hosts.

The problem with Class B networks is that even though they are much smaller than Class A networks, they still allocate far too many host IDs. Very few networks have tens of thousands of hosts. Thus, careless assignment of Class B addresses can lead to a large percentage of the available host addresses being wasted on organizations that don't need them.

Class C addresses

In a Class C address, the first three octets are used for the network ID, and the fourth octet is used for the host ID. With only eight bits for the host ID, each Class C network can accommodate only 254 hosts. However, with 24 network ID bits, Class C addresses allow for more than 2 million networks.

The problem with Class C networks is that they're too small. Although few organizations need the tens of thousands of host addresses provided by a Class B address, many organizations need more than a few hundred. The large discrepancy between Class B networks and Class C networks is what led to the development of *subnetting,* which I describe in the next section.

Subnetting

Subnetting is a technique that lets network administrators use the 32 bits available in an IP address more efficiently by creating networks that aren't limited to the scales provided by Class A, B, and C IP addresses. With subnetting, you can create networks with more realistic host limits.

Subnetting provides a more flexible way to designate which portion of an IP address represents the network ID and which portion represents the host ID. With standard IP address classes, only three possible network ID sizes exist: 8 bits for Class A, 16 bits for Class B, and 24 bits for Class C. Subnetting lets you select an arbitrary number of bits to use for the network ID.

Two reasons compel people to use subnetting. The first is to allocate the limited IP address space more efficiently. If the Internet were limited to Class A, B, or C addresses, every network would be allocated 254, 64 thousand, or

**Book IV
Chapter 2**

**Understanding IP
Addresses**

16 million IP addresses for host devices. Although many networks with more than 254 devices exist, few (if any) exist with 64 thousand, let alone 16 million. Unfortunately, any network with more than 254 devices would need a Class B allocation and probably waste tens of thousands of IP addresses.

The second reason for subnetting is that even if a single organization has thousands of network devices, operating all those devices with the same network ID would slow the network to a crawl. The way TCP/IP works dictates that all the computers with the same network ID must be on the same physical network. The physical network comprises a single *broadcast domain,* which means that a single network medium must carry all the traffic for the network. For performance reasons, networks are usually segmented into broadcast domains that are smaller than even Class C addresses provide.

Subnets

A *subnet* is a network that falls within a Class A, B, or C network. Subnets are created by using one or more of the Class A, B, or C host bits to extend the network ID. Thus, instead of the standard 8-, 16-, or 24-bit network ID, subnets can have network IDs of any length.

Figure 2-3 shows an example of a network before and after subnetting has been applied. In the unsubnetted network, the network has been assigned the Class B address `144.28.0.0`. All the devices on this network must share the same broadcast domain.

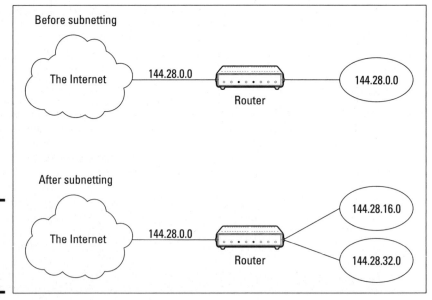

Figure 2-3: A network before and after subnetting.

In the second network, the first four bits of the host ID are used to divide the network into two small networks, identified as subnets 16 and 32. To the outside world (that is, on the other side of the router), these two networks still appear to be a single network identified as 144.28.0.0. For example, the outside world considers the device at 144.28.16.22 to belong to the 144.28.0.0 network. As a result, a packet sent to this device will be delivered to the router at 144.28.0.0. The router then considers the subnet portion of the host ID to decide whether to route the packet to subnet 16 or subnet 32.

Subnet masks

For subnetting to work, the router must be told which portion of the host ID should be used for the subnet network ID. This little sleight of hand is accomplished by using another 32-bit number, known as a *subnet mask*. Those IP address bits that represent the network ID are represented by a 1 in the mask, and those bits that represent the host ID appear as a 0 in the mask. As a result, a subnet mask always has a consecutive string of ones on the left, followed by a string of zeros.

For example, the subnet mask for the subnet shown in Figure 2-3, where the network ID consists of the 16-bit network ID plus an additional 4-bit subnet ID, would look like this:

```
11111111 11111111 11110000 00000000
```

In other words, the first 20 bits are ones, and the remaining 12 bits are zeros. Thus, the complete network ID is 20 bits in length, and the actual host ID portion of the subnetted address is 12 bits in length.

To determine the network ID of an IP address, the router must have both the IP address and the subnet mask. The router then performs a bitwise operation called a *logical AND* on the IP address in order to extract the network ID. To perform a logical AND, each bit in the IP address is compared with the corresponding bit in the subnet mask. If both bits are 1, the resulting bit in the network ID is set to 1. If either of the bits are 0, the resulting bit is set to 0.

For example, here's how the network address is extracted from an IP address using the 20-bit subnet mask from the previous example:

```
                144  .    28   .   16   .    17
IP address:   10010000 00011100 00010000 00010001
Subnet mask:  11111111 11111111 11110000 00000000
Network ID:   10010000 00011100 00010000 00000000
                144  .    28   .   16   .    0
```

Thus, the network ID for this subnet is 144.28.16.0.

The subnet mask itself is usually represented in dotted-decimal notation. As a result, the 20-bit subnet mask used in the previous example would be represented as 255.255.240.0:

```
Subnet mask:  11111111 11111111 11110000 00000000
                 255  .   255  .   240  .    0
```

Don't confuse a subnet mask with an IP address. A subnet mask doesn't represent any device or network on the Internet. It's just a way of indicating which portion of an IP address should be used to determine the network ID. (You can spot a subnet mask right away because the first octet is always 255, and 255 is not a valid first octet for any class of IP address.)

Network prefix notation

Because a subnet mask always begins with a consecutive sequence of ones to indicate which bits to use for the network ID, you can use a shorthand notation — a *network prefix* — to indicate how many bits of an IP address represent the network ID. The network prefix is indicated with a slash immediately after the IP address, followed by the number of network ID bits to use. For example, the IP address 144.28.16.17 with the subnet mask 255.255.240.0 can be represented as 144.28.16.17/20 because the subnet mask 255.255.240.0 has 20 network ID bits.

Network prefix notation is also called *classless interdomain routing* notation (*CIDR,* for short) because it provides a way of indicating which portion of an address is the network ID and which is the host ID without relying on standard address classes.

Default subnets

The *default subnet masks* are three subnet masks that correspond to the standard Class A, B, and C address assignments. These default masks are summarized in Table 2-5.

Table 2-5		The Default Subnet Masks	
Class	*Binary*	*Dotted-Decimal*	*Network Prefix*
A	11111111 00000000 00000000 00000000	255.0.0.0	/8
B	11111111 11111111 00000000 00000000	255.255.0.0	/16
C	11111111 11111111 11111111 00000000	255.255.255.0	/24

Keep in mind that a subnet mask is not actually required to use one of these defaults because the IP address class can be determined by examining the first three bits of the IP address. If the first bit is 0, the address is Class A, and the subnet mask 255.0.0 is applied. If the first two bits are 10, the address is Class B, and 255.255.0.0 is used. If the first three bits are 110, the Class C default mask 255.255.255.0 is used.

The great subnet roundup

You should know about a few additional restrictions that are placed on subnets and subnet masks. In particular

✦ **The minimum number of network ID bits is eight.** As a result, the first octet of a subnet mask is always 255.

✦ **The maximum number of network ID bits is 30.** You have to leave at least two bits for the host ID portion of the address to allow for at least two hosts. If you use all 32 bits for the network ID, that leaves no bits for the host ID. Obviously, that won't work. Leaving just one bit for the host ID won't work, either, because a host ID of all ones is reserved for a broadcast address, and all zeros refers to the network itself. Thus, if you use 31 bits for the network ID and leave only 1 for the host ID, host ID 1 would be used for the broadcast address, and host ID 0 would be the network itself, leaving no room for actual hosts. That's why the maximum network ID size is 30 bits.

✦ **Because the network ID portion of a subnet mask is always composed of consecutive bits set to 1, only eight values are possible for each octet of a subnet mask:** 0, 128, 192, 224, 248, 252, 254, and 255.

✦ **A subnet address can't be all zeros or all ones.** Thus, the number of unique subnet addresses is two less than two raised to the number of subnet address bits. For example, with three subnet address bits, six unique subnet addresses are possible ($2^3 - 2 = 6$). This implies that you must have at least two subnet bits. (If a single-bit subnet mask were allowed, it would violate the "can't be all zeros or all ones" rule because the only two allowed values would be 0 or 1.)

IP block parties

A subnet can be thought of as a range or block of IP addresses that have a common network ID. For example, the CIDR 192.168.1.0/28 represents the following block of 14 IP addresses:

```
192.168.1.1    192.168.1.2    192.168.1.3    192.168.1.4
192.168.1.5    192.168.1.6    192.168.1.7    192.168.1.8
192.168.1.9    192.168.1.10   192.168.1.11   192.168.1.12
192.168.1.13   192.168.1.14
```

Given an IP address in CIDR notation, it's useful to be able to determine the range of actual IP addresses that the CIDR represents. This matter is straightforward when the octet within which the network ID mask ends happens to be 0, as in the preceding example. You just determine how many host IDs are allowed based on the size of the network ID and count them off.

However, what if the octet where the network ID mask ends is not 0? For example, what are the valid IP addresses for 192.168.1.100 when the subnet mask is 255.255.255.240? In that case, the calculation is a little harder. The first step is to determine the actual network ID. You can do that by converting both the IP address and the subnet mask to binary and then extracting the network ID as in this example:

```
              192  .   168  .    1 .   100
IP address:   11000000 10101000 00000001 01100100
Subnet mask:  11111111 11111111 11111111 11110000
Network ID:   11000000 10101000 00000001 01100000
              192  .   168  .    1 .   96
```

As a result, the network ID is 192.168.1.96.

Next, determine the number of allowable hosts in the subnet based on the network prefix. You can calculate this by subtracting the last octet of the subnet mask from 254. In this case, the number of allowable hosts is 14.

To determine the first IP address in the block, add 1 to the network ID. Thus, the first IP address in my example is 192.168.1.97. To determine the last IP address in the block, add the number of hosts to the network ID. In my example, the last IP address is 192.168.1.110. As a result, the 192.168.1.100 with subnet mask 255.255.255.240 designates the following block of IP addresses:

```
192.168.1.97   192.168.1.98   192.168.1.99    192.168.1.100
192.168.1.101 192.168.1.102 192.168.1.103    192.168.1.104
192.168.1.105 192.168.1.106 192.168.1.107    192.168.1.108
192.168.1.109 192.168.1.110
```

Private and public addresses

Any host with a direct connection to the Internet must have a globally unique IP address. However, not all hosts are connected directly to the Internet. Some are on networks that aren't connected to the Internet. Some hosts are hidden behind firewalls, so their Internet connection is indirect.

Several blocks of IP addresses are set aside just for this purpose, for use on private networks that are not connected to the Internet or to use on networks that are hidden behind a firewall. Three such ranges of addresses exist, summarized in Table 2-6. Whenever you create a private TCP/IP network, you should use IP addresses from one of these ranges.

Table 2-6	**Private Address Spaces**	
CIDR	*Subnet Mask*	*Address Range*
10.0.0.0/8	255.0.0.0	10.0.0.1–10.255.255.254
172.16.0.0/12	255.255.240.0	172.16.1.1–172.31.255.254
192.168.0.0/16	255.255.0.0	192.168.0.1–192.168.255.254

Network Address Translation

Many firewalls use a technique called *network address translation* (NAT) to hide the actual IP address of a host from the outside world. When that's the case, the NAT device must use a globally unique IP to represent the host to the Internet. Behind the firewall, though, the host can use any IP address it wants. When packets cross the firewall, the NAT device translates the private IP address to the public IP address and vice versa.

One of the benefits of NAT is that it helps to slow down the rate at which the IP address space is assigned. That's because a NAT device can use a single public IP address for more than one host. It does so by keeping track of outgoing packets so that it can match incoming packets with the correct host. To understand how this works, consider the following sequence of steps:

1. A host whose private address is 192.168.1.100 sends a request to 216.239.57.99, which happens to be www.google.com. The NAT device changes the source IP address of the packet to 208.23.110.22, the IP address of the firewall. That way, Google will send its reply back to the firewall router. The NAT records that 192.168.1.100 sent a request to 216.239.57.99.

2. Now another host, at address 192.168.1.107, sends a request to 207.46.134.190, which happens to be www.microsoft.com. The NAT device changes the source of this request to 208.23.110.22 so that Microsoft will reply to the firewall router. The NAT records that 192.168.1.107 sent a request to 207.46.134.190.

3. A few seconds later, the firewall receives a reply from 216.239.57.99. The destination address in the reply is 208.23.110.22, the address of the firewall. To determine to whom to forward the reply, the firewall checks its records to see who is waiting for a reply from 216.239.57.99. It discovers that 192.168.1.100 is waiting for that reply, so it changes the destination address to 192.168.1.100 and sends the packet on.

**Book IV
Chapter 2**

Understanding IP Addresses

Actually, the process is a little more complicated than that, because it's very likely that two or more users may have pending requests from the same public IP. In that case, the NAT device uses other techniques to figure out to which user each incoming packet should be delivered.

Chapter 3: Using DHCP

In This Chapter

✓ Discovering the basics of DHCP

✓ Exploring scopes

✓ Configuring a DHCP server

✓ Setting up a DHCP client

*E*very host on a Transmission Control Protocol/Internet Protocol (TCP/IP) network must have a unique IP address. Each host must be properly configured so that it knows its IP address. When a new host comes online, it must be assigned an IP address that's within the correct range of addresses for the subnet but not already in use. Although you can manually assign IP addresses to each computer on your network, that task quickly becomes overwhelming if the network has more than a few computers.

That's where DHCP — Dynamic Host Configuration Protocol — comes into play. *DHCP* automatically configures the IP address for every host on a network, thus assuring that each host has a valid, unique IP address. DHCP even automatically reconfigures IP addresses as hosts come and go. As you can imagine, DHCP can save a network administrator many hours of tedious configuration work.

In this chapter, you discover the ins and outs of DHCP: what it is, how it works, and how to set it up.

Understanding DHCP

DHCP allows individual computers on a TCP/IP network to obtain their configuration information — in particular, their IP address — from a server. The DHCP server keeps track of which IP addresses are already assigned so that when a computer requests an IP address, the DHCP server offers it an IP address that's not already in use.

Configuration information provided by DHCP

Although the primary job of DHCP is to dole out IP addresses and subnet masks, DHCP actually provides more configuration information than just the IP address to its clients. The additional configuration information are DHCP options. The following is a list of some common DHCP options that can be configured by the server:

✦ The router address, also known as the Default Gateway address

✦ The expiration time for the configuration information

✦ Domain name

✦ Domain Name Server (DNS) server address

✦ Windows Internet Name Service (WINS) server address

DHCP servers

A DHCP server can be a server computer located on the TCP/IP network. All modern server operating systems have a built-in DHCP server. To set up DHCP on a network server, all you have to do is enable the server's DHCP function and configure its settings. In the upcoming section, "Working with a DHCP Server," I show you how to configure a DHCP server for Windows Server 2012. (The procedure for Windows Server 2008 is similar.)

A server computer running DHCP doesn't have to be devoted entirely to DHCP unless the network is very large. For most networks, a file server can share duty as a DHCP server. This is especially true if you provide long leases for your IP addresses. (*Lease* is the term used by DHCP to indicate that an IP address has been temporarily given out to a particular computer or other device.)

Many multifunction routers also have built-in DHCP servers. If you don't want to burden one of your network servers with the DHCP function, you can enable the router's built-in DHCP server. An advantage of allowing the router to be your network's DHCP server is that you rarely need to power-down a router. In contrast, you occasionally need to restart or power-down a file server to perform system maintenance, apply upgrades, or perform troubleshooting.

Most networks require only one DHCP server. Setting up two or more servers on the same network requires that you carefully coordinate the IP address ranges (known as *scopes*) for which each server is responsible. If you accidentally set up two DHCP servers for the same scope, you may end up with duplicate address assignments if the servers attempt to assign the same IP address to two different hosts. To prevent this from happening, just set up one DHCP server unless your network is so large that one server can't handle the workload.

How DHCP actually works

You can configure and use DHCP without knowing the details of how DHCP client configuration actually works. However, a basic understanding of the process can help you to understand what DHCP is actually doing. Not only is this understanding enlightening, but it can also help when you're troubleshooting DHCP problems.

The following paragraphs contain a blow-by-blow account of how DHCP configures TCP/IP hosts. This procedure happens every time you boot up a host computer. It also happens when you release an IP lease and request a fresh lease.

1. When a host computer starts up, the DHCP client software sends a special broadcast packet, known as a *DHCP Discover message.*

   This message uses the subnet's broadcast address (all host ID bits set to one) as the destination address and `0.0.0.0` as the source address.

   The client has to specify `0.0.0.0` as the source address because it doesn't yet have an IP address, and it specifies the broadcast address as the destination address because it doesn't know the address of any DHCP servers. In effect, the DHCP Discover message is saying, "Hey! I'm new here. Are there any DHCP servers out there?"

2. The DHCP server receives the broadcast DHCP Discover message and responds by sending a *DHCP Offer message.*

   The DHCP Offer message includes an IP address that the client can use.

   Like the DHCP Discover message, the DHCP Offer message is sent to the broadcast address. This makes sense because the client to which the message is being sent doesn't yet have an IP address and won't have one until it accepts the offer. In effect, the DHCP Offer message is saying, "Hello there, whoever you are. Here's an IP address you can use, if you want it. Let me know."

   What if the client never receives a DHCP Offer message from a DHCP server? In that case, the client waits for a few seconds and tries again. The client will try four times — at 2, 4, 8, and 16 seconds. If it still doesn't get an offer, it will try again after five minutes.

3. The client receives the DHCP Offer message and sends back a message known as a *DHCP Request message.*

   At this point, the client doesn't actually own the IP address: It's simply indicating that it's ready to accept the IP address that was offered by the server. In effect, the DHCP Request message says, "Yes, that IP address would be good for me. Can I have it, please?"

4. When the server receives the DHCP Request message, it marks the IP address as assigned to the client and broadcasts a *DHCP Ack message.*

The DHCP Ack message says, in effect, "Okay, it's all yours. Here's the rest of the information you need to use it."

5. When the client receives the DHCP Ack message, it configures its TCP/IP stack by using the address it accepted from the server.

Understanding Scopes

A *scope* is simply a range of IP addresses that a DHCP server is configured to distribute. In the simplest case, where a single DHCP server oversees IP configuration for an entire subnet, the scope corresponds to the subnet. However, if you set up two DHCP servers for a subnet, you can configure each with a scope that allocates only one part of the complete subnet range. In addition, a single DHCP server can serve more than one scope.

You must create a scope before you can enable a DHCP server. When you create a scope, you can provide it with the following properties:

✦ A **scope name,** which helps you to identify the scope and its purpose

✦ A **scope description,** which lets you provide additional details about the scope and its purpose

✦ A **starting IP address** for the scope

✦ An **ending IP address** for the scope

✦ A **subnet mask** for the scope

You can specify the subnet mask with dotted-decimal notation or with network prefix notation.

✦ **One or more ranges of excluded addresses**

These addresses won't be assigned to clients. For more information, see the section "Feeling excluded?" later in this chapter.

✦ **One or more reserved addresses**

These are addresses that will always be assigned to particular host devices. For more information, see the section "Reservations suggested" later in this chapter.

✦ The **lease duration,** which indicates how long the host will be allowed to use the IP address

The client will attempt to renew the lease when half of the lease duration has elapsed. For example, if you specify a lease duration of eight days, the client will attempt to renew the lease after four days. This allows the host plenty of time to renew the lease before the address is reassigned to some other host.

✦ The **router address** for the subnet

This value is also known as the Default Gateway address.

✦ The **domain name and the IP address of the network's DNS servers and WINS servers**

Feeling excluded?

Everyone feels excluded once in awhile. With a wife, three daughters, and a female dog, I know how it feels. Sometimes, however, being excluded is a good thing. In the case of DHCP scopes, exclusions can help you to prevent IP address conflicts and can enable you to divide the DHCP workload for a single subnet among two or more DHCP servers.

An *exclusion* is a range of addresses that are not included in a scope. The exclusion range falls within the range of the scope's starting and ending addresses. In effect, an exclusion range lets you punch a hole in a scope. The IP addresses that fall within the hole won't be assigned.

Here are a few reasons for excluding IP addresses from a scope:

✦ **The computer that runs the DHCP service itself must usually have a static IP address assignment.** As a result, the address of the DHCP server should be listed as an exclusion.

✦ **Some hosts may not be able to support DHCP.** In that case, the host will require a static IP address. For example, you may have a really old MS-DOS computer that doesn't have a DHCP client. By excluding its IP address from the scope, you can prevent that address from being assigned to any other host on the network.

Reservations suggested

In some cases, you may want to assign a particular IP address to a particular host. One way to do this is to configure the host with a static IP address so that the host doesn't use DHCP to obtain its IP configuration. However, here are two major disadvantages to that approach:

✦ **TCP/IP configuration supplies more than just the IP address.** If you use static configuration, you must manually specify the subnet mask, the Default Gateway address, the DNS server address, and other configuration information required by the host. If this information changes, you have to change it not only at the DHCP server, but also at each host that you configured statically.

✦ **You must remember to exclude the static IP address from the DHCP server's scope.** Otherwise, the DHCP server won't know about the static address and may assign it to another host. Then, you'll have two hosts with the same address on your network.

What about BootP?

BootP — Bootstrap Protocol — is an Internet protocol that enables diskless workstations to boot themselves over the Internet or local network. Like DHCP, BootP allows a computer to receive an IP address assigned from a server. However, unlike DHCP, BootP also enables the computer to download a *boot image file,* which the computer can then use to boot itself from. A significant difference between BootP and DHCP is that BootP comes into play before the computer actually loads an operating system. In contrast, DHCP is used after an operating system has been loaded, during the configuration of network devices.

Most DHCP servers can also support BootP. If your network has diskless workstations, you can use the DHCP server's BootP support to boot those computers. At one time, diskless workstations were all the rage because network administrators thought they'd be easier to manage. Users hated them, however. Most diskless workstations have now been buried in landfills, and BootP isn't used much.

A better way to assign a fixed IP address to a particular host is to create a DHCP reservation. A *reservation* simply indicates that whenever a particular host requests an IP address from the DHCP server, the server should provide it the address that you specify in the reservation. The host won't receive the IP address until the host requests it from the DHCP server, but whenever the host does request IP configuration, it will always receive the same address.

To create a reservation, you associate the IP address that you want assigned to the host with the host's Media Access Control (MAC) address. As a result, you need to get the MAC address from the host before you create the reservation. You can get the MAC address by running the command `ipconfig / all` from a command prompt.

If you set up more than one DHCP server, each should be configured to serve a different range of IP addresses. Otherwise, the servers might assign the same address to two different hosts.

How long to lease?

One of the most important decisions that you'll make when you configure a DHCP server is the length of time to specify for the lease duration. The default value is eight days, which is appropriate in many cases. However, you may encounter situations in which a longer or shorter interval may be appropriate:

✦ **The more stable your network,** the longer the lease duration can safely exist. If you only periodically add new computers to the network or replace existing computers, you can safely increase the lease duration past eight days.

✦ **The more volatile the network,** the shorter the lease duration should be. For example, a wireless network in a university library is used by students who bring their laptop computers into the library to work for a few hours at a time. For this network, a duration such as one hour may be appropriate.

Don't configure your network to allow infinite duration leases. Some administrators feel that this cuts down the workload for the DHCP server on stable networks. However, no network is permanently stable. Whenever you find a DHCP server that's configured with infinite leases, look at the active leases. I guarantee you'll find IP leases assigned to computers that no longer exist.

Working with a DHCP Server

The exact steps that you should follow when configuring and managing a DHCP server depend on the network operating system that you're using. The following procedures show you how to work with a DHCP server in Windows Server 2012. The procedures for other operating systems are similar.

Installing a Windows Server 2012 DHCP server

To install the DHCP server role on Windows Server 2012, follow these steps:

1. **Click Server Manager in the taskbar.**

The Server Manager application appears.

2. **Choose Manage⊏⟩Add Roles and Features.**

The Add Roles and Features Wizard appears.

3. **Choose Role-Based or Feature-Based Installation and then click Next.**

The wizard displays a list of available servers.

4. **Select the server on which you want to install the DHCP role on; then click Next.**

The wizard displays a list of available server roles.

5. **Select DHCP Server from the list of roles and then click Next.**

The wizard displays a list of required features that must also be installed to support DHCP.

6. **Click Next.**

The wizard displays a page describing what the DHCP role entails.

7. **Click Next.**

The wizard displays a confirmation screen.

8. **Click Install.**

   The wizard installs the DHCP role, which may take a few minutes. When the installation completes, a results page is displayed to summarize the results of the installation.

9. **Click Close.**

   You're done!

Configuring a new scope

After you installed the DHCP role on Windows Server 2012, you'll need to create at least one scope so the server can start handing out IP addresses. Here are the steps:

1. **In Server Manager, choose Tools⇨DHCP.**

   This brings up the DHCP management console, shown in Figure 3-1.

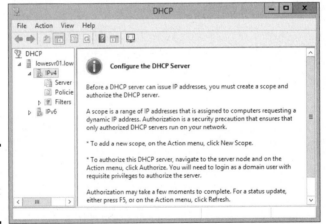

Figure 3-1:
The DHCP management console.

2. **Select the DHCP server you want to define the scope for, click IPv4, and then click the New Scope button on the toolbar.**

   This brings up the New Scope Wizard dialog box, as shown in Figure 3-2.

Figure 3-2:
The New
Scope
Wizard
comes to
life.

3. **Click Next.**

   You're prompted for the name of the scope, as shown in Figure 3-3.

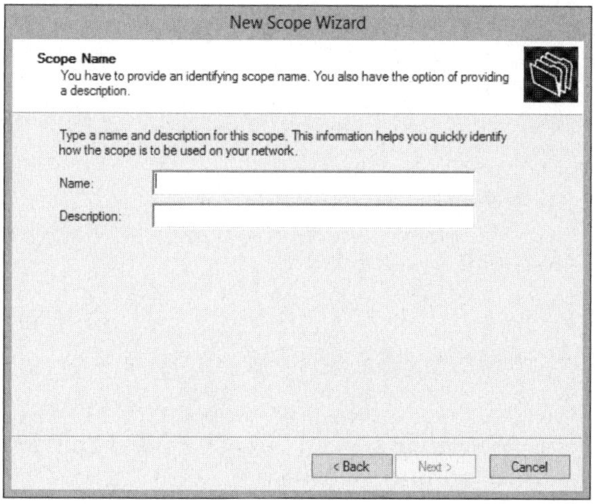

Figure 3-3:
The wizard
asks for a
name for the
new scope.

4. **Enter a name and optional description, and then click Next.**

   The wizard asks for information required to create the scope, as shown
   in Figure 3-4.

**Book IV
Chapter 3**

Using DHCP

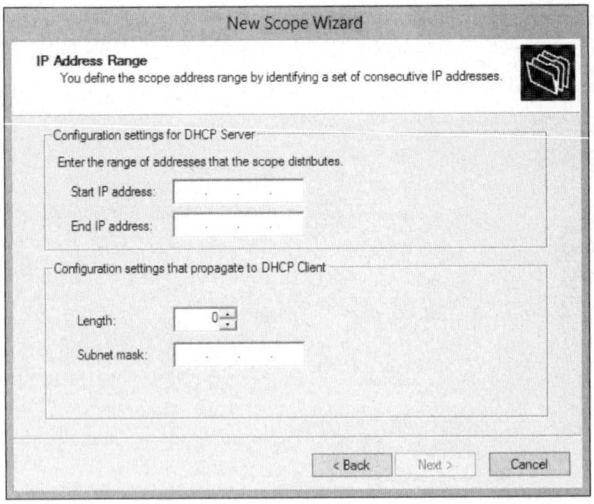

Figure 3-4:
The wizard
asks for
scope
information.

5. **Enter the information for the new scope.**

   You must enter the following information:

   • *Start IP Address:* This is the lowest IP address that will be issued for this scope.

   • *End IP Address:* This is the highest IP address that will be issued for this scope.

   • *Subnet Mask:* This is the subnet mask issued for IP addresses in this scope.

6. **Click Next.**

   The wizard asks whether you want to exclude any ranges from the scope range, as shown in Figure 3-5.

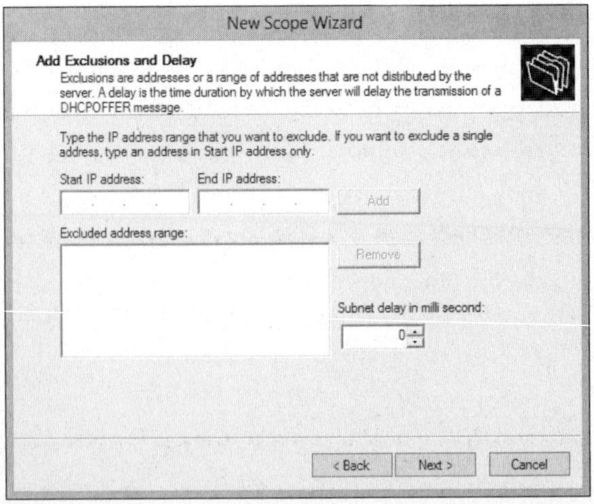

Figure 3-5:
Do you want
to create
exclusions?

7. **(Optional) To create an exclusion, enter the IP address range to exclude and then click Add.**

   You can repeat this step as many times as necessary to add any excluded addresses.

8. **Click Next.**

   The wizard asks for the lease duration, as shown in Figure 3-6.

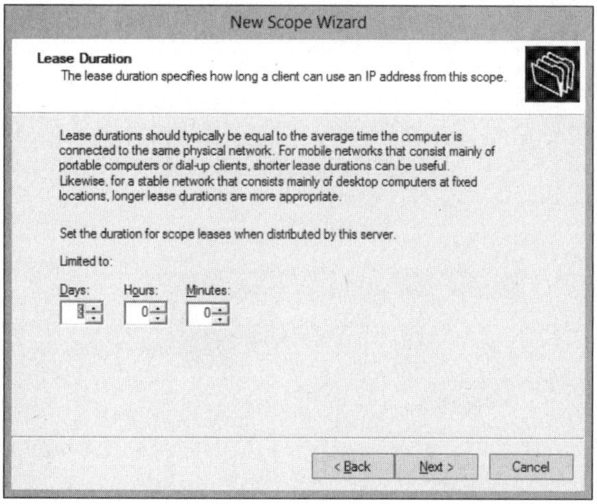

   New Scope Wizard

   Lease Duration
   The lease duration specifies how long a client can use an IP address from this scope.

   Lease durations should typically be equal to the average time the computer is connected to the same physical network. For mobile networks that consist mainly of portable computers or dial-up clients, shorter lease durations can be useful. Likewise, for a stable network that consists mainly of desktop computers at fixed locations, longer lease durations are more appropriate.

   Set the duration for scope leases when distributed by this server.

   Limited to:

   Days: Hours: Minutes:

   < Back   Next >   Cancel

Figure 3-6:
Set the
lease
duration.

9. **(Optional) Change the lease duration; then click Next.**

   When the wizard asks whether you want to configure additional DHCP options, leave this option set to Yes to complete your DHCP configuration now.

10. **Click Next.**

    The wizard asks for the default gateway information, as shown in Figure 3-7.

11. **Enter the address of your network's router; then click Next**.

    The wizard now asks for additional DNS information, as shown in Figure 3-8.

12. **(Optional) If you want to add a DNS server, enter its address and then click Add.**

    Repeat this step as many times as necessary to add any additional DNS servers.

13. **Click Next.**

    The wizard next asks for WINS configuration information.

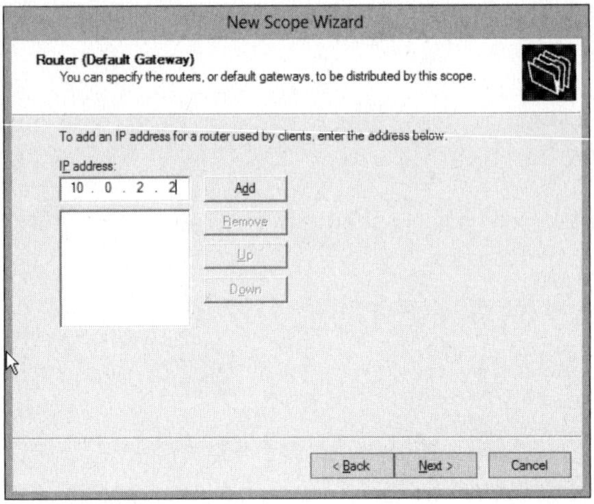

Figure 3-7:
Provide
the default
gateway
address.

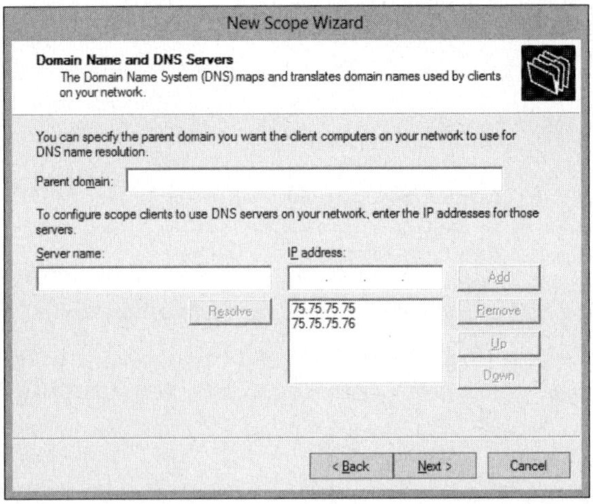

Figure 3-8:
Provide
additional
DNS
information.

14. **(Optional) If you want to enable WINS, enter the WINS server configuration.**

WINS isn't required for most modern networks, so you can usually just leave this page blank.

15. **Click Next.**

The wizard now asks whether you want to activate the scope.

16. **Select Yes, I Want to Activate This Scope and then click Next.**

A final confirmation page is displayed.

17. **Click Finish.**

The scope is created.

How to Configure a Windows DHCP Client

Configuring a Windows client for DHCP is easy. The DHCP client is automatically included when you install the TCP/IP protocol, so all you have to do is configure TCP/IP to use DHCP. And in nearly all cases, DHCP is configured automatically when you install Windows.

If you must configure DHCP manually, bring up the Network Properties dialog box by choosing Network or Network Connections from Control Panel (depending on which version of Windows the client is running). Then, select the Internet Protocol Version 4 and click the Properties button. This brings up the dialog box shown in Figure 3-9. To configure the computer to use DHCP, select the Obtain an IP Address Automatically option and the Obtain DNS Server Address Automatically option.

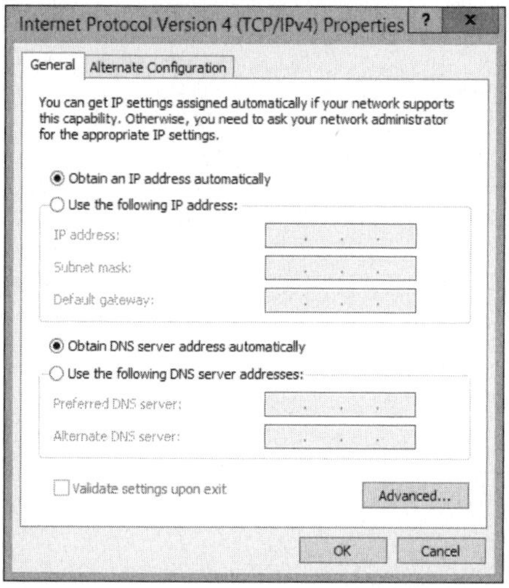

Figure 3-9:
Configuring a Windows client to use DHCP.

Automatic private IP addressing

If a Windows computer is configured to use DHCP but the computer can't obtain an IP address from a DHCP server, the computer automatically assigns itself a private address by using a feature called Automatic Private IP Addressing (APIPA). APIPA assigns a private address from the $169.254.x.x$ range and uses a special algorithm to ensure that the address is unique on the network. As soon as the DHCP server becomes available, the computer requests a new address, so the APIPA address is used only while the DHCP server is unavailable.

Renewing and releasing leases

Normally, a DHCP client attempts to renew its lease when the lease is half-way to the point of being expired. For example, if a client obtains an eight-day lease, it attempts to renew the lease after four days. However, you can renew a lease sooner by issuing the `ipconfig /renew` command at a command prompt. You may want to do this if you changed the scope's configuration or if the client's IP configuration isn't working correctly.

You can also release a DHCP lease by issuing the `ipconfig /release` command at a command prompt. When you release a lease, the client computer no longer has a valid IP address. This is shown in the output from the `ipconfig /release` command:

```
C:\>ipconfig /release
Windows IP Configuration
Ethernet adapter Local Area Connection:
        Connection-specific DNS Suffix  . :
        IP Address. . . . . . . . . . . : 0.0.0.0
        Subnet Mask . . . . . . . . . . : 0.0.0.0
        Default Gateway . . . . . . . . :
```

Here, you can see that the IP address and subnet masks are set to `0.0.0.0` and that the Default Gateway address is blank. When you release an IP lease, you can't communicate with the network by using TCP/IP until you issue an `ipconfig /renew` command to renew the IP configuration or restart the computer.

Chapter 4: Using DNS

In This Chapter

✔ Discovering the basics of DNS

✔ Exploring zones

✔ Examining resource records

✔ Configuring a DNS server

✔ Setting up a DNS client

Domain Name Server — DNS — is the TCP/IP facility that lets you use names rather than numbers to refer to host computers. Without DNS, you'd buy books from `207.171.166.252` instead of from `www.amazon.com`, you'd sell your used furniture at `66.211.160.87` instead of on `www.ebay.com`, and you'd search the Web at `74.125.19.147` instead of at `www.google.com`.

Understanding how DNS works and how to set up a DNS server is crucial to setting up and administering a Transmission Control Protocol/Internet Protocol (TCP/IP) network. (For more on that, see Chapter 1 of this mini-book.) This chapter introduces you to the basics of DNS, including how the DNS naming system works and how to set up a DNS server.

If you want to review the complete official specifications for DNS, look up RFC 1034 and 1035 at `www.ietf.org/rfc/rfc1034.txt` and `www.ietf.org/rfc/rfc1035.txt`, respectively.

Understanding DNS Names

DNS is a name service that provides a standardized system for providing names to identify TCP/IP hosts as well as a way to look up the IP address of a host, given the host's DNS name. For example, if you use DNS to look up the name `www.ebay.com`, you get the IP address of the eBay web host: `66.135.210.61`. Thus, DNS allows you to access the eBay website by using the DNS name `www.ebay.com` instead of the site's IP address.

The following sections describe the basic concepts of DNS.

Domains and domain names

To provide a unique DNS name for every host computer on the Internet, DNS uses a time-tested technique: Divide and conquer. DNS uses a hierarchical naming system that's similar to how folders are organized hierarchically on a Windows computer. Instead of folders, however, DNS organizes its names into domains. Each domain includes all the names that appear directly beneath it in the DNS hierarchy.

For example, Figure 4-1 shows a small portion of the DNS domain tree. At the very top of the tree is the *root domain,* which is the anchor point for all domains. Directly beneath the root domain are four top-level domains, named edu, com, org, and gov.

In reality, many more top-level domains than this exist in the Internet's root domain. For more information, see the section "Top-Level Domains" later in this chapter.

Beneath the com domain in Figure 4-1 is another domain called LoweWriter, which happens to be my own personal domain. (Pretty clever, eh?) To completely identify this domain, you have to combine it with the name of its *parent domain* (in this case, com) to create the complete domain name: LoweWriter.com. Notice that the parts of the domain name are separated from each other with periods, which are called dots. As a result, when you read this domain name, you pronounce it *LoweWriter dot com.*

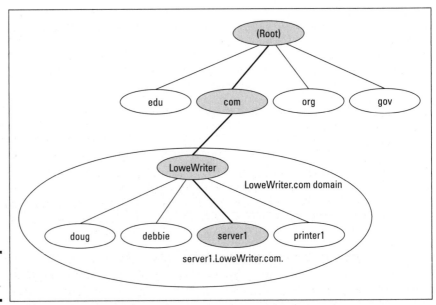

Figure 4-1:
DNS names.

Beneath the `LoweWriter` node are four host nodes, named `doug`, `debbie`, `server1`, and `printer1`. Respectively, these correspond to three computers and a printer on my home network. You can combine the host name with the domain name to get the complete DNS name for each of my network's hosts. For example, the complete DNS name for my server is `server1.LoweWriter.com`. Likewise, my printer is `printer1.LoweWriter.com`.

Here are a few additional details that you need to remember about DNS names:

+ **DNS names are not case sensitive.** As a result, `LoweWriter` and `Lowewriter` are treated as the same name, as are `LOWEWRITER`, `LOWEwriter`, and `LoWeWrItEr`. When you use a domain name, you can use capitalization to make the name easier to read, but DNS ignores the difference between capital and lowercase letters.

+ **The name of each DNS node can be up to 63 characters long (not including the dot) and can include letters, numbers, and hyphens.**

    No other special characters are allowed.

+ **A *subdomain* is a domain that's beneath an existing domain.** For example, the `com` domain is actually a subdomain of the root domain. Likewise, `LoweWriter` is a subdomain of the `com` domain.

+ **DNS is a hierarchical naming system that's similar to the hierarchical folder system used by Windows.**

    However, one crucial difference exists between DNS and the Windows naming convention. When you construct a complete DNS name, you start at the bottom of the tree and work your way up to the root. Thus, `doug` is the lowest node in the name `doug.LoweWriter.com`. In contrast, Windows paths are the opposite: They start at the root and work their way down. For example, in the path `\Windows\System32\dns`, `dns` is the lowest node.

+ **The DNS tree can be up to 127 levels deep.** However, in practice, the DNS tree is pretty shallow. Most DNS names have just three levels (not counting the root). And although you'll sometimes see names with four or five levels, you'll rarely see more levels than that.

+ **Although the DNS tree is shallow, it's very broad.** In other words, each of the top-level domains has a huge number of second-level domains immediately beneath it. For example, at the time of this writing, the `com` domain had well over a million second-level domains beneath it.

Fully qualified domain names

If a domain name ends with a trailing dot, that trailing dot represents the root domain, and the domain name is said to be a *fully qualified domain name* (also known as an FQDN). A fully qualified domain name is also called an *absolute name*. A fully qualified domain name is unambiguous because it identifies itself all the way back to the root domain. In contrast, if a domain name doesn't end with a trailing dot, the name may be interpreted in the context of some other domain. Thus, DNS names that don't end with a trailing dot are called *relative names*.

This is similar to how relative and absolute paths work in Windows. For example, if a path begins with a backslash, such as `\Windows\System32\dns`, the path is absolute. However, a path that doesn't begin with a backslash, such as `System32\dns`, uses the current directory as its starting point. If the current directory happens to be `\Windows`, then `\Windows\System32\dns` and `System32\dns` refer to the same location.

In many cases, relative and fully qualified domain names are interchangeable because the software that interprets them always interprets relative names in the context of the root domain. That's why, for example, you can type `www.wiley.com` (without the trailing dot) — not `www.wiley.com.` — to go to the Wiley home page in a web browser. Some applications, such as DNS servers, may interpret relative names in the context of a domain other than the root.

Top-Level Domains

A *top-level domain* appears immediately beneath the root domain. Top-level domains come in two categories: generic domains and geographic domains. These categories are described in the following sections. (Actually, a third type of top-level domain exists, which is used for reverse lookups. I describe it later in this chapter, in the section "Reverse Lookup Zones.")

Generic domains

Generic domains are the popular top-level domains that you see most often on the Internet. Originally, seven top-level organizational domains existed. In 2002, seven more were added to help ease the congestion of the original seven — in particular, the `com` domain.

Table 4-1 summarizes the original seven generic top-level domains. Of these, you can see that the `com` domain is far and away the most populated, with nearly 1.9 million second-level domains beneath it.

The Size column in this table indicates approximately how many second-level domains existed under each top-level domain as of January 2012, according to an Internet Software Consortium survey, found at `www.isc.org`.

Table 4-1   The Original Seven Top-Level Domains

Domain	Description	Size
com	Commercial organizations	156,860,679
edu	Educational institutions	12,587,684
gov	Government institutions	2,387,387
int	International treaty organizations	19,435
mil	Military institutions	2,613,099
net	Network providers	319,311,234
org	Noncommercial organizations	2,078,160

Because the com domain ballooned to an almost unmanageable size in the late 1990s, the Internet authorities approved seven new top-level domains in an effort to take some of the heat off of the com domain. Most of these domains, listed in Table 4-2, became available in 2002. As you can see, they haven't really caught on yet even though they've been around for several years.

Table 4-2   The New Seven Top-Level Domains

Domain	Description	Size
aero	Aerospace industry	2,735
biz	Business	111,801
coop	Cooperatives	19,671
info	Informational sites	473,096
museum	Museums	38
name	Individual users	4,104
pro	Professional organizations	1,719

Geographic domains

Although the top-level domains are open to anyone, U.S. companies and organizations dominate them. An additional set of top-level domains corresponds to international country designations. Organizations outside the United States often use these top-level domains to avoid the congestion of the generic domains.

**Book IV
Chapter 4**

Using DNS

Table 4-3 lists those geographic top-level domains with more than 200 registered subdomains at the time of this writing, in alphabetical order. In all, about 150 geographic top-level domains exist. The exact number varies from time to time as political circumstances change.

Table 4-3   **Geographic Top-Level Domains with More Than 200 Subdomains**

Domain	Description	Domain	Description
ac	Ascension Island	ie	Ireland
ae	United Arab Emirates	in	India
ag	Antigua and Barbuda	is	Iceland
am	Armenia	it	Italy
an	Netherlands Antilles	jp	Japan
as	American Samoa	kz	Kazakhstan
at	Austria	la	Lao People's Democratic Republic
be	Belgium	li	Liechtenstein
bg	Bulgaria	lk	Sri Lanka
br	Brazil	lt	Lithuania
by	Belarus	lu	Luxembourg
bz	Belize	lv	Latvia
ca	Canada	ma	Morocco
cc	Cocos (Keeling) Islands	md	Moldova
ch	Switzerland	nl	Netherlands
cl	Chile	no	Norway
cn	China	nu	Niue
cx	Christmas Island	pl	Poland
cz	Czech Republic	pt	Portugal
de	Germany	ro	Romania
dk	Denmark	ru	Russian Federation
ee	Estonia	se	Sweden
es	Spain	si	Slovenia
eu	European Union	sk	Slovakia
fi	Finland	st	São Tomé and Principe

Domain	Description	Domain	Description
fm	Micronesia	su	Soviet Union
fo	Faroe Islands	to	Tonga
fr	France	tv	Tuvalu
ge	Georgia	tw	Taiwan
gr	Greece	ua	Ukraine
hr	Croatia	us	United States
hu	Hungary	ws	Samoa

The Hosts File

Long ago, in a network far, far away, the entire Internet was small enough that network administrators could keep track of it all in a simple text file. This file, called the *Hosts file,* simply listed the name and IP address of every host on the network. Each computer had its own copy of the Hosts file. The trick was keeping all those Hosts files up to date. Whenever a new host was added to the Internet, each network administrator would manually update his copy of the Hosts file to add the new host's name and IP address.

As the Internet grew, so did the Hosts file. In the mid-1980s, it became obvious that a better solution was needed. Imagine trying to track the entire Internet today by using a single text file to record the name and IP address of the millions of hosts on the Internet! DNS was invented to solve this problem.

Understanding the Hosts file is important for two reasons:

✦ **The Hosts file is not dead.** For small networks, a Hosts file may still be the easiest way to provide name resolution for the network's computers. In addition, a Hosts file can coexist with DNS. The Hosts file is always checked before DNS is used, so you can even use a Hosts file to override DNS if you want.

✦ **The Hosts file is the precursor to DNS.** DNS was devised to circumvent the limitations of the Hosts file. You'll be in a better position to appreciate the benefits of DNS when you understand how the Hosts file works.

The Hosts file is a simple text file that contains lines that match IP addresses with host names. You can edit the Hosts file with any text editor, including Notepad or by using the MS-DOS EDIT command. The exact location of the Hosts file depends on the client operating system, as listed in Table 4-4.

Table 4-4	Location of the Hosts File
Operating System	*Location of Hosts File*
Windows 9x/Me	`c:\windows\hosts`
Windows NT/2000	`c:\winnt\system32\drivers\etc\hosts`
Windows XP and later	`c:\windows\system32\drivers\etc\hosts`
Unix/Linux	`/etc/hosts`

All TCP/IP implementations are installed with a starter Hosts file. For example, Listing 4-1 shows a typical Windows TCP/IP Hosts file. As you can see, the starter file begins with some comments that explain the purpose of the file.

The Hosts file ends with comments, which show the host mapping commands used to map for the host name `localhost`, mapped to the IP address `127.0.0.1`. The IP address `127.0.0.1` is the standard loopback address. As a result, this entry allows a computer to refer to itself by using the name `localhost`.

Note that after the `127.0.0.1 localhost` entry, another `localhost` entry defines the standard IPv6 loopback address (`::1`). This is required because unlike previous versions of Windows, Vista provides built-in support for IPv6.

Prior to Windows 7, these lines were not commented out in the Hosts file. But beginning with Windows 7, the name resolution for localhost is handled by DNS itself, so its definition isn't required in the Hosts file.

Listing 4-1: A Sample Hosts File

```
# Copyright (c) 1993-2009 Microsoft Corp.
#
# This is a sample HOSTS file used by Microsoft TCP/IP for Windows.
#
# This file contains the mappings of IP addresses to host names. Each
# entry should be kept on an individual line. The IP address should
# be placed in the first column followed by the corresponding host name.
# The IP address and the host name should be separated by at least one
# space.
#
# Additionally, comments (such as these) may be inserted on individual
# lines or following the machine name denoted by a '#' symbol.
#
# For example:
#
#      102.54.94.97     rhino.acme.com          # source server
#       38.25.63.10     x.acme.com              # x client host

# localhost name resolution is handled within DNS itself.
#127.0.0.1       localhost
#::1             localhost
```

To add an entry to the Hosts file, simply edit the file in any text editor. Then, add a line at the bottom of the file, after the `localhost` entry. Each line that you add should list the IP address and the host name that you want to use for the address. For example, to associate the host name `server1.LoweWriter.com` with the IP address `192.168.168.201`, you add this line to the Hosts file:

```
192.168.168.201 server1.LoweWriter.com
```

Then, whenever an application requests the IP address of the host name `server1.LoweWriter.com`, the IP address `192.168.168.201` is returned.

You can also add an alias to a host mapping. This enables users to access a host by using the alias as an alternative name. For example, consider the following line:

```
192.168.168.201 server1.LoweWriter.com s1
```

Here, the device at address `192.168.168.201` can be accessed as `server1.LoweWriter.com` or just `s1`.

Listing 4-2 shows a Hosts file with several hosts defined.

Listing 4-2: A Hosts File with Several Hosts Defined

```
# Copyright (c) 1993-2009 Microsoft Corp.
#
# This is a sample HOSTS file used by Microsoft TCP/IP for Windows.
#
# This file contains the mappings of IP addresses to host names. Each
# entry should be kept on an individual line. The IP address should
# be placed in the first column followed by the corresponding host name.
# The IP address and the host name should be separated by at least one
# space.
#
# Additionally, comments (such as these) may be inserted on individual
# lines or following the machine name denoted by a '#' symbol.
#
# For example:
#
#      102.54.94.97     rhino.acme.com        # source server
#       38.25.63.10     x.acme.com            # x client host

# localhost name resolution is handled within DNS itself.
# 127.0.0.1       localhost
# ::1             localhost

192.168.168.200 doug.LoweWriter.com         #Doug's computer
192.168.168.201 server1.LoweWriter.com s1   #Main server
192.168.168.202 debbie.LoweWriter.com       #Debbie's computer
192.168.168.203 printer1.LoweWriter.com p1  #HP Laser Printer
```

Book IV
Chapter 4

Using DNS

Even if your network uses DNS, every client still has a Hosts file that defines at least `localhost`.

Understanding DNS Servers and Zones

A *DNS server* is a computer that runs DNS server software, helps to maintain the DNS database, and responds to DNS name resolution requests from other computers. Although many DNS server implementations are available, the two most popular are BIND and the Windows DNS service. BIND runs on Unix-based computers (including Linux computers), and Windows DNS (naturally) runs on Windows computers. Both provide essentially the same services and can interoperate.

The key to understanding how DNS servers work is to realize that the DNS database — that is, the list of all the domains, subdomains, and host mappings — is a massively distributed database. No single DNS server contains the entire DNS database. Instead, authority over different parts of the database is delegated to different servers throughout the Internet.

For example, suppose that I set up a DNS server to handle name resolutions for my `LoweWriter.com` domain. Then, when someone requests the IP address of `doug.LoweWriter.com`, my DNS server can provide the answer. However, my DNS server wouldn't be responsible for the rest of the Internet. Instead, if someone asks my DNS server for the IP address of some other computer, such as `coyote.acme.com`, my DNS server will have to pass the request on to another DNS server that knows the answer.

Zones

To simplify the management of the DNS database, the entire DNS namespace is divided into zones, and the responsibility for each zone is delegated to a particular DNS server. In many cases, zones correspond directly to domains. For example, if I set up a domain named `LoweWriter.com`, I can also set up a DNS zone called `LoweWriter.com` that's responsible for the entire `LoweWriter.com` domain.

However, the subdomains that make up a domain can be parceled out to separate zones, as shown in Figure 4-2. Here, a domain named `LoweWriter.com` has been divided into two zones. One zone, `us.LoweWriter.com`, is responsible for the entire `us.LoweWriter.com` subdomain. The other zone, `LoweWriter.com`, is responsible for the entire `LoweWriter.com` domain except for the `us.LoweWriter.com` subdomain.

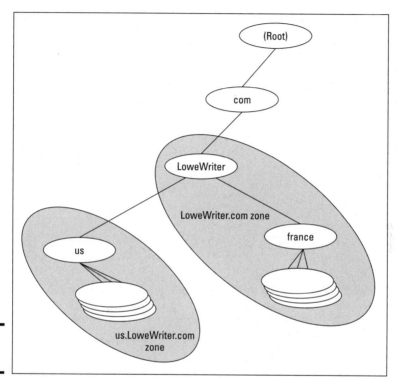

Figure 4-2:
DNS zones.

Why would you do that? The main reason is to delegate authority for the zone to separate servers. For example, Figure 4-2 suggests that part of the `LoweWriter.com` domain is administered in the United States and that part of it is administered in France. The two zones in the figure allow one server to be completely responsible for the U.S. portion of the domain, and the other server handles the rest of the domain.

The following are the two basic types of zones:

+ A **primary zone** is the master copy of a zone. The data for a primary zone is stored in the local database of the DNS server that hosts the primary zone. Only one DNS server can host a particular primary zone. Any updates to the zone must be made to the primary zone.

+ A **secondary zone** is a read-only copy of a zone. When a server hosts a secondary zone, the server doesn't store a local copy of the zone data. Instead, it obtains its copy of the zone from the zone's primary server by using a process called *zone transfer*. Secondary servers must periodically check primary servers to see whether their secondary zone data is still current. If not, a zone transfer is initiated to update the secondary zone.

The old phony Hosts file trick

The Hosts file can be the basis of a fun, practical joke. Of course, neither I nor my editors or publishers recommend that you actually do this. If it gets you into trouble, don't send your lawyers to me. This sidebar is here only to let you know what to do if it happens to you.

The idea is to edit your poor victim's Hosts file so that whenever the user tries to access his favorite website, a site of your choosing comes up instead. For example, if you're trying to get your husband to take you on a cruise, add a line to his Hosts file that replaces his favorite website with the website for a cruise line. For example, this line should do the trick:

```
151.124.250.181 www.espn.com
```

Now, whenever your husband tries to call up the ESPN website, he'll get the Carnival Cruise Lines home page instead.

Of course, to actually pull a stunt like this would be completely irresponsible, especially if you didn't first make a backup copy of the Hosts file, just in case it somehow gets messed up.

Be warned: If the wrong websites suddenly start coming up, check your Hosts file to see whether it's been tampered with.

Primary and secondary servers

Each DNS server is responsible for one or more zones. The following are the two different roles that a DNS server can take:

✦ **Primary server for a zone,** which means that the DNS server hosts a primary zone. The data for the zone is stored in files on the DNS server. Every zone must have one primary server.

✦ **Secondary server for a zone,** which means that the DNS server obtains the data for a secondary zone from a primary server. Every zone should have at least one secondary server. That way, if the primary server goes down, the domain defined by the zone can be accessed via the secondary server or servers.

A secondary server should be on a different subnet than the zone's primary server. If the primary and secondary servers are on the same subnet, both servers will be unavailable if the router that controls the subnet goes down.

Note that a single DNS server can be the primary server for some zones and a secondary server for other zones. A server is said to be *authoritative* for the primary and secondary zones that it hosts because it can provide definitive answers for queries against those zones.

Root servers

The core of DNS comprises the *root servers,* which are authoritative for the entire Internet. The main function of the root servers is to provide the address of the DNS servers that are responsible for each of the top-level domains. These servers, in turn, can provide the DNS server address for sub-domains beneath the top-level domains.

The root servers are a major part of the glue that holds the Internet together. As you can imagine, they're swamped with requests day and night. A total of 13 root servers are located throughout the world. Table 4-5 lists the IP address and the organization that oversees the operation of each of the 13 root servers.

Table 4-5		The 13 Root Servers
Server	*IP Address*	*Operator*
A	198.41.0.4	VeriSign Global Registry Services
B	192.228.79.201	Information Sciences Institute
C	192.33.4.12	Cogent Communications
D	128.8.10.90	University of Maryland
E	192.203.230.10	NASA Ames Research Center
F	192.5.5.241	Internet Systems Consortium
G	192.112.36.4	U.S. DOD Network Information
H	128.63.2.53	U.S. Army Research Lab
I	192.36.148.17	Autonomica
J	192.58.128.30	VeriSign Global Registry Services
K	193.0.14.129	Reseaux IP Europeens Network
L	199.7.83.42	ICANN
M	202.12.27.33	WIDE Project

DNS servers learn how to reach the root servers by consulting a *root hints* file that's located on the server. In the Unix/Linux world, this file is known as `named.root` and can be found at `/etc/named.root`. For Windows DNS servers, the file is called `cache.dns` and can be found in `\windows\system32\dns\` or `\winnt\system32\dns\`, depending on the Windows version. Listing 4-3 shows the file itself.

**Book IV
Chapter 4**

Using DNS

Listing 4-3: The `named.root` File

```
;       This file holds the information on root name servers needed to
;       initialize cache of Internet domain name servers
;       (e.g. reference this file in the "cache  .  <file>"
;       configuration file of BIND domain name servers).
;
;       This file is made available by InterNIC
;       under anonymous FTP as
;           file                /domain/named.root
;           on server           FTP.INTERNIC.NET
;       -OR-                    RS.INTERNIC.NET
;
;       last update:    Dec 12, 2008
;       related version of root zone:   2008121200
;
; formerly NS.INTERNIC.NET
;
.                           3600000  IN  NS   A.ROOT-SERVERS.NET.
A.ROOT-SERVERS.NET.         3600000      A    198.41.0.4
A.ROOT-SERVERS.NET.         3600000      AAAA 2001:503:BA3E::2:30
;
; FORMERLY NS1.ISI.EDU
;
.                           3600000      NS   B.ROOT-SERVERS.NET.
B.ROOT-SERVERS.NET.         3600000      A    192.228.79.201
;
; FORMERLY C.PSI.NET
;
.                           3600000      NS   C.ROOT-SERVERS.NET.
C.ROOT-SERVERS.NET.         3600000      A    192.33.4.12
;
; FORMERLY TERP.UMD.EDU
;
.                           3600000      NS   D.ROOT-SERVERS.NET.
D.ROOT-SERVERS.NET.         3600000      A    128.8.10.90
;
; FORMERLY NS.NASA.GOV
;
.                           3600000      NS   E.ROOT-SERVERS.NET.
E.ROOT-SERVERS.NET.         3600000      A    192.203.230.10
;
; FORMERLY NS.ISC.ORG
;
.                           3600000      NS   F.ROOT-SERVERS.NET.
F.ROOT-SERVERS.NET.         3600000      A    192.5.5.241
F.ROOT-SERVERS.NET.         3600000      AAAA 2001:500:2F::F
;
; FORMERLY NS.NIC.DDN.MIL
;
.                           3600000      NS   G.ROOT-SERVERS.NET.
G.ROOT-SERVERS.NET.         3600000      A    192.112.36.4
;
; FORMERLY AOS.ARL.ARMY.MIL
;
.                           3600000      NS   H.ROOT-SERVERS.NET.
H.ROOT-SERVERS.NET.         3600000      A    128.63.2.53
H.ROOT-SERVERS.NET.         3600000      AAAA 2001:500:1::803F:235
;
```

```
; FORMERLY NIC.NORDU.NET
;
.                          3600000      NS     I.ROOT-SERVERS.NET.
I.ROOT-SERVERS.NET.        3600000      A      192.36.148.17
;
; OPERATED BY VERISIGN, INC.
;
.                          3600000      NS     J.ROOT-SERVERS.NET.
J.ROOT-SERVERS.NET.        3600000      A      192.58.128.30
J.ROOT-SERVERS.NET.        3600000      AAAA   2001:503:C27::2:30
;
; OPERATED BY RIPE NCC
;
.                          3600000      NS     K.ROOT-SERVERS.NET.
K.ROOT-SERVERS.NET.        3600000      A      193.0.14.129
K.ROOT-SERVERS.NET.        3600000      AAAA   2001:7FD::1
;
; OPERATED BY ICANN
;
.                          3600000      NS     L.ROOT-SERVERS.NET.
L.ROOT-SERVERS.NET.        3600000      A      199.7.83.42
L.ROOT-SERVERS.NET.        3600000      AAAA   2001:500:3::42
;
; OPERATED BY WIDE
;
.                          3600000      NS     M.ROOT-SERVERS.NET.
M.ROOT-SERVERS.NET.        3600000      A      202.12.27.33
M.ROOT-SERVERS.NET.        3600000      AAAA   2001:DC3::35
; End of File
```

Caching

DNS servers don't really like doing all that work to resolve DNS names, but they're not stupid. They know that if a user visits www.wiley.com today, he'll probably do it again tomorrow. As a result, name servers keep a cache of query results. The next time the user visits www.wiley.com, the name server is able to resolve this name without having to query all those other name servers.

The Internet is constantly changing, however, so cached data can quickly become obsolete. For example, suppose that Wiley Publishing, Inc., switches its website to a different server? It can update its name servers to reflect the new IP address, but any name servers that have a cached copy of the query will be out of date.

To prevent this from being a major problem, DNS data is given a relatively short expiration time. The expiration value for DNS data is called the *TTL* (Time to Live). TTL is specified in seconds. Thus, a TTL of 60 means the data is kept for one minute.

Understanding DNS Queries

When a DNS client needs to resolve a DNS name to an IP address, it uses a library routine — a *resolver* — to handle the query. The resolver takes care of sending the query message over the network to the DNS server, receiving and interpreting the response, and informing the client of the results of the query.

A DNS client can make two basic types of queries: recursive and iterative. The following list describes the difference between these two query types. (The following discussion assumes that the client is asking the server for the IP address of a host name, which is the most common type of DNS query. You find out about other types of queries later; they, too, can be either recursive or iterative.)

✦ **Recursive queries:** When a client issues a *recursive DNS query,* the server must reply with either the IP address of the requested host name or an error message indicating that the host name doesn't exist. If the server doesn't have the information, it asks another DNS server for the IP address. When the first server finally gets the IP address, it sends it back to the client. If the server determines that the information doesn't exist, it returns an error message.

✦ **Iterative queries:** When a server receives an iterative query, it returns the IP address of the requested host name if it knows the address. If the server doesn't know the address, it returns a *referral,* which is simply the address of a DNS server that should know. The client can then issue an iterative query to the server to which it was referred.

Normally, DNS clients issue recursive queries to DNS servers. If the server knows the answer to the query, it replies directly to the client. If not, the server issues an iterative query to a DNS server that it thinks should know the answer. If the original server gets an answer from the second server, it returns the answer to the client. If the original server gets a referral to a third server, the original server issues an iterative query to the third server. The original server keeps issuing iterative queries until it either gets the answer or an error occurs. It then returns the answer or the error to the client.

A real-life DNS example

Confused? I can understand why. An example may help to clear things up. Suppose that a user wants to view the web page `www.wiley.com`. The following sequence of steps occurs to resolve this address:

1. The browser asks the client computer's resolver to find the IP address of `www.wiley.com`.

2. The resolver issues a recursive DNS query to its name server.

   In this case, I'll call the name server `ns1.LoweWriter.com`.

3. The name server `ns1LoweWriter.com` checks whether it knows the IP address of `www.wiley.com`.

   It doesn't, so the name server issues an iterative query to one of the root name servers to see whether it knows the IP address of `www.wiley.com`.

4. The root name server doesn't know the IP address of `www.wiley.com`, so it returns a list of the name servers that are authoritative for the `com` domain.

5. The `ns1.LoweWriter.com` name server picks one of the `com` domain name servers and sends it an iterative query for `www.wiley.com`.

6. The `com` name server doesn't know the IP address of `www.wiley.com`, so it returns a list of the name servers that are authoritative for the `wiley.com` domain.

7. The `ns1.LoweWriter.com` name server picks one of the name servers for the `wiley.com` domain and sends it an iterative query for `www.wiley.com`.

8. The `wiley.com` name server knows the IP address for `www.wiley.com`, so the name server returns it.

9. The `ns1.LoweWriter.com` name server shouts with joy for having finally found the IP address for `www.wiley.com`. It gleefully returns this address to the client. It also caches the answer so that the next time the user looks for `www.wiley.com`, the name server won't have to contact other name servers to resolve the name.

10. The client also caches the results of the query.

    The next time the client needs to look for `www.wiley.com`, the client can resolve the name without troubling the name server.

Zone Files and Resource Records

Each DNS zone is defined by a *zone file* (also known as a *DNS database* or a *master file*). For Windows DNS servers, the name of the zone file is *domain*.zone. For example, the zone file for the `LoweWriter.com` zone is named `LoweWriter.com.zone`. For Bind DNS servers, the zone files are named db.*domain*. Thus, the zone file for the `LoweWriter.com` domain would be `db.LoweWriter.com`. The format of the zone file contents is the same for both systems, however.

A zone file consists of one or more resource records. Creating and updating the resource records that comprise the zone files is one of the primary tasks of a DNS administrator. The Windows DNS server provides a friendly graphical interface to the resource records. However, you should still be familiar with how to construct resource records.

Resource records are written as simple text lines, with the following fields:

```
Owner    TTL    Class    Type    RDATA
```

These fields must be separated from each other by one or more spaces. The following list describes the five resource record fields:

+ **Owner:** The name of the DNS domain or the host that the record applies to. This is usually specified as a fully qualified domain name (with a trailing dot) or as a simple host name (without a trailing dot), which is then interpreted in the context of the current domain.

   You can also specify a single @ symbol as the owner name. In that case, the current domain is used.

+ **TTL:** Also known as *Time to Live;* the number of seconds that the record should be retained in a server's cache before it's invalidated. If you omit the TTL value for a resource record, a default TTL is obtained from the Start of Authority (SOA) record.

+ **Class:** Defines the protocol to which the record applies. You should always specify IN, for the Internet protocol. If you omit the class field, the last class field that you specified explicitly is used. As a result, you'll sometimes see zone files that specify IN only on the first resource record (which must be an SOA record) and then allow it to default to IN on all subsequent records.

+ **Type:** The resource record type. The most commonly used resource types are summarized in Table 4-6 and are described separately later in this section. Like the Class field, you can also omit the Type field and allow it to default to the last specified value.

+ **RDATA:** Resource record data that is specific to each record type.

Table 4-6		Common Resource Record Types
Type	*Name*	*Description*
SOA	Start of Authority	Identifies a zone
NS	Name Server	Identifies a name server that is authoritative for the zone
A	Address	Maps a fully qualified domain name to an IP address

(continued)

Type	Name	Description
CNAME	Canonical Name	Creates an alias for a fully qualified domain name
MX	Mail Exchange	Identifies the mail server for a domain
PTR	Pointer	Maps an IP address to a fully qualified domain name for reverse lookups

Most resource records fit on one line. If a record requires more than one line, you must enclose the data that spans multiple lines in parentheses.

You can include comments to clarify the details of a zone file. A comment begins with a semicolon and continues to the end of the line. If a line begins with a semicolon, the entire line is a comment. You can also add a comment to the end of a resource record. You see examples of both types of comments later in this chapter.

SOA records

Every zone must begin with an SOA record, which names the zone and provides default information for the zone. Table 4-7 lists the fields that appear in the RDATA section of an SOA record. Note that these fields are positional, so you should include a value for all of them and list them in the order specified. Because the SOA record has so many RDATA fields, you'll probably need to use parentheses to continue the SOA record onto multiple lines.

Table 4-7	RDATA Fields for an SOA Record
Name	*Description*
MNAME	The domain name of the name server that is authoritative for the zone.
RNAME	An e-mail address (specified in domain name format; not regular e-mail format) of the person responsible for this zone.
SERIAL	The serial number of the zone. Secondary zones use this value to determine whether they need to initiate a zone transfer to update their copy of the zone.
REFRESH	A time interval that specifies how often a secondary server should check whether the zone needs to be refreshed. A typical value is 3600 (one hour).
RETRY	A time interval that specifies how long a secondary server should wait after requesting a zone transfer before trying again. A typical value is 600 (ten minutes).

(continued)

Book IV
Chapter 4

Using DNS

Table 4-7 *(continued)*

Name	Description
EXPIRE	A time interval that specifies how long a secondary server should keep the zone data before discarding it. A typical value is 86400 (one day).
MINIMUM	A time interval that specifies the TTL value to use for zone resource records that omit the TTL field. A typical value is 3600 (one hour).

Note two things about the SOA fields:

✦ **The e-mail address of the person responsible for the zone is given in DNS format, not in normal e-mail format.** Thus, you separate the user from the mail domain with a dot rather than an @ symbol. For example, doug@LoweWriter.com would be listed as doug.lowewriter.com.

✦ **The serial number should be incremented every time you change the zone file.** If you edit the file via the graphic interface provided by Windows DNS, the serial number is incremented automatically. However, if you edit the zone file via a simple text editor, you have to manually increment the serial number.

Here's a typical example of an SOA record, with judicious comments to identify each field:

```
lowewriter.com. IN  SOA (
    ns1.lowewriter.com         ; authoritative name server
    doug.lowewriter.com        ; responsible person
    148                        ; version number
    3600                       ; refresh (1 hour)
    600                        ; retry (10 minutes)
    86400                      ; expire (1 day)
    3600 )                     ; minimum TTL (1 hour)
```

NS records

Name server (NS) records identify the name servers that are authoritative for the zone. Every zone must have at least one NS record. Using two or more NS records is better so that if the first name server is unavailable, the zone will still be accessible.

The owner field should either be the fully qualified domain name for the zone, with a trailing dot, or an @ symbol. The RDATA consists of just one field: the fully qualified domain name of the name server.

The following examples show two NS records that serve the `lowewriter.com` domain:

```
lowewriter.com.   IN  NS  ns1.lowewriter.com.
lowewriter.com.   IN  NS  ns2.lowewriter.com.
```

A records

Address (A) records are the meat of the zone file: They provide the IP addresses for each of the hosts that you want to make accessible via DNS. In an A record, you usually list just the host name in the owner field, thus allowing DNS to add the domain name to derive the fully qualified domain name for the host. The RDATA field for the A record is the IP address of the host.

The following lines define various hosts for the `LoweWriter.com` domain:

```
doug       IN  A  192.168.168.200
server1    IN  A  192.168.168.201
debbie     IN  A  192.168.168.202
printer1   IN  A  192.168.168.203
router1    IN  A  207.126.127.129
www        IN  A  64.71.129.102
```

Notice that for these lines, I don't specify the fully qualified domain names for each host. Instead, I just provide the host name. DNS will add the name of the zone's domain to these host names in order to create the fully qualified domain names.

If I wanted to be more explicit, I could list these A records like this:

```
doug.lowewriter.com.       IN  A  192.168.168.200
server1.lowewriter.com.    IN  A  192.168.168.201
debbie.lowewriter.com.     IN  A  192.168.168.202
printer1.lowewriter.com.   IN  A  192.168.168.203
router1.lowewriter.com     IN  A  207.126.127.129
www.lowewriter.com.        IN  A  64.71.129.102
```

Book IV
Chapter 4

Using DNS

However, all this does is increase the chance for error. Plus, it creates more work for you later if you decide to change your network's domain.

CNAME records

A *Canonical Name* (CNAME) record creates an alias for a fully qualified domain name. When a user attempts to access a domain name that is actually an alias, the DNS system substitutes the real domain name — known as the *Canonical Name* — for the alias. The owner field in the CNAME record provides the name of the alias that you want to create. Then, the RDATA field provides the Canonical Name — that is, the real name of the host.

For example, consider these resource records:

```
ftp.lowewriter.com.      IN  A      207.126.127.132
files.lowewriter.com.    IN  CNAME  www1.lowewriter.com.
```

Here, the host name of an FTP server at `207.126.127.132` is `ftp.lowewriter.com`. The CNAME record allows users to access this host as `files.lowewriter.com` if they prefer.

PTR records

A *Pointer* (PTR) record is the opposite of an address record: It provides the fully qualified domain name for a given address. The owner field should specify the reverse lookup domain name, and the RDATA field specifies the fully qualified domain name. For example, the following record maps the address `64.71.129.102` to `www.lowewriter.com`:

```
102.129.71.64.in-addr.arpa. IN  PTR  www.lowewriter.com.
```

PTR records don't usually appear in normal domain zones. Instead, they appear in special reverse lookup zones. For more information, see the section "Reverse Lookup Zones," later in this chapter.

MX records

Mail Exchange (MX) records identify the mail server for a domain. The owner field provides the domain name that users address mail to. The RDATA section of the record has two fields. The first is a priority number used to determine which mail servers to use when several are available. The second is the fully qualified domain name of the mail server itself.

For example, consider the following MX records:

```
lowewriter.com.      IN  MX  0   mail1.lowewriter.com.
lowewriter.com.      IN  MX  10  mail2.lowewriter.com.
```

In this example, the `lowewriter.com` domain has two mail servers, named `mail1.lowewriter.com` and `mail2.lowewriter.com`. The priority numbers for these servers are 0 and 10. Because it has a lower priority number, mail will be delivered to `mail1.lowewriter.com` first. The `mail2.lowewriter.com` server will be used only if `mail1.lowewriter.com` isn't available.

The server name specified in the RDATA section should be an actual host name, not an alias created by a CNAME record. Although some mail servers can handle MX records that point to CNAMEs, not all can. As a result, you shouldn't specify an alias in an MX record.

Be sure to create a reverse lookup record (PTR, described in the next section) for your mail servers. Some mail servers won't accept mail from a server that doesn't have valid reverse lookup entries.

Reverse Lookup Zones

Normal DNS queries ask a name server to provide the IP address that corresponds to a fully qualified domain name. This kind of query is a *forward lookup*. A *reverse lookup* is the opposite of a forward lookup: It returns the fully qualified domain name of a host based on its IP address.

Reverse lookups are possible because of a special domain called the `in-addr.arpa` domain, which provides a separate fully qualified domain name for every possible IP address on the Internet. To enable a reverse lookup for a particular IP address, all you have to do is create a PTR record in a reverse lookup zone (a zone that is authoritative for a portion of the `in-addr.arpa` domain). The PTR record maps the `in-addr.arpa` domain name for the address to the host's actual domain name.

The technique used to create the reverse domain name for a given IP address is pretty clever. It creates subdomains beneath the `in-addr.arpa` domain by using the octets of the IP address, listing them in reverse order. For example, the reverse domain name for the IP address `207.126.67.129` is `129.67.126.207.in-addr.arpa`.

Why list the octets in reverse order? Because that correlates the network portions of the IP address (which work from left to right) with the subdomain structure of DNS names (which works from right to left). The following description should clear this up:

✦ The 255 possible values for the first octet of an IP address each have a subdomain beneath the `in-addr.arpa` domain. For example, any IP address that begins with `207` can be found in the `207.in-addr.arpa` domain.

✦ Within this domain, each of the possible values for the second octet can be found as a subdomain of the first octet's domain. Thus, any address that begins with `207.126` can be found in the `126.207.in-addr.arpa` domain.

✦ The same holds true for the third octet, so any address that begins with `207.126.67` can be found in the `67.126.207.in-addr.arpa` domain.

✦ By the time you get to the fourth octet, you've pinpointed a specific host. The fourth octet completes the fully qualified reverse domain name. Thus, `207.126.67.129` is mapped to `129.67.126.207.in-addr.arpa`.

As a result, to determine the fully qualified domain name for the computer at `207.126.67.129`, the client queries its DNS server for the FQDN that corresponds to `129.67.126.207.in-addr.arpa`.

Working with the Windows DNS Server

Installing and managing a DNS server depends on the network operating system (NOS) that you're using. The following sections are specific to working with a DNS server in Windows Server 2012. Working with Bind in a Unix/Linux environment is similar but without the help of a graphical user interface (GUI).

You can install the DNS server on Windows Server 2012 from the Server Manager application. Open the Server Manager and choose Manage➪Add Roles and Features. Then, follow the wizard's instructions to add the DNS Role.

After you set up a DNS server, you can manage the DNS server from the DNS management console, as shown in Figure 4-3. From this management console, you can perform common administrative tasks, such as adding additional zones, changing zone settings, adding A or MX records to an existing zone, and so on. The DNS management console hides the details of the actual resource records from you, thus allowing you to work with a friendly GUI instead.

To add a new host (that is, an A record) to a zone, right-click the zone in the DNS management console and choose the Add New Host command. This brings up the New Host dialog box, as shown in Figure 4-4. From this dialog box, specify the following information.

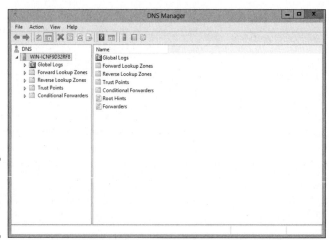

Figure 4-3:
The DNS
management
console.

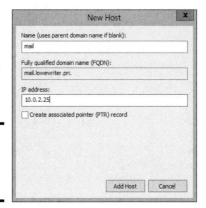

Figure 4-4:
The New
Host dialog
box.

+ **Name:** The host name for the new host.

+ **IP Address:** The host's IP address.

+ **Create Associated Pointer (PTR) Record:** Automatically creates a PTR record in the reverse lookup zone file. Select this option if you want to allow reverse lookups for the host.

You can add other records, such as MX or CNAME records, in the same way.

How to Configure a Windows DNS Client

Client computers don't need much configuration in order to work properly with DNS. The client must have the address of at least one DNS server. Usually, this address is supplied by DHCP, so if the client is configured to obtain its IP address from a DHCP server, it will also obtain the DNS server address from DHCP.

To configure a client computer to obtain the DNS server location from DHCP, bring up the Network Properties dialog box by choosing Network or Network Connections in Control Panel (depending on which version of Windows the client is running). Then, select the Internet Protocol Version 4 (TCP/IPv4) protocol and click the Properties button. This summons the dialog box shown in Figure 4-5. To configure the computer to use Dynamic Host Configuration Protocol (DHCP), select the Obtain an IP Address Automatically and the Obtain DNS Server Address Automatically options.

If the computer doesn't use DHCP, you can use this same dialog box to manually enter the IP address of your DNS server.

**Book IV
Chapter 4**

Using DNS

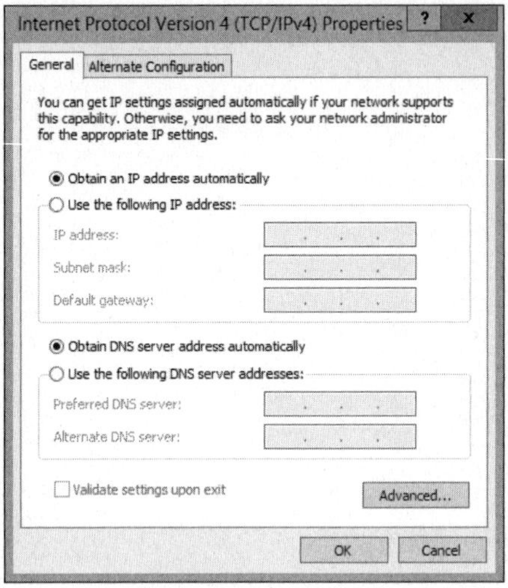

Figure 4-5:
Configuring
a Windows
client to
obtain
its DNS
address
from DHCP.

Internet Protocol Version 4 (TCP/IPv4) Properties

General | Alternate Configuration

You can get IP settings assigned automatically if your network supports this capability. Otherwise, you need to ask your network administrator for the appropriate IP settings.

○ Obtain an IP address automatically
○ Use the following IP address:

IP address:
Subnet mask:
Default gateway:

○ Obtain DNS server address automatically
○ Use the following DNS server addresses:

Preferred DNS server:
Alternate DNS server:

☐ Validate settings upon exit

Advanced...

OK   Cancel

Chapter 5: Using FTP

In This Chapter

✓ **Figuring out the basics of FTP**

✓ **Setting up an FTP server**

✓ **Retrieving files from an FTP server**

✓ **Using FTP commands**

*F*ile Transfer Protocol (FTP) is the basic method for exchanging files over the Internet. If you need to access files from someone's FTP site, this chapter shows you how to do so by using a web browser or a command line FTP client. If you need to set up your own FTP server to share files with other users, this chapter shows you how to do that, too.

Discovering FTP

FTP is as old as the Internet. The first versions of FTP date to the early 1970s, and even the current FTP standard (RFC 959) dates to 1985. You can use FTP with the command line FTP client (which has a decidedly 1980s feel to it), or you can access FTP sites with most modern web browsers if you prefer a graphic interface. Old computer hounds prefer the FTP command line client, probably for nostalgic reasons.

In spite of its age, FTP is still commonly used on the Internet. For example, InterNIC (the organization that manages Internet names) maintains an FTP site at `ftp://ftp.rs.internic.net`. There, you can download important files, such as `named.root`, which provides the current location of the Internet's root name servers. Many other companies maintain FTP sites from which you can download software, device drivers, documentation, reports, and so on. FTP is also one of the most common ways to publish HTML files to a web server. Because FTP is still so widely used, it pays to know how to use it from both the command line and from a browser.

In the Windows world, an FTP server is integrated with the Microsoft web server, Internet Information Services (IIS). As a result, you can manage FTP from the IIS management console along with other IIS features. Note that the FTP component is an optional part of IIS, so you may need to install it separately if you opted to not include it when you first installed IIS.

On Unix and Linux systems, FTP isn't usually integrated with a web server. Instead, the FTP server is installed as a separate program. You're usually given the option to install FTP when you install the operating system. If you choose not to, you can always install it later.

When you run an FTP server, you expose a portion of your file system to the outside world. As a result, you need to be careful about how you set up your FTP server so that you don't accidentally allow hackers access to the bowels of your file server. Fortunately, the default configuration of FTP is pretty secure. You shouldn't tinker much with the default configuration unless you know what you're doing.

Configuring an FTP Server

In the following sections, I show you how to configure FTP services in Microsoft IIS. The examples show IIS version 8 running on Windows Server 2012, but the procedures are essentially the same for other IIS versions.

Installing FTP

Although FTP is integrated with IIS, FTP is not installed by default when you install IIS. As a result, if you didn't specifically select FTP when you installed IIS, you need to install FTP before you can set up an FTP site. Here are the procedures for Windows Server 2003, 2008, and 2012:

✦ **Windows Server 2003:** Install the FTP protocol by choosing Control Panel➪Add or Remove Programs➪Add/Remove Windows Components. Then, select Application Server from the list of components, click Details, and choose Internet Information Services (IIS). Click Details again and then select File Transfer Protocol (FTP) from the list of IIS subcomponents. Finally, click OK to install FTP. If asked, you'll need to insert the Windows Server 2003 setup disc.

✦ **Windows Server 2008:** Choose Start➪Server Manager and select the Web Server (IIS) role. Scroll down to the Role Services section and then click Add Role Services. Select the FTP Server role, click Next, and then click Install.

✦ **Windows Server 2012:** Start Server Manager and choose Manage➪Add Roles and Features. When you get to the page that lists the server roles, expand the Web Server (IIS) node and select the FTP Server role. Then complete the wizard to install the FTP service.

Creating an FTP site

After you install FTP, you must create at least one FTP site. Here are the steps for Windows Server 2012, and the procedure for earlier versions is similar:

1. **Open Server Manager and choose Tools⇨Internet Information Services (IIS) Manager.**

This launches the IIS Manager console, as shown in Figure 5-1.

2. **Right-click the Sites node and choose Add FTP Site.**

The first page of the Add FTP Site Wizard appears, as shown in Figure 5-2.

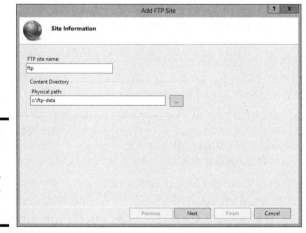

Book IV
Chapter 5

Using FTP

3. Enter your site information.

a. *Enter a name for your FTP site.*

b. *Enter the path to the folder that will hold the FTP site's data.*

This field determines the location on the server where the data stored on the FTP site will be located. If you don't know the exact path, click the Browse button and browse to the folder location.

4. Click Next.

The second page of the Add FTP Site Wizard appears, as shown in Figure 5-3. On this page, you set the IP address and port number that the FTP site will use.

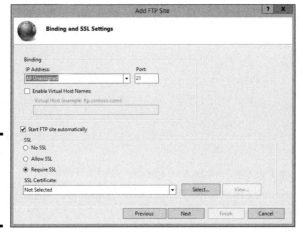

Figure 5-3:
Set the port and SSL security here.

a. *Leave the IP Address and Port fields unchanged unless you want to use a nonstandard port.*

By default, the FTP site will use port 21, which is the standard port for the FTP protocol.

b. *Select the SSL security option you want to use.*

If you have an SSL certificate and want to use SSL security, select either Allow SSL or Require SSL. If you select Allow SSL, users can access your site with or without SSL security. If you select Require SSL, users must always use SSL security to access the FTP site.

If you don't have a certificate available or if the site will contain data that doesn't require tight security, select No SSL.

5. **Click Next.**

   The third page of the Add FTP Site Wizard appears, as shown in
   Figure 5-4, where you set authentication and authorization to be used
   for the site.

Figure 5-4:
Set basic
login
security
here.

- *Anonymous:* Select the Anonymous option if you want to allow anonymous users to access your FTP site.

  If you select this option, users can access your FTP site without providing any login information. You should specify this option only for
  sites that have no security requirements.

- *Basic:* Select the Basic option if you want to allow Basic authentication.

  This option allows users to log in using a Windows username and
  password. Note that because this option transmits the password in
  unencrypted form, you should use it only when you know that the
  connection between the user and the FTP server is secure.

- *Select the user access permissions you want to grant.*

  You can grant Read and Write permissions to All Users (as shown in
  the figure), to anonymous users, and to individual users or groups.

  Do not grant Write permissions to anonymous users. If you do, your
  FTP site will quickly become a dumping ground for all kinds of trash
  as word gets out about your totally unsecured FTP site.

6. **Click Finish.**

   Your FTP site is created!

**Book IV
Chapter 5**

Using FTP

Changing the FTP site properties

You can change the properties for an FTP site by selecting the site in IIS Manager. This brings up a page with several icons that let you change various settings for the site, as shown in Figure 5-5.

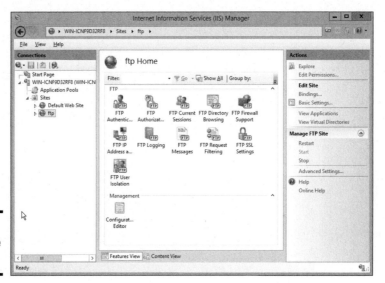

Figure 5-5:
The FTP site page.

The following are the more important icons found on the FTP Site Properties page for configuring the properties of your FTP site:

✦ **FTP Authentication:** Enable or disable Anonymous and Basic authentication for the FTP site.

✦ **FTP Authorization:** Grant access rights to individual users, groups of users, anonymous users, or all users.

✦ **FTP Current Sessions:** Display a list of users who are currently accessing the FTP site.

✦ **FTP Directory Browsing:** Set several options that determine how users can browse the data directories in the FTP site.

✦ **FTP Firewall Support:** Set several advanced options for working with firewalls. Best leave these settings alone unless you're a firewall guru.

✦ **FTP IPv4 Address and Domain Restrictions:** Grant or deny access to users based on their IP addresses or domain names. This page is useful if you want to restrict access to a specific set of users.

✦ **FTP Logging:** Control logging for the site.

✦ **FTP Messages:** Create four customized messages that appear when users access the site, as shown in Figure 5-6.

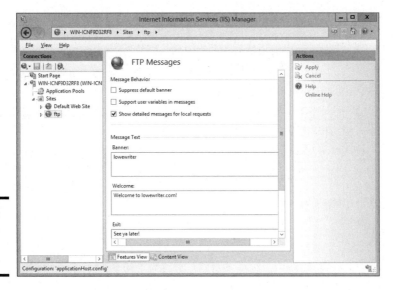

Figure 5-6:
Customize
the site's
messages.

The four messages you can configure are:

- The *Banner message* appears when a user first accesses the site, before he or she has logged on. If the site allows anonymous logons, you may mention that in the Banner message.

- The *Welcome message* appears after the user has successfully logged on to your site.

- The *Exit message* appears when the user leaves the site.

- The *Maximum Connections message* appears when the connection limit has been exceeded.

Adding content to your FTP site

When you set up an FTP site, the data for the site is stored in a folder on one of the server's disks. To make your FTP site useful, you'll need to add files to this folder. Those files will then be available for download on the site. The easiest way to do that is to simply open Windows Explorer, browse to the folder, and copy the files you want to include. If you're not sure where the site's home folder is located, you can find it by opening the site in IIS Manager and choosing the site in the IIS Manager and clicking Basic Settings in the task pane on the right side of the screen.

The following list offers some useful tips for setting up FTP site content:

✦ **Create a `readme.txt` file in the FTP site's home directory that describes the content and rules for your site.** Hopefully, users will view this file when they visit your site. There's no guarantee that they will, but you can always hope.

✦ **If your site has a lot of files, organize them into subdirectories beneath the home directory.**

✦ **Stick to short filenames.** Users working with command line clients appreciate brevity because they'll have to type the filenames accurately to retrieve your files.

✦ **Don't use spaces in filenames.** Some clients balk at names that include spaces.

Accessing an FTP Site with a Browser

Modern web browsers include built-in support for FTP. Internet Explorer lets you access an FTP site almost as if it were a local disk. You can even drag and drop files to and from an FTP site.

To access an FTP site in a web browser, just type the name of the site in the address bar. If you want, you can explicitly specify the FTP protocol by typing **ftp://** before the FTP site name, but that's usually not necessary. The browser determines that the name you type is an FTP site and invokes the FTP protocol automatically.

Figure 5-7 shows you how a typical FTP site appears when accessed with Windows Explorer on a Windows 7 system. As you can see, the files and folders appear as if they were on a local disk. Double-click a folder to display the files contained in that folder; download files by dragging them from the browser window to the desktop or to another window. You can also upload files by dragging them from the desktop or another window into the FTP browser window.

If the contents of an FTP site don't appear in the browser window, you may need to log on to the site. Choose File⇨Login As to display the Log On As dialog box. If the site administrator has given you a name and password, you can enter it here to access the site. Otherwise, select the Log On Anonymously check box and then click the Log On button.

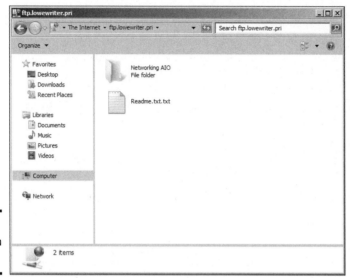

Figure 5-7:
Browsing an
FTP site.

Using an FTP Command Line Client

If you're a command line junkie, you'll appreciate the FTP command that comes with Windows. It isn't pretty, but it gets the job done. At the end of this chapter, you can find a command reference that details all the subcommands you can use with the FTP command. In this section, I just show you a typical session in which I sign on to an FTP server named ftp. lowewriter.com, switch to a directory named pics, download a file, and then log off.

First, open a command window: Choose Start➪Run, type **Command** in the text box, and then click OK. Navigate to the directory to where you want to download files. This step is important because although you can change the local working directory from within the FTP command, it's much easier to just start FTP from the right directory.

To start FTP, type **ftp** with the name of the FTP server as the parameter, like this:

```
C:\>ftp ftp.lowewriter.com
```

Assuming that you typed the site name correctly, the FTP command con-nects to the site, displays the banner message, and prompts you to log on:

```
Connected to ftp.lowewriter.com.
220-Microsoft FTP Service
220 We have 999 spooks here, but there's always room for one
    more! To volunteer, log in as Anonymous.
User (ftp.lowewriter.com:(none)):
```

To log on anonymously, type **Anonymous** and then press Enter. The server responds by telling you that Anonymous access is allowed and asks for your e-mail address as a password:

```
331 Anonymous access allowed, send identity (e-mail name) as
    password.
Password:
```

Type your e-mail address as the password and then press Enter. The Welcome message appears, followed by the ftp> prompt:

```
230-Welcome to my FTP site! For spooky Halloween pictures,
    check out the Pics folder.
230 Anonymous user logged in.
ftp>
```

Whenever you see the ftp> prompt, the FTP command is waiting for you to enter a subcommand. Start by entering **dir** to see a directory listing:

```
200 PORT command successful.
150 Opening ASCII mode data connection for /bin/ls.
06-30-07  08:05PM       <DIR>          pics
06-30-07  07:55PM                 2365 readme.txt
06-30-07  07:55PM       <DIR>          sounds
06-30-07  07:56PM       <DIR>          videos
226 Transfer complete.
ftp: 190 bytes received in 0.00Seconds 190000.00Kbytes/sec.
ftp>
```

As you can see, the response from the dir command isn't quite as clean as the display from an MS-DOS command. Still, you can pick out that the direc-tory includes three subdirectories — pics, sounds, and videos — and a single file, named readme.txt. The size of the file is 2,365 bytes.

Here's a good question: If you enter a dir command, why does the response read 200 PORT command successful? The answer has to do with how the FTP protocol works. When you enter a dir command, the FTP client for-wards a PORT command to the server that opens a data transfer port that is then used to return the resulting directory listing. The server replies that the PORT command has successfully opened a data transfer port. Then, it sends back the directory listing. Finally, it sends two more lines: one to indicate that the transfer is complete (that is, that the `dir` output has been success-fully sent), and the other to summarize the number of bytes of data that were sent and the data transfer rate.

The files that I want to download are located in the `pics` subdirectory, so the next command to issue is `cd pics`. This results in the following output:

```
250 CWD command successful.
ftp>
```

Once again, the command's output isn't exactly what you'd expect. The FTP protocol doesn't actually have a CD command. Instead, it uses a command named CWD, which stands for *change working directory,* to change the direc-tory. The Windows FTP client uses command CD instead of CWD to be more consistent with the Windows/MS-DOS user interface, which uses the com-mand CD to change directories. When you type a CD command at the `ftp>` prompt, the FTP client sends a CWD command to the FTP server. The server then replies with the message CWD command successful to indicate that the directory has been changed.

Next, type **dir** again. The FTP server displays the directory listing for the `pics` directory:

```
200 PORT command successful.
150 Opening ASCII mode data connection for /bin/ls.
06-27-07  10:04PM              123126 door.jpg
06-27-07  10:06PM              112457 echair.jpg
06-27-07  10:06PM               81610 fence.jpg
06-27-07  10:09PM              138102 fog.jpg
06-27-07  10:09PM               83712 gallows.jpg
06-27-07  10:10PM              166741 ghost.jpg
06-27-07  09:58PM              119859 skel01.jpg
06-27-07  10:05PM               87720 wall.jpg
226 Transfer complete.
ftp: 400 bytes received in 0.00Seconds 400000.00Kbytes/sec.
ftp>
```

Here, you can see that the `pics` directory contains eight files. To download a file, you use the GET command, specifying the name of the file that you want to download. For example, to download the `door.jpg` file, type **get door.jpg**. The FTP server transfers the file to your computer and displays the following response:

```
200 PORT command successful.
150 Opening ASCII mode data connection for door.jpg(123126 bytes).
226 Transfer complete.
ftp: 123126 bytes received in 0.13Seconds 985.01Kbytes/sec.
ftp>
```

**Book IV
Chapter 5**

Using FTP

Notice again that the response indicates that the command actually processed by the server is a PORT command. The file is transferred in ASCII mode. The entire transfer takes 0.13 seconds, which works out to a transfer rate of about 985K per second.

After you download the file, you can end the session by typing **bye**. FTP responds by displaying the site's goodbye message; then it returns you to the MS-DOS command prompt:

```
221 Hurry back...
C:\>
```

Of course, FTP is a lot more involved than this simple session suggests. Still, the most common use of FTP is to download files, and most downloads are no more complicated than this example.

FTP Command and Subcommand Reference

The rest of this chapter is an FTP command reference. In the following sections, you can find complete reference information for the FTP command and all its subcommands. The first command described is the FTP command itself. After that, all the FTP command subcommands are listed in alphabetical order.

The FTP command

What it does: Starts the FTP client so that you can transfer files to and from an FTP server

Syntax: **ftp** [**-v**] [**-d**] [**-i**] [**-n**] [**-g**] [-s:*filename*] [**-a**] [**-w:***windowsize*] [**-A**] [*host*]

Parameters:

-v	Turns off Verbose mode.
-d	Turns on Debug mode.
-i	Turns off Prompt mode.
-n	Forces manual logon.
-g	Turns off Glob mode.
-s	Specifies a script file that contains FTP commands.
-a	Specifies that any network interface can be used to bind the data connection.

-w	Specifies the size of the transmission buffer. The default is 4K.
-A	Automatically logs on as Anonymous.

Host: The FTP server to which you want to connect. This can be the server's DNS name or an IP address.

Examples: **ftp ftp.lowewriter.com**
ftp ftp.lowewriter.com -A

More info: Unlike most Windows commands, the switches for this command begin with a hyphen, not a slash.

If you want to script subcommands, use the -s switch. Input redirection doesn't work with FTP.

When FTP is running, the prompt ftp> appears. When this prompt is displayed, you can enter any of the FTP subcommands described in the rest of this chapter.

! (Escape)

What it does: Escape to a command shell

Syntax: !

More info: This command brings up a temporary command prompt so that you can enter commands. To return to the ftp> prompt, type **exit**.

? (Help)

What it does: Displays Help information

Syntax: ? [*command*]

help [*command*]

Example: **help mput**

More info: ? and help are interchangeable. If you enter **?** or **help** by itself, a list of FTP commands appears. If you enter **?** or **help** followed by a command name, a summary of that command's function appears.

Book IV
Chapter 5

Using FTP

append

What it does: Uploads a file and appends it to the end of an existing file on the remote system

Syntax: **append** *localfile* [*remotefile*]

Example: **append extra.txt start.txt**

More info: If you omit the `remotefile` parameter, the remote file is assumed to have the same name as the local file.

ascii

What it does: Sets the ASCII transfer mode

Syntax: **ascii**

More info: This command sets the transfer type of ASCII, which is best suited for text files. ASCII is the default transfer type.

bell

What it does: Causes the FTP client to beep when each transfer is complete

Syntax: **bell**

More info: This command is useful when you're downloading long files and want to take a nap during the download. Unfortunately, it doesn't beep when it sees your boss approaching your office, so you'll need some other alarm system to cover that contingency.

binary

What it does: Sets the binary transfer type

Syntax: **binary**

More info: The binary file type is best for executable files and other nontext files.

bye

What it does: Ends the FTP session and exits the FTP client

Syntax: **bye**

More info: This is the command to use when you're done. It's the same as the `quit` command.

cd

What it does: Changes the working directory on the remote computer

Syntax: **cd** *remotedirectory*

Example: **cd pics**

More info: Use this to change to the directory that contains the files you want to download or the directory to which you want to upload files.

Type **cd ** to go to the root directory.

close

What it does: Closes the session with the remote computer but doesn't leave the FTP program

Syntax: **close**

More info: You can use this command if you want to switch to another FTP server without leaving and restarting the FTP program. This command is the same as the `disconnect` command.

debug

What it does: Toggles Debug mode

Syntax: **debug**

More info: When Debug mode is on, the FTP client displays the actual `FTP` commands that are sent to the FTP server. This can be useful if you're an FTP guru trying to diagnose a problem with a server or a client, but it can also be fun if you just want to see how FTP client commands (like `CD`) get translated into FTP server commands (like `CWD`).

Book IV
Chapter 5

Using FTP

delete

What it does: Deletes the specified file on the remote computer

Syntax: **delete** *remotefile*

Example: **delete fright.txt**

More info: You can delete only one file at a time with this command. To delete more than one file in a single command, use the `mdelete` command.

dir

What it does: Lists contents of remote directory

Syntax: **dir** [*remotedirectory*] [*localfile*]

Examples: **dir**
dir \pics
dir \pics picdir.txt

More info: The first parameter lets you list a directory other than the current working directory. The second parameter lets you capture the output to a file on the local computer.

disconnect

What it does: Disconnects from the remote computer but doesn't leave the FTP program

Syntax: **disconnect**

More info: You can use this command if you want to switch to another FTP server without leaving and restarting the FTP program. This command is the same as the `close` command.

get

What it does: Downloads a file from the remote computer

Syntax: **get** *remotefile* [*localfile*]

Examples: **get boo.exe**
get boo.exe bar.exe

More info:	This command downloads the specified file from the current working directory on the remote system to the current directory on the local system. The second parameter lets you save the file using a different name than the name used on the remote system.
	You can use this command to download only one file at a time. To download multiple files, use the mget command.
	This command is the same as the recv command.

glob

What it does:	Toggles the use of wildcards for local filenames
Syntax:	**glob**
More info:	If globbing is on, you can use * and ? characters in local filenames. Globbing is on by default.

hash

What it does:	Toggles the display of hash marks (#) to indicate transfer progress
Syntax:	**hash**
More info:	Hash is off by default. If you turn it on by issuing the hash command, a hash mark (#) appears each time a 2K data block is transferred. This helps you track the progress of transfers.

help

What it does:	Displays Help information
Syntax:	**?** [*command*]
	help [*command*]
Example:	**help mput**
More info:	? and help are interchangeable. If you enter **?** or **help** by itself, a list of FTP commands appears. If you enter **?** or **help** followed by a command name, a summary of that command's function appears.

**Book IV
Chapter 5**

Using FTP

lcd

What it does:	Changes the working directory on the local computer
Syntax:	**lcd** *localdirectory*
Example:	**lcd \docs**
More info:	Use this to change to the directory you want to download files to or that contains files you want to upload.

literal

What it does:	Sends a native FTP command directly to the server
Syntax:	**literal** *arguments* . . .
Example:	**literal cwd pics**
More info:	Use this command if you're an FTP guru and you want to send a native FTP command to the server. It's the same as the quote command.

ls

What it does:	List contents of remote directory
Syntax:	**ls** [*remotedirectory*] [*localfile*]
Examples:	**ls** **ls \pics** **ls \pics picdir.txt**
More info:	The first parameter lets you list a directory other than the current working directory. The second parameter lets you capture the output to a file on the local computer.

mdelete

What it does:	Delete multiple files
Syntax:	**mdelete** *remotefile* . . .
Examples:	**mdelete file1.txt** **mdelete file1.txt file2.txt file3.txt**
More info:	This command deletes one or more files from the current working directory on the remote system.

mdir

What it does: Lists the contents of multiple remote directories

Syntax: **mdir** *remotedirectory* . . . [*localfile*]

Example: **mdir pics videos**

More info: Specify a hyphen as the last parameter to display the output on the screen. Otherwise, the last parameter will be interpreted as the name of the local file you want the directory listing captured to.

mget

What it does: Downloads multiple files

Syntax: **mget** *remotefile* . . .

Example: **mget file1.txt**
mget file1.txt file2.txt file3.txt

More info: This command downloads one or more files from the current working directory on the remote system to the current directory on the local computer.

mkdir

What it does: Creates a directory on the remote system

Syntax: **mkdir** *remotedirectory*

Example: **mdir plans**

More info: The new subdirectory is created in the current working directory on the remote system.

mls

What it does: Lists the contents of multiple remote directories

Syntax: **mls** *remotedirectory* . . . [*localfile*]

Example: **mls pics videos**

More info: Specify a hyphen as the last parameter to display the output on the screen. Otherwise, the last parameter will be interpreted as the name of the local file you want the directory listing captured to.

**Book IV
Chapter 5**

Using FTP

mput

What it does:	Uploads multiple files
Syntax:	**mput** *localfile* . . .
Examples:	**mput file1.txt** **mput file1.txt file2.txt file3.txt**
More info:	This command uploads one or more files from the current directory on the local system to the current working directory on the remote system.

open

What it does:	Connects to an FTP server
Syntax:	**open** *remotesystem* [*port*]
Examples:	**open ftp.microsoft.com** **open ftp.weirdport.com 1499**
More info:	Specify the port number only if the remote system does not use the standard FTP ports (20 and 21).

prompt

What it does:	Toggles prompting for multiple transfers
Syntax:	**prompt**
More info:	When Prompt mode is on, you're prompted for each file before the file is transferred. Prompt mode is on by default.

put

What it does:	Uploads a file to the remote computer
Syntax:	**put** *localfile* [*remotefile*]
Examples:	**put boo.exe** **put boo.exe bar.exe**
More info:	This command uploads the specified file from the current directory on the local system to the current working directory on the remote system. The second parameter lets you save the file with a different name than the name used on the local system.

You can use this command to upload only one file at a time. To upload multiple files, use the `mput` command.

This command is the same as the `send` command.

pwd

What it does: Displays the current working directory on the remote computer

Syntax: **pwd**

More info: If you aren't sure what the current directory is on the remote system, use this command to find out.

quit

What it does: Ends the FTP session and quits the FTP program

Syntax: **quit**

More info: This is the command to use when you're done. It's the same as the `bye` command.

quote

What it does: Sends a native `FTP` command directly to the server

Syntax: **quote** *arguments* . . .

Example: **quote cwd pics**

More info: Use this command if you're an FTP guru and you want to send a native `FTP` command to the server. It's the same as the `literal` command.

recv

What it does: Downloads a file from the remote computer

Syntax: **recv** *remotefile* [*localfile*]

Examples: **recv boo.exe**
recv boo.exe bar.exe

More info: This command downloads the specified file from the current working directory on the remote system to the current directory on the local system. The second parameter lets you save the file with a different name than the name used on the remote system.

You can use this command to download only one file at a time. To download multiple files, use the `mget` command.

This command is the same as the `get` command.

remotehelp

What it does: Displays help for remote commands

Syntax: **remotehelp** [*command*]

Example: **remotehelp cwd**

More info: If you enter `remotehelp` by itself, a list of FTP commands is displayed. If you enter `remotehelp` followed by a command name, a summary of that command's function appears.

rename

What it does: Renames a file on the remote system

Syntax: **rename** *filename newfilename*

Example: **rename door.jpg doorway.jpg**

More info: Use this command to change the name of a file on the remote system.

rmdir

What it does: Removes a directory on the remote system

Syntax: **rmdir** *directoryname*

Example: **rmdir oldpics**

More info: This command removes a directory and all the files in it, so use it with caution!

send

What it does:	Uploads a file to the remote computer
Syntax:	**send** *localfile* [*remotefile*]
Examples:	**send boo.exe** **send boo.exe bar.exe**
More info:	This command uploads the specified file from the current directory on the local system to the current working directory on the remote system. The second parameter lets you save the file with a different name than the name used on the local system.
	You can use this command to upload only one file at a time. To upload multiple files, use the mput command.
	This command is the same as the put command.

status

What it does:	Displays the current status of the FTP client
Syntax:	**status**
More info:	Use this command to display the current settings of options, such as bell, prompt, and verbose, as well as the current connection status.

trace

What it does:	Activates Trace mode
Syntax:	**trace**
More info:	When Trace mode is on, detailed information about each packet transmission is displayed. trace is off by default and should be left off unless you're digging deep into the bowels of FTP or just want to show off.

**Book IV
Chapter 5**

Using FTP

type

What it does:	Sets the transfer type to ASCII or binary or displays the current mode
Syntax:	**type [ascii or binary]**
Examples:	**type ascii** **type binary** **type**
More info:	Use ASCII transfers for text files, and use binary transfers for nontext files.

If you don't specify a type, the current transfer type appears.

You can also use the ascii or binary command to switch the transfer type.

user

What it does:	Logs you on to a remote system
Syntax:	**user** *username* [*password*]
Examples:	**user doug** **user doug notmypw**
More info:	This command logs you on to the remote system by using the username and password you provide. If you omit the password, you're prompted to enter it.

verbose

What it does:	Toggles Verbose mode
Syntax:	**verbose**
More info:	When Verbose mode is on, FTP responses appear. Verbose mode is on by default.

Chapter 6: TCP/IP Tools and Commands

In This Chapter

✔ Recognizing tools and commands

✔ Making all your hosts sing with `IPConfig` and `Ping`

Most client and server operating systems that support Transmission Control Protocol/Internet Protocol (TCP/IP) come with a suite of commands and tools that are designed to let you examine TCP/IP configuration information and diagnose and correct problems. Although the exact form of these commands varies between Windows and Unix/Linux, most are surprisingly similar. This chapter is a reference to the most commonly used TCP/IP commands.

Using the arp Command

Using the `arp` command allows you to display and modify the Address Resolution Protocol (ARP) cache, which is a simple mapping of IP addresses to MAC addresses. Each time a computer's TCP/IP stack uses ARP to determine the Media Access Control (MAC) address for an IP address, it records the mapping in the ARP cache so that future ARP lookups go faster.

If you use the `arp` command without any parameters, you get a list of the command's parameters. To display the ARP cache entry for a specific IP address, use an `-a` switch followed by the IP address. For example:

```
C:\>arp -a 192.168.168.22
Interface: 192.168.168.21 --- 0x10004
  Internet Address      Physical Address      Type
  192.168.168.22        00-60-08-39-e5-a1     dynamic
C:\>
```

You can display the complete ARP cache by using `-a` without specifying an IP address, like this:

```
C:\>arp -a
Interface: 192.168.168.21 --- 0x10004
  Internet Address      Physical Address      Type
  192.168.168.9         00-02-e3-16-e4-5d     dynamic
```

```
192.168.168.10      00-50-04-17-66-90     dynamic
192.168.168.22      00-60-08-39-e5-a1     dynamic
192.168.168.254     00-40-10-18-42-49     dynamic
C:\>
```

ARP is sometimes useful when diagnosing duplicate IP assignment problems. For example, suppose you can't access a computer that has an IP address of `192.168.168.100`. You try to ping the computer, expecting the ping to fail, but lo and behold — the ping succeeds. One possible cause for this may be that two computers on the network have been assigned the address `192.168.168.100`, and your ARP cache is pointing to the wrong one. The way to find out is to go to the `192.168.168.100` computer that you want to access, run `ipconfig /all`, and make a note of the physical address. Then return to the computer that's having trouble reaching the `192.168.168.100` computer, run `arp -a`, and compare the physical address with the one you noted. If they're different, that two computers are assigned the same IP address. You can then check the Dynamic Host Configuration Protocol (DHCP) or static TCP/IP configuration of the computers involved to find out why.

Using the hostname Command

The `hostname` command is the simplest of all the TCP/IP commands presented in this chapter. It simply displays the computer's host name. For cxample:

```
C:\>hostname
doug
C:\>
```

Here, the host name for the computer is `doug`. The Windows version of the `hostname` command has no parameters. However, the Unix/Linux versions of `hostname` let you set the computer's host name as well as display it. You do that by specifying the new host name as an argument.

Using the ipconfig Command

Using the `ipconfig` command displays information about a computer's TCP/IP configuration. It can also be used to update DHCP and Domain Name Server (DNS) settings.

Displaying basic IP configuration

To display the basic IP configuration for a computer, use the `ipconfig` command without any parameters, like this:

```
C:\>ipconfig

Windows IP Configuration


Ethernet adapter Local Area Connection:

   Connection-specific DNS Suffix  . :
   Link-local IPv6 Address . . . . . : fe80::cca:9067:9427:a911%8
   IPv4 Address. . . . . . . . . . . : 192.168.1.110
   Subnet Mask . . . . . . . . . . . : 255.255.255.0
   Default Gateway . . . . . . . . . : 192.168.1.1

Tunnel adapter Local Area Connection* 6:

   Connection-specific DNS Suffix  . :
   IPv6 Address. . . . . . . . . . . : 2001:0:4136:e38c:2c6c:670:3f57:fe91
   Link-local IPv6 Address . . . . . : fe80::2c6c:670:3f57:fe91%9
   Default Gateway . . . . . . . . . : ::

Tunnel adapter Local Area Connection* 7:

   Connection-specific DNS Suffix  . :
   Link-local IPv6 Address . . . . . : fe80::5efe:192.168.1.110%10
   Default Gateway . . . . . . . . . :
C:\>
```

When you use `ipconfig` without parameters, the command displays the name of the adapter, the domain name used for the adapter, the IP address, the subnet mask, and the default gateway configuration for the adapter. This is the easiest way to determine a computer's IP address.

If your computer indicates an IP address in the `169.254.x.x` block, odds are good that the DHCP server isn't working. `169.254.x.x` is the Class B address block that Windows uses when it resorts to IP Autoconfiguration. This usually happens only when the DHCP server can't be reached or isn't working.

Displaying detailed configuration information

You can display detailed IP configuration information by using an `/all` switch with the `ipconfig` command, like this:

```
C:\>ipconfig /all

Windows IP Configuration

   Host Name . . . . . . . . . . . . : WK07-001
   Primary Dns Suffix  . . . . . . . :
   Node Type . . . . . . . . . . . . : Hybrid
   IP Routing Enabled. . . . . . . . : No
   WINS Proxy Enabled. . . . . . . . : No

Ethernet adapter Local Area Connection:

   Connection-specific DNS Suffix  . :
   Description . . . . . . . . . . . : Intel(R) PRO/100 VE Network Connection
```

```
Physical Address. . . . . . . . . : 00-12-3F-A7-17-BA
DHCP Enabled. . . . . . . . . . . : No
Autoconfiguration Enabled . . . . : Yes
Link-local IPv6 Address . . . . . : fe80::cca:9067:9427:a911%8(Preferred)
IPv4 Address. . . . . . . . . . . : 192.168.1.110(Preferred)
Subnet Mask . . . . . . . . . . . : 255.255.255.0
Default Gateway . . . . . . . . . : 192.168.1.1
DNS Servers . . . . . . . . . . . : 192.168.1.10
                                    68.87.76.178
NetBIOS over Tcpip. . . . . . . . : Enabled

C:\>
```

You can determine a lot of information about the computer from the
`ipconfig /all` command. For example:

- ✦ The computer's host name is `WK07-001`.

- ✦ The computer's IPv4 address is `192.168.1.110`, and the subnet mask
  is `255.255.255.0`.

- ✦ The default gateway is a router located at `192.168.1.1`.

- ✦ The DNS servers are at 192.168.1.10 and `68.87.76.178`.

Renewing an IP lease

If you're having an IP configuration problem, you can often solve it by renew-
ing the computer's IP lease. To do that, use a `/renew` switch, like this:

```
C:\>ipconfig /renew
Windows IP Configuration
Ethernet adapter Local Area Connection:
        Connection-specific DNS Suffix  . :
        IP Address. . . . . . . . . . . . : 192.168.1.110
        Subnet Mask . . . . . . . . . . . : 255.255.255.0
        Default Gateway . . . . . . . . . : 192.168.1.1
C:\>
```

When you renew an IP lease, the `ipconfig` command displays the new lease
information.

This command won't work if you configured the computer to use a static IP
address.

Releasing an IP lease

You can release an IP lease by using an `ipconfig` command with the `/`
`release` parameter, like this:

```
C:\>ipconfig /release
Windows IP Configuration
Ethernet adapter Local Area Connection:
        Connection-specific DNS Suffix  . :
```

```
               IP Address. . . . . . . . . . . . : 0.0.0.0
               Subnet Mask . . . . . . . . . . . : 0.0.0.0
               Default Gateway . . . . . . . . . :
C:\>
```

As you can see, the DNS suffix and default gateway for the computer are blank, and the IP address and subnet mask are set to `0.0.0.0`.

After you release the DHCP lease, you can use an `ipconfig /renew` command to obtain a new DHCP lease for the computer.

Flushing the local DNS cache

You probably won't need to do this unless you're having DNS troubles. If you've been tinkering with your network's DNS configuration, though, you may need to flush the cache on your DNS clients so that they'll be forced to reacquire information from the DNS server. You can do that by using a `/flushdns` switch:

```
C:\>ipconfig /flushdns
Windows IP Configuration
Successfully flushed the DNS Resolver Cache.
C:\>
```

Even if you don't need to do this, it's fun just to see the computer read `flushed`. If I worked at Microsoft, you'd be able to revert Windows Vista computers back to XP by using a `/flushVista` switch.

Using the nbtstat Command

`nbtstat` is a Windows-only command that can help solve problems with NetBIOS name resolution. (*nbt* stands for *NetBIOS over TCP/IP*.) You can use any of the switches listed in Table 6-1 to specify what `nbtstat` output you want to display. For example, you can use an `-a` switch to display the cached name table for a specified computer, like this:

```
C:\>nbtstat -a WK07-001

Local Area Connection:
Node IpAddress: [192.168.1.110] Scope Id: []

         NetBIOS Remote Machine Name Table

    Name               Type         Status
    ---------------------------------------------
    WK07-001     <00>  UNIQUE       Registered
    WORKGROUP    <00>  GROUP        Registered
    WK07-001     <20>  UNIQUE       Registered
```

```
WORKGROUP        <1E>   GROUP        Registered
WORKGROUP        <1D>   UNIQUE       Registered
..__MSBROWSE__.<01>     GROUP        Registered

MAC Address = 00-12-3F-A7-17-BAC:\>
C:\>
```

Table 6-1 lists the switches that you can use with nbtstat and explains the function of each switch.

Table 6-1	nbtstat Command Switches
Switch	*What It Does*
-a name	Lists the specified computer's name table given the computer's name
-A IP-address	Lists the specified computer's name table given the computer's IP address
-c	Lists the contents of the NetBIOS cache
-n	Lists locally registered NetBIOS names
-r	Displays a count of the names resolved by broadcast and via WINS
-R	Purges and reloads the cached name table from the LMHOSTS file
-RR	Releases and then reregisters all names
-S	Displays the sessions table using IP addresses
-s	Displays the sessions table and converts destination IP addresses to computer NetBIOS names

Using the netstat Command

Using the netstat command displays a variety of statistics about a computer's active TCP/IP connections. It's a useful tool to use when you're having trouble with TCP/IP applications, such as File Transfer Protocol (FTP), HyperText Transport Protocol (HTTP), and so on.

Displaying connections

If you run netstat without specifying any parameters, you get a list of active connections, something like this:

```
C:\>netstat
Active Connections
  Proto  Local Address  Foreign Address              State
```

```
TCP     Doug:1463       192.168.168.10:1053        ESTABLISHED
TCP     Doug:1582       192.168.168.9:netbios-ssn  ESTABLISHED
TCP     Doug:3630       192.168.168.30:9100        SYN_SENT
TCP     Doug:3716       192.168.168.10:4678        ESTABLISHED
TCP     Doug:3940       192.168.168.10:netbios-ssn ESTABLISHED
C:\>
```

This list shows all the active connections on the computer and indicates the local port used by the connection, as well as the IP address and port number for the remote computer.

You can specify the -n switch to display both local and foreign addresses in numeric IP form:

```
C:\>netstat -n
Active Connections
  Proto  Local Address          Foreign Address        State
  TCP    192.168.168.21:1463    192.168.168.10:1053    ESTABLISHED
  TCP    192.168.168.21:1582    192.168.168.9:139      ESTABLISHED
  TCP    192.168.168.21:3658    192.168.168.30:9100    SYN_SENT
  TCP    192.168.168.21:3716    192.168.168.10:4678    ESTABLISHED
  TCP    192.168.168.21:3904    207.46.106.78:1863     ESTABLISHED
  TCP    192.168.168.21:3940    192.168.168.10:139     ESTABLISHED
C:\>
```

Finally, you can specify the -a switch to display all TCP/IP connections and ports that are being listened to. I won't list the output from that command here because it would run several pages, and I want to do my part for the rainforests. Suffice it to say that it looks a lot like the netstat output shown previously, but a lot longer.

Displaying interface statistics

If you use an -e switch, netstat displays various protocol statistics, like this:

```
C:\>netstat -e
Interface Statistics
                           Received            Sent
Bytes                     672932849       417963911
Unicast packets             1981755         1972374
Non-unicast packets          251869           34585
Discards                          0               0
Errors                            0               0
Unknown protocols              1829
C:\>
```

REMEMBER

The items to pay attention to in this output are the Discards and Errors. These numbers should be zero, or at least close to it. If they're not, the network may be carrying too much traffic or the connection may have a physical problem. If no physical problem exists with the connection, try segmenting the network to see whether the error and discard rates drop.

Book IV
Chapter 6

TCP/IP Tools and
Commands

You can display additional statistics by using an -s switch, like this:

```
C:\>netstat -s

IPv4 Statistics

    Packets Received               = 9155
    Received Header Errors         = 0
    Received Address Errors        = 0
    Datagrams Forwarded            = 0
    Unknown Protocols Received     = 0
    Received Packets Discarded     = 0
    Received Packets Delivered     = 14944
    Output Requests                = 12677
    Routing Discards               = 0
    Discarded Output Packets       = 71
    Output Packet No Route         = 0
    Reassembly Required            = 0
    Reassembly Successful          = 0
    Reassembly Failures            = 0
    Datagrams Successfully Fragmented = 0
    Datagrams Failing Fragmentation  = 0
    Fragments Created              = 0


IPv6 Statistics

    Packets Received               = 3
    Received Header Errors         = 0
    Received Address Errors        = 0
    Datagrams Forwarded            = 0
    Unknown Protocols Received     = 0
    Received Packets Discarded     = 0
    Received Packets Delivered     = 345
    Output Requests                = 377
    Routing Discards               = 0
    Discarded Output Packets       = 0
    Output Packet No Route         = 0
    Reassembly Required            = 0
    Reassembly Successful          = 0
    Reassembly Failures            = 0
    Datagrams Successfully Fragmented = 0
    Datagrams Failing Fragmentation  = 0
    Fragments Created              = 0


ICMPv4 Statistics

                              Received      Sent
    Messages                  6             14
    Errors                    0             0
    Destination Unreachable   6             14
    Time Exceeded             0             0
    Parameter Problems        0             0
    Source Quenches           0             0
    Redirects                 0             0
    Echo Replies              0             0
    Echos                     0             0
    Timestamps                0             0
    Timestamp Replies         0             0
    Address Masks             0             0
    Address Mask Replies      0             0
    Router Solicitations      0             0
    Router Advertisements     0             0
```

```
ICMPv6 Statistics

                                  Received      Sent
        Messages                  3             7
        Errors                    0             0
        Destination Unreachable   0             0
        Packet Too Big            0             0
        Time Exceeded             0             0
        Parameter Problems        0             0
        Echos                     0             0
        Echo Replies              0             0
        MLD Queries               0             0
        MLD Reports               0             0
        MLD Dones                 0             0
        Router Solicitations      0             6
        Router Advertisements     3             0
        Neighbor Solicitations    0             1
        Neighbor Advertisements   0             0
        Redirects                 0             0
        Router Renumberings       0             0

TCP Statistics for IPv4

        Active Opens                   = 527
        Passive Opens                  = 2
        Failed Connection Attempts     = 1
        Reset Connections              = 301
        Current Connections            = 1
        Segments Received              = 8101
        Segments Sent                  = 6331
        Segments Retransmitted         = 301

TCP Statistics for IPv6

        Active Opens                   = 1
        Passive Opens                  = 1
        Failed Connection Attempts     = 0
        Reset Connections              = 1
        Current Connections            = 0
        Segments Received              = 142
        Segments Sent                  = 142
        Segments Retransmitted         = 0

UDP Statistics for IPv4

        Datagrams Received   = 6703
        No Ports             = 0
        Receive Errors       = 0
        Datagrams Sent       = 6011

UDP Statistics for IPv6

        Datagrams Received   = 32
        No Ports             = 0
        Receive Errors       = 0
        Datagrams Sent       = 200
C:\>
```

**Book IV
Chapter 6**

**TCP/IP Tools and
Commands**

Using the nslookup Command

The `nslookup` command is a powerful tool for diagnosing DNS problems. You know you're experiencing a DNS problem when you can access a resource by specifying its IP address but not its DNS name. For example, if you can get to www.ebay.com by typing **66.135.192.87** in your browser's address bar but not by typing **www.ebay.com**, you have a DNS problem.

Looking up an IP address

The simplest use of `nslookup` is to look up the IP address for a given DNS name. For example, how did I know that 66.135.192.87 was the IP address for www.ebay.com? I used `nslookup` to find out:

```
C:\>nslookup ebay.com
Server:    ns1.orng.twtelecom.net
Address:   168.215.210.50
Non-authoritative answer:
Name:      ebay.com
Address:   66.135.192.87
C:\>
```

As you can see, just type **nslookup** followed by the DNS name you want to look up, and `nslookup` issues a DNS query to find out. This DNS query was sent to the server named ns1.orng.twtelecom.net at 168.215.210.50. It then displayed the IP address that's associated with ebay.com: namely, 66.135.192.87.

In some cases, you may find that using an `nslookup` command gives you the wrong IP address for a host name. To know that for sure, of course, you have to know with certainty what the host IP address *should* be. For example, if you know that your server is 203.172.182.10 but `nslookup` returns a completely different IP address for your server when you query the server's host name, something is probably wrong with one of the DNS records.

Using nslookup subcommands

If you use `nslookup` without any arguments, the `nslookup` command enters a subcommand mode. It displays a prompt character (>) to let you know that you're in `nslookup` subcommand mode rather than at a normal Windows command prompt. In subcommand mode, you can enter various subcommands to set options or to perform queries. You can type a question mark (?) to get a list of these commands. Table 6-2 lists the subcommands you'll use most.

Get me out of here!

One of my pet peeves is that it seems as if every program that uses subcommands chooses a different command to quit the application. I can never remember whether the command to get out of `nslookup` is `quit`, `bye`, or `exit`. I usually end up trying them all. And no matter what program I'm using, I always seem to choose the one that works for some other program first. When I'm in `nslookup`, I use `bye` first. When I'm in FTP, I try `exit` first. Arghh! If I were King of the Computer Hill, every program that had subcommands would respond to the following commands by exiting the program and returning to a command prompt:

```
Quit        Sayonara

Exit        Ciao

Bye         Mañana

Leave       Makelikeatree
```

Of course, the final command to try would be `Andgetouttahere` (in honor of Biff from the *Back to the Future* movies).

Table 6-2   The Most Commonly Used `nslookup` Subcommands

Subcommand	*What It Does*
`name`	Queries the current name server for the specified name.
`server name`	Sets the current name server to the server you specify.
`root`	Sets the root server as the current server.
`set type=x`	Specifies the type of records to be displayed, such as A, CNAME, MX, NS, PTR, or SOA. Specify ANY to display all records.
`set debug`	Turns on Debug mode, which displays detailed information about each query.
`set nodebug`	Turns off Debug mode.
`set recurse`	Enables recursive searches.
`set norecurse`	Disables recursive searches.
`exit`	Exits the `nslookup` program and returns you to a command prompt.

Book IV
Chapter 6

TCP/IP Tools and
Commands

Displaying DNS records

One of the main uses of `nslookup` is to examine your DNS configuration to make sure that it's set up properly. To do that, follow these steps:

1. **At a command prompt, type** nslookup **without any parameters.**

`nslookup` displays the name of the default name server and displays the > prompt.

```
C:\>nslookup
Default Server:  ns1.orng.twtelecom.net
Address:  168.215.210.50
>
```

2. **Type the subcommand** set type=any.

`nslookup` silently obeys your command and displays another prompt:

```
> set type=any
>
```

3. **Type your domain name.**

`nslookup` responds by displaying the name servers for your domain:

```
> lowewriter.com
Server:  ns1.orng.twtelecom.net
Address:  168.215.210.50
Non-authoritative answer:
lowewriter.com  nameserver = NS000.NS0.com
lowewriter.com  nameserver = NS207.PAIR.com
lowewriter.com  nameserver = NS000.NS0.com
lowewriter.com  nameserver = NS207.PAIR.com
>
```

4. **Use a `server` command to switch to one of the domain's name servers.**

For example, to switch to the first name server listed in Step 3, type **server NS000.NS0.com**. `nslookup` replies with a message that indicates the new default server:

```
> server ns000.ns0.com
Default Server:  ns000.ns0.com
Address:  216.92.61.61
>
```

5. **Type your domain name again.**

This time, `nslookup` responds by displaying the DNS information for your domain:

```
> lowewriter.com
Server:  ns000.ns0.com
Address:  216.92.61.61
lowewriter.com
```

```
                    primary name server = ns207.pair.com
                    responsible mail addr = root.pair.com
                    serial  = 2001121009
                    refresh = 3600 (1 hour)
                    retry   = 300 (5 mins)
                    expire  = 604800 (7 days)
                    default TTL = 3600 (1 hour)
        lowewriter.com  nameserver = ns000.ns0.com
        lowewriter.com  nameserver = ns207.pair.com
        lowewriter.com  MX preference = 50, mail exchanger =
            sasi.pair.com
        lowewriter.com  internet address = 209.68.34.15
        >
```

6. **Type** exit **to leave the** **Nslookup** **program.**

You return to a command prompt.

```
    > exit
    C:\>
```

Wasn't that fun?

Locating the mail server for an e-mail address

If you're having trouble delivering mail to someone, you can use `nslookup`
to determine the IP address of the user's mail server. Then, you can use the
`ping` command to see whether you can contact the user's mail server. If
not, you can use the `tracert` command to find out where the communication breaks down. (See "Using the tracert Command" later in this chapter for
more information.)

To find a user's mail server, start `nslookup` and enter the command **set
type=MX**. Then, enter the domain portion of the user's e-mail address.
For example, if the user's address is Doug@LoweWriter.com, enter
LoweWriter.com. `nslookup` will display the MX (Mail eXchange) information for the domain, like this:

```
C:\>nslookup
Default Server:  ns7.attbi.com
Address:  204.127.198.19
> set type=mx
> lowewriter.com
Server:  ns7.attbi.com
Address:  204.127.198.19
lowewriter.com  MX preference = 50, mail exchanger = sasi.pair.com
lowewriter.com  nameserver = ns000.ns0.com
lowewriter.com  nameserver = ns207.pair.com
ns000.ns0.com   internet address = 216.92.61.61
ns207.pair.com  internet address = 209.68.2.52
>
```

Here, you can see that the name of the mail server for the `LoweWriter.com` domain is `sasi.pair.com`.

Taking a ride through DNS-Land

Ever find yourself wondering how DNS really works? I mean, how is it that you can type a DNS name like `www.disneyland.com` into a web browser and you're almost instantly transported to the Magic Kingdom? Is it really magic?

Nope. It isn't magic; it's DNS. In Book IV, Chapter 4, I present a somewhat dry and theoretical overview of DNS. After you have the `nslookup` command in your trusty TCP/IP toolbox, take a little trip through the Internet's maze of DNS servers to find out how DNS gets from `www.disneyland.com` to an IP address in just a matter of milliseconds.

DNS does its whole name resolution thing so fast that it's easy to take it for granted. If you follow this little procedure, you'll gain a deeper appreciation for what DNS does literally tens of thousands of times every second of every day.

1. **At a command prompt, type** nslookup **without any parameters.**

`nslookup` displays the name of the default name server and displays the > prompt.

```
C:\>nslookup
Default Server:  ns1.orng.twtelecom.net
Address:  168.215.210.50
>
```

2. **Type** root **to switch to one of the Internet's root servers.**

`nslookup` switches to one of the Internet's 13 root servers and then displays the > prompt.

```
> root
Default Server:  A.ROOT-SERVERS.NET
Address:  198.41.0.4
```

3. **Type** www.disneyland.com**.**

`nslookup` sends a query to the root server to ask if it knows the IP address of `www.disneyland.com`. The root server answers with a referral, meaning that it doesn't know about `www.disneyland.com`, but you should try one of these servers because they know all about the `com` domain.

```
> www.disneyland.com
Server:  A.ROOT-SERVERS.NET
Address:  198.41.0.4
Name:    www.disneyland.com
Served by:
```

```
       - A.GTLD-SERVERS.NET
               192.5.6.30
               com
       - G.GTLD-SERVERS.NET
               192.42.93.30
               com
       - H.GTLD-SERVERS.NET
               192.54.112.30
               com
       - C.GTLD-SERVERS.NET
               192.26.92.30
               com
       - I.GTLD-SERVERS.NET
               192.43.172.30
               com
       - B.GTLD-SERVERS.NET
               192.33.14.30
               com
       - D.GTLD-SERVERS.NET
               192.31.80.30
               com
       - L.GTLD-SERVERS.NET
               192.41.162.30
               com
       - F.GTLD-SERVERS.NET
               192.35.51.30
               com
       - J.GTLD-SERVERS.NET
               192.48.79.30
               com
    >
```

4. **Type** server **followed by the name or IP address of one of the** com **domain name servers.**

   It doesn't really matter which one you pick. nslookup switches to that server. (The server may spit out some other information besides what I've shown here; I left it out for clarity.)

   ```
   > server 192.48.79.30
   Default Server:  [192.5.6.30]
   Address:   192.5.6.30
   >
   ```

5. **Type** www.disneyland.com **again.**

   nslookup sends a query to the com server to ask whether it knows where the Magic Kingdom is. The com server's reply indicates that it doesn't know where www.disneyland.com is, but it does know which server is responsible for disneyland.com.

   ```
   Server:   [192.5.6.30]
   Address:   192.5.6.30
   Name:     www.disney.com
   ```

```
Served by:
- huey.disney.com
            204.128.192.10
            disney.com
- huey11.disney.com
            208.246.35.40
            disney.com
>
```

It figures that Disney's name server is huey.disney.com. There's probably also a dewey.disney.com and a louie.disney.com.

6. **Type** server **followed by the name or IP address of the second-level domain name server.**

   nslookup switches to that server:

   ```
   > server huey.disney.com
   Default Server:  huey.disney.com
   Address:  204.128.192.10
   >
   ```

7. **Type** www.disneyland.com **again.**

   Once again, nslookup sends a query to the name server to find out whether it knows where the Magic Kingdom is. Of course, huey.disney.com *does* know, so it tells us the answer:

   ```
   > www.disneyland.com
   Server:  huey.disney.com
   Address:  204.128.192.10
   Name:    disneyland.com
   Address:  199.181.132.250
   Aliases:  www.disneyland.com
   >
   ```

8. **Type** Exit, **and then shout like Tigger in amazement at how DNS queries work.**

   And be glad that your DNS resolver and primary name server do all this querying for you automatically.

Okay, maybe that wasn't an E Ticket ride, but it never ceases to amaze me that the DNS system can look up any DNS name hosted anywhere in the world almost instantly.

Using the pathping Command

pathping is an interesting command that's unique to Windows. It's sort of a cross between the ping command and the tracert command, combining the features of both into one tool. When you run pathping, it first traces the route to the destination address much the way tracert does. Then, it launches into a 25-second test of each router along the way, gathering statistics on the rate of data loss to each hop. If the route has a lot of hops, this can take a long time. However, it can help you to spot potentially unreliable hops. If you're having intermittent trouble reaching a particular destination, using `pathping` may help you pinpoint the problem.

The following command output is typical of the `pathping` command. Using an -n switch causes the display to use numeric IP numbers only, instead of DNS host names. Although fully qualified host names are convenient, they tend to be very long for network routers, which makes the `pathping` output very difficult to decipher.

```
C:\>pathping -n www.lowewriter.com
Tracing route to lowewriter.com [209.68.34.15]
over a maximum of 30 hops:
  0  192.168.168.21
  1  66.193.195.81
  2  66.193.200.5
  3  168.215.55.173
  4  168.215.55.101
  5  168.215.55.77
  6  66.192.250.38
  7  66.192.252.22
  8  208.51.224.141
  9  206.132.111.118
 10  206.132.111.162
 11  64.214.174.178
 12  192.168.1.191
 13  209.68.34.15
Computing statistics for 325 seconds...
            Source to Here   This Node/Link
Hop  RTT Lost/Sent = Pct  Lost/Sent = Pct  Address
 0                                          192.168.168.21
                             0/ 100 =   0%   |
 1    1ms   0/ 100 =   0%    0/ 100 =   0%  66.193.195.81]
                             0/ 100 =   0%   |
 2   14ms   0/ 100 =   0%    0/ 100 =   0%  66.193.200.5
                             0/ 100 =   0%   |
 3   10ms   0/ 100 =   0%    0/ 100 =   0%  168.215.55.173
                             0/ 100 =   0%   |
 4   10ms   0/ 100 =   0%    0/ 100 =   0%  168.215.55.101
                             0/ 100 =   0%   |
 5   12ms   0/ 100 =   0%    0/ 100 =   0%  168.215.55.77
                             0/ 100 =   0%   |
 6   14ms   0/ 100 =   0%    0/ 100 =   0%  66.192.250.38
                             0/ 100 =   0%   |
 7   14ms   0/ 100 =   0%    0/ 100 =   0%  66.192.252.22
                             0/ 100 =   0%   |
 8   14ms   0/ 100 =   0%    0/ 100 =   0%  208.51.224.141
                             0/ 100 =   0%   |
 9   81ms   0/ 100 =   0%    0/ 100 =   0%  206.132.111.118
                             0/ 100 =   0%   |
10   81ms   0/ 100 =   0%    0/ 100 =   0%  206.132.111.162]
                             0/ 100 =   0%   |
11   84ms   0/ 100 =   0%    0/ 100 =   0%  64.214.174.178]
                             0/ 100 =   0%   |
12   --- 100/ 100 =100%   100/ 100 =100%  192.168.1.191
                             0/ 100 =   0%   |
13   85ms   0/ 100 =   0%    0/ 100 =   0%  209.68.34.15
Trace complete.
```

Using the ping Command

`ping` is probably the most basic TCP/IP command line tool. Its main purpose is to determine whether you can reach another computer from your computer. It uses Internet Control Message Protocol (ICMP) to send mandatory `ECHO_REQUEST` datagrams to the specified host computer. When the reply is received back from the host, the `ping` command displays how long it took to receive the response.

You can specify the host to ping by using an IP address, as in this example:

```
C:\>ping 192.168.168.10
Pinging 192.168.168.10 with 32 bytes of data:
Reply from 192.168.168.10: bytes=32 time<1ms TTL=128
Reply from 192.168.168.10: bytes=32 time<1ms TTL=128
Reply from 192.168.168.10: bytes=32 time<1ms TTL=128
Reply from 192.168.168.10: bytes=32 time<1ms TTL=128
Ping statistics for 192.168.168.10:
    Packets: Sent = 4, Received = 4, Lost = 0 (0% loss),
Approximate round trip times in milli-seconds:
    Minimum = 0ms, Maximum = 0ms, Average = 0ms
C:\>
```

By default, the `ping` command sends four packets to the specified host. It displays the result of each packet sent. Then it displays summary statistics: how many packets were sent, how many replies were received, the error loss rate, and the approximate round-trip time.

You can also ping by using a DNS name, as in this example:

```
C:\>ping www.lowewriter.com
Pinging lowewriter.com [209.68.34.15] with 32 bytes of data:
Reply from 209.68.34.15: bytes=32 time=84ms TTL=53
Reply from 209.68.34.15: bytes=32 time=84ms TTL=53
Reply from 209.68.34.15: bytes=32 time=84ms TTL=53
Reply from 209.68.34.15: bytes=32 time=84ms TTL=53
Ping statistics for 209.68.34.15:
    Packets: Sent = 4, Received = 4, Lost = 0 (0% loss),
Approximate round trip times in milli-seconds:
    Minimum = 84ms, Maximum = 84ms, Average = 84ms
C:\>
```

The `ping` command uses a DNS query to determine the IP address for the specified host, and then pings the host based on its IP address.

The `ping` command has a number of other switches that you'll use rarely, if ever. Some of these switches are available only for some operating systems. To find out which switches are available for your version of Ping, type **ping /?** (Windows) or **man ping** (Unix/Linux).

You can find a very interesting story about the creation of the `ping` command written by the command's author, Mike Muus, at his website at `http://ftp.arl.mil/~mike/ping.html`. (Sadly, Mr. Muus was killed in an automobile accident in November, 2000.)

Using the route Command

Using the `route` command displays or modifies the computer's routing table. For a typical computer that has a single network interface and is connected to a local area network (LAN) that has a router, the routing table is pretty simple and isn't often the source of network problems. Still, if you're having trouble accessing other computers or other networks, you can use the `route` command to make sure that a bad entry in the computer's routing table isn't the culprit.

For a computer with more than one interface and that's configured to work as a router, the routing table is often a major source of trouble. Setting up the routing table properly is a key part of configuring a router to work.

Displaying the routing table

To display the routing table (both IPv4 and IPv6) in Windows, use the `route print` command. In Unix/Linux, you can just use `route` without any command line switches. The output displayed by the Windows and Unix/Linux commands are similar. Here's an example from a typical Windows client computer:

```
C:\>route print
===========================================================================
Interface List
  8 ...00 12 3f a7 17 ba ...... Intel(R) PRO/100 VE Network Connection
  1 ........................ Software Loopback Interface 1
  9 ...02 00 54 55 4e 01 ...... Teredo Tunneling Pseudo-Interface
 10 ...00 00 00 00 00 00 00 e0  isatap.{D0F85930-01E2-402F-B0FC-31DFF887F06F}
===========================================================================

IPv4 Route Table
===========================================================================
Active Routes:
Network Destination        Netmask          Gateway       Interface  Metric
          0.0.0.0          0.0.0.0      192.168.1.1    192.168.1.110    276
        127.0.0.0        255.0.0.0          On-link        127.0.0.1    306
        127.0.0.1  255.255.255.255          On-link        127.0.0.1    306
  127.255.255.255  255.255.255.255          On-link        127.0.0.1    306
      192.168.1.0    255.255.255.0          On-link    192.168.1.110    276
    192.168.1.110  255.255.255.255          On-link    192.168.1.110    276
    192.168.1.255  255.255.255.255          On-link    192.168.1.110    276
        224.0.0.0        240.0.0.0          On-link        127.0.0.1    306
        224.0.0.0        240.0.0.0          On-link    192.168.1.110    276
  255.255.255.255  255.255.255.255          On-link        127.0.0.1    306
  255.255.255.255  255.255.255.255          On-link    192.168.1.110    276
===========================================================================
```

```
Persistent Routes:
  Network Address           Netmask  Gateway Address  Metric
          0.0.0.0           0.0.0.0      192.168.1.1  Default
===========================================================================

IPv6 Route Table
===========================================================================
Active Routes:
 If Metric Network Destination      Gateway
  9     18 ::/0                      On-link
  1    306 ::1/128                   On-link
  9     18 2001::/32                 On-link
  9    266 2001:0:4136:e38c:2c6c:670:3f57:fe91/128
                                     On-link
  8    276 fe80::/64                 On-link
  9    266 fe80::/64                 On-link
 10    281 fe80::5efe:192.168.1.110/128
                                     On-link
  8    276 fe80::cca:9067:9427:a911/128
                                     On-link
  9    266 fe80::2c6c:670:3f57:fe91/128
                                     On-link
  1    306 ff00::/8                  On-link
  9    266 ff00::/8                  On-link
  8    276 ff00::/8                  On-link
===========================================================================
Persistent Routes:
  None
C:\>
```

For each entry in the routing table, five items of information are listed:

+ **The destination IP address**

  Actually, this is the address of the destination subnet, and must be interpreted in the context of the subnet mask.

+ **The subnet mask that must be applied to the destination address to determine the destination subnet**

+ **The IP address of the gateway to which traffic intended for the destination subnet will be sent**

+ **The IP address of the interface through which the traffic will be sent to the destination subnet**

+ **The *metric,* which indicates the number of hops required to reach destinations via the gateway**

Each packet that's processed by the computer is evaluated against the rules in the routing table. If the packet's destination address matches the destination subnet for the rule, the packet is sent to the specified gateway via the specified network interface. If not, the next rule is applied.

The computer on which I ran the route command in this example is on a private 192.168.1.0 subnet. The computer's IP address is 192.168.1.100, and the default gateway is a router at 192.168.1.1.

Here's how the rules shown in this example are used. Notice that you have to read the entries from the bottom up:

✦ **The first rule is for packets sent to 255.255.255.255, with subnet mask 255.255.255.255.** This special IP address is for broadcast packets. The rule specifies that these broadcast packets should be delivered to the local network interface (192.168.1.100).

✦ **The next rule is for packets sent to 192.168.1.255, again with subnet mask 255.255.255.255.** These are also broadcast packets and are sent to the local network interface.

✦ **The next rule is for packets sent to 192.168.1.100, again with subnet mask 255.255.255.255.** This is for packets that the computer is sending to itself via its own IP address. This rule specifies that these packets will be sent to the local loopback interface on 127.0.0.1.

✦ **The next rule is for packets sent to 192.168.1.0, with subnet mask 255.255.255.0.** These are packets intended for the local subnet. They're sent to the subnet via the local interface at 192.169.1.100.

✦ **The next rule is for packets sent to the loopback address (127.0.0.1, subnet mask 255.0.0.0).** These packets are sent straight through to the loopback interface, 127.0.0.1.

✦ **The last rule is for everything else.** All IP addresses will match the destination IP address 0.0.0.0 with subnet mask 0.0.0.0 and will be sent to the default gateway router at 192.168.1.1 via the computer's network interface at 192.168.1.100.

One major difference between the Windows version of route and the Unix/Linux version is the order in which they list the routing table. The Windows route command lists the table starting with the most general entry and works toward the most specific. The Unix/Linux version is the other way around: It starts with the most specific and works toward the more general. The Unix/Linux order makes more sense — the Windows route command displays the routing list upside down.

Modifying the routing table

Besides displaying the routing table, the route command also lets you modify it by adding, deleting, or changing entries.

Don't try this unless you know what you're doing. If you mess up the routing table, your computer may not be able to communicate with anyone.

The syntax for the route command for adding, deleting, or changing a route entry is

```
route [-p] command dest [mask subnet] gateway [-if interface]
```

The following list describes each of the `route` command's parameters:

+ –p: Makes the entry persistent. If you omit –p, the entry will be deleted the next time you reboot. (Use this only with `add` commands.)

+ *command*: Add, delete, or change.

+ *dest*: The IP address of the destination subnet.

+ `mask` *subnet*: The subnet mask. If you omit the subnet mask, the default is 255.255.255.255, meaning that the entry will apply only to a single host rather than a subnet. You usually want to include the mask.

+ *gateway*: The IP address of the gateway to which packets will be sent.

+ `if` *interface*: The IP address of the interface through which packets will be sent. If your computer has only one network interface, you can omit this.

Suppose that your network has a second router that serves as a link to another private subnet, 192.168.2.0 (subnet mask 255.255.255.0). The interface on the local side of this router is at 192.168.1.200. To add a static route entry that sends packets intended for the 192.168.2.0 subnet to this router, use a command like this:

```
C:\>route -p add 192.168.2.0 mask 255.255.255.0 192.168.1.200
```

Now, suppose that you later change the IP address of the router to 192.168.1.222. You can update this route with the following command:

```
C:\>route change 192.168.2.0 mask 255.255.255.0 192.168.1.222
```

Notice that I specify the mask again. If you omit the mask from a `route change` command, the command changes the mask to 255.255.255.255!

Finally, suppose that you realize that setting up a second router on this network wasn't such a good idea after all, so you want to just delete the entry. The following command will do the trick:

```
C:\>route delete 192.168.2.0
```

Using the tracert Command

The `tracert` command (`traceroute` in Unix/Linux implementations) is one of the key diagnostic tools for TCP/IP. It displays a list of all the routers that a packet must go through to get from the computer where `tracert` is run to any other computer on the Internet. Each one of these routers is called a *hop,* presumably because the original designers of the IP protocol played a lot of hopscotch when they were young. If you can't connect to another computer, you can use `tracert` to find out exactly where the problem is occurring.

`tracert` makes three attempts to contact the router at each hop and displays the response time for each of these attempts. Then, it displays the DNS name of the router (if available) and the router's IP address.

To use `tracert`, type the `tracert` command followed by the host name of the computer to which you want to trace the route. For example, suppose that you're having trouble sending mail to a recipient at `wiley.com`. You've used `nslookup` to determine that the mail server for `wiley.com` is `xmail.wiley.com`, so now you can use `tracert` to trace the routers along the path from your computer to `xmail.wiley.com`:

```
C:\>tracert xmail.wiley.com
Tracing route to xmail.wiley.com [208.215.179.78]
over a maximum of 30 hops:
  1    27 ms    14 ms    10 ms  10.242.144.1
  2    11 ms    43 ms    10 ms  bar01-p5-0-0.frsnhe4.ca.attbb.net [24.130.64.125]
  3     9 ms    14 ms    12 ms  bar01-p4-0-0.frsnhe1.ca.attbb.net [24.130.0.5]
  4    25 ms    30 ms    29 ms  bic01-p6-0.elsgrdc1.ca.attbb.net [24.130.0.49]
  5    25 ms    29 ms    43 ms  bic02-d4-0.elsgrdc1.ca.attbb.net [24.130.0.162]
  6    21 ms    19 ms    20 ms  bar01-p2-0.lsanhe4.ca.attbb.net [24.130.0.197]
  7    37 ms    38 ms    19 ms  bic01-p2-0.lsanhe3.ca.attbb.net [24.130.0.193]
  8    20 ms    22 ms    21 ms  12.119.9.5
  9    21 ms    21 ms    22 ms  tbr2-p012702.la2ca.ip.att.net [12.123.199.241]
 10    71 ms   101 ms    62 ms  tbr2-p013801.sl9mo.ip.att.net [12.122.10.13]
 11    68 ms    77 ms    71 ms  tbr1-p012401.sl9mo.ip.att.net [12.122.9.141]
 12    79 ms    81 ms    83 ms  tbr1-cl4.wswdc.ip.att.net [12.122.10.29]
 13    83 ms   107 ms   103 ms  tbr1-p012201.n54ny.ip.att.net [12.122.10.17]
 14   106 ms    85 ms   105 ms  gbr6-p30.n54ny.ip.att.net [12.122.11.14]
 15   104 ms    96 ms    88 ms  gar3-p370.n54ny.ip.att.net [12.123.1.189]
 16    98 ms    86 ms    83 ms  12.125.50.162
 17    85 ms    90 ms    87 ms  xmail.wiley.com [208.215.179.78]
Trace complete.
```

Wow, when I send mail to my editors at Wiley, the mail travels through 17 routers along the way. No wonder I'm always missing deadlines!

The most likely problem that you'll encounter when you use `tracert` is a timeout during one of the hops. Timeouts are indicated by asterisks where you'd expect to see a time. For example, the following `tracert` output shows the fourth hop timing out on all three attempts:

```
C:\>tracert xmail.wiley.com
Tracing route to xmail.wiley.com [208.215.179.78]
over a maximum of 30 hops:
  1    27 ms    14 ms    10 ms  10.242.144.1
  2    11 ms    43 ms    10 ms  bar01-p5-0-0.frsnhe4.ca.attbb.net [24.130.64.125]
  3     9 ms    14 ms    12 ms  bar01-p4-0-0.frsnhe1.ca.attbb.net [24.130.0.5]
  4     *        *        *     Request timed out.
```

**Book IV
Chapter 6**

TCP/IP Tools and Commands

Understanding how tracert works

Understanding how `tracert` works can provide some insight that may help you to interpret the results it provides. Plus, you can use this knowledge to impress your friends, who probably don't know how it works.

The key to `tracert` is a field that's a standard part of all IP packets called TTL, which stands for *Time to Live.* In most other circumstances, a value called TTL would be a time value — not in IP packets, however. In an IP packet, the TTL value indicates how many routers a packet can travel through on its way to its destination. Every time a router forwards an IP packet, it subtracts one from the packet's TTL value. When the TTL value reaches zero, the router refuses to forward the packet.

The `tracert` command sends a series of special messages called ICMP Echo Requests to the destination computer. The first time it sends this message, it sets the TTL value of the packet to 1. When the packet arrives at the first router along the path to the destination, that router subtracts one from the TTL value, sees that the TTL value has become 0, so it sends a Time Exceeded message back to the original host. When the `tracert` command receives this Time Exceeded message, it extracts the IP address of the router from it, calculates the time it took for the message to return, and displays the first hop.

Then the `tracert` command sends another Echo Request message: this time, with the TTL value set to 2. This message goes through the first router to the second router, which sees that the TTL value has been decremented to 0 and then sends back a Time Exceeded message. When `tracert` receives the Time Exceeded message from the second router, it displays the line for the second hop. This process continues, each time with a greater TTL value, until the Echo Request finally reaches the destination.

Pretty clever, eh?

(Note that the Unix/Linux `traceroute` command uses a slightly different set of TCP/IP messages and responses to accomplish the same result.)

Sometimes, timeouts are caused by temporary problems, so you should try the `tracert` again to see if the problem persists. If you keep getting timeouts at the same router, the router could be having a genuine problem.

Book V

Wireless Networking

The 5th Wave   By Rich Tennant

"Good news! I found a place where the router works with the PC upstairs and the one in the basement."

Contents at a Glance

Chapter 1: Setting Up a Wireless Network

In This Chapter

✔ Looking at wireless network standards

✔ Reviewing some basic radio terms

✔ Considering infrastructure and ad-hoc networks

✔ Working with a wireless access point

✔ Configuring Windows for wireless networking

Since the beginning of Ethernet networking, cable has been getting smaller and easier to work with. The original Ethernet cable was about as thick as your thumb, weighed a ton, and was difficult to bend around tight corners. Then came coaxial cable, which was lighter and easier to work with. Coaxial cable was supplanted by unshielded twisted-pair (UTP) cable, which is the cable used for most networks today.

Although cable through the years has become smaller, cheaper, and easier to work with, it is still *cable*. So you have to drill holes in walls, pull cable through ceilings, and get insulation in your hair to wire your entire home or office.

That's why wireless networking has become so popular. With wireless networking, you don't need cables to connect your computers. Instead, wireless networks use radio waves to send and receive network signals. As a result, a computer can connect to a wireless network at any location in your home or office.

Wireless networks are especially useful for notebook computers. After all, the main benefit of a notebook computer is that you can carry it around with you wherever you go. At work, you can use your notebook computer at your desk, in the conference room, in the break room, or even out in the parking lot. At home, you can use it in the bedroom, kitchen, den, or game room, or out by the pool. With wireless networking, your notebook computer can be connected to the network, no matter where you take it.

Wireless networks have also become extremely useful for other types of mobile devices, such as smartphones and tablet computers. These devices can connect via a cell network, but such connections can be expensive. With a wireless network, you can connect your smart phone or tablet without having to pay your cell-phone company for the connection time.

This chapter introduces you to the ins and outs of setting up a wireless network. I tell you what you need to know about wireless networking standards, how to plan a wireless network, how to install and configure wireless network components, and how to create a network that mixes wireless and cabled components.

Diving into Wireless Networking

A *wireless network* is a network that uses radio signals rather than direct cable connections to exchange information. A computer with a wireless network connection is like a cell phone. Just as you don't have to be connected to a phone line to use a cell phone, you don't have to be connected to a network cable to use a wireless networked computer.

The following paragraphs summarize some of the key concepts and terms that you need to understand to set up and use a basic wireless network:

✦ A wireless network is often referred to as a *WLAN,* for *wireless local area network.* Some people prefer to switch the acronym around to *local area wireless network,* or *LAWN.* The term *Wi-Fi* is often used to describe wireless networks, although it technically refers to just one form of wireless network: the 802.11b standard. (See the section "Eight-Oh-Two-Dot-Eleventy Something? [Or, Understanding Wireless Standards]" later in this chapter for more information.)

✦ A wireless network has a name, known as a SSID. *SSID* stands for *service set identifier.* (Wouldn't that make a great *Jeopardy!* question? I'll take obscure four-letter acronyms for $400, please!) All the computers that belong to a single wireless network must have the same SSID.

✦ Wireless networks can transmit over any of several channels. For computers to talk to one another, they must be configured to transmit on the same channel.

✦ The simplest type of wireless network consists of two or more computers with wireless network adapters. This type of network is called an *ad-hoc mode network.*

✦ A more complex type of network is an *infrastructure mode network.* All this really means is that a group of wireless computers can be connected not only to one another, but also to an existing cabled network via a device called a *wireless access point,* or *WAP.* (I tell you more about ad-hoc and infrastructure networks later in this chapter.)

A Little High School Electronics

I was a real nerd in high school: I took three years of electronics. The electronics class at my school was right next door to the auto shop. All the cool kids took auto shop, of course, and only nerds like me took electronics. We hung in there, though, and learned all about capacitors and diodes while the cool kids were learning how to raise their cars and install 2-gigawatt stereo systems.

It turns out that a little of that high school electronics information proves useful when it comes to wireless networking — not much, but a little. You'll understand wireless networking much better if you know the meanings of some basic radio terms.

Waves and frequencies

For starters, *radio* consists of electromagnetic waves that are sent through the atmosphere. You can't see or hear them, but radio receivers can pick them up and convert them to sounds, images, or — in the case of wireless networks — data. Radio waves are actually cyclical waves of electronic energy that repeat at a particular rate called the *frequency.*

Figure 1-1 shows two frequencies of radio waves. The first is one cycle per second; the second is two cycles per second. (Real radio doesn't operate at that low a frequency, but I figured that one and two cycles per second would be easier to draw than 680,000 and 2.4 million cycles per second.)

The measure of a frequency is *cycles per second,* which indicates how many complete cycles the wave makes in 1 second (duh). In honor of Heinrich Hertz — who didn't invent catsup, but was the first person to successfully send and receive radio waves (it happened in the 1880s) — *cycles per second* is usually referred to as *Hertz,* abbreviated *Hz.* Thus, 1 Hz is one cycle per second. Incidentally, when the prefix *K* (for *kilo,* or 1,000), *M* (for *mega,* 1 million), or *G* (for *giga,* 1 billion) is added to the front of Hz, the *H* is still capitalized. Thus, 2.4 MHz is correct (not 2.4 Mhz).

The beauty of radio frequencies is that transmitters can be tuned to broadcast radio waves at a precise frequency. Likewise, receivers can be tuned to receive radio waves at a precise frequency, ignoring waves at other frequencies. That's why you can tune the radio in your car to listen to dozens of radio stations: Each station broadcasts at its own frequency.

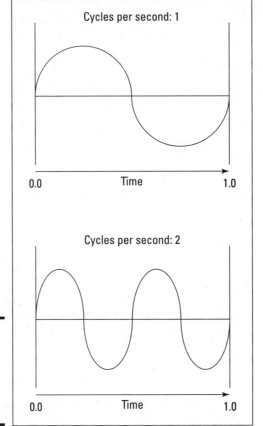

Figure 1-1:
Radio
waves
frequently
have
frequency.

Wavelength and antennas

A term related to frequency is *wavelength*. Radio waves travel at the speed of light. The term *wavelength* refers to how far the radio signal travels with each cycle. Because the speed of light is roughly 182,282 miles per second, for example, the wavelength of a 1 Hz radio wave is about 182,282 miles. The wavelength of a 2 Hz signal is about half that, a mere 91,141 miles.

As you can see, the wavelength decreases as the frequency increases. The wavelength of a typical AM radio station broadcasting at 580 KHz is about 522 yards. For a TV station broadcasting at 100 MHz, it's about 3 yards. For a wireless network broadcasting at 2.4 GHz, the wavelength is just under 5 inches.

It turns out that the shorter the wavelength, the smaller the antenna needs to be to adequately receive the signal. As a result, higher-frequency transmissions need smaller antennas. You may have noticed that AM radio stations usually have huge antennas mounted on top of tall towers, but cellphone transmitters are much smaller, and their towers aren't nearly as tall. That's because cell phones operate on a higher frequency than AM radio stations do. So who decides what type of radio gets to use specific frequencies? That's where spectrums and the FCC come in.

Spectrums and the FCC

The term *spectrum* refers to a continuous range of frequencies on which radio can operate. In the United States, the Federal Communications Commission (FCC) regulates not only how much of Janet Jackson can be shown at the Super Bowl, but also how various portions of the radio spectrum can be used. Essentially, the FCC has divided the radio spectrum into dozens of small ranges called *bands* and restricted certain uses to certain bands. AM radio, for example, operates in the band from 535 KHz to 1,700 KHz.

Table 1-1 lists some of the most popular bands. Note that some of these bands are wide — UHF television begins at 470 MHz and ends at 806 MHz — but other bands are restricted to a specific frequency. The difference between the lowest and highest frequency within a band is called the *bandwidth*.

And now, a word from the irony department

I was an English-literature major in college, so I like to use literary devices such as irony. I don't get to use it much in the computer books I write, so when I get the chance to use irony, I like to jump on it like a hog out of water.

So here's my juicy bit of irony for today: The very first Ethernet system was actually a wireless network. Ethernet traces its roots to a network called AlohaNet, developed at the University of Hawaii in 1970. This network transmitted its data by using small radios. If two computers tried to broadcast data at the same time, the computers detected the collision and tried again after a short, random delay. This technique was the inspiration for the basic technique of Ethernet, now called *carrier sense multiple access with collision detection,* or *CSMA/CD.* The wireless AlohaNet was the network that inspired Robert Metcalfe to develop his cabled network, which he called *Ethernet,* as his doctoral thesis at Harvard in 1973.

For the next 20 years or so, Ethernet was pretty much a cable-only network. It wasn't until the mid-1990s that Ethernet finally returned to its wireless roots.

Table 1-1	Popular Bands of the Radio Spectrum
Band	*Use*
535 KHz–1,700 KHz	AM radio
5.9 MHz–26.1 MHz	Shortwave radio
26.96 MHz–27.41 MHz	Citizens Band (CB) radio
54 MHz–88 MHz	Television (VHF channels 2 through 6)
88 MHz–108 MHz	FM radio
174 MHz–220 MHz	Television (VHF channels 7 through 13)
470 MHz–806 MHz	Television (UHF channels)
806 MHz–890 MHz	Cellular networks
900 MHz	Cordless phones
1850 MHz–1990 MHz	PCS cellular
2.4 GHz–2.4835 GHz	Cordless phones and wireless networks (802.11b and 802.11n)
4 GHz–5 GHz	Large-dish satellite TV
5 GHz	Wireless networks (802.11a)
11.7 GHz–12.7 GHz	Small-dish satellite TV

Two of the bands in the spectrum are allocated for use by wireless networks: 2.4 GHz and 5 GHz. Note that these bands aren't devoted exclusively to wireless networks. In particular, the 2.4 GHz band shares its space with cordless phones. As a result, cordless phones sometimes interfere with wireless networks.

Eight-Oh-Two-Dot-Eleventy Something? (Or, Understanding Wireless Standards)

The most popular standards for wireless networks are the IEEE 802.11 standards. These standards are essential wireless Ethernet standards and use many of the same networking techniques that the cabled Ethernet standards (in other words, 802.3) use. Most notably, 802.11 networks use the same CSMA/CD technique as cabled Ethernet to recover from network collisions.

The 802.11 standards address the bottom two layers of the IEEE seven-layer model: The Physical layer and the Media Access Control (MAC) layer. Note that TCP/IP protocols apply to higher layers of the model. As a result, TCP/IP runs just fine on 802.11 networks.

The original 802.11 standard was adopted in 1997. Two additions to the standard, 802.11a and 802.11b, were adopted in 1999. The latest and greatest versions are 802.11g and 802.11n.

Table 1-2 summarizes the basic characteristics of the four variants of 802.11.

Table 1-2	802.11 Variations		
Standard	Speeds	Frequency	Typical Range (Indoors)
802.11a	Up to 54 Mbps	5 GHz	150 feet
802.11b	Up to 11 Mbps	2.4 GHz	300 feet
802.11g	Up to 54 Mbps	2.4 GHz	300 feet
802.11n	Up to 600 Mbps (but most devices are in the 100 Mbps range)	2.4 GHz	230 feet

Currently, most wireless networks are based on the 802.11n standard.

Home on the Range

The maximum range of an 802.11g wireless device indoors is about 300 feet. This can have an interesting effect when you get a bunch of wireless computers together — such that some of them are in range of one another, but others are not. Suppose that Wally, Ward, and the Beaver all have wireless notebooks. Wally's computer is 200 feet away from Ward's computer, and Ward's computer is 200 feet away from Beaver's in the opposite direction (see Figure 1-2). In this case, Ward is able to access both Wally's and Beaver's computers, but Wally can access only Ward's computer, and Beaver can access only Ward's computer. In other words, Wally and Beaver won't be able to access each other's computers because they're outside the 300-feet range limit. (This is starting to sound suspiciously like an algebra problem. Now suppose that Wally starts walking toward Ward at 2 miles per hour, and Beaver starts running toward Ward at 4 miles per hour. . . .)

Although the normal range for 802.11g is 300 feet, the range may be less in actual practice. Obstacles such as solid walls, bad weather, cordless phones, microwave ovens, backyard nuclear reactors, and so on can all conspire to reduce the effective range of a wireless adapter. If you're having trouble connecting to the network, sometimes just adjusting the antenna helps.

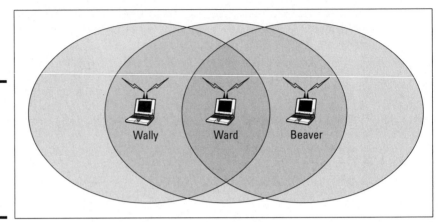

Figure 1-2:
Wally,
Ward, and
the Beaver
playing
with their
wireless
network.

Also, wireless networks tend to slow down when the distance increases. 802.11g network devices claim to operate at 54 Mbps, but they usually achieve that speed only at ranges of 100 feet or less. At 300 feet, they often slow to a crawl. You should also realize that when you're at the edge of the wireless device's range, you're more likely to lose your connection suddenly due to bad weather.

Wireless Network Adapters

Each computer that will connect to your wireless network needs a *wireless network adapter,* which is similar to the network interface card (NIC) that's used for a standard Ethernet connection. Instead of having a cable connector on the back, however, a wireless network adapter has an antenna.

Just about all notebook computers come with wireless networking built in, so you don't have to add a separate wireless network adapter to a notebook computer. Desktop computers are a different story. They typically don't have built-in wireless networking, so you'll need to purchase one of two types of wireless adapters:

✦ **A wireless PCI card** is a wireless network adapter that you install in an available slot inside a desktop computer. To install this type of card, you need to take your computer apart, so use this type of card only if you have the expertise and the nerves to dig into your computer's guts.

✦ **A wireless USB adapter** is a separate box that plugs into a USB port on your computer. Because the USB adapter is a separate device, it takes up extra desk space. You can install it without taking your computer apart, however.

You can purchase a combination 802.11b/g PCI adapter for less than $50.
USB versions cost about $10 more.

> **TIP**
>
> At first, you may think that wireless network adapters are prohibitively
> expensive. After all, you can buy a regular Ethernet adapter for as little as
> $20. When you consider that you don't have to purchase and install cable to
> use a wireless adapter, however, the price of wireless networking becomes
> more palatable. Also, if you shop around, sometimes you can find wireless
> adapters for as little as $19.95.

Figure 1-3 shows a typical wireless network adapter. This one is a Linksys
WUSB11, which sells for about $50. To install this device, you simply con-
nect it to one of your computer's USB ports with the included USB connector. Then you install the driver software that comes on the CD, and you're
ready to network. The device is relatively small. You'll find a little strip of
Velcro on the back so you can mount the adapter on the side of your computer or desk, if you want. The adapter gets its power from the USB port
itself, so there's no separate power cord to plug in.

Figure 1-3:
A typical
wireless
networking
adapter.

Wireless Access Points

Unlike cabled networks, wireless networks don't need a hub or switch. If all
you want to do is network a group of wireless computers, you just purchase
a wireless adapter for each computer, put them all within 300 feet of one
another, and voilà! — instant network.

But what if you already have an existing cabled network? Suppose that you work at an office with 15 computers all cabled up nicely, and you just want to add a couple of wireless notebook computers to the network. Or suppose that you have two computers in your den connected with network cable, but you want to link up a computer in your bedroom without pulling cable through the attic.

That's where a *wireless access point,* also known as a *WAP,* comes in. A WAP performs two functions:

✦ It acts as a central connection point for all your computers that have wireless network adapters. In effect, the WAP performs essentially the same function that a hub or switch performs for a wired network.

✦ It links your wireless network to your existing wired network so that your wired computer and your wireless computers get along like one big happy family. This sounds like the makings of a Dr. Seuss story. ("Now the wireless sneeches had hubs without wires. But the twisted-pair sneeches had cables to thires. . . .")

Wireless access points are sometimes just called *access points,* or *APs.* An access point is a box that has an antenna (or often a pair of antennae) and an RJ-45 Ethernet port. You just plug the access point into a network cable and then plug the other end of the cable into a hub or switch, and your wireless network should be able to connect to your cabled network.

Figure 1-4 shows how an access point acts as a central connection point for wireless computers and how it bridges your wireless network to your wired network.

Infrastructure mode

When you set up a wireless network with an access point, you're creating an *infrastructure mode* network. It's called *infrastructure mode* because the access point provides a permanent infrastructure for the network. The access points are installed at fixed physical locations, so the network has relatively stable boundaries. Whenever a mobile computer wanders into the range of one of the access points, it has come into the sphere of the network and can connect.

An access point and all the wireless computers that are connected to it are referred to as a *Basic Service Set,* or *BSS.* Each BSS is identified by a *Service Set Identifier,* or *SSID.* When you configure an access point, you specify the SSID that you want to use. The SSID is often a generic name such as *wireless,* or it can be a name that you create. Some access points use the MAC address of the WAP as the SSID.

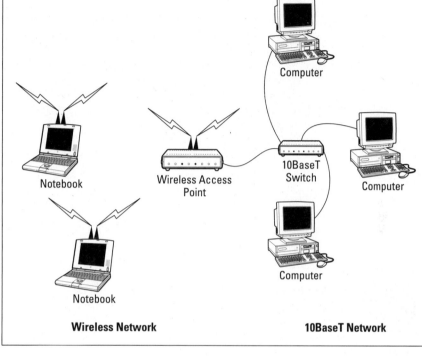

Figure 1-4:
A wireless
access
point
connects
a wireless
network to
a cabled
network.

Multifunction WAPs

Wireless access points often include other built-in features. Some access points double as Ethernet hubs or switches, and in that case, the access point will have more than one RJ-45 port. In addition, some access points include broadband cable or DSL firewall routers that enable you to connect to the Internet. Figure 1-5 shows a Linksys BEFW11S4 wireless access point router. I have one of these little guys in my home. This inexpensive (about $60) device includes the following features:

✦ An 802.11b wireless access point that lets me connect a notebook computer and a computer located on the other side of the house because I didn't want to run cable through the attic.

✦ A four-port 10/100 MHz switch that I can use to connect up to four computers via twisted-pair cable.

✦ A DSL/cable router that I connect to my cable modem. This router enables all the computers on the network (cabled and wireless) to access the Internet.

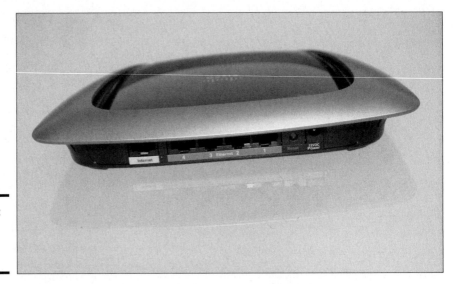

Figure 1-5:
A typical
wireless
router.

A multifunction access point that's designed to serve as an Internet gateway for home networks sometimes is called a *residential gateway*.

Roaming

You can use two or more wireless access points to create a large wireless network in which computer users can roam from area to area and still be connected to the wireless network. As the user moves out of the range of one access point, another access point automatically picks up the user and takes over without interrupting the user's network service.

To set up two or more access points for roaming, you must carefully place the WAPs so that all areas of the office or building that are being networked are in range of at least one of the WAPs. Then just make sure that all the computers and access points use the same SSID.

Two or more access points joined for the purposes of roaming, along with all the wireless computers connected to any of the access points, form what's called an *Extended Service Set,* or *ESS.* The access points in the ESS are usually connected to a wired network.

One of the current limitations of roaming is that each access point in an ESS must be on the same TCP/IP subnet. That way, a computer that roams from one access point to another within the ESS retains the same IP address. If the access points had a different subnet, a roaming computer would have to change IP addresses when it moved from one access point to another.

Wireless bridging

Another use for wireless access points is to bridge separate subnets that can't easily be connected by cable. Suppose that you have two office buildings that are only about 50 feet apart. To run cable from one building to the other, you'd have to bury conduit — a potentially expensive job. Because the buildings are so close, though, you can probably connect them with a pair of wireless access points that function as a *wireless bridge* between the two networks. Connect one of the access points to the first network and the other access point to the second network. Then configure both access points to use the same SSID and channel.

Ad-hoc networks

A wireless access point isn't necessary to set up a wireless network. Any time two or more wireless devices come within range of each other, they can link up to form an *ad-hoc network*. If you and a few of your friends all have notebook computers with 802.11b/g or 802.11/n wireless network adapters, for example, you can meet anywhere and form an ad-hoc network.

All the computers within range of one another in an ad-hoc network are called an *Independent Basic Service Set,* or *IBSS.*

Configuring a Wireless Access Point

The physical setup for a wireless access point is pretty simple: You take it out of the box, put it on a shelf or on top of a bookcase near a network jack and a power outlet, plug in the power cable, and plug in the network cable.

The software configuration for an access point is a little more involved but still not very complicated. It's usually done via a web interface. To get to the configuration page for the access point, you need to know the access point's IP address. Then you just type that address in the address bar of a browser on any computer on the network.

Multifunction access points usually provide DHCP and NAT services for the networks and double as the network's gateway router. As a result, they typically have a private IP address that's at the beginning of one of the Internet's private IP address ranges, such as 192.168.0.1 or 10.0.0.1. Consult the documentation that came with the access point to find out more.

If you use a multifunction access point that is both your wireless access point and your Internet router, and you can't remember the IP address, run the IPCONFIG command at a command prompt on any computer on the network. The Default Gateway IP address should be the IP address of the access point.

Basic configuration options

Figure 1-6 shows the main configuration screen for a Linksys BEFW11S4 wireless access point router that is pictured in Figure 1-5. I called up this configuration page by entering **192.168.1.1** in the address bar of a web browser and then supplying the login password when prompted.

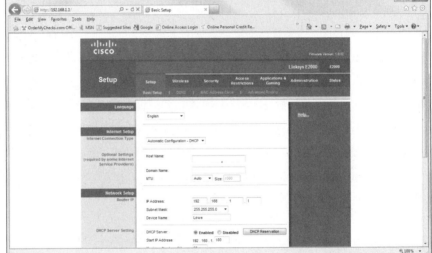

Figure 1-6:
The main configuration page for a Linksys wireless router.

The main setup page of this router lets you figure information such as the hostname and IP address of the router and whether the router's DHCP server should be enabled. Options that are found on additional tabs let you configure wireless settings such as the network name (also called the SSID), the type of security to enforce, and a variety of other settings.

DHCP configuration

You can configure most multifunction access points to operate as a DHCP server. For small networks, it's common for the access point to also be the DHCP server for the entire network. In that case, you need to configure the access point's DHCP server. Figure 1-7 shows the DHCP configuration page for the Linksys WAP router. To enable DHCP, you select the Enable option and then specify the other configuration options to use for the DHCP server.

Larger networks that have more demanding DHCP requirements are likely to have a separate DHCP server running on another computer. In that case, you can defer to the existing server by disabling the DHCP server in the access point.

Figure 1-7:
Configuring
DHCP for
a Linksys
wireless
router.

For more information on configuring a DHCP server, please refer to Book IV, Chapter 3.

Configuring Windows XP for Wireless Networking

The first step in configuring Windows XP for wireless networking is installing the appropriate device driver for your wireless network adapter. To do that, you need the installation CD that came with the adapter. Follow the instructions that came with the adapter to install the drivers.

Windows XP has some nice built-in features for working with wireless networks. You can configure these features by opening the Network Connections folder. Choose Start➪Control Panel and then double-click the Network Connections icon. Right-click the wireless network connection, and choose Properties from the contextual menu to bring up the Properties dialog box. Then click the Wireless Networks tab to display the wireless networking options shown in Figure 1-8.

Each time you connect to a wireless network, Windows XP adds that network to this dialog box. Then you can juggle the order of the networks in the Preferred Networks section to indicate which network you prefer to join if you find yourself within range of two or more networks at the same time. You can use the Move Up and Move Down buttons next to the Preferred Networks list to change your preferences.

Figure 1-8:
Configuring
wireless
networking
in
Windows XP.

To add a network that you haven't yet actually joined, click the Add button. This brings up the dialog box shown in Figure 1-9. Here, you can type the SSID value of the network that you want to add. You can also specify other information, such as whether to use data encryption, how to authenticate yourself, and whether the network is an ad-hoc rather than an infrastructure network.

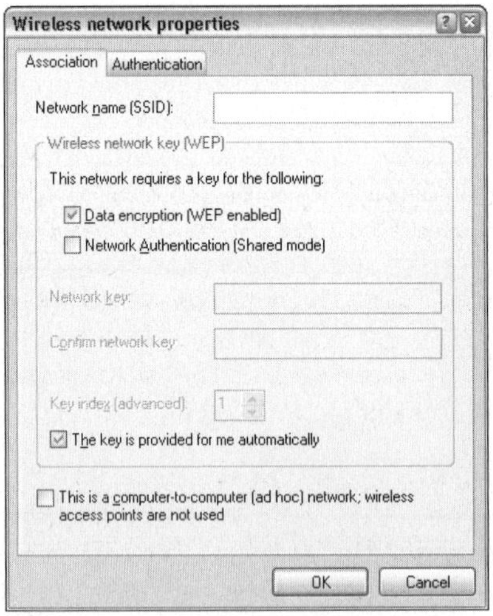

Figure 1-9:
Adding a
wireless
network in
Windows XP.

Using a Wireless Network with Windows XP

Windows XP also has some nice built-in features that simplify the task of using a wireless network. When your computer comes within range of a wireless network, for example, a pop-up balloon appears in the taskbar, indicating that a network is available.

If one of your preferred networks is within range, clicking the balloon automatically connects you to that network. If Windows XP doesn't recognize any of the networks, clicking the balloon displays the dialog box shown in Figure 1-10. With this dialog box, you can choose the network that you want to join (if more than one network is listed) and then click Connect to join the selected network.

Figure 1-10: Joining a wireless network in Windows XP.

After you've joined a wireless network, a network status icon appears in the notification area of the taskbar. You can see the network status quickly by hovering the mouse cursor over this icon; a balloon appears to indicate the state of the connection. For more detailed information, you can click the status icon to display the Wireless Network Connection Status dialog box, shown in Figure 1-11.

This dialog box provides the following items of information:

+ **Status:** Indicates whether you're connected.

+ **Duration:** Indicates how long you've been connected.

+ **Speed:** Indicates the current network speed. Ideally, this setting should say 11 Mbps for an 802.11b network, or 54 Mbps for an 802.11a or 802.11g network. If the network connection isn't of the highest quality, however, the speed may drop to a lower value.

✦ **Signal Strength:** Displays a graphic representation of the quality of the signal.

✦ **Packets Sent and Received:** Indicates how many packets of data you've sent and received over the network.

Figure 1-11:
The
Wireless
Network
Connection
Status
dialog box
(Windows
XP).

You can click the Properties button to bring up the Connection Properties dialog box for the wireless connection.

Connecting to a Wireless Network with Windows Vista

Wireless networking in Windows Vista is considerably simpler than in Windows XP. When Windows Vista detects that a wireless network is within range, a balloon notification appears on the screen to indicate that one or more wireless networks are available. You can double-click this balloon to summon the dialog box shown in Figure 1-12. Then you can double-click the network you want to connect to.

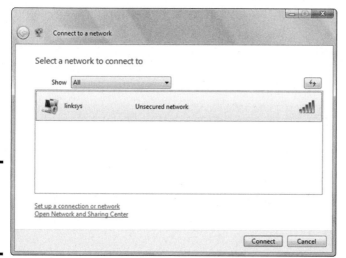

Figure 1-12:
Choosing
a wireless
network in
Vista.

Connecting to a Wireless Network with Windows 7

Wireless networking in Windows 7 is similar to networking in Windows Vista. When Windows Vista detects a nearby wireless network, it displays a balloon notification in the Windows taskbar. You can click the balloon to display the dialog box shown in Figure 1-13, which lists the available networks. Then double-click the network you want to connect to.

Figure 1-13:
Choosing
a wireless
network in
Windows 7.

Chapter 2: Securing a Wireless Network

In This Chapter

✔ Reviewing the threats posed by wireless networks

✔ Enabling the basic security features of a wireless network

✔ Locking down your network with MAC address filtering

*B*efore you dive headfirst into the deep end of the wireless networking pool, you should consider the inherent security risks in setting up a wireless network. With a cabled network, the best security tool that you have is the lock on the front door of your office. Unless someone can physically get to one of the computers on your network, he or she can't get into your network. (Well, I'm sort of ignoring your wide-open broadband Internet connection for the sake of argument.)

If you go wireless, an intruder doesn't have to get into your office to hack into your network. He or she can do it from the office next door. Or the lobby. Or the parking garage below your office. Or the sidewalk outside. In short, when you introduce wireless devices into your network, you usher in a whole new set of security issues to deal with.

This chapter explores some of the basic security issues that come with the territory when you go wireless.

Understanding Wireless Security Threats

Wireless networks have the same basic security considerations as wired networks. As a network administrator, you need to balance the need of legitimate users to access network resources against the risk of illegitimate users breaking into your network. That's the basic dilemma of network security. Whether the network uses cables, wireless devices, kite strings and tin cans, or smoke signals, the basic issues are the same.

At one extreme of the wireless network security spectrum is the totally open network, in which anyone within range of your wireless transmissions can log on as an administrator and gain full access to every detail of your network. At the other end is what I call the "cone-of-silence syndrome," in which the network is so secure that no one can gain access to the network — not even legitimate users.

The goal of securing a wireless network is to find the happy medium between these two extremes that meets the access and risk-management needs of your organization.

The following sections describe the types of security threats that wireless networks are most likely encounter. You should take each of these kinds of threats into consideration when you plan your network's security.

Intruders

With a wired network, an intruder usually must gain access to your facility to physically connect to your network. That's not so with a wireless network. In fact, hackers equipped with notebooks that have wireless network capability can gain access to your network if they can place themselves physically within range of your network's radio signals. Consider these possibilities:

✦ If you share a building with other tenants, the other tenants' offices may be within range.

✦ If you're in a multifloor building, the floor immediately above or below you may be in range.

✦ The lobby outside your office may be within range of your network.

✦ The parking lot outside or the parking garage in the basement may be in range.

If a would-be intruder can't get within normal broadcast range, he or she may try one of several tricks to increase the range:

✦ A would-be intruder can switch to a bigger antenna to extend the range of his or her wireless computer. Some experiments have shown that big antennas can receive signals from wireless networks miles away. In fact, I once read about someone who listened in on wireless networks based in San Francisco from the Berkeley hills, across San Francisco Bay.

✦ If a would-be intruder is serious about breaking into your network, he or she may smuggle a wireless repeater device into your facility — or near it — to extend the range of your wireless network to a location that he or she *can* get to.

A *physical* connection to your network isn't the only way an intruder can gain access, of course. You must still take steps to prevent an intruder from sneaking into your network through your Internet gateway. In most cases, this means that you need to set up a firewall to block unwanted and unauthorized traffic.

Freeloaders

Freeloaders are intruders who want to piggyback on your wireless network to get free access to the Internet. If they manage to gain access to your wireless network, they probably won't do anything malicious: They'll just fire up their web browsers and surf the Internet. These are folks who are too cheap to spend $40 per month on their own broadband connection at home, so they'd rather drive into your parking lot and steal yours.

Even though freeloaders may be relatively benign, they can be a potential source of trouble. In particular:

✦ Freeloaders use bandwidth that you're paying for. As a result, their mere presence can slow down Internet access for your legitimate users.

✦ After freeloaders gain Internet access through your network, they can potentially cause trouble for you or your organization. They may use your network to download illegal pornography, or they may try to send spam via your mail server. Most ISPs will cut you off cold if they catch you sending spam, and they won't believe you when you tell them that the spam came from a kid parked in a Pinto out in your parking lot.

✦ If you're in the business of *selling* access to your wireless network, obviously, freeloaders are a problem.

✦ Freeloaders may start out innocently looking for free Internet access. Once they get in, though, curiosity may get the better of them, leading them to snoop around your network.

✦ If freeloaders can get in, so can malicious intruders.

Eavesdroppers

Eavesdroppers just like to listen to your network traffic. They don't actually try to gain access via your wireless network — at least, not at first. They just listen.

Unfortunately, wireless networks give them plenty to listen to:

✦ Most wireless access points regularly broadcast their Service Set Identifiers (SSIDs) to anyone who's listening.

✦ When a legitimate wireless network user joins the network, an exchange of packets occurs as the network authenticates the user. An eavesdropper can capture these packets and, if security isn't set up right, determine the user's logon name and password.

✦ An eavesdropper can steal files that are opened from a network server. If a wireless user opens a confidential sales report that's saved on the network, the sales-report document is broken into packets that are sent over the wireless network to the user. A skilled eavesdropper can copy those packets and reconstruct the file.

✦ When a wireless user connects to the Internet, an eavesdropper can see any packets that the user sends to or receives from the Internet. If the user purchases something online, the transaction may include a credit card number and other personal information. (Ideally, these packets will be encrypted so that the eavesdropper won't be able to decipher the data.)

Spoilers

A *spoiler* is a hacker who gets kicks from jamming networks so that they become unusable. A spoiler usually accomplishes this act by flooding the network with meaningless traffic so that legitimate traffic gets lost in the flow. Spoilers may also try to place viruses or worm programs on your network via an unsecured wireless connection.

Rogue access points

One of the biggest problems that network administrators have to deal with is the problem of rogue access points. A *rogue access point* is an access point that suddenly appears on your network out of nowhere. What usually happens is that an employee decides to connect a notebook computer to the network via a wireless computer. So this user stops at Computers R Us on the way home from work one day, buys a Fisher-Price wireless access point for $25, and plugs it into the network without asking permission.

Now, in spite of all the elaborate security precautions you've taken to fence in your network, this well-meaning user has opened the barn door. It's *very* unlikely that the user will enable the security features of the wireless access point; in fact, he or she probably isn't even aware that wireless access devices *have* security features.

Unless you take some kind of action to find it, a rogue access point can operate undetected on your network for months or even years. You may not discover it until you report to work one day and find that your network has been trashed by an intruder who found his or her way into your network via an unprotected wireless access point that you didn't even know existed.

Here are some steps you can take to reduce the risk of rogue access points appearing on your system:

✦ Establish a policy prohibiting users from installing wireless access points on their own. Then make sure that you inform all network users of the policy, and let them know why installing an access point on their own can be such a major problem.

✦ If possible, establish a program that quickly and inexpensively grants wireless access to users who want it. Rogue access points show up in the first place for two reasons: (1) Users need the access, and (2) The access is hard to get through existing channels. If you make it easier for users to get legitimate wireless access, you're less likely to find wireless access points hidden behind file cabinets or in flower pots.

✦ Once in a while, take a walk through the premises, looking for rogue access points. Take a look at every network outlet in the building; see what's connected to it.

✦ Turn off all your wireless access points and then walk around the premises with a wireless-equipped notebook computer that has scanning software, such as NetStumbler (www.netstumbler.com), looking for wireless access. (Just because you detect a wireless network, of course, doesn't mean you have found a rogue access point; you may have stumbled onto a wireless network in a nearby office or home.)

✦ If your network is large, consider using a software tool such as AirWave (www.airwave.com) to snoop for unauthorized access points.

Securing Your Wireless Network

I hope you're convinced that wireless networks do indeed pose many security risks. In the following sections, I describe some steps that you can take to help secure your wireless network.

Changing the password

Probably the first thing you should do when you install a wireless access point is change its administrative password. Most access points have a built-in, web-based setup page that you can access from any web browser to configure the access point's settings. The setup page is protected by a username and password, but the username and password are initially set to default values that are easy to guess.

For Linksys access points, for example, the default username is blank, and the password is admin. If you leave the username and password set to their default values, anyone can access the access point and change its configuration settings, thus bypassing any other security features that you enable for the access point.

So the first step in securing your wireless access point is changing the setup password to a value that can't be guessed. I suggest that you use a random combination of numerals and both uppercase and lowercase letters. Be sure to store the password in a secure location. (If you forget the password, you can press the Reset button on the router to restore it to its factory default. Then you can log on by using the default password, which you can find with the documentation that came with the router.)

Securing the SSID

The next step is to secure the SSID that identifies the network. A client must know the access point's SSID to join the wireless network. If you can prevent unauthorized clients from discovering the SSID, you can prevent them from accessing your network.

Securing the SSID isn't a complete security solution, so you shouldn't rely on it as your only security mechanism. SSID security can slow down casual intruders and wardrivers who are just looking for easy and free Internet access, but it isn't possible to prevent serious hackers from discovering your SSID.

You can do three things to secure your SSID:

✦ **Change the SSID from the default.** Most access points come preconfigured with well-known default SSIDs, such as those listed in Table 2-1. By changing your access point's SSID, you can make it more difficult for an intruder to determine your SSID and gain access.

Table 2-1	Common Default SSID Values
SSID	*Manufacturer*
3com	3Com
Compaq	Compaq
Linksys	Linksys
Tsunami	Cisco
Wireless	NetGear
WLAN	DLink
WLAN	SMC

✦ **Disable SSID broadcast.** Most access points frequently broadcast their SSIDs so that clients can discover the network when they come within range. Clients that receive this SSID broadcast can use the SSID to join the network.

You can increase network security somewhat by disabling the SSID broadcast feature. That way, clients won't automatically learn the access point's SSID. To join the network, a client computer must figure out the SSID on its own. Then you can tell your wireless network users the SSID to use when they configure their clients.

Unfortunately, when a client computer connects to a wireless network, it sends the SSID to the access point in an unencrypted packet. So a sophisticated intruder who's using a packet sniffer to eavesdrop on your wireless network can determine your SSID as soon as any legitimate computer joins the network.

✦ **Disable guest mode.** Many access points have a guest-mode feature that enables client computers to specify a blank SSID or to specify "any" as the SSID. If you want to ensure that only clients that know the SSID can join the network, you must disable this feature.

Enabling WEP

WEP stands for *wired equivalent privacy* and is designed to make wireless transmission as secure as transmission over a network cable. WEP encrypts your data by using either a 40-bit key or a 128-bit key. Keep in mind that 40-bit encryption is faster than 128-bit encryption and is adequate for most purposes. So unless you work for the Central Intelligence Agency, I suggest that you enable 40-bit encryption.

Note: To use WEP, both the client and the server must know the encryption keys being used. So a client that doesn't know the access point's encryption keys won't be able to join the network.

You can specify encryption keys for WEP in two ways. The first way is to create the ten-digit key manually by making up a random number. The second method, which I prefer, is to use a *passphrase,* which can be any word or combination of numerals and letters that you want. WEP automatically converts the passphrase to the numeric key used to encrypt data. If the client knows the passphrase used to generate the keys on the access point, the client will be able to access the network.

As it turns out, security experts have identified several flaws in WEP that compromise its effectiveness. As a result, with the right tools, a sophisticated intruder can get past WEP. So although it's a good idea to enable WEP, you shouldn't count on it for complete security.

Besides just enabling WEP, you should take two steps to increase its effectiveness:

✦ **Make WEP mandatory.** Some access points have a configuration setting that enables WEP but makes it optional. This setting may prevent eavesdroppers from viewing the data transmitted on WEP connections, but it doesn't prevent clients that don't know your WEP keys from accessing your network.

✦ **Change the encryption keys.** Most access points come preconfigured with default encryption keys that make it easy for even casual hackers to defeat your WEP security. You should change the default keys, either by using a passphrase or by specifying your own key. Figure 2-1 shows the WEP key configuration page for a typical access point (in this case, a Linksys BEFW11).

Figure 2-1:
Changing
the WEP
settings on
a Linksys
wireless
router.

Using WPA and WPA2

WPA, which stands for *Wi-Fi Protected Access,* is a newer form of security for wireless networks that's designed to plug some of the holes of WEP. WPA is similar in many ways to WEP. The big difference is that when you use WPA, the encryption key is automatically changed at regular intervals, thus thwarting all but the most sophisticated efforts to break the key. Most newer wireless devices support WPA. If your equipment supports it, I suggest that you use it.

Here are a few additional things to know about WPA:

✦ A small office and home version of WPA, called WPA-PSK, bases its encryption keys on a passkey value that you supply. True WPA devices, however, rely on a special authentication server to generate the keys.

✦ All versions of Windows since Windows XP Service Pack 2 have built-in support for WPA.

✦ official IEEE standard for WPA is 802.11i. WPA devices were widely available before the 802.11i standard was finalized, however; as a result, not all WPA devices implement every aspect of 802.11i.

✦ The original version of WAP has been superseded by a newer version, named WPA2.

Using MAC address filtering

MAC address filtering allows you to specify a list of MAC addresses for the devices that are allowed to access the network or are prohibited from accessing the network. If a computer with a different MAC address tries to join the network via the access point, the access point will deny access.

MAC address filtering is a great idea for wireless networks with a fixed number of clients. If you set up a wireless network at your office so that a few workers can connect their notebook computers, you can specify the MAC addresses of those computers in the MAC filtering table. Then other computers won't be able to access the network via the access point.

Don't neglect the basics

The security techniques described in this chapter are specific to wireless networks. They should be used alongside the basic security techniques that are presented in Book III. In other words, don't forget the basics, such as these:

✔ Use strong passwords for your user accounts.

✔ Apply security patches to your servers.

✔ Change default server account information (especially the administrator password).

✔ Disable unnecessary services.

✔ Check your server logs regularly.

✔ Install virus protection.

✔ Back up!

Unfortunately, it isn't difficult to configure a computer to lie about its MAC address. Thus, after a potential intruder determines that MAC filtering is being used, he or she can just sniff packets to determine an authorized MAC address and then configure his or her computer to use that address. (This practice is called *MAC spoofing.*) So you shouldn't rely on MAC address filtering as your only means of security.

Figure 2-2 shows the screen used to edit the MAC address table for a Linksys wireless access point.

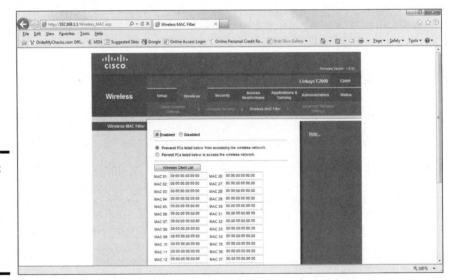

Figure 2-2:
A MAC
address
table for
a Linksys
wireless
router.

Placing your access points outside the firewall

The most effective security technique for wireless networking is placing all your wireless access points *outside* your firewall. That way, all network traffic from wireless users will have to travel through the firewall to access the network.

As you can imagine, doing this can significantly limit network access for wireless users. To get around those limitations, you can enable a virtual private network (VPN) connection for your wireless users. The VPN will allow full network access to authorized wireless users.

Obviously, this solution requires a bit of work to set up and can be a little inconvenient for your users, but it's an excellent way to fully secure your wireless access points.

Chapter 3: Hotspotting

*W*ireless networks aren't just for private use within your home or at your place of work. Nowadays, many public places, such as airports, libraries, hotels, restaurants, and coffeehouses, host public-access wireless networks, called *hotspots*. If you visit one of these establishments with a wireless-equipped laptop computer in tow, you can use its hotspot to access the Internet.

In this chapter, you read about these public hotspots and find out how to use them.

As you read this chapter, keep in mind that public hotspots use the same 802.11 technology as private wireless networks described in the first two chapters of this minibook. So the techniques that you use to connect to a hotspot are the same as those you use to connect to any wireless network. The security implications are the same, too.

What Is a Hotspot?

A *hotspot* is an area that has wireless networking available to the public. The first public hotspots were in airports and hotels, where business travelers could connect to the Internet with their laptop computers to pick up e-mail while on the road. Soon, libraries jumped on the bandwagon, providing Internet access to anyone who brought in a wireless-equipped laptop.

Many hotels, restaurants, and coffeehouses provide wireless hotspots so that you can stream music and video or play an online game while sipping a vanilla latte. Starbucks is probably the best-known trendy hotspot, but many others are joining in. Many Schlotzsky's Deli locations have free hotspot access, and even McDonald's is equipping many of its restaurants with hotspots. Barnes & Noble bookstores also provide access.

A *personal hotspot* is a wireless network, created by a smartphone or another mobile device that has a cellular connection to the Internet. A personal hotspot has a small range and allows a limited number of computers to connect. If your device can create a personal hotspot, you don't need to locate a public hotspot to connect.

What's So Great about Hotspots?

If you're puzzled about why so many businesses are getting into the hotspotting business, the following paragraphs offer some of the most common reasons:

✦ **To increase traffic and, therefore, business.** The chief executive officer of Schlotzsky's Deli (`www.schlotzskys.com`) has said that free Internet access results in 15,000 additional visits to each store every year. And those people who come in simply to use the free Internet access usually buy something, even if it's just a soda and a bag of chips.

✦ **To identify the business as hip or trendy.**

✦ **To make money directly from the hotspot.** Note that just because a business charges for its wireless access doesn't mean it's making a significant amount of money from the hotspot. Some businesses must charge fees to help cover the costs because they can't justify the expense of commercial-quality broadband access simply on the basis of goodwill and a little increased traffic.

Safe Hotspotting

To simplify the connection process, most hotspots — both free and fee-based — disable the security features that are available for wireless networks. As a result, you should take some basic precautions when you use a public hotspot:

✦ Make sure that you have a firewall installed and running. If you don't have a separate firewall program, enable the Windows Firewall that's built into Windows.

✦ Disable file sharing on your laptop computer.

✦ Avoid sites that ask for confidential information but don't use the secure HTTPS protocol.

✦ Use a VPN if you plan on accessing your company's network.

✦ Disconnect from the wireless network when you finish using it.

Free Hotspots

Many hotspots are free of charge. The hotspots at Schlotzsky's Deli are free, and hotspots at libraries typically are free.

To use a free hotspot, all you have to do is turn on your wireless-equipped laptop computer in the vicinity of the hotspot access point. Then, when you see the notification bubble in the bottom-right corner indicating that a wireless network is in range, click it to connect to the network, and fire up your web browser to surf the web.

Connecting to a free hotspot is easy. The hard part is finding an available hotspot to connect to, especially a free one. If you happen to live across the street from a library or a Schlotzsky's Deli, you're in luck. Otherwise, you'll have to search for a hotspot. Fortunately, you can consult several websites to locate hotspots in your area:

+ `www.freenetworks.org`: An organization of free networks around the world

+ `www.wififreespot.com`: A directory of free wireless networks around the world

+ `www.socalfreenet.org`: Free networks in Southern California

With Google and a little perseverance, you may be able to find a website devoted to your city. Note, however, that you're much more likely to find free hotspot access in a big city than in Mayberry.

Fee-Based Hotspots

Although some hotspots are free, most charge a fee. Although some charge for hourly use, others offer subscriptions that give you unlimited use for a monthly fee, usually in the neighborhood of $30 per month.

When you connect to a fee-based hotspot, a logon page is displayed. On this logon page, you can enter your user ID and password if you're already a subscriber. If not, you can join on the spot; just have your credit card handy. After you've joined and logged on, you can access the Internet by using your web browser.

Many fee-based providers have roaming agreements with one another that effectively increase the number of locations that are available. You may have to pay an additional surcharge if you use roaming, however.

Just a few years ago, the most popular fee-based hotspot services were T-Mobile and Boingo. These hotspot services are still very popular, but when you subscribe to one of these services, you're confined to a relatively limited number of hotspot locations. A newer alternative is purchasing a personal hotspot device from a cell-phone carrier such as Verizon or AT&T. These devices provide a short-range wireless hotspot that enables one or more computers to connect, and they work wherever you have a viable 3G or 4G cell-phone connection.

Setting Up Your Own Hotspot

So you own a little cafe and think it would be cool to set up a hotspot for your customers to use, eh? If you want to set up a free hotspot, here's all you need:

✦ A reliable broadband Internet connection. DSL, cable, or T1 will work nicely.

✦ A wireless access point. For a small hotspot, a simple consumer-grade access point (like a Linksys wireless router) will do fine.

✦ A sign that tells your customers about the hotspot and how to connect to it.

There's a lot more to it, of course. Consider a few additional issues:

✦ You need a firewall to prevent your customers from poking around inside your private network. The wireless access point should be *outside* the firewall.

✦ No matter how good your sign is, your customers will have questions about how to connect. So in addition to showing them how to make a mocha latte, you need to teach your employees how to help customers connect to your hotspot.

✦ Your broadband provider may not appreciate it if you let the general public access the Internet through your wireless access point. In fact, your service contract may prohibit it. As a result, you probably need to pay a bit more to share your broadband connection with the general public.

If you want to charge for hotspot access, you have a lot more work to do. In particular, you need to devise a way to charge your customers. The easiest way to do this is to purchase a single-box solution that includes the necessary wireless devices, as well as software that handles the authentication and billing.

Chapter 4: Troubleshooting a Wireless Network

In This Chapter

✓ Isolating the cause of wireless problems

✓ Changing channels

✓ Hardware that can improve wireless connections

✓ Resetting your access point/router password

*W*ireless networks are great until something goes haywire. When a regular network doesn't work, you usually know about it right away because the network simply becomes unavailable. You can't display web pages, read e-mail, or access files on shared drives. The troubleshooting chapters in Book III address the most common problems encountered on cabled networks.

But wireless networks can cause problems of their own. And to add to the frustration, wireless networks tend to degrade rather than completely fail. Performance gets slower. Web pages that usually pop up in a second or two take 15 to 20 seconds to appear. Or sometimes they don't appear at all, but if you try again a few minutes later, they download fine.

This chapter offers some troubleshooting tips that can help you restore normalcy to a failing wireless network.

Checking for Obvious Problems

Before you roll up your sleeves and take drastic corrective action, you should check for a few obvious things if you're having wireless network trouble. The following list highlights some basic things you should check for:

✦ Is everything turned on? Make sure you have lights on your wireless access point/router, as well as on your cable or DSL modem.

✦ Many access point/routers use a power supply transformer that plugs into the wall. Make sure that the transformer is plugged into the wall outlet and that the small cable that comes out of the transformer is plugged into the power connector on the access point/router.

✦ Are the cables connected? Check the network cable that connects your access point/router to the cable or DSL modem.

✦ Try restarting everything. Turn off the computer, the access point/ router, and your cable or DSL modem. Leave everything off for at least two minutes. Then turn everything back on. Sometimes, simply cycling the power off and back on clears up a connection problem.

Pinpointing the Problem

If you can't connect to the Internet, one of the first steps (after you've made sure that everything is turned on) is finding out whether the problem is with your access point/router or with your broadband connection. Here is one way you can check to find out whether your wireless connection is working:

1. **Open a command prompt window by choosing Start⇨Run, typing** cmd, **and pressing Enter.**

2. **At the command prompt, type** ipconfig, **and press Enter.**

   You should get a display similar to this:

   ```
   Ethernet adapter Wireless Network Connection:
           Connection-specific DNS Suffix  . : hsd1.ca.comcast.net)).
           IP Address. . . . . . . . . . . : 192.168.1.101
           Subnet Mask . . . . . . . . . . : 255.255.255.0
           Default Gateway . . . . . . . . : 192.168.1.1
   ```

If the display resembles this but with different numbers, you're connected to the wireless network, and the problem most likely lies with your broadband modem.

But if the IP Address, Subnet Mask, and Default Gateway indicate 0.0.0.0 instead of valid IP addresses, you have a problem with your wireless network.

Changing Channels

One of the most common sources of wireless network trouble is interference from other wireless devices. The culprit might be a cordless phone, or it could be a neighbor who also has a wireless network.

The simplest solution to this type of interference is changing channels. 802.11b access points let you select 1 of 11 different channels to broadcast on. If you're having trouble connecting to your access point, try changing the channel. To do that, you must log on to the router with the administrator password. Then hunt around the router's administrator pages until you find the controls that let you change the channel.

You may have to try changing the channel several times before you solve the problem. Unfortunately, 802.11b channels overlap slightly, which means that broadcasts on one channel may interfere with broadcasts on adjacent channels. Thus, if you're having trouble connecting on channel 1, don't bother switching to channel 2. Instead, try switching to channel 5 or 6. If that doesn't work, switch to channel 10 or 11.

Fiddling with the Antennas

Sometimes, you can fix intermittent connection problems by fiddling with the antennas on the access point and your computer's wireless adapter. This procedure is similar to playing with old-fashioned rabbit-ear antennas on a TV to get the best reception.

The angles of the antennas sometimes make a difference, so try adjusting the antenna angles. In addition, you usually have better results if you place the access point at a high location, such as on top of a bookshelf.

In some cases, you may actually need to add a high-gain antenna to the access point to increase its range. A high-gain antenna simply snaps or screws onto the access point to provide a bigger antenna. Figure 4-1 shows high-gain antennas that are designed to work with Linksys access points. Antennas such as these cost about $70 for the pair.

Figure 4-1:
High-gain
antennas
for a Linksys
wireless
router.

Photo courtesy of Linksys.

A more drastic fix is to add a signal booster to your access point. A *signal booster* is a power amplifier that increases the transmission power of most wireless devices by a factor of five. A typical signal booster costs about $100.

Adding Another Access Point

If you have a computer that's out of range of your access point, one solution is to add a second access point closer to the problematic computer. Most likely, the only difficulty will be getting an Ethernet cable to the location where you want to put your second access point.

If possible, you can simply run a length of cable through your walls or attic to the second access point. If that solution isn't feasible, you can use a HomePlug or Phone (HPNA) network connection for the second access point.

An alternative to a second access point is simply adding a repeater, such as the Linksys Wireless-G Range Expander shown in Figure 4-2. All you have to do is place this device midway between your access point and the computer that's having trouble connecting.

Figure 4-2:
A wireless repeater such as this one from Linksys can help increase the range of your wireless network.

Photo courtesy of Linksys.

Help! 1 Forgot My Router's Password!

I mention many times throughout this book that you should always change the default passwords that come with computer and operating systems to more secure passwords, usually consisting of a random combination of letters, digits, and special symbols.

Ideally, you've already taken my sage advice and changed the password on your combination wireless access point/router. Good for you. But what if you forget the password later? Is there any way to get back into your access point/router then?

Fortunately, there is. Most access point/routers have a reset button. It's usually located on the back or on the bottom of the router's case. Press this button to restore the access point/router to its factory default settings. That action resets the administrator password to the factory default — and also resets any other custom settings you've applied, so you may have to reconfigure your router to get it working again.

Chapter 5: Wireless Networking with Bluetooth

In This Chapter

✔ Discovering how Bluetooth works

✔ Digging into some of Bluetooth's technical issues

✔ Installing a USB Bluetooth adapter

✔ Using Bluetooth in Windows

*A*vast! If 'twere up to me, the name *Bluetooth* surely would be the proud name of a pirate, not some lily-livered computer network gadget. Aye, and make no mistake. Blame it on those scurvy bilge rats whats call themselves Engineers. The next landlubber Engineer whats wastes a perfectly good pirate name on some network gadget will soon be feeding fish in Davy Jones' locker, says I. Alas, me hearties, the deed is done, so forevermore, *Bluetooth* shall be the topic of a chapter in blaggard books about computers instead of proper books about piracy.

Arrrrr!

Understanding Bluetooth

Bluetooth is the name of a short-range wireless network technology that's designed to let devices connect to each other without need for cables or a Wi-Fi network access point. The two main uses for Bluetooth are to connect peripheral devices such as keyboards or mice to a computer and to connect handheld devices such as phones and PDAs (personal digital assistants) to computers.

Here are just a few of the many uses of Bluetooth:

✦ Wirelessly connecting a keyboard and mouse to a computer so that you don't have to fuss with cables. This is marginally useful for desktop computers because it eliminates the need for cables. But it's even more useful for laptop computers because it lets you use a keyboard and mouse simply by placing them next to the laptop.

✦ Synchronizing the address book in your cell phone with your computer's address book, with no cables.

✦ Exchanging files between your Pocket PC or Palm PDA and your laptop or desktop computers.

✦ Using a cord-free headset with your cell phone.

✦ Connecting a Global Positioning System (GPS) device to a computer so that it can track your location. This is especially useful when used in your car with a laptop, Pocket PC, or Palm PDA.

✦ Swapping electronic business cards between handheld computers.

Bluetooth Technical Stuff

For you technical enthusiasts out there, here's a whole section that gets the Technical Stuff icon. The following paragraphs point out some of the important and obscure technical highlights of Bluetooth:

✦ Bluetooth was developed in 1998 by a consortium of companies including IBM, Intel, Ericsson, Nokia, and Toshiba. Not wanting to be left out of the action, IEEE turned Bluetooth into a standard called 802.15.

✦ Bluetooth operates in the same 2.4 GHz bandwidth as 802.11 Wi-Fi networks. Although it's possible for Bluetooth and Wi-Fi networks to interfere with one another, Bluetooth includes features that usually minimize or eliminate this interference.

✦ The original version of Bluetooth was slow — about 721 Kbps, way slower than Wi-Fi networks. Newer versions can transmit data as fast as 3 Mbps. Still, Bluetooth isn't designed to transport large amounts of data, such as huge video files. For that, you should use Wi-Fi.

✦ Bluetooth devices periodically "sniff" the air to see whether other Bluetooth devices are nearby so that they can automatically hook up.

✦ Bluetooth has very low power requirements. As a result, it's ideal for battery-powered devices such as cell phones and PDAs.

✦ Bluetooth comes in three flavors, as described in Table 5-1. Class 1 is the most powerful form of Bluetooth and the most commonly used. Class 2 is ideal for devices such as wireless mice or keyboards and wireless cell-phone headsets, which need to communicate only at close range. Class 3 is for devices that operate at even closer range, but few Bluetooth devices actually implement Class 3.

Table 5-1	Bluetooth Classes	
Class	*Power*	*Range*
Class 1	100 mW	300 feet (100 meters)
Class 2	10 mW	30 feet (10 meters)
Class 3	1 mW	< 30 feet (10 meters)

♦ Bluetooth was originally conceived by cell-phone giant Ericsson as a way to connect a wireless earpiece to a cell phone. As the developers worked on the idea, they soon realized that the technology had uses far beyond wireless earpieces for cell phones.

♦ The name *Bluetooth* is an English translation of *Blatand* — as in Harald Blatand, a Viking king who united Denmark and Norway in the 10th century.

How to Add Bluetooth to Your Computer

Many computers sold today — especially laptop computers and PDAs — come equipped with Bluetooth technology. If your computer doesn't already support Bluetooth, you can easily add Bluetooth support. Just purchase a USB Bluetooth adapter, which is a small device that plugs into any available USB port on your computer. After you plug it in, your computer is Bluetooth-enabled and can connect to any other Bluetooth device that's in range.

Many companies make Bluetooth USB adapters, most of which look and work similarly. Figure 5-1 shows an adapter made by Linksys that sells for about $40.

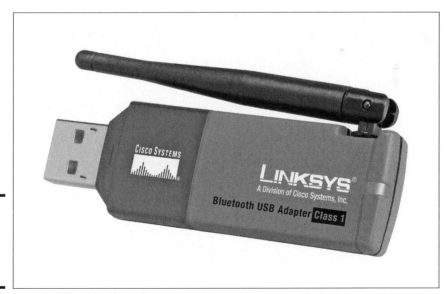

Figure 5-1:
A typical
USB
Bluetooth
adapter.

Photo courtesy of Linksys.

Using Bluetooth in Windows

Windows Vista, Windows 7, and Windows 8 all include excellent built-in support for Bluetooth. If your computer has Bluetooth, a special Bluetooth icon appears in the system tray (the panel at the right end of the taskbar). You can click this icon to bring up a menu with the following choices:

✦ Add a Bluetooth Device

✦ Show Bluetooth Devices

✦ Send a File

✦ Receive a File

✦ Join a Personal Area Network

✦ Open Bluetooth Settings

✦ Remove Bluetooth Icon

Installing a USB Bluetooth Adapter

Installing a USB Bluetooth adapter is easy. All you have to do is install the software provided with the adapter and plug the adapter into a free USB port. Usually, you can start the installation process by inserting the CD that comes with the adapter into your CD drive. Then the installation program automatically starts. After the installation program starts, follow its steps, and plug the adapter in when the program instructs you to.

Be sure to follow the installation instructions that come with the adapter. In most cases, you should install the software that comes with the adapter *before* you plug in the adapter.

Enabling Discovery

By default, your computer remains hidden from other Bluetooth devices. If you want other Bluetooth devices to be able to recognize your computer, you need to enable a feature called *discovery*. Here are the steps:

1. **Right-click the Bluetooth icon in the system tray, and choose Open Bluetooth Settings from the contextual menu.**

2. **In the Bluetooth Properties dialog box that appears, click the Options tab.**

3. **Select the Turn Discovery On check box.**

4. **Select the Allow Bluetooth Devices to Connect to This Computer check box.**

5. **Select the Alert Me When a New Bluetooth Device Wants to Connect check box.**

6. **Click OK.**

Installing a Bluetooth Mouse or Keyboard

Installing a Bluetooth-enabled mouse or keyboard is easy. The only trick, ironically, is that you have to have a normal mouse or keyboard installed before you can install a Bluetooth mouse or keyboard. After you install the Bluetooth mouse or keyboard, however, you can unplug the normal mouse or keyboard.

The main trick in installing a Bluetooth mouse or keyboard is that you must first enable discovery on the mouse or keyboard. Most Bluetooth mice and keyboards have a button on the bottom that does this. After Bluetooth is enabled, you can install the mouse or keyboard by right-clicking the Bluetooth icon in the system and choosing the Add a Bluetooth Device command from the contextual menu. Then follow the wizard's steps to install the mouse or keyboard.

Book VI

Mobile Networking

Contents at a Glance

Chapter 1: Managing Mobile Devices

In This Chapter

✔ Looking at mobile devices

✔ Configuring Windows Mobile devices for Exchange access

✔ Examining BlackBerry and BlackBerry Enterprise Server (BES)

✔ Considering security implications

A computer consultant once purchased a used BlackBerry device on eBay for $15.50. When he put in a new battery and turned on the device, he discovered that it contained confidential e-mails and personal contact information for executives of a well-known financial institution.

Oops!

It turns out that a former executive with the company sold his old BlackBerry on eBay a few months after he left the firm. He'd assumed that because he'd removed the battery, everything on the BlackBerry had been erased.

The point of this true story is that mobile devices such as smartphones and tablet computers pose a special set of challenges for network administrators. These challenges are now being faced even by administrators of small networks. Just a few years ago, only large companies had BlackBerry or other mobile devices that integrated with Exchange e-mail, for example. Now it isn't uncommon for companies with just a few employees to have mobile devices connected to the company network.

This chapter is a brief introduction to mobile devices and the operating systems they run. In the remaining chapters of this minibook, you find some specifics for working with three of the most common types of mobile devices: BlackBerry, iOS (such as the iPhone and iPad), and Android.

The Many Types of Mobile Devices

Once upon a time, there were mobile phones and PDAs. A mobile phone was just that: a handheld telephone you could take with you. The good ones had nice features such as a call log, an address book, and perhaps a crude game but not much else. PDAs — *Personal Digital Assistants* — were little handheld computers designed to replace the old-fashioned Day-Timer books people used to carry around with them to keep track of their appointment calendars and address books.

All that changed when cellular providers began adding data capabilities to their networks. Now, cell phones can have complete mobile Internet access. This fact has resulted in the addition of sophisticated PDA features to mobile phones and phone features to PDAs so that the distinctions are blurred.

The term *mobile device* is used to describe a wide assortment of devices that you can hold in one hand and that are connected through a wireless network. The term *handheld* is a similar generic name for such devices. The following list describes some of the most common specifics of mobile devices:

✦ **Mobile phone:** A *mobile phone* (or *cell phone)* is a mobile device whose primary purpose is to enable phone service. Most mobile phones include features such as text messaging, address books, appointment calendars, and games, and they may provide Internet access.

✦ **Smartphone:** A *smartphone* is a mobile phone with advanced features that aren't typically found on mobile phones. There's no clearly drawn line between mobile phones and smartphones. One distinction is whether the phone can provide integrated access to corporate e-mail. The screen on a smartphone is typically bigger than the screen on a traditional cell phone, and the most popular models (such as the iPhone and most Android devices) do not have a keyboard at all.

✦ **BlackBerry:** BlackBerry devices are sophisticated PDAs made by Research In Motion (RIM) that have cell-phone capabilities. The most distinctive feature of BlackBerry devices is their capability to synchronize with Exchange e-mail servers to provide instant access to your corporate e-mail. Typically, this synchronization requires a special server called *BlackBerry Enterprise Server* (BES) running on the corporate network. BlackBerry devices use a proprietary operating system developed by RIM.

For more information about working with BlackBerry devices, see Book VI, Chapter 2.

✦ **iPhone and iPad:** Apple's iPhone has taken the smartphone market by storm. Unlike a BlackBerry, an iPhone doesn't require a separate server to enable full Exchange mailbox synchronization.

For more information, see Book VI, Chapter 3.

✦ **Android:** Android is an open-source operating system for smartphones developed by Google. Android is designed in many ways to mimic the features of the iPhone, so experienced iPhone users will find Android phones to be very similar.

At the time I wrote this chapter, the overwhelming majority of new smartphones being sold were Android devices. But Apple had just won a patent infringement lawsuit claiming that Android devices (specifically, the Samsung Galaxy) had illegally copied many of the features of the iPhone.

For more information about Android devices, see Book VI, Chapter 4.

Considering Security for Mobile Devices

As a network administrator, one of your main responsibilities regarding mobile devices is to keep them secure. Unfortunately, that's a significant challenge. Here are some of the reasons why:

✦ **Mobile devices connect to your network via other networks that are out of your control.** You can go to great lengths to set up firewalls, encryption, and a host of other security features, but mobile devices connect via public networks whose administrators may not be as conscientious as you.

✦ **Mobile devices are easy to lose.** A user might leave her smartphone at a restaurant or hotel, or it might fall out of his pocket on the subway.

✦ **Mobile devices run operating systems that aren't as security-conscious as Windows.**

✦ **Users who wouldn't dare install renegade software on their desktop computers think nothing of downloading free games or other applications to their handheld devices.** Who knows what kinds of viruses or Trojans these downloads carry?

✦ **Inevitably, someone will buy his own handheld device and connect it to your network without your knowledge or permission.**

Here are some recommendations for beefing up security for your mobile devices:

✦ Establish clear, consistent policies for mobile devices, and enforce them.

✦ Make sure employees understand that they aren't allowed to bring their own devices into your network. Allow only company-owned devices to connect.

✦ Train your users in the security risks associated with using mobile devices.

✦ Implement antivirus protection for your mobile devices.

Chapter 2: Managing BlackBerry Devices

In This Chapter

✔ Looking at how the BlackBerry infrastructure works

✔ Setting up new BlackBerry users

✔ Locking or disabling a BlackBerry device

*B*lackBerry devices were once the most popular type of smartphones in use. BlackBerry became popular because of its seamless integration with corporate e-mail accounts — specifically, its capability to synchronize with Microsoft Exchange. Now that other smartphones such as the iPhone and Android devices offer similar capabilities, BlackBerry has lost most of its popularity. But there are still many loyal BlackBerry users out there.

The BlackBerry devices themselves are made by a company called RIM, which stands for *Research In Motion.* RIM has arrangements with a variety of cell-phone providers, so you can get BlackBerry devices from AT&T, Verizon, and Sprint, as well as other major providers.

This chapter begins with an overview of how the BlackBerry works — not just how the BlackBerry phone itself works, but also how the entire BlackBerry architecture works to provide its legendary e-mail integration over cellular networks. Then it presents a few basic procedures for working with the server-side BlackBerry software, known as BlackBerry Enterprise Server (BES).

Understanding BlackBerry

BlackBerry is more than just a phone; it's a complete integrated system of hardware and software devices designed to provide smooth and nearly instantaneous integration with Microsoft Exchange Server. You may be surprised to discover just how complex this infrastructure actually is. Figure 2-1 shows a simplified diagram of its major components.

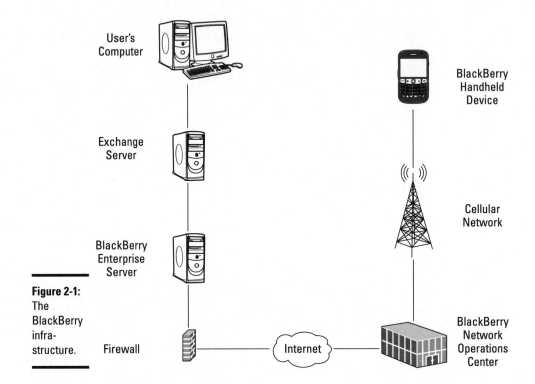

Figure 2-1:
The
BlackBerry
infra-
structure.

User's Computer

Exchange Server

BlackBerry Enterprise Server

Firewall

Internet

BlackBerry Handheld Device

Cellular Network

BlackBerry Network Operations Center

The following paragraphs describe several of the components pictured in Figure 2-1:

✦ **BlackBerry handheld device:** The BlackBerry handheld device itself is a combination of a cell phone and a handheld computer. The cell phone has the ability to handle not only voice communications, but also data communications over the provider's cellular network. Most BlackBerry devices include a small LCD screen and a keyboard, though the BlackBerry Storm model doesn't have a separate keyboard; instead, it uses a touch-sensitive screen.

✦ **Cellular network:** The cellular network is how the BlackBerry device communicates with the rest of the world. This part of the BlackBerry infrastructure is provided and managed by the cell-phone provider you purchase the BlackBerry from. Because different providers have different coverage areas, you should choose the provider that has the best coverage for the areas you visit most often.

✦ **BlackBerry Network Operations Center:** The BlackBerry Network Operations Center (NOC) handles the routing of data between the Internet and the cell network. RIM maintains several NOC locations throughout the country (actually, throughout the world) to ensure that data can be efficiently routed between the Internet and its handheld devices via the cell network.

✦ **BlackBerry Enterprise Server:** Also known as BES, this key piece of software makes BlackBerries do their magic. BES is a software server that runs one of the server computers within your network. The main purpose of BES is to act as an interface between e-mail servers (most often, Microsoft Exchange Server) and the BlackBerry NOC. Simply put, BES monitors all activity on a user's Exchange mailbox and sends periodic updates over the Internet to the BlackBerry NOC, which relays the updates to the handheld device via the cellular network.

As a network administrator, you'll find that BES is the critical piece of the BlackBerry puzzle. Most of the time you spend administering BlackBerry users, you spend in BES. Here are some additional details you should know about BES:

**Book VI
Chapter 2**

**Managing
BlackBerry Devices**

✦ Although it's possible to run BES on the same computer that you run Exchange on, this configuration isn't recommended. Instead, BES should be run on its own dedicated server computer.

✦ A free version of BES called BlackBerry Enterprise Server Express is available for smaller systems with fewer than 75 users of handheld devices. For larger organizations, you need to purchase the Enterprise edition of BES.

✦ BES works like a client as far as Microsoft Exchange is concerned. BES logs on to Exchange via a special account called BESAdmin and uses this account to access the data in BlackBerry users' mailboxes. BES retrieves the data from these mailboxes and then sends it over the Internet to the BlackBerry NOC.

✦ For BES to work, you must grant the BESAdmin account full mailbox rights for each BlackBerry user. Without this right, the BESAdmin account won't be able to access each BlackBerry user's mailbox.

✦ To connect a BlackBerry handheld device with a BES server, you must go through a process called *Enterprise Activation.*

✦ BES uses sophisticated encryption techniques to ensure that the data sent over the Internet to the BlackBerry NOC and then from the BlackBerry NOC to the handheld device is secure. Thus, you can be confident that no one can intercept your Exchange data as it travels from your Exchange server, through the Internet, and over the cellular network to your BlackBerry.

One final note before I get into the details of working with BES: The server was developed at a time when the bandwidth capacity of cellular networks was very limited. As a result, BES goes to great lengths to optimize the delivery of data over the cell network. This effort is most evident in the way that BES handles attachments. Instead of sending the attachment directly to the handheld device, BES creates a compressed JPEG image of the attachment and sends the image. Initially, this image is scaled to keep the file as small as possible. Even this small image is sent only when the BlackBerry user requests it. The viewer built into the BlackBerry device allows the user to zoom in for a closer look at the image. When the user zooms in, the device requests a more detailed JPEG rendering of the attachment. Then BES creates and sends the requested detail. This arrangement may seem to be cumbersome, especially with high-capacity 3G or 4G cellular networks being available in many areas now, but it's very efficient.

Adding a BES User

One of the most common BES administration tasks is adding new BlackBerry users. To do this, follow these steps:

1. **Open Active Directory Users and Computers (found under Start➪ Management), right-click the user you want to add, and choose Properties from the contextual menu.**

   The Properties page for the user appears.

2. **Select the Exchange Advanced tab, and click the Mailbox Rights button.**

   The Permissions dialog box appears. This dialog box lets you grant mailbox rights for the user's mailbox.

3. **Click Add, type** BESAdmin, **and click OK.**

   BES adds the BESAdmin account for the user you selected in Step 1 to the list of users who have mailbox rights, but it doesn't actually grant any permissions.

4. **Select the Full Mailbox Access check box, and click OK.**

   BES grants full mailbox access rights to the BESAdmin account for the BlackBerry user.

5. **Click OK again to dismiss the Properties dialog box.**

   You're done with Active Directory Users and Computers; you can close it if you want.

6. **Open the BlackBerry Manager by clicking the BlackBerry Manager icon on the desktop.**

   BlackBerry Manager comes to life, as shown in Figure 2-2.

7. **In the Explorer View pane, navigate to the server you're managing.**

   In Figure 2-2, I've navigated to the server BCFWEB01.

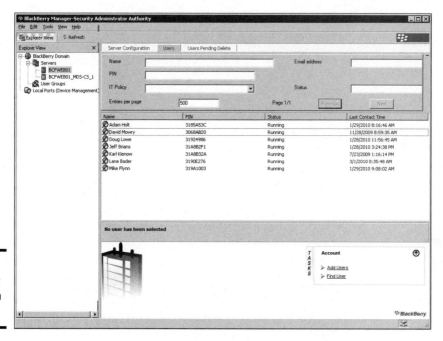

Figure 2-2:
BlackBerry
Manager in
action.

8. Click a blank area within the list of BlackBerry users, and choose Add Users.

A dialog box named Select Mailbox appears. This dialog box lists all the Active Directory users who have Exchange mailboxes.

9. Select the user you want to add and then click OK.

The Select Mailbox dialog box vanishes, and the user is added to the list of BlackBerry users.

10. Right-click the user and then choose Generate an Email Activation Password from the contextual menu.

This action initiates the Enterprise Activation process by generating an activation password and e-mailing it to the user, as shown in Figure 2-3. This e-mail provides not only the password, but also the instructions the user needs to follow to activate his or her BlackBerry device.

You're done!

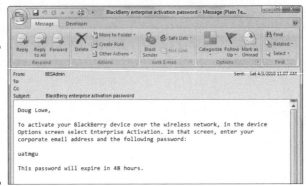

Figure 2-3:
This e-mail is sent to invite a BlackBerry user to Enterprise Activation.

After you've created the activation password, it's up to the user to activate the BlackBerry device. The user does this by navigating to the Options screen and selecting Enterprise Activation. Then the user enters his or her e-mail address and the activation password that was generated and sent via e-mail. After the e-mail address and password are verified, the activation process begins. It should take 10–15 minutes to complete. When the activation is complete, the phone should begin receiving e-mails, contacts, and calendar items from the user's Exchange mailbox.

Locking and Erasing a Handheld Device

After adding new BlackBerry users, the next-most-common BES administration tasks are locking and erasing a missing handheld device. If a user complains that his or her BlackBerry is missing, I usually start by locking the device. That way, if the device has fallen into the wrong hands, the finder won't be able to access the device without the correct password.

If the BlackBerry doesn't turn up within a few days, the next step is to erase the BlackBerry entirely so that even if the new owner manages to get past the password lock, he or she won't find any useful information on the phone.

Both of these tasks are handled via the BlackBerry Manager. Right-click the user whose phone you want to lock or erase and then choose one of the following commands from the contextual menu:

✦ **Set Password and Lock Handheld:** This command displays the dialog box shown in Figure 2-4. This dialog box lets you set a new password for the handheld device. It also lets you change the owner information that's displayed when the handheld device is locked. When you click OK, a message is sent to the handheld device, directing it to change the password and (optionally) the owner information and then to lock the keyboard. After the keyboard is locked, a user can unlock it only by entering the password.

✦ **Erase Data and Disable Handheld:** This command is more drastic: It erases all the contents of the handheld device, including any stored e-mails, contacts, calendar items, and other files. It also disables Enterprise Activation. This command effectively restores the device to its original, factory-new state.

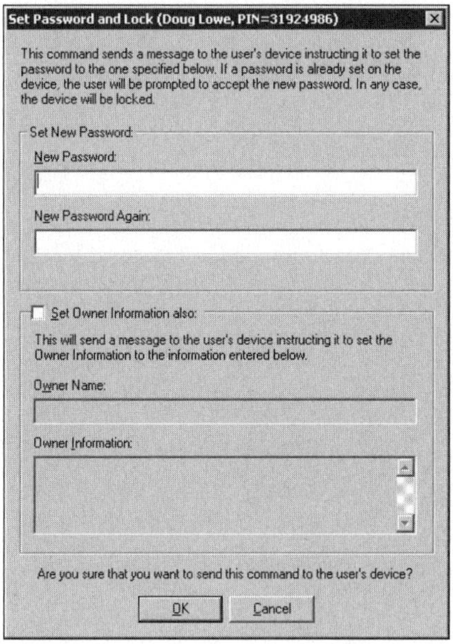

Figure 2-4:
Remotely
locking a
BlackBerry
handheld
device.

Chapter 3: Managing iOS Devices

In This Chapter

✔ **Looking at how the iPhone works**

✔ **Enabling ActiveSync for iPhone users**

✔ **Configuring an Exchange e-mail account**

*I*n 2007, the Apple iPhone, one of the most innovative little gadgets in many, many years, hit the technology market. As a result, in just a few short years, the iPhone captured a huge slice of a market that was previously owned almost exclusively by Research In Motion (RIM) and its BlackBerry devices. Since then, the iPhone's share of the mobile-phone market has grown beyond that of the former king, BlackBerry.

The success of the iPhone was due in large part to the genius of its operating system, called iOS. In 2010, Apple released the iPad, a tablet computer that runs the same iOS operating system as the iPhone. Together, iPhone and iPad devices are commonly known as iOS devices.

This chapter covers both iOS devices: the iPhone and the iPad. You get a brief overview of what the iPhone and iPad actually are, as well as simple procedures for setting them up to access enterprise e-mail.

Understanding the iPhone

The iPhone is essentially a combination of four devices:

✦ A cell phone

✦ An iPod with a memory capacity of 8GB to 64GB

✦ A digital camera

✦ An Internet device with its own web browser (named Safari) and applications such as e-mail, calendar, and contact management

The most immediately noticeable feature of the iPhone is its lack of a keyboard. Instead, nearly the entire front surface of the iPhone is occupied by a high-resolution, touch-sensitive LCD display. The display is not only the main output device of the iPhone, but also its main input device. When necessary, the display becomes either a keypad input for dialing a telephone number or a keyboard for entering text. You can also use various *finger gestures,* such as tapping icons to start programs or pinching to zoom in the display.

The iPhone has several other innovative features:

✦ An accelerometer tracks the motion of the iPhone in three directions. The main use of the accelerometer is to adjust the orientation of the display from landscape to portrait based on how the user is holding the phone. Some other applications — mostly games — use the accelerometer as well.

✦ A Wi-Fi interface lets the iPhone connect to local Wi-Fi networks for faster Internet access.

✦ GPS capability provides location awareness for many applications, including Google Maps.

✦ The virtual private network (VPN) client lets you connect to your internal network.

Of all the unique features of the iPhone, probably the most important is its huge collection of third-party applications that can be downloaded from a special web portal called the App Store. Many of these applications are free or cost just a few dollars. (Many are just 99 cents or $1.99.) At the time I wrote this chapter (August 2012), more than 500,000 applications — everything from business productivity to games — were available in the App Store.

Understanding the iPad

The iPad is essentially an iPhone without the phone but with a larger screen. The iPhone comes with a 3.5-inch screen; the iPad has a 9.7-inch screen.

Apart from these basic differences, an iPad is nearly identical to an iPhone. Any application that can run on an iPhone can also run on an iPad, and many applications are designed to take special advantage of the iPad's larger screen.

All the information that follows in this chapter applies equally to iPhones and iPads.

Integrating iOS Devices with Exchange

An iOS device can integrate with Microsoft Exchange e-mail. You must follow three procedures to make that integration possible:

1. **Enable the Mobile Services feature of Microsoft Exchange.**

2. **Enable ActiveSync for the user's mailbox.**

3. **Configure the iPhone to connect to the user's Exchange mailbox.**

The following sections describe these procedures.

Enabling Exchange Mobile Services

To enable an Exchange mailbox for an iOS device, you must enable the Exchange Mobile Services feature on the Exchange server. You must complete this procedure just once for each Exchange server. Here are the steps:

1. **Log on to the Exchange server with an Exchange Administrator account.**

2. **Choose Start⇨Administrative Tools⇨Exchange System Manager.**

3. **In the navigation pane of Exchange System Manager, expand the Global Settings node.**

4. **Right-click Mobile Services and then choose Properties from the contextual menu.**

The dialog box shown in Figure 3-1 appears.

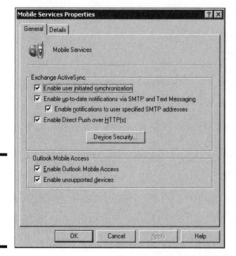

Figure 3-1:
Enabling
Outlook
Mobile
Access.

5. **Select all the check boxes on the General tab.**

This step enables all the capabilities of Outlook Mobile Access.

6. **Click OK.**

7. **Close Exchange System Manager.**

   You're done!

Enabling ActiveSync for a user's mailbox

After you've enabled Exchange Mobile Services for your Exchange server, you can enable ActiveSync for the user's Exchange mailbox. Enabling ActiveSync allows the mailbox to be synchronized with a remote mail client such as an iPhone. Here are the steps:

1. **Choose Start➪Administrative Tools➪Active Directory Users and Computers.**

   The Active Directory Users and Computers console opens.

2. **Expand the domain, and locate the user you want to enable mobile access for.**

3. **Right-click the user, and choose Properties from the contextual menu.**

4. **Click the Exchange Features tab.**

   The Exchange Features options are displayed, as shown in Figure 3-2.

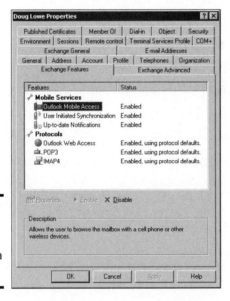

Figure 3-2:
Enabling mobile access for a user.

5. **Enable all three options listed under Mobile Services.**

   If the options aren't already enabled, right-click each option and choose Enable from the contextual menu.

6. **Click OK.**

7. **Repeat Steps 5 and 6 for any other users you want to enable mobile access for.**

8. **Close Active Directory Users and Computers.**

That's all there is to it. After you've enabled these features, any users running Windows Mobile will be able to synchronize their handheld devices with their Exchange mailboxes.

Configuring an iOS Device for Exchange e-mail

After ActiveSync is enabled for the mailbox, you can configure an iPhone or iPad to tap into the Exchange account by following these steps:

1. **On the iPhone or iPad, tap Settings; tap Mail, Contacts, Calendars; and then tap Add Account.**

   The screen shown in Figure 3-3 appears.

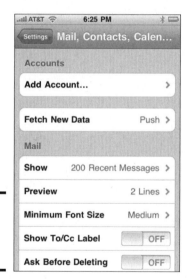

Figure 3-3:
Adding
an e-mail
account.

2. **Tap Add Account.**

   The screen shown in Figure 3-4 appears, allowing you to choose the type of e-mail account you want to add.

3. **Tap Microsoft Exchange.**

   The screen shown in Figure 3-5 appears, allowing you to enter the basic information for your Exchange account.

Figure 3-4:
The iPhone can support many types of e-mail accounts.

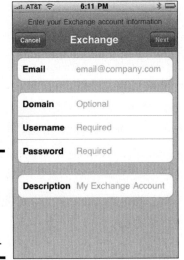

Figure 3-5:
Entering your e-mail address and logon information.

4. **Enter your e-mail address, Windows username, and password.**

   For most installations, you should leave the Domain field empty. (If the e-mail configuration doesn't work, come back to this screen, and enter your domain name here.)

5. **Tap Next.**

   The screen shown in Figure 3-6 appears.

Figure 3-6:
Entering
your
Exchange
server.

6. Enter either the DNS name or the IP address of your Exchange server.

I entered **smtp.lowewriter.com** for my Exchange server, for example.

7. Tap Next.

The screen shown in Figure 3-7 appears. This screen lets you select which mailbox features you want to synchronize: Mail, Contacts, or Calendars.

Figure 3-7:
Selecting
the
features to
synchronize.

8. **Select the features you want to synchronize and then tap Done.**

   The e-mail account is created.

After the e-mail account has been configured, the user can access it via the Mail icon on the iPhone's home screen.

Chapter 4: Managing Android Devices

In This Chapter

✔ Looking at how Android phones work

✔ Touring the Android operating system

✔ Examining the Android's core applications

✔ Working with Exchange e-mail accounts

*F*or the better part of a year, Apple had the touchscreen smartphone market all to itself. But in late 2008, T-Mobile released the touchscreen smartphone named the Dream, made by HTC. This smartphone was the first of many phones based on an operating system named Android, developed by Google. Like the iPhone, Android phones do not have physical keyboards. Instead, you interact with an Android phone by using fingertip gestures on the touch screen.

This chapter is a brief introduction to the Android platform. You find out a bit about what Android actually is, and you discover the procedures for setting up Exchange e-mail access on an Android phone.

Understanding Android Phones

In many ways, Android phones are similar to iPhones. Like iPhones, Android phones feature a touchscreen display, have built-in MP3 music players, and provide access to a large library of downloadable third-party applications. In essence, Android phones are competitors with iPhones.

Crucial differences exist between Android phones and iPhones, however. The most important difference — in many ways the *only* important difference — is that Android phones are based on an open-source operating system derived from Linux, which can be extended and adapted to work on a wide variety of hardware devices from different vendors. With the iPhone, though, you're locked into Apple hardware. With an Android phone, you can buy hardware from a variety of manufacturers, and you can use the phone on a variety of cellular networks.

Looking at the Android Operating System

Most people associate the Android operating system with Google, and it's true that Google is the driving force behind Android. The Android operating system is an open-source operating system managed by an organization called the Open Handset Alliance (OHA). Google still plays a major role in the development of Android, but more than 50 companies are involved in the OHA, including hardware manufacturers such as HTC, Intel, and Motorola; software companies such as Google and eBay; and mobile-phone operators such as T-Mobile and Sprint-Nextel.

Technically speaking, Android is more than just an operating system. It's also a complete *software stack,* which consists of several key components that work together to create the complete Android platform:

✦ **The operating-system core,** which is based on the popular Linux operating system.

✦ **A middleware layer,** which provides drivers and other support code to enable the operating-system core to work with the hardware devices that make up a complete phone, such as a touch-sensitive display, the cell-phone radio, the speaker and microphone, Bluetooth or Wi-Fi networking components, and so on.

✦ **A set of core applications** that the user interacts with to make phone calls, read e-mail, send text messages, take pictures, and so on.

✦ **A Software Developers Kit (SDK)** that lets third-party software developers create their own applications to run on an Android phone, as well as a marketplace where the applications can be marketed and sold, much as the App Store lets iPhone developers market and sell applications for the iPhone.

Besides the basic features provided by all operating systems, here are a few bonus features of the Android software stack:

✦ An optimized graphical display engine that can produce sophisticated 2D and 3D graphics

✦ GPS capabilities that provide location awareness that can be integrated with applications such as Google Maps

✦ Compass and accelerometer capabilities that can determine whether the phone is in motion and in which direction it's pointed

✦ A built-in SQL database server for data storage

✦ Support for several network technologies, including 3G, Bluetooth, and Wi-Fi

✦ Built-in media support, including common formats for still images, audio, and video files

Perusing Android's Core Applications

The Android operating system comes preconfigured with several standard applications, which provide the functionality that most people demand from a modern smartphone. These applications include

+ **Dialer:** Provides the basic cell-phone function that lets users make calls.

+ **Browser:** A built-in web browser that's similar to Google's Chrome browser.

+ **Messaging:** Provides text (SMS) and multimedia (MMS) messaging.

+ **Email:** A basic e-mail client that works best with Google's Gmail but that can be configured to work with other e-mail servers, including Exchange.

+ **Contacts:** Provides a contacts list that integrates with the Dialer and Email applications.

+ **Camera:** Lets you use the phone's camera hardware (if any) to take pictures.

+ **Calculator:** A simple calculator application.

+ **Alarm Clock:** A basic alarm clock that lets you set up to three different alarms.

+ **Maps:** An integrated version of Google Maps.

+ **YouTube:** An integrated version of YouTube.

+ **Music:** An MP3 player similar to the iPod. You can purchase and download music files from Amazon.

+ **Market:** Lets you purchase and download third-party applications for the Android phone.

+ **Settings:** Lets you control various settings for the phone.

Integrating Android with Exchange

The Android's core Email application can integrate with Microsoft Exchange e-mail. To do that, you must enable ActiveSync on the Exchange server. I won't go over the details of configuring Microsoft Exchange for ActiveSync here; instead, I refer you to Book VI, Chapter 3.

After you've enabled Exchange Mobile Services and ActiveSync on your Exchange server, you can easily configure the Android phone for e-mail access. Just run the Email application on the Android phone, and follow the configuration steps, which ask you for basic information such as your e-mail address, username, password, and Exchange mail server.

Chapter 5: Managing Netbooks

In This Chapter

✔ Checking out typical specifications for netbooks

✔ Understanding how networks connect

✔ Getting tips for working with netbooks

*O*ne of the newest trends in mobile computing is the use of *netbook computers,* or just *netbooks,* instead of traditional notebook or laptop computers. A netbook is like a cross between a smartphone and a laptop, with a strange blend of the strengths and weaknesses of both devices.

This chapter is a brief overview of what netbooks are and what factors you should take into consideration when incorporating them into your mobile network plans.

Understanding Netbook Computers

As you probably know, a netbook looks like a notebook computer that got run through the wash with hot water and shrank to about half of its original size. This small size makes it an ideal companion for many mobile users: It's larger than a smartphone, so it can be used for ordinary computer tasks like word processing or spreadsheet analysis, but it's much smaller than a notebook computer, so it's easier to take with you.

Figure 5-1 shows a typical netbook computer — in this case, an HP Mini 311. This computer comes with the following features:

✦ An 11.6-inch display (which is actually on the large size for a netbook; most netbook displays are closer to 10 inches).

✦ Intel Atom processor, which chugs along at 1.6 GHz. The Atom is a single-core processor that's optimized for very low power use.

✦ Up to 3GB of RAM.

✦ 160GB, 250GB, or 320GB hard drive.

✦ Built-in wireless 802.11g or 802.11n network interface (or both).

✦ Built-in mobile broadband compatible with Sprint, AT&T, or Verizon.

✦ Windows 7 Home Premium edition (32-bit).

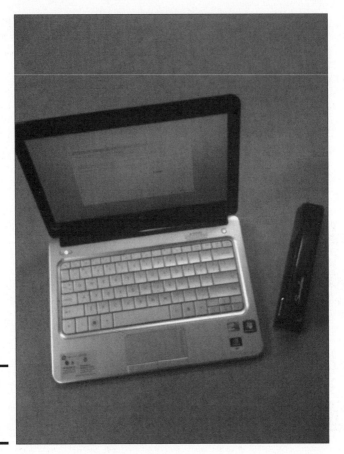

Figure 5-1:
A typical
netbook
computer.

The entire system is about 8×11 inches and about ¾ inch thick — about the size of a small hardcover book. It weighs just over 3 pounds.

Connecting with a Netbook

Other than its small size, the most distinguishing characteristic of a netbook computer is the built-in mobile broadband Internet connection from a mobile-phone provider such as AT&T, Sprint, Verizon, or T-Mobile. In fact, these companies typically discount the purchase price of the netbook to $100 or $200 if you sign up for a two-year network plan, which typically costs about $50 per month.

The built-in mobile broadband network connection means that no matter where you are, you can access the network, provided that you're within range of one of your provider's cell towers. With a traditional laptop computer, you have to find an available Wi-Fi network to connect to. With a netbook, you can connect from almost anywhere — a restaurant, a street corner, even riding on a bus.

Unfortunately, the service plans available for netbook computers don't provide for unlimited data transfer. Most plans are limited to 5GB per month; after that, you're charged an additional overage fee. As a result, you want to make sure that your users are careful about the amount of data they transfer. A 5GB limit is plenty for most legitimate business uses, but if your users spend their free time watching videos on YouTube, they'll quickly exceed the 5GB limit.

The mobile broadband provider provides software that connects to its broadband network. Figure 5-2 shows the software provided by Verizon.

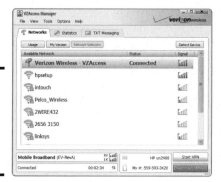

Figure 5-2:
Connecting
via
broadband
with
Verizon.

Here are a few tips that may help your users keep their usage under the maximum:

✦ Besides a mobile broadband connection, all netbooks include a built-in Wi-Fi interface. You should encourage your users to use the Wi-Fi connection rather than the mobile broadband connection whenever possible. Any data transferred over the Wi-Fi connection doesn't count against the 5GB maximum imposed by the mobile broadband connection.

✦ Similarly, all netbook computers include an RJ45 connector for a standard Ethernet cable connection. Your users should use this connection whenever possible — when they're using the netbook on a desk or in a home office, for example.

✦ Be sure to disable Windows Update. Otherwise, whenever an update is available, Windows Update downloads it regardless of the type of connection that's in place. Instead, your users should check for Windows updates manually on a regular basis when using a Wi-Fi or cabled network connection.

✦ Educate your users about the differences among mobile broadband, Wi-Fi, and cabled network connections to be sure that they understand the appropriate use of each type.

Tips for Using a Netbook Effectively

In this section, I offer some random suggestions that I've found useful for working with netbooks. Here they are, in no particular order:

✦ **Carry a standard-size keyboard and mouse in your car.** The keyboard on a netbook computer is pretty small, and the touchpad mouse is also small. You may not want to lug the keyboard and mouse into a restaurant or coffee shop, but it's handy to have when you take the netbook into your hotel room and want to do some real work.

✦ **Consider disabling the tap feature of the netbook's touchpad.** Because of the netbook's small size, the touchpad usually is located uncomfortably close to the keyboard. I end up tapping it with the base of my thumbs when I type, which causes the mouse pointer to jump all over the place almost at random. I solved this problem by disabling the tap feature of the touchpad.

✦ **Create a desktop icon that will take your users directly to your Office Web Access (OWA) site.** That way, your users can easily access their e-mail whenever they have an Internet connection.

✦ **Install virtual private network (VPN) client software to allow your users to tunnel in to your network.** For more information, refer to Book III, Chapter 5.

✦ **Because netbook computers usually run one of the Home editions of Windows 7, netbooks can't join your domain.** That's probably for the best, though, because most users will use the netbook mostly for web browsing and e-mail — which, as mentioned earlier in this list, can be easily accomplished with OWA.

✦ **Keep in mind that even though the netbook computer can't join the domain, it can still access network shares.** The user has to provide a valid username and password each time he or she tries to open a network share.

Book VII

Windows Server 2012 Reference

The 5th Wave   By Rich Tennant

"Well, the first level of Windows security seems
good - I can't get the shrink-wrapping off."

Contents at a Glance

Chapter 1: Installing and Configuring Windows Server 2012

In This Chapter

✔ Making sure you have everything you need

✔ Planning how to install Windows Server 2012

✔ Installing Windows Server 2012

*T*his chapter presents the procedures that you need to follow to install Windows Server — specifically, Windows Server 2012. Note that although the specific details provided are for Windows Server 2012, installing the previous version (just plain Windows Server 2008) is very similar, as is installing the older Windows Server 2003. So you won't have any trouble adapting these procedures if you're installing Windows Server 2012 or Windows Server 2008.

Planning a Windows Server Installation

Before you begin the Setup program to actually install a Windows Server operating system, you need to make several preliminary decisions, as the following sections describe.

Checking system requirements

Before you install a Windows Server operating system, you should make sure that the computer meets the minimum requirements. Table 1-1 lists the official minimum requirements for Windows Server 2012. (The minimums for Windows Server 2008 are the same.) Table 1-1 also lists what I consider to be more realistic minimums if you expect satisfactory performance from the server as a moderately used file server.

Table 1-1	Minimum Hardware Requirements for Windows Server 2012 (Standard Edition)	
Item	*Official Minimum*	*A More Realistic Minimum*
CPU	1.4 GHz	3 GHz
RAM	512MB	4GB
Free disk space	32GB	100GB

Note, however, that there is no 32-bit version of Windows Server 2012. A 64-bit processor is required, but that shouldn't be a problem, as nearly all computers manufactured since around 2007 have 64-bit processors.

Reading the release notes

The Windows Server 2012 distribution DVD includes a file called readme. rtf, located in the Sources folder. You should read this file before you start Setup, just to check whether any of the specific procedures or warnings it contains applies to your situation.

Deciding whether to upgrade or install

Windows offers two installation modes: full installation or upgrade installation.

A *full installation* deletes any existing operating system(s) it finds on the computer and configures the new operating system from scratch. If you do a full installation onto a disk that already has an operating system installed, the full installation offers to keep any existing data files that it finds on the disk.

An *upgrade installation* assumes that you already have a previous Windows Server (Windows Server 2012 or Windows Server 2008) installation in place. The operating system is upgraded to Windows Server 2012, preserving as many settings from the previous installation as possible.

Here are some points to ponder before you perform an upgrade installation:

✦ You can't upgrade a client version of Windows to a server version.

✦ With an upgrade installation, you don't have to reinstall any applications that were previously installed on the disk.

✦ Always perform a full backup before doing an upgrade installation!

Considering your licensing options

Two types of licenses are required to run a Windows Server operating system: a *server license,* which grants you permission to run a single instance of the server, and *Client Access Licenses* (CALs), which grant users or devices permission to connect to the server. When you purchase Windows Server, you ordinarily purchase a server license plus some number of CALs.

To complicate matters, there are two distinct types of CALs: per-user and per-device. *Per-user* CALs limit the number of users who can access a server simultaneously, regardless of the number of devices (such as client computers) in your organization. By contrast, *per-device* CALs limit the number of unique devices that can access the server, regardless of the number of users in your organization.

Thinking about multiboot

Windows includes a *multiboot* feature that lets you set up the computer so that it has more than one operating system. When you boot up the computer, you can select the operating system you want to boot up from a menu.

If you're a software developer or a network manager who needs to make sure that software is compatible with multiple operating systems, the multiboot feature can be useful. For most servers, however, you want to install just one operating system.

TIP

A much better alternative to a multiboot installation is to use virtual-machine software such as VMware. This software allows you to install a development version of an operating system such as Windows Server 2012 within an already-installed operating system. For more information, see www.vmware.com.

Book VII
Chapter 1

Installing and
Configuring
Windows
Server 2012

Planning your partitions

Partitioning enables you to divide a physical disk into one or more separate units called *partitions.* Each disk can have up to four partitions. All four of the partitions can be primary partitions. A *primary partition* contains one — and only one — file system. Alternatively, you can create up to three primary partitions and one extended partition, which can be subdivided into one or more logical drives. Then each logical drive can be formatted with a file system.

Windows Server 2012 offers you two file systems: NTFS and ReFS. NTFS is the tried-and-true file system that has been the standard file system for going on 20 years. The partition that Windows Server 2012 boots from must be NTFS. ***However, other partitions can*** be either NTFS or ReFS.

Although you can set up partitions for a Windows server in many ways, the following two approaches are the most common:

✦ **Allocate the entire disk as a single partition that will be formatted with NTFS.** The operating system is installed into this partition, and disk space that isn't needed by the operating system or other network applications can be shared.

✦ **Divide the disk into two partitions.** Install the operating system and any other related software (such as Exchange Server or a backup utility) on the first partition. If the first partition will contain just the operating system, 10GB is a reasonable size, although you can get by with as little as 4GB if space is at a premium. Then use the second partition for application data or network file shares.

Note that the disk partitioning scheme is independent of any hardware-based RAID configuration your server may employ. Your server may actually include five physical hard drives that are combined by the hardware disk controller to form a single logical drive, for example. Within this logical drive, you can create one or more operating-system partitions.

Deciding your TCP/IP configuration

Before you install the operating system, you should have a plan for implementing TCP/IP on the network. Here are some of the things you need to decide or find out:

✦ What are the IP subnet address and mask for your network?

✦ What is the domain name for the network?

✦ What is the host name for the server?

✦ Will the server obtain its address from DHCP?

✦ Will the server have a static IP address? If so, what?

✦ Will the server be a DHCP server?

✦ What is the Default Gateway for the server (that is, what is the IP address of the network's Internet router)?

✦ Will the server be a DNS server?

In almost all cases, you should assign the server a static IP address.

For more information about planning your TCP/IP configuration, see Book IV.

Choosing workgroups or domains

A *domain* is a method of placing user accounts and various network resources under the control of a single directory database. Domains ensure that security policies are applied consistently throughout a network and greatly simplify the task of managing user accounts on large networks.

A *workgroup* is a simple association of computers on a network that makes it easy to locate shared files and printers. Workgroups don't have sophisticated directory databases, so they can't enforce strict security.

Microsoft says that workgroups should be used only for very small networks with just a few users. In fact, any network that is large enough to have a dedicated server running Windows Server 2012 is too large to use workgroups. As a result, if you're installing a Windows server, you should always opt for domains.

After you decide to use domains, you have to make two basic decisions:

✦ **What will the domain name be?** If you have a registered Internet domain name, such as mydomain.com, you may want to use it for your network's domain name. Otherwise, you can make up any name you want.

✦ **What computer or computers will be the domain controllers for the domain?** If this server is the first server in a domain, you must designate it as a domain controller. If you already have a server acting as a domain controller, you can either add this computer as an additional domain controller or designate it a member server.

 You can always change the role of a server from a domain controller to a member server, and vice versa, if the needs of your network change. If your network has more than one server, it's always a good idea to create at least two domain controllers. That way, if one fails, the other one can take over.

Before You Install . . .

After you've made the key planning decisions for your Windows server installation, but before you actually start the Setup program, you should take a few precautionary steps. The following sections describe what you should do before you perform an upgrade installation.

Note: All these steps except the last one apply only to upgrades. If you're installing a Windows server on a new system, you can skip the first steps.

**Book VII
Chapter 1**

Installing and
Configuring
Windows
Server 2012

Backing up

Do a complete backup of the server before you begin. Although Windows Setup is reliable, sometimes, something serious goes wrong, and data is lost.

You don't have to back up the drive to external media, such as tape. If you can find a network disk share with enough free space, back up to it.

Checking the event logs

Look at the event logs of the existing server computer to check for recurring errors. You may discover that you have a problem with a SCSI device or your current TCP/IP configuration. It's better to find out now rather than in the middle of setup.

Uncompressing data

If you've used DriveSpace or any other disk compression software to compress a drive, you have to uncompress the drive before you run Setup. Neither Windows 2003 Server nor Windows Server 2012 supports DriveSpace or other disk compression programs.

Disconnecting UPS devices

If you've installed an uninterruptible power supply (UPS) device on the server and connected it to your computer via a serial cable, you should temporarily disconnect the serial cable before you run Setup. When Setup is complete, you can reconnect the serial cable.

Running Setup

Now that you've planned your installation and prepared the computer, you're ready to run the Setup program. The following procedure describes the steps that you must follow to install Windows Server 2012 on a new computer that has a bootable DVD drive:

1. **Insert the distribution CD into the DVD drive, and restart the computer.**

   After a few moments, the Windows Setup Wizard fires up, as shown in Figure 1-1.

2. **Click Install Now to start the installation.**

   Windows asks which edition of the operating system you want to install, as shown in Figure 1-2.

Figure 1-1:
Welcome
to Windows
Setup!

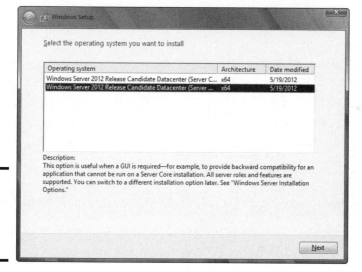

Figure 1-2:
Selecting
the OS
edition to
install.

Book VII
Chapter 1

Installing and
Configuring
Windows
Server 2012

3. Select the edition you want to install and then click Next.

The Setup Wizard displays the License Agreement information. Read it if you enjoy legalese.

4. Click I Accept the License Terms and then click Next.

The Setup Wizard asks whether you want to perform an upgrade installation or a full installation.

5. **Click the installation option you want to use.**

   Setup continues by displaying the computer's current partition information. You can select the partition that you want to use for the installation. If necessary, you can reconfigure your partitions from this screen by deleting existing partitions or creating new ones. I assume here that you want to create a single partition that uses all available space on the drive.

6. **Select the partition on which you want to install Windows and then click Next.**

   Setup formats the drive and then copies files to the newly formatted drive. This step usually takes a while. I suggest you bring along your favorite book. Start reading at Chapter 1.

   After all the files have been copied, Setup reboots your computer. Then Setup examines all the devices on the computer and installs any necessary device drivers. You can read Chapter 2 of your book during this time.

   When Setup finishes installing drivers, it asks for the password you want to use for the computer's Administrator account, as shown in Figure 1-3.

Figure 1-3:
Setting the
Administrator password.

7. **Enter the Administrator password twice and then click Finish.**

   Be sure to write this password down somewhere and keep it in a secure place. If you lose this password, you won't be able to access your server.

   After you've set the Administrator password, Windows displays the login screen shown in Figure 1-4.

8. **Press Ctrl+Alt+Del, and log in using the Administrator account.**

   You have to enter the password you created in Step 7 to gain access.

   When you're logged in, Windows displays the Server Manager Dashboard, as shown in Figure 1-5.

Figure 1-4:
Press
Ctrl+Alt+Del
to log in.

Book VII
Chapter 1

Installing and
Configuring
Windows
Server 2012

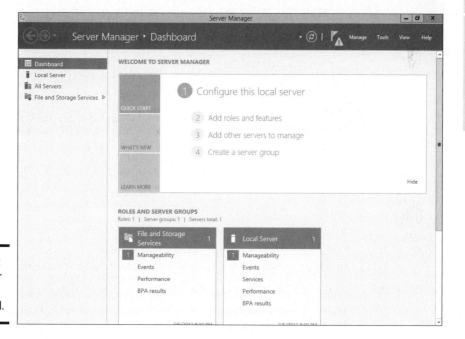

Figure 1-5:
The Server
Manager
Dashboard.

The Server Manager Dashboard provides links that let you complete the configuration of your server. Specifically, you can

- Click Configure This Local Server to configure server settings such as the computer's name and the domain it belongs to, network settings such as the static IP address, and so on.

- Click Add Roles and Features to add server roles and features. (For more information, see "Adding Server Roles and Features," later in this chapter.)

- Click Add Other Servers to Manage to manage other servers in your network.

- Click Create a Server Group if you have a large number of servers on your network and want to divide them into separate groups that you can manage separately.

Adding Server Roles and Features

Server roles are the roles that your server can play on your network — roles such as file server, web server, or DHCP or DNS server. *Features* are additional capabilities of the Windows operating system itself, such as the .NET Framework or Windows Backup. Truthfully, the distinctions between roles and features are a bit arbitrary. The web server is considered to be a role, for example, but the Telnet server is a feature. Go figure.

The following procedure describes how to install server roles. The procedure for installing server features is similar.

1. **Click Add Roles and Features on the Server Manager Dashboard. (Refer to Figure 1-6.)**

   The Add Roles and Features Wizard appears, as shown in Figure 1-6.

2. **Click Next.**

   The wizard asks which of two installation types you want to perform. In most cases, you want to leave the default choice (Role-Based or Feature-Based Installation) selected. Select the alternative (Remote Desktop Services Installation) only if you're configuring a remote virtual server.

3. **Click Next.**

   The wizard lets you select the server you want to install roles or features for, as shown in Figure 1-7. In this example, only one server is listed. If you'd chosen Add Other Servers to Manage in the Server Manager Dashboard to add other servers, those servers would appear on this page as well.

Figure 1-6:
The Add
Roles and
Features
Wizard.

Figure 1-7:
Selecting
the server to
manage.

Book VII
Chapter 1

Installing and
Configuring
Windows
Server 2012

4. **Select the server you want to manage and then click Next.**

   The Select Server Roles page, shown in Figure 1-8, appears. This page
   lets you select one or more roles to add to your server.

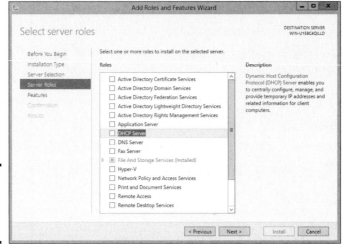

Figure 1-8:
The Select
Server
Roles page.

5. Select one or more roles to install.

You can click each role to display a brief description of it. If you click DHCP Server, for example, the following text is displayed:

```
Dynamic Host Configuration Protocol (DHCP) Server enables you to
     centrally configure, manage, and provide temporary IP addresses and
     related information for client computers.
```

6. Click Next.

The Select Features page appears, as shown in Figure 1-9. This page lists additional server features that you can install.

Figure 1-9:
The Select
Features
page.

7. **Select the features you want to install.**

   Again, you can select each feature to see a brief text description of the service.

8. **Click Next.**

   A confirmation page appears, listing the roles and features you've selected.

9. **Click Install.**

   Windows installs the server role and its features. A progress screen is displayed during the installation so that you can gauge the installation's progress. When the installation finishes, a final results page is displayed.

10. **Click OK.**

    You're done!

Book VII
Chapter 1

Installing and
Configuring
Windows
Server 2012

Chapter 2: Managing Windows Server 2012

This chapter provides an introduction to the most important tools that you'll use to administer Windows Server 2012.

Using the Administrator Account

Windows comes with a built-in account named *Administrator* that has complete access to all the features of the server. As a network administrator, you frequently log on using the Administrator account to perform maintenance chores.

Because the Administrator account is so powerful, you should always enforce good password practices for it. In other words, don't use your dog's name as the Administrator account password. Instead, pick a random combination of letters and numbers. Then change the password periodically.

Write down the Administrator account password, and keep it in a secure location. Note that by *secure location,* I don't mean taped to the front of the monitor. Keep it in a safe place where you can retrieve it if you forget it, but where it won't easily fall into the hands of someone who's looking to break into your network.

Note that you cannot delete or disable the Administrator account. If Windows allowed you to do that, you could potentially find yourself locked out of your own system.

As much as possible, you should avoid using the Administrator account. Instead, you should create accounts for each of your system administrators and grant them administrator privileges by assigning their accounts to the Administrators group.

Although you can't delete or disable the Administrator account, you can rename it. Some network managers use this ability to hide the true Administrator account. To do this, just follow these steps:

1. **Rename the Administrator account.**

   Write down the new name you use for the Administrator account, along with the password, and store it in a top-secret secure location.

2. **Create a new account named Administrator, and assign it a strong password, but don't give this account any significant privileges.**

   This new account will become a "decoy" Administrator account. The idea is to get hackers to waste time trying to crack this account's password. Even if a hacker does manage to compromise this account, he won't be able to do anything when he gets in.

Using Remote Desktop Connection

One of the most useful tools available to system administrators is a program called *Remote Desktop Connection,* or *RDC* for short. RDC lets you connect to a server computer from your own computer and use it as though you were actually sitting at the server. In short, RDC lets you administer your server computers from your own office.

Enabling remote access

Before you can use Remote Desktop Connection to access a server, you must enable remote access on the server. To do that, follow these steps (on the server computer, not your desktop computer):

1. **Open the Control Panel and then double-click System.**

   This step brings up the System applet.

2. **Click the Remote tab.**

   This step brings up the remote access options, as shown in Figure 2-1.

3. **Select the Allow Remote Connections to This Computer radio button.**

4. **Click OK.**

Figure 2-1:
Configuring
remote
access.

You're done! Repeat this procedure for each server computer you want to allow access to.

Here are a few other points to ponder concerning remote access:

✦ You can click the Select Users button to create a list of users who are authorized to access the computer remotely. Note that all members of the Administrators group are automatically granted access, so you don't have to add administrators to this list.

✦ There's no question that RDC is convenient and useful. It's also inherently dangerous, however. Don't enable it unless you've taken precautions to secure your Administrator accounts by using strong passwords; also, you should already have a firewall installed to keep unwanted visitors out of your network. For more information on account security, see Book VII, Chapter 6.

Connecting remotely

After you've enabled remote access on a server, you can connect to the server by using the Remote Desktop Client that's automatically installed with Windows. Here's the procedure for Windows 7:

1. **Choose Start➪All Programs➪Accessories➪Remote Desktop Connection.**

The Remote Desktop Connection client comes to life, as shown in Figure 2-2.

Figure 2-2:
Connecting
with Remote
Desktop
Connection.

2. **Enter the name of the computer you want to connect to.**

   Alternatively, you can use the drop-down list to select the computer
   from the list of available computers.

3. **Click the Connect button.**

   You're connected to the computer you selected, and the computer's
   logon screen is displayed.

4. **Log on, and use the computer.**

   After you log on, you can use the computer as though you were sitting
   right in front of it.

Here are a few other tips for working with the Remote Desktop Connection
client:

✦ When you're using the Remote Desktop Connection client, you can't just
   Alt+Tab to another program running on the client computer. Instead,
   you must first minimize the RDC client's window by clicking its minimize
   button. Then you can access other programs running on your computer.

✦ If you minimize the RDC client window, you have to provide your logon
   credentials again when you return. This security feature is there in case
   you forget that you have an RDC session open.

✦ If you use RDC a lot on a particular computer (such as your own desktop
   computer), I suggest that you create a shortcut to RDC and place it on
   the desktop, at the top of the Start menu, or in the Quick Launch portion
   of the taskbar.

✦ RDC has several useful configuration options that you can access by
   clicking the Options button.

Using Microsoft Management Console

Microsoft Management Console, also known as *MMC,* is a general-purpose management tool that's used to administer many different types of objects on a Windows system. Throughout this minibook, you see many examples of MMC for working with objects such as user accounts, disk drives, event logs, and so on. This section provides a general overview of how to use MMC.

By itself, MMC doesn't actually manage anything. Instead, it's a framework that accepts management snap-ins, which do the actual managing. The main point of MMC is that it provides a consistent framework for building management snap-ins so that all the snap-ins behave in similar ways. As a result, you don't have to struggle to learn completely different tools to manage various aspects of Windows Server 2012.

Another advantage of MMC is that you can create your own custom management consoles with just the right combination of snap-ins. Suppose that you spend most of your time managing user accounts, disk devices, and IIS (Internet Information Services, the web server that comes with Windows Server 2012), and studying event logs. You can easily craft a management console with just these four snap-ins. For more information, see the section "Customizing MMC," later in this chapter.

Working with MMC

There are several ways to open a Microsoft Management Console window. The easiest is to open one of the predefined consoles that come with Windows Server 2012. To access these consoles, press the Windows key and then select Administrative Tools.

You can also start MMC from a command prompt. To start MMC without opening a snap-in, just type **mmc** at a command prompt. To open a specific console, type the path to the console file after mmc. The following command, for example, opens the Computer Management console:

```
mmc \Windows\System32\compmgmt.msc
```

Figure 2-3 shows a typical Microsoft Management Console window, displaying the Active Directory Users and Computers snap-in. As you can see, the MMC window consists of two panes. The pane on the left is a tree pane that displays a hierarchical tree of the objects that you can manage. The pane on the right is a Details pane that shows detailed information about the object that's selected in the tree pane.

**Book VII
Chapter 2**

Managing Windows
Server 2012

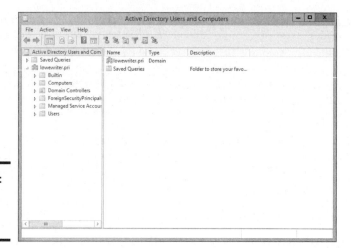

Figure 2-3:
A typical
MMC
window.

The procedures for working with the information in the Details pane vary depending on the console you're viewing. Most of the consoles, however, display lists of some kind, such as settings or user accounts. Double-clicking an item usually brings up a Properties dialog box that lets you view or set properties for the object. In most cases, you can click the column headings at the top of the list to change the order in which the list items are displayed.

MMC also includes a menu and toolbar with commands and buttons that vary depending on the item selected in the tree. In particular, the Action menu contains commands that apply to the current item. The Action menu includes a New User command when you're working with the Active Directory Users and Computers console, for example, and a Defragment command when you view the Disk Defragmenter item in the Computer Management Console. As you work with different items within the different consoles, be sure to check the Action menu frequently to find out what commands are available.

Taking an overview of the MMC consoles

The Tools menu in Server Manager Dashboard gives you direct access to many useful management consoles. You find detailed descriptions of several of these tools later in this minibook. The following paragraphs give you a brief overview of the most important of these consoles:

✦ **Active Directory Domains and Trusts:** Manages the domain and trust relationships for the server.

✦ **Active Directory Sites and Services:** Manages Active Directory services.

✦ **Active Directory Users and Computers:** Lets you create and modify user accounts.

✦ **Component Services:** Lets you manage how COM+ (Component Object Model) services work on the server. You mess with this console only if you're involved in developing applications that use COM+ services.

✦ **Computer Management:** Provides access to several useful tools for managing a server. In particular, the Computer Management console provides the following management tools:

- *Event Viewer:* Lets you view event logs.

- *Shared Folders:* Lets you manage shared folders for a file server. In addition to finding out what shares are available, you can use this tool to find out which users are connected to the server and which files are open.

- *Local Users and Groups* (available only on servers that aren't domain controllers): Lets you manage local user and group accounts. For a domain controller, you use the Active Directory Users and Computers console to manage user accounts.

- *Performance:* Lets you monitor system performance counters.

- *Device Manager:* Lets you manage the hardware devices connected to a server. You'll probably use it only if you're having a problem with the server that you suspect may be hardware-related.

- *Disk Management:* Lets you view the physical disks and volumes that are available to the system. You can also use this tool to create and delete partitions, set up RAID volumes, format disks, and so on.

- *Services:* Lets you manage system services. You can use this tool to start or stop services such as Exchange e-mail services, TCP/IP services such as DNS and DHCP, and so on.

- *WMI Control:* Lets you configure *Windows Management Instrumentation services,* which track management data about computers, users, applications, and other objects in large Enterprise networks.

✦ **DHCP:** Manages the DHCP server.

✦ **DNS:** Manages the DNS server.

✦ **Domain Controller Security Policy:** Lets you set security policy for a domain controller.

✦ **Event Viewer:** Lets you view event logs.

✦ **Group Policy Management:** Lets you set system policies that can be applied to objects such as users and groups.

✦ **Internet Information Services (IIS) Manager:** Lets you manage the services provided by IIS (Microsoft's web server) if IIS is installed on the server.

✦ **ODBC Data Sources:** Manages database connections that use ODBC. You'll probably use this console only if you're a developer or database administrator.

✦ **Performance Monitor:** Lets you monitor a server's performance and twiddle with various settings that can have positive or negative effects on performance.

✦ **Services:** Lets you start and stop Windows services. (It's also available via the Computer Management console.)

Customizing MMC

One of the best things about Microsoft Management Console is that you can customize it so that the tools you use most often are grouped together in whatever combination you choose. To create a custom console, first start Microsoft Management Console without loading a console by pressing the Windows key, typing **cmd** and pressing Enter to open a command prompt, and then entering the command **mmc**. This action creates an empty console, as shown in Figure 2-4.

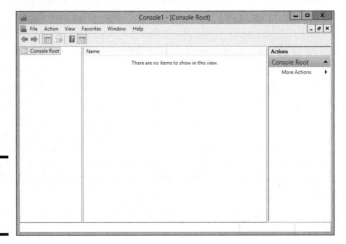

Figure 2-4:
An empty
MMC
console.

Adding snap-ins

After you've created an empty console, you can customize it by adding whatever snap-ins you want to make use of in the console. To add a snap-in, follow these steps:

1. **Choose File➪Add/Remove Snap-In.**

This command brings up the Add or Remove Snap-Ins dialog box, shown in Figure 2-5.

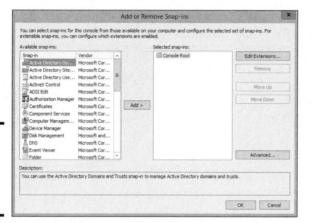

Figure 2-5:
The Add
or Remove
Snap-Ins
dialog box.

2. Select the snap-in you want to add and then click the Add button.

Depending on which snap-in you select, a dialog box appears, asking whether you want to use the add-in to manage settings on your own computer or on a local computer.

3. Repeat Step 2 if you want to add other snap-ins to the console.

4. Click OK.

The console is equipped with the snap-ins you've selected.

Adding taskpads

A *taskpad* is a customized page that's displayed within a console. Taskpads are designed to provide quick access to the most common chores for a particular snap-in. A taskpad can display shortcuts that run programs, execute menu commands, open web pages, or open folders. Figure 2-6 shows a simple taskpad that I created for managing local user accounts. As you can see, it includes icons that let you quickly add an account, delete an account, and change an account's password.

To add a taskpad, follow these steps:

1. Select the tree node where you want the taskpad to appear.

Each taskpad you create is specific to a tree node. The taskpad shown in Figure 2-6, for example, is displayed only when you select a user account. To create this taskpad, I opened the Local Users and Groups node and selected the Users node.

**Book VII
Chapter 2**

**Managing Windows
Server 2012**

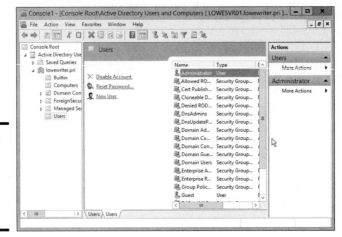

Figure 2-6:
A taskpad
for
managing
user
accounts.

2. **Choose Action⇨New Taskpad View.**

   This step brings up the New Taskpad View Wizard, as shown in Figure 2-7.

Figure 2-7:
The New
Taskpad
View
Wizard.

3. **Click Next.**

   The Taskpad Style page appears, as shown in Figure 2-8.

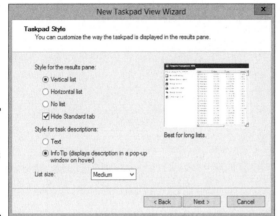

Figure 2-8:
Setting the style options for a new taskpad page.

This page provides the following options for formatting the taskpad display:

- *Vertical List:* If you want to include the list from the details page, you can select this option to place taskpad icons to the left of the list. I selected this option for the taskpad shown in Figure 2-6.

- *Horizontal List:* This option places the taskpad icons below the details-page list.

- *No List:* This option creates a taskpad with no list, just taskpad icons.

- *Hide Standard Tab:* Each taskpad can have a standard view, which simply lists all the items in the taskpad without showing custom tasks. The Hide Standard Tab check box, which is selected by default, hides this tab. Most of the time, you'll want to leave this check box selected.

- *Text:* This option displays descriptive information below each task-pad icon.

- *InfoTip:* This option displays descriptive information as a pop-up tip that appears when you hover the mouse over the icon.

- *List Size:* This drop-down list lets you select how much of the taskpad area should be devoted to the list. The options are Small, Medium, and Large.

It's a good thing that this wizard wasn't designed by a fast-food company. If it had been, the options for List Size would be Large, Extra Large, and MegaSuperKing.

4. Select the taskpad options you want and then click Next.

The next page of the wizard presents two options that let you control when the taskpad should be displayed:

Book VII
Chapter 2

Managing Windows
Server 2012

- *Selected Tree Item:* The taskpad is displayed only for the specific tree item that you selected in Step 1.

- *All Tree Items That Are the Same Type As the Selected Item:* The taskpad is displayed not only for the selected tree item, but also for other items of the same type. This option is the more common choice.

5. **Select the taskpad display option and then click Next.**

   The next page of the wizard asks for a name and description for the taskpad.

6. **Type a name and description for the taskpad, and then click Next.**

   The final page of the New Taskpad View Wizard is displayed, as shown in Figure 2-9.

Figure 2-9:
The final
page of
the New
Taskpad
View
Wizard.

7. **Select the Add New Tasks to This Taskpad After the Wizard Closes check box and then click Finish.**

   This step completes the New Taskpad View Wizard but automatically launches the New Task Wizard so that you can begin adding tasks to the taskpad. The New Task Wizard begins by displaying a typical greeting page.

8. **Click Next.**

   The page shown in Figure 2-10 is displayed. This page lets you select one of three types of shortcuts to create on the taskpad:

   - *Menu Command:* Lets you choose one of the console's menu commands. All three of the shortcuts shown in the taskpad in Figure 2-6 are menu commands.

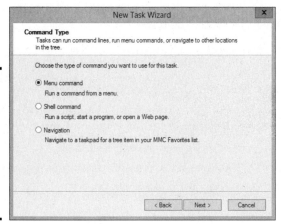

- *Shell Command:* Lets you run another program, start a batch file, or open a web page.

- *Navigation:* Lets you go to one of the views you've added to the Favorites menu. (If you want to add shortcuts that navigate to different taskpads in a console, first add each taskpad view to your Favorites menu by navigating to the taskpad and choosing Favorites⇨Add to Favorites.)

9. **Choose the type of shortcut command you want to create and then click Next.**

The page that's displayed next depends on which option you selected in Step 8. The rest of this procedure assumes that you selected the Menu Command option, which displays the page shown in Figure 2-11.

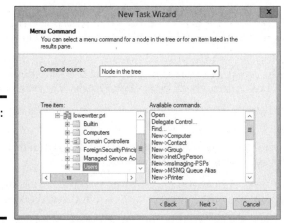

10. **Choose the command you want to use and then click Next.**

The available commands are listed in the Available Commands list box. Note that you can bring up several different lists of available commands by choosing an option from the Command Source drop-down list.

When you click Next, the wizard asks for a name and description for the command you've selected.

11. **Enter a name and description for the command and then click Next.**

This step brings up the page shown in Figure 2-12.

Figure 2-12:
Selecting an
icon.

12. **Choose the icon you want to use and then click Next.**

Note that in many cases, the New Task Wizard suggests an appropriate icon. If you select a Delete command, for example, the standard Delete icon will be selected.

When you click Next, the final page of the wizard is displayed, as shown in Figure 2-13.

13. **If you want to create additional tasks, select the When I Click Finish, Run This Wizard Again check box; click Finish; and repeat Steps 8–13.**

You can run the wizard as many times as necessary to add tasks to your taskpad.

14. **When you're finished adding tasks, deselect the When I Click Finish, Run This Wizard Again check box, and click Finish.**

You're done!

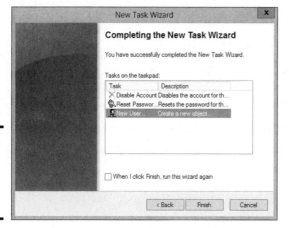

Figure 2-13:
The final
page of the
New Task
Wizard.

Here are a few other pointers for working with taskpads:

✦ You can edit an existing taskpad by selecting the tree node that displays
   the taskpad and choosing Action➪Edit Taskpad View. This command
   brings up a Properties dialog box that lets you change the taskpad
   layout options and add or remove tasks.

✦ To delete a taskpad, select the tree node that displays the taskpad, and
   choose Action➪Delete Taskpad View.

✦ Don't forget to save (File➪Save) often while you're creating custom
   taskpads.

Chapter 3: Dealing with Active Directory

Active Directory is among the most important features of Windows Server, and much of your time as a network administrator will be spent keeping Active Directory neat and tidy. In Book VII, Chapter 4, I discuss the details of working with the most common and troublesome types of Active Directory objects, users, and groups. First, this chapter lays some foundation by explaining what Active Directory is and how it works.

What Directories Do

Everyone uses directory services of one type or another every day. When you look up someone's name in a phone book, you're using a directory service. But you're also using a directory service when you make a call: When you enter someone's phone number into your touch-tone phone, the phone system looks up that number in its directory to locate that person's phone.

Almost from the very beginning, computers have had directory services. When I got started in the computer business back in the 1970s, I used IBM mainframe computers and a transaction-processing system called CICS that's still in widespread use today. CICS relied on many different directories to track such things as files available to the system, users that were authorized to access the system, and application programs that could be run.

But the problem with this directory system, and with most other directory systems that were popular in those days, is that it was made up of many small directory systems that didn't know how to talk to one another. I have the very same problem at home. I have my own little personal address book that has phone numbers and addresses for my friends and family members. I have a Day-Timer book with a bunch of other phone numbers and addresses. Then I have a church directory that lists everyone who goes to my church. Oh, and there's the list of players on the softball team I coach, and of course, my cell phone has a directory.

All counted, I probably have a dozen sources for phone numbers that I routinely call. So when I need to look up someone's phone number, I first have to decide which directory to look in. Some of my friends are listed in two or three of these sources, which raises the possibility that their listings are out of sync.

That's exactly the type of problem that Active Directory is designed to address. Before I get into the specifics of Active Directory, however, I show you the directory system that Microsoft used on Windows networks before Active Directory became available.

Remembering the Good Ol' Days of NT Domains

Active Directory was introduced with Windows 2000 Server. Before then, the directory management system in a Windows network was managed by Windows NT domains, which stored directory information in a database called the Security Account Manager (SAM) database.

PDCs and BDCs

The most important thing to know about NT domains is that they are *servercentric* — that is, every Windows NT domain is under the control of a Windows NT server computer that hosts the primary copy of the SAM database. This server is called the *Primary Domain Controller (PDC)*.

Large networks couldn't work efficiently if all directory access had to be channeled through a single computer, of course. To solve that bottleneck problem, Windows NT domains can also be serviced by one or more *Backup Domain Controllers (BDCs)*. Each BDC stores a read-only copy of the SAM database, and any changes made to the SAM database on the PDC must be propagated down to the BDC copies of the database.

Note that although any of the BDC servers can service access requests such as user logons, all changes to the SAM database must be made via the PDC. Then those changes are copied to the BDC servers. Naturally, this arrangement raises the possibility that the PDC and BDC database are out of sync.

If the PDC should fail for some reason, one of the BDCs can be promoted so that it becomes the PDC for the domain. This promotion allows the domain to continue to function while the original PDC is repaired. Because the BDC is an important backup for the PDC, it's important that all NT networks have at least one BDC.

Trusts

Many organizations have directory needs that are too complicated to store on just one NT domain PDC. In that case, the organization can create two or more separate domains for its network, each with its own PDC and BDCs. Then the organization can set up trusts among its domains.

Simply put, a *trust* is a relationship in which one domain trusts the directory information stored in another domain. The domain that does the trusting is called — you guessed it — the *trusting domain,* and the domain that contains the information being trusted is called the *trusted domain.*

Trust relationships work in one direction. Suppose that you have two domains, named DomainA and DomainB, and a trust relationship is set up so that DomainA trusts DomainB. That means that users whose accounts are defined in DomainB can log on to DomainA and access resources. The trust relationship doesn't work in the other direction, however: Users in DomainA can't log on and access resources defined in DomainB.

Also, trust relationships aren't *transitive.* (There's a word that takes you back to high-school algebra.) That means that even if DomainA trusts DomainB and DomainB trusts DomainC, DomainA doesn't automatically trust DomainC. For DomainA to trust DomainC, you'd have to create a separate trust relationship between DomainA and DomainC.

NetBIOS names

One other important characteristic of Windows NT domains is that they use NetBIOS names. Thus, NT names such as computer names and domain names are limited to 15 characters.

Actually, NetBIOS names are 16 characters long. But NT uses the last character of the 16-character NetBIOS name for its own purposes, so that character isn't available for use. As a result, NT names can be only 15 characters long.

Active Directory to the Rescue

Active Directory solves many of the inherent limitations of Windows NT domains by creating a distributed directory database that keeps track of every conceivable type of network object.

Active Directory is a comprehensive directory management system that tracks just about everything worth tracking in a Windows network, including users, computers, files, folders, applications, and much more. Much of your job as a network administrator involves working with Active Directory, so it's vital that you have a basic understanding of how it works.

One of the most important differences between Active Directory and NT domains is that Active Directory isn't servercentric. In other words, Active Directory isn't tied to a specific server computer, the way a Windows NT domain is. Although Active Directory still uses domains and domain controllers, these concepts are much more flexible in Active Directory than they are in Windows NT.

Another important difference between Active Directory and NT domains is that Active Directory uses the same naming scheme that's used on the Internet: Domain Name System (DNS). Thus, an Active Directory domain might have a name like `sales.mycompany.com`.

Understanding How Active Directory Is Structured

Like all directories, Active Directory is essentially a database management system. The Active Directory database is where the individual objects tracked by the directory are stored. Active Directory uses a *hierarchical* database model, which groups items in a treelike structure.

The terms *object, organizational unit, domain, tree,* and *forest* are used to describe the way Active Directory organizes its data. The following sections explain the meaning of these important Active Directory terms.

Objects

The basic unit of data in Active Directory is called an *object.* Active Directory can store information about many kinds of objects. The objects you work with most are users, groups, computers, and printers.

Figure 3-1 shows the Active Directory Manager displaying a list of built-in objects that come preconfigured with Windows Server 2012 R2. To get to this management tool, choose Start⇨Administrative Tools⇨Active Directory Users and Computers. Then click the Builtin node to show the built-in objects.

Objects have descriptive characteristics called *properties* or *attributes.* You can call up the properties of an object by double-clicking the object in the management console.

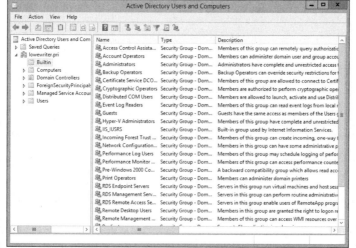

Figure 3-1:
Objects displayed by the Active Directory Manager console.

Domains

A *domain* is the basic unit for grouping related objects in Active Directory. Typically, domains correspond to departments in a company. A company with separate Accounting, Manufacturing, and Sales departments might have domains named (you guessed it) `Accounting`, `Manufacturing`, and `Sales`. Or the domains may correspond to geographical locations. A company with offices in Detroit, Dallas, and Denver might have domains named `det`, `dal`, and `den`.

Note that because Active Directory domains use DNS naming conventions, you can create subdomains that are considered to be child domains. You should always create the top-level domain for your entire network before you create any other domain. If your company is named Nimbus Brooms, and you've registered `NimbusBroom.com` as your domain name, you should create a top-level domain named `NimbusBroom.com` before you create any other domains. Then you can create subdomains such as `Accounting.NimbusBroom.com`, `Manufacturing.NimbusBroom.com`, and `Sales.NimbusBroom.com`.

If you have Microsoft Visio, you can use it to draw diagrams for your Active Directory domain structure. Visio includes several templates that provide cool icons for various types of Active Directory objects. Figure 3-2 shows a diagram that shows an Active Directory with four domains created with Visio.

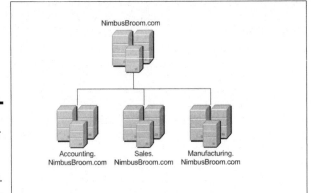

Figure 3-2:
Domains for
a company
with three
departments.

Note that these domains have little to do with the physical structure of your network. In Windows NT, domains usually are related to the network's physical structure.

Every domain must have at least one *domain controller,* which is a server that's responsible for the domain. Unlike a Windows NT PDC, however, an Active Directory domain controller doesn't have unique authority over its domain. In fact, a domain can have two or more domain controllers that share administrative duties. A feature called *replication* works hard at keeping all the domain controllers in sync.

Organizational units

Many domains have too many objects to manage together in a single group. Fortunately, Active Directory lets you create one or more *organizational units,* also known as OUs. OUs let you organize objects within a domain, without the extra work and inefficiency of creating additional domains.

One reason to create OUs within a domain is to assign administrative rights to each OU of different users. Then these users can perform routine administrative tasks such as creating new user accounts or resetting passwords.

Suppose that the domain for the Denver office, named den, houses the Accounting and Legal departments. Rather than create separate domains for these departments, you could create organizational units for the departments.

Trees

A *tree* is a set of Active Directory names that share a namespace. The domains NimbusBroom.com, Accounting.NimbusBroom.com, Manufacturing. NimbusBroom.com, and Sales.NimbusBroom.com make up a tree that's derived from a common root domain, NimbusBroom.com.

The domains that make up a tree are related to one another through *transitive trusts.* In a transitive trust, if DomainA trusts DomainB and DomainB trusts DomainC, DomainA automatically trusts DomainC.

Note that a single domain all by itself is still considered to be a tree.

Forests

As its name suggests, a *forest* is a collection of trees. In other words, a forest is a collection of one or more domain trees that do *not* share a common parent domain.

Suppose that Nimbus Brooms acquires Tracorum Technical Enterprises, which already has its own root domain named `TracorumTech.com`, with several subdomains of its own. You can create a forest from these two domain trees so that the domains can trust each other. Figure 3-3 shows this forest.

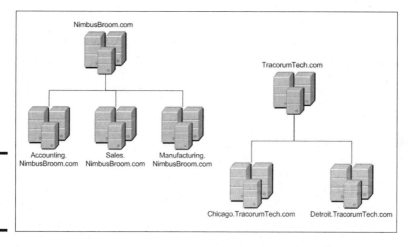

Figure 3-3: A forest with two trees.

The key to Active Directory forests is a database called the global catalog. The *global catalog* is sort of a superdirectory that contains information about all the objects in a forest, regardless of the domain. If a user account can't be found in the current domain, the global catalog is searched for the account. The global catalog provides a reference to the domain in which the account is defined.

Creating a New Domain

To create a domain, you start by designating a Windows Server 2012 R2 system to be the new domain's controller. You can do that by using the Server Manager to install Active Directory services as described in Book VII, Chapter 1. After you've installed Active Directory services, click the Notifications icon near the top-right corner of the Server Manager, and choose Promote This Server to a Domain Controller. This command launches the wizard shown in Figure 3-4.

Figure 3-4:
Creating
a domain
controller.

This wizard lets you designate the server as a domain controller. As you can see, the wizard gives you three options:

✦ **Add a Domain Controller to an Existing Domain:** Choose this option if you've already created the domain and want to add this server as a domain controller.

✦ **Add a New Domain to an Existing Forest:** If you've already created a forest but want to create a new domain within the existing forest, choose this option.

✦ **Add a New Forest:** This option is the one to choose if you're setting up a new domain in a brand-new forest.

When you create a new domain, the configuration wizard asks you for a name for the new domain. If you're creating the first domain for your network, use your company's domain name, such as NimbusBroom.com. If you're creating a subdomain, use a name such as Sales.NimbusBroom.com.

Creating an Organizational Unit

Organizational units can simplify the task of managing large domains by dividing users, groups, and other objects into manageable collections. By default, Active Directory domains include several useful OUs. The Domain Controllers OU, for example, contains all the domain controllers for the domain.

If you want to create additional organizational units to help manage a domain, follow these steps:

1. **In Server Manager, choose Tools ➪Active Directory Users and Computers.**

The Active Directory Users and Computers console appears, as shown in Figure 3-5.

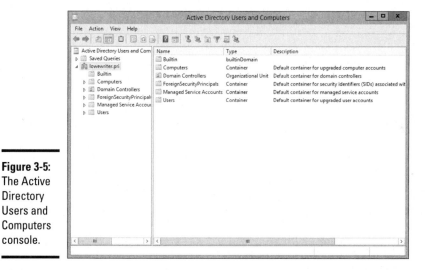

Figure 3-5:
The Active Directory Users and Computers console.

Book VII Chapter 3

Dealing with Active Directory

2. **Right-click the domain you want to add the OU to, and choose New➪Organizational Unit from the contextual menu.**

The New Object – Organizational Unit dialog box appears, as shown in Figure 3-6.

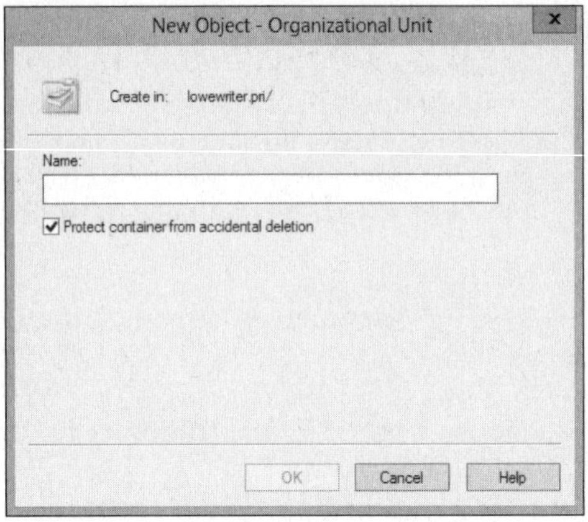

Figure 3-6:
Creating
a new
organiza-
tional unit.

3. **Type a name for the new organization unit.**

4. **Click OK.**

   You're done!

Here are just a few more thoughts about OUs to ponder as you drift off to sleep:

✦ You can delegate administrative authority for an OU to another user by right-clicking the OU and choosing Select Delegate Control from the contextual menu. Then you can select the user or group that will have administrative authority over the OU. You can also choose which administrative tasks will be assigned to the selected user or group.

✦ Remember that OUs aren't the same as groups. *Groups* are security principals, which means that you can assign them rights. Thereafter, when you assign a user to a group, the user is given the rights of the group. By contrast, an OU is merely an administrative tool that lets you control how user and group accounts are managed.

✦ For more information about how to create user and group accounts as well as other Active Directory objects, turn to Book VII, Chapter 4.

Chapter 4: Managing Windows User Accounts

In This Chapter

✓ Understanding user accounts

✓ Creating user accounts

✓ Setting account options

✓ Working with groups

✓ Creating a roaming profile

*E*very user who accesses a network must have a *user account.* User accounts let you control who can access the network and who can't. In addition, user accounts let you specify what network resources each user can use. Without user accounts, all your resources would be open to anyone who casually dropped by your network.

Understanding Windows User Accounts

User accounts are among the basic tools for managing a Windows server. As a network administrator, you'll spend a large percentage of your time dealing with user accounts — creating new ones, deleting expired ones, resetting passwords for forgetful users, granting new access rights, and so on. Before I get into the specific procedures of creating and managing user accounts, this section presents an overview of user accounts and how they work.

Local accounts versus domain accounts

A *local account* is a user account that's stored on a particular computer and applies only to that computer. Typically, each computer on your network will have a local account for each person who uses that computer.

By contrast, a *domain account* is a user account that's stored by Active Directory and can be accessed from any computer that's a part of the domain. Domain accounts are centrally managed. This chapter deals primarily with setting up and maintaining domain accounts.

User account properties

Every user account has several important account properties that specify the characteristics of the account. The three most important account properties are

✦ **Username:** A unique name that identifies the account. The user must enter the username when logging on to the network. The username is public information. In other words, other network users can (and often should) find out your username.

✦ **Password:** A secret word that must be entered to gain access to the account. You can set up Windows so that it enforces password policies, such as the minimum length of the password, whether the password must contain a mixture of letters and numerals, and how long the password remains current before the user must change it.

✦ **Group membership:** The group or groups to which the user account belongs. Group memberships are the key to granting access rights to users so that they can access various network resources, such as file shares or printers, or perform certain network tasks, such as creating new user accounts or backing up the server.

Many other account properties record information about the user, such as the user's contact information, whether the user is allowed to access the system only at certain times or from certain computers, and so on. I describe some of these features in later sections of this chapter, and some are described in more detail in Book VII, Chapter 6.

Creating a New User

To create a new domain user account in Windows Server 2008, follow these steps:

1. **Choose Start⇨Administrative Tools⇨Active Directory Users and Computers.**

    This command fires up the Active Directory Users and Computers management console, as shown in Figure 4-1.

2. **Right-click the domain that you want to add the user to and then choose New⇨User from the contextual menu.**

    This command summons the New Object – User Wizard, as shown in Figure 4-2.

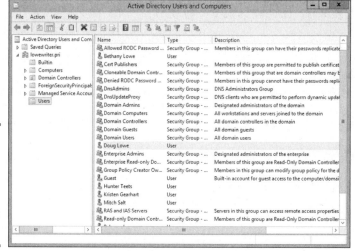

Figure 4-1:
The Active
Directory
Users and
Computers
management
console.

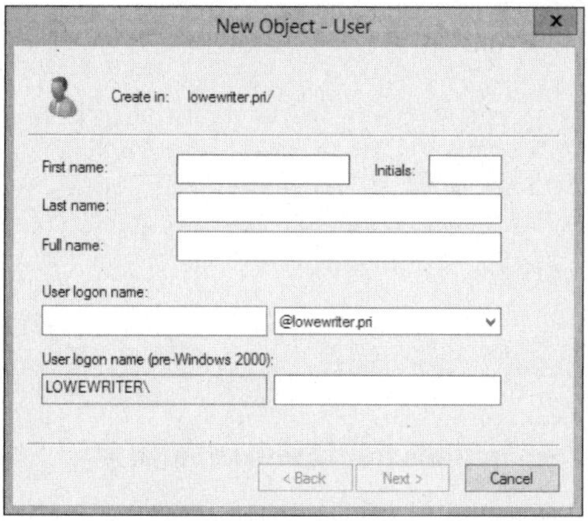

Figure 4-2:
Creating a
new user.

3. **Type the user's first name, middle initial, and last name.**

   As you type the name, the New Object Wizard automatically fills in the Full Name field.

4. **Change the Full Name field if you want it to appear different from what the wizard proposes.**

   You may want to reverse the first and last names so the last name appears first, for example.

5. **Type the user logon name.**

   This name must be unique within the domain.

Pick a naming scheme to follow when creating user logon names. You can use the first letter of the first name followed by the complete last name, the complete first name followed by the first letter of the last name, or any other scheme that suits your fancy.

6. **Click Next.**

The second page of the New Object – User Wizard appears, as shown in Figure 4-3.

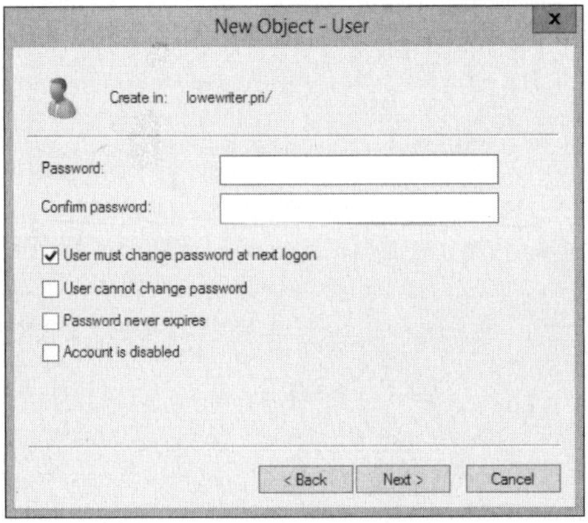

New Object - User

Create in: lowewriter.pri/

Password:

Confirm password:

☑ User must change password at next logon
☐ User cannot change password
☐ Password never expires
☐ Account is disabled

< Back   Next >   Cancel

Figure 4-3:
Setting
the user's
password.

7. **Type the password twice.**

You're asked to type the password twice, so type it correctly. If you don't type it identically in both boxes, you're asked to correct your mistake.

8. **Specify the password options that you want to apply.**

The following password options are available:

• User Must Change Password at Next Logon.

• User Cannot Change Password.

• Password Never Expires.

• Account Is Disabled.

For more information about these options, see the section "Setting account options," later in this chapter.

9. **Click Next.**

You're taken to the final page of the New Object – User Wizard, as shown in Figure 4-4.

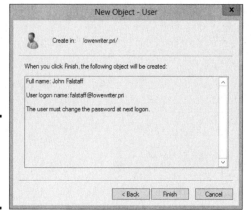

Figure 4-4:
Verifying
the user
account
information.

10. **Verify that the information is correct and then click Finish to create the account.**

   If the account information isn't correct, click the Back button, and correct the error.

   You're done! Now you can customize the user's account settings. At minimum, you'll probably want to add the user to one or more groups. You may also want to add contact information for the user or set up other account options.

Setting User Properties

After you've created a user account, you can set additional properties for the user by right-clicking the new user and choosing Properties from the contextual menu. This command brings up the User Properties dialog box, which has about a million tabs that you can use to set various properties for the user. Figure 4-5 shows the General tab, which lists basic information about the user, such as the user's name, office location, and phone number.

The following sections describe some of the administrative tasks that you can perform via the various tabs of the User Properties dialog box.

Figure 4-5:
The General
tab.

Changing the user's contact information

Several tabs of the User Properties dialog box contain contact information
for the user:

✦ **Address:** Lets you change the user's street address, post office box, city,
state, zip code, and so on.

✦ **Telephones:** Lets you specify the user's phone numbers.

✦ **Organization:** Lets you record the user's job title and the name of his or
her boss.

Setting account options

The Account tab of the User Properties dialog box, shown in Figure 4-6,
features a variety of interesting options that you can set for the user. From
this dialog box, you can change the user's logon name. In addition, you can
change the password options that you set when you created the account,
and you can set an expiration date for the account.

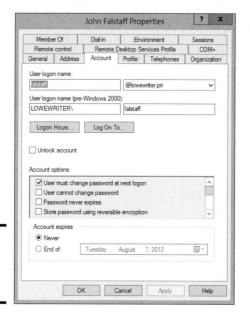

Figure 4-6:
The
Account
tab.

The following account options are available in the Account Options list box:

+ **User Must Change Password at Next Logon:** This option, which is selected by default, allows you to create a one-time-only password that can get the user started with the network. The first time the user logs on to the network, he or she is asked to change the password.

+ **User Cannot Change Password:** Use this option if you don't want to allow users to change their passwords. (Obviously, you can't use this option and the preceding one at the same time.)

+ **Password Never Expires:** Use this option if you want to bypass the password-expiration policy for this user so that the user will never have to change his or her password.

+ **Store Password Using Reversible Encryption:** This option stores passwords by using an encryption scheme that hackers can easily break, so you should avoid it like the plague.

+ **Account Is Disabled:** This option allows you to create an account that you don't yet need. As long as the account remains disabled, the user won't be able to log on. See the section "Disabling and Enabling User Accounts," later in this chapter, to find out how to enable a disabled account.

+ **Smart Card Is Required for Interactive Logon:** If the user's computer has a smart card reader to read security cards automatically, check this option to require the user to use it.

✦ **Account Is Trusted for Delegation:** This option indicates that the account is trustworthy and can set up delegations. This advanced feature usually is reserved for Administrator accounts.

✦ **Account Is Sensitive and Cannot Be Delegated:** This option prevents other users from impersonating this account.

✦ **Use DES Encryption Types for This Account:** This option beefs up the encryption for applications that require extra security.

✦ **Do Not Require Kerberos Preauthentication:** Select this option if you use a different implementation of the Kerberos protocol.

Specifying logon hours

You can restrict the hours during which the user is allowed to log on to the system by clicking the Logon Hours button on the Account tab of the User Properties dialog box. This button brings up the Logon Hours for [User] dialog box, shown in Figure 4-7.

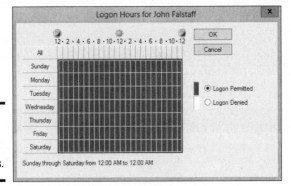

Figure 4-7:
Restricting
the user's
logon hours.

Initially, the Logon Hours dialog box is set to allow the user to log on at any time of day or night. To change the hours that you want the user to have access, click a day and time or a range of days and times; choose either Logon Permitted or Logon Denied; and click OK.

Restricting access to certain computers

Normally, a user can use his or her user account to log on to any computer that's part of the user's domain. You can restrict a user to certain computers, however, by clicking the Log On To button on the Account tab of the User Properties dialog box. This button brings up the Logon Workstations dialog box, as shown in Figure 4-8.

To restrict the user to certain computers, select the radio button labeled The Following Computers. Then, for each computer you want to allow the user to log on from, type the computer's name in the text box, and click Add.

Figure 4-8:
Restricting
the user
to certain
computers.

If you make a mistake, you can select the incorrect computer name and then click Edit to change the name or Remove to delete the name.

Setting the user's profile information

The Profile tab, shown in Figure 4-9, lets you configure the user's profile information. This dialog box lets you configure three bits of information related to the user's profile:

Figure 4-9:
The Profile
tab.

✦ **Profile Path:** This field specifies the location of the user's roaming profile. For more information, see the section "Working with User Profiles," later in this chapter.

✦ **Logon Script:** This field is the name of the user's logon script. A *logon script* is a batch file that's run whenever the user logs on. The main purpose of the logon script is to map the network shares that the user requires access to. Logon scripts are carryovers from early versions of Windows NT Server. In Windows Server 2008, profiles are the preferred way to configure the user's computer when the user logs on, including setting up network shares. Many administrators still like the simplicity of logon scripts, however. For more information, see the section "Creating a Logon Script," later in this chapter.

✦ **Home Folder:** This section is where you specify the default storage location for the user.

The Profile tab lets you specify the location of an existing profile for the user, but it doesn't actually let you set up the profile. For more information about setting up a profile, see the section "Working with User Profiles," later in this chapter.

Resetting User Passwords

By some estimates, the single most time-consuming task of most network administrators is resetting user passwords. It's easy to think that users are forgetful idiots, but put yourself in their shoes. We insist that they set their passwords to something incomprehensible, such as 94kD82leL384K; that they change it a week later to something more unmemorable, such as dJUQ63DWd8331; and that they don't write it down. Then we get mad when they forget their passwords.

So when a user calls and says that he or she forgot his or her password, the least we can do is be cheerful when we reset it. After all, the user probably spent 15 minutes trying to remember it before finally giving up and admitting failure.

Here's the procedure to reset the password for a user domain account:

1. **Log on as an administrator.**

You must have administrator privileges to perform this procedure.

2. **In Server Manager, choose Tools⇨Active Directory Users and Computers.**

The Active Directory Users and Computers management console appears.

3. **Click Users in the console tree.**

4. **In the Details pane, right-click the user who forgot his or her password, and choose Reset Password from the contextual menu.**

5. **Type the new password in both password boxes.**

   You have to type the password twice to ensure that you type it correctly.

6. **If desired, select the User Must Change Password at Next Logon option.**

   If you select this option, the password that you assign will work for only one logon. As soon as the user logs on, he or she will be required to change the password.

7. **Click OK.**

   That's all there is to it! The user's password is reset.

Disabling and Enabling User Accounts

If you want to temporarily prevent a user from accessing the network, you can disable his or her account. Then you can enable the account later, when you're ready to restore the user to full access. Here's the procedure:

1. **Log on as an administrator.**

   You must have administrator privileges to perform this procedure.

2. **From Server Manager, choose Tools⇨Active Directory Users and Computers.**

   The Active Directory Users and Computers management console appears.

3. **Click Users in the console tree.**

4. **In the Details pane, right-click the user that you want to enable or disable; then choose either Enable Account or Disable Account from the contextual menu to enable or disable the user.**

Deleting a User

Deleting a user account is surprisingly easy. Just follow these steps:

1. **Log on as an administrator.**

   You must have administrator privileges to perform this procedure.

2. **Choose Start⇨Administrative Tools⇨Active Directory Users and Computers.**

The Active Directory Users and Computers management console appears.

3. **Click Users in the console tree.**

4. **In the Details pane, right-click the user that you want to delete and then choose Delete from the contextual menu.**

   Windows asks whether you really want to delete the user, just in case you're kidding.

5. **Click Yes.**

   Poof! The user account is deleted.

Deleting a user account is a permanent, nonreversible action. Do it only if you're absolutely sure that you'll never want to restore the user's account. If there's any possibility of restoring the account later, you should disable the account instead of delete it.

Working with Groups

A *group* is a special type of account that represents a set of users who have common network access needs. Groups can dramatically simplify the task of assigning network access rights to users. Rather than assign access rights to each user individually, you can assign rights to the group itself. Then those rights automatically extend to any user you add to the group.

The following sections describe some of the key concepts that you need to understand to use groups, along with some of the most common procedures you'll employ when setting up groups for your server.

Group types

Two distinct types of groups exist:

+ **Security groups:** Most groups are security groups, which extend access rights to members of the group. If you want to allow a group of users to access your high-speed color laser printer, for example, you can create a group called ColorPrintUsers. Then you can grant permission to use the printer to the ColorPrintUsers group. Finally, you can add individual users to the ColorPrintUsers group.

+ **Distribution groups:** Distribution groups aren't used as much as security groups are. They're designed as a way to send e-mail to a group of users by specifying the group as the recipient.

Group scope

A group can have any of three distinct *scopes,* which determine what domains the group's members can belong to. Three distinct scopes exist:

+ **Domain local:** A group with *domain local scope* can have members from any domain. The group can be granted permissions only from the domain in which the group is defined, however.

+ **Global:** A group with *global scope* can have members only from the domain in which the group is defined. The group can be granted permissions in any domain in the forest, however. (For more information about forests, refer to Book VII, Chapter 3.)

+ **Universal scope:** Groups with *universal scope* are available in all domains that belong to the same forest.

    As you can probably guess, universal scope groups are usually used only on very large networks.

One common way you can use domain local and global groups is as follows:

1. **Use domain local groups to assign access rights for network resources.**

    To control access to a high-speed color printer, for example, create a domain local group for the printer. Grant the group access to the printer, but don't add any users to the group.

2. **Use global groups to associate users with common network access needs.**

    Create a global group for users who need to access color printers, for example. Then add each user who needs access to a color printer membership to the group.

3. **Finally, add the global group to the domain local group.**

    That way, access to the printer is extended to all members of the global group.

This technique gives you the most flexibility when your network grows.

Default groups

Windows Server 2008 comes with several predefined groups that you can use. Although you shouldn't be afraid to create your own groups when you need them, there's no reason to create your own group if you find a default group that meets your needs.

**Book VII
Chapter 4**

Managing Windows
User Accounts

Some of these groups are listed in the Builtin container in the Active Directory Users and Computers management console. Others are listed in the Users container. Table 4-1 lists the most useful default groups in Builtin, and Table 4-2 lists the default groups in the Users container.

Table 4-1   Default Groups Located in the Builtin Container

Group	Description
Account Operators	This group is for users who should be allowed to create, edit, or delete user accounts but shouldn't be granted full administrator status.
Administrators	This group is for the system administrators who have full control of the domain. The Administrator account is a default member of this group. You should create only a limited number of accounts that belong to this group.
Backup Operators	This group is for users who need to perform backup operations. Because this group must have access to the files that are backed up, it presents a security risk, so you should limit the number of users that you add to this group.
Guests	This group allows members to log on but little else. The default Guest account is a member of this group.
Network Configuration	This group is allowed to twiddle with network configuration settings, including releasing and renewing DHCP leases.
Print Operators	This group grants users access to printers, including the ability to create and share new printers and to manage print queues.
Remote Desktop Users	This group can remotely log on to domain controllers in the domain.
Replicator	This group is required to support directory replication. Don't add users to this group.
Server Operators	These users can log on locally to a domain controller.
Users	These users can perform common tasks, such as running applications and using local and network printers.

Table 4-2 Default Groups Located in the Users Container

Group	Description
Cert Publishers	These users can publish security certificates for users and computers.
DnsAdmins	This group is installed if you install DNS. It grants administrative access to the DNS Server service.
DnsUpdateProxy	This group is installed if you install DNS. It allows DNS clients to perform dynamic updates on behalf of other clients, such as DHCP servers.
Domain Admins	These users have complete control of the domain. By default, this group is a member of the Administrators group on all domain controllers, and the Administrator account is a member of this group.
Domain Computers	This group contains all computers that belong to the domain. Any computer account created becomes a member of this group automatically.
Domain Controllers	This group contains all domain controllers in the domain.
Domain Guests	This group contains all domain guests.
Domain Users	This group contains all domain users. Any user account created in the domain is added to this group automatically.
Group Policy	These users can modify group policy for the domain.
IIS_WPG	This group is created if you install IIS. It's required for IIS to operate properly.
RAS and IAS Servers	This group is required for RAS and IAS servers to work properly.

**Book VII
Chapter 4**

Managing Windows
User Accounts

Creating a group

If none of the built-in groups meets your needs, you can create your own group by following these steps:

1. **Log on as an administrator.**

You must have administrator privileges to perform this procedure.

2. **From Server Manager, choose Tools⇨Active Directory Users and Computers.**

The Active Directory Users and Computers management console appears.

3. **Right-click the domain to which you want to add the group and then choose New➪Group from the contextual menu.**

   The New Object – Group dialog box appears, as shown in Figure 4-10.

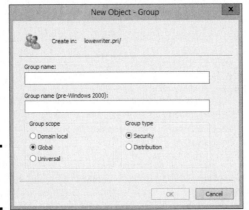

Figure 4-10:
Creating a
new group.

4. **Type the name for the new group.**

   Enter the name in both text boxes.

5. **Choose the group scope.**

   The choices are Domain Local, Global, and Universal. For groups that will be granted access rights to network resources, choose Domain Local. Use Global for groups to which you'll add users and Domain Local groups. Use Universal groups only if you have a large network with multiple domains.

6. **Choose the group type.**

   The choices are Security and Distribution. In most cases, choose Security.

7. **Click OK.**

   The group is created.

Adding a member to a group

Groups are collections of objects, called *members*. The members of a group can be user accounts or other groups. When you create a group, it has no members. As a result, the group isn't useful until you add at least one member.

Follow these steps to add a member to a group:

1. **Log on as an administrator.**

   You must have administrator privileges to perform this procedure.

2. **Choose Start⇨Administrative Tools⇨Active Directory Users and Computers.**

   The Active Directory Users and Computers management console appears.

3. **Open the folder that contains the group to which you want to add members and then double-click the group.**

   The Group Properties dialog box appears.

4. **Click the Members tab.**

   The members of the group are displayed, as shown in Figure 4-11.

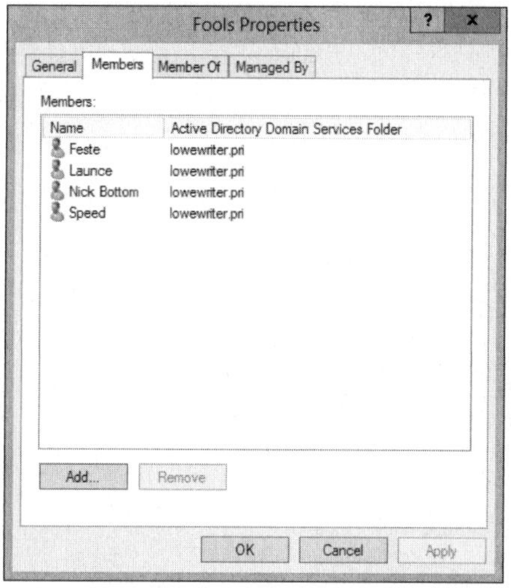

Figure 4-11:
Adding
members to
a group.

Book VII
Chapter 4

Managing Windows
User Accounts

5. **Click Add, type the name of a user or another group that you want to add to this group, and click OK.**

   The member is added to the list.

6. **Repeat Step 5 for each user or group that you want to add.**

   Keep going until you've added everyone!

7. **Click OK.**

That's all there is to it.

The Group Properties dialog box also has a Member Of tab that lists each group that the current group is a member of.

Adding members to a group is only half the process of making a group useful. The other half is adding access rights to the group so that the members of the group can actually *do* something. The procedures for doing that are covered in Book VII, Chapter 5.

Working with User Profiles

User profiles automatically maintain desktop settings for Windows users. By default, a user profile is stored on the user's local computer. The following items are just some of the settings that are stored as part of the user profile:

✦ **Desktop settings** in the Display Properties dialog box, including wallpaper, screen savers, and color schemes

✦ **Start-menu programs** and Windows toolbar options

✦ **Favorites,** which provide easy access to the files and folders that the user accesses frequently

✦ **Application Data,** such as option settings, custom dictionaries, and so on

✦ **Cookies,** used for Internet browsing

✦ **My Recent Documents,** which keeps shortcuts to the documents most recently accessed by the user

✦ **Templates,** which stores user templates

✦ **Network Neighborhood,** which keeps shortcuts to the user's network locations

✦ **Send To,** which keeps shortcuts to document-handling utilities

✦ **Local Settings,** such as history and temporary files

✦ **Printers,** which keeps shortcuts to the user's printers

✦ **My Documents,** which stores the user's local documents

Types of user profiles

Four types of user profiles exist:

✦ **Local user profile:** A local user profile is stored on the user's local computer and is applied only when the user logs on to that computer. A local user profile is created automatically when a new user logs on.

✦ **Roaming user profile:** A roaming user profile is created on a network share. That way, the user can access the roaming profile when he or she logs on to any computer on the network.

✦ **Mandatory user profile:** A mandatory user profile is a roaming user profile that the user is not allowed to change. One benefit of mandatory user profiles is that users can't mess up their desktop settings. Another benefit is that you can create a single mandatory profile that can be used by multiple users.

✦ **Temporary user profile:** If a roaming or mandatory profile isn't available for some reason, a temporary user profile is automatically created for the user. The temporary profile is deleted when the user logs off, so any changes that the user makes while using a temporary profile are lost at the end of the session.

Roaming profiles

A *roaming user profile* is simply a user profile that has been copied to a network share so that it can be accessed from any computer on the network.

Before you can create roaming user profiles, you should create a shared folder on the server to hold the profiles. You can name the shared folder anything you like, but most administrators call it Users. For information on the procedure to create a shared folder, see Book VII, Chapter 3.

**Book VII
Chapter 4**

After you've created the shared Users folder, you can copy the profile to the server by following these steps at the user's local computer (Windows 7 or Vista):

1. **Log on to the computer by using an account other than the one you want to make a user account.**

Windows won't let you copy the profile that you're logged on with.

2. **Click the Start button, type the word** Profile, **and choose the Configure Advanced User Profile Properties option from the menu that appears.**

This step brings up the User Profiles dialog box, shown in Figure 4-12.

3. **Select the profile that you want to copy and then click Copy To.**

A Copy To dialog box appears.

4. **Type the path and name for the roaming profile in the Copy Profile To box.**

To copy a profile named Doug to the Users share on a server named Server01, for example, type **\\Server01\Users\Doug**.

5. **Click OK.**

The profile is copied.

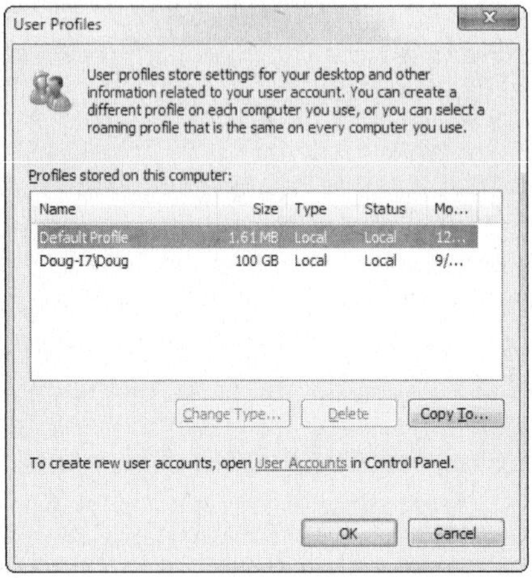

Figure 4-12:
The User
Profiles
dialog box.

Now you can go back to the server, log on as an administrator, and follow these steps to designate a roaming profile for the user's domain account:

1. **From the Server Manager, choose Tools⇨Active Directory Users and Computers.**

The Active Directory Users and Computers management console appears.

2. **Right-click the user account, and choose Properties from the contextual menu.**

The User Properties dialog box appears.

3. **Click the Profile tab.**

The Profile tab appears. (This tab is shown in Figure 4-9, earlier in this chapter, so I won't repeat it here.)

4. **Type the path and name of the profile in the Profile Path text box.**

The path and name that you type here should be the same path and name that you used to copy the profile to the server.

5. **Click OK.**

Creating a Logon Script

A *logon script* is a batch file that's run automatically whenever a user logs on. The most common reason for using a logon script is to map the network shares that the user needs access to. Here's a simple logon script that maps three network shares:

```
echo off
net use m: \\server1\shares\admin
net use n: \\server1\shares\mktg
net use o: \\server2\archives
```

Here, two shares on server1 are mapped to drives M and N, and a share on server2 is mapped as drive O.

If you want, you can use the special variable `%username%` to get the user's username. This variable is useful if you've created a folder for each user, and you want to map a drive to each user's folder, as follows:

```
net use u: \\server1\users\%username%
```

If a user logs on with the username `dlowe`, for example, drive U is mapped to `\\server1\users\dlowe`.

Scripts should be saved in the Scripts folder, which is buried deep in the bowels of the SYSVOL folder — typically, `c:\Windows\SYSVOL\Sysvol\` *domainname*`\Scripts`, where *domainname* is your domain name. Because you need to access this folder frequently, I suggest creating a shortcut to it on your desktop.

After you've created a logon script, you can assign it to a user by using the Profile tab of the User Properties dialog box. For more information, see the section "Setting the user's profile information," earlier in this chapter.

Book VII
Chapter 4

Managing Windows User Accounts

Chapter 5: Managing a File Server

*1*n this chapter, you discover how to set up and manage file and print servers for Windows Server 2012. Because the features for file and print servers are essentially the same for both operating systems, the techniques presented in this chapter should work for either system.

Understanding Permissions

Before I get into the details of setting up a file server, you need to have a solid understanding of the concept of permissions. *Permissions* allow users to access shared resources on a network. Simply sharing a resource such as a disk folder or a printer doesn't guarantee that a given user is able to access that resource. Windows makes this decision based on the permissions that have been assigned to various groups for the resource and group memberships of the user. If the user belongs to a group that has been granted permission to access the resource, the access is allowed. If not, access is denied.

In theory, permissions sound pretty simple. In practice, however, they can get pretty complicated. The following paragraphs explain some of the nuances of how access control and permissions work:

✦ Every object — that is, every file and folder — on an NTFS volume has a set of permissions called the *Access Control List (ACL)* associated with it.

✦ The ACL identifies the users and groups who can access the object and specifies what level of access each user or group has. A folder's ACL may specify that one group of users can read files in the folder, whereas another group can read and write files in the folder, and a third group is denied access to the folder.

✦ Container objects — files and volumes — allow their ACLs to be inherited by the objects that they contain. As a result, if you specify permissions for a folder, those permissions extend to the files and child folders that appear within it.

✦ Table 5-1 describes the six permissions that can be applied to files and folders on an NTFS volume.

Table 5-1	File and Folder Permissions
Permission	*Description*
Full Control	The user has unrestricted access to the file or folder.
Modify	The user can change the file or folder's contents, delete the file or folder, read the file or folder, or change the attributes of the file or folder. For a folder, this permission allows you to create new files or subfolders within the folder.
Read & Execute	For a file, this permission grants the right to read or execute the file. For a folder, this permission grants the right to list the contents of the folder or to read or execute any of the files in the folder.
List Folder Contents	This permission applies only to folders; it grants the right to list the contents of the folder.
Read	This permission grants the right to read the contents of a file or folder.
Write	This permission grants the right to change the contents of a file or its attributes. For a folder, this permission grants the right to create new files and subfolders within the folder.

✦ Actually, the six file and folder permissions comprise various combinations of *special permissions* that grant more detailed access to files or folders. Table 5-2 lists the special permissions that apply to each of the six file and folder permissions.

✦ It's best to assign permissions to groups rather than to individual users. Then if a particular user needs access to a particular resource, add that user to a group that has permission to use the resource.

Table 5-2		Special Permissions				
Special Permission	*Full Control*	*Modify*	*Read & Execute*	*List Folder Contents*	*Read*	*Write*
Traverse Folder/ Execute File	*	*	*	*		
List Folder/Read Data	*	*	*	*	*	

Special Permission	Full Control	Modify	Read & Execute	List Folder Contents	Read	Write
Read Extended Attributes	*	*	*	*	*	
Create Files/ Write Data	*	*				*
Create Folders/ Append Data	*	*				*
Write Attributes	*	*				*
Write Extended Attributes	*	*				*
Delete Subfolders and Files	*					
Delete	*	*				
Read Permissions	*	*	*	*	*	*
Change Permissions	*					
Take Ownership	*					
Synchronize	*	*	*	*	*	*

Understanding Shares

A *share* is simply a folder that is made available to other users via the network. Each share has the following elements:

+ **Share name:** The name by which the share is known over the network. To make the share name compatible with older computers, you should stick to eight-character share names whenever possible.

+ **Path:** The path to the folder on the local computer that's being shared, such as `C:\Accounting`.

+ **Description:** A one-line description of the share.

+ **Permissions:** A list of users or groups who have been granted access to the share.

When you install Windows and configure various server roles, special shared resources are created to support those roles. You shouldn't disturb these special shares unless you know what you're doing. Table 5-3 describes some of the most common special shares.

Table 5-3	Special Shares
Share Name	*Description*
`drive$`	The root directory of a drive.
`ADMIN$`	Used for remote administration of a computer. This share points to the operating system folder (usually, `C:\Windows`).
`IPC$`	Used by named pipes, a programming feature that lets processes communicate with one another.
`NETLOGON`	Required for domain controllers to function.
`SYSVOL`	Another required domain controller share.
`PRINT$`	Used for remote administration of printers.
`FAX$`	Used by fax clients.

Notice that some of the special shares end with a dollar sign ($). These shares are *hidden shares* that aren't visible to users. You can still access them, however, by typing the complete share name (including the dollar sign) when the share is needed. The special share C$, for example, is created to allow you to connect to the root directory of the C: drive from a network client. You wouldn't want your users to see this share, would you? (Shares such as C$ are also protected by privileges, of course, so if an ordinary user finds out that C$ is the root directory of the server's C: drive, he or she still can't access it.)

Managing Your File Server

To manage shares on a Windows Server 2012 system, open the Server Manager, and select File and Storage Services in the task pane on the left side of the window. Then click Shares to reveal the management console shown in Figure 5-1.

The following sections describe some of the most common procedures that you'll use when managing your file server.

Using the New Share Wizard

To be useful, a file server should offer one or more *shares* — folders that have been designated as publicly accessible via the network. To create a new share, use the New Share Wizard, as described in the following procedure:

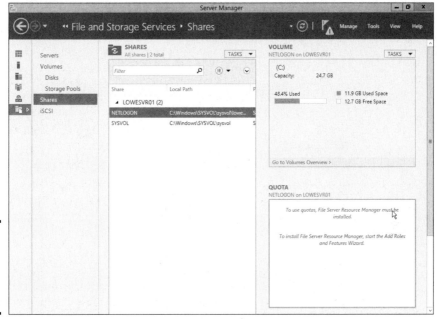

Figure 5-1:
Managing
shares in
Windows
Server 2012.

1. **In Server Manager, click File and Storage Services, click Shares, and
then choose New Share from the Tasks drop-down menu.**

The opening screen of the New Share Wizard appears, as shown in
Figure 5-2. Here, the wizard asks you what folder you want to share.

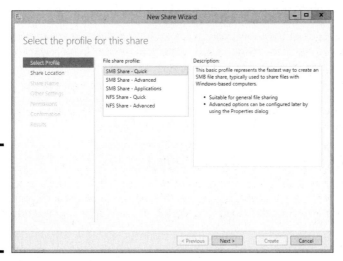

Figure 5-2:
The New
Share
Wizard
comes to
life.

2. Select SMB Share – Quick in the list of profiles and then click Next.

Next, the New Share Wizard asks for the location of the share, as shown in Figure 5-3.

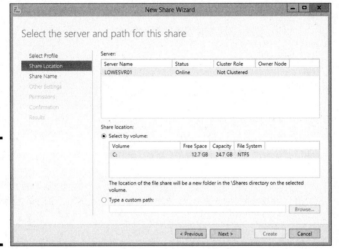

Figure 5-3:
The wizard asks where you'd like to locate the share.

3. Select the server you want the share to reside on.

4. Select the location of the share by choosing one of these two options:

- *Select by Volume:* This option selects the volume on which the shared folder will reside while letting the New Share Wizard create a folder for you. If you select this option, the wizard will create the shared folder on the designated volume. Use this option if the folder doesn't yet exist and you don't mind Windows placing it in the default location, which is inside a folder called Shares on the volume you specify.

- *Type a Custom Path:* Use this option if the folder exists or if you want to create one in a location other than the Shares folder.

5. Click Next.

The dialog box shown in Figure 5-4 appears.

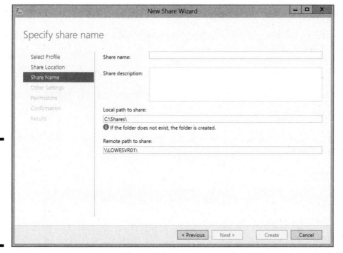

Figure 5-4:
The wizard
asks for
the share
name and
description.

6. **Type the name that you want to use for the share in the Share Name box.**

   The default name is the name of the folder being shared. If the folder name is long, you can use a more succinct name here.

7. **Enter a description for the share.**

8. **Click Next.**

   The dialog box shown in Figure 5-5 appears.

Figure 5-5:
Specifying
the share
settings.

9. **Select the share settings you'd like to use:**

   - *Enable Access-Based Enumeration:* Hides files that the user does not have permission to access

   - *Allow Caching of Share:* Makes the files available to offline users

   - *Encrypt Data Access:* Encrypts files accessed via the share

10. **Click Next.**

    The wizard displays the default permissions that will be used for the new share, as shown in Figure 5-6.

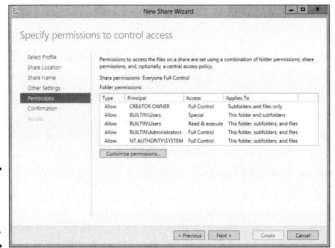

Figure 5-6:
Setting
the share
permissions.

11. **If you want to customize the permissions, click Customize Permissions.**

    This button summons the Advanced Security Settings for Data dialog box, which lets you customize both the NTFS and the share permissions.

12. **Click Next.**

    The confirmation page appears, as shown in Figure 5-7.

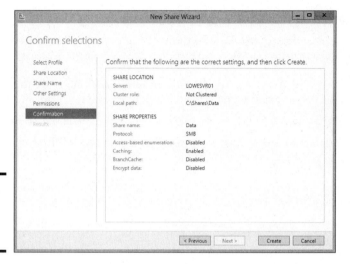

Figure 5-7:
Confirming
your share
settings.

13. Verify that all the settings are correct and then click Create.

The share is created, and a results dialog box is displayed, as shown in
Figure 5-8.

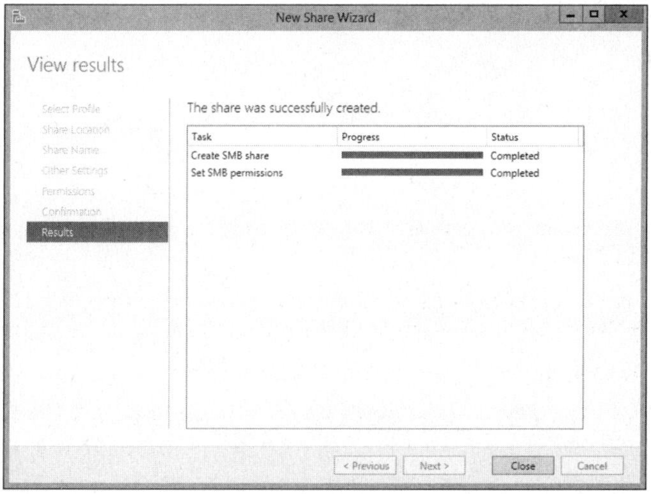

Figure 5-8:
You're
done!

Sharing a folder without the wizard

If you think wizards should be confined to *Harry Potter* movies, you can set up a share without bothering with the wizard. Just follow these steps:

1. **Press the Windows key, click Computer, and navigate to the folder that you want to share.**

2. **Right-click the folder, and choose Properties from the contextual menu.**

This action brings up the Properties dialog box for the folder.

3. **Click the Sharing tab.**

The Sharing tab comes to the front, as shown in Figure 5-9.

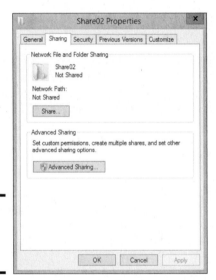

Figure 5-9:
Manually
sharing a
folder.

4. **Click the Advanced Sharing button.**

The dialog box shown in Figure 5-10 appears.

5. **Select the Share This Folder check box to designate the folder as shared.**

The rest of the controls in this dialog box will be unavailable until you select this check box.

6. **Type the name that you want to use for the share in the Share Name box, and type a description of the share in the Comments box.**

The default name is the name of the folder being shared. If the folder name is long, you can use a more succinct name here.

Figure 5-10:
Setting the
share name.

The description is strictly optional but sometimes helps users determine the intended contents of the folder.

7. **If you want to specify permissions now, click Permissions.**

This button brings up a dialog box that lets you create permissions for the
share. For more information, see the next section, "Granting permissions."

8. **Click OK.**

The folder is now shared.

Granting permissions

When you first create a file share, all users are granted read-only access to
the share. If you want to allow users to modify files in the share or allow
them to create new files, you need to add permissions. Here's how to do this
via the Share and Storage Management console:

1. **Open Windows Explorer by pressing the Windows key and clicking
Computer; then browse to the folder whose permissions you want
to manage.**

2. **Right-click the folder you want to manage, and choose Properties from
the contextual menu.**

The Properties dialog box for the folder appears.

3. **Click the Sharing tab; then click Advanced Sharing.**

The Advanced Sharing dialog box appears.

4. **Click Permissions.**

The dialog box shown in Figure 5-11 appears. This dialog box lists all
the users and groups to whom you've granted permission for the folder.
When you select a user or group from the list, the check boxes at the

bottom of the list change to indicate which specific permissions you've assigned to each user or group.

Figure 5-11:
Setting
the share
permissions.

5. **Click Add.**

The dialog box shown in Figure 5-12 appears.

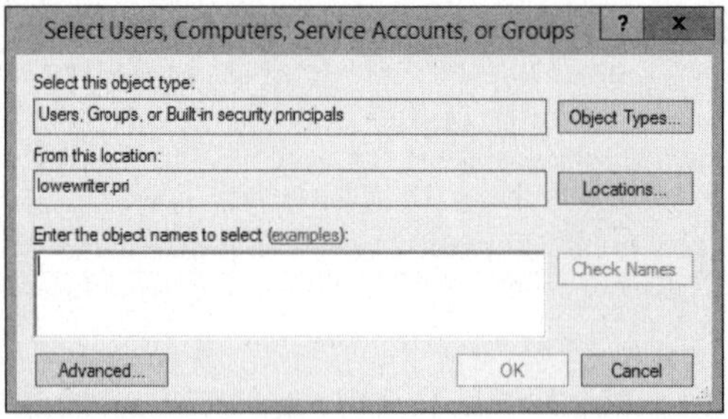

Figure 5-12:
The Select
Users,
Computers,
Service
Accounts,
or Groups
dialog box.

6. **Type the name of the user or group to whom you want to grant permission and then click OK.**

If you're not sure of the name, click Advanced. This action brings up a dialog box that lets you search for existing users. You can click the Find Now button to display a list of all users and groups in the domain. Alternatively, you can enter the first part of the name that you're looking for before you click Find Now to search more specifically.

When you click OK, you return to the Share Permissions tab, with the new user or group added.

7. **Select the appropriate Allow and Deny check boxes to specify which permissions to allow for the user or group.**

8. **Repeat Steps 5 through 7 for any other permissions that you want to add.**

9. **When you're done, click OK.**

Here are a few other thoughts to ponder concerning adding permissions:

+ If you want to grant full access to everyone for this folder, don't bother adding another permission. Instead, select the Everyone group and then select the Allow check box for each permission type.

+ You can remove a permission by selecting the permission and then clicking Remove.

+ If you'd rather not fuss with the Share and Storage Management console, you can set the permissions from My Computer. Right-click the shared folder, choose Sharing and Security from the contextual menu, and then click Permissions. Then you can follow the preceding procedure, picking up at Step 5.

+ The permissions assigned in this procedure apply only to the share itself. The underlying folder can also have permissions assigned to it. If that's the case, whichever of the restrictions is most restrictive always applies. If the share permissions grant a user Full Control permission but the folder permission grants the user only Read permission, for example, the user has only Read permission for the folder.

Chapter 6: Using Group Policy

In This Chapter

✔ Looking at group policy concepts

✔ Enabling group policy on a Windows Server

✔ Editing group policy objects

*G*roup policy refers to a feature of Windows operating systems that lets you control how certain aspects of Windows and other Microsoft software work throughout your network. Many features that you might expect to find in a management console, such as Active Directory Users and Computers, are controlled by group policy instead. You must use group policy to control how often users must change their passwords, for example, and how complicated their passwords must be. As a result, group policy is an important tool for any Windows network administrator.

Unfortunately, group policy can be a confusing beast. In fact, it's one of the most confusing aspects of Windows network administration. So don't be put off if you find this chapter more confusing than other chapters in this minibook. Group policy becomes clear after you spend some time actually working with it.

Understanding Group Policy

Here it is in a nutshell: Group policy consists of a collection of *group policy objects* (also called *GPOs*) that define individual policies. These policy objects are selectively applied to both users and computers. Each policy object specifies how some aspect of Windows or some other Microsoft software should be configured. A group policy object might specify the home page that's initially displayed when any user launches Internet Explorer, for example. When a user logs on to the domain, that policy object is retrieved and applied to the user's Internet Explorer configuration.

Group policy objects can apply to either computers or users. A policy that applies to a computer will be enforced for any user of the computer, and a policy that applies to a user will be enforced for that user no matter what computer he or she logs on to. As a network administrator, you'll be concerned mostly with policies that apply to users. But computer policies are useful from time to time as well.

To use group policy, you have to know how to do two things: (1) create individual group policy objects, and (2) apply — or *link* — those objects to user and computer objects. Both tasks can be a little tricky.

The trick to creating group policy objects is finding the particular setting you want to employ. Trying to find a specific group policy among the thousands of available policies can be frustrating. Suppose that you want to force all network users to change their passwords every 30 days. You know that a group policy controls the password-expiration date. But where is it? You'll find help with this aspect of working with group policy in the section titled "Creating Group Policy Objects," later in this chapter.

After you've created a group policy object, you then are faced with the task of linking it to the users or computers you want it to apply to. Creating a policy that applies to all users or computers is simple enough. But things get more complicated if you want to be more selective — for example, if you want the policy to apply only to users in a particular organizational unit (OU) or to users that belong to a particular group. You'll find help for this aspect of working with group policy in the section "Filtering Group Policy Objects," later in this chapter.

Enabling Group Policy Management on Windows Server 2012

Before you can work with group policy on a Windows Server 2012, you must enable group policy on the server. The procedure is simple enough and needs to be done only once for each server. Here are the steps:

1. **In the Server Manager, click Add Roles and Features.**

2. **Follow the wizard until you get to the Select Features page, which is shown in Figure 6-1.**

3. **Select the Group Policy Management check box and then click Next.**

4. **When the confirmation page appears, click Install.**

   Be patient again; installation may take a few minutes.

5. **Click Close.**

   You're done!

After you've completed this procedure, a new command titled Group Policy Management appears on the Tools menu in the Server Manager.

Figure 6-1:
Enabling
group policy
management
on Windows
Server 2012.

Creating Group Policy Objects

The easiest way to create group policy objects is to use the Group Policy
Management Console, which you can run from the Server Manager by choosing Tools⬩Group Policy Management.

A single group policy object can consist of one setting or many individual
group policy settings. The Group Policy Management Console presents the
thousands of group policy settings that are available for your use in several
categories. The more you work with group policy, the more these categories
will begin to make sense. When you get started, you can expect to spend a
lot of time hunting through the lists of policies to find the specific one you're
looking for.

The easiest way to learn how to use the Group Policy Management Console
is to use it to create a simple group policy object. In the following procedure, I show you how to create a GPO that defines a group policy enabling
Windows Update for all computers in a domain so that users can't disable
Windows Update.

1. **In the Server Manager, choose Tools⬩Group Policy Management.**

   The Group Policy Management console appears, as shown in Figure 6-2.

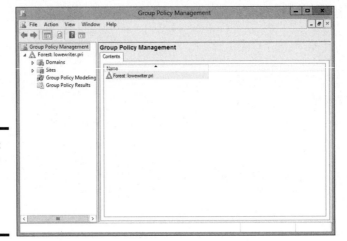

Figure 6-2:
The Group
Policy
Manage-
ment
console.

2. **In the Navigation pane, drill down through the Domains node to the node for your domain, then select the Group Policy Objects node for your domain.**

3. **Right-click the Group Policy Objects node and then choose New from the contextual menu that appears.**

   This command brings up the dialog box shown in Figure 6-3.

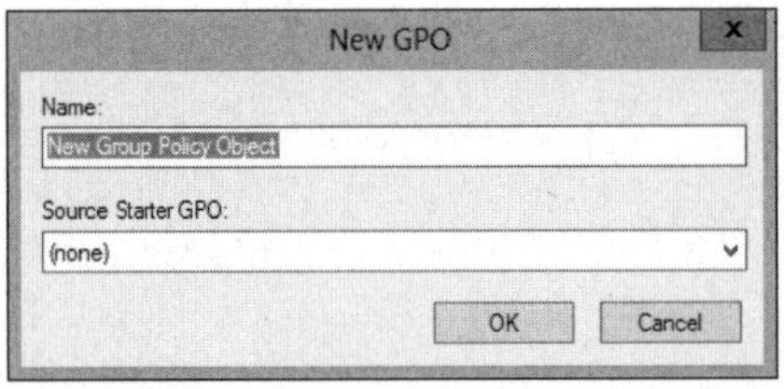

Figure 6-3:
Creating a
new group
policy
object.

4. **Type a name for the group policy object and then click OK.**

   For this example, type something like **Windows Update** for a policy that will manage the Windows Update feature.

   When you click OK, the group policy object is created.

5. **Double-click the new group policy.**

   The group policy opens, as shown in Figure 6-4. Note that at this stage, the Location section of the group policy doesn't list any objects. As a result, this policy is not yet linked to any Active Directory domains or groups. I get to that topic in a moment. First, I create the policy settings.

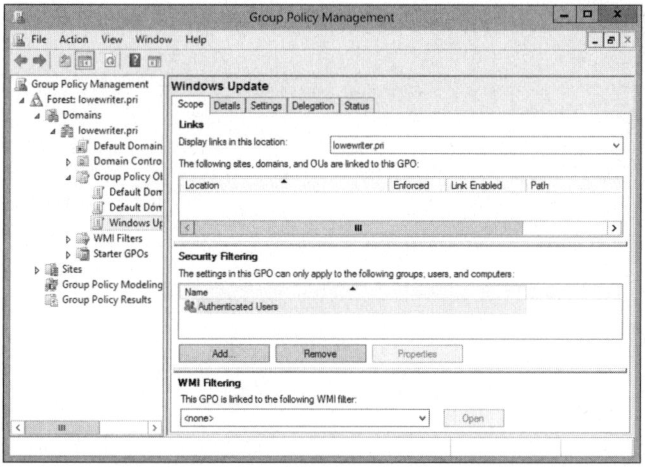

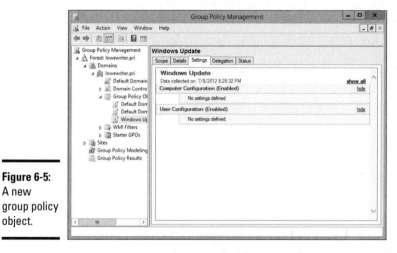

Figure 6-4:
A new
group policy
object.

6. Click the Settings tab.

The group policy settings are displayed, as shown in Figure 6-5.

Figure 6-5:
A new
group policy
object.

7. Right-click Computer Configuration and then choose Edit from the contextual menu.

This command opens the Group Policy Management Editor, as shown in Figure 6-6, where you can edit the Computer Configuration policies.

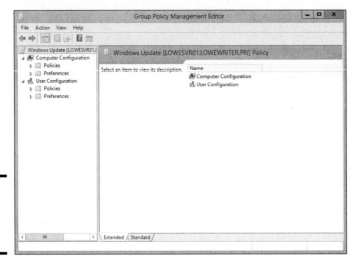

Figure 6-6:
Editing
group
policy.

8. **In the Navigation pane, navigate to Computer Configuration⇨ Policies⇨Administrative Templates⇨Windows Components⇨ Windows Update.**

   This step brings up the Windows Update policy settings, as shown in Figure 6-7.

Figure 6-7:
The
Windows
Update
policy
settings.

9. **Double-click Configure Automatic Updates.**

   This step brings up the Configure Automatic Updates dialog box, as shown in Figure 6-8.

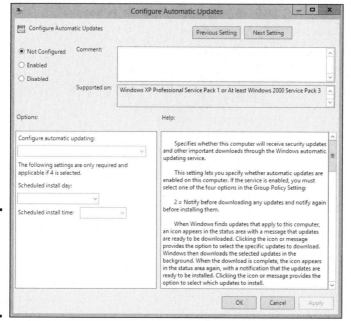

Figure 6-8:
The
Configure
Automatic
Updates
dialog box.

10. **Select Enabled to enable the policy.**

11. **Configure the Windows Update settings however you want.**

For this example, I configure Windows Update so that updates are automatically downloaded every day at 3 a.m.

12. **Click OK.**

You return to the Group Policy Management Editor.

13. **Close the Group Policy Management Editor window.**

This step returns you to the Group Policy Management settings window, which you opened in Step 6.

14. **Right-click User Configuration, and choose Refresh from the contextual menu.**

The Windows Update policy is visible, as shown in Figure 6-9.

15. **In the Navigation pane, drag the new Windows Update policy object to the top-level domain (in this case, LoweWriter.pri).**

When you release the mouse button, the dialog box shown in Figure 6-10 appears.

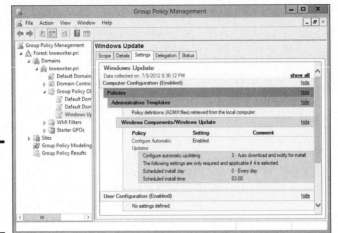

Figure 6-9:
The
Windows
Update
policy.

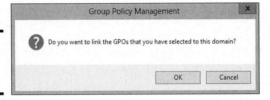

Figure 6-10:
Confirming
the scope.

16. **Click OK.**

The domain is added to the scope, as shown in Figure 6-11.

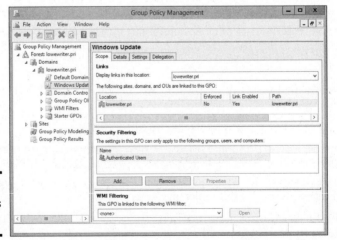

Figure 6-11:
The policy is
finished.

17. **Close the Group Policy Management window.**

The new group policy is now active.

Filtering Group Policy Objects

One of the most confusing aspects of group policy is that even though it applies to users and computers, you don't associate group policy objects with users or computers. Instead, you link GPOs to sites, domains, or organizational units (OUs). At first glance, this aspect may seem to limit the usefulness of group policy. For most simple networks, you'll work with group policy mostly at the domain level and occasionally at the OU level. Site-level group policy objects are used only for very large or complex networks.

Group policy wouldn't be very useful if you had to assign exactly the same policy to every user or computer within a domain. And although OUs can help break down group policy assignments, even that capability is limiting, because a particular user or computer can be a member of only one OU. Fortunately, group policy objects can have *filters* that further refine which users or computers the policy applies to. Although you can filter policy objects so that they apply only to individual users or computers, you're more likely to use groups to apply your group policy objects.

Suppose that you want to use group policy to assign two different default home pages for Internet Explorer. For the Marketing department, you want the default home page to be www.dummies.com, but for the Accounting department, you'd like the default home page to be www.beancounters.com. You can easily accomplish this task by creating two groups named Marketing and Accounting in Active Directory Users and Computers, and assigning the marketing and accounting users to the appropriate groups. Next, you can create two group policy objects: one for the Marketing department's home page and the other to assign the Accounting department's home page. Then you can link both of these policy objects to the domain and use filters to specify which group each policy applies to.

For the following procedure, I've created two group policies, named IE Home Page Dummies and IE Home Page Beancounter, as well as two Active Directory groups, named Marketing and Accounting. Here are the steps for filtering these policies to link correctly to the groups:

1. **Choose Start⇨Administrative Tools⇨Group Policy Management.**

The Group Policy Management console appears. (Refer to Figure 6-2 for a refresher on what it looks like.)

2. **In the Navigation pane, navigate to the group policy object you want to apply the filter to.**

For this example, I navigated to the IE Home Page Dummies policy, as shown in Figure 6-12.

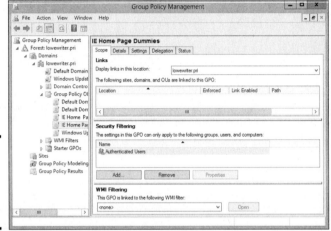

Figure 6-12:
The IE Home Page Dummies policy.

3. **In the Security Filtering section, click Authenticated Users and then click Remove.**

   This step removes Authenticated Users so that the policy won't be applied to all users.

4. **Click Add.**

   This step brings up the Select User, Computer, or Group dialog box, as shown in Figure 6-13.

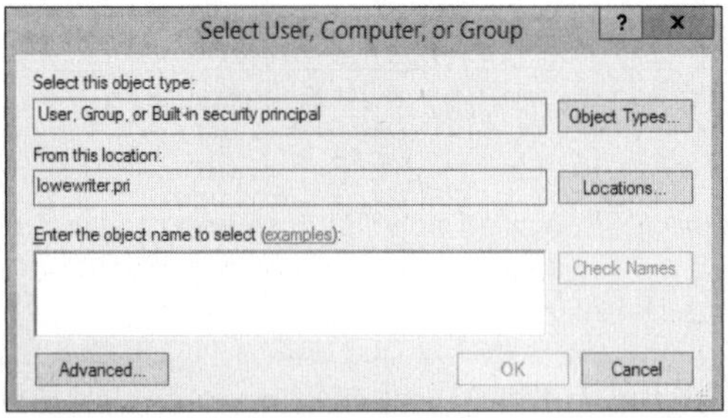

Figure 6-13:
The Select User, Computer, or Group dialog box.

5. **Type** Marketing **in the text box and then click OK.**

   The policy is updated to indicate that it applies to members of the Marketing group, as shown in Figure 6-14.

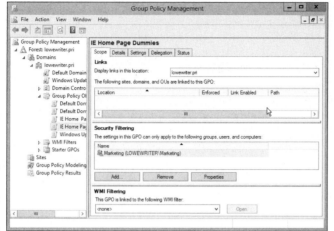

Figure 6-14:
A policy that
uses a filter.

6. Repeat Steps 2 through 5 for the IE Home Page Beancounter policy, applying it to the Accounting group.

You're done!

Chapter 7: Troubleshooting

In This Chapter

✔ Examining the Event Viewer

✔ Perusing the Performance console

✔ Checking out the Computer Management console

✔ Surveying the Services console

Both Windows Server 2008 and Windows Server 2012 are extremely reliable. Get them configured right in the first place, and they'll chug along without incident — that is, at least until something goes wrong, which is inevitable.

In this chapter, I review some of the tools that Windows provides to help you diagnose trouble. Before I start, however, I want to point you to a few other chapters that also contain troubleshooting information. This chapter deals only with those tools that apply specifically to Windows servers. You can find other information in these chapters:

✦ Book II, Chapter 7 gives you some guidance on verifying that the network is functioning.

✦ Book III, Chapter 6 gives some basic performance management tips.

✦ Book III, Chapter 7 gives some basic network troubleshooting tips.

✦ Book IV, Chapter 6 explains how to use the TCP/IP troubleshooting tools, such as `ping` and `ipconfig`.

Working with the Event Viewer

Windows has a built-in event-tracking feature that automatically logs a variety of interesting system events. Usually, when something goes wrong with your server, you can find at least one and maybe dozens of events in one of the logs. All you have to do is open the Event Viewer and check the logs for suspicious-looking entries.

Using the Event Viewer

To display the event logs, open the Server Manager, and choose Tools⇨ Event Viewer. This command brings up the Event Viewer, as shown in Figure 7-1. The tree on the left side of the Event Viewer lists the various categories of events that are tracked:

✦ **Application:** Lists events that were generated by application programs. In most cases, the application's developers purposely wrote these events to the event log to inform you of error conditions or developing trouble.

✦ **Security:** Lists security-related events, such as unsuccessful logon attempts, changes to security policy, and so on.

✦ **Setup:** Lists events generated during operating-system setup.

✦ **System:** Lists events related to hardware or operating-system failures. If you're having trouble with a hard drive, for example, you should check here for events related to the hard drive.

✦ **Forwarded Events:** Lists other events that were forwarded to this server.

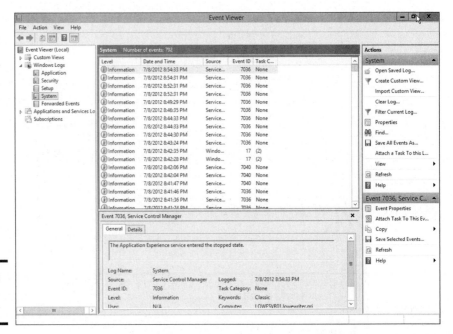

Figure 7-1:
The Event
Viewer.

Note that you may find other categories in this list, depending on the roles you've configured for the server.

Select one of these options to see the log that you want to view. In Figure 7-1, I clicked the System events log.

Notice the cute little icons next to the items in the log. Table 7-1 summarizes the meanings of these icons.

Table 7-1		Icons Used in the Event Log
Icon	*Name*	*Description*
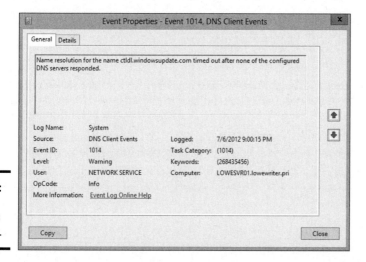 Information	Information	A noteworthy operation completed successfully.
Warning	Warning	An event developed a problem that wasn't fatal, though a problem may be looming on the horizon.
Error	Error	Something has gone wrong.

To see the details for a particular event, double-click the event to bring up the Event Properties dialog box, shown in Figure 7-2. Here, you can see the details of the event. In some cases, you may be able to diagnose a problem just by reading the error message displayed in this dialog box. In other cases, this information just points you in the right direction; it tells you *what* went wrong, but you still have to figure out *why*.

Figure 7-2:
The Event
Properties
dialog box.

Setting event log policies

To set default policies that affect how application, security, and system event logs are kept. open the Group Policy Management Editor by choosing Tools⇨Group Policy Management from Server Manager (see Figure 7-3). You can find the event log policies in the Navigation pane by navigating to Computer Configuration⇨Policies⇨Windows Settings⇨Security Settings.

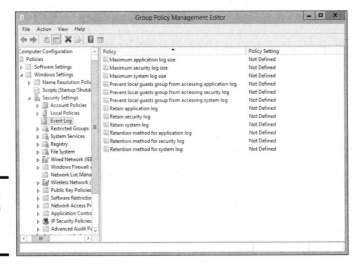

Figure 7-3:
Setting the event log policies.

You can use these policies to specify the following options for the Application, Security, and System logs:

✦ **Maximum Log Size:** This policy lets you specify the maximum size of the log in kilobytes (KB).

✦ **Prevent Local Guests Group from Accessing Log:** This policy prevents users who are logged on via a guest account from viewing the logs. Enabling this policy is a good security precaution.

✦ **Retain Log:** This policy looks as though it might let you disable the log, but it doesn't. Instead, it specifies the number of days that log data should be kept if you specify By Days as the Retention Method policy.

✦ **Retention Method for Log:** This policy specifies how log events should be overwritten when the log becomes full. Options are By Days, As Needed, and Do Not Overwrite.

Monitoring Performance

The Performance Monitor console is a troubleshooting tool that can help you track down nasty and elusive problems — particularly the type that don't cause the server to crash but just cause it to run slowly. With the Performance Monitor console, you can look at many aspects of system performance to figure out why your system is dragging.

Using the Reliability and Performance Monitor

To run the Performance Monitor console, choose Start⇨Administrative Tools⇨Performance Monitor. The Performance Monitor comes to life, as shown in Figure 7-4.

The display in Figure 7-4 shows essential performance data for the server, including memory and network interface utilization, disk access, and so on.

If you want, you can click the Open Resource Monitor link to display the Resource Monitor, which graphically displays utilization information, as shown in Figure 7-5. This display resembles something that you'd expect to see in a hospital.

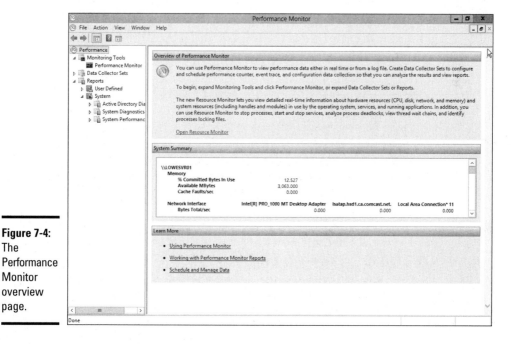

**Book VII
Chapter 7**

Troubleshooting

Figure 7-4:
The
Performance
Monitor
overview
page.

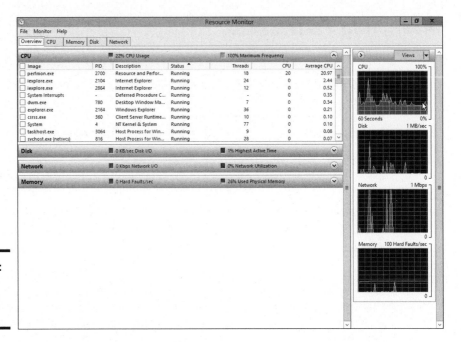

Figure 7-5:
The
Resource
Monitor.

You can summon more-specific performance information by clicking Performance Monitor in the console tree of the Performance Monitor console. This action brings up the Performance Monitor, as shown in Figure 7-6.

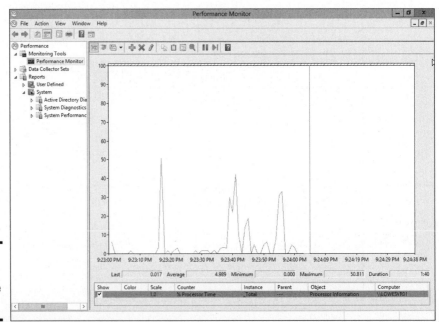

Figure 7-6:
The
Performance
Monitor.

The Performance Monitor lets you keep track of several aspects of system performance at the same time. You track each performance aspect by setting up a counter. You can choose among hundreds of counters. Table 7-2 describes some of the most commonly used counters. Notice that each counter refers to a server object, such as physical disk, memory, or the processor.

Table 7-2	Commonly Used Performance Counters	
Object	*Counter*	*Description*
Physical Disk	% Free Space	The percentage of free space on the server's physical disks. It should be at least 15.
Physical Disk	Average Queue Length	The number of disk operations that are waiting while the disk is busy servicing other disk operations. It should be 2 or less.
Memory	Pages/second	The number of pages retrieved per second from the virtual-memory page files. A typical value is about 2,500.
Processor	% Processor Time	The percentage of the processor's time that it's busy doing work rather than sitting idle. It should be 85 or less.

To add a counter, click the Add button (the one with the green plus sign) to bring up the Add Counters dialog box, as shown in Figure 7-7. Then select the object that you want to track from the drop-down list, choose the counter that you want to add from the list, and click Add. You can add more than one counter from this dialog box; when you're finished adding counters, click OK to dismiss the Add Counters dialog box.

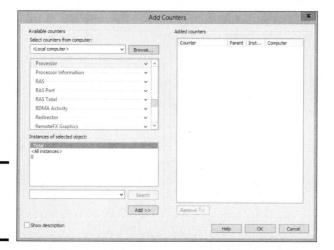

Figure 7-7:
The Add
Counters
dialog box.

The act of gathering performance data slows your server, so don't leave performance logging turned on all the time. Use it only occasionally when you want to gather baseline data or when you're experiencing a performance problem.

Creating performance logs

Instead of staring at the Performance Monitor for hours on end, waiting for a performance glitch to occur, you can create a performance log — which in Windows Server 2012 is called a *Data Collector Set.* (In Windows Server 2003, it was called a *Performance Log.* I guess the intellectuals at Microsoft think the term *Data Collector Set* is more meaningful than *Performance Log.* I disagree, but they didn't ask for my opinion.)

When the network is running well, you can collect data to act as a baseline so you'll know whether performance has slipped. When the network isn't acting well, you can collect data to help isolate the problem.

To set up a performance log, follow these steps:

1. **Open the Data Collector Sets node in the Performance Monitor's console tree.**

2. **Right-click the User Defined node, and choose New⇨Data Collector Set from the contextual menu.**

   This action brings up a wizard that steps you through the process of creating a new log, as shown in Figure 7-8.

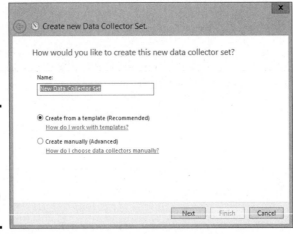

Figure 7-8: Creating a new Data Collector Set (er, Performance Log).

3. **Type a name for your log, choose whether you want to use a pre-defined template or create your own custom log, and then click Next.**

For this example, I use one of the templates. The dialog box shown in Figure 7-9 lists the available templates.

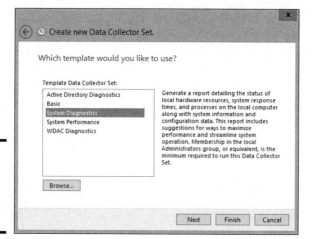

Figure 7-9:
Data
Collector
Set
templates.

4. **Select System Performance and then click Finish.**

Note that creating the log doesn't actually start the logging activity. To start the log, right-click it, and choose Start from the contextual menu. Alternatively, you can click the big green Start button on the toolbar. When you want to stop the log, select the log and click the Stop button, or right-click the log and choose Stop from the contextual menu.

To display the data accumulated by a performance log, right-click the log, and choose Latest Report from the contextual menu. A summary of the logged data is displayed, as shown in Figure 7-10.

Book VII
Chapter 7

Troubleshooting

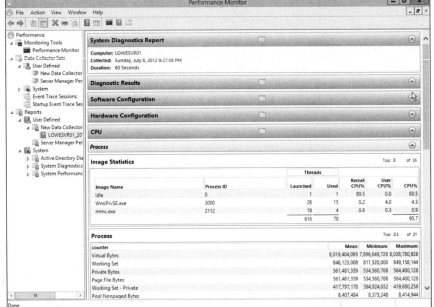

Figure 7-10:
Data
collected
by a
performance
log.

Using the Computer Management Console

The Server Manager's Tools⇨Computer Management command leads you
to the Computer Management console, a tool that's often useful for tracking
down problems in a Windows Server 2012 system. Poke around the console
tree in Computer Management, and you'll find the following:

✦ **Event Viewer:** Refer to the section "Using the Event Viewer," earlier in
this chapter, for more information.

✦ **Shared Folders:** Here, you can manage your shared folders, current sessions, and open files. For more information, see Book VII, Chapter 4.

✦ **Performance Logs and Alerts:** Refer to the section "Using the Reliability
and Performance Monitor," earlier in this chapter, for more information.

✦ **Device Manager:** This tool is handy for diagnosing problems with hardware devices. Device Manager lists all the hardware devices currently
installed on the computer, as shown in Figure 7-11. You can double-click
a device to bring up a Properties dialog box that displays information
about the status of the device and lets you change drivers or configuration settings.

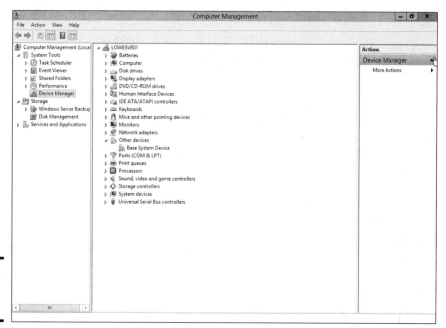

Figure 7-11:
Device
Manager.

**Book VII
Chapter 7**

Troubleshooting

- ✦ **Removable Storage:** This tool lets you track removable storage media, such as tapes and CDs, as well as manage tape and CD libraries.

- ✦ **Disk Defragmenter:** This tool lets you optimize the way data is stored on your disks.

- ✦ **Disk Management:** This tool lets you work with disk partitions, format disks, create mirror sets, and perform other disk operations.

- ✦ **Services and Applications:** Here, you can manage services and applications that you've installed on the computer, such as DHCP, DNS, IIS, and so on.

Working with Services

The last troubleshooting tool I want to describe in this chapter is the Services console, which you can access by choosing Start⇨Administrative Tools⇨Services. As Figure 7-12 shows, the Services console displays a list of all the services that are currently running on your system.

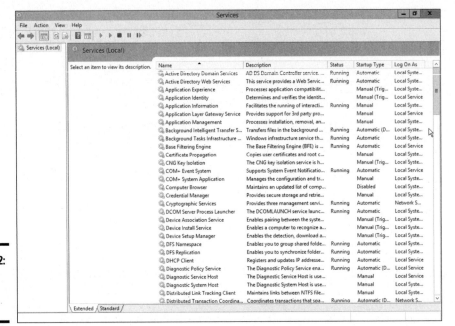

Figure 7-12:
The
Services
console.

If a Windows server feature isn't working properly, the problem often is that
something caused one of the services associated with the feature to stop.
You may be able to correct the problem by calling up the Services console
and restarting the service. To do that, just select the service and then click
the Start the Service link.

This action doesn't correct the underlying cause of the problem, of course.
If the service stopped because of a one-time error, simply restarting the service may be all that you need to do. In many cases, though, the problem that
caused the service to start will resurface and cause the service to stop again.

So if you fix a problem by restarting a service, you must keep an eye out for
the problem's resurgence. Usually, if the problem doesn't recur within a
few days, you can safely assume that you encountered a one-time glitch and
fixed it by restarting the service. But if the problem happens again, you'll
need to investigate more to get to the bottom of the problem.

Chapter 8: Windows Commands

In This Chapter

✔ Getting started with a command window

✔ Taking advantage of command tricks and techniques

✔ Looking at batch files

✔ Using the amazing Net commands

Although Windows sports a fancy graphical interface that makes it possible to perform most network management tasks by pointing and clicking, you can also do almost any network management task from a command prompt. Whether you choose to do so is largely a matter of personal style. Some network administrators pride themselves on being able to type Windows commands blindfolded and with two fingers on each hand tied behind their backs. Others have fully embraced the graphical user interface and think the command line is for administrators with Unix envy.

So the choice is yours. Skip this chapter if the thought of typing commands causes you to lose sleep. If you're willing to venture forth, this chapter begins with an overview of working from the command prompt. Then it describes some of the more useful Windows commands. Finally, this chapter introduces the fine (and almost lost) art of writing batch files.

 Windows Server 2012 includes a brand-new command environment known as PowerShell. *PowerShell* is an advanced command processor that has many sophisticated features that are designed especially for creating powerful scripts. For more information, see Microsoft's PowerShell site at www. microsoft.com/powershell.

Using a Command Window

Command prompts are even older than video monitors. The first computer I worked on used a teletype machine as its terminal, so the command prompt was printed on paper rather than displayed onscreen. Surprisingly, though, the concept of the command prompt hasn't changed much since those days. The system displays a prompt to let you know it's waiting for a command. When you type the command and press the Enter key, the system reads your command, interprets it, executes it, displays the results, and then displays the prompt again so that you can enter another command.

Opening and closing a command window

To get to a command prompt on a Windows server, follow these steps:

1. **Press the Windows key on your keyboard, and then type** cmd.

2. **Press the Enter key.**

   The command prompt window appears, as shown in Figure 8-1.

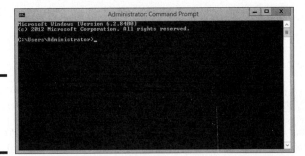

You can type any commands you want in the window.

To exit the command prompt, type **Exit**, and press Enter. This action properly terminates cmd.exe and closes the command prompt window. If you try to close the command prompt window by clicking its Close button, Windows is forced to shut down cmd.exe. The process works, but you have to click your way through an intervening dialog box and wait a few seconds while Windows terminates cmd.exe. Entering the Exit command is a much faster method.

Editing commands

Most of the time, you just type commands by using the keyboard. If you make a mistake, you just retype the command, being careful not to repeat the mistake. cmd.exe, however, has several built-in editing features that can simplify the task of correcting a mistaken command or entering a sequence of similar commands:

✦ Press the right-arrow key to recall the text of the last command that you entered, one letter at a time. When you get to the spot where the new command should differ from the previous command, start typing.

✦ Press F3 to recall all the previous commands from the current cursor position to the end of the line.

✦ If you want to repeat a command that you've used recently, press the up-arrow key. This action recalls up to 50 of the most recently executed commands. You can press Enter to execute a command as is, or you can edit the command before you execute it.

Using the Control menu

Although the command window has no menu bar, it does have a menu that you can access via the control box in the top-left corner of the window. Besides the commands found on this menu for all windows (such as Move, Size, and Minimize), this menu includes three additional commands:

✦ **Edit:** The Edit command leads to a submenu with several choices. Several of these commands work together so that you can copy information from the command window to the Clipboard, and vice versa. If you choose Edit➪Mark, you're placed in a special editing mode that lets you highlight text in the command window with the mouse. (Normally, the mouse doesn't do anything in the command window.) Then you can choose Edit➪Copy or just press Enter to copy the text that you selected to the Clipboard.

You can also use the Edit menu to paste text from the Clipboard, to scroll the window, and to search the window for text.

✦ **Default:** This command lets you set default properties for the command window.

✦ **Properties:** This command displays a Properties dialog box that you can use to change the appearance of the window. You can change the font size, choose background colors, and make other adjustments to make the command window look good on your computer.

**Book VII
Chapter 8**

**Windows
Commands**

Special Command Tricks

Before I get into the details of using specific commands, I want to describe some techniques you should familiarize yourself with. In many cases, these techniques can let you accomplish in a single command what would otherwise take dozens of separate commands.

Wildcards

Wildcards are among the most compelling reasons to use the command prompt. With wildcards, you can process all the files that match a particular naming pattern with a single command. Suppose that you have a folder containing 500 files, and you want to delete all the files that contain the letters *Y2K* and end with the extension `.doc`, which happens to be 50 files. If you open a My Documents window, you'll spend ten minutes picking these files out from the list. From a command window, you can delete them all with the single command `del *Y2K*.doc`.

You can use two wildcard characters. An asterisk stands for any number of characters, including zero, and an exclamation point stands for just one character. Thus, `!Text.doc` would match files with names like `aText.doc`, `xText.doc`, and `4Text.doc`, but not `abcText.doc` or just `Text.doc`. `*Text.doc`, however, would match any of the names mentioned in the previous sentence.

Wildcards work differently in Windows than they did in MS-DOS. In MS-DOS, anything you typed after an asterisk was ignored. Thus, `ab*cd.doc` was the same as `ab*.doc`. In Windows, the asterisk wildcard can come before static text, so `ab*cd.doc` and `ab*.doc` are *not* the same.

Chaining commands

You can enter two or more commands on the same line by separating the commands with an ampersand (`&`), like this:

```
C:\>copy *.doc a: & del *.doc
```

Here, the `copy` command copies all the `.doc` files to the A: drive. Then, the `del` command deletes the `.doc` files.

Although that technique may be convenient, it's also dangerous. What if the A: drive fills up so that all the files can't be copied? In that case, the `del` command executes anyway, deleting the files that didn't get copied.

A safer alternative is to use two ampersands, telling Windows to execute the second command only if the first command finishes successfully:

```
C:\>copy *.doc a: && del *.doc
```

Now the `del` command will be executed only if the `copy` command succeeds.

You can also use two pipe characters (the *pipe* is the vertical bar character that's above the backslash on the keyboard) to execute the second command only if the first command fails. Thus,

```
C:\>copy *.doc a: || echo Oops!
```

displays the message `Oops!` if the `copy` command fails.

Finally, you can use parentheses to group commands. Then you can use the other symbols in combination:

```
C:\>(copy *.doc a: && del *.doc) || echo Oops!
```

Here, the files are copied and then deleted if the copy was successful. If either command fails, the message is displayed.

Redirection and piping

Redirection and piping are related techniques. *Redirection* lets you specify an alternative destination for output that will be displayed by a command or an alternative source for input that should be fed into a command. You can save the results of an `ipconfig /all` command to a file named `myconfig.txt` like this:

```
C:\>ipconfig /all > myconfig.txt
```

Here, the greater-than sign (>) is used to redirect the command's console output.

If a command accepts input from the keyboard, you can use input redirection to specify a file that contains the input you want to feed to the command. You can create a text file named `lookup.txt` with subcommands for a command such as `nslookup`. Then you can feed those scripted subcommands to the `nslookup` command, like this:

```
C:\>nslookup < lookup.txt
```

Piping is a similar technique. It takes the console output from one command and feeds it into the next command as input. Piping is often used with special commands called *filters,* which are designed to read input from the console, modify the data in some way, and then write it to the console.

Suppose that you want to display the contents of a file named `users.txt` sorted into alphabetical order. You can use the `Type` command, which displays a file on the console, and then pipe the output into the `Sort` command, a filter that sorts its input and displays the sorted output on the console. The resulting command looks like this:

```
C:\>type users.txt | sort
```

The vertical bar is often called the *pipe character* because it's the symbol used to indicate piping.

Environment variables

The command shell makes several *environment variables* available to commands. Environment variables all begin and end with percent signs. You can use an environment variable anywhere in a command. The command

```
C:\>echo %OS% running on a %PROCESSOR_IDENTIFIER%
```

displays a line such as this:

```
Windows_NT running on an x86 Family 15 Model 2 Stepping 8, GenuineIntel
```

Interestingly, Windows NT, Windows 2000 Server, Windows Server 2003, and Windows Server 2008 all display `Windows_NT` for the operating-system name.

If the environment variable represents a path, you may need to enclose it in quotation marks, like this:

```
C:\>dir "%HOMEPATH%"
```

This command displays the contents of the user's home directory. The quotation marks are required here because the environment variable expands to a pathname that may include spaces, and the command shell requires that long filenames that include spaces be enclosed in quotation marks.

Table 8-1 lists the environment variables that are available to you and your commands.

Table 8-1	Environment Variables
Variable	*Description*
`%ALLUSERSPROFILE%`	The location of the All Users profile
`%APPDATA%`	The path where applications store data by default
`%CD%`	The path to the current directory
`%CMDCMDLINE%`	The command line that was used to start the command shell
`%CMDEXTVERSION%`	The version number of the command shell
`%COMPUTERNAME%`	The computer's name
`%COMSPEC%`	The path to the command shell executable (`cmd.exe`)
`%DATE%`	The current date in the format generated by the `date /t` command
`%ERRORLEVEL%`	The error returned by the most recent command
`%HOMEDRIVE%`	The drive letter of the user's home directory
`%HOMEPATH%`	The path to the user's home directory
`%HOMESHARE%`	The network path to the user's shared home directory
`%LOGONSERVER%`	The name of the domain controller the user logged on to
`%NUMBER_OF_PROCESSORS%`	The number of processors on the computer

Variable	Description
%OS%	The name of the operating system
%PATH%	The current search path
"%PATHEXT%"	A list of the extensions the operating system treats as executable files
%PROCESSOR_ARCHITECTURE%	The chip architecture of the processor
%PROCESSOR_IDENTIFIER%	A description of the processor
%PROCESSOR_REVISION%	The revision level of the processor
%PROMPT%	The current prompt string
%RANDOM%	A random number between 1 and 32,767
%SYSTEMDRIVE%	The drive containing the operating system
%SYSTEMROOT%	The path to the operating system
%TEMP%	The path to a temporary folder for temporary files
%TMP%	Same as %TEMP%
%TIME%	The time in the format produced by the time /t command
%USERDOMAIN%	The name of the user's domain
%USERNAME%	The user's account name
%USERPROFILE%	The path to the user's profile
%WINDIR%	The path to the operating-system directory

Book VII Chapter 8

Windows Commands

Batch files

A *batch file* is simply a text file that contains one or more commands. Batch files are given the extension .bat and can be run from a command prompt as though they were commands or programs. You can also run a batch file from the Start menu by choosing Start⇨Run, typing the name of the batch file, and clicking OK.

As a network administrator, you'll find plenty of uses for batch files. Most of them won't be very complicated. Here are some examples of very simple batch files I've used:

✦ I once used a one-line file to copy the entire contents of an important shared network drive to a user's computer every night at 10 p.m. The user had just purchased a new Dell computer with a 100GB drive, and the server had only a 20GB drive. The user wanted a quick-and-dirty backup solution that would complement the regular tape backups that ran every night.

✦ I've also used a pair of short batch files to stop and then restart an Exchange server before and after nightly backups.

✦ If I frequently need to work with several related folders at the same time, I create a short batch file that opens Explorer windows for each of the folders. (You can open an Explorer window from a batch file simply by typing the path to the folder that you want to open as a command.) Then I place the batch file on my desktop so that I can get to it quickly.

You can also use batch files to create logon scripts that are executed whenever a user logs on. Microsoft keeps trying to get users to use profiles instead of logon scripts, but many networks still use logon scripts.

The EventCreate Command

The `EventCreate` command lets you create an event that's added to one of the Windows event logs. This command can be useful if you want to make a note of something unusual that's happened. It's often used in batch files to mark the start or completion of a task such as a nightly backup.

Here's the basic syntax:

```
eventcreate [options]
eventcreate /T type /D "description" /ID eventide
    [/L logname] [/SO sourcename]
    [/S system [/U username [/P password]]]
```

Here's a description of the options:

✦ **/T:** Specifies the type. The options are `Information`, `Warning`, and `Error`.

✦ **/D:** Provides a descriptive message that's saved in the log. Use quotes if the message contains more than one word.

✦ **/ID:** A number from 1 to 1000.

✦ **/L:** The name of the log to write the event to. The default is `Application`.

✦ **/SO:** A string that represents the source of the event. The default is `EventCreate`. If you specify this option, you must also specify the `/L` option.

✦ **/S:** The name of the system on which the event should be recorded.

✦ **/U:** The user account to use when logging the event. You can specify this option only if you also specify `/S`.

✦ **/P:** The password. You can specify this option only if you also specify `/U`.

Here's an example that writes an informational message to the Application log:

```
eventcreate /t information /id 100 /d "Nightly processing completed" /L
    Application /SO Nightly
```

Figure 8-2 shows an event created by the preceding command.

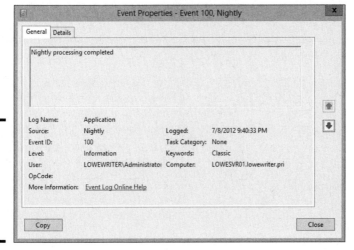

Figure 8-2:
An event
generated
by the
Event
Create
command.

**Book VII
Chapter 8**

**Windows
Commands**

Net Commands

Among the most useful commands for network administrators are the Net Services commands. All these commands are two-word commands beginning with Net — such as Net Use and Net Start. In the following sections, I present the Net commands in alphabetical order for handy reference. First, though, I want to point out a few details about the Net commands:

✦ You can get a quick list of the available Net commands by typing **net /?** at a command prompt.

✦ You can get brief help for any Net command by typing **net help *command***. To display help for the Net Use command, for example, type **net help use**. (Yes, we all could use some help.)

✦ Many of the Net commands prompt you for confirmation before completing an operation. For these commands, you can specify /Y or /N to bypass the confirmation prompt. You'll want to do that if you include these commands in a batch file that runs unattended. Note that you can use /Y or /N on any Net command, even if it doesn't prompt you for confirmation. So I suggest that you place /Y on every Net command in a batch file that you intend to run unattended.

The Net Accounts command

This command updates user account policies for password requirements. Here's the command syntax:

```
net accounts [/forcelogoff:{minutes | no}]
    [/minpwlen:length] [/maxpwage:{days | unlimited}]
    [/minpwage:days] [/uniquepw:number]
    [/domain]
```

The following paragraphs describe the parameters for the Net Accounts command:

- ✦ **forcelogoff:** Specifies how long to wait before forcing a user off the system when the user's logon time expires. The default value, no, prevents users from being forced to log off. If you specify a number, the user will be warned a few minutes before being forcibly logged off.

- ✦ **minpwlen:** Specifies the minimum length for the user's password. *Length* can be 0 through 127. The default is 6.

- ✦ **maxpwage:** Specifies the number of days a user's password is considered to be valid. Unlimited means that the password will never expire. *Days* can be from 1 through 49,710, which is about 135 years. The default is 90.

- ✦ **minpwage:** Specifies the minimum number of days after a user changes a password before the user can change it again. The default value is 0. You usually should set this value to 1 day to prevent users from bypassing the Uniquepw policy.

- ✦ **uniquepw:** Indicates how many different passwords the user must use before he or she is allowed to reuse the same password. The default setting is 5. The range is 0 through 24.

- ✦ **domain:** Specifies that the operation should be performed on the primary domain controller rather than on the local computer.

If you enter Net Accounts without any parameters, the command simply displays the current policy settings.

Here's an example that sets the minimum and maximum password ages:

```
C:\>net accounts /minpwage:7 /maxpwage:30
```

The Net Computer command

This command creates or deletes a computer account. Here's the syntax:

```
net computer \\computername {/add | /del}
```

The following paragraphs describe the parameters for the Net Computer command:

✦ **Computername:** Specifies the computer to add or delete

✦ **add:** Creates a computer account for the specified computer

✦ **del:** Deletes the specified computer account

Here's an example that adds a computer named Theodore:

```
C:\>net computer \\theodore /add
```

The Net Config command

This command lets you view or configure various network services. Here's the syntax:

```
net config [{server|workstation}] [options]
```

To configure server settings, use this syntax:

```
net config server [/autodisconnect:time]                [/srvcomment:"text"] [/
    hidden:{yes | no}]
```

The following paragraphs describe the parameters for the Net Config command:

✦ **server:** Lets you display and configure the Server service while it's running.

✦ **workstation:** Lets you display and configure the workstation service while it's running.

✦ **autodisconnect:** Specifies how long a user's session can be inactive before it's disconnected. Specify –1 to never disconnect. The range is –1 to 65535 minutes, which is about 45 days. The default is 15 minutes.

✦ **srvcomment:** Specifies a description of the server. The comment can be up to 48 characters long and should be enclosed in quotation marks.

✦ **hidden:** Specifies whether the server appears in screens that display available servers. Hiding a server doesn't make the server unavailable; it just means that the user will have to know the name of the server to access it. The default is No.

Here's an example that sets a server's descriptive comment:

```
C:\>net config server /srvcomment:"DHCP Server"
```

The Net Continue command

This command continues a service you've suspended with the `net pause` command. Here's the syntax:

```
net continue service
```

Here are some typical services that you can pause and continue:

+ **netlogon:** The Net Logon service.
+ **schedule:** The Task Scheduler service.
+ **server:** The Server service.
+ **workstation:** The Workstation service.

Here's an example that continues the Workstation service:

```
C:>net continue workstation
```

If the service name has embedded spaces, enclose the service name in quotation marks. This command continues the NT LM Security Support Provider service:

```
C:\>net continue "nt lm security support provider"
```

The Net File command

This command lists all open shared files and the number of file locks placed on each file. You can also use this command to close files and remove locks, which is a useful procedure when a user manages to accidentally leave a file open or locked. Here's the syntax:

```
C:\>net file [id [/close]]
```

The following paragraphs describe the `Net File` command's parameters:

+ ***id:*** The file's identification number.
+ **close:** Closes an open file and releases any locks that were placed on the file.

To close a file, you must issue the command from the server where the file is shared.

`net files` works, too.

To close an open file, first run `net file` without any parameters to list the open files. Here's a sample of the output that you can expect from `net file`:

```
File      Path                  Username    #locks
--------------------------------------------------
0         C:\BUDGET.DOC         WARD        0
1         C:\RECIPE.MDF         JUNE        4
```

Next, run `net file` again, specifying the file number displayed for the file that you want to close. To close the `RECIPE.MDF` file, for example, use this command:

```
C:\>net file 1 /close
```

The Net Group command

This command lets you add, display, or change global groups. This command has several different syntaxes, depending on how you intend to use it.

To display information about a group or to change a group's comment, use this syntax:

```
net group groupname [/comment:"text"] [/domain]
```

To create a new group, use this syntax:

```
net group groupname /add [/comment:"text"] [/domain]
```

To delete a group, use this syntax:

```
net group groupname /delete [/domain]
```

Finally, to add or remove users from a group, use this syntax:

```
net group groupname username[ ...] {/add | /delete} [/domain]
```

The following paragraphs describe the parameters that you can use with the `net group` command:

**Book VII
Chapter 8**

**Windows
Commands**

✦ **groupname:** Specifies the name of the group to add, change, or delete. If you specify this parameter and no others, a list of users in the group appears.

✦ **comment:** Specifies a comment for the group. The comment can be up to 48 characters in length and should be enclosed in quotation marks.

✦ **domain:** Specifies that the operation should be performed on the primary domain controller rather than on the local computer.

✦ **add:** Creates a new group or adds users to an existing group. Before you add a user to a group, you must create a user account for the user.

✦ **delete:** Removes a group or removes users from the group.

✦ *username:* Specifies one or more usernames to be added to or removed from the group. If you list more than one name, separate the names with spaces.

Windows isn't picky: You can specify `net groups` rather than `net group` if you want.

This example lists all the groups on a server:

```
C:\>net group
```

This example adds a group named Admin:

```
C:\>net group Admin /add
```

This example adds three users to the Admin group:

```
C:\>net group Admin Ward Wally June /add
```

This example lists the users in the Admin group:

```
C:\>net group Admin
```

The Net Help command

This command displays help for the `net` command or for a specific net subcommand. Here's the basic syntax:

```
net help [command]
```

The *command* parameter can be any of the following commands:

accounts	help	share
computer	helpmsg	start
config	localgroup	statistics
config server	name	stop
config workstation	pause	time
continue	print	use
file	send	user
group	session	view

You can type **net help services** to display a list of services that you can start via the Net Start command.

The Net Helpmsg command

This command displays an explanation of network error codes. Here's the syntax:

```
net helpmsg message#
```

The *message#* parameter should be the four-digit number displayed when the error occurred. If you get an error with message 2180, for example, use this command to see an explanation of the error:

```
C:\>net helpmsg 2180
The service database is locked.
EXPLANATION
Another program is holding the service database lock.
ACTION
Wait for the lock to be released and try again later. If it is possible to
     determine which program is holding the lock, then end that program.
```

The Net Localgroup command

This command lets you add, display, or change local groups. This command has several different syntaxes, depending on how you intend to use it.

To display information about a local group or to change a local group's comment, use this syntax:

```
net localgroup groupname [/comment:"text"] [/domain]
```

To create a new group, use this syntax:

```
net localgroup groupname /add [/comment:"text"] [/domain]
```

To delete a group, use this syntax:

```
net localgroup groupname /delete [/domain]
```

Finally, to add users to or remove users from a group, use this syntax:

```
net localgroup groupname username[ ...] {/add | /delete}            [/domain]
```

The following paragraphs describe the parameters that you can use with the net localgroup command:

✦ ***groupname*:** Specifies the name of the group to add, change, or delete. If you specify this parameter and no others, a list of users in the group appears.

✦ **comment:** Specifies a comment for the group. The comment can be up to 48 characters in length and should be enclosed in quotation marks.

✦ **domain:** Specifies that the operation should be performed on the primary domain controller rather than on the local computer.

✦ **add:** Creates a new group or adds users to an existing group. Before you add a user to a group, you must create a user account for the user.

✦ **delete:** Removes a group or removes users from the group.

✦ *username:* Specifies one or more usernames to be added to or removed from the group. If you list more than one name, separate the names with spaces.

This example lists all the local groups:

```
C:\>net localgroup
```

This example adds a local group named Admin:

```
C:\>net localgroup Admin /add
```

This example adds three users to the Admin local group:

```
C:\>net localgroup Admin Ward Wally June /add
```

This example lists the users in the Admin group:

```
C:\>net localgroup Admin
```

The Net Name command

This command creates or removes an alias that can be used to send messages to the computer, or it lists any existing aliases. Here's the syntax:

```
net name [name {/add|/delete}]
```

You can use the following parameters with the net name command:

✦ *name:* The name of the alias to create or remove.

✦ **add:** Creates the alias.

✦ **delete:** Removes the alias.

Use net name to specify a name for receiving messages. You must start the Messenger service before you can use net name. Each messaging name must be unique on the network. Names created with net name are strictly for messaging — not for group names. Windows XP uses three name types.

To list the current names for a computer, use the `net name` command like this:

```
C:\>net name
Name
--------------------------------------------------------------
DOUG
DOUG LOWE
The command completed successfully.
```

To add the name T1000 to your computer, use this command:

```
C:\>net name T1000 /add
```

To delete the name, use this command:

```
C:\>net name T1000 /delete
```

The Net Pause command

This command temporarily pauses a service. It's a good idea to pause a service for a while before you stop the service altogether. That gives users who are currently using the service a chance to finish any pending tasks, while at the same time preventing other users from beginning new sessions with the service. To reactivate the service later, use the `net continue` command.

The syntax to pause a service is

```
net pause service
```

Here are some typical services that you can pause:

+ **netlogon:** The Net Logon service.
+ **schedule:** The Task Scheduler service.
+ **server:** The Server service.
+ **workstation:** The Workstation service.

Here's an example that pauses the Workstation service:

```
CL>net pause workstation
```

If the service name has embedded spaces, enclose the service name in quotation marks. This command pauses the NT LM Security Support Provider service, for example:

```
C:\>net pause "nt lm security support provider"
```

The Net Print command

This command displays information about print jobs and shared print queues. To display information about a print queue, use this syntax:

```
net print \\computername\sharename
```

To display information about a specific print job or to change the status of a print job, use this syntax:

```
net print [\\computername] job#
    [/hold | /release | /delete]
```

The following paragraphs describe the parameters of the Net Print command:

+ **\\computername:** Specifies the name of the computer sharing the printer.

+ **sharename:** Lists the name of the shared printer.

+ **job#:** Lists the identification number for the print job.

+ **hold:** Prevents a job in a queue from printing. The job remains in the queue but isn't printed until it's released from the queue.

+ **release:** Releases a job that was held.

+ **delete:** Removes a job from the print queue.

To display the status of the print queue for a printer named LASER1 on a computer named PSERVER, use this command:

```
C:\>net print \\PSERVER\LASER1
Printers at \\PSERVER
Name                 Job #      Size      Status
-------------------------------------------------------
LASER1Queue          3 jobs               *Printer Active*
    Ward             54         43546     Printing
    Wally            55         13565     Waiting
    Beaver           56         18321     Waiting
```

Now suppose that you happen to be user Beaver, and you want to crowd ahead of Wally's print job. All you have to do is issue this command:

```
C:\>net print \\PSERVER 55 /hold
```

The Net Send command

This command lets you send messages to other users on the network. The message pops up, interrupting whatever the user is doing. Use this command sparingly, or you'll lose friends quickly. Here's the syntax:

```
net send {name | * | /domain[:name] | /users} message
```

Here's what the parameters do:

+ **name:** Provides the name of the user or computer to whom you want to send the message. (This paramter can also be an alias created by the Net Name command.) If the name includes spaces, enclose it in quotes.

+ ***:** Sends the message to all computers in the domain or workgroup.

+ **domain:** Sends the message to everyone in the computer's domain or workgroup. If you specify a domain name, the message is sent to all users in the specified domain or workgroup.

+ **users:** Sends the message to all users who are currently connected to the server.

+ **message:** Provides the message to be sent. Interestingly, you don't have to enclose the message in quotes, even if it contains spaces.

To send the message `I'm shutting down the server in 10 minutes` to everyone on the network, use this command:

```
C:\>net send * I'm shutting down the server in 10 minutes
```

To send the message `How about lunch?` to a user named Pooh, use this command:

```
C:\>net send pooh How about lunch?
```

The Net Session command

This command lets you view current server connections and kick users off, if you feel inclined. Here's the syntax:

```
net session [\\ComputerName] [/delete]
```

Here's what the parameters do:

+ **computerName:** Indicates which computer's session you want to view or disconnect. If you omit this parameter, all sessions are listed.

+ **delete:** Disconnects the computer's session. Any open files are immediately closed. If you use this parameter without specifying a computer name, all computers currently connected to the server are disconnected.

**Book VII
Chapter 8**

**Windows
Commands**

This command is an obviously dangerous one. If you disconnect users while they're updating files or before they have a chance to save their work, they'll be hopping mad.

To find out who is connected to a computer, use this command:

```
C:\>net session
Computer      User name        Client type     Opens  Idle time
-----------------------------------------------------------------
\\DEN         Ward             Windows XP      1      00:00:4
\\BEDROOM     Administrator    Windows 2008    0      02:15:17
```

The Net Share command

This command lets you manage shared resources. To display information about all shares or a specific share, use this syntax:

```
net share [ShareName]
```

To create a new share, use this syntax:

```
net share ShareName=path          [{/users:number|/unlimited}]          [/
    remark:"text"] [/cache: {manual|automatic|no}]
```

To change the properties of an existing share, use this syntax:

```
net share ShareName [{/users:number|unlimited}]                        [/
    remark:"text"] [/cache: {manual|automatic|no}]
```

To delete an existing share, use this syntax:

```
net share {ShareName|drive:path} /delete
```

Here's what the parameters do:

✦ *ShareName:* Specifies the share name. Use this parameter by itself to display information about the share.

✦ *path:* Specifies the path to the folder to be shared. The path should include a drive letter. If the path includes spaces, enclose it in quotation marks.

✦ *users:* Specifies how many users can access the share concurrently.

✦ *unlimited:* Specifies that an unlimited number of users can access the share concurrently.

✦ *remark:* Creates a descriptive comment for the share. The comment should be enclosed in quotation marks.

✦ **cache:** Specifies the caching option for the share.

✦ **delete:** Stops sharing the folder.

If you use `net share` without any parameters, all the current shares are listed, as shown in this example:

```
C:\>net share
Sharename   Resource              Remark
-------------------------------------------------------
ADMIN$      C:\WINNT              Remote Admin
C$          C:\                   Default Share
print$      C:\WINNT\SYSTEM\SPOOL
IPC$                              Remote IPC
LASER       LPT1                  Spooled Laser printer
```

The following example creates a share named Docs:

```
C:\>net share Docs=C:\SharedDocs /remark:"Shared documents"
```

The Net Start command

This command lets you start a networking service or display a list of all the services that are currently running. The syntax is

```
net start [service]
```

In most cases, you'll use this command to start a service that you've previously stopped with the `net stop` command. In that case, you should first run the `net start` command without any parameters to find the name of the service that you want to stop. Make a note of the exact spelling of the service that you want to stop. Then use the `net stop` command to stop the service. When you want to restart the service, use the `net start` command again — this time specifying the service to start.

Suppose that you need to stop your DNS server. Using `net start`, you discover that the name of the service is DNS Server, so you use the following command to stop it:

```
C:\>net stop "DNS Server"
```

Later, you can use this command to restart the service:

```
C:\>net start "DNS Server"
```

The Net Statistics command

This command lists the statistics log for the local Workstation or Server service. The syntax is

```
net statistics [{workstation | server}]
```

You can specify `workstation` or `server` to indicate the service for which you'd like to view statistics.

If you use `net statistics workstation`, the following information appears:

+ The computer name
+ The date and time when the statistics were last updated
+ The number of bytes and server message blocks (SMB) received and transmitted
+ The number of read and write operations that succeeded or failed
+ The number of network errors
+ The number of sessions that failed, disconnected, or were reconnected
+ The number of connections to shared resources that succeeded or failed

If you use `Net Statistics Server`, the following information is listed:

+ The computer name
+ The date and time when the statistics were last updated
+ The number of sessions that have been started, disconnected automatically, and disconnected because of errors
+ The number of kilobytes sent and received, and the average response time
+ The number of password and permission errors and violations
+ The number of times the shared files, printers, and communication devices were used
+ The number of times the size of the memory buffer was exceeded

The Net Stop command

This command lets you stop a networking service. The syntax is

```
net stop service
```

To use this command, first run the `net start` command to determine the exact spelling of the service that you want to stop. If the service name includes spaces, enclose it in quotation marks.

You can restart the service later by using the `net start` command.

The following example stops the DNS Server service:

```
C:\>net stop "DNS Server"
```

The Net Time command

This command synchronizes the computer's clock with the clock on another computer. To access a clock on another computer in the same domain or workgroup, use this form:

```
net time \\ComputerName [/set]
```

To synchronize time with a domain, use this form:

```
net time /domain[:DomainName] [/set]
```

To use an RTS time server, use this syntax:

```
net time /rtsdomain[:DomainName] [/set]
```

To specify the computer to use for Network Time Protocol, use this syntax:

```
net time [\\ComputerName] [/querysntp] [/setsntp[:NTPServerList]]
```

To set the computer's clock to match the Server01 clock, use this command:

```
C:\>net time \\Server01 /set
```

The Net Use command

This command connects to or disconnects from a shared resource on another computer and maps the resource to a drive letter. Here's the complete syntax:

```
net use [{drive | *}]
        [{\\computername\sharename]
        [{password | *}]]
        [/user:[domainname\]username]
        [/savecred]
        [/smartcard]
        [{/delete | /persistent:{yes | no}}]
```

**Book VII
Chapter 8**

**Windows
Commands**

To set up a home directory, use this syntax:

```
net use [drive [/home[{password | *}]
        [/delete:{yes | no}]]
```

And to control whether connections should be persistent, use this:

```
net use [/persistent:{yes | no}]
```

Here's what the parameters do:

✦ *drive*: Specifies the drive letter. (Note that for a printer, you should specify a printer device such as LPT1: here instead of a drive letter.) If you specify an asterisk, Windows will determine what drive letter to use.

✦ *computername**sharename*: Specifies the server and share name to connect to.

✦ *password*: Provides the password needed to access the shared resource. If you use an asterisk, you're prompted for the password.

✦ **user**: Specifies the username to use for the connection.

✦ **savecred**: Saves the credentials for reuse later if the user is prompted for a password.

✦ **smartcard**: Specifies that the connection should use a smart card for authorization.

✦ **delete**: Deletes the specified connection. If you specify an asterisk (*), all network connections are canceled.

✦ **persistent**: Specifies whether connections should be persistent.

✦ **home**: Connects to the home directory.

To display all current connections, type **net use** with no parameters.

The following example shows how to create a persistent connection to a drive named Acct on a server named Server01, using drive K:

```
C:\>net use k: \\Server01\Acct /persistent: yes
```

The following example drops the connection:

```
C:\>net use k: /delete
```

The Net User command

This command creates or changes user accounts. To display a user's information, use this form:

```
net user username
```

To update user information, use this form:

```
net user [username [password | *] [options]] [/domain]
```

To add a new user, use this form:

```
net user username [password | *] /add [options] [/domain]
```

To delete a user, use this form:

```
net user username /delete [/domain]
```

Most of the parameters for this command are straightforward. The `options` parameters, however, can have a variety of settings. Table 8-2 lists the descriptions of these options as presented by the `Net Help Users` command.

Table 8-2	The Options Parameters
Options	*Description*
`/ACTIVE:{YES	NO}`	Activates or deactivates the account. If the account isn't active, the user can't access the server. The default is YES.
`/COMMENT:"text"`	Provides a descriptive comment about the user's account (maximum of 48 characters). Enclose the text in quotation marks.
`/COUNTRYCODE:nnn`	Uses the operating-system country code to implement the specified language files for a user's help and error messages. A value of 0 signifies the default country code.
`/EXPIRES:{date	NEVER}`	Causes the account to expire if date is set. NEVER sets no time limit on the account. An expiration date is in the form *mm/dd/yy* or *dd/mm/yy*, depending on the country code. The month can be a number, spelled out, or abbreviated with three letters. The year can be two or four numbers. Use slashes (/), not spaces, to separate parts of the date.

(continued)

Table 8-2 *(continued)*

Options	Description
/FULLNAME:" name"	Is a user's full name (rather than a username). Enclose the name in quotation marks.
/HOMEDIR:pathname	Sets the path for the user's home directory. The path must exist.
/PASSWORDCHG:{YES | NO}	Specifies whether users can change their own passwords. The default is YES.
/PASSWORDREQ:{YES | NO}	Specifies whether a user account must have a password. The default is YES.
/PROFILEPATH[:path]	Sets a path for the user's logon profile.
/SCRIPTPATH:pathname	Is the location of the user's logon script.
/TIMES:{times | ALL}	Is the logon hours. TIMES is expressed as day[-day][,day[-day]],time[-time] [,time[-time]], limited to 1-hour increments. Days can be spelled out or abbreviated. Hours can be 12- or 24-hour notation. For 12-hour notation, use am or pm (without periods) or a.m. or p.m. ALL means that a user can always log on, and a blank value means that a user can never log on. Separate day and time entries with a comma, and separate multiple day and time entries with a semicolon.
/USERCOMMENT:"text"	Lets an administrator add or change the User Comment for the account.
/WORKSTATIONS:	Lists as many as eight computers from which a user {ComputerName[,...] | *} can log on to the network. If /WORKSTATIONS has no list or if the list is *, the user can log on from any computer.

To display information for a particular user, use the command like this:

```
C:\>net user Doug
```

To add a user account for Theodore Cleaver with the username Beaver, use this command:

```
C:\>net user Beaver /add /fullname:"Theodore Cleaver"
```

The Net View command

This command displays information about your network. If you use it without parameters, it displays a list of the computers in your domain. You can use parameters to display resources that are being shared by a particular computer. Here's the syntax:

```
net view [\\computername] [/domain[:domainname]]
net view /network:nw [\\computername]
```

Here's what the parameters do:

✦ **computername:** Specifies the computer whose shared resources you want to view.

✦ **domainname:** Specifies the domain you want to view, if it's other than the current domain.

Here's typical output from a net view command:

```
C:\>net view
Server Name              Remark
-------------------------------------------------
\\Server01               Main file server
\\Print01                Main print server
```

The RunAs Command

The runas command lets you run a program from a command prompt by using the credentials of another user account. Here's the basic syntax:

```
runas /user:username [other parameters] program
```

To run the Microsoft Management Console with the dom1 domain's administrator account, for example, you can use this command:

```
runas /user:dom1\administrator mmc
```

Assuming that the username is valid, you'll be prompted for the user's password. Then the program will be run using the specified user's account.

Here are some of the parameters you can use with the RunAs command:

✦ **/user:** Specifies the domain and username. You can use either of two forms to specify the domain and username: *domain\username* or *username@domain*.

✦ **/profile:** Specifies that the user's profile should be loaded. (This option is on by default, so you don't have to specify it explicitly.)

✦ **/noprofile:** Doesn't load the user's profile. Although this parameter can cause the application to load faster, it can also prevent some applications from functioning properly.

✦ **/env:** Uses the current environment instead of the user's.

✦ **/netonly:** Indicates that the user account isn't valid in the current domain. (If you use /netonly, the username must be specified in the form *domain\username*; the *username@domain* form won't work.)

✦ **/savecred:** Saves the password so that it has to be entered only the first time the RunAs command is used.

Using the /savecred parameter is an extremely bad idea, as it creates a gaping security hole. In short, after you've used /savecred, any user at the computer can use the RunAs command to run any program with administrator privileges.

✦ **/smartcard:** Specifies that the user's credentials will be supplied by a smart card device.

Book VIII

Using Other Windows Servers

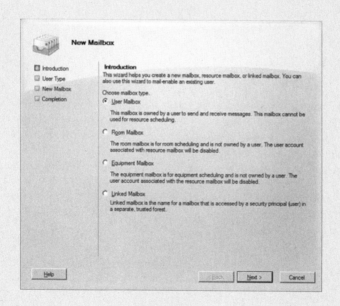

Contents at a Glance

Chapter 1: Using Internet Information System (IIS)

In This Chapter

✔ Configuring a server to use IIS

✔ Working with the default website

✔ Creating your own websites

*I*nternet Information Services, also known as *IIS*, is the web server that comes with Windows Server. It's an essential piece of software for hosting public websites, and it's also a must for any network that includes an intranet with web pages designed to be used by your network users.

In this chapter, you find out how to set up IIS and perform the most common types of maintenance chores, such as creating new websites.

Installing IIS

IIS is a free component of Windows Server 2003 and 2012, but it's not installed by default. After you've completed the installation of Windows Server, you must add the Web Server role to enable IIS. The following procedure is for Windows Server 2012, but the procedure for Windows Server 2008 (or 2003, for that matter) is similar:

1. **Open the Server Manager; then choose Add Roles and Features.**

   The Add Roles and Features Wizard comes to life.

2. **Follow the steps of the Add Roles and Features Wizard up to the Select Server Roles step.**

   The Select Server Roles page is shown in Figure 1-1.

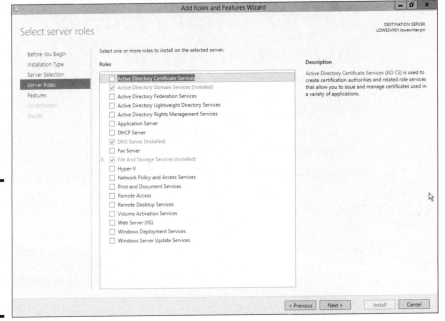

Figure 1-1:
The Select
Server
Roles page
of the Add
Roles and
Features
Wizard.

3. **Select the Web Server (IIS) check box and then click Next.**

   The Add Roles and Features Wizard asks whether you want to install the related IIS Management Console, as shown in Figure 1-2.

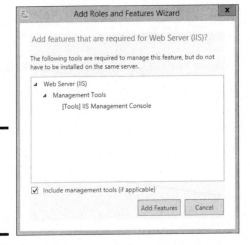

Figure 1-2:
Installing
the IIS
Manage-
ment
Console.

4. **Click Add Features; then click Next.**

   The Select Features page appears.

5. **Click Next.**

   The Web Server Role (IIS) page appears, as shown in Figure 1-3.

6. **Click Next.**

   The Select Role Services page appears, as shown in Figure 1-4. This page lists a variety of optional services that can be configured for IIS.

7. **Select the services you want to configure for IIS.**

   If you want, you can study this list and try to anticipate which features you think you'll need. Or you can just leave the default options selected.

   You can always return to the Add Roles and Features Wizard to add features you leave out here.

8. **Click Next.**

   A confirmation page appears.

9. **Click Install.**

   The features you selected are installed. This may take a few minutes, so now would be a good time to take a walk.

   When the installation finishes, an Installation Results page is displayed to verify that IIS was properly installed.

10. **Click Close.**

    IIS is now installed and ready to use!

Figure 1-3:
The Web Server Role (IIS) page of the Add Roles and Features Wizard.

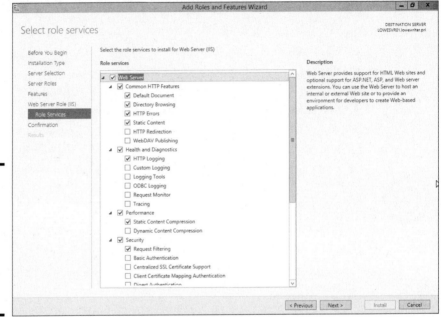

Figure 1-4:
The Select
Role
Services
page of
the Add
Roles and
Features
Wizard.

Understanding the Default Website

Initially, IIS is configured with a single website, called the *default website*.
You can test that IIS is up and running by opening a browser window on the
server and typing **localhost** in the address bar. You can also reach this page
by entering your local domain name in the address bar, such as **lowewriter.
pri**. Figure 1-5 shows the standard welcome page that appears when you
browse to the default site.

The actual files that make up the default website are stored on the server's
C: drive in a folder named \inetpub\wwwroot. When you browse to the
default website without requesting a specific file (simply by **localhost** in the
address bar, for example), IIS looks for the following files, in this order:

✦ default.htm

✦ default.asp

✦ index.htm

✦ index.html

✦ iisstart.htm

✦ default.aspx

Figure 1-5:
The default
website.

Initially, `c:\inetpub\wwwroot` contains just two files: `iisstart.htm` and `welcome.png`. The `iisstart.htm` file is the file that's displayed when you browse to the website; it contains the HTML markup necessary to display the image contained in the `welcome.png` file, which is the image you actually see on the page.

You can preempt the standard page for the default website by providing your own file one of the preceding names. You can follow these steps, for example, to create a simple `default.htm` file that displays the words *Hello World!* as the start page for the default website:

1. **Open an Explorer window, and browse to `c:\inetpub\wwwroot`.**

2. **Choose File⇨New⇨Text Document, type** default.htm **for the filename, and press Enter.**

3. **Right-click the `default.htm` file you just created, and choose Open With⇨Notepad from the contextual menu.**

4. **Enter the following text in the Notepad window:**

```
<HTML>
<BODY>
<H1>Hello World!</H1>
</BODY>
</HTML>
```

5. **Choose File⇨Save to save the file and then choose File⇨Exit to quit Notepad.**

6. **Open a browser window.**

7. **Type** localhost **in the address bar, and press Enter.**

   The page shown in Figure 1-6 appears.

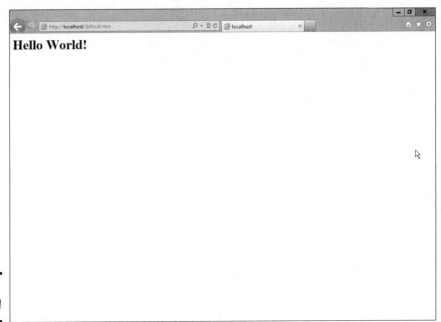

Figure 1-6:
Hello World!

Creating Websites

IIS has the ability to host multiple websites. This is an extremely useful feature not only for web servers that host public sites, but also for web servers that host internal (intranet) sites. You might create a separate intranet website for Human Resources and assign it the website name hr. Then, assuming that the domain name is lowewriter.pri, users can browse to the website by using the address hr.lowewriter.pri.

Here are the steps:

1. **Using Windows Explorer, create a folder in which you will save the files for the new website.**

   For this example, I created a folder named c:\HR-Web-Site.

2. **In Server Manager, choose Tools⇨Internet Information Services (IIS) Manager.**

   The IIS Manager springs to life, as shown in Figure 1-7.

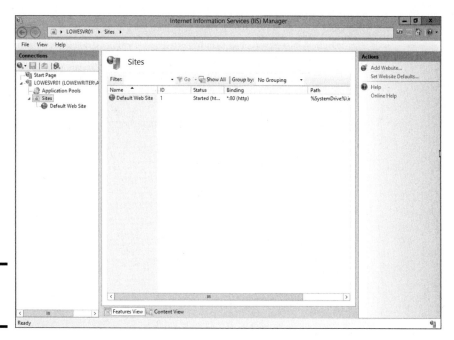

Figure 1-7:
The IIS
Manager.

3. **Right-click Sites and then choose Add Website from the contextual menu.**

   The Add Website dialog box appears, as shown in Figure 1-8.

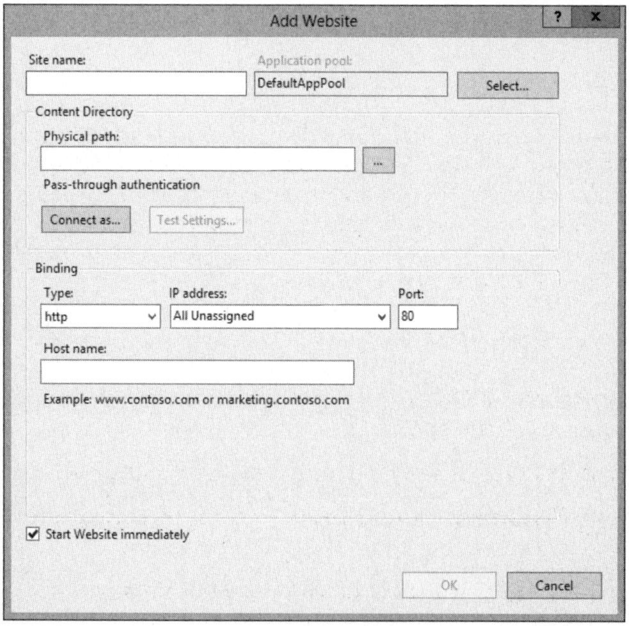

Figure 1-8:
The Add
Website
dialog box.

4. **Enter a name for the website in the Site Name text box.**

   For this example, I used HR.

5. **Click the Browse button (the one with the ellipsis), browse to the folder you created in Step 1, and then click OK.**

   For this example, I browsed to `C:\HR-Web-Site`.

6. **In the Host Name text box, enter the exact DNS name you want to use for the site.**

   For this example, I entered `hr.lowewriter.pri`.

7. **Click OK.**

   The newly created website appears below the Sites node in the IIS Manager, as shown in Figure 1-9.

8. **Close the IIS Manager.**

9. **Create a web page to display in the folder you created in Step 1.**

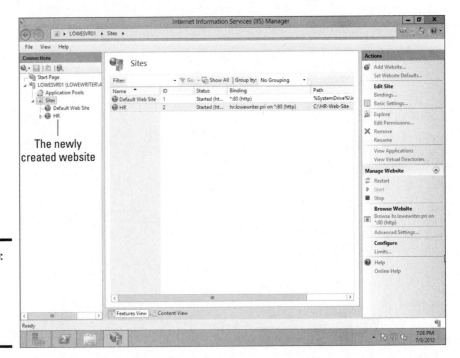

Figure 1-9:
The HR website appears in the IIS Manager.

For this example, I used Notepad to create a text file named `default.htm`, with the following text:

```
<HTML>
<BODY>
<H1>Welcome to the HR Website!</H1>
</BODY>
</HTML>
```

10. In Server Manager, choose Tools⇨DNS.

This brings up the DNS Manager console, as shown in Figure 1-10.

11. In the navigation pane, navigate to the node for your domain.

In this example, I navigated to `lowewriter.pri`.

12. Choose Action⇨New Alias (CNAME).

The New Resource Record dialog box appears, as shown in Figure 1-11.

13. Enter the alias name you want to use in the Alias Name text box.

For this example, I entered simply `hr`.

14. Enter the computer name of your web server in the text box labeled Fully Qualified Domain Name (FQDN) for Target Host.

For this example, I entered `lserver01`.

15. Click OK.

The DNS alias is created.

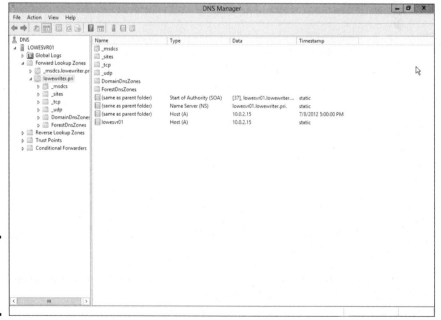

Figure 1-10:
The DNS Manager console.

Book VIII Chapter 1

Using Internet Information System (IIS)

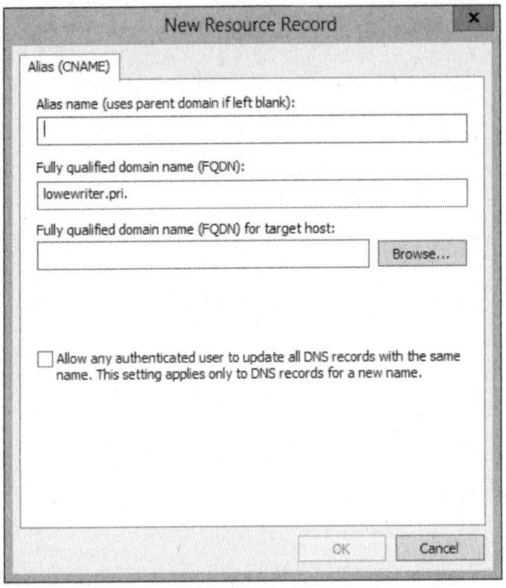

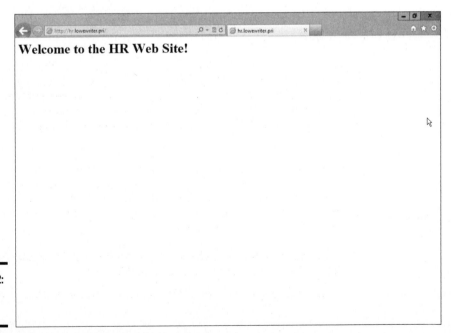

Figure 1-11:
Creating
a CNAME
record.

16. **Close the DNS Manager console.**

17. **Open a browser window.**

18. **Browse to the alias address you just created.**

    For this example, I browsed to `hr.lowewriter.pri`. Figure 1-12 shows
    the resulting page.

Welcome to the HR Web Site!

Figure 1-12:
Viewing a
website.

Chapter 2: Managing Exchange Server 2010

In This Chapter

✔ **Working with the Exchange Server consoles**

✔ **Managing mailboxes**

✔ **Granting mailbox access**

Although not strictly a part of Windows Server 2012, Exchange Server 2010 is the mail server software that's used on most Windows networks. Yes, I know Microsoft doesn't call Exchange Server a *mail server*. It's a *messaging and collaboration server*. But the basic reason for Exchange Server's existence is e-mail. The other messaging and collaboration features are just icing on the cake.

In this chapter, you discover how to perform the most commonly requested maintenance chores for Exchange Server, such as how to create a new mailbox, grant a user access to an additional mailbox, and deal with mailbox size limits.

Creating a Mailbox

In previous versions of Exchange, you created user mailboxes using Active Directory Users and Computers (ADUC). With Exchange 2010, however, Microsoft has removed the Exchange management features of ADUC. So instead, you create and manage user mailboxes using Exchange Management Console, which you can find in Server Manager on the Tools menu.

The Exchange Management Console lets you create a mailbox for an existing Active Directory user. Or you can use Exchange Management Console to create a new user with a mailbox. Because that's the most likely case, the following procedure describes the steps you should follow to create a new Active Directory user with a mailbox:

1. **From Server Manager, choose Tools⇨Microsoft Exchange Server 2010⇨Exchange Management Console.**

This fires up the Exchange Management Console, as shown in Figure 2-1.

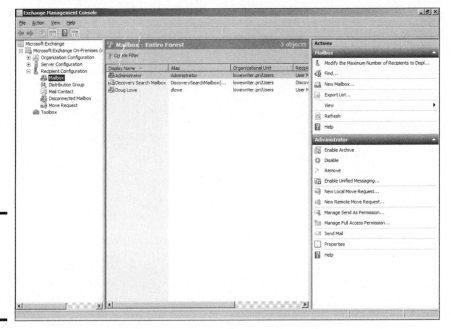

Figure 2-1:
The
Exchange
Manage-
ment
Console.

2. **In the Navigation pane on the left side of the window, navigate to Microsoft Exchange⇨Microsoft Exchange On-Premises⇨Recipient Configuration.**

   If you have more than one Exchange server, pick the Microsoft Exchange On-Premises node for the server you want to add the user to.

3. **Right-click the Mailbox node in the navigation pane and choose New Mailbox.**

   This summons the New Mailbox Wizard, as shown in Figure 2-2. The first page of the wizard lets you choose among several different types of mailbox accounts you can create.

4. **Choose User Mailbox and then click Next.**

   This brings up the User Type page, shown in Figure 2-3. The User Type page lets you indicate whether you want to create a new user account or add a mailbox for an existing Active Directory user.

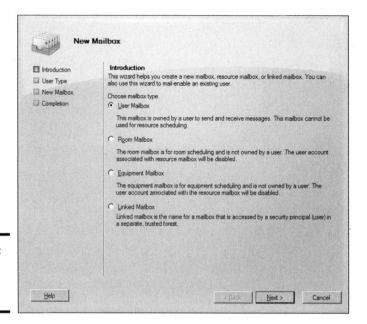

Figure 2-2:
Creating
a user
mailbox.

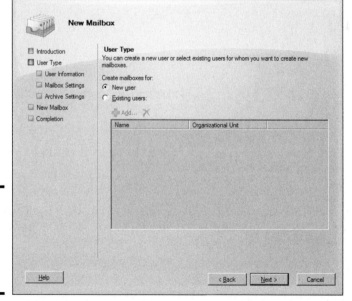

Figure 2-3:
The User
Type page
of the New
Mailbox
Wizard.

5. **Select New User and then click Next.**

   The User Information page is displayed, as shown in Figure 2-4.

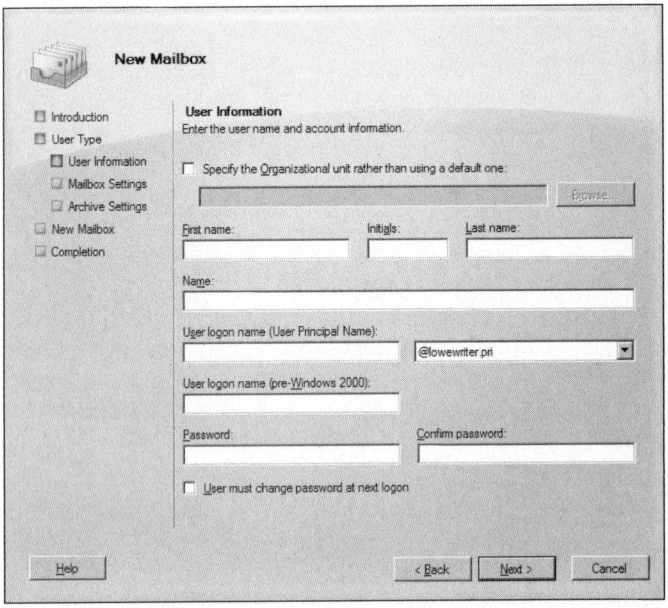

Figure 2-4:
The User
Information
page of
the New
Mailbox
Wizard.

6. **Type the user's first name, middle initial, and last name.**

As you type the name, the New Object Wizard automatically fills in the Name field.

7. **Change the Name field if you want it to appear different from what was proposed.**

You may want to reverse the first and last names so the last name appears first, for example.

8. **Enter the user logon name.**

This name must be unique within the domain and will be used to form the user's e-mail address.

9. **Enter the password twice.**

You're asked to type the password twice, so type it correctly. If you don't type it identically in both boxes, you're asked to correct your mistake.

10. **If the password is temporary, select the User Must Change Password at Next Logon check box.**

This setting requires the user to change the temporary password the first time he or she logs on.

11. Click Next.

The Mailbox Settings page is displayed, as shown in Figure 2-5. This page lets you create an alias for the user's account name and also lets you set several Exchange options for the user's mailbox.

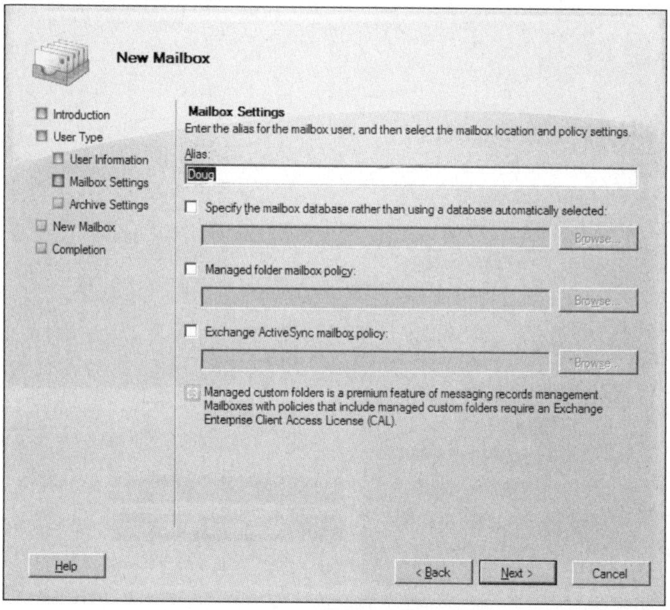

Figure 2-5:
The Mailbox
Settings
page of
the New
Mailbox
Wizard.

12. Enter an alias for the user and then click Next.

The alias can be the same as the name that was used in the Name field on the previous page of the wizard, or you can type a different name if you want.

When you click Next, the page shown in Figure 2-6 is displayed.

13. If you want to create an archive mailbox for the user, select the Create an Archive Mailbox for This Account check box; otherwise, leave the option deselected.

Archive mailboxes are available only with the Enterprise Edition of Exchange Server 2010, so don't even think about this option unless you've shelled out the money for Enterprise Edition.

14. Click Next.

You're taken to the final page of the New Mailbox Wizard, as shown in Figure 2-7.

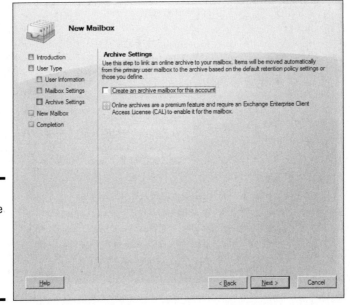

Figure 2-6:
The Archive
Settings
page of
the New
Mailbox
Wizard.

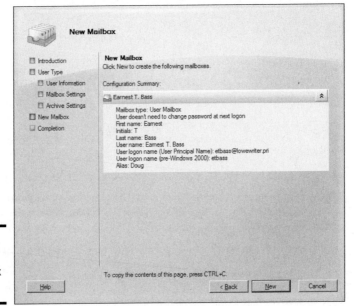

Figure 2-7:
Verifying
the mailbox
settings.

15. **Verify that the information is correct and then click New to create the mailbox.**

If the account information is not correct, click the Back button and correct the error.

When you click Next, Exchange Management Console displays various and sundry messages and progress bars as it creates the user account and its mailbox. When it's finished, the Completion page shown in Figure 2-8 is displayed.

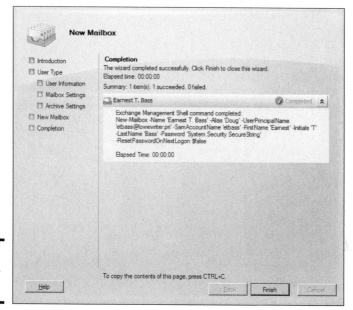

Figure 2-8: Congratulations!

16. **Pat yourself on the back; then click Finish.**

You're done!

Managing Mailboxes

After you've set up a mailbox, you can use the Exchange Management Console to manage the basic settings of the mailbox. To do that, just right-click the mailbox you want to manage, and choose the Properties command from the contextual menu. This action brings up the Properties dialog box, which is the portal that grants access to many of the most frequently used features of Exchange.

The following sections describe several commonly used features that are controlled via this dialog box.

Enabling mailbox features

Exchange Mailbox Features refers to several features of Exchange mailboxes that are controlled via the Mailbox Features tab of the mailbox Properties dialog box. This tab is shown in Figure 2-9.

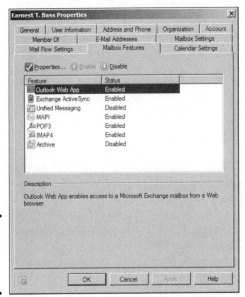

Figure 2-9: The Mailbox Features tab.

The following paragraphs describe the features that are controlled from this tab:

✦ **Outlook Web App:** Lets the user access his or her Exchange mailbox from a web browser rather than from an Outlook client. With this feature enabled, the user can read e-mail from any computer that has an Internet connection. Note that this feature used to be called *Outlook Web Access.*

✦ **Exchange ActiveSync:** Activates the ActiveSync feature, which allows Exchange data to synchronize with mobile devices such as iPhones or Windows Mobile phones.

✦ **Unified Messaging:** Enables a premium feature (available only with Enterprise Edition) that integrates voice mail and fax messages with Exchange mailboxes.

✦ **MAPI:** Enables e-mail using the MAPI protocol.

✦ **POP3:** Enables e-mail using the POP3 protocol.

✦ **IMAP4:** Enables e-mail using the IMAP4 protocol.

+ **Archive:** Enables the Exchange Archive feature, which is available only with the Enterprise edition of Exchange.

Creating a forwarder

A *forwarder* is a feature that automatically forwards any incoming e-mail to another e-mail address. This feature is most often used when an employee is on vacation or leave and the employee's manager has requested that someone else temporarily handle the absent employee's e-mail.

To configure a forwarder, follow these steps:

1. **In Server Manager, choose Tools⇨Microsoft Exchange Server 2010⇨Exchange Management Console.**

   This command fires up the Exchange Management Console (refer to Figure 2-1).

2. **In the Navigation pane, navigate to Microsoft Exchange⇨Microsoft Exchange On-Premises⇨Recipient Configuration.**

3. **Right-click the mailbox for the user whose e-mail you want to forward, and choose Properties from the contextual menu.**

   This summons the mailbox Properties dialog box.

4. **Click the Mail Flow Settings tab.**

   The Mail Flow settings are displayed, as shown in Figure 2-10.

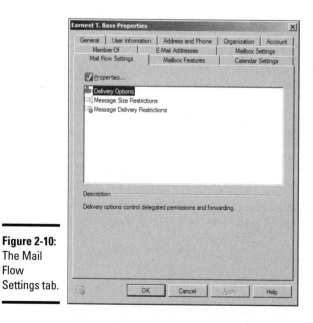

Figure 2-10:
The Mail Flow Settings tab.

Book VIII
Chapter 2

Managing
Exchange Server
2010

5. **Double-click Delivery Options.**

The Delivery Options dialog box appears, as shown in Figure 2-11.

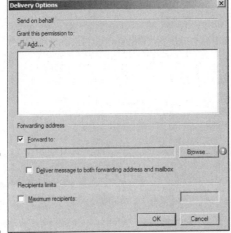

Figure 2-11:
The Delivery
Options
dialog box.

6. **Select the Forward To check box.**

7. **Click the Browse button.**

The Select Recipient dialog box appears, as shown in Figure 2-12.

Figure 2-12:
The Select
Recipient
dialog box.

8. **Select the recipient you want to forward the e-mail to and then click OK.**

   The name you selected is displayed in the text box next to the Browse button in the Delivery Options dialog box (refer to Figure 2-11).

9. **If you want the e-mail to be delivered to this user's mailbox in addition to the forwarding address, select the Deliver Message to Both Forwarding Address and Mailbox check box.**

   If you leave this option deselected, only the forwarding address will receive the e-mail; the mail won't be delivered to this user's mailbox.

10. **Click OK to close the Delivery Options dialog box.**

    You return to the mailbox Properties dialog box.

11. **Click OK to dismiss the Properties dialog box.**

Setting mailbox storage limits

Exchange lets you set a limit on the size of each user's mailbox. In a very small organization, you can probably get away without imposing strict mailbox size limits. But if your organization has 20 or more users, you need to limit the size of each user's mailbox to prevent the Exchange private mail store from getting out of hand.

Exchange provides three kinds of storage limits for user mailboxes:

✦ **Issue Warning At:** When this limit is exceeded, an e-mail warning is sent to the user to let him know that his mailbox is getting large.

✦ **Prohibit Send At:** When this limit is reached, the user can't send e-mail, but the mailbox continues to receive e-mail. The user won't be able to send e-mails again until she deletes enough e-mails to reduce the mailbox size below the limit.

✦ **Prohibit Send and Receive At:** When this limit is reached, the mailbox shuts down and can neither send nor receive e-mails.

You can (and should) set a default storage limit that applies to all mailboxes in your organization. You can also override these limits for specific users.

To configure the default storage limits for all mailboxes, follow these steps:

1. **In Server Manager, choose Tools⇨Microsoft Exchange Server 2010⇨Exchange Management Console.**

   This command fires up the Exchange Management Console (refer to Figure 2-1).

2. **In the Navigation pane, navigate to Microsoft Exchange⇨Microsoft Exchange On-Premises⇨Organization Configuration⇨Mailbox.**

   The organization's mailbox configuration displays, as shown in Figure 2-13.

3. **In the list of mailbox databases, right-click the mailbox database, and choose Properties from the contextual menu.**

   Usually, only one mailbox database is listed; the mailbox database is highlighted in Figure 2-13.

   When you choose Properties, the Mailbox Database Properties dialog box is displayed.

4. **Click the Limits tab.**

   The Limits tab is displayed, as shown in Figure 2-14.

5. **Change the Storage Limits settings to meet your needs.**

   By default, the storage limits are set quite high: Warnings are issued at about 1.9GB, send permission is revoked at 2GB, and both send and receive permissions are revoked at about 2.4GB. A 2GB allowance for each user's mailbox is generous, but bear in mind that if you have 100 users, your mailbox database may grow to 200GB. You may want to set lower limits.

6. **Click OK.**

   The limits you set take effect immediately.

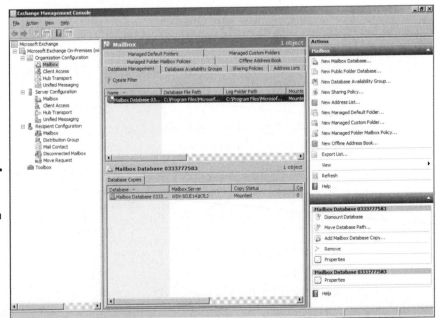

Figure 2-13: The Organization Mailbox page of the Exchange Management Console.

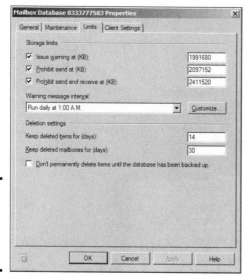

Figure 2-14:
Setting
the default
storage
limits.

If you impose restrictive default storage limits for your users, you may want to relax the limits on a case-by-case basis. Some users may require a larger mailbox because of the type of work they do, and you probably don't want to impose a tight limit on your boss.

Fortunately, it's easy to override the default limits for a specific user. Here are the steps:

1. **In Exchange Management Console, navigate to Microsoft Exchange⇨Microsoft Exchange On-Premises⇨Recipient Configuration⇨Mailbox.**

2. **Right-click the user for whom you want to override the limits and choose Properties.**

This summons the Mailbox Properties dialog box.

3. **Click the Mailbox Settings tab.**

4. **Double-click Storage Quotas.**

The Storage Quotas dialog box appears, as shown in Figure 2-15.

5. **Deselect the Use Mailbox Database Defaults check box.**

This option enables the controls that let you set the Issue Warning, Prohibit Send, and Prohibit Send and Receive limits.

6. **Set the appropriate limits for the user.**

7. **Click OK.**

The storage limits are configured.

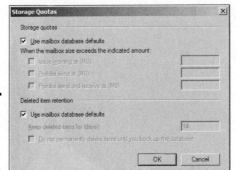

Figure 2-15:
The Storage
Quotas
dialog box.

You can configure many other features of Exchange via the Exchange
Management Console. You should take some time to explore all of the nodes
in the navigation pane and to examine the Properties dialog boxes for the
various types of Exchange objects that appear when you select each node.

Configuring Outlook for Exchange

After you've created an Exchange mailbox for a user, you can configure that
user's Outlook client software to connect to the user's account. Although
you can do this configuration directly within Outlook, it's better to do it outside Outlook, using the Control Main Mail applet. Here are the steps:

1. **Open Control Panel, and open the Mail applet.**

The dialog box shown in Figure 2-16 appears.

Figure 2-16:
The Mail
Setup dialog
box.

2. **Click the Show Profiles button.**

The dialog box shown in Figure 2-17 appears, listing the mail profiles
that already exist on the computer.

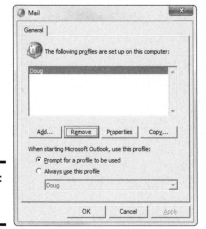

Figure 2-17:
The mail
profiles.

3. Double-click the user's profile.

The Mail Setup dialog box shown in Figure 2-18 appears.

Figure 2-18:
The Mail
Setup dialog
box.

4. Click the E-mail Accounts button.

The Account Settings dialog box appears, as shown in Figure 2-19.

Book VIII
Chapter 2

Managing
Exchange Server
2010

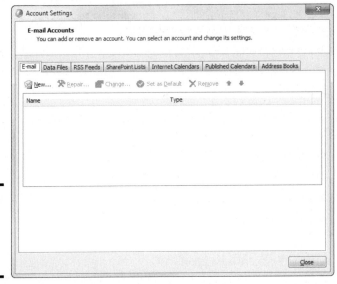

5. Click the New icon.

An Add E-mail Account dialog box appears. Don't enter your e-mail address as prompted in this dialog box; instead, proceed to Step 6.

6. Click the Manually Configure Server Settings or Additional Server Types option and then click Next.

A dialog box asks you what type of e-mail account you want to create. The choices are Internet E-mail, Microsoft Exchange, and Other.

7. Select the Microsoft Exchange option and then click Next.

The dialog box shown in Figure 2-20 appears.

8. **Enter the name of the Exchange server and the username in the appropriate text boxes; then click Next.**

   A dialog box displays the following message:

   ```
   The E-Mail account you have just added will not start until you choose
        Exit from the File menu, and then restart Microsoft Outlook.
   ```

9. **Click OK.**

   The message dialog box disappears, and the last page of the E-Mail Accounts Wizard appears.

10. **Click the Finish button.**

    The wizard is dismissed.

11. **Choose File⇨Exit to close Outlook.**

12. **Restart Outlook.**

    The mailbox should be configured.

Viewing Another Mailbox

Sometimes, you want to set up Outlook so that in addition to the user's main mailbox, he or she has access to another user's mailbox. Suppose that you create a user named Support so that your customers can send e-mail to Support@YourCompany.com to ask technical support questions. If you don't set up at least one of your users so that he or she can read the Support mailbox, any mail sent to Support@YourCompany.com will languish unanswered. Assuming that this situation isn't what you want, you can set up one or more of your users to access the Support mailbox so that those users can read and respond to the mail.

First, you must configure the Support user account's mailbox so that it grants access rights to each user whom you want to access the account. To do that, follow these steps:

1. **On the server, open Exchange Management Console and then select the mailbox you want to access from another user's Outlook.**

2. **In the Actions pane (on the right side of the Exchange Management Console window), click Manage Full Access Permission.**

   The Manage Full Access Permission Wizard appears, as shown in Figure 2-21.

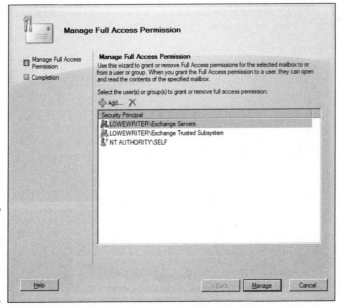

Figure 2-21:
The Manage
Full Access
Permission
Wizard.

3. **Click the Add icon.**

A dialog box titled Select User or Group opens.

4. **Select the user you want to grant access to; then click OK.**

You're returned to the wizard. The user you added is selected in the list of users who have access to the mailbox.

5. **Click the Manage button.**

The mailbox rights are updated. The wizard displays a summary page to let you know that the change was successfully made.

6. **Click Finish.**

The Manage Full Access Permission Wizard is dismissed.

After you've granted access to the account, you can configure the user's Outlook to read the Support account. Follow these steps:

1. **On the user's computer, start Outlook, and choose Tools⇨Account.**

The Account Settings dialog box is displayed.

2. **Select your main e-mail account and then click Change.**

The Server Settings dialog box appears, as shown in Figure 2-22.

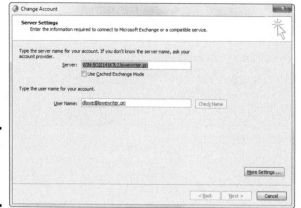

Figure 2-22:
The Server
Settings
dialog box.

3. **Click the More Settings button to open the Microsoft Exchange dialog box and then click the Advanced tab.**

   The Advanced tab is shown in Figure 2-23.

Figure 2-23:
The
Advanced
tab.

4. **Click the Add button.**

   A dialog box appears, prompting you for the name of the mailbox you want to add.

5. **Type the name of the mailbox you want to add and then click OK.**

   The mailbox is added to the list box in the Microsoft Exchange dialog box (refer to Figure 2-23).

6. **Click OK.**

   You're returned to the Server Settings dialog box.

7. **Click Next and then click Finish.**

   You're done! Now you can view the Support mailbox.

To view the mailbox, you need to open the Folder List window in Outlook (by choosing View⇨Folder List). Then you can double-click the Support mailbox in the list to open it.

Chapter 3: Using SQL Server 2012

SQL Server 2012 is the latest and greatest version of the most common database server used on Microsoft networks.

This chapter introduces you to the basics of installing and running SQL Server 2012. It begins with a basic introduction to relational databases and SQL. Then it shows you how to install SQL Server 2012.

Note: The information in this chapter applies to SQL Server 2005 as well.

What Is a Database?

A *database* is simply an organized collection of information. Here are some examples of databases from everyday life:

✦ Your personal address book

✦ The shoebox that contains your tax records for the year

✦ Your baseball card collection

✦ All those parking tickets conveniently stuffed into your car's glove compartment

✦ The phone book

✦ That pile of score cards that has been accumulating in the bottom of your golf bag for 15 years

You can think of each of these databases as a collection of records. In database lingo, a *record* consists of all the useful information that you can gather about a particular thing. In your address book, each record represents one of your friends (or enemies). For your tax records database, each receipt in the shoebox is a record.

Each snippet of information that makes up a record is called a *field.* Using the address book as an example once again, each person's record (that is, each entry in your address book) consists of several fields: name; street address; city; state; zip code; phone number; e-mail address; and other information that may be optional, such as the person's birthday, whether you sent a Christmas card to the person last year, or how much money the person owes you.

SQL Server is designed to create and manage computerized databases that are similar to these noncomputerized databases. Like your address book or shoebox full of tax records, a SQL Server database is a collection of records, and each record is a collection of fields. The biggest difference is that in a SQL Server database, the information is stored on a server computer's hard drive rather than in a shoebox.

What Is a Relational Database?

SQL Server is a database management server that creates and maintains relational databases. Unfortunately, the term *relational database* is one of the most used and abused buzzwords in the computer business. The term has at least three meanings. A *relational database* can be

+ **A database in which data is stored in tables:** In a relational database, groups of similar records are called *tables.* A database usually consists of more than one table; in fact, it isn't uncommon for a single database to have dozens of tables. You can establish relationships between and among these tables based on common information. A sales database, for example, might contain a table of customer information and a table of invoices, with both tables containing a customer-number column that establishes a relationship between the tables.

+ **A database model based on a Coneheads branch of mathematics called Set Theory:** This is actually the most technically precise definition of a relational database, but only computer geeks know or care. Contrary to popular belief, the term *relational database* is derived not from the ability to create relationships among tables, but from the term *relation,* a mathematical term that refers to the way data is arranged into tables of rows and columns.

   (It's a little-known fact that relational-database theory was developed at around the same time that the Coneheads from the planet Remulak first visited Earth, back in the 1970s. I've always suspected that these two developments are — dare I say it? — related.)

+ **A database that's accessed via SQL:** *SQL,* which stands for *Structured Query Language,* provides a practical way to access data stored in relational tables. A database that's based on SQL is inherently relational because SQL stores its data in tables and is based on Set Theory. SQL Server, as its name implies, is based on SQL.

How do you pronounce SQL?

Here's something you've probably wondered ever since you first saw the letters *SQL:* How do you pronounce it? Two schools of thought exist on the subject:

✔ Spell out the letters: *S-Q-L.*

✔ Pronounce it like the word *sequel.*

Either way is acceptable, but *sequel* is hipper.

You can always tell how a writer pronounces *SQL* by checking to see whether the author writes "a SQL query" or "an SQL query."

You can impress even the staunchest SQL expert by pointing out that originally, the language was called SEQUEL by the IBM engineers who created the first version way back in the 1970s. *SEQUEL* stood for *Structured English Query Language.* Someone must have correctly pointed out that aside from borrowing a few words from English, such as `select` and `CREATE`, SEQUEL actually bore no resemblance whatsoever to English. So *English* was dropped from the name, and the acronym was shortened from SEQUEL to SQL.

From a practical point of view, the third definition is the most important: A relational database is a database that you can access via SQL. Thus, SQL Server is used for relational databases. The next section dives a little more deeply into what SQL is.

What Is SQL?

SQL, which stands for *Structured Query Language,* is a language designed to extract, organize, and update information in relational databases. Originally, SQL was envisioned as an English-like query language that untrained end users could use to access and update relational database data. In reality, SQL is nothing like English, and it's far too complicated and esoteric for untrained users, but it has become the overwhelming favorite among programmers who develop applications that access relational databases.

SQL dialects

Like most computer languages, SQL has several dialects. In fact, each major brand of SQL database server has its own dialect of SQL. These dialects are 95 percent the same, so a basic SQL statement is likely to work the same way regardless of the database server you use it with. But the ways that the more advanced features of SQL work have many variations.

The version of SQL used by Microsoft's SQL Server is known as *T-SQL.*

SQL statements

Like other programming languages, SQL uses statements to get its work done. Table 3-1 lists the most commonly used statements.

Table 3-1	Common SQL Statements
SQL Statement	*What It Does*
Use	Identifies the name of the database that subsequent SQL statements apply to.
select	Retrieves data from one or more tables. This is the SQL statement that's used the most.
Insert	Inserts one or more rows into a table.
delete	Deletes one or more rows from a table.
update	Updates existing rows in a table.
create	Creates tables and other database objects.
alter	Alters the definition of a table or other database object.
drop	Deletes a table or other database object.

Using the select statement

As the name *Structured Query Language* suggests, queries are what SQL is all about. Thus, the select statement is the most important of the SQL statements. A select statement extracts data from one or more tables in a database and creates a *result set* containing the selected rows and columns.

In a select statement, you list the table or tables from which you want to retrieve the data; the specific columns you want to retrieve (you may not be interested in everything that's in the table); and other clauses that indicate which specific rows should be retrieved, what order the rows should be presented in, and so on.

Here's a simple select statement that retrieves data from a table named movie, which contains information about your favorite movies:

```
select title, year
    from movie
    order by year
```

Now take this statement apart piece by piece:

✦ select title, year names the columns you want included in the query result (title and year).

✦ `from movie` names the table you want the rows retrieved from (`movie`).

✦ `order by year` indicates that the result should be sorted in sequence by the `year` column so that the oldest movie appears first.

In other words, this `select` statement retrieves the title and date for all the rows in the `movie` table and sorts them into `year` sequence.

If you want the query to retrieve all the columns in each row, you can use an asterisk instead of naming the individual columns:

```
select * from movie order by year;
```

Both examples so far include an `order by` clause. In a SQL database, the rows stored in a table are not assumed to be in any particular sequence. As a result, if you want to display the results of a query in sequence, you must include an `order by` clause in the `select` statement.

Suppose that you want to find information about one particular video title. To select certain rows from a table, use the `where` clause in a `select` statement:

```
select title, year from movie
    where year <= 1980
    order by year
```

Here, the `select` statement selects all rows in which the `year` column is less than or equal to 1980. The results are ordered by the `year` column.

Perhaps you want to retrieve all rows except those that match certain criteria. Here's a query that ignores movies made in the 1970s (which is probably a good idea, with exceptions like *The Godfather* and *Young Frankenstein*):

```
select title, year from movie
    where year < 1970 or year > 1979
    order by year;
```

You can do much more with `select` statements, of course. But this chapter isn't about SQL itself; it's about installing and using SQL Server. So get ready to move on to the good stuff.

Using SQL Server 2012 Management Studio

SQL Server Management Studio is a component of SQL Server 2012 that runs on workstation computers and lets you manage any or all of the SQL Server instances on your network. You run it by choosing Start➪SQL Server Management Studio on any computer on which you have installed the Management Studio. SQL Server Management Studio begins by displaying a

Connect to Server dialog box, as shown in Figure 3-1. You can use this dialog box to connect to any SQL Server instance on your network.

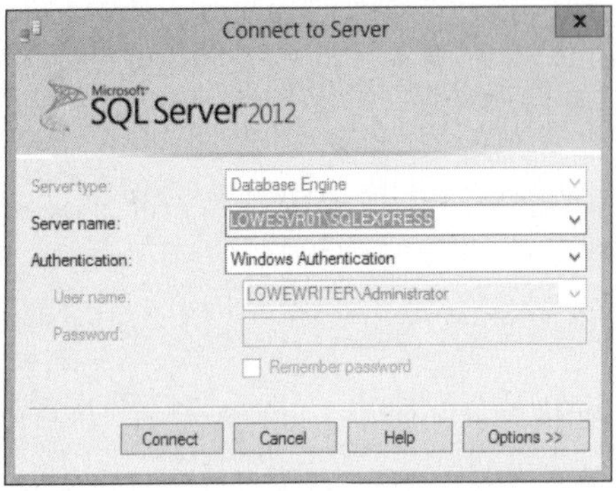

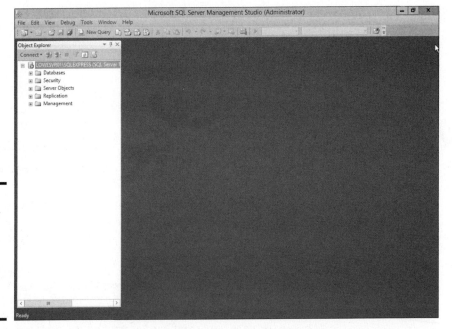

Figure 3-1:
Connecting
to a SQL
Server
instance.

To connect to a SQL Server instance, specify the instance name and your logon credentials, and then click Connect. After you've connected, SQL Server Management Studio displays the screen shown in Figure 3-2.

Figure 3-2:
SQL Server
Manage-
ment
Studio has
connected
to an
instance!

The following sections explain how to perform some of the most common SQL Server chores: creating databases and tables, viewing database data, and so on.

Creating a New Database

To create a new database, follow these steps:

1. **Right-click the Databases node in the Navigation pane (on the left side of SQL Server Management Studio window), and choose New Database from the contextual menu that appears.**

This brings up the New Database dialog box, shown in Figure 3-3.

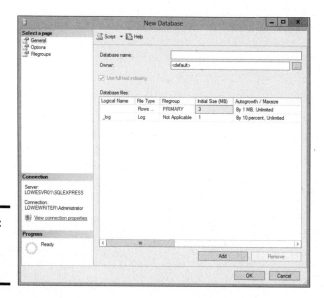

Figure 3-3:
Creating
a new
database.

2. **Type a name for the new database in the Database Name field.**

3. **In the Owner field, enter the domain username of the user who is responsible for the database.**

You can leave this field set to the default if you want to be listed as the owner.

4. **If you want, change the settings for the database and log files.**

You can change the following settings:

- *Initial Size:* This setting refers to the amount of disk space initially allocated to the files. The defaults are a ridiculously small 2MB for the database and 1MB for the log files. Unless your databases are going to be extremely small, you probably should increase these defaults.

- *Autogrowth:* This setting sets the incremental amount by which the database grows when it exceeds the allocated capacity. Again, you'll probably want to change these amounts for any but the smallest databases.

- *Path:* This setting points the way to the folder where the files are stored. By default, the files are created under the Program Files folder on the server's C: drive. You may want to change this setting to a more appropriate location. (You'll have to scroll the database files section of the NewDatabase dialog to the right to see this setting.)

- *File Name:* You can change this setting if you want to use a filename that's different from the database name. (You'll have to scroll the database files section of the NewDatabase dialog to the right to see this setting.)

Note that you can change additional options by clicking Options or Filegroups in the top-left corner of the New Database dialog box. These pages link to additional pages of options you can set to tweak the behavior of the database.

5. **Click OK.**

SQL Server grinds and whirs for a few moments while it creates the new database. When it's finished, the database appears below the Databases node, as shown in Figure 3-4.

That's all!

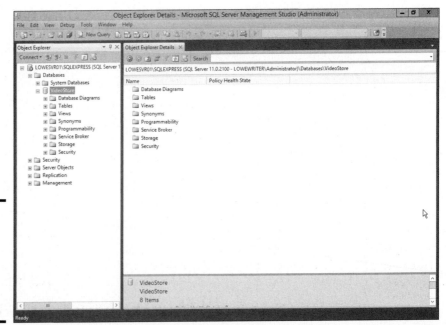

Figure 3-4:
A new database named VideoStore has been created.

The new database is ready to use. It won't be very useful until you define some tables, of course, so read on.

Creating Tables

A database is nothing more than a container for various types of database objects. The most important of these objects are *tables,* which hold the actual data that makes up the database. A database isn't very useful without at least one table. Most real-world databases have more than one table; in fact, many databases have dozens of tables.

To create a table, follow these steps:

1. **Right-click the Tables node for the database, and choose New Table from the contextual menu.**

The window shown in Figure 3-5 appears.

2. **Type the name of the first column of the table and then press the Tab key.**

3. **Choose the data type for the column and then press the Tab key.**

SQL Server has several data types to choose among for each column. Use the drop-down list to choose the appropriate type.

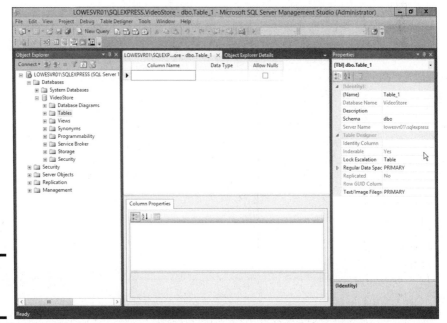

Figure 3-5:
Creating a
new table.

4. **Use the Allow Nulls check box to indicate whether the column should allow null values; then press the Tab key.**

   Nulls are among the most confusing aspects of database design and programming. In a SQL database, *null* means that the item doesn't have a value. It's different from zero (for numbers) or an empty string (for text). Allowing a column to have null values introduces programming complexities, because when you retrieve the value of a column, the program has to anticipate that the value may be missing. But prohibiting nulls (by deselecting the check box) also introduces complexities, because you have to make sure that you provide an explicit value for every column.

   The phrase *null value* is actually an oxymoron. Because *null* means the absence of a value, it doesn't make sense to say that a column can have a null value or that the value of a column is null.

5. **Repeat Steps 2 through 4 to create additional columns.**

   Figure 3-6 shows how the table looks after several columns have been defined.

6. **When all the columns have been created, select the column you want to use as a key field for the table, right-click the column, and choose Set Primary Key from the contextual menu.**

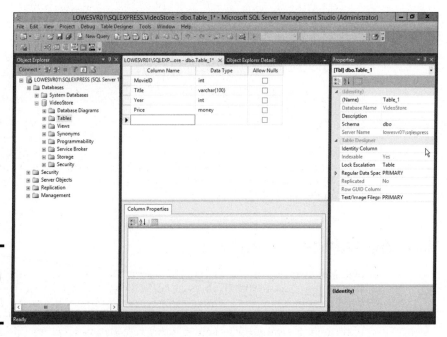

Figure 3-6:
A table with several columns.

A little key icon appears next to that column to indicate that it's the primary key.

(The *primary key* provides a unique value that can be used to identify each row in the table. Most tables use a single column, such as Customer Number or Invoice Number, as the primary key. But some tables create the primary key by combining two or more columns. This type of key is called a *composite key.*)

7. **Right-click the table-name tab that appears above the list of columns, and choose Save from the contextual menu.**

   A Save dialog box appears, prompting you to enter a name for the table.

8. **Type a name for the table and then click OK.**

   The table is created.

Note that each column has a properties page that appears when you select the column. You can set a variety of properties for each column, including the following:

✦ **Default Value:** A value that's supplied for the column if no value is provided when a row is created. This property is especially useful for columns that don't allow null values.

✦ **Description:** A text description that you can use to explain the purpose of the column.

✦ **Identity Specification:** Used to create an *identity field,* which is a field whose value is generated automatically when rows are created. Often, an identity field is used as the primary key field for a table when it's desirable for the table to have a primary key, but no other column in the table provides a unique value for each row.

   When you create an identity field, you can specify two settings that affect how the values are generated: the seed and the increment. The *seed* is the value used for the first row in the table. The *increment* is a value that's added to the seed for each subsequent row. If you specify 1000 for the seed and 1 for the increment, the rows in the table will be numbered 1001, 1002, 1003, and so on.

Editing Tables

SQL Management Studio includes a spreadsheetlike feature that lets you edit the contents of database tables directly. To use it, right-click the table you want to edit, and choose Open Table from the contextual menu. The table opens in a spreadsheetlike window. Then you can add data to the table by entering table values for each row. Figure 3-7 shows a table after some data has been added via the Open Table command.

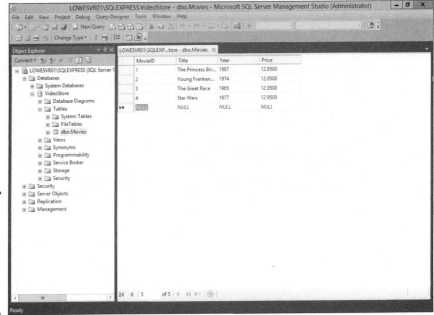

Figure 3-7:
A table with several rows added via the Open Table command.

Note that in addition to inserting new rows, you can edit existing rows. You can also delete one or more rows by selecting the rows you want to delete and pressing the Delete key.

Working with Queries

SQL Management Studio includes a query tool that lets you type SQL commands and execute them. You can type any SQL statement you want in a query window and then click the Execute button to execute the query.

There are two important rules to follow when you work with queries:

✦ Each SQL statement in the query should end with a semicolon.

✦ You must begin the query with a use statement that provides the name of the database.

Here's an example of a query that follows these two rules:

```
use VideoStore;
select * from movies;
```

The `use` statement indicates that the query applies to the `VideoStore` database, and the `select` statement retrieves all the data from the `movies` table.

To use the query tool, click the New Query button on the toolbar. Then enter the statements for your query in the window, and click the Execute button on the toolbar. The results of the query are displayed in the window, as shown in Figure 3-8.

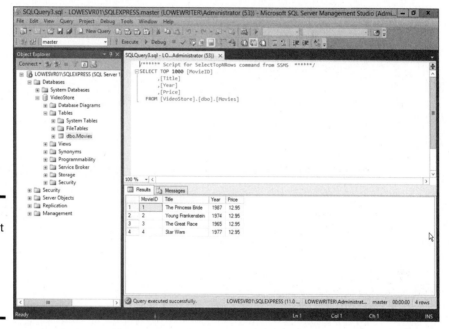

Figure 3-8:
A query that retrieves data from the `Movies` table.

Working with Scripts

One final feature of SQL Management Studio I want to cover in this chapter is the use of scripts. Although you can create databases by using the graphical features presented earlier in this chapter (in the sections "Creating a New Database" and "Creating Tables"), it's actually much better practice to write SQL scripts that contain the `CREATE` commands necessary to create the database, as well as its tables and other objects. That's because during the development and operation of any database application, you often need to delete the database and re-create it from scratch. By scripting these actions, you can delete the database and re-create it simply by running a script.

Fortunately, SQL Management Studio can generate scripts from existing databases and tables. Thus, you can use the visual design features of SQL Management Studio to create your databases initially; then you can generate scripts that let you delete and re-re-create the database easily.

To create a script for a database or table, just right-click the database or table and choose one of the Script As commands from the contextual menu. Figure 3-9 shows the script that results when I right-click the movies table and choose Script Table As➪CREATE To➪New Query Window. As you can see, this command generated a CREATE TABLE statement along with other advanced SQL statements to create the Movies table automatically.

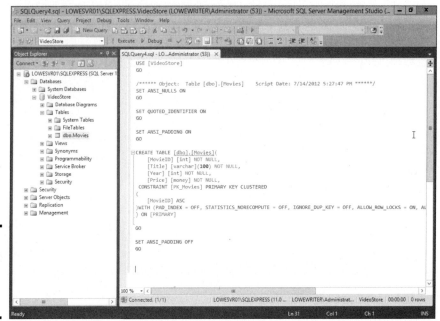

Figure 3-9:
A script that creates the Movies table.

After you've created the script, you can save it to a text file by clicking the Save button. Then you can run the script at any time by following these steps:

1. **Choose File➪Open➪File.**

2. **Select the file you saved the script to.**

3. **Click Open.**

4. **Click the Execute button to run the script.**

The only limitation of this technique is that although you can generate scripts to define your databases and tables, you can't automatically generate scripts to insert data into your tables. If you want scripts that insert data, you have to manually create the INSERT statements to insert the data.

Chapter 4: Using SharePoint

This chapter covers the basics of working with SharePoint 2010 in Windows Server 2012. For more detailed information about SharePoint Portal Server, please refer to *SharePoint 2010 For Dummies,* 2nd Edition, written by Vanessa L. Williams and published by Wiley, of course.

What Is SharePoint?

SharePoint is a web application that lets you create team websites designed to let your network users work together on projects. Among other things, these team websites can include the following features:

✦ Announcements and news

✦ Document libraries that can store and track documents

✦ Discussion forums where team members can discuss issues

✦ Task lists that help keep track of things that need to be done

✦ Contact lists

✦ *Wikis,* which are collections of pages where users can work together to build a repository of interlinked articles

Connecting to a SharePoint Site

Users access SharePoint sites by opening a web browser and browsing to the server that hosts SharePoint. Figure 4-1 shows the default home page of the SharePoint site on a server named `sharepoint.lowewriter.pri`.

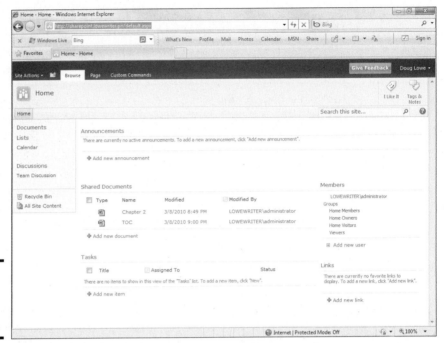

Figure 4-1:
A
SharePoint
site.

The default SharePoint site consists of the following pages:

✦ A home page with announcements, a reminder of upcoming events on the site's calendar, and an area where you can add favorite links

✦ A document library named Shared Documents, where you can store files that can be accessed by other SharePoint users

✦ A calendar

✦ A task list

✦ A discussion area named *Team Discussion*

All the pages on a SharePoint site have several elements in common, including the following:

✦ Near the top left is a title area that displays the name of the SharePoint site — in this case, simply *Home.*

✦ At the top left (above the title area) is a button labeled Site Actions. When you click this button, a menu appears, with commands that let you create additional pages, edit the current page, or manage site settings.

✦ At the top right is a logon control that displays the name of the current user and includes a drop-down menu that lets you sign out, change users, or update your user settings.

✦ Below the logon control is a Help button (with a question-mark icon) that displays useful information about how to use SharePoint.

✦ To the left of the Help button is a search box that lets you search the entire site for specific text. Just enter the text you want to search for and then click the magnifying-glass icon.

✦ Below the title area is a series of one or more tabs called the Top Link Bar. Initially, the Top Link Bar contains a single tab named Home, which takes you to the home page for the site. But you can add links.

✦ A navigation menu called *Quick Launch* runs down the left side of the window. It provides quick access to the individual pages on the site.

✦ The main display area, in the center of each SharePoint page, contains one or more gadgets called *web parts.* SharePoint comes with a collection of web parts that can be added to this area, and additional web parts are available from various sources. If you're handy with ASP.NET web programming, you can even create your own web parts.

Adding Users

One of the first things you'll want to do after you create a SharePoint site is add one or more users for the site. SharePoint recognizes three different *types,* also called *groups,* of users:

✦ **Owners** have full control of the site. Owners can add or remove pages, change the look and feel of pages, manage site settings, and perform any other administrative tasks necessary to keep the site running well. You should create a limited number of owners.

✦ **Members** can add content to the site but can't change the site's overall structure or modify its settings. Most of your users should be Team Site Members.

✦ **Visitors** have read-only access to the site: They can view the site's pages but cannot add content of their own.

Here's the procedure for adding a new member:

1. **Log on to the site as an Owner.**

Only an Owner can manage users. If you created the site yourself, you're already designated as an owner.

2. **Click the Site Actions button and then choose Site Settings.**

This brings up the Site Settings page, shown in Figure 4-2. As you can see, this page contains links that lead to various site administration pages.

3. **Below the Users and Permissions heading, click the People and Groups link.**

This brings up the People and Groups page, as shown in Figure 4-3.

**Book VIII
Chapter 4**

Using SharePoint

Figure 4-2:
The Site
Settings
page.

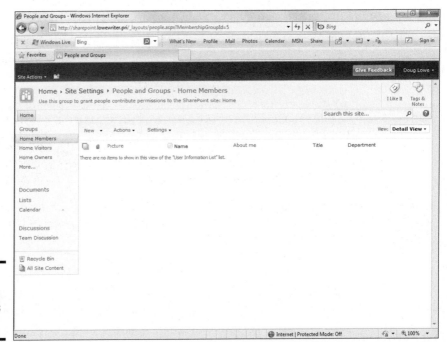

Figure 4-3:
The People
and Groups
page.

4. **Select the group to which you want to add the new user.**

The site groups are listed in the Quick Launch area on the left side of the page. In Figure 4-3, the Members group is selected.

5. **Click the New drop-down list and then choose Add Users.**

The Grant Permissions dialog box appears, as shown in Figure 4-4.

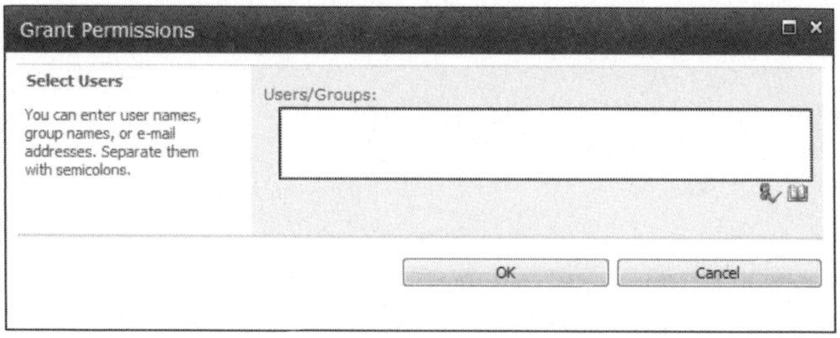

Figure 4-4:
Adding
users.

Grant Permissions

Select Users

You can enter user names,
group names, or e-mail
addresses. Separate them
with semicolons.

Users/Groups:

OK   Cancel

6. **Type the name of the user you want to add in the Users/Groups text box.**

You must type the actual domain account name. To add more than one user, separate the names with semicolons. If you want, you can click the Browse button (represented by an address-book icon) to browse for names.

7. **Click OK.**

The user is created. You're returned to the People and Groups page, where the new user account is now listed (see Figure 4-5).

After you've created a new user, you can edit the user's settings by clicking the user's name. This brings up the User Information page, shown in Figure 4-6. Initially, there isn't much user information — just the user's name and Active Directory account. You can rectify that situation by clicking Actions➪Edit Item, which brings up a form that lets you enter the user's e-mail address, descriptive About Me information, a picture, and so on.

Any SharePoint user can access his or her own User Information page by choosing My Settings from the logon control that appears in the top-right section of each SharePoint page.

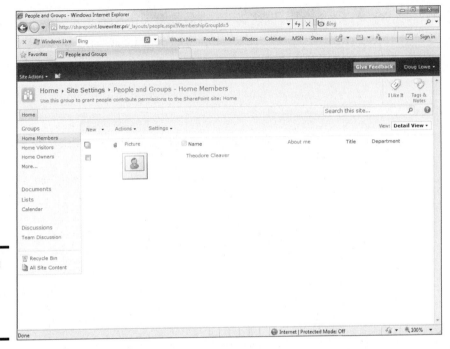

Figure 4-5:
A user
account
has been
created.

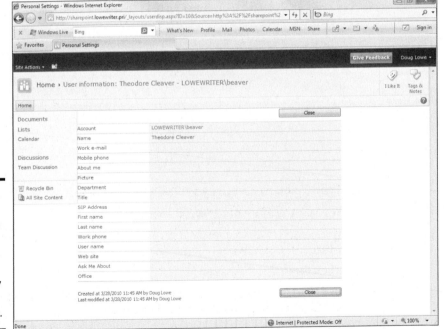

Figure 4-6:
The User
Information
page for a
new user
doesn't
contain any
interesting
information.

Adding and Removing Announcements

The home page includes an area for announcements. As the site owner, you'll want to periodically add new announcements to this page and remove old ones. Here are the steps for adding a new announcement:

1. **Click the Add New Announcement link.**

If you don't see an Add New Announcement link (refer to Figure 4-1), you don't have adequate permissions to add new announcements. You can skip the rest of this procedure.

Assuming that you have adequate permissions, the page shown in Figure 4-7 appears.

Figure 4-7:
The Announcements page.

Book VIII
Chapter 4

Using SharePoint

2. **Type a subject and body for the announcement.**

3. **Set an expiration date, if you want.**

When you set an expiration date, the message is automatically removed when it has expired.

4. **Click Save.**

The new announcement is added to the top of the list of announcements on the home page, as shown in Figure 4-8.

You're done! You and the site's users can now view and enjoy your latest announcement.

Figure 4-8:
The home page with a new announcement.

To edit or remove the announcement, click the announcement's title. This displays a page that lets you modify or delete the announcement.

Creating New Pages

The default SharePoint site consists of several standard pages, including a document library, calendar, and a discussion forum. You can add pages to your SharePoint site to customize it as needed. Many SharePoint sites have multiple document libraries to store different types of documents, for example.

To create a new SharePoint page, click Site Actions and then click More Options. The Create page is displayed, as shown in Figure 4-9.

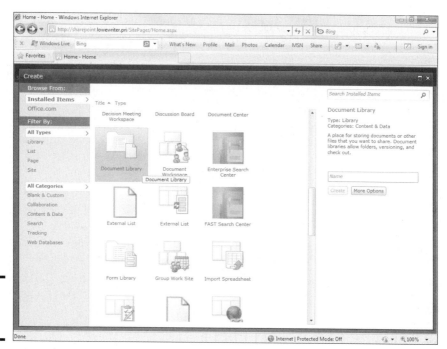

Figure 4-9:
Creating a
new page.

As you can see, SharePoint lets you add many types of pages and sites to your portal. Here are some of the most commonly used ones:

✦ **Announcements:** A list of news items and other short bits of information.

✦ **Basic Meeting Workspace:** An entire site (not just a single page) that lets you plan, organize, and record the results of a meeting. The site includes lists for managing the agenda, meeting attendees, and documents.

✦ **Blank Meeting Workspace:** A blank meeting site, similar to the basic meeting workspace but without the predefined lists.

✦ **Blank Site:** A site (not just a single page) that doesn't add any content.

✦ **Blog:** A blog page.

✦ **Calendar:** A group calendar. SharePoint calendar pages track events related to the SharePoint site, but they can be integrated with users' personal calendar managers, such as Microsoft Outlook.

✦ **Charitable Contributions Web:** Tracks information about fundraising campaigns.

✦ **Contacts:** A contact list. Here, you can find a list of names and addresses that can be integrated with other contact managers, including Outlook and Exchange.

✦ **Content Page:** A page that you can edit any way you want.

✦ **Custom List:** A list in which you can specify the data to be recorded for each item in the list.

✦ **Discussion Board:** A message forum where users can post messages and post replies to other user's messages.

✦ **Document Library:** A repository of document files in a system of folders and subfolders. Document libraries can track multiple versions of documents, and they give users the ability to check documents in and out. For more information about document libraries, see "Working with Document Libraries," later in this chapter.

✦ **Document Workspace:** A collaboration center where users can work together on shared documents. Document workspaces are nicely integrated with Microsoft Office 2010.

✦ **Form Library:** A repository of XML-based business forms. Form libraries are designed to work with a forms editor such as Microsoft's InfoPath.

✦ **Group Work Site:** A site designed for groups working together on a project. The site includes a group calendar, circulation list, phone-call memo, document library, and other lists.

✦ **Issue Tracking:** Tracks problems associated with a project or item.

✦ **Links:** A list of links to other web pages.

✦ **Picture Library:** A collection of pictures. Picture libraries can offer users the ability to view thumbnails, download picture files, and easily create slideshows.

✦ **Project Tasks:** A list of project-management tasks that can be viewed as a Gantt chart.

✦ **Survey:** A list of questions that can be answered by users.

✦ **Web Part Page:** A web page to which you can add standard or customized web parts.

✦ **Wiki Page Library:** A collection of interconnected articles.

When you click one of the page types on the Create page, SharePoint prompts you for the basic options for the page — typically, just the name of the page — in the pane on the right side of the window, as shown earlier in Figure 4-9. To create the item, type a name in the text box, and click Create.

If you want to set additional options, you can click the More Options button in the pane on the right side of the page to display a new page that asks for the additional information. The More Options page for a Document Library, for example (shown in Figure 4-10), asks you to enter the name and description for the document library, and lets you choose whether to include the library in the Quick Launch menu, choose whether to track version history for documents in the library, and specify the default file type for new documents added to the library. After you enter the requested information, click the Create button to create the page.

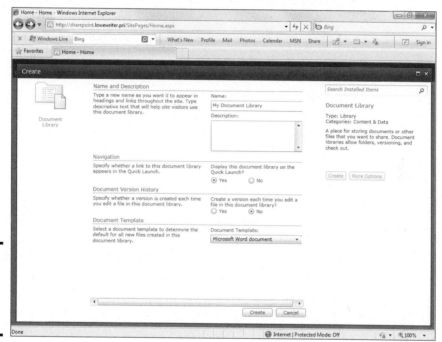

Figure 4-10:
Creating
a new
document
library.

Editing the Quick Launch Menu

The Quick Launch menu is the menu that appears on the left side of SharePoint pages. It provides one-click access to the most important pages on the site.

In most cases, you'll want to include any new pages you add to a SharePoint site to the Quick Launch menu. Otherwise, the site's users will have difficulty locating those pages. You can specify that a new page is added to the Quick Launch menu when you create the page, or you can add the page later if you forget.

To modify the Quick Launch menu, click Site Actions, choose Site Settings, and then click the Quick Launch link. This displays the page shown in Figure 4-11, which lets you modify the way that items appear in the Quick Launch menu. You can use this page to add or remove items, change the order in which items appear, or add or change existing headings.

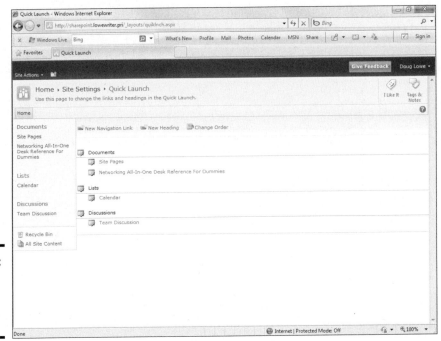

Figure 4-11:
Editing
the Quick
Launch
menu.

Working with Document Libraries

In many ways, document libraries are the heart of SharePoint. They're often the most important and most frequently used pages on a SharePoint site. In fact, the purpose of many SharePoint sites is to enable a team of people to collaborate on the creation of the documents stored in a document library.

Figure 4-12 shows a document library named *Networking All-in-One For Dummies,* which I might use if I wanted to use SharePoint to help with the development of a book such as this. As you can see, I've added three Microsoft Word documents to the library so far.

As a network administrator, you need to know the single most important thing about SharePoint document libraries (and maybe about SharePoint in general): Documents stored in a SharePoint library aren't stored as separate files on the server computer's file system. Instead, they're stored in a SQL database. The bottom-line result of this fact is this: After you (or a user) create a document in a SharePoint library, that document can be accessed and managed only from SharePoint. You can't open Windows Explorer and navigate to the file via the Windows folder structure.

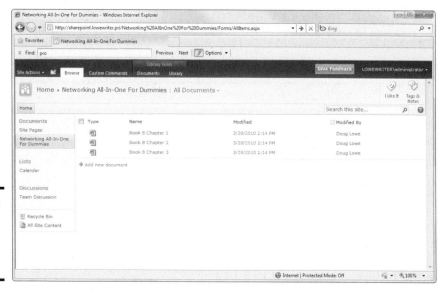

Figure 4-12:
A
SharePoint
document
library.

The following paragraphs describe some things you can do with documents in SharePoint document libraries:

✦ **To add an existing file to a document library,** click the Upload button and then choose Upload Document. This brings up the page shown in Figure 4-13, from which you can upload an existing file. Just type the file-name (with path) for the file, or click the Browse button and browse for the file; then click OK to upload the file.

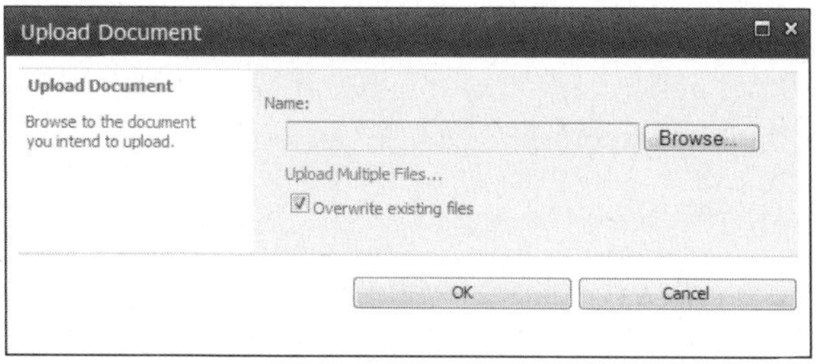

Figure 4-13:
Uploading
an existing
file to a
SharePoint
document
library.

**Book VIII
Chapter 4**

Using SharePoint

✦ **To open a file,** just click the filename in the document library. The application associated with the file launches and opens the document.

✦ **To display a shortcut menu with useful commands,** hover the mouse over a document name. In a moment, a border appears around the file-name, with a drop-down arrow at the right. Click this arrow to reveal the shortcut menu.

✦ **To check out a document,** right-click it and choose Check Out from the contextual menu. This prevents other users from changing the file until you check the file back in by right-clicking it and choosing Check In from the contextual menu.

✦ **To organize documents in document libraries,** create folders. To create a folder, click the New button and then choose the New Folder command.

Book IX

Managing Linux Systems

The 5th Wave   By Rich Tennant

"They can predict earthquakes and seizures, why <u>not</u> server failures?"

Contents at a Glance

Chapter 1: Installing a Linux Server

In This Chapter

✔ Getting ready to install Linux

✔ Installing Linux

✔ Adding additional packages after installation

his chapter presents the procedures that you need to follow to install Linux on a server computer. The details provided are specifically for Fedora 17, a free Linux distribution sponsored by Red Hat. However, the procedures for installing other distributions of Linux are similar, so you won't have any trouble adapting these procedures if you're using a different distribution.

Planning a Linux Server Installation

Before you begin the installation program, you need to make a number of preliminary decisions. The following sections describe the decisions that you need to make before you install Linux.

Checking system requirements

Before you install Linux, make sure that the computer meets the minimum requirements. Although the minimum requirements for Linux are considerably less than those for the latest version of Windows Server, you can't run Linux on an abacus. The following paragraphs summarize the minimum capabilities you need:

✦ **A Pentium-based computer:** Even an ancient and slow Pentium 3 system will run some builds of Linux although performance will be slow. The minimum recommended for Fedora 17 is a Pentium 4.

✦ **768MB of RAM or more:** Of course, the more the better, but Linux can make do with much less RAM than Windows.

✦ **A hard drive with enough free space to hold the packages that you need to install:** A suitable minimum is 10GB.

✦ **A DVD-ROM drive from which to install the operating system**

✦ **Just about any video card and monitor combination:** You don't need anything fancy for a server. In fact, fancy video cards often lead to hardware compatibility issues. Stick to a basic video card.

✦ **An extra mouse:** If you're converting an old junker computer to a Linux server and you've lost the mouse (that seems to happen a lot), pick one up at your local office supply store. A cheap one costs only about $15.

✦ **A network interface card (NIC)**

Choosing a distribution

Because the *kernel* (that is, the core operating functions) of the Linux operating system is free, several companies have created their own *distributions* of Linux, which include the Linux OS along with a bundle of packages, such as administration tools, web servers, and other useful utilities, as well as printed documentation.

The following are some of the more popular Linux distributions:

✦ **Fedora:** One of the popular Linux distributions. You can download Fedora free from `http://fedoraproject.org`. You can also obtain it by purchasing any of several books on Fedora that include the Fedora distribution on DVD or CD-ROM.

All the examples in this book are based on Fedora 17.

✦ **Mandriva Linux:** Another popular Linux distribution, one that is often recommended as the easiest for first-time Linux users to install. This distribution was formerly known as *Mandrake Linux.* Go to `www.mandriva.com` for more information.

✦ **Ubuntu:** A Linux distribution that has gained popularity in recent years. It focuses on ease of use. For more information, go to `www.ubuntu.com`.

✦ **SUSE:** Pronounced *SOO-zuh,* like the name of the famous composer of marches; a popular Linux distribution sponsored by Novell. You can find more information at `www.suse.com`.

✦ **Slackware:** One of the oldest Linux distributions and still popular, especially among Linux old-timers. A full installation of Slackware gives you all the tools that you need to set up a network or Internet server. See `www.slackware.com` for more information.

All distributions of Linux include the same core components: the Linux kernel, an X Server, popular windows managers such as GNOME and KDE, compilers, Internet programs such as Apache, Sendmail, and so on. However, not all Linux distributions are created equal. In particular, the manufacturer of each distribution creates its own installation and configuration programs to install and configure Linux.

I can't see my C: drive!

Linux and Windows have a completely different method of referring to your computer's hard drives and partitions. The differences can take some getting used to for experienced Windows users.

Windows uses a separate letter for each drive and partition on your system. For example, if you have a single drive formatted into three partitions, Windows identifies the partitions as drives C:, D:, and E:. Each of these drives has its own root directory, which can, in turn, contain additional directories used to organize your files. As far as Windows is concerned, drives C:, D:, and E: are completely separate drives even though the drives are actually just partitions on a single drive.

Linux doesn't use drive letters. Instead, Linux combines all the drives and partitions into a single directory hierarchy. In Linux, one of the partitions is designated as the *root* partition. The root partition is roughly analogous to the root directory of the C: drive on a Windows system. Then, the other partitions can be *mounted* on the root partition and treated as if they were directories on the root partition. For example, you may designate the first partition as the root partition and then mount the second partition as /user and the third

partition as /var. Then, any files stored in the /user directory would actually be stored in the second partition, and files stored in the /var directory would be stored in the third partition.

The directory to which a drive mounts is called the drive's *mount point*.

Notice that Linux uses regular forward slash characters (/) to separate directory names rather than the backward slash characters (\) used by Windows. Typing backslashes instead of regular slashes is one of the most common mistakes made by new Linux users.

While I'm on the subject, Linux uses a different convention for naming files, too. In Windows, filenames end in a three- or four-letter extension that's separated from the rest of the filename by a period. The extension is used to indicate the file type. For example, files that end in .exe are program files, but files that end in .doc are word-processing documents.

Linux doesn't use file extensions, but periods are often used in Linux filenames to separate different parts of the name — and the last part often indicates the file type. For example, ldap.conf and pine.conf are both configuration files.

The installation program is what makes or breaks a Linux distribution. All the distributions I list in this section have easy-to-use installation programs that automatically detect the hardware that's present on your computer and configure Linux to work with that hardware, thus eliminating most — if not all — manual configuration chores. The installation programs also let you select the Linux packages that you want to install and let you set up one or more user accounts besides the root account.

Thinking about multiboot

Linux comes with a boot loader program called *GRUB* that lets you choose from several installed operating systems when you start your computer. GRUB makes it possible to keep your existing Windows system on a computer and install Linux into a separate partition. Then, each time you start the computer, you can decide whether to start Windows or Linux.

If you're new to Linux and want to experiment with it a bit before you commit to it, multiboot is a good way to go. But if you're setting up a production server on a machine that will be devoted to Linux, there's no reason to mess around with multiboot.

Going virtual

Another common way to install Linux is in a virtual machine running within the Windows operating system. In fact, all the examples in this minibook were tested using Oracle VM VirtualBox, a free virtualization platform you can download from `www.virtualbox.org`. For more information, see Chapter 8 of Book II.

Deciding on your TCP/IP configuration

Before you install the OS, you should have a plan for how you will implement TCP/IP on the network. Here are some of the things you need to decide or find out:

✦ The public IP subnet address and mask for your network

✦ The domain name for the network

✦ The host name for the server?

✦ Whether the server obtain its address from DHCP

✦ Whether the server have a static IP address — and if so, what?

✦ Whether the server be a DHCP server

✦ The default gateway for the server — that the IP address of the network's Internet router

✦ Whether the server be a DNS server

If the server will host TCP/IP servers (such as DHCP or DNS), you'll probably want to assign the server a static IP address.

For more information about planning your TCP/IP configuration, see Book IV.

Installing Fedora 17

After you plan your installation and prepare the computer, you're ready
to actually install Linux. The following procedure describes the steps you
must follow to install Fedora 17 on a computer that has a bootable DVD-
ROM drive:

1. **Insert the Fedora 17 CD in the DVD drive and restart the computer.**

The computer boots from the DVD drive and displays a Linux boot
prompt, which looks like this:

    Boot:

If you don't have the installation DVD, download the DVD images from
`http://fedoraproject.org`. Then, use DVD-burning software to
create a DVD from the image.

2. **Press Enter.**

The computer starts Linux from the installation disk. The screen shown
in Figure 1-1 soon appears.

3. **Press Enter.**

A bunch of text messages fly by your screen as Linux starts up.
Eventually, the screen shown in Figure 1-2 appears, asking you which
language you'd like to use.

4. **Choose your language and then click Next.**

The Keyboard Configuration screen appears, as shown in Figure 1-3. It
lets you choose from about 55 different keyboard styles.

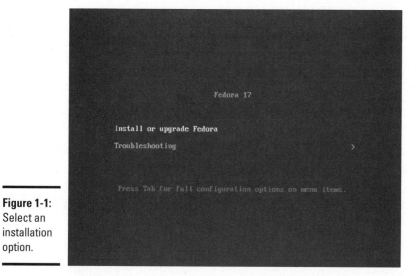

Figure 1-1:
Select an
installation
option.

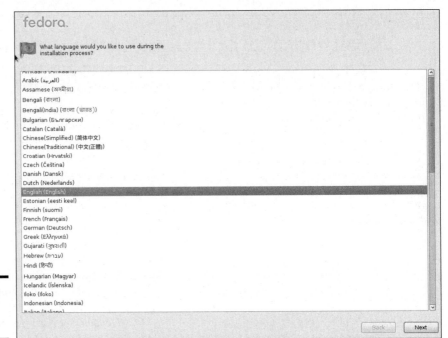

Figure 1-2:
Choose a
language.

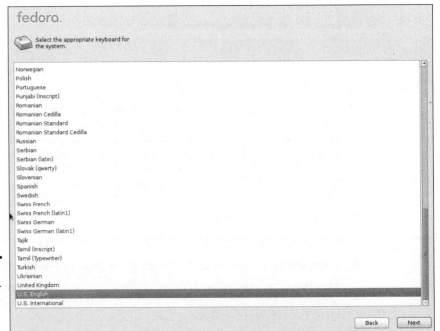

Figure 1-3:
Choose your
keyboard
here.

Virtual consoles and the installation program

Linux is inherently a command line–oriented OS. Graphical user interfaces — including the installation program's GUI — are provided by an optional component called *X Window System*. However, while you're working with the GUI of the installation program, Linux keeps several additional command line consoles open. Normally, you don't need to use every one of these consoles during installation. However, if something goes wrong during installation, these consoles may be useful:

✔ **Console 1: The Installation dialog box.** This is the main installation console. You see it when Setup first starts. After the GUI takes over, it's hidden in the background. You can call it up by pressing Ctrl+Alt+F1.

✔ **Console 2: Shell prompt.** This console provides you with a shell prompt, from which you can enter Linux commands. If you need to do something manually during installation,

you can do it from this console. The keyboard shortcut is Ctrl+Alt+F2.

✔ **Console 3: Install log.** This console lists messages generated by the installation program. You can get to it by pressing Ctrl+Alt+F3.

✔ **Console 4: System log.** This console displays system-related messages. You can get to it by pressing Ctrl+Alt+F4.

✔ **Console 5: Other messages.** Still more messages may appear in this console, which you can open by pressing Ctrl+Alt+F5.

✔ **Console 6: X graphical display.** This is the console where the GUI of the installation program is displayed. If you use a Ctrl+Alt keyboard combination to view any of the other logs, press Ctrl+Alt+F7 to return to the installation GUI.

---

5. **Choose your keyboard type and then click Next.**

6. **Click Next.**

   The Setup program checks the disk. If existing partitions are found, Setup will ask which partition you want to install Linux into. If there are no partitions on the disk, Setup displays the warning screen shown in Figure 1-4. This screen indicates that because Setup doesn't see any partitions, it can't be certain that the disk is empty. In most cases, the disk is empty, so you can continue with the installation by clicking the Yes, Discard Any Data button.

7. **Click the Yes, Discard Any Data button.**

   Fedora asks for the host name for the computer, as shown in Figure 1-5.

8. **Enter the name you want to assign this computer and then click Next.**

   The Time Zone Selection screen appears, as shown in Figure 1-6. On this screen is a map of the world with dots representing about 500 different locations throughout the world.

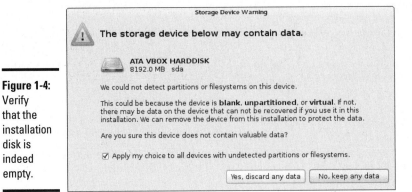

Figure 1-4:
Verify that the installation disk is indeed empty.

Figure 1-5:
Choose the host name.

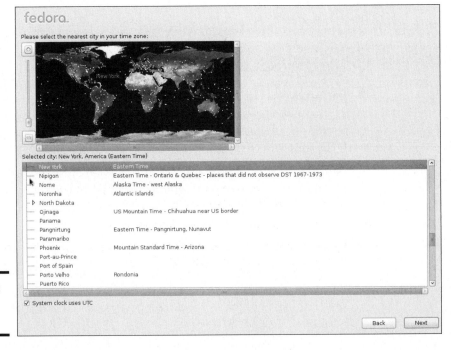

Figure 1-6:
Choose a time zone.

9. **Click the location that's closest to you and then click Next.**

The Set Root Password screen appears, as shown in Figure 1-7. This screen lets you enter the all-important root account password. It's vital that this account be protected by a strong password, so choose a good one. Write down the password somewhere and store it in a secure location away from the computer.

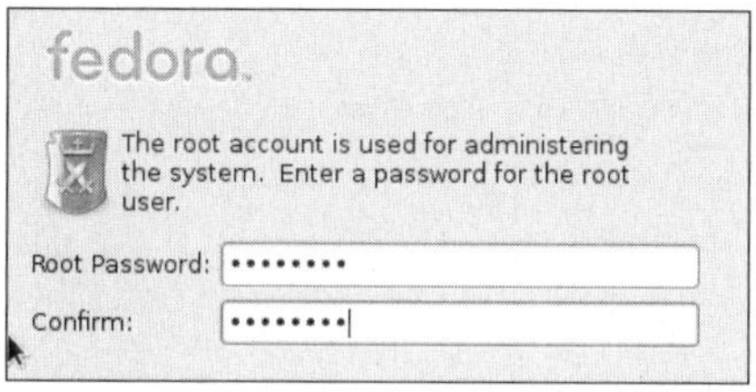

Figure 1-7:
Set the root
password.

fedora.

The root account is used for administering
the system. Enter a password for the root
user.

Root Password: ••••••••

Confirm: ••••••••|

The screen shown in Figure 1-8 displays, providing several options for how you want to install Linux into partitions on the installation disk. The alternatives are

- *Use All Space:* This option removes all existing partitions from the disk drive and creates one large partition for the new Linux installation.

- *Replace Existing Linux System(s):* This option removes any existing Linux partitions but leaves other partitions in place. Then, a single partition is created for the new Linux installation. This is the preferred option.

- *Shrink Current System:* This option reduces the size of existing partitions as much as possible and then creates a new partition from the free space thus created.

- *Use Free Space:* This option creates a new Linux partition in any existing free space on the disk.

- *Create Custom Layout:* If none of the above options work for your situation, you can select this option. Then, you'll be prompted to create a new partition for the Linux installation.

10. **Select your partitioning option and then click Next.**

Fedora warns you that it is about to wipe out any existing data on your hard disk, as shown in Figure 1-9.

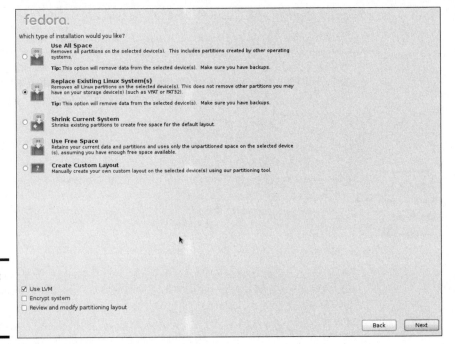

Figure 1-8:
Select a
partition
option.

Figure 1-9:
Fedora
warns you
that existing
data will be
lost.

11. **Click the Write Changes to Disk button.**

The installation program displays a bunch of progress boxes as it creates various components of the Linux system. When everything has
been created, the screen shown in Figure 1-10 is displayed, where you
can choose the optional features that you want to install.

12. **Select the Web Server and the Customize Now radio buttons and then
click Next.**

The screen shown in Figure 1-11 appears. This screen allows you to further customize the packages to be installed.

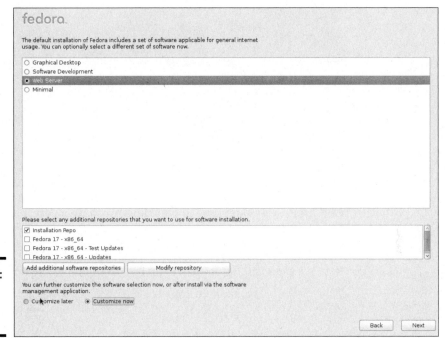

Figure 1-10:
Choose
optional
features.

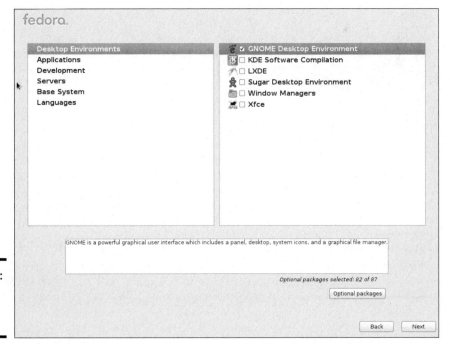

Figure 1-11:
Select
additional
packages.

13. **Click Servers.**

A list of optional server packages appears.

14. **Select the server packages you want to install and then click Next.**

For example, to add the DNS server function to your Linux server, choose DNS Server.

After you click Next, the installation program does some double-checking to make sure that none of the packages you chose depend on other packages that you haven't chosen. If it finds such a dependency, it adds the dependent package so that your system will function properly.

After these dependencies have been verified, the installation program begins installing Linux. This will take a while — maybe a long while — so now would be a good time to grab a book or take a nap.

When the installation finishes, the screen shown in Figure 1-12 is shown. Pat yourself on the back for your ingenuity and perseverance.

15. **Remove the installation disk from the drive and then click Reboot.**

The system is rebooted. Installation is done!

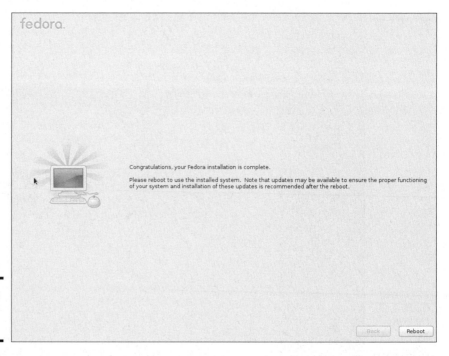

fedora.

Congratulations, your Fedora installation is complete.

Please reboot to use the installed system. Note that updates may be available to ensure the proper functioning of your system and installation of these updates is recommended after the reboot.

Back   Reboot

Figure 1-12:
Congratula-
tions!

Using the Setup Agent

When Fedora restarts the first time after completing the installation program, it launches a handy Setup Agent, as shown in Figure 1-13. (*Note:* The Setup Agent runs only if you installed a GUI.) The Setup Agent resembles the installation program, but it asks a few questions that the installation program forgot to ask.

When the Setup Agent starts, follow these steps to see it through to completion:

1. **On the Welcome screen, click Forward to get started.**

The Setup Agent displays the License Agreement, as if after going through the previous 15 steps to install Fedora, you're now going to decide you don't agree to their terms. It's useless to resist.

2. **Click Forward to confirm your acceptance of the license agreement.**

The Setup Agent asks you to create a user account so that you don't have to access the system by using the root account, as shown in Figure 1-14.

Figure 1-13:
The Setup
Agent.

Welcome

> Welcome
> License
> Information
> Create User
> Date and Time
> Hardware Profile

Welcome

There are a few more steps to take before your system is ready to use. The Setup Agent will now guide you through some basic configuration. Please click the "Forward" button in the lower right corner to continue

fedora

Back   Forward

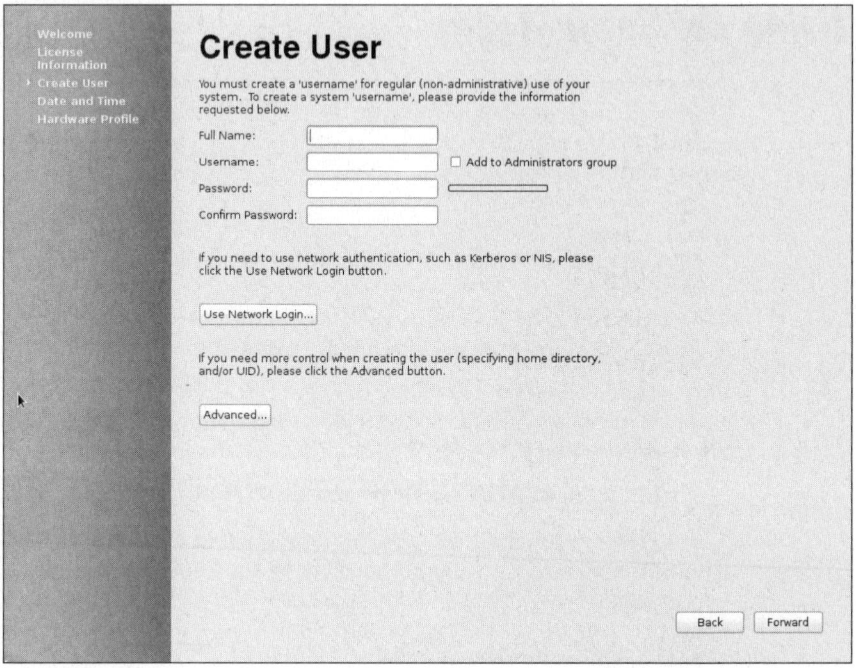

Figure 1-14:
Create
a user
account.

3. **Type a name and password for the user account and then click Forward.**

   The Setup Agent now asks you to set the date and time.

4. **Select the correct date and time and then click Forward.**

   The Setup Agent asks whether you want to submit details about your hardware configuration as part of an effort to improve Linux's support for various hardware devices.

5. **Click Send Profile or Do Not Send Profile and then click Finish.**

That's all there is. Your Linux system is now set up and ready to go.

Chapter 2: Getting Used to Linux

In This Chapter

✔ Getting used to the Linux way of thinking

✔ Logging on and off Linux

✔ Using a GUI

✔ Working with commands

✔ Setting up user accounts

*B*efore you can set up Linux to do serious networking, you need to discover the basics of getting around Linux. In this chapter, you find out those basics. You see how to log on and off Linux, how the Linux file system works, and how to use commands. I also introduce you to GNOME, the graphical user interface (GUI) that's used most with Fedora and many other Linux distributions. Finally, I show you the basics of setting up a Linux user account.

In this chapter, I assume that you have plenty of experience with Windows, so I focus mostly on the differences between Linux and Windows — which, unfortunately, are myriad.

Linux: It Isn't Windows

Before I get into the details of actually using a Linux system, you need to understand some basic differences between Linux and Windows that will puzzle you at first. Linux looks a lot like Windows, but underneath, it's very different. You won't have any trouble finding out how to point and click your way through the GNOME user interface, but before long, you'll run into Linux file-naming conventions, terminal windows, configuration files, and a host of other significant differences.

The following sections describe some of the more important differences between Linux and Windows.

X Window

Linux doesn't have a built-in graphical user interface (GUI) as Windows does. Instead, the GUI in Linux is provided by an optional component called *X Window System.* You can run Linux without X Window, in which case you interact with Linux by typing commands. If you prefer to use a GUI, you must install and run X Window.

X Window is split into two parts:

✦ A server component, called an **X Server,** handles the basic chores of managing multiple windows and providing graphics services for application programs.

✦ A user interface (UI) component, called a **window manager,** provides UI features such as menus, buttons, toolbars, a taskbar, and so on. Several different window managers are available, each with a different look and feel. The most popular is GNOME. I describe it in more detail later in this chapter, in the section "Using GNOME."

Virtual consoles

Linux is a true multiuser OS. This means that you can log on to Linux by using one user account and then log on by using a different account, so that you're logged on twice at the same time. You switch back and forth between the different user sessions, and actions that you take in one session don't affect any of your other sessions.

In addition to an X Window client such as GNOME, Linux provides a traditional text-based environment — a *console* — through which you can enter Linux commands to perform any function available in Linux. The more you work with Linux, the more you'll discover the limitations of even a sophisticated GUI such as GNOME. When that happens, you'll turn to a console where you can enter brute-force commands.

Because Linux is a multiuser system, it lets you work with more than one console. In fact, you actually have six virtual consoles at your disposal. You can switch to a particular virtual console by pressing Ctrl+Alt+F1 through F6. For example, to switch to virtual console 3, press Ctrl+Alt+F3.

When a GUI such as GNOME is running, you can switch to it by pressing Ctrl+Alt+F7.

Understanding the file system

The Linux file system is a bit different from the Windows file system. Two of the most obvious differences are actually superficial:

✦ Linux uses forward slashes rather than backward slashes to separate directories. Thus, /home/doug is a valid path in Linux; \Windows\System32 is a valid path in Windows.

✦ Linux filenames don't use extensions. You can use periods within a filename, but unlike Windows, the final period doesn't identify a file extension.

The fundamental difference between the Linux and Windows file system is that Linux treats everything in the entire system as a file, and it organizes everything into one gigantic tree that begins at a single root. When I say, "Everything is treated as a file," I mean that hardware devices such as floppy drives, serial ports, and Ethernet adapters are treated as files.

The root of the Linux file system is the root partition from which the OS boots. Additional partitions, including other devices that support file systems such as CD-ROM drives, floppy drives, or drives accessed over the network, can be grafted into the tree as directories called *mount points*. Thus, a directory in the Linux file system may actually be a separate hard drive.

Another important aspect of the Linux file system is that the directories that compose a Linux system are governed by a standard called the Filesystem Hierarchy Standard (FHS). This standard spells out which directories a Linux file system should have. Because most Linux systems conform to this standard, you can trust that key files will always be found in the same place.

Table 2-1 lists the top-level directories that are described in the FHS.

Table 2-1   Top-Level Directories in a Linux File System

Directory	Description
/bin	Essential command binaries
/boot	Static files of the boot loader
/dev	Devices
/etc	Configuration files for the local computer
/home	Home directories for users
/lib	Shared libraries and kernel modules
/mnt	Mount point for file systems mounted temporarily
/opt	Add-on applications and packages
/root	Home directory for the root user
/sbin	Essential system binaries
/tmp	Temporary files
/usr	Read-only, shared files such as binaries for user commands and libraries
/var	Variable data files

On Again, Off Again

Any user who accesses a Linux system, whether locally or over a network, must be authenticated by a valid user account on the system. In the following sections, you find out how to log on and off of a Linux system and how to shut down the system.

Logging on

When Linux boots up, it displays a series of startup messages as it starts the various services that compose a working Linux system. Assuming that you selected X Window when you installed Linux, you're eventually greeted by the screen shown in Figure 2-1. To log on to Linux, click your user name, then type your password and press Enter. (Note that this logon procedure is for Fedora. Other distributions have similar logon procedures.)

As a part of the installation process (described in Chapter 1 of this mini-book), the Setup Agent created a user account for you. You should use this user account rather than the root user account whenever possible. Use the root account only when you are making major changes to the system's configuration. When you're doing routine work, log on as an ordinary user in order to avoid accidentally corrupting your system.

Figure 2-1:
Begin by
logging on.

When you log on, Linux grinds its gears for a moment and then displays the GNOME desktop, which I describe later in this chapter.

Logging off

After you've logged on, you'll probably want to know how to log off. To do so, click your username in the upper right corner of the screen, and then choose Log Out. A dialog box asks whether you're sure that you want to log out. Click Log Out.

Shutting down

As with any OS, you should never turn off the power to a Linux server without first properly shutting down the system. You can shut down a Linux system by using one of these two techniques:

✦ Press Ctrl+Alt+Delete.

✦ Click on your user name in the upper right corner of the screen, then choose Shut Down.

Using GNOME

Figure 2-2 shows a typical GNOME desktop with the Text Editor application open. Although the GNOME desktop looks a lot different from the Windows desktop, many of the basic skills used for working with Microsoft Windows — such as moving or resizing windows, minimizing or maximizing windows, and using drag-and-drop to move items between windows — are almost exactly the same in GNOME.

Figure 2-2:
The
desktop.

The following paragraphs describe some of the key features of the GNOME desktop:

✦ The Activities Overview provides a single access point for all GNOME applications. It provides fast access to common functions, such as Internet browsing, e-mail, or file management, as well as desktop access to other applications. You can access Activities Overview by pressing the Windows key on the keyboard or clicking Activities in the top-left corner. (The screen in Figure 2-2 shows the Activities Overview open.)

✦ The search box in the top-right corner is the easiest way to find things in GNOME. For example, if you want to run the gedit program to edit a text file, search for "gedit." Or if you want to fiddle with network settings, search for "Network."

✦ To manage your system or user settings, click your name at the top right of the screen. This reveals a menu with options for various settings.

Getting to a Command Shell

You can get to a command shell in one of two basic ways when you need to run Linux commands directly. The first is to press Ctrl+Alt+Fx to switch to one of the virtual consoles, where Fx is one of the function keys, from F1 through F12. (If you aren't sure which function key to use to open a virtual console, refer to the "Virtual consoles" section in this chapter.) Then, you can log on and run commands to your heart's content. When you're done, press Ctrl+Alt+F7 to return to GNOME.

Alternatively, you can open a command shell directly in GNOME by opening the Activities Overview, clicking Applications, and then clicking the Terminal icon. This opens a command shell in a window right on the GNOME desktop, as shown in Figure 2-3. Because this shell runs within the user account that GNOME is logged on as, you don't have to log on. You can just start typing commands. When you're done, type **Exit** to close the window.

Figure 2-3:
A terminal
window.

Managing User Accounts

One of the most common network administration tasks is adding a user account. The Setup Agent prompts you to create a user account the first time you start Linux after installing it. However, you'll probably need to create additional accounts.

Each Linux user account has the following information associated with it:

✦ **Username:** The name the user types to log on to the Linux system.

✦ **Full name:** The user's full name.

✦ **Home directory:** The directory that the user is placed in when he or she logs on. In Fedora, the default home directory is `/home/username`. For example, if the username is `blowe`, the home directory will be `/home/blowe`.

✦ **Shell:** The program used to process Linux commands. Several shell programs are available. In most distributions, the default shell is `/bin/bash`.

✦ **Group:** You can create group accounts, which make it easy to apply identical access rights to groups of users.

✦ **User ID:** The internal identifier for the user.

You can add a new user by using the `useradd` command. For example, to create a user account named `slowe`, using default values for the other account information, open a Terminal window or switch to a virtual console and type this command:

```
# useradd slowe
```

The `useradd` command has many optional parameters that you can use to set account information, such as the user's home directory and shell.

Fortunately, most Linux distributions come with special programs that simplify routine system management tasks. Fedora is no exception. It comes with a program called User Manager, shown in Figure 2-4. To start this program, click Activities, click Applications, and then double-click Users and Groups (scroll down to find it).

To create a user with User Manager, click the Add User button. This brings up a dialog box that asks for the user's name, password, and other information. Fill out this dialog box and then click OK.

The User Manager also lets you create groups. You can simplify the task of administering users by applying access rights to groups rather than individual users. Then, when a user needs access to a resource, you can add the user to the group that has the needed access.

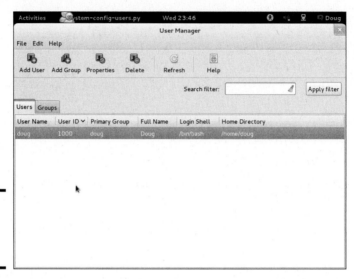

Figure 2-4:
Managing
users and
groups.

To create a group, click the Add Group button. A dialog box appears, asking for the name of the new group. Type the name you want and then click OK.

To add a user to a group, click the Groups tab in the User Manager. Then, double-click the group to which you want to add users. This brings up the Group Properties dialog box. Click the Group Users tab and then select the users that you want to belong to the group.

Chapter 3: Basic Linux Network Configuration

In This Chapter

✓ **Configuring network interfaces**

✓ **Looking directly at network configuration files**

✓ **Using the ifconfig command to display network status**

*I*n many cases, configuring a Linux server for networking is a snap. When you install Linux, the installation program automatically detects your network adapters and installs the appropriate drivers. Then, you're prompted for basic network configuration information, such as the computer's IP address, host name, and so on.

However, you may need to manually change your network settings after installation. You may also need to configure advanced networking features that aren't configured during installation. In this chapter, you discover the basic procedures for configuring Linux networking services.

Using the Network Configuration Program

Before you can use a network interface to access a network, you have to configure the interface's basic TCP/IP options, such as its IP address, host name, Domain Name System (DNS) servers, and so on. This configuration is automatically set up when you install Linux, but you may need to change it later on. In this section, I show you how to do that by using Fedora's Network settings program. You can access this program by clicking your name in the top-right corner of the screen, choosing Settings, and then choosing Network.

If you prefer a more masochistic approach to configuring your network, see the section "Working with Network Configuration Files," later in this chapter.

The Network Configuration program lets you configure the basic TCP/IP settings for a network interface by pointing and clicking your way through tabbed windows. Here are the steps:

1. **Click your user name at the top-right of the screen, select System Settings, and then click Network.**

The Network application appears, as shown in Figure 3-1.

Figure 3-1:
The
Network
application.

2. **Select the network interface that you want to configure and then click Options.**

This summons the Editing window, as shown in Figure 3-2.

Figure 3-2:
Editing a
network
connection.

3. **Click the IPv4 Settings tab.**

The screen shown in Figure 3-3 is displayed.

Figure 3-3:
Configuring
IPv4
settings.

4. **To configure the device to use DHCP, select Automatic (DHCP) in the Method drop-down.**

If you plan on setting up this computer to be your network's DHCP or DNS server, you shouldn't select this check box. Instead, you should assign a static IP address as described in Step 5.

5. **To configure the device with a static IP address, select Manual in the Method drop-down.**

This enables the controls shown in Figure 3-4.

6. **Click the Add button to enter an IP address for the network interface, and then enter the address, netmask, and gateway addresses.**

The IP address should be located on one of the standard private sub-nets. Typically, you'll use an address in the form 192.168.*x.x*.

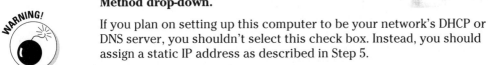

If you're setting up this computer to be the gateway router that will manage traffic between your local network and the Internet, use a static address that's easy to remember, such as 192.168.1.1.

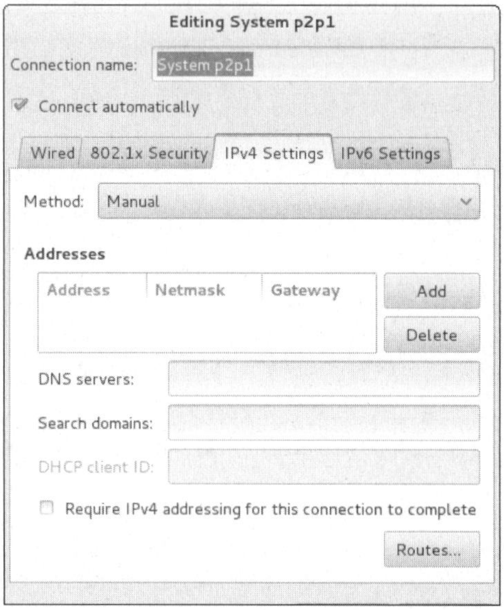

Figure 3-4:
Manual IP
configuration.

The subnet mask should be the mask that's appropriate for the IP address you choose. For a 192.168.*x.x* address, use 255.255.255.0.

The default gateway address should be the address of the gateway router that links your network to the Internet. If this computer *is* the gateway router, specify the gateway address provided to you by your Internet service provider (ISP).

7. **Enter the IP addresses for the DNS servers that you want to use in the DNS Servers text box.**

   If your network runs its own DNS server, you can specify its address here. Otherwise, you have to get the DNS server addresses from your ISP.

8. **Click Save.**

   Any changes you made to the network configuration are saved, and you return to the Network application.

9. **Restart the network services.**

   For the gory details on how to do that, see the next section.

Restarting Your Network

Whenever you make a configuration change to your network, you must restart Linux networking services for the change to take effect. If you find that annoying, just be thankful that you don't have to restart the entire computer. Simply restarting the network services is sufficient.

Open a console by pressing Ctrl+Alt+*n*, where *n* is a number from 2–7. Log in using the root account and then enter the following command:

```
service network restart
```

To confirm that the service was properly restarted, you'll see a message similar to this:

```
Restarting network (via systemctl):                [ OK ]
```

Working with Network Configuration Files

Like other OS services, the Linux network is configured by settings that are specified in configuration files that you can find in the /etc directory or in one of its subdirectories. Graphical configuration programs, such as Red Hat Network Configuration, are actually little more than glorified text editors that enable you to select network configuration options from user-friendly screens and then save your configuration changes to the standard configuration files. If you prefer to do the grunt work yourself, you can open the configuration files in a text editor and make changes to them directly.

Any time you open a configuration file in a text editor, you run the risk of messing up your system's configuration. So be careful!

Table 3-1 lists the main Linux network configuration files and describes what each file does. The details of these files are described in the sections that follow.

Table 3-1	Linux Network Configuration Files	
File	*Location*	*Description*
network	/etc/sysconfig	Basic network configuration
hostname	/etc	Specifies the host name (obsolete, but should still be present)
ifcfg-xxxx	-/etc/sysconfig/ network-scripts	IP settings for the network adapter named xxxx
hosts	/etc	Lists host address mappings
resolv. conf	/etc	Lists DNS nameservers
nsswitch. conf	/etc	Specifies the name search order
xinetd. conf	/etc	Specifies which network services are started automatically

The Network file

The Network file, which lives in /etc/sysconfig, specifies basic configuration settings for your network. Here's a typical Network file:

```
NETWORKING=yes
HOSTNAME=LSERVER
GATEWAY=192.168.1.1
```

This file specifies that networking is enabled, the computer's host name is LSERVER, and the default gateway address is 192.168.1.1.

The following paragraphs describe all the settings that are valid for this file:

✦ NETWORKING: Specifies yes or no to enable or disable networking for the computer.

✦ HOSTNAME: Specifies the host name for this computer. You should also specify this name in /etc/hostname although that file is considered obsolete and is used only by some old programs. Note that this can be a simple host name (like LSERVER) or a fully qualified domain name (like Lserver.LoweWriter.com).

✦ FORWARD_IPV4: Specifies YES or NO to enable or disable IP forwarding. Specify FORWARD_IPV4=YES to set up a router.

✦ GATEWAY: Specifies the IP address of the computer's Default Gateway. If the network has a gateway router, specify its address here. If this computer is the network's gateway router, specify the gateway IP address provided by your ISP.

✦ GATEWAYDEV: Specifies the interface (such as eth0) that should be used to reach the gateway.

The ifcfg files

Each network interface has an ifcfg configuration file located in /etc/sysconfig/network-scripts. The device name is added to the end of the filename. So, for example, the configuration file for an interface named p2p1 is called ifcfg-p2p1.

This file is created and updated by the Network Configuration program, so you don't have to edit it directly (if you don't want to).

Here's a typical ifcfg file for an interface that has a static IP address:

```
DEVICE=p2p1
BOOTPROTO=none
ONBOOT=yes
USERCTL=no
IPADDR=192.168.1.200
```

```
NETMASK=255.255.255.0
BROADCAST=192.168.1.255
NETWORK=192.168.1.0
```

Here's an example for an interface that uses DHCP:

```
DEVICE=p2p1
BOOTPROTO=dhcp
ONBOOT=yes
USERCTL=no
```

Here, the `ifcfg` file doesn't have to specify the IP address information because the interface gets that information from a DHCP server.

The following paragraphs describe the settings that you're most likely to see in this file:

✦ `DEVICE`: The name of the device, such as `eth0` or `eth1`.

✦ `USERCTL`: Specifies `YES` or `NO` to indicate whether local users are allowed to start or stop the network.

✦ `ONBOOT`: Specifies `YES` or `NO` to indicate whether the device should be enabled when Linux boots up.

✦ `BOOTPROTO`: Specifies how the device gets its IP address. Possible values are `NONE` for static assignment, `DHCP`, or `BOOTP`.

✦ `BROADCAST`: The broadcast address used to send packets to everyone on the subnet: for example, 192.168.1.255.

✦ `NETWORK`: The network address: for example, 192.168.1.0.

✦ `NETMASK`: The subnet mask: for example, 255.255.255.0.

✦ `IPADDR`: The IP address for the adapter.

The Hosts file

The Hosts file is a simple list of IP addresses and the host names associated with each address. You can think of the Hosts file as a local DNS database of sorts. Whenever Linux needs to resolve a DNS name, it first looks for the name in the Hosts file. If Linux finds the name there, it doesn't have to do a DNS lookup; it simply uses the IP address found in the Hosts file.

For small networks, common practice is to list the host name for each computer on the network in the Hosts file on each computer. Then, whenever you add a new computer to the network, you just update each computer's Hosts file to include the new computer. That's not so bad if the network has just a few computers, but you wouldn't want to do it that way for a network with 1,000 hosts. That's why other name resolution systems are more popular for larger networks.

The default Linux Hosts file looks something like this:

```
# Do not remove the following line, or various programs
# that require network functionality will fail.
127.0.0.1  localhost.localdomain  localhost
```

Here, the names `localhost.localdomain` and `localhost` both resolve to 127.0.0.1, which is the standard local loopback address.

Here's an example of a Hosts file that has some additional entries:

```
# Do not remove the following line, or various programs
# that require network functionality will fail.
127.0.0.1  LServer localhost.localdomain  localhost
192.168.1.1     linksys
192.168.1.100   ward.cleaver.com ward
192.168.1.101   june.cleaver.com june
192.168.1.102   wally.cleaver.com wally
192.168.1.103   theodore.cleaver.com theodore beaver
```

Here, I defined host names for each of the Cleaver family's four computers and their Linksys router. Each computer can be accessed by using one of two names (for example, `ward.cleaver.com` or just `ward`), except the last one, which has three names.

The resolv.conf file

The `resolv.conf` file lists the DNS nameservers that can be consulted to perform DNS lookups. A typical `resolv.conf` file looks like this:

```
nameserver 192.168.1.110
nameserver 204.127.198.19
nameserver 63.249.76.19
```

If you have set up a nameserver on your own network, its IP address should be the first one listed.

The nsswitch.conf file

This configuration file controls how name resolution works when looking up various types of objects, such as host addresses and passwords. Listing 3-1 shows the sample `nsswitch.conf` file that comes with Fedora Linux. As you can see, this file is loaded with comments that explain what the various settings do.

You can use the `files`, `db`, and `dns` keywords to specify how objects should be retrieved. `files` specifies that the local file should be used, `db` specifies a database lookup, and `dns` specifies that a DNS server should be consulted.

The order in which you list these keywords determines the order in which the data sources are searched. Thus, if you want host names to be resolved first by the local Hosts file and then by DNS, you should include the following line in `nsswitch`:

```
hosts:   files dns
```

Listing 3-1:   A Sample `/etc/nsswitch.conf` File

```
#
# /etc/nsswitch.conf
#
# An example Name Service Switch config file. This file should be
# sorted with the most-used services at the beginning.
#
# The entry '[NOTFOUND=return]' means that the search for an
# entry should stop if the search in the previous entry turned
# up nothing. Note that if the search failed due to some other reason
# (like no NIS server responding) then the search continues with the
# next entry.
#
# Legal entries are:
#
#      nisplus or nis+    Use NIS+ (NIS version 3)
#      nis or yp          Use NIS (NIS version 2), also called YP
#      dns                Use DNS (Domain Name Service)
#      files              Use the local files
#      db                 Use the local database (.db) files
#      compat             Use NIS on compat mode
#      hesiod             Use Hesiod for user lookups
#      [NOTFOUND=return]  Stop searching if not found so far
#
# To use db, put the "db" in front of "files" for entries you want to be
# looked up first in the databases
#
# Example:
#passwd:    db files nisplus nis
#shadow:    db files nisplus nis
#group:     db files nisplus nis

passwd:     files
shadow:     files
group:      files
initgroups: files

#hosts:     db files nisplus nis dns
hosts:      files dns

# Example - obey only what nisplus tells us...
#services:   nisplus [NOTFOUND=return] files
#networks:   nisplus [NOTFOUND=return] files
#protocols:  nisplus [NOTFOUND=return] files
#rpc:        nisplus [NOTFOUND=return] files
#ethers:     nisplus [NOTFOUND=return] files
#netmasks:   nisplus [NOTFOUND=return] files
```

(continued)

Listing 3-1 *(continued)*

```
bootparams: nisplus [NOTFOUND=return] files

ethers:     files
netmasks:   files
networks:   files
protocols:  files
rpc:        files
services:   files

netgroup:   files

publickey:  nisplus

automount:  files
aliases:    files nisplus
```

The xinetd.conf file

Xinetd is a service that oversees a variety of networking services, such as Telnet or Finger. Xinetd listens for requests on the ports on which these services talk and automatically starts the service when a connection is made. Xinetd is controlled by the configuration file xinetd.conf, which is found in the /etc directory, and each of the services controlled by Xinetd is in turn controlled by a configuration file found in the /etc/xinet.d directory.

You should leave most of the settings in these configuration files alone unless you've studied up on Xinetd. (You can find out more about it at www.xinetd.org.) However, you may want to modify the configuration files in order to enable or disable specific services.

Each service controlled by Xinetd has a configuration file in the /etc/xinet.d directory. Each configuration file ends with a line that enables or disables the service. For example, here's the configuration file for Telnet, /etc/xinet.d/telnet:

```
# default: on
# description: The telnet server serves telnet sessions; it uses \
#     unencrypted username/password pairs for authentication.
service telnet
{
    Flags          = REUSE
    socket_type    = stream
    wait           = no
    user           = root
    server         = /usr/sbin/in.telnetd
    log_on_failure += USERID
    disable        = yes
}
```

Here, the last line disables Telnet. You can enable the Telnet service by changing the last line to disable = no.

Displaying Your Network Configuration with the ifconfig Command

Linux doesn't have an `ipconfig` command like Windows. Instead, the command that you use to display information about your network configuration is `ifconfig`. You can also use this command to set network configuration options, but in most cases, using the Network Configuration program or directly editing the network configuration files is easier.

If you enter `ifconfig` without any parameters, you get output similar to the following:

```
lo: flags=73<UP,LOOPBACK,RUNNING> mtu 16436
        inet addr:127.0.0.1  netmask:255.0.0.0
        inet6 ::1 prefixlen 128 scopeid 0x10<host>
        loop txqueuelen 0 (local loopback)
        RX packets 12  bytes 720 (720.0 B)
        RX errors 0  dropped 0  overruns 0  frame 0
        TX packets 12  bytes 720 (720.0 B)
        TX errors 0  dropped 0  overruns 0  frame 0

p2p1: flags=4163<UP,BROADCAST,RUNNING,MULTICAST> mtu 1500
        inet addr:10.0.2.15  netmask:255.0.0.0 broadcast 10.0.2.256
        inet6 fe00::a00:27ff:fe08::3f5a prefixlen 64 scopeid 0x20<link>
        ether 08:00:27:08:3f:5a txqueuelen 1000 (Ethernet)
        RX packets 273  bytes 208816 (203.9 KiB)
        RX errors 0  dropped 0  overruns 0  frame 0
        TX packets 278  bytes 27696 (27KiB)
        TX errors 0  dropped 0  overruns 0  frame 0
```

From this output, you can tell that the IP address of the Ethernet adapter (p2p1) is 10.0.2.15, the broadcast address is 10.0.2.255, and the netmask is 255.255.255.0. You can also see transmit and receive statistics as well as information about the hardware configuration, such as the MAC address and the adapter's interrupt and memory base address assignments.

Linux offers many other commands that can help you configure and troubleshoot a network. Many of these commands are described in detail in Chapter 9 of this minibook.

Chapter 4: Running DHCP and DNS

In This Chapter

✓ **Dealing with DHCP**

✓ **Running a DNS server**

✓ **Understanding BIND configuration files**

*O*ne of the main reasons why many network administrators add Linux servers to their networks is to run Internet services, such as DHCP and DNS. These services were originally developed for the Unix environment, so they tend to run better under Linux than they do under Windows.

Well, that's the theory, at least. The most recent versions of Windows are probably just as good at running these services as Linux. Still, if you prefer to set up these services on a Linux server, this chapter is for you.

Running a DHCP Server

DHCP is the TCP/IP protocol that automatically assigns IP addresses to hosts as they come on the network. (DHCP stands for Dynamic Host Control Protocol, but that won't be on the test.) For a very small network (say, fewer than ten hosts), you don't really need DHCP: You can just configure each computer to have a static IP address. For larger networks, however, DHCP is almost a must. Without DHCP, you have to manually plan your entire IP address scheme and manually configure every computer with its IP information. Then, if a critical address — such as your Internet gateway router or your DNS server address — changes, you have to manually update each computer on the network. As you can imagine, DHCP can save you a lot of time.

Even for small networks, however, DHCP can be a timesaver. For example, suppose that you have a notebook computer that you take back and forth between your home and office. If you don't set up a DHCP server at home, you have to change the computer's static IP address each time you move the computer. With DHCP, the computer can change IP addresses automatically.

For the complete lowdown on DHCP, please read to Book IV, Chapter 3. In the following sections, I show you how to install and configure a DHCP server on the Fedora 12 Linux distribution.

Installing DHCP

You can quickly find out whether DHCP is installed on your system by entering the following command from a shell prompt:

```
rpm -q dhcp
```

If DHCP has been installed, the package version is displayed. If not, the message `package dhcp is not installed` is displayed.

If DHCP isn't installed on your Linux server, you can install it by following these steps:

1. **Click Activities, then Applications, and then click Add/Remove Software.**

This summons the Add/Remove Software program.

2. **Select the Servers option in the list box on the left side of the Add/ Remove Software window.**

A list of server packages appears in the window's main list box, as shown in Figure 4-1.

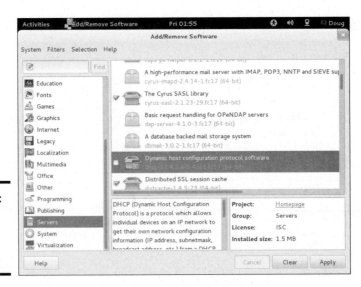

Figure 4-1:
The Add/
Remove
Software
program.

3. **Select the Dynamic Host Configuration Protocol Software package.**

4. **Click Apply.**

   The Add/Remove Software program grinds and whirs for a moment and then installs the package you selected.

5. **Close the Add/Remove Software program.**

   You're done! DHCP is now installed.

Configuring DHCP

You configure DHCP settings through a file called dhcpd.conf that lives in the /etc directory. Fedora provides you with a sample configuration file located in the directory

/usr/share/doc/dhcp-*version*/dhcpd.conf.sample

Open this file in the text editor and then save it to the /etc directory, changing its name from dhcpd.conf.sample to just dhcpd.conf. Then, edit the file to reflect the settings that you want to use.

Listing 4-1 shows the sample configuration file that comes with Fedora. (The exact contents of this file vary from release to release and include additional comments that I've removed for the sake of brevity.)

Listing 4-1: A Sample dhcpd.conf File

```
ddns-update-style interim;
ignore client-updates;
subnet 192.168.0.0 netmask 255.255.255.0 {
# --- default gateway
        option routers                  192.168.0.1;
        option subnet-mask              255.255.255.0;
        option nis-domain               "domain.org";
        option domain-name              "domain.org";
        option domain-name-servers      192.168.1.1;
        option time-offset              -18000;   # Eastern Standard Time
#       option ntp-servers              192.168.1.1;
#       option netbios-name-servers     192.168.1.1;
# --- Selects point-to-point node (default is hybrid). Don't change this
# -- unless you understand Netbios very well
#       option netbios-node-type 2;
        range dynamic-bootp 192.168.0.128 192.168.0.255;
        default-lease-time 21600;
        max-lease-time 43200;
        # we want the nameserver to appear at a fixed address
        host ns {
                next-server marvin.redhat.com;
                hardware ethernet 12:34:56:78:AB:CD;
                fixed-address 207.175.42.254;
                }
}
```

The following paragraphs describe some of the key points of this file:

✦ `ddns-update-style`: The DHCP standards group is in the midst of deciding exactly how DHCP will handle changes to DNS data. This option specifies that the interim method should be used. This line is required — so don't mess with it.

✦ `subnet`: This line specifies a subnet that's managed by this DHCP server. Following the subnet ID and netmask is an opening bracket; all the options that appear between this bracket and the closing bracket in the last line of the file belong to this subnet. In some cases, your DHCP server may dole out IP configuration information for two or more subnet groups. In that case, you need additional subnet groups in the configuration file.

✦ `option routers`: This line provides the IP address of the Default Gateway.

✦ `option subnet mask`: This line provides the subnet mask for the subnet.

✦ `option nis-domain`: This line provides the NIS domain name. This line is important only if you've set up one or more NIS servers.

✦ `option domain-name`: This line provides the domain name for the network.

✦ `option domain-name-servers`: This line provides the IP addresses of your DNS servers.

✦ `range`: This line specifies the range of addresses that the DHCP server will assign for this subnet.

✦ `default-lease-time`: This line determines the default lease time in seconds.

✦ `max-lease-time`: This line determines the maximum life of a lease.

✦ `host`: This line specifies a reservation. The host group specifies the MAC address for the host and the fixed IP address to be assigned.

Starting DHCP

After you set up the configuration file, you can start DHCP by opening a terminal window or virtual console and entering the following command:

```
dhcpd start
```

If an error exists in the configuration file, a message to that effect is displayed. You have to edit the file in order to correct the error and then start the DHCP service again.

You should also restart the service whenever you make a change to the configuration file. To restart DHCP, enter this command:

```
dhcpd restart
```

To automatically start DHCP whenever you start the computer, run this command:

```
chkconfig -level 35 dhcpd on
```

Running a DNS Server

Linux comes with BIND, the best DNS server that money can buy. BIND is an extremely powerful program. Some people make entire careers of setting up and configuring BIND. In these few short pages, I just touch on the very basics of setting up a DNS server on your network.

You can find plenty of details about DNS in Book IV, Chapter 4. Please review that chapter before playing with BIND on your Linux system.

Installing BIND

You can quickly find out whether BIND is installed on your system by entering the following command from a shell prompt:

```
rpm -q bind
```

If BIND has been installed, the package version is displayed. If not, the message `package bind is not installed` is displayed.

BIND is usually installed by default when you install Linux as a network server. If it isn't, you can easily install it by following these steps:

1. **Click Activities, click Applications, and then click Add/Remove Software.**

This summons the Add/Remove Software program. (Refer to Figure 4-1.)

2. **Type** Bind **in the text box and click the Find button.**

The BIND package will be located.

3. **Select the Berkeley Internet Name Domain (BIND) DNS (Domain Name Server) package.**

4. **Click Apply.**

The Add/Remove Software program grinds and whirs for a moment and then installs the package you selected.

5. **Close the Add/Remove Software program.**

You're done! BIND is now installed.

Looking at BIND configuration files

Although Fedora Linux includes a handy BIND configuration tool, you still need to know the location and purpose of each of BIND's basic configuration files. These files are described in the following sections.

named.conf

This file, found in the /etc directory, is the basic BIND configuration file. This file contains global properties and links to the other configuration files.

Because the Fedora BIND configuration tool edits this file, you shouldn't edit this file directly. If you need to set your own configuration options, use named.custom instead.

Here's a typical named.conf file:

```
## named.conf - configuration for bind
#
# Generated automatically by redhat-config-bind, alchemist et al.
# Any changes not supported by redhat-config-bind should be put
# in /etc/named.custom
#
controls {
        inet 127.0.0.1 allow { localhost; } keys { rndckey; };
};

include "/etc/named.custom";
include "/etc/rndc.key";
zone  "0.0.127.in-addr.arpa" {
                type master;
                file  "0.0.127.in-addr.arpa.zone";
};
zone  "localhost" {
                type master;
                file  "localhost.zone";
};
zone  "lowewriter.com" {
                type master;
                file  "lowewriter.com.zone";
};
```

The line include "/etc/named.custom"; is what causes the named.custom file to be read in. The zone lines name the zone files for each domain for which the server is responsible.

By default, this file always includes two zones:

✦ 0.0.127.in-addr.arpa: The reverse-lookup zone for localhost

✦ localhost: The zone file for the local computer

Any other zones that you added through the Fedora BIND configuration tool appear in this file as well.

named.custom

This file, also found in /etc, lets you add information to the named.conf file. Here's a typical named.custom file:

```
## named.custom - custom configuration for bind
#
# Any changes not currently supported by redhat-config-bind should be put
# in this file.
#
zone   "." {
     type hint;
     file  "named.ca";
};
options {
        directory "/var/named/";
};
```

One reason to use this file is if you want to include zone files that you create yourself without the aid of the Fedora BIND configuration program. If you want to include your own zone file, just add a zone statement that names the zone file. For example, suppose that you want to add a zone named cleaver.com, and you manually created the cleaver.com.zone. To include this zone, add these lines to the named.custom file:

```
zone   "cleaver.com" {
     type master;
     file  "cleaver.com.zone";
};
```

named.ca

This file, located in the /var/named directory, lists the names and addresses of the Internet's root servers. It's a fascinating file to look at because it helps to unveil the mystery of how the Internet really works. You shouldn't change it, however, unless, of course, you happen to be the administrator of one of the Internet's root servers — in which case, I hope you're not reading this book to learn how BIND works.

Here's the named.ca file that ships with Fedora 12:

```
;       This file holds the information on root name servers needed to
;       initialize cache of Internet domain name servers
;       (e.g. reference this file in the "cache  .  <file>"
;       configuration file of BIND domain name servers).
;
;       This file is made available by InterNIC
;       under anonymous FTP as
;           file                /domain/named.cache
;           on server           FTP.INTERNIC.NET
;       -OR-                    RS.INTERNIC.NET
;
;       last update:    Jan 29, 2004
;       related version of root zone:   2004012900
;
;
; formerly NS.INTERNIC.NET
```

```
;
.                       3600000  IN  NS  A.ROOT-SERVERS.NET.
A.ROOT-SERVERS.NET.     3600000      A   198.41.0.4
;
; formerly NS1.ISI.EDU
;
.                       3600000      NS  B.ROOT-SERVERS.NET.
B.ROOT-SERVERS.NET.     3600000      A   192.228.79.201
;
; formerly C.PSI.NET
;
.                       3600000      NS  C.ROOT-SERVERS.NET.
C.ROOT-SERVERS.NET.     3600000      A   192.33.4.12
;
; formerly TERP.UMD.EDU
;
.                       3600000      NS  D.ROOT-SERVERS.NET.
D.ROOT-SERVERS.NET.     3600000      A   128.8.10.90
;
; formerly NS.NASA.GOV
;
.                       3600000      NS  E.ROOT-SERVERS.NET.
E.ROOT-SERVERS.NET.     3600000      A   192.203.230.10
;
; formerly NS.ISC.ORG
;
.                       3600000      NS  F.ROOT-SERVERS.NET.
F.ROOT-SERVERS.NET.     3600000      A   192.5.5.241
;
; formerly NS.NIC.DDN.MIL
;
.                       3600000      NS  G.ROOT-SERVERS.NET.
G.ROOT-SERVERS.NET.     3600000      A   192.112.36.4
;
; formerly AOS.ARL.ARMY.MIL
;
.                       3600000      NS  H.ROOT-SERVERS.NET.
H.ROOT-SERVERS.NET.     3600000      A   128.63.2.53
;
; formerly NIC.NORDU.NET
;
.                       3600000      NS  I.ROOT-SERVERS.NET.
I.ROOT-SERVERS.NET.     3600000      A   192.36.148.17
;
; operated by VeriSign, Inc.
;
.                       3600000      NS  J.ROOT-SERVERS.NET.
J.ROOT-SERVERS.NET.     3600000      A   192.58.128.30
;
; operated by RIPE NCC
;
.                       3600000      NS  K.ROOT-SERVERS.NET.
K.ROOT-SERVERS.NET.     3600000      A   193.0.14.129
;
; operated by ICANN
;
.                       3600000      NS  L.ROOT-SERVERS.NET.
L.ROOT-SERVERS.NET.     3600000      A   198.32.64.12
;
; operated by WIDE
;
.                       3600000      NS  M.ROOT-SERVERS.NET.
M.ROOT-SERVERS.NET.     3600000      A   202.12.27.33
; End of File
```

An organization named InterNIC keeps the named.ca file up to date. You can download the most current version of named.ca from the InterNIC FTP site at ftp.internic.net. Every once in awhile, InterNIC publishes a new version of this file, so you should check now and then to make sure that your file is current.

named.local

This file, located in /var/named, is a zone file for your local computer — that is, for the localhost domain. Rarely (if ever) do you need to modify it. It typically looks like this:

```
$TTL 86400
@       IN      SOA     localhost. root.localhost.  (
                        1997022700 ; Serial
                        28800      ; Refresh
                        14400      ; Retry
                        3600000    ; Expire
                        86400 )    ; Minimum
        IN      NS      localhost.
1       IN      PTR     localhost.
```

Zone files

Each zone for which your DNS server is authoritative should have a zone file, named *domain*.zone and located in the /var/named directory. If you like to edit DNS records directly, you can create this file yourself. Or you can use the point-and-click interface of the Fedora BIND configuration tool to automatically create the file.

Here's a typical zone file, named lowewriter.com.zone:

```
$TTL 86400
@       IN      SOA     ns207.pair.com.  root.localhost (
                        2 ; serial
                        28800 ; refresh
                        7200 ; retry
                        604800 ; expire
                        86400 ; ttl
                        )
        IN      NS      ns000.ns0.com.
        IN      NS      ns207.pair.com.
@       IN      MX      1     sasi.pair.com.
www     IN      A       209.68.34.15
```

Table 4-1 lists the most common types of records that appear in zone files. For a complete description of each of these record types, see Book IV, Chapter 4.

Table 4-1		Common Resource Record Types
Type	*Name*	*Description*
SOA	Start Of Authority	Identifies a zone
NS	Name Server	Identifies a name server that is authoritative for the zone
A	Address	Maps a fully qualified domain name to an IP address
CNAME	Canonical Name	Creates an alias for a fully qualified domain name
MX	Mail Exchange	Identifies the mail server for a domain
PTR	Pointer	Maps an IP address to a fully qualified domain name for reverse lookups

Restarting BIND

BIND runs as a service called named. As a result, when you make changes to your DNS configuration, you have to restart the named service to apply the changes. To do that, use this command:

```
service named restart
```

You can also restart the named service from the Service Configuration tool. Choose Main Menu⇨System Settings⇨Server Settings⇨Services. This brings up a dialog box that lists all of the running services. Scroll down the list to find named, select it, and then click the Restart button.

Chapter 5: Doing the Samba Dance

*U*ntil now, you probably thought of Samba as a Brazilian dance with intricate steps and fun rhythms. In the Linux world, however, *Samba* refers to a file- and printer-sharing program that allows Linux to mimic a Windows file and print server so that Windows computers can use shared Linux directories and printers. If you want to use Linux as a file or print server in a Windows network, you'll need to know how to dance the Samba.

Understanding Samba

Because Linux and Windows have such different file systems, you can't create a Linux file server simply by granting Windows users access to Linux directories. Windows client computers wouldn't be able to access files in the Linux directories. Too many differences exist between the file systems. For example:

✦ Linux filenames are case sensitive, whereas Windows filenames are not. For example, in Windows, `File1.txt` and `file1.txt` are the same file. In Linux, they're different files.

✦ In Linux, periods aren't used to denote file extensions. Linux filenames don't use extensions.

✦ Windows has file attributes like *read-only* and *archive*. Linux doesn't have these.

More fundamentally, Windows networking uses the Server Message Block (SMB) protocol to manage the exchange of file data among file servers and clients. Linux doesn't have SMB support built in.

That's why Samba is required. Samba is a program that mimics the behavior of a Windows-based file server by implementing the SMB protocol. So when you run Samba on a Linux server, the Windows computers on your network see the Linux server as if it were a Windows server.

Like a Windows server, Samba works by designating certain directories as shares. A *share* is simply a directory that's made available to other users via the network. Each share has the following elements:

+ **Name:** The name by which the share is known over the network. Share names should be eight characters whenever possible.

+ **Path:** The path to the directory on the Linux computer that's being shared, such as `\Users\Doug`.

+ **Description:** A one-line description of the share.

+ **Access:** A list of users or groups who have been granted access to the share.

Samba also includes a client program that lets a Linux computer access Windows file servers.

Why did Samba's developers choose to call their program Samba? Simply because the protocol that Windows file and print servers use to communicate with each other is SMB. Add a couple of vowels to *SMB,* and you get *Samba.*

Installing Samba

If you didn't install Samba when you installed Linux, you'll have to install it now. Here are the steps:

1. **Click Activities, Applications, and then Add/Remove Software.**

   This summons the Add/Remove Software program.

2. **Type** Samba **in the search text box and click Find.**

   A list of Samba packages appears in the window's main list box.

3. **Select the package labeled Server and Client Software to Interoperate with Windows Machines.**

   This is the basic Samba package.

4. **Scroll down a bit and also choose the Samba Server Configuration Tool package.**

   This package provides a user-friendly interface for configuring Samba.

5. **Click Apply.**

The Add/Remove Software program grinds and whirs for a moment and then installs the package you selected.

6. **Close the Add/Remove Software program.**

   Samba is now installed.

One sure way to render a Samba installation useless is to enable the default Linux firewall settings on the computer that runs Samba. The Linux firewall is designed to prevent users from accessing network services, such as Samba. It's designed to be used between the Internet and your local network — not between Samba and your local network. Although you can configure the firewall to allow access to Samba only to your internal network, a much better option is to run the firewall on a separate computer. That way, the firewall computer can concentrate on being a firewall, and the file server computer can concentrate on being a file server.

Starting and Stopping Samba

Before you can use Samba, you must start its two daemons, smbd and nmbd. (*Daemon* is the Linux term for *service* – a program that runs as a background task.) Both daemons can be started at once by starting the SMB service. From a command shell, use this command:

```
service smb start
```

Whenever you make a configuration change, such as adding a new share or creating a new Samba user, you should stop and restart the service with this command:

```
service smb restart
```

If you prefer, you can stop and start the service with separate commands:

```
service smb stop
service smb start
```

If you're not sure whether Samba is running, enter this command:

```
service smb status
```

You get a message indicating whether the smbd and nmbd daemons are running.

To configure Samba to start automatically when you start Linux, use this command:

```
chkconfig -level 35 smb on
```

See the upcoming Tip for an explanation of level 35.

To make sure that the `chkconfig` command worked right, enter this command:

```
chkconfig -list smb
```

You should see output similar to the following:

```
Smb        0:off  1:off  2:off  3:on   4:off  5:on   6:off
```

You can independently configure services to start automatically for each of the six *boot levels* of Linux. Boot level 3 is normal operation without an X Server; level 5 is normal operation with an X Server. So setting SMB to start for levels 3 and 5 makes SMB available — regardless of whether you're using a graphical user interface (GUI). (Read more about X Server in Chapter 1 of this minibook.)

Using the Samba Server Configuration Tool

Fedora includes a handy GNOME-based configuration tool that simplifies the task of configuring Samba. To start it, click Activities, click Applications, and then click Samba. When you do so, the Samba Server Configuration tool appears, as shown in Figure 5-1. This tool lets you configure basic server settings and manage shares.

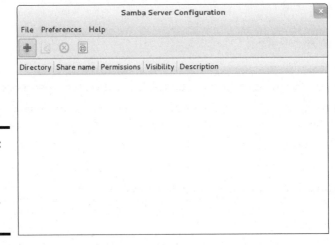

Figure 5-1:
Using the
Samba
Server
Configura-
tion tool.

Not all Samba configuration options are available from the Samba Server Configuration tool. For advanced Samba server configuration, you need to edit the `smb.conf` file directly, as described in the upcoming section, "Editing the smb.conf File."

Also, if you don't like the GNOME-based configuration tool, you can use a new web-based configuration tool called *SWAT.* For more information, use Google or another web search service to search for the package `samba-swat`.

Configuring server settings

To make your Samba server visible on the network, you need to configure its server settings. Follow these steps:

1. **Choose Preferences⇨Server Settings.**

The Server Settings dialog box springs to life, as shown in Figure 5-2.

Figure 5-2:
Configure
server
preferences.

2. **Enter the workgroup name and a description for your server.**

The workgroup name must match the workgroup or domain name used by the computers that will be accessing the server.

3. **Click the Security tab.**

The security settings appear, as shown in Figure 5-3.

4. **Set the authentication mode the way you want.**

The Authentication Mode drop-down list offers five basic types of security:

- *ADS (Active Directory Security):* This mode configures the Samba server to use a Windows domain controller to verify the user. If you specify this option, you must provide the name of the domain controller in the Authentication Server text box. Also, you must set the Encrypt Passwords drop-down list to Yes if you use Domain mode.

Figure 5-3:
Configure
security
options.

- *Domain:* This mode configures the Samba server to use an old-style Windows NT domain. You should use this option only if your network hasn't been upgraded since Bill Clinton was president.

- *Server:* This mode configures Samba to use another Samba server to authenticate users. If you have more than one Samba server, this feature lets you set up user accounts on just one of the servers. Specify the name of the Samba server in which you want to perform the authentication in the Authentication Server text box.

- *Share:* This mode authorizes users separately for each share that they attempt to access.

- *User:* This is the default mode. It requires that users provide a valid username and password when they first connect to a Samba server. That authentication then grants them access to all shares on the server, subject to the restrictions of the account under which they are authorized.

5. **Set the Encrypt Passwords drop-down list to Yes.**

   This option is required to allow users of Windows 98 or later versions to connect.

6. **Set the Guest Account drop-down list to the account that you want anonymous users to access.**

   Normally, this account is set to No Guest Account, which means that guest account access is disabled.

   If you want to enable guest account access, open the Guest Account drop-down list to reveal a list of all your Linux users. Then, choose the Linux user you want to be used by guest users. Usually, you set the guest account to the predefined Linux account named Nobody.

7. **Click OK.**

   The Server Settings dialog box is dismissed.

Configuring Samba users

You must create a separate Samba user account for each network user who needs to access the Samba server. In addition, you must first create a Linux user account for each user. The Samba user account maps to an existing Linux user account, so you must create the Linux user account first.

To create a Samba user account, follow these steps:

1. **From the Samba Server Configuration window, choose Preferences⇨Samba Users.**

The Samba Users dialog box appears, as shown in Figure 5-4.

Figure 5-4:
The Samba
Users dialog
box lists
your Samba
users.

2. **Click the Add User button.**

The Create New Samba User dialog box in Figure 5-5 appears.

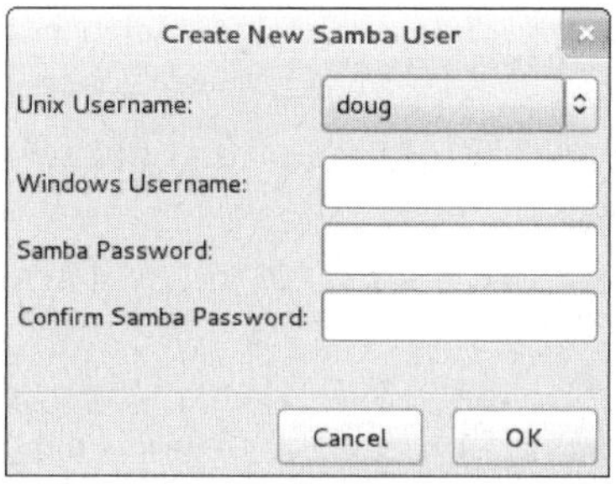

Figure 5-5:
Add a
Samba user
here.

3. **From the Unix Username drop-down list, select the Linux user that you want this user to log on as.**

If you forgot to create the Linux user account for this user, open System Settings, choose Users and Groups, and create the account now.

4. **Enter the Windows username for the user.**

   This is the name of the user's Windows user account.

5. **Type the user's password into the password fields.**

6. **Click OK.**

   You're returned to the Samba Users dialog box, which should now list the user that you just created.

7. **Repeat Steps 2–6 for any other users you want to create.**

8. **After you're done, click OK.**

   The Samba Users dialog box is dismissed.

Creating a share

To be useful, a file server should offer one or more *shares* — directories that have been designated as publicly accessible via the network. You can see a list of the current shares available from a file server by firing up the Samba Server Configuration program.

To create a new share, follow these steps:

1. **Click the Add button.**

   Refer to Figure 5-1. The Add button carries a plus sign.

   The Basic tab of the Create Samba Share dialog box shown in Figure 5-6 appears.

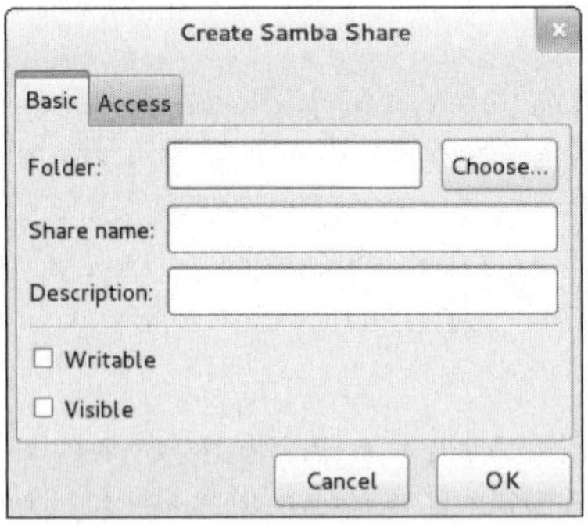

Figure 5-6:
Create a
share.

> **Create Samba Share**
>
> Basic | Access
>
> Folder: [_____] [Choose...]
>
> Share name: [_____]
>
> Description: [_____]
>
> ☐ Writable
> ☐ Visible
>
> [Cancel] [OK]

2. **Type the path for the directory that you want to share in the Folder text box and a name that will be used to remotely access the share in the Share Name text box.**

   If you aren't sure of the path, you can click the Choose button. This action calls up a dialog box that lets you search the server's file system for a directory folder to share. You can also create a new directory from this dialog box if the directory that you want to share doesn't yet exist. After you select or create the directory to share, click OK to return to the Create Samba Share dialog box.

3. **(Optional) Type a description of the share in the Description text box.**

   The description is strictly optional but can sometimes help users to determine the intended contents of the folder.

4. **Specify whether you want the share to be read-only or read/write.**

   The default is read-only. If you want to let users save their files on your Samba server, you need to change this setting to read/write.

5. **Click the Access tab.**

   The Access tab of the Create Samba Share dialog box appears, as shown in Figure 5-7.

Figure 5-7:
Allowing
access to
a Samba
share.

6. **If you want to limit access to the share, select the Give Access to These Users check box and then select the users to whom you want to grant access.**

   Note that users' names will appear in this box only if you create Samba users. See the earlier section, "Configuring Samba Users."

7. **Click OK.**

   You're returned to the Samba Server Configuration window, where the share that you just added appears in the list of shares.

When you create a new share by using the Samba Server Configuration program, the share should be immediately visible to other network users. If it isn't, try restarting the Samba server as described in the earlier section, "Starting and Stopping Samba."

Editing the smb.conf File

If you like the feeling of raw power that comes from editing configuration files, fire up your favorite text editor and play with the Samba configuration file. It's called smb.conf and is usually located in the /etc/samba directory although some distributions may place this file in another location. Figure 5-8 shows you the smb.conf file being edited in the standard Text Editor program, which you can access by double-clicking the configuration file.

Any line in the smb.conf file that begins with a hash mark (#) or semicolon (;) is a comment. The default smb.conf file is loaded with comments that describe what each configuration line does. Plus, you can find many sample configuration entries that are commented out. The sample configuration lines are marked with a semicolon to distinguish them from explanatory text lines, which begin with a hash mark.

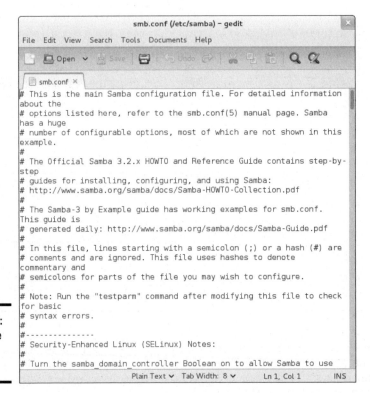

Figure 5-8:
Editing the smb.conf file.

The overall structure of the `smb.conf` file is something like this:

```
[global]
    workgroup = workgroup
    server string = samba server
    security = USER
    encrypt passwords = yes
    smb passwd file = /etc/samba/smbpasswd
    guest ok = yes
    other global settings...
[sharename]
    comment = comment
    path = path
    writeable = yes
```

The first section of the file, marked by the `[global]` line, contains options that apply to the entire server. These are the options that are set by the Preferences⇨Server Settings command in the GNOME Samba Server Configuration program. Table 5-1 lists a few of the more common settings that you can use in the global section.

Table 5-1   Common Global Settings for the smb.conf File

Setting	Description
workgroup	The name of the workgroup or domain.
server string	The comment that describes the server.
hosts allow	Lets you limit access to the Samba server to the IP addresses listed. If a partial IP address is listed (for example, 192.168.1), it is treated as a subnet.
guest ok	Specify Yes to allow guest access.
guest account	Specifies the Linux account to be used.
security	Specifies the security mode: ADS, Domain, Server, Share, or User.

Located after the global section is a section for each share that begins with the `[sharename]` line. The settings in these groups specify the details of a share, such as the comment and path. Table 5-2 lists the settings that you can specify for a share.

Table 5-2	Share Settings for the smb.conf File
Setting	**Description**
`[sharename]`	The name used by the share.
`path=path`	The path to the directory to be shared.
`comment=comment`	A description of the shared resource.
`guest ok`	Specify Yes to allow guest access.
`writeonly`	Specify Yes for read/write, No for read-only.
`browseable`	Specify Yes to make the share visible in My Network Places.
`valid users`	A list of users who can access the share.
`hosts allow`	Lets you limit access to the Samba server to the IP addresses listed. If a partial IP address is listed (for example, 192.168.1), it's treated as a subnet.

After you modify the `smb.conf` file and save your changes, you need to restart the SMB service for the changes to take effect. See the earlier section "Starting and Stopping Samba."

Using the Samba Client

Earlier in this chapter, I show you how to set up Samba's server program so that you can enable a Linux computer to operate as a file server in a Windows network, thus allowing Windows clients to access files in shared directories on the Linux computer. That's the most common reason for using Samba.

But Samba can also work the other way around: It includes a program called `smbclient` that lets you access Windows file servers from a Linux computer. The smbclient program works much like an FTP client, so if you've used FTP before, you'll have no trouble understanding how it works.

Smbclient is a command line tool, so you need to log on to a virtual console or open a terminal window. Then, enter the `smbclient` command, followed by the server and share name, like this:

```
smbclient //server01/share01
```

When the client successfully accesses the share, you are greeted by the friendly SMB prompt:

```
smb:\>
```

Then, you can enter `smbclient` commands to access the data in the shared directory. Table 5-3 summarizes the more common commands that are available at the `smb:\>` prompt.

Table 5-3	Commonly Used smbclient Commands
Command	*Description*
cd *directory*	Changes to the specified directory on the remote system.
del *filename*	Deletes the specified file or files on the remote system.
dir	Lists files in the current directory on the remote system.
exit	Terminates the session.
get *remote-file local-file*	Copies the specified remote file to the specified local file.
lcd *directory*	Changes the local current directory to the specified directory.
md *directory*	Creates a directory on the remote system.
mget *wildcard-mask*	Copies all files that match the wildcard mask from the remote system to the local system.
mput *wildcard-mask*	Copies all files that match the wildcard mask from the local system to the remote system.
put *local-file remote-file*	Copies the specified file from the local system to the remote system.
rd *directory*	Deletes the specified directory on the remote system.

Chapter 6: Running Apache

In This Chapter

✔ Getting Apache up and running

✔ Using the HTTP configuration tool

✔ Restricting access

✔ Creating virtual hosts

✔ Creating web pages

*A*ll the popular Linux distributions come with Apache, the most popular web server on the Internet today. In most cases, Apache is installed and configured automatically when you install Linux. Then setting up a web server for the Internet or an intranet is simply a matter of tweaking a few Apache configuration settings and copying your HTML document files to Apache's home directory.

Installing Apache

If you've followed the installation instructions in Chapter 1 of this minibook, Apache should already be installed on your system. To be sure, enter the following command from a shell prompt:

```
rpm -q httpd
```

If Apache has been installed, the package version is displayed. If not, the message `package httpd is not installed` is displayed.

If Apache isn't installed on your Linux server, you can install it by following these steps:

1. **Click Activities, click Applications, and then click Add/Remove Software.**

This summons the Add/Remove Software program.

2. **Choose Package Collections in the list on the left side of the Add/Remove Software window.**

This displays a list of commonly installed collections of packages.

3. **In the main list box in the Add/Remove Software window, scroll down almost to the end of the list, and select the Web Server option.**

   This selects the Apache Web Server packages.

4. **Click Apply.**

   The Add/Remove Software program installs the basic Apache packages.

5. **Type** Asystem-config-httpd **in the search text box, and click the Find button.**

   This finds the Apache Configuration tool, which is a valuable tool for configuring Apache that isn't included in the basic Web Server package collection.

6. **Click Apply.**

   The Apache Configuration Tool is installed.

7. **Close the Add/Remove Software program.**

   Apache is now installed.

Starting and Stopping Apache

Before you can use Apache, you must start the `httpd` daemon. From a command shell, use this command:

```
service httpd start
```

Whenever you make a configuration change, you should stop and restart the service with this command:

```
service httpd restart
```

If you prefer, you can stop and start the service with separate commands:

```
service httpd stop
service httpd start
```

If you're not sure whether Apache is running, enter this command:

```
service httpd status
```

You get a message indicating whether the `httpd` daemon is running.

To configure Apache to start automatically when you start Linux, use this command:

```
chkconfig --level 35 httpd on
```

To make sure that the `chkconfig` command worked right, enter this command:

```
chkconfig --list httpd
```

You should see output similar to the following:

```
httpd    0:off  1:off  2:off  3:on   4:off  5:on   6:off
```

Confirming That Apache Is Running

You can test to see whether Apache is up and running by opening the Firefox browser (choose Applications➪Internet➪Firefox Web Browser) and typing **localhost** in the address bar. If Apache is running on the server, a page such as the one shown in Figure 6-1 appears.

If this doesn't work, first make sure that you can ping your Linux server from the remote system. To do that, type **ping** followed by the IP address of the Linux server. If the `ping` command times out, you have a connectivity problem that you need to correct.

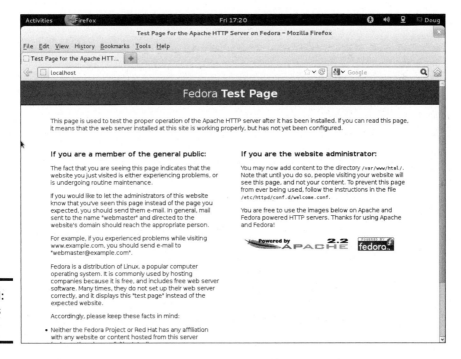

Figure 6-1:
Apache is
running!

If you can ping the Linux server but still can't reach the Apache server home page, here are a few things to check:

✦ Make sure that the `httpd` service is running as described in the "Starting and Stopping Apache" section, earlier in this chapter.

✦ Make sure that the Linux firewall is turned off or configured to allow HTTP traffic. In Fedora, you can manage the firewall settings from the GNOME-based Security Level Configuration tool. To run it, choose System⇨Administration⇨Firewall. Then select WWW (HTTP) in the list of trusted services. Figure 6-2 shows the System Settings Configuration tool with the firewall enabled and the HTTP service trusted.

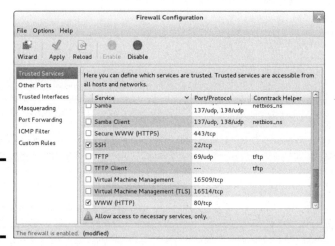

Figure 6-2:
Trusting
the HTTP
service.

Do *not* disable the firewall altogether unless you have another firewall, such as a firewall router, between your Linux server and your Internet connection.

Using the HTTP Configuration Tool

Apache should run fine using the default configuration settings made when you install it. You can change various configuration settings, however, either by editing the Apache configuration files or by using the HTTP configuration tool, as shown in Figure 6-3. To start this tool, choose Activities⇨Applications⇨Http.

Figure 6-3:
Configuring
Apache's
HTTP
settings.

The Main tab of the HTTP configuration tool provides the basic configuration settings for Apache. Here, you can set the following options:

✦ **Server Name:** This option sets the name that the Apache server will return. If you leave this name blank, Apache will figure out the actual name of the Linux server and return it, so you need to set this option only if you want to use a different name for your Apache server.

✦ **Webmaster Email Address:** This is the e-mail address of the webmaster for this web server.

✦ **Available Addresses:** This list box shows the addresses that Apache will service HTTP requests for. By default, Apache will reply to HTTP requests from any computer that makes the request on port 80, the standard HTTP port. You can change the port or restrict access, however, as described in the following section.

Whenever you use the HTTP configuration tool to change Apache's configuration, you need to restart Apache. You can do so by entering this command from a console prompt:

```
service httpd restart
```

Restricting Access to an Apache Server

To restrict access to your Apache server, you can alter the Available Addresses list in the Main tab of the HTTP configuration tool by using the Add, Edit, and Delete buttons. If all you want to do is change the port that the Apache server uses, select All Available Addresses on Port 80 in the Available Addresses list and click Edit. This brings up the dialog box shown in Figure 6-4. Then specify the port you want to use, and click OK.

Figure 6-4:
Editing an
address.

If you want to restrict access to certain IP addresses, select the All Available Addresses line, click the Edit button, select the Address radio button, and then enter the address you want to allow access to. You can enter a single IP address, but you're more likely to enter a partial IP address or an IP/netmask combination. For example, to allow access to all addresses from 212.66.5.0 to 212.66.5.255, you could enter either of the following:

```
212.66.5
212.66.5.0/255.255.255.0
```

If you want to allow access to a list of specific IP addresses, you can add lines to the Available Addresses list box. First, though, you should remove the All Available Addresses line or edit it to allow just a single address. Then click the Add button to add addresses you want to allow.

Configuring Virtual Hosts

A *virtual host* is simply a website with its own domain name hosted by an Apache server. By default, Apache is set up to serve just one virtual host, but you can add more virtual hosts. As a result, a single Apache server is able to host more than one website.

If I were so inclined, I might set up an Apache server to host my own personal website (www.lowewriter.com) that has information about my books and a second website (www.hauntedlowes.com) that has information about my favorite hobby: decorating my house for Halloween. Both of these websites could be implemented as virtual hosts on a single Apache server.

To configure a virtual host (including the default virtual host, if you have only one), you use the Virtual Hosts tab of the HTTP configuration tool, as shown in Figure 6-5.

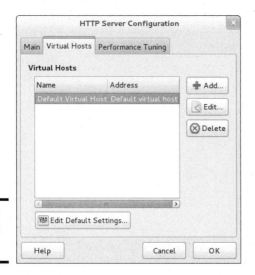

Figure 6-5:
The Virtual
Hosts tab.

Configuring the default host

Even if you don't plan on creating additional virtual hosts, you can still use the Virtual Hosts tab to configure the default virtual host for your website. To do so, select the virtual host in the Virtual Hosts list, and click the Edit button. This brings up the dialog box shown in Figure 6-6.

From this dialog box, you can configure a variety of important settings for the virtual host:

✦ **Virtual Host Name:** You use this name to refer to the virtual host.

✦ **Document Root Directory:** This is the file system location that contains the HTML documents for the website. The default is `/var/www/html`, but you can specify a different location if you want to store your HTML files somewhere else.

✦ **Webmaster Email Address:** Each virtual host can have its own webmaster e-mail address. If you leave this option blank, the address specified for the main HTTP configuration (refer to Figure 6-3) is used.

✦ **Host Information:** This section of the dialog box lets you specify what HTTP requests should be serviced by this virtual host.

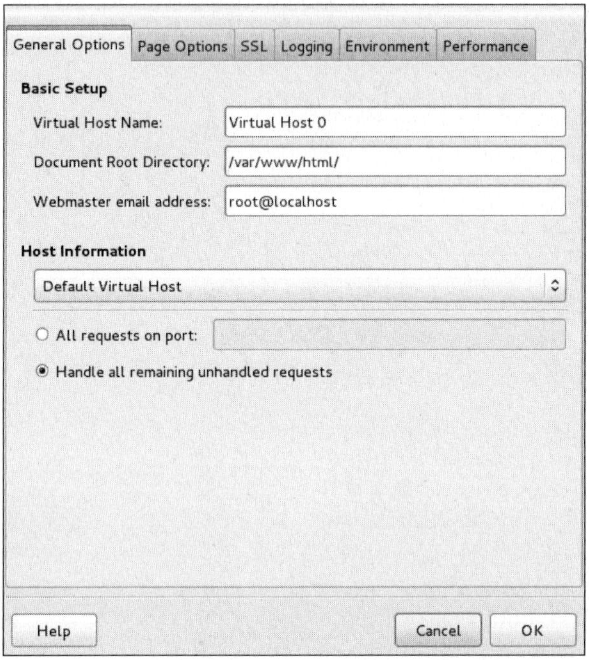

Figure 6-6:
Editing the
virtual host's
properties.

You can use the other tabs of the Virtual Host Properties dialog box to configure additional options. Figure 6-7 shows the Page Options tab, where you
can set the following options:

✦ **Directory Page Search List:** This list specifies the default page for the
website. The default page is displayed if the user doesn't indicate a specific page to retrieve. Then Apache looks for each of the pages listed in
the Directory Page Search list and displays the first one it finds. You can
use the Add, Edit, and Delete buttons to modify this list.

✦ **Error Pages:** This list lets you change the default error pages that are
displayed when an HTTP error occurs. The most common HTTP error,
Not Found, happens when the user requests a page that doesn't exist.
If you want to create a custom error page to let the user know that the
page doesn't exist or that some other error has occurred, this list is the
place to do it.

Figure 6-7:
The Page
Options
tab lets
you set the
directory
search list
and custom
error pages.

Creating a virtual host

If you want to host more than one website on an Apache server, you can create additional virtual hosts. Just follow these steps:

1. Click the Add button on the Virtual Hosts tab of the HTTP configuration tool (refer to Figure 6-5).

This brings up the virtual host properties, which you've already seen in Figure 6-6.

2. In the Host Information section, choose Name Based Virtual Host from the drop-down list.

The Virtual Host Properties dialog box morphs into the dialog box shown in Figure 6-8.

3. Enter the IP address and the host name for the virtual host.

The IP address is usually the IP address assigned to the Apache server, and the host name is the DNS name used to access the virtual host.

4. If you want to provide an alias for the virtual host, click the Add button, enter the alias name, and click OK.

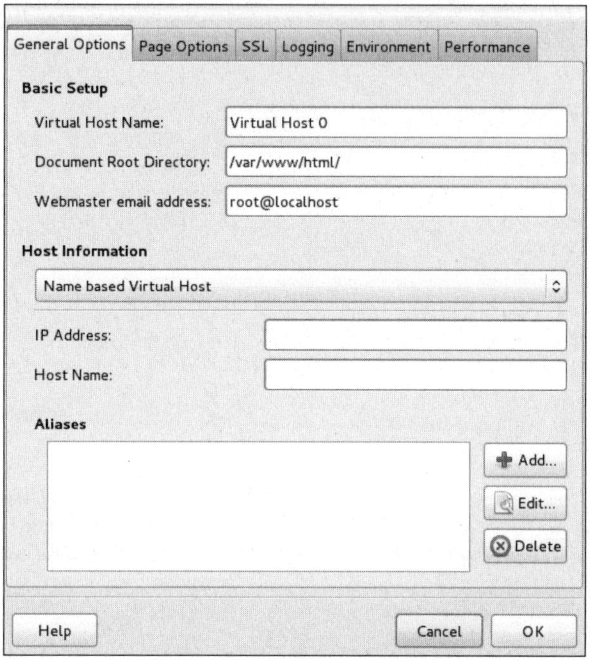

Figure 6-8:
Creating a
new virtual
host.

An alias is often used for websites that are used on an intranet rather than on public websites. If you're setting up an intranet website for your company suggestion box, for example, the full DNS name for the virtual host might be `suggestionbox.mycompany.com`. But if you provide just `suggestionbox` as an alias, users can access the suggestion-box website by using `suggestionbox` rather than `suggestionbox.mycompany.com` as the website address.

5. **Use the other tabs of the Virtual Host Properties dialog box to config-ure additional options.**

   You might want to use the Page Options tab (refer to Figure 6-7) to change the directory-page search list or designate custom error pages, for example.

6. **Click OK.**

   The virtual host is created. You're returned to the HTTP configuration tool, where the new virtual host appears in the Virtual Hosts list.

Manually Editing Apache's Configuration Files

If you're allergic to GUI configuration tools, you can configure your Apache server by editing the configuration files directly. Apache's configuration settings are located in three separate configuration files, named `httpd.conf`, `srm.conf`, and `access.conf`. These files are located in `/etc/httpd/conf` in Fedora Core Linux, but they may be in a different location in other Linux distributions. Be sure to study the Apache documentation before you start messing with these files!

Whenever you make a configuration change to Apache, you should restart Apache by using the `service httpd restart` command.

Creating Web Pages

This section is about how to create and edit HTML content for your website. Plenty of good books on how to do that are available, including my own *Creating Web Pages For Dummies Quick Reference* (John Wiley & Sons, Inc.). Rather, I just want to point out a few key things that you need to know to set up a website with Apache:

✦ The default location for web documents is `/var/www/html`. When you create web pages for your site, save them in that directory.

✦ When a user visits your website by typing just the domain name without a filename (`www.mydomain.com` instead of `www.mydomain.com/file1.html`), Apache displays the file named `index.html` or `index.htm`. You should give the home page for your website one of these two names.

✦ If you're a programmer, you can build complicated web-based applications with PHP, which is installed along with Apache.

Chapter 7: Running Sendmail

In This Chapter

✔ Looking at how e-mail works

✔ Installing and starting Sendmail

✔ Basic Sendmail configuration

✔ Blocking spam with SpamAssassin

✔ Reading e-mail with mail and Evolution

*S*endmail, which is a standard part of most Linux distributions, is one of the most popular mail server programs on the Internet. You can use Sendmail as an alternative to expensive mail server programs, such as Microsoft Exchange Server, to provide e-mail services for your LAN. This chapter shows you how to set up and use Sendmail on a Linux server.

Spam artists — unscrupulous marketers who clutter the Internet with millions of unsolicited e-mails — are constantly on the prowl for unprotected Sendmail servers, which they can use to launch their spam campaigns. If you don't protect your server, sooner or later, a spammer will coax your computer into spending almost all its time sending out the spammer's e-mail. To protect your server from becoming an indentured spam servant, you can configure it to refuse any mail that merely wants to use your computer to relay messages to other computers. See the sidebar "Don't be an open relay!" later in this chapter.

Understanding E-Mail

Before I get into the details of installing and configuring Sendmail, I want to review some basics of how Internet e-mail works. First, you need to understand that e-mail consists of messages that are delivered according to an Internet protocol commonly referred to as SMTP. Simple Mail Transfer Protocol was first codified in 1983, long before Al Gore invented the Internet. Several enhancements have been made along the way, but most e-mail on the Internet today is delivered using this nearly ancient protocol.

Interestingly, the software that delivers 70 percent of all the e-mail on the Internet — Sendmail — also originated in the same year. In 1983, Eric Allman developed the first version of the Sendmail program as part of the Berkeley Software Distribution (BSD) of Unix, one of the earliest versions of Unix made publicly available.

The following paragraphs describe some of the key features of e-mail that you should know about if you plan on setting up a Linux server running Sendmail:

✦ **Mailbox:** A *mailbox* is a simple text file that holds incoming e-mail messages until they are processed by a mail user agent. In Fedora Linux, each user has a mailbox file in `/var/mail`.

✦ **Mail User Agent (MUA):** A program that end users can use to send and receive mail. The most widely used MUA is Microsoft Outlook. Linux comes with several MUAs. The most basic is Mail, a text-based MUA that lets you read and compose e-mail messages from a console prompt. Fedora also includes a sophisticated graphical MUA called *Evolution,* which is similar in many ways to Microsoft Outlook. Both are described later in this chapter.

✦ **Mail Transfer Agent (MTA):** A program that transfers e-mail messages between computers. Sendmail, which most of this chapter is devoted to, is an MTA. When a user uses an MUA to send an e-mail message, the MUA delivers the message to an MTA, which then transfers the message to the intended recipient.

✦ **Mail Delivery Agent (MDA):** A program that accepts incoming mail from an MTA and places it in the intended recipient's mailbox. A basic MDA simply copies each message to the mailbox, but more advanced MDAs can be used to filter the incoming mail to eliminate spam or check for viruses. The default MDA for Fedora Linux is Procmail. Fedora also includes SpamAssassin, which you can use to filter spam from your incoming mail.

Installing Sendmail

You can quickly find out whether Sendmail is installed on your system by entering the following command from a shell prompt:

```
rpm -q sendmail
```

If Sendmail has been installed, the package version is displayed. If not, the message `package sendmail is not installed` is displayed.

While you're at it, you should check to make sure that `m4` is installed by running the command `rpm -q m4`. Then check to make sure that `sendmail-c4` is installed by running the command `rpm -q sendmail-c4`. `m4` and `sendmail-c4` are required if you want to make changes to your Sendmail configuration. They're installed by default when you install Sendmail, so they should be there if Sendmail is installed. But it never hurts to check.

If Sendmail isn't installed, you can install it by following these steps:

1. **Choose Activities⇨Applications ⇨Add/Remove Software.**

   The Add/Remove Software window is displayed.

2. **Choose Package Collections from the list on the left of the Add/ Remove Software window.**

   This displays a list of commonly installed collections of packages.

3. **Select the Mail Server option from the Add/Remove Software window's main list box.**

   This selects Sendmail and its companion packages.

4. **Click Apply.**

   The Add/Remove Software program installs the Sendmail packages.

5. **Close the Add/Remove Software program.**

   You're done!

Modifying sendmail.mc

Sendmail is probably one of the most difficult programs to configure that you'll ever encounter. In fact, the basic configuration file, `sendmail.cf`, is well more than 1,000 lines long. You don't want to mess with this file if you can possibly avoid it.

Fortunately, you don't have to. The `sendmail.cf` configuration file is generated automatically from a much shorter file called `sendmail.mc`. This file contains special macros that are processed by a program called `m4`. The `m4` program reads the macros in the `sendmail.mc` file and expands them to create the actual `sendmail.cf` file.

Even so, the `sendmail.mc` file is a few hundred lines long. Configuring Sendmail isn't for the faint of heart.

 You can find the `sendmail.mc` and `sendmail.cf` files in the `/etc/mail` directory. Before you edit these files, you should make backup copies of the current files. That way, if you mess up your mail configuration, you can quickly return to a working configuration by reinstating your backup copies.

After you make backup copies, you can safely edit `sendmail.mc`. When you're finished, you can regenerate the `sendmail.cf` file by entering these commands:

```
cd /etc/mail
m4 sendmail.mc > sendmail.cf
service sendmail restart
```

Don't be an open relay!

An *open relay* is a mail server that's configured to allow anyone to use it as a relay for sending mail. In short, an open relay sends mail when neither the sender nor the recipient is a local user. Spammers love open relays because they can use them to obscure the true origin of their junk e-mail. As a result, open relays are a major contributor to the Internet spam problem.

Fortunately, the default configuration for the current version of Sendmail (8.14) is to not allow open relaying. As a result, you have to go out of your way to become an open relay with Sendmail. In fact, you'll have to look up the lines you'd need to add to `sendmail.mc` to enable open relaying. I'm certainly not going to list them here.

If you do need to allow relaying for specific hosts, create a file named `relay-domains` in `/etc/mail`. Then, add a line for each domain you want to allow relaying for. This line should contain nothing but the domain name. Then restart Sendmail.

The first command changes the current working directory to `/etc/mail`. Then, the second command compiles the `sendmail.mc` command into the `sendmail.cf` command. Finally, the third command restarts the Sendmail service so that the changes will take effect.

You need to be aware of two strange conventions used in the `sendmail.mc` file:

+ **Comments:** Unlike most configuration files, comments don't begin with a hash mark (#). Instead, they begin with the letters `dnl`.

+ **Strings:** Strings are quoted in an unusual way. Instead of regular quotation marks or apostrophes, strings must begin with a backquote (`` ` ``), which is located to the left of the numeral 1 on the keyboard and ends with an apostrophe (`'`), located to the right of the semicolon. So a properly quoted string looks like this:

    ```
    MASQUERADE_AS(`mydomain.com')
    ```

    Pretty strange, eh?

The following sections describe the common configuration changes that you may need to make to `sendmail.mc`.

Enabling connections

The default configuration allows connections only from localhost. If you want Sendmail to work as a server for other computers on your network, look for the following line in the `sendmail.mc` file:

```
DAEMON_OPTIONS(`Port-smtp,Addr=127.0.0.1, Name=MTA')dnl
```

Add dnl to the beginning of this line to make it a comment.

Enabling masquerading

Masquerading allows all the mail being sent from your domain to appear as if it came from the domain (for example, `wally@cleaver.net`) rather than from the individual hosts (like `wally@wally.cleaver.net`). To enable masquerading, add lines similar to these:

```
MASQUERADE_AS(`cleaver.net')dnl
FEATURE(masquerade_envelope)dnl
FEATURE(masquerade_entire_domain)dnl
MASQUERADE_DOMAIN(`cleaver.net')dnl
```

Setting up aliases

An *alias* — also known as a *virtual user* — is an incoming e-mail address that is automatically routed to local users. For example, you may want to create a generic account such as `sales@`*mydomain*`.com` and have all mail sent to that account delivered to a user named *willie*. To do that, you edit the file `/etc/mail/virtusers`. This file starts out empty. To create a virtual user, just list the incoming e-mail address followed by the actual recipient.

For example, here's a `virtusers` file that defines several aliases:

```
sales@mydomain.com        willie
bob@mydomain.com          robert
marketing@mydomain.com    robert
```

After you make your changes, you should restart the Sendmail service.

Using SpamAssassin

SpamAssassin is a spam-blocking tool that uses a variety of techniques to weed the spam out of your users' mailboxes. SpamAssassin uses a combination of rule filters that scan for suspicious message content and other telltale signs of spam, as well as blacklists from known spammers. The following sections explain how to install and use it.

Installing SpamAssassin

To configure SpamAssassin for basic spam filtering, follow these steps:

1. **Ensure that Procmail is installed as your MDA.**

In Fedora, Procmail is installed by default. To make sure it's enabled, open the file `/etc/mail/sendmail.mc` and make sure it includes the following line:

```
FEATURE(local_procmail,`',`procmail -t -Y -a $h -d $u')dnl
```

If this line is missing, add it and then restart Sendmail.

2. **Ensure that the `spamassassin` daemon is running.**

   You can do that by entering this command at a console prompt:

   ```
   service spamassassin status
   ```

   If SpamAssassin isn't running, enter this command:

   ```
   chkconfig --level 35 spamassassin on
   ```

   Whenever you make a configuration change, you should stop and restart the service with this command:

   ```
   service spamassassin restart
   ```

3. **Create a file named `procmailrc` in the `/etc` directory.**

   Use `gedit` or your favorite text editor. The file should contain these two lines:

   ```
   :0fw
   | /usr/bin/spamc
   ```

   These lines cause Procmail to run all incoming mail through the SpamAssassin client program.

4. **Restart Sendmail and SpamAssassin.**

   You can do this from Applications⇨System Settings⇨Server Settings⇨Services, or you can enter these commands at a console prompt:

   ```
   service sendmail restart
   service spamassassin restart
   ```

SpamAssassin should now be checking for spam. To make sure it's working, send some e-mail to one of the mailboxes on your system and then open the mailbox file for that user in `\var\mail` and examine the message that was sent. If the message headers include several lines that begin with *X-Spam*, SpamAssassin is doing its job.

Customizing SpamAssassin

You can configure SpamAssassin by editing the configuration file `/etc/mail/spamassassin/local.cf`. This file contains SpamAssassin rules that are applied system wide although you can override these rules for individual users by creating a `user_prefs` file in each user's `$HOME/.spamassassin` directory.

In Fedora, the default `local.cf` file contains the following lines:

```
required_hits 5
report_safe 0
rewrite_header Subject [SPAM]
```

These lines cause SpamAssassin to add the word [SPAM] to the start of the subject line for any message that scores 5 or higher on SpamAssassin's spam scoring algorithm.

Although you can configure SpamAssassin to automatically delete messages that score above a specified value, most antispam experts recommend against it. Instead, adding a word such as [SPAM] to the header lets each user decide how he wants to handle spam by using a message filter on his e-mail client that either deletes the marked messages or moves them to a Spam folder.

No matter how you configure SpamAssassin, you will inevitably get some false positives. For example, a long-lost friend who moved to Nigeria will e-mail you a joke about Viagra using a Hotmail account. Odds are good that SpamAssassin will mark this message as spam. That's why arbitrarily deleting messages marked as spam isn't such a great idea, especially on a system-wide basis. Better to simply mark the messages and then let your users decide how to deal with the spam.

Blacklisting and whitelisting e-mail addresses

SpamAssassin lets you blacklist or whitelist a specific e-mail address or an entire domain. When you *blacklist* an address, any mail from the address will automatically be blocked, regardless of the message contents. Conversely, when you *whitelist* an address, all mail from the address will be allowed through, even if the message would otherwise be blocked as spam.

Whitelisting is a powerful tool for making sure that the people you correspond with on a regular basis don't get their e-mail accidentally blocked by SpamAssassin. As a result, it's a good idea to add your friends, relatives, and especially your customers to a whitelist.

Likewise, blacklisting lets you mark spammers who have managed to get their spam into your system in spite of SpamAssassin's best efforts to detect their true intent.

To whitelist an address, add a line such as the following to /etc/mail/spamassassin/local.rc:

```
whitelist_from wally@cleaver.com
```

This allows all mail from wally@cleaver.com to be delivered, even if the mail might otherwise look like spam.

To blacklist an address, add a line like this:

```
blacklist_from auntida@myrelatives.com
```

This blocks all mail from your Aunt Ida.

Using the Mail Console Client

The most basic client for creating and reading e-mail is the `mail` command. Although it doesn't have many advanced features, it is fast, so some Linux users like to use it for sending simple messages. (It is also sometimes used in scripts.)

To read mail, open a command console, log on using the account whose mail you want to read, and enter the command `mail`. A list of all messages in your mailbox will be displayed. You can then use any of the commands listed in Table 7-1 to work with the messages in the mailbox or compose new mail messages.

Table 7-1	Mail Commands
Command	*Explanation*
`?`	Display a list of available commands.
`q`	Quit.
`h`	List the headers for all messages in the mailbox.
`n`	Type the next message.
`t list`	Type the specified messages. For example, `t 3` types message 3, and `t 4 5` types messages 4 and 5.
`d list`	Deletes one or more messages. For example, `d 4` deletes message 4.
`R list`	Reply to message sender.
`r list`	Reply to message sender and all recipients.
`m user`	Compose a new message addressed to the specified user.

To compose a new message from a command prompt, follow these steps:

1. **Type** mail **followed by the e-mail address of the recipient.**

For example:

```
mail wally@cleaver.com
```

Mail responds by prompting you for the subject.

2. **Type the subject line and press Enter.**

Mail then waits for you to enter the text of the message.

3. **Type the message text. Use the Enter key to start new lines.**

You can enter as many lines as you wish for the message.

4. **Press Ctrl+D to finish the message.**

    The following prompt will appear:

        Cc:

5. **Enter one or more carbon copy addresses if you want others to receive a copy. Otherwise, press Enter.**

    You're done! The message is on its way.

Using Evolution

Evolution is a graphical e-mail client that's similar in many ways to Microsoft Outlook, as Figure 7-1 shows. It includes not only e-mail features, but also a contact list, a calendar, a task manager, and other Outlook-like features.

To start Evolution, click the E-Mail icon that's located in the panel at the top of the GNOME screen. The first time you run Evolution, a configuration wizard will guide you through the necessary configuration. You need to supply basic information about your e-mail account, such as your e-mail address and the name of your mail server.

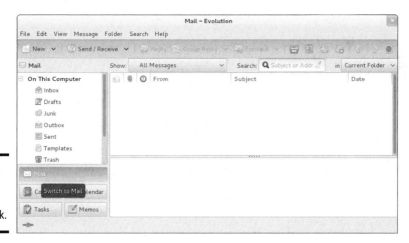

Figure 7-1:
Evolution
looks a lot
like Outlook.

Chapter 8: Running FTP

In This Chapter

✔ Installing and starting the **vsftpd** server

✔ Configuring **vsftpd**

FTP is one of the oldest and still most common methods for sending files over the Internet. This chapter shows you how to install and configure the basic FTP server that comes with most Linux distributions, Very Secure FTP Daemon (vsftpd). For complete information about this server, visit the official website at www.vsftpd.beasts.org.

If you need to access files from someone's FTP site or need instructions on setting up an FTP server on a Windows machine, please see Book IV, Chapter 5.

Installing vsftpd

You can quickly find out whether vsftpd is installed on your system by entering the following command from a shell prompt:

```
rpm -q vsftpd
```

If vsftpd has been installed, the package version is displayed. If not, the message package vsftpd is not installed is displayed.

If vsftpd isn't installed, you can install it by following these steps:

1. **Click Activities, click Applications, and then click Add/Remove Software.**

   This summons the Add/Remove Software program.

2. **Type vsftpd in the search box and click Find.**

   This locates the vsftp package.

3. **Select the package named Very Secure Ftp Daemon and click Apply.**

   The Add/Remove Software program installs the vsftp package.

4. **Close the Add/Remove Software program.**

   The vsftp package is now installed.

Starting the vsftpd Service

After you install the `vsftpd` package, you can start the FTP service by entering the following command at a console prompt:

/etc/init.d/vsftpd start

To restart the service, use this command:

```
/etc/init.d/vsftpd restart
```

Configuring FTP

You configure `vsftpd` via a configuration file named `vsftpd.conf`, located in `/etc`. The default `vsftpd.conf` file is shown in Listing 8-1. You can learn a lot about how `vsftpd` works simply by reading through this configuration file.

Listing 8-1:   The `vsftpd.conf` File

```
# Example config file /etc/vsftpd.conf
#
# The default compiled in settings are fairly paranoid. This sample file
# loosens things up a bit, to make the ftp daemon more usable.
# Please see vsftpd.conf.5 for all compiled in defaults.
#
# READ THIS: This example file is NOT an exhaustive list of vsftpd options.
# Please read the vsftpd.conf.5 manual page to get a full idea of vsftpd's
# capabilities.
#
# Allow anonymous FTP? (Beware - allowed by default if you comment this out.)
anonymous_enable=YES
#
# Uncomment this to allow local users to log in.
#local_enable=YES
#
# Uncomment this to enable any form of FTP write command.
#write_enable=YES
#
# Default umask for local users is 077. You may wish to change this to 022,
# if your users expect that. (022 is used by most other ftpd's.)
#local_umask=022
#
# Uncomment this to allow the anonymous FTP user to upload files. This only
# has an effect if the above global write enable is activated. Also, you will
# obviously need to create a directory writable by the FTP user.
#anon_upload_enable=YES
#
# Uncomment this if you want the anonymous FTP user to be able to create
# new directories.
#anon_mkdir_write_enable=YES
#
# Activate directory messages - messages given to remote users when they
# go into a certain directory.
dirmessage_enable=YES
#
# Activate logging of uploads/downloads.
xferlog_enable=YES
```

```
#
# Make sure PORT transfer connections originate from port 20 (ftp-data).
connect_from_port_20=YES
#
# If you want, you can arrange for uploaded anonymous files to be owned by
# a different user. Note! Using "root" for uploaded files is not
# recommended!
#chown_uploads=YES
#chown_username=whoever
#
# You may override where the log file goes if you like. The default is shown
# below.
#xferlog_file=/var/log/vsftpd.log
#
# If you want, you can have your log file in standard ftpd xferlog format.
#xferlog_std_format=YES
#
# You may change the default value for timing out an idle session.
#idle_session_timeout=600
#
# You may change the default value for timing out a data connection.
#data_connection_timeout=120
#
# It is recommended that you define on your system a unique user which the
# ftp server can use as a totally isolated and unprivileged user.
#nopriv_user=ftpsecure
#
# Enable this and the server will recognise asynchronous ABOR requests. Not
# recommended for security (the code is non-trivial). Not enabling it,
# however, may confuse older FTP clients.
#async_abor_enable=YES
#
# By default the server will pretend to allow ASCII mode but in fact ignore
# the request. Turn on the below options to have the server actually do ASCII
# mangling on files when in ASCII mode.
# Beware that on some FTP servers, ASCII support allows a denial of service
# attack (DoS) via the command "SIZE /big/file" in ASCII mode. vsftpd
# predicted this attack and has always been safe, reporting the size of the
# raw file.
# ASCII mangling is a horrible feature of the protocol.
#ascii_upload_enable=YES
#ascii_download_enable=YES
#
# You may fully customise the login banner string:
#ftpd_banner=Welcome to blah FTP service.
#
# You may specify a file of disallowed anonymous e-mail addresses. Apparently
# useful for combatting certain DoS attacks.
#deny_email_enable=YES
# (default follows)
#banned_email_file=/etc/vsftpd.banned_emails
#
# You may specify an explicit list of local users to chroot() to their home
# directory. If chroot_local_user is YES, then this list becomes a list of
# users to NOT chroot().
#chroot_list_enable=YES
# (default follows)
#chroot_list_file=/etc/vsftpd.chroot_list
#
# You may activate the "-R" option to the builtin ls. This is disabled by
# default to avoid remote users being able to cause excessive I/O on large
# sites. However, some broken FTP clients such as "ncftp" and "mirror" assume
# the presence of the "-R" option, so there is a strong case for enabling it.
#ls_recurse_enable=YES
```

You can edit this file via the text editor. (Choose Applications⇨Accessories⇨ Text Editor.) After you save your changes, you'll need to restart the `vsftpd` service for the changes to take effect, as described in the previous section.

The following paragraphs describe some of the more common modifications to the `vsftpd.conf` file:

✦ **Anonymous access:** By default, anonymous access is allowed. To prevent users from accessing the FTP site anonymously, change the `anonymous_enable` line to

    anonymous_enable=NO

If you disable anonymous access, your users will have to have a Linux account on the server to access the FTP site. By default, each user will be directed to his or her home directory.

✦ **Allowing local users:** By default, local users are allowed to access the FTP site. To prevent local users from accessing the FTP site, change the `local_enable` line to

    local_enable=NO

You can disable either anonymous users or local users, but do *not* disable both!

✦ **Creating a read-only FTP site:** If you want to make your FTP site read-only so that users can download files but not upload, change the `write_enable` line to

    write_enable=NO

✦ **Customizing the welcome banner:** You can customize the welcome banner by uncommenting the `ftpd_banner` line and adding your banner. For example

    Ftpd_banner=Welcome to my FTP site!

Chapter 9: Linux Commands

In This Chapter

✔ Discovering the basics of command shells

✔ Identifying file and directory commands

✔ Discovering commands that help with packages and services

✔ Figuring out commands for managing users and groups

✔ Becoming familiar with networking commands

*L*inux has several nice graphical user interfaces (GUI) to choose from, and many of the more common Linux networking functions have graphical configuration utilities. Still, many Linux configuration tasks can be done only from a command shell. In many cases, though, the configuration utility provides access only to the most basic configuration parameters, so if you want to configure advanced features, you have to use commands. In fact, some network features don't even have a graphical configuration utility, so you have no choice but to use commands.

Even when GNOME-based alternatives are available, you'll often resort to using commands because frankly, that's what Linux was built to do. Unlike Windows, Linux relies on commands as its primary means of getting things done. If you're going to work with Linux, knowing the basic commands presented in this chapter is a must.

Command Shell Basics

A *shell* is a program that accepts commands from a command prompt and executes them. The shell displays a prompt to let you know it's waiting for a command. When you type the command and press Enter, the system reads your command, interprets it, executes it, displays the results, and then displays the prompt again so that you can enter another command.

Linux commands are case-sensitive, so be careful about capitalization when you type Linux commands.

Getting to a shell

You can work with Linux commands directly from one of the six virtual consoles. If you like the responsiveness of text mode, virtual consoles are for you. To switch to a virtual console, press Ctrl+Alt+F*x*. For example, press Ctrl+Alt+F1 to switch to virtual console 1. When you're in a virtual console, you have to answer the logon prompt with a valid username and password. To return to GNOME, press Ctrl+Alt+F7.

The alternative is to work in a terminal window within the GNOME environment. If you have an older computer, you may find that the terminal window is a little unresponsive. If your computer is relatively new, however, the terminal window will be just as responsive as the text-mode virtual console. Plus, you'll have the benefit of a scroll bar that lets you scroll to see text that otherwise would have flown off the screen.

To open a terminal window, click Activities, click Applications, then click the Terminal icon. This opens a command shell in a window right on the GNOME desktop, as shown in Figure 9-1. Because this shell runs within the user account GNOME is logged on as, you don't have to log on. You can just start typing commands. When you're done, type **Exit** to close the window.

For normal Linux users, the command shell prompt character is a dollar sign ($). If you see a hash mark (#) as the prompt character, it means you're logged on as `root`. Whenever you see a hash prompt, you should be extra careful about what you do because you can easily get yourself into trouble by deleting important files or otherwise corrupting the system.

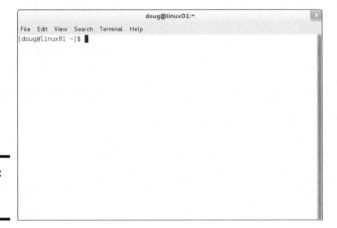

Figure 9-1:
A terminal
window.

Editing commands

Most of the time, you just type commands using the keyboard. If you make a mistake, you just type the command again, being careful not to repeat the mistake. However, Linux shells have several built-in editing features that can simplify the task of correcting a mistaken command or entering a sequence of similar commands:

✦ **Repeat:** If you want to repeat a command that you've used recently, press the up-arrow key. This action recalls your most recently executed commands. You can press Enter to execute a command as is, or you can edit the command before you execute it.

✦ **Autocomplete:** The shell has a handy autocomplete feature that can finish partially spelled directory, file, or command names. Just type part of the name and then press Tab. If you've typed enough for the shell to figure out what you mean, the shell finishes the name for you. Otherwise, it just beeps, in which case you can type a few more letters and try again. In some cases, the shell displays a list of items that match what you've typed so far to help you know what to type next.

Wildcards

Wildcards are one of the most powerful features of command shells. With wildcards, you can process all the files that match a particular naming pattern with a single command. For example, suppose that you have a folder with 500 files in it, and you want to delete all the files that contain the letters Y2K and end with `.doc`, which happens to be 50 files. If you try to do this in GNOME, you'll spend ten minutes picking these files out from the list. From a shell, you can delete them all with the single command `rm *Y2K*.doc`.

You can use two basic wildcard characters. An asterisk (`*`) stands for any number of characters, including zero, and an exclamation mark (`!`) stands for just one character. Thus, `!Text.doc` matches files with names like `aText.doc`, `xText.doc`, and `4Text.doc`, but not `abcText.doc` or just `Text.doc`. However, `*Text.doc` would match any of those filenames.

You can also use brackets to indicate a range of characters to choose from. For example, `report[123]` matches the files `report1`, `report2`, or `report3`. You can also specify `report[1-5]` to match `report1`, `report2`, `report3`, `report4`, or `report5`. The wildcard `r[aeiou]port` matches files named `raport`, `report`, `riport`, `roport`, or `ruport`. As you can see, the possibilities are almost endless.

Redirection and piping

Redirection and piping are related techniques. *Redirection* lets you specify an alternative destination for output that will be displayed by a command or specify an alternative source for input that should be fed into a command. For example, you can save the results of an `ifconfig` command to `/home/doug/myconfig` like this:

```
$ ifconfig > /home/doug/myconfig
```

Here, the greater-than sign (>) is used to redirect the command's console output.

If a command accepts input from the keyboard, you can use input redirection to specify a file that contains the input that you want to feed to the command. For example, you can create a text file named `lookup.commands` with subcommands for a command such as `nslookup`. Then, you can feed those scripted subcommands to the `nslookup` command, like this:

```
$ nslookup < /home/doug/lookup.commands
```

Piping is a similar technique. It takes the console output from one command and feeds it into the next command as input. One of the most common uses of piping is to send the output of a command that displays a lot of information to the `more` program, which displays the output one page at a time. For example:

```
$ ifconfig | more
```

The vertical bar (|) is often called the *pipe character* because it's the symbol used to indicate piping.

Environment variables

The shell makes several environment variables available to commands. An *environment variable* is a predefined value you can use in your commands to provide commonly used information, such as the name of the current user or the operating system version. You can use an environment variable anywhere in a command by typing **$** (dollar sign) followed by the environment variable name. For example, this command

```
$ echo This is $HOSTNAME running on an $HOSTTYPE
```

displays a line such as

```
This is LSERVER running on an i386
```

Table 9-1 lists some of the more useful environment variables that are available to you and your commands.

Table 9-1	Environment Variables
Variable	*Description*
HOME	The current user's home directory
HOSTNAME	The computer's host name
HOSTTYPE	The host computer type
OSTYPE	The operating system
PATH	The search order for executable programs
PROMPT_COMMAND	The command used to generate the prompt
PWD	The present working directory
SHELL	The shell being used
USERNAME	The current username

Shell scripts

A *shell script* is simply a text file that contains one or more commands which you can execute in sequence by running the script. The simplest shell scripts are just lists of commands, but advanced shell scripts can include complicated scripting statements that border on a full-featured programming language.

You can create shell scripts by using any text editor. The easiest text editor to use is gedit, which you can access from the GNOME desktop by choosing Activities➪Applications➪gedit. If you want your friends to think you're a Linux guru, however, take a few moments to learn how to use vi, a powerful text mode editor. To create or edit a file in vi, type the command **vi** followed by a filename. Then, type away. To use a vi command, press Esc(ape) and then type one of the commands listed in Table 9-2.

Table 9-2	Common vi Commands
Command	*Explanation*
i	Enters insert mode so that you can enter text at the cursor location. Move the cursor to the point where you want to enter the text first. When you're finished inserting text, press Esc to return to command mode.
:w	Saves the file. (w stands for write.)
:q	Quit.
:wq	Write and then quit.

(continued)

Table 9-2 *(continued)*

Command	Explanation
:q!	Quit without saving.
/string	Search forward for string.
?string	Search backward for string.
n	Repeat the last search.
u	Undo the previous command.

After you create a shell script, you have to grant yourself execute permission to run the script. For example, to grant yourself permission to run a script named myscript, use this command:

```
$ chmod 755 myscript
```

To run a shell script, you use the sh command and provide the name of the script file. For example:

```
$ sh myscript
```

Directory- and File-Handling Commands

Because much of Linux administration involves working with configuration files, you frequently need to use the basic directory-and file-handling commands presented in this section.

The pwd command

This command displays the current directory, which is called the *present working directory* — hence the command name pwd. Here's the syntax:

```
pwd
```

Enter this command, and you get output similar to the following:

```
$ pwd
/home/doug
```

The cd command

The cd command changes the current working directory. The syntax is as follows:

```
cd directory
```

You may want to follow the cd command with a pwd command to make sure that you changed to the right directory. For example:

```
$ cd /etc/mail
$ pwd
/etc/mail
```

To change to a subdirectory of the current directory, omit the leading slash from the directory name. For example:

```
$ pwd
/home
$ cd doug
$ pwd
/home/doug
```

You can also use the double-dot (. .) to represent the parent of the current directory. Thus, to move up one level, use the command cd . . as follows:

```
$ pwd
/home/doug
$ cd ..
$ pwd
/home
```

The mkdir command

To create a new directory, use the mkdir command. It has the following syntax:

```
mkdir directory
```

Here's an example that creates a subdirectory named images in the current directory:

```
$ mkdir images
```

This example creates a directory named /home/doug/images:

```
$ mkdir /home/doug/images
```

The rmdir command

The rmdir command removes a directory. It has the following syntax:

```
rmdir directory
```

Here's an example:

```
$ rmdir /home/doug/images
```

Here, the `/home/doug/images` directory is deleted. Note that the directory must be empty to be removed, so you have to first delete any files in the directory.

The ls command

The `ls` command lists the contents of the current directory. Here's the syntax:

```
ls [options] directory
```

The following paragraphs describe the more important options for the `ls` command:

+ `-a`: Lists all the files in the directory, including files that start with a period

+ `-c`: Sorts entries by the time the files were last modified

+ `-d`: Lists only directory names

+ `-l`: Displays in long format

+ `-r`: Displays files in reverse order

+ `-R`: Lists the contents of all subdirectories, and subdirectories of subdirectories, and subdirectories of subdirectories of subdirectories; in other words, lists subdirectories recursively

+ `-s`: Displays file sizes

+ `-S`: Sorts files by size

+ `-t`: Sorts files by timestamp.

+ `-u`: Sorts files by the time the files were last accessed.

+ `-X`: Sorts files by their extensions.

Without arguments, the `ls` command lists all the files in the current directory, like this:

```
$ pwd
/etc/mail
$ ls
access            helpfile          Makefile        submit.cf        virtusertable
access.db         local-host-names  sendmail.cf     submit.cf.bak    virtusertable.db
domaintable       mailertable       sendmail.mc     submit.mc
domaintable.db    mailertable.db    statistics      trusted-users
```

You can limit the display to certain files by typing a filename, which can include wildcards. For example:

```
$ ls a*
access            access.db
```

You can also specify the directory that you want to display, like this:

```
$ ls /etc/httpd
conf   conf.d   logs   modules   run
```

To display detailed information about the files in the directory, use the -l switch, as in this example:

```
$ ls /etc/mail/s* -l
-rw-r--r--   1 root     root         57427 Jul 19 16:35 sendmail.cf
-rw-r--r--   1 root     root          5798 Feb 24 16:15 sendmail.mc
-rw-------   1 root     root           628 Jul 24 17:21 statistics
-rw-r--r--   1 root     root         39028 Jul 19 17:28 submit.cf
-r--r--r--   1 root     root         39077 Feb 24 16:15 submit.cf.bak
-rw-r--r--   1 root     root           953 Feb 24 16:15 submit.mc
```

The cp command

The cp command copies files. Here's the basic syntax:

```
cp [options] source-file destination-file
```

The following list describes the more important options for the ls command:

+ -a: The same as -dpR.

+ -b: Makes backup copies of existing files before they're overwritten. Sounds like a good plan to me.

+ -d: Copies links rather than the files the links point to.

+ -f: Removes files that will be overwritten.

+ -i: Interactively prompts for each file to be overwritten.

+ -l: Creates links to files rather than actually copying file contents.

+ -p: Preserves ownership and permissions.

+ -R: Copies the contents of subdirectories recursively.

+ -s: Creates symbolic links to files rather than actually copying file contents.

+ -u: Replaces destination files only if the source file is newer.

To make a copy of a file within the same directory, use cp like this:

```
$ cp sendmail.cf sendmail.cf.backup
```

If you want to copy a file to another directory without changing the filename, use cp like this:

```
$ cp sendmail.cf /home/doug
```

You can use wildcards to copy multiple files:

```
$ cp send* /home/doug
```

To include files in subdirectories of the source file, use the -R switch, like this:

```
$ cp -R /etc/*.cf /home/doug
```

In this example, all files in the /etc directory or any of its subdirectories that end with .cf are copied to /home/doug.

The rm command

The rm command deletes files. The syntax is as follows:

```
rm [options] file
```

The options are described in the following paragraphs:

✦ -f: Removes files that will be overwritten

✦ -i: Interactively prompts for each file to be overwritten

✦ -R: Copies the contents of subdirectories recursively

To delete a single file, use it like this:

```
$ rm any.old.file
```

To delete multiple files, use a wildcard:

```
$ rm any.*
```

To delete an entire directory, use the -r switch:

```
$ rm -r /doug/old.files
```

The mv command

The mv command moves files or renames them. In Linux, moving and renaming a file is essentially the same thing. Moving a file changes the file's directory location but leaves its name the same. Renaming a file leaves the file in the same directory but changes the file's name.

The syntax of the mv command is

```
mvp [options] source-file destination
```

The following paragraphs describe the options:

✦ –b: Makes backup copies of existing files before they're overwritten. Still sounds like a good plan to me.

✦ –f: Removes files that will be overwritten.

✦ –i: Interactively prompts for each file to be overwritten.

✦ –u: Replaces destination files only if the source file is newer.

To move a file to another directory, provide a filename for the first argument and a directory for the second, like this:

```
$ mv monthly.report /home/Debbie/
```

To rename a file, provide filenames for both arguments:

```
$ mv monthly.report august.monthly.report
```

The touch command

The `touch` command is one of the more interesting Linux file management commands. Here's the syntax:

```
touch [options] file
```

Here are some of the options that you can use:

✦ –a: Changes the access time only

✦ –c: Doesn't create files that don't exist

✦ –m: Changes the modification time only

The basic form of the `touch` command looks like this:

```
$ touch monthly.report
```

If you use `touch` on an existing file, the `touch` command changes the modification date of the file. If you use it on a command that doesn't exist, the `touch` command creates a new, empty file.

The cat command

The `cat` command displays the contents of a file. It has the following syntax:

```
cat [options] [filename...]
```

The filename is optional. If you omit the filename, the `cat` command obtains its input from the console, which you can redirect if you want.

And, you can specify more than one filename. If you do, the files are combined to create a single output stream.

Here are some of the options you can use:

✦ -A: Displays new line characters as $, tab characters as ^I, and control characters with a caret (^)

✦ -b: Numbers all nonblank lines as they're displayed

✦ -e: Displays new line characters as $ and control characters with a caret (^)

✦ -E: Displays new line characters as $

✦ -n: Numbers lines as they are displayed

✦ -s: Squeezes multiple spaces down to a single space

✦ -t: Displays tab characters as ^I and control characters with a caret (^)

✦ -T: Displays tab characters as ^I

✦ -v: Shows nonprinting control characters with a caret (^)

Here's a basic example:

```
$ cat /etc/hosts
# Do not remove the following line, or various programs
# that require network functionality will fail.
127.0.0.1       LSERVER localhost.localdomain    localhost
$
```

If you don't provide any filename arguments, the cat command copies text from the keyboard and displays it on the console. You can use the cat command along with output redirection to quickly create a short text file, like this:

```
$ cat >mytext
This is line one.
This is line two.
This is line three.
<ctrl+D>
```

For the last line, press Ctrl+D. This signals the end of the input to the cat command.

Commands for Working with Packages and Services

As a Linux administrator, you frequently need to start and stop services and check the status of installed packages or install new packages. The following sections describe the Linux commands that help you to perform these tasks.

The service command

You use the service command to check the status of services and to start, stop, or restart services. You need to restart a service whenever you make a configuration change in order for your changes to take effect. Here's the basic syntax:

```
service [service] [ start | stop | restart ]
```

The following paragraphs describe some typical uses of the service command:

✦ To check the status of the httpd service (Apache), use this command:

```
$ service httpd status
```

✦ To stop the httpd service:

```
$ service httpd stop
```

✦ To start the httpd service:

```
$ service httpd start
```

✦ To restart the httpd service:

```
$ service httpd restart
```

The only trick to using the service command is that you have to know the name of the service. If you're not sure of the name, you can run the service command to display the status of all services, like this:

```
$ service --status-all
```

It will take a few moments to list all the services, but after the command is done, you can scroll through the list to find the service that you're looking for.

Table 9-3 lists some of the more common services.

Table 9-3   Common Linux Services

Service	Description
atd	Runs commands scheduled by the at command
autof	Automatically mounts file systems
crond	Runs programs at specified times
dhcpd	The DHCP server
finger	The Internet finger service
httpd	The Apache web server
imap	The IMAP mail protocol
imaps	Secure IMAP service (SSL)
ipop3	The POP3 mail protocol
iptables	Automatic packet filtering for firewalls
isdn	ISDN services
named	The BIND DNS server
netf	The network file system
network	Activates and deactivates all network interfaces
nfs	Native Unix/Linux network file sharing
pop3s	Secure POP3 service (SSL)
sendmail	The Sendmail service
smb	The Samba file- and printer-sharing service
snmpd	SNMP
telnet	The Telnet server

The rpm command

The rpm command is the Red Hat Package Manager, a tool that simplifies the task of managing packages on your Linux system. Although rpm was originally developed for Red Hat Linux, it's now found on many Linux distributions, including Fedora (which is, of course, based on the Red Hat distribution).

Here's the basic syntax for querying the status of a package:

```
rpm -q [options] package
```

To install, upgrade, or remove a package, the basic syntax is more like this:

```
rpm [ -i | -u | -e ] [options] package-file
```

You can use quite a few options with the rpm command, but the most common are

✦ -v: Displays verbose output. You may as well know what rpm is doing while it chugs along.

✦ -h: Displays hash marks (#) periodically to reassure you that the program hasn't died.

You can use rpm to determine the status of installed packages on your system by using the -q switch. For example, to find out what version of Sendmail is installed, use this command:

```
$ rpm -q send*
Sendmail-8.12.8-4
```

Notice that you can use a wildcard with the package name. If you don't have a package whose name matches the package name you supply, you get the message package not installed.

To install a package, you use the -i switch and specify a wildcard filename that indicates the location of the package file. It's also a good idea to use the -v and -h switches so that you can monitor the installation's progress. For example, to install Sendmail from a mounted CD-ROM drive, you use this command:

```
$ rpm -ivh /mnt/cdrom/Fedora/Packages/sendmail*
```

If you want to update to a newer version of a package, you can use the -u switch instead of the -i switch:

```
$ rpm -uvh /mnt/cdrom/Fedora/Packages/sendmail*
```

Finally, you can remove a package by using the -e switch:

```
$ rpm -e send*
```

To use the rpm command, you must log on as root.

The yum command

yum, which stands for *Yellowdog Updater Modified*, is an improvement over the rpm command. One of the biggest drawbacks of using the rpm command is that when you install a package with it, rpm does not automatically detect and install any dependent packages that may be required. In contrast, yum searches for and automatically installs dependent packages.

Although `yum` has many command line options, the most common way to use it is as follows:

```
yum install package-name
```

For example, to install a package named `sendmail`, you would use this command:

```
yum install sendmail
```

Commands for Administering Users

The following sections describe the Linux commands that you can use to create and manage user accounts from a command shell.

You should log on as `root` to perform these tasks.

The useradd command

The `useradd` command creates a user account. Here's the basic syntax for adding a new user:

```
useradd [options] username
```

You can also use this command to change the default options for new users. In that case, the syntax is more like this:

```
useradd -D [options]
```

If you use –D with no options, a list of the current default settings will be shown.

The options are as follows:

+ `-c comment`: Typically the user's full name
+ `-d home-dir`: The home directory of the new user
+ `-e date`: The expiration date for the user
+ `-f time`: The number of days between logons before the user is considered expired
+ `-g group`: The initial logon group for the user
+ `-G groups`: Additional groups the user should belong to
+ `-m`: Creates the new user's home directory if it doesn't exist already
+ `-s shell-path`: Specifies the user's logon shell

The following option is valid only with –D (which sets a default option):

✦ **-b** *base-dir*: Provides the default base directory if a home directory is not specified

Its most basic form, the useradd command creates a user with default option settings:

```
$ useradd theodore
```

This command creates a user named theodore.

Here's a command that specifies the user's full name in the comment option:

```
$ useradd -c 'Theodore Cleaver' theodore
```

The following command creates a temporary account named ghost that expires on Halloween 2012:

```
$ useradd -e 2012-10-31 ghost
```

If you want to see what the default values are for account options, use the –D option without any other parameters:

```
$ useradd -D
GROUP=100
HOME=/home
INACTIVE=-1
EXPIRE=
SHELL=/bin/bash
SKEL=/etc/skel
```

The usermod command

The usermod command modifies an existing user. It has the following syntax:

```
usermod [options] username
```

The options are as follows:

✦ c *comment*: Typically the user's full name

✦ **-d** *home-dir*: The home directory of the new user

✦ **-e** *date*: The expiration date for a logon

✦ **-f** *time*: The number of days between logons before the user is considered expired

✦ **-g** *group*: The initial logon group for the user

✦ -G *groups*: Additional groups the user should belong to

✦ -m: Creates the new user's home directory if it doesn't exist already

✦ -s *shell-path*: Specifies the user's logon shell

✦ -l: Locks an account

✦ -u: Unlocks an account

Here's an example that changes a user's full name:

```
$ usermod -c 'The Beave' theodore
```

The userdel command

The userdel command deletes a user. It has a simple syntax:

```
userdel [-r] username
```

If you specify -r, the user's home directory is deleted along with the account.

The chage command

The chage command modifies date policies for a user's passwords. It has the following syntax:

```
chage [options] username
```

The following paragraphs describe the options you can use:

✦ -m *days*: Specifies the minimum number of days allowed between password changes.

✦ -M *days*: Specifies the maximum number of days allowed between password changes.

✦ -d *date*: The date of the last password change.

✦ -E *date*: The date on which the account will expire.

✦ -W *days*: The number of days prior to the password expiring that the user will be warned the password is about to expire.

✦ -I *days*: The number of days of inactivity after the password has expired that the account is locked out. Specify 0 to disable this feature.

Here's an example that sets an account to expire on Halloween 2016:

```
$ chage -E 2016-10-31 ghost
```

If you specify a username but no other options, you're prompted to enter each option. This is a lot easier than trying to remember all the switches!

The passwd command

The passwd command changes the password for a user account. Its syntax is

```
passwd [user]
```

If you don't supply a user, the password for the current user is changed.

The passwd command prompts you to enter the new password twice to prevent the possibility of mistyping the password.

The newusers command

The newusers command provides an easy way to create a group of new user accounts. It reads a text file that contains one line for each new user, listing the user's name and password.

Here's the syntax of the newusers command:

```
newusers [filename]
```

If you omit the filename, newusers accepts input from the console.

Suppose that you have a file named /root/island.users that contains these lines:

```
gilligan    ml9jiedr
skipper     1hiecr8u
professor   dr0uxiaf
maryann     choe7rlu
ginger      jiuqled5
mrhowell    j1emoaf1
lovie       zo2priak
```

You can then create these seven stranded user accounts by issuing this command:

```
$ newusers /root/island.users
```

Because the newusers file contains unencrypted passwords, you shouldn't leave it lying around. Require these new users to change their passwords immediately and delete the file you used to create the users.

The groupadd command

The `groupadd` command creates a new group. It has the following syntax:

```
groupadd [options] group
```

Although you have several possible options to use, the only one you're likely to need is `-r`, which creates a system group that has special privileges.

Here's an example that creates a group named castaways:

```
$ groupadd castaways
```

That's all you have to do to create a new group. To administer the group, you use the `gpasswd` command.

The groupdel command

The `groupdel` command deletes a group. It has the following syntax:

```
groupdel group
```

Here's an example that deletes a group named castaways:

```
$ groupdel castaways
```

Poof! The group is gone.

The gpasswd command

You use the `gpasswd` command to administer a group. This command has several different syntax options.

To change the group password:

```
gpasswd [ -r | -R ] group
```

To add a user:

```
gpasswd -a user group
```

To remove a user:

```
gpasswd -d user group
```

To create group administrators and/or members:

```
gpasswd [-A administrators...] [-M members... ] group
```

The options are as follows:

- ✦ -r: Removes the password from the group.

- ✦ -R: Disables access to the group via the newgrp command.

- ✦ -a: Adds the specified user to the group.

- ✦ -d: Deletes the specified user from the group.

- ✦ -A: Specifies one or more group administrators. Use commas with no intervening spaces to separate the administrators from each other. Each administrator must be an existing user.

- ✦ -M: Specifies one or more group members. Use commas with no intervening spaces to separate the members from each other. Each member must be an existing user.

The following example adds seven group members and one administrator to a group called castaways:

```
$ gpasswd -A skipper -M skipper,gilligan,professor,maryann,
ginger,mrhowell,lovie castaways
```

If the rest of the group finally decides to throw Gilligan off the island, they can remove him from the group with this command:

```
$ gpasswd -d gilligan castaways
```

Commands for Managing Ownership and Permissions

This section presents the details of the chown and chmod commands, which are the essential tools for assigning file system rights in the Linux environment.

The chown command

The chown command changes the owner of a file. Typically, the user who creates a file is the owner of the file. However, the owner can transfer the file to someone else via this command. The basic syntax of this command is

```
chown user file
```

For example, to change the owner of a file named rescue.plans to user professor, use this command:

```
$ chown professor rescue.plans
```

To change ownership of all the files in the directory named /home/island to professor, use this command:

```
$ chown professor /home/island
```

Issuing the following command would be a really bad idea:

```
$ chown gilligan rescue.plans
```

The chgrp command

Every file has not only an individual owner, but also a group owner. You can change the group ownership by using the chgrp command, which has the following basic syntax:

```
chgrp group file
```

For example, to grant the castaways group ownership of the file rescue. plans, use this command:

```
$ chgrp castaways rescue.plans
```

To change group ownership of all the files in the directory named /home/ island to castaways, use this command:

```
$ chgrp castaways /home/island
```

The chmod command

The chmod command lets you change the permissions for a Linux file. Before explaining the syntax of the chmod command, you need to look at the cryptic way that Linux reports file permissions. Linux grants three different types of permissions — read, write, and execute — for three different scopes: owner, group, and everyone. That's a total of nine permissions.

When you use the ls command with the -l option, the permissions are shown as a ten-character string that begins with a hyphen if the entry is for a file or a d if the entry is for a directory. Then, the next nine letters are the nine permissions, in this order:

✦ Read, write, execute for the owner

✦ Read, write, execute for the group

✦ Read, write, execute for everyone

The letters r, w, or x appear if the permission has been granted. If the permission is denied, a hyphen appears.

For example, suppose the `ls -l` command lists these permissions:

```
-rw-r--r--
```

You interpret this permission string like this:

✦ The first hyphen indicates that this is a file, not a directory.

✦ The next three positions are `rw-`. Therefore, the owner has read and write permission on this file, but not execute permission.

✦ The next three positions are `r--`. That means the group owner has read permissions but not write or execute permission.

✦ The last three positions are also `r--`. That means that everyone else has read permission but not write or execute permission.

The full syntax of the `chmod` command is pretty complex. However, you can do most of what you need to do with this form:

```
chmod specification file
```

Here, `specification` is in the form `u=rwx`, `g=rwx`, or `o=rwx` to set the permissions for the user (owner), group, and others (everyone). You don't have to specify `r`, `w`, and `x`; you just list the permissions that you want to grant. For example, to grant read and write permission for the user to a file named `rescue.plans`, use this command:

```
$ chmod u=rw rescue.plans
```

You can also combine specifications, like this:

```
$ chmod u=rw,g=rw,o=r rescue.plans
```

To revoke all rights for the user, group, or others, don't type anything after the equal sign. For example, this command revokes all rights for others:

```
$ chmod o= rescue.plans
```

Networking Commands

The following sections present Linux commands that are used to display information about the network or configure its settings.

You can find more detail about some of these commands in Book IV, Chapter 6.

The hostname command

The `hostname` command simply displays the computer's host name. It has the following syntax:

```
hostname [name]
```

If you use this command without any parameters, the computer's host name is displayed. If you specify a name, the computer's host name is changed to the name you specify.

The ifconfig command

`ifconfig` displays and sets configuration options for network interfaces. Although you can configure an Ethernet adapter using this command, you'll rarely have to. Linux does a pretty good job of automatically configuring network adapters, and the GNOME-based Network Configuration tool supplied with the Red Hat distribution should be able to handle most network configuration chores. So you'll use `ifconfig` mostly to display network configuration settings.

The basic syntax for `ifconfig` is

```
ifconfig interface [address] [netmask mask]
        [broadcast broadcast]
```

Here are the options that you can use on the `ifconfig` command:

✦ *interface*: The symbolic name for your network adapter. It's typically `eth0` for the first Ethernet adapter or `eth1` for the second adapter.

✦ *address*: The IP address you want to assign to the interface, such as 192.168.1.100.

✦ *netmask*: The subnet mask to use, such as 255.255.255.0.

✦ *broadcast:* The broadcast, which should be the highest address on the subnet. For example: 192.168.1.255.

If you enter `ifconfig` without any parameters, the `ifconfig` command displays the current status of your network adapters, like this:

```
eth0     Link encap:Ethernet  HWaddr 00:20:78:16:E0:6A
         UP BROADCAST RUNNING MULTICAST  MTU:1500  Metric:1
         RX packets:0 errors:0 dropped:0 overruns:0 frame:0
         TX packets:11 errors:0 dropped:0 overruns:0 carrier:0
         collisions:0 txqueuelen:100
         RX bytes:0 (0.0 b)  TX bytes:2916 (2.8 Kb)
         Interrupt:11 Base address:0xd000
eth1     Link encap:Ethernet  HWaddr 00:40:05:80:51:F3
         inet addr:192.168.3.100  Bcast:192.168.3.255  Mask:255.255.255.0
         UP BROADCAST RUNNING MULTICAST  MTU:1500  Metric:1
```

```
            RX packets:2358 errors:0 dropped:0 overruns:0 frame:0
            TX packets:1921 errors:0 dropped:0 overruns:0 carrier:0
            collisions:0 txqueuelen:100
            RX bytes:265194 (258.9 Kb)  TX bytes:424467 (414.5 Kb)
            Interrupt:3 Base address:0xc000
lo          Link encap:Local Loopback
            inet addr:127.0.0.1  Mask:255.0.0.0
            UP LOOPBACK RUNNING  MTU:16436  Metric:1
            RX packets:93707 errors:0 dropped:0 overruns:0 frame:0
            TX packets:93707 errors:0 dropped:0 overruns:0 carrier:0
            collisions:0 txqueuelen:0
            RX bytes:6393713 (6.0 Mb)  TX bytes:6393713 (6.0 Mb)
```

To change the IP address of an adapter, use `ifconfig` like this:

```
$ ifconfig eth0 192.168.1.200
```

The netstat command

The `netstat` command lets you monitor just about every aspect of a Linux server's network functions. This command can generate page after page of interesting information — if you know what it all means.

The two most common reasons to use `netstat` are to display the routing table and to display open TCP/IP connections. The syntax for displaying the routing table is

```
netstat -r
```

This results in a display similar to this:

```
Kernel IP routing table
Destination     Gateway         Genmask         Flags   MSS Window  irtt Iface
192.168.1.0     *               255.255.255.0   U         0 0          0 eth1
192.168.1.0     *               255.255.255.0   U         0 0          0 eth0
127.0.0.0       *               255.0.0.0       U         0 0          0 lo
```

To display TCP/IP connections, use this syntax:

```
netstat -l
```

This results in a display similar to the following:

```
Active Internet connections (only servers)
Proto Recv-Q Send-Q Local Address           Foreign Address         State
tcp        0      0 *:1024                   *:*                     LISTEN
tcp        0      0 LSERVER:1025             *:*                     LISTEN
tcp        0      0 *:netbios-ssn            *:*                     LISTEN
tcp        0      0 *:sunrpc                 *:*                     LISTEN
tcp        0      0 *:http                   *:*                     LISTEN
tcp        0      0 *:x11                    *:*                     LISTEN
tcp        0      0 *:ssh                    *:*                     LISTEN
tcp        0      0 LSERVER:ipp              *:*                     LISTEN
tcp        0      0 LSERVER:smtp             *:*                     LISTEN
tcp        0      0 *:https                  *:*                     LISTEN
```

```
udp       0       0 *:1024                *:*
udp       0       0 LSERVER:1026          *:*
udp       0       0 192.168.1.20:netbios-ns *:*
udp       0       0 192.168.1.20:netbios-ns *:*
udp       0       0 *:netbios-ns          *:*
udp       0       0 192.168.1.2:netbios-dgm *:*
udp       0       0 192.168.1.2:netbios-dgm *:*
udp       0       0 *:netbios-dgm         *:*
udp       0       0 *:940                 *:*
udp       0       0 *:sunrpc              *:*
udp       0       0 *:631                 *:*
  .
  .
  .
```

From this display, you can tell which Linux services are actively listening on TCP/IP ports.

The ping command

The `ping` command is the basic troubleshooting tool for TCP/IP. You use it to determine whether basic TCP/IP connectivity has been established between two computers. If you're having any kind of network trouble between two computers, the first troubleshooting step is almost always to see whether the computers can ping each other.

The basic syntax of `ping` is straightforward:

```
ping [options] address
```

The options can be

- ✦ `-c`: The number of packets to send. If you omit this, `ping` continues to send packets until you interrupt it.

- ✦ `-d`: Floods the network with packets, as many as 100 per second. Use with care!

- ✦ `-i`: Specifies how many seconds to wait between sending packets. The default is one second. If you're having intermittent connection problems, you may try letting `ping` run for a while with this option set to a higher value, such as `60`, to send a packet every minute.

- ✦ `-R`: Displays the route the packets take to get to the destination computer.

`ping` will continue to ping the destination computer until you interrupt it by pressing Ctrl+Z.

You can specify the host to ping by using an IP address, as in this example:

```
$ ping 192.168.1.100
PING 192.168.1.100 (192.168.1.100) 56(84) bytes of data.
```

```
64 bytes from 192.168.1.100: icmp_seq=1 ttl=128 time=0.382 ms
64 bytes from 192.168.1.100: icmp_seq=2 ttl=128 time=0.345 ms
64 bytes from 192.168.1.100: icmp_seq=3 ttl=128 time=0.320 ms
64 bytes from 192.168.1.100: icmp_seq=4 ttl=128 time=0.328 ms
```

You can also ping by using a DNS name, as in this example:

```
$ ping www.lowewriter.com
PING www.lowewriter.com (209.68.34.15) 56(84) bytes of data.
64 bytes from www.lowewriter.com (209.68.34.15): icmp_seq=1 ttl=47 time=88.9 ms
64 bytes from www.lowewriter.com (209.68.34.15): icmp_seq=2 ttl=47 time=87.9 ms
64 bytes from www.lowewriter.com (209.68.34.15): icmp_seq=3 ttl=47 time=88.3 ms
64 bytes from www.lowewriter.com (209.68.34.15): icmp_seq=4 ttl=47 time=87.2 ms
```

The route command

The `route` command displays or modifies the computer's routing table.
To display the routing table, use `route` without any parameters. To add an
entry to the routing table, use this syntax:

```
route add [ -net | -host ] address [options]
```

To delete an entry, use this syntax:

```
route del [ -net | -host ] address [options]
```

The available options are as follows:

✦ `netmask` *mask*: Specifies the subnet mask for this entry

✦ `gw` *address*: Specifies the gateway address for this entry

✦ `dev` *if*: Specifies an interface (such as `eth0` or `eth1`) for this entry

If you enter `route` by itself, with no parameters, you'll see the routing table,
as in this example:

```
$ route
Kernel IP routing table
Destination     Gateway         Genmask         Flags Metric Ref    Use Iface
192.168.1.0     *               255.255.255.0   U     0      0        0 eth1
192.168.1.0     *               255.255.255.0   U     0      0        0 eth1
169.254.0.0     *               255.255.0.0     U     0      0        0 eth1
127.0.0.0       *               255.0.0.0       U     0      0        0 lo
default         192.168.1.1     0.0.0.0         UG    0      0        0 eth1
```

Suppose that your network has a second router that serves as a link to
another private subnet, 192.168.2.0 (subnet mask 255.255.255.0). The interface on the local side of this router is at 192.168.1.200. To add a static route
entry that sends packets intended for the 192.168.2.0 subnet to this router,
use a command like this:

```
$ route add 192.168.2.0 netmask 255.255.255.0 gw 192.168.1.200
```

The traceroute command

The `traceroute` command displays a list of all the routers that a packet must go through to get from the local computer to a destination on the Internet. Each one of these routers is a *hop*. If you're unable to connect to another computer, you can use `traceroute` to find out exactly where the problem is occurring.

Here's the syntax:

```
traceroute [-i interface] host
```

Although several options are available for the `traceroute` command, the one you're most likely to use is `-i`, which lets you specify an interface. This is useful if your computer has more than one network adapter.

Appendix A: Directory of Useful Websites

*T*hroughout this book, I mention many websites that you can visit to glean more information about various networking topics. This appendix gathers those sites into one convenient location and adds a bunch more that are also worth visiting from time to time. Happy surfing!

Certification

Here are the sites to check out for official certification information:

- ✦ `www.microsoft.com/learning/mcp`: Microsoft's certification headquarters
- ✦ `www.comptia.org`: Independent certification, including A+, Network+, and Security+
- ✦ `www.novell.com/training/certinfo`: The home page for Novell certification
- ✦ `www.ibm.com/certify`: IBM's certification home page
- ✦ `www.cisco.com/certification`: Cisco's certification home page
- ✦ `www.vmware.com/certification`: The place to go for information about certification in VMware tools
- ✦ `www.redhat.com/training/certification`: Red Hat's Linux certification home page

Hardware

The following websites are general resources for researching computer hardware:

- ✦ `http://reviews.cnet.com`: CNET's reviews section offers reviews on all types of computer hardware, with a special section devoted to networking.
- ✦ `www.hardwarecentral.com`: HardwareCentral is another good source for general computer hardware information, reviews, and advice.
- ✦ `www.tomshardware.com`: Tom's Hardware Guide is the place to go if you want detailed information about the latest in computer components.

The following manufacturers offer high-end networking products, including servers, routers, switches, and so on:

✦ `www.ibm.com/systems/networking`: IBM's networking portal is a must-see site.

✦ `www.hp.com/servers`: This page is the home page for Hewlett-Packard's server products.

✦ `www.dell.com/servers`: This page is the home page for Dell server products.

✦ `www.oracle.com/servers`: This page is the home page for Sun servers.

Home and Small-Business Networking

The following websites have general information about home and small-business networking:

✦ `www.homenethelp.com`: This excellent website is devoted to helping people get their home networks up and running. The site is loaded with step-by-step procedures and flowcharts.

✦ `www.practicallynetworked.com`: This site is a great source of information for home networking, with general networking information, technology backgrounders, product reviews, troubleshooting advice, and more.

✦ `www.hometoys.com`: This site provides information on all sorts of gadgets for the home, including networks.

✦ `www.ehpub.com`: This page is the home page of EH Publishing, which publishes several magazines about home technology.

✦ `www.homepna.org`: This page is the home page of the HomePNA Alliance.

✦ `www.homeplug.org`: This page is the home page of the HomePlug Powerline Alliance, which promotes Powerline networking.

✦ `www.linksys.com`: This page is the home page of Linksys, one of the most popular manufacturers of networking devices for homes and small offices, including 10/100BaseT, wireless, and even phone and Powerline devices.

✦ `www.netgear.com`: This page is the home page of NETGEAR, which makes home and small-office networking devices, including 10/100BaseT adapters and switches, wireless devices, and phone-line systems.

Linux

The following website has general information about Linux:

+ www.linux.org: One of the best overall websites for everything Linux. It's a central source of Linux information and news, and includes many links to Linux distributions and downloadable applications.

Here are the home pages for some of the most popular distributions:

+ www.redhat.com: The website of the most popular Linux distribution
+ www.redhat.com/Fedora: The home page of the Fedora project
+ www.ubuntu.com: The website of the popular Ubuntu Linux distribution
+ www.suse.com: The SUSE distribution
+ www.caldera.com: The Caldera distribution from SCO
+ www.mandriva.com: The Mandriva Linux distribution (formerly called *Mandrake Linux)*
+ www.slackware.com: Slackware, one of the oldest Linux distributions

Here are the home pages for some popular Linux networking software:

+ www.isc.org/software/BIND: The official page for BIND, the most popular DNS nameserver on the Internet
+ www.sendmail.org: Official site for Sendmail, the SMTP mail exchange server
+ www.apache.org: Official site for the Apache HTTP server
+ www.samba.org: Official site for the Samba file and print server

Magazines

Here are some links to various magazines on networking topics:

+ www.informationweek.com: *InformationWeek*
+ www.infoworld.com: *InfoWorld*
+ www.networkcomputing.com: *Network Computing*
+ www.windowsitpro.com: *Windows IT Pro Magazine*
+ www.2600.com: *2600 Magazine*
+ www.linuxjournal.com: *Linux Journal*
+ www.linux-mag.com: *Linux Magazine*

Microsoft

Microsoft's website is vast. Here are some links to a few useful areas within this huge website:

✦ `www.microsoft.com/windows`: The home page for the Windows family of products

✦ `www.microsoft.com/windowsserver2008`: The home page for Windows Server 2008

✦ `www.microsoft.com/windowsserver2012`: The home page for Windows Server 2012

✦ `www.microsoft.com/windowsxp`: The home page for Windows XP

✦ `www.microsoft.com/windowsvista`: The home page for Windows Vista

✦ `www.microsoft.com/windows7`: The home page for Windows 7

✦ `www.microsoft.com/servers`: The home page for Microsoft server products

✦ `www.microsoft.com/exchange`: The home page for Exchange

✦ `www.microsoft.com/sqlserver`: The home page for SQL Server

✦ `www.microsoft.com/iis`: The home page for Internet Information Services (IIS)

✦ `www.microsoft.com/sharepoint`: The home page for SharePoint

✦ `http://technet.microsoft.com`: TechNet, a great source for technical information on Microsoft technologies

✦ `http://support.microsoft.com`: Microsoft's general support site

Network Standards Organizations

The following websites are useful when you're researching network standards:

✦ `www.ansi.org`: The American National Standards Institute (ANSI), the official standards organization in the United States

✦ `www.ieee.org`: The Institute of Electrical and Electronics Engineers (IEEE), an international organization that publishes several key networking standards, including the official Ethernet standards (known as *IEEE 802.3)*

✦ www.iso.org: The International Organization for Standardization (ISO), a federation of more than 100 standards organizations throughout the world

✦ www.isoc.org: The Internet Society, an international organization for global coordination and cooperation on the Internet

✦ www.ietf.org: The Internet Engineering Task Force (IETF), responsible for the protocols that drive the Internet

✦ www.iana.org: The Internet Assigned Numbers Authority, which has responsibility for the IP address space

✦ www.w3c.org: The World Wide Web Consortium (W3C), an international organization that handles the development of standards for the World Wide Web

✦ www.rfc-editor.org: The official repository of RFCs (requests to create new standards), which includes a search facility that lets you look up RFCs by name or keyword

Reference

Several general-purpose and computer-specific reference sites provide encyclopedia-style articles or simple definitions of computer and networking terms. If you aren't sure what some new technology is, start at one of these sites:

✦ www.webopedia.com: Webopedia is a great online dictionary of computer and Internet terms. Not sure what *direct sequence spread spectrum* means? Look it up at Webopedia!

✦ www.wikipedia.org: Wikipedia is a huge, user-written online encyclopedia.

✦ www.whatis.com: Whatis.com is another great dictionary of computer and networking terms.

✦ www.howstuffworks.com: This site has general information about many types of technology: computers, automobiles, electronics, science, and more. The computer section provides good low-level introductions to various computer topics, including computer hardware, the Internet, and security.

Search

Search engines are often the first places you turn when you're trying to solve a network problem and need information fast:

✦ www.google.com: Google is the most popular search site on the Internet today, with a huge database of websites and newsgroup articles that's constantly updated. Google has a powerful keyword search feature that lets you refine your search as you go.

✦ www.bing.com: Microsoft's own search engine is designed to compete with Google.

✦ www.yahoo.com: Yahoo!, one of the original website catalogs, is still the best place to go if you want to browse categories rather than search for keywords.

✦ www.webfetch.com: Webfetch is a meta-search tool that searches multiple search engines at the same time.

✦ www.dogpile.com: Dogpile is another search-engine aggregator that searches multiple search engines at the same time.

TCP/IP and the Internet

The following sites have interesting information about the Internet:

✦ www.internic.net: The InterNIC website is a central point of information for domain registration. Check here for a list of accredited domain registrars.

✦ www.networksolutions.com: This site is the home of Network Solutions, the most popular site for registering domain names.

✦ www.register.com: Register.com is another domain registration site.

✦ www.isc.org: Members of the Internet Systems Consortium are the folks who do the twice-a-year domain survey to try to estimate how big the Internet really is.

For DNS information, try www.dnsstuff.com, which lets you perform a variety of DNS lookups to make sure that your DNS zones are set up correctly.

Check these sites to find information about web browsers:

✦ www.microsoft.com/ie: The official home page for Internet Explorer.

✦ www.mozilla.org: The home of Firefox, a popular alternative Web browser. Many users consider Firefox to be the best web browser around.

+ www.opera.com: The home of Opera, another alternative to Internet Explorer.

+ chrome.google.com: The home of Google Chrome, Google's popular web browser.

Wireless Networking

Here are some websites with general information about wireless networking:

+ www.wi-fiplanet.com: Wi-Fi Planet is a large site devoted to news, information, and product reviews for wireless networking.

Here are the websites for the most popular brands of wireless networking products:

+ www.linksys.com: Linksys is a manufacturer of wireless network cards and access points.

+ www.netgear.com: NETGEAR is another manufacturer of wireless components.

+ www.dlink.com: D-Link is yet another manufacturer of inexpensive wireless products.

+ www.smc.com: The home page for SMC, another manufacturer of wireless network products.

+ www.cisco.com: Cisco is the place to go for high-end wireless networking.

+ www.3com.com: 3Com is another good place to go for wireless networking components.

The following websites have interesting information about wireless network security:

+ www.netstumbler.com: The maker of NetStumbler, software that detects wireless network access and security problems

+ www.airwave.com: The maker of AirWave, a software-based tool that snoops for unauthorized access points

+ www.wardriving.com: An extensive site devoted to the practice of wardriving

Smartphones

The following websites contain useful information about various smartphone platforms:

◆ www.blackberry.com: The main website for Research In Motion's BlackBerry platform

◆ www.blackberryforums.com: A popular discussion-forum website for the BlackBerry platform

◆ www.microsoft.com/windowsphone: The home page for the Windows Phone platform

◆ www.android.com: The home page for Google's Android platform

◆ www.apple.com/iphone: The home page for Apple's iPhone

Appendix B: Glossary

10Base2: A type of coax cable that was once the most often used cable for Ethernet networks; also known as *thinnet* or *cheapernet*. The maximum length of a single segment is 185 meters (600 feet). 10base2 is now all but obsolete.

10Base5: The original Ethernet coax cable, now pretty much obsolete; also known as *yellow cable* or *thick cable*. The maximum length of a single segment is 500 meters (1,640 feet).

10BaseT: Twisted-pair cable, commonly used for Ethernet networks; also known as *UTP, twisted pair,* or *twisted sister* (just kidding!). The maximum length of a single segment is 100 meters (330 feet). Of the three Ethernet cable types, this one is the easiest to work with.

100BaseFX: The Ethernet standard for high-speed fiber-optic connections.

100BaseT4: An alternative standard for 100 Mbps Ethernet using four-pair Category-3 cable.

100BaseTX: The leading standard for 100 Mbps Ethernet, which uses two-pair, Category-5 twisted-pair cable.

100VG AnyLAN: A standard for 100 Mbps Ethernet that isn't as popular as 100BaseT. Like 100BaseT, 100VG AnyLAN uses twisted-pair cable.

1000BaseT: A new standard for 1,000 Mbps Ethernet using four-pair, Category-5, unshielded twisted-pair cable. 1000BaseT is also known as *Gigabit Ethernet.*

1000000000000BaseT: Well, not really. But if current trends continue, we'll get there soon.

802.2: The forgotten IEEE standard. The more glamorous 802.3 standard relies on 802.2 for moral support.

802.3: The IEEE standard known in the vernacular as *Ethernet.*

802.11: The IEEE standard for wireless networking. Popular variants include 802.11a, 802.11ab, 802.11g, and 802.11n.

8088 processor: The microprocessor chip around which IBM designed its original PC, marking the transition from the Bronze Age to the Iron Age.

80286 processor: *Computo-habilis,* an ancient ancestor of today's modern computers.

80386 processor: The first 32-bit microprocessor chip used in personal computers, long since replaced by newer, better designs.

80486 processor: The last of Intel's CPU chips to have a number instead of a name. It was replaced years ago by the Pentium processor.

AAUI: *Apple Attachment Unit Interface,* a type of connector used in some Apple Ethernet networks.

access rights: A list of rights that tells you what you can and can't do with network files or directories.

account: The way by which the network knows who you are and what rights you have on the network. You can't get into the network without one.

acronym: An abbreviation made up of the first letters of a series of words.

Active Directory: The directory service in Windows networks.

Active Server Pages: An Internet feature from Microsoft that enables you to create web pages with scripts that run on the server rather than on the client; also known as *ASP.* The newest version is called *ASP.NET.*

ActiveSync: A Windows component used to synchronize data between computers.

adapter card: An electronic card that you can plug into one of your computer's adapter slots to give it some new and fabulous capability, such as displaying 16 million colors, talking to other computers over the phone, or accessing a network.

address book: In an e-mail system, a list of users with whom you regularly correspond.

administrator: The big network cheese who's responsible for setting things up and keeping them running. Pray that it's not you. The administrator is also known as the *network manager.*

AFP: *Apple Filing Protocol,* a protocol for filing used by Apple. (That helps a lot, doesn't it?)

AGP: *Advanced Graphics Port,* a high-speed graphics interface used on most new computer motherboards.

allocation unit: Windows allocates space to files one allocation unit at a time; the allocation unit typically is 2,048 or 4,096 bytes, depending on the size of the disk. An allocation unit is also known as a *cluster.* Windows Server uses allocation schemes that are more efficient than those in standard Windows.

Android: A popular open-source mobile phone and tablet platform developed by Google.

antivirus program: A program that sniffs out viruses on your network and sends them into exile.

Apache: The most popular web server on the Internet. It comes free with most versions of Linux and Windows.

Application layer: The highest layer of the OSI reference model, which governs how software communicates with the network.

archive bit: A flag that's kept for each file to indicate whether the file has been modified since it was last backed up.

ARCnet: An ancient network topology developed by Datapoint and now found only in history books.

Athlon: A competitor to Intel's Pentium CPU chip manufactured by AMD.

attributes: Characteristics that are assigned to files. DOS alone provides four attributes: system, hidden, read-only, and archive. Network operating systems generally expand the list of file attributes.

AUI: *Attachment Unit Interface,* the big connector on older network cards and hubs that's used to attach yellow cable via a transceiver.

auto attendant: A feature of PBX systems that eliminates or reduces the need for human operators.

AUTOEXEC.BAT: A batch file that DOS executes automatically every time you start your computer.

backbone: A trunk cable used to tie sections of a network together.

BackOffice: A suite of Microsoft programs designed to run on a Windows server.

backup: A copy of your important files made for safekeeping in case something happens to the original files — something you should make every day.

banner: A fancy page that's printed between print jobs so that you can easily separate jobs from one another.

batch file: A file that contains one or more commands that are executed together as a set. You create the batch file by using a text editor and run the file by typing its name at the command prompt.

benchmark: A repeatable test you use to judge the performance of your network. The best benchmarks are the ones that closely duplicate the type of work you routinely do on your network.

BES: See *BlackBerry Enterprise Server (BES).*

BlackBerry: A popular smartphone made by Research In Motion (RIM).

BlackBerry Enterprise Server (BES): Software that runs on a Windows server to enable BlackBerry devices to synchronize with Microsoft Exchange.

Bluetooth: (1) A Viking king who united Denmark and Norway in the tenth century. (2) A wireless networking protocol for short-range networks, used mostly for devices such as wireless keyboards, mice, and cell phones.

bottleneck: The slowest link in your network, which causes work to get jammed up. The first step in improving network performance is identifying the bottlenecks.

bridge: Not the popular card game, but a device that enables you to link two networks together. Bridges are smart enough to know which computers are on which side of the bridge, so they allow only those messages that need to get to the other side to cross the bridge. This device improves performance on both sides of the bridge.

broadband: A high-speed connection used for wide-area networking.

buffer: An area of memory that holds data en route to somewhere else. A hard drive buffer, for example, holds data as it travels between your computer and the hard drive.

bus: A type of network topology in which network nodes are strung out along a single run of cable called a *segment.* 10Base2 networks used a bus topology. *Bus* also refers to the row of expansion slots within your computer.

cable tie: Little strips of plastic that are especially handy for securing cables or bundling them together.

cache: A sophisticated form of buffering in which a large amount of memory is set aside to hold data so that it can be accessed quickly.

Category 3: An inexpensive form of unshielded twisted-pair (UTP) cable that is suitable only for 10 Mbps networks (10BaseT). Avoid using Category 3 cable for new networks.

Category 5: The higher grade of UTP cable that is suitable for 100 Mbps networks (100BaseTX) and Gigabit Ethernet (1000BaseT).

Category 6: An even higher grade of UTP cable that's more reliable than Category 5 cable for Gigabit Ethernet.

CD-ROM: A high-capacity disc that uses optical technology to store data in a form that can be read but not written over.

CD-RW drive: A CD drive that can read, write, and then rewrite CDs.

Centrex: A type of phone system similar to a PBX, except that the system is located on the phone company's premises, not on a customer's premises.

Certified NetWare Engineer: Someone who has studied hard and passed the official exam offered by Novell; also known as *CNE*.

Certified Network Dummy: Someone who knows nothing about networks but nevertheless gets the honor of installing one; also known as *CND*.

chat: What you do on the network when you talk live with another network user.

Chaucer: A dead English dude.

cheapernet: See *10Base2*.

CHKDSK: A DOS command that checks the recordkeeping structures of a DOS hard drive for errors.

circuit: An end-to-end connection between transmitters and receivers, typically in phone systems.

click: What you do in Windows to get things done.

client: A computer that has access to the network but doesn't share any of its own resources with the network. See also *server*.

client/server: A vague term meaning roughly that the workload is split between a client computer and a server computer.

cloud computing: An approach to networking in which certain elements of a network that were traditionally implemented within a LAN (such as file storage, backup, or e-mail services) are instead implemented remotely via the Internet.

Clouseau: The most dangerous man in all of France. Some people say he only plays the fool.

cluster: See *allocation unit.*

coaxial cable: A type of cable that contains two conductors. The center conductor is surrounded by a layer of insulation, which is then wrapped by a braided-metal conductor and an outer layer of insulation.

Com1, Com2: The first two serial ports on a computer.

computer name: A unique name assigned to each computer on a network.

Cone of Silence: A running gag on the old TV series *Get Smart* in which a security device would be lowered over two people who needed to have a secure conversation. Unfortunately, the Cone of Silence worked so well that the people in it couldn't hear each other. (Anyone outside the Cone of Silence, however, could easily hear what the people in the cone were saying.)

CONFIG.SYS: A file on old-style Windows computers that contains configuration information. CONFIG.SYS is processed every time you start your computer.

console: In Linux, a text-mode command prompt.

Control Panel: In Windows, an application that enables you to configure various aspects of the Windows operating system.

CPU: *Central processing unit,* the brains of the computer.

crimp tool: A special tool used to attach connectors to cables. No network manager should be without one. Try not to get your fingers caught in it.

crossover cable: A cable used to daisy-chain two hubs or switches together.

CSMA/CD: *Carrier Sense Multiple Access with Collision Detection,* the traffic-management technique used by Ethernet.

daisy-chain: A way of connecting computer components in which the first component is connected to the second, which is connected to the third, and so on. In Ethernet, you can daisy-chain hubs together.

DAT: *Digital audiotape,* a type of tape often used for network backups.

Data Link layer: The second layer of the OSI model, responsible for transmitting bits of data over the network cable.

dedicated server: A computer used exclusively as a network server.

delayed write: A hard-drive-caching technique in which data written to the hard drive is placed in cache memory and actually written to the hard drive later.

dial tone: The distinctive tone produced on a phone system to indicate that the system is ready to accept a call.

DID: *Direct Inward Dialing,* a feature of PBX systems that lets you associate an external phone number with an extension on the PBX system.

differential backup: A type of backup in which only the files that have changed since the last full backup are backed up.

DIP switch: A bank of switches used to configure an old-fashioned adapter card. Modern cards configure themselves automatically, so DIP switches aren't required. See also *jumper block.*

Direct Inward Dialing: See *DID.*

directory hash: A popular breakfast food enjoyed by Linux administrators.

disk: A device (also known as a *hard drive)* that stores information magnetically. A hard drive is permanently sealed in an enclosure and has a capacity usually measured in thousands of megabytes, also known as *gigabytes.*

distribution: A publicly available version of the Linux operating system. There are many distributions. One of the most popular is Fedora.

DNS: See *Domain Name System (DNS).*

domain: (1) In a Windows network, one or more network servers that are managed by a single network directory. (2) In the Internet, a name assigned to a network.

Domain Name System (DNS): The naming system used on the Internet, in which a network is given a domain name and individual computers are given host names.

DOS: *Disk Operating System,* the original operating system for IBM and IBM-compatible computers.

dot-matrix printer: A prehistoric type of printer that works by applying various-colored pigments to the walls of caves. Once the mainstay printer for PCs, dot-matrix printers have given way to laser printers and inkjet printers. High-speed matrix printers still have their place on the network, though, and matrix printers have the advantage of being able to print multipart forms.

dumb terminal: Back in the heyday of mainframe computers, a monitor and keyboard attached to the central mainframe. All the computing work occurred at the mainframe; the terminal only displayed the results and sent input typed at the keyboard back to the mainframe.

DVD drive: A type of optical drive similar to a CD-ROM drive but with much higher storage capacity.

Eddie Haskell: The kid who's always sneaking around, poking his nose into other people's business, and generally causing trouble. Every network has one.

editor: A program for creating and changing text files.

e-mail: Messages that are exchanged with other network users.

emoticon: A shorthand way of expressing emotions in e-mail and chats by combining symbols to create smiles, frowns, and so on.

encryption: A security technique in which data is stored in an encoded (encrypted) form that can be decoded (or decrypted) only if the key used to encrypt the data is known.

enterprise computing: A trendy term that refers to a view of an organization's complete computing needs rather than just a single department's or group's needs.

Ethernet: The World's Most Popular Network Standard.

ETLA: *Extended Three-Letter Acronym,* an acronym with four letters. See also *TLA.*

Exchange Server: The software that handles e-mail services on a Windows server.

Fast Ethernet: 100 Mbps Ethernet; also known as *100BaseT* or *100BaseTX.*

FAT: *File Allocation Table,* a recordkeeping structure once used on DOS and Windows computers to keep track of the location of every file on a hard drive.

FAT32: An improved way of keeping track of hard drive files that can be used with Windows 98 and later.

FDDI: *Fiber Distributed Data Interface,* a 100 Mbps network standard used with fiber-optic backbone. When FDDI is used, FDDI/Ethernet bridges connect Ethernet segments to the backbone.

Fedora: A popular distribution of Linux.

fiber-optic cable: A blazingly fast network cable that transmits data using light rather than electricity. Fiber-optic cable is often used as the backbone in large networks, especially where great distances are involved.

file rights: The capability of a particular network user to access specific files on a network server.

file server: A network computer containing hard drives that are available to network users.

firewall: A special type of router that connects a LAN to the Internet while preventing unauthorized Internet users from accessing the LAN.

fish tape: A gadget that helps you pull cable through walls.

forest: A group of Active Directory domains.

FTP: *File Transfer Protocol,* a method for retrieving files from the Internet.

full backup: A backup of all the files on a hard drive, whether or not the files have been modified since the last backup. See also ***differential backup.***

gateway: A device that connects dissimilar networks. Gateways often connect Ethernet networks to mainframe computers or to the Internet.

GB: Gigabyte, roughly a billion bytes of hard drive storage (1,024MB, to be precise). See also *K, MB,* and *TB.*

generation backup: A backup strategy in which several sets of backup disks or tapes are retained; sometimes called *grandfather-father-son.*

generation gap: What happens when you skip one of your backups.

glass house: The room where the mainframe computer is kept. It's symbolic of the mainframe mentality, which stresses bureaucracy, inflexibility, and heavy iron.

GNOME: A graphical user interface that's popular on Linux systems.

group account: A type of security account that lets you group user accounts that have similar access rights.

groupware: An application that enables collaborative work.

guest: A user account that has no privileges. The guest account is designed to provide minimal network access to users who don't have a regular network account.

guru: Anyone who knows more about computers than you do.

hotspot: An area that has access to a public wireless network. Hotspots are commonly found in airports, hotels, and trendy coffee shops.

HTML: *Hypertext Markup Language,* the language used to compose pages that can be displayed via the World Wide Web.

HTTP: *Hypertext Transfer Protocol,* the protocol used by the World Wide Web for sending HTML pages from a server computer to a client computer.

HTTPS: A secure form of HTTP used to transmit sensitive data such as credit-card numbers.

hub: In Ethernet, a now obsolete device that is used with 10BaseT and 100BaseT cabling to connect computers to the network. Hubs have been replaced by switches. See also *switch.*

I/O port address: Every I/O device in a computer — including network interface cards — must be assigned a unique address. In the old days, you had to configure the port address by using DIP switches or jumpers. Newer network cards automatically configure their own port addresses so that you don't have to mess with switches or jumper blocks.

i7 processor: A popular multicore processor made by Intel. (Variants include i3 and i5.)

IACI: Acronym for *International Association of the Computer Impaired.*

IEEE: *Institute of Electrical and Electronics Engineers,* where they send computer geeks who've had a few too many parity errors.

IIS: *Internet Information Services,* Microsoft's web server. IIS is included with all versions of Windows Server.

incremental backup: A type of backup in which only the files that have changed since the last backup are backed up. Unlike a differential backup, an incremental backup resets each file's archive bit as it backs it up. See also *archive bit, differential backup,* and *full backup.*

inkjet printer: A type of printer that creates full-color pages by spraying tiny jets of ink onto paper.

Internet: A humongous network of networks that spans the globe and gives you access to just about anything you could ever hope for, provided that you can figure out how to work it.

Internet Explorer: Microsoft's popular web browser.

interoperability: Providing a level playing field for incompatible networks to work together, kind of like NAFTA.

intranet: A network that resembles the Internet but is accessible only within a company or organization. Most intranets use the familiar World Wide Web interface to distribute information to company employees.

IP address: A string of numbers used to address computers on the Internet. If you enable TCP/IP on your network, you must provide an IP address for each computer on the network.

iPhone: A popular smartphone developed by Apple, best known for popularizing the trendy business of capitalizing the sEcond letter of words instead of the first.

IPX: A transport protocol used by NetWare.

ISA bus: *Industry Standard Architecture,* a once-popular type of expansion bus for accommodating adapter cards, now replaced by PCI.

ISDN: A digital telephone connection that lets you connect to the Internet at about twice the speed of a regular phone connection. It was once popular, but now, more cost-effective forms of high-speed Internet connections are available.

ISO: Acronym for *International Organization for Standardization.* Don't ask why the abbreviation is *ISO* instead of *IOS.*

ISP: *Internet service provider,* a company that provides access to the Internet for a fee.

Java: A programming language popular on the Internet.

JavaScript: A popular scripting language that can be used on web pages.

jumper block: A device used to configure an old-fashioned adapter card. To change the setting of a jumper block, you remove the jumper from one set of pins and place it on another.

K: Kilobytes, roughly one thousand bytes (1,024, to be precise). See also *GB, MB,* and *TB.*

Kerberos: (1) The mythical three-headed dog that guards the gates of Hades. (2) A network security protocol that authenticates users when they log on and grants the user a ticket that allows him or her to access resources throughout the network.

LAN: *Local area network* — what this book is all about.

LAN Manager: An obsolete network operating system that Microsoft used to sell. Microsoft long ago put all its networking eggs in the Windows basket, so LAN Manager exists only on isolated islands along with soldiers who are still fighting World War II.

LAN Server: IBM's version of LAN Manager.

LANcache: The disk caching program that comes with LANtastic.

laser printer: A high-quality printer that uses lasers and photon torpedoes to produce beautiful output.

LATA: *Local Access Transport Area,* an area within which a local carrier provides service. Calls between phones in different LATAs require the use of a long distance carrier.

LEC: See *local carrier.*

Lemon-Pudding layer: A layer near the middle of the OSI reference model that provides flavor and moistness.

Linux: An open-source version of the Unix operating system that's popular as a network server.

LLC sublayer: The *logical link control sublayer* of layer 2 of the OSI model. The LLC is addressed by the IEEE 802.2 standard.

local area network: See *LAN.*

local resources: Disk drives, printers, and other devices that are attached directly to a workstation rather than accessed via the network.

log in: Same as *log on.*

log on: The process of identifying oneself to the network (or a specific network server) and gaining access to network resources.

log out: The process of leaving the network. When you log out, any network drives or printers you were connected to become unavailable to you.

logon name: In a Windows network, the name that identifies a user uniquely to the network; same as *username* or *user ID*.

logon script: A batch file that is executed when a user logs on to a Windows domain.

LPT1: The first printer port on a PC. If a computer has a local printer, it more than likely is attached to this port. That's why you should set up printer redirections using LPT2 and LPT3.

Macintosh: A popular alternative to Windows, made by Apple.

Mac OS X: The latest and greatest operating system for Macintoshes.

Mac OS X Server: Apple's most powerful server operating system for Macintosh computers.

MAC sublayer: The *media access control* sublayer of layer 2 of the OSI model. The MAC is addressed by the IEEE 802.3 standard.

mail server: The server computer on which e-mail messages are stored. This same computer also may be used as a file and print server, or it may be dedicated as a mail server.

mainframe: A huge computer kept in a glass house on raised floors and cooled with liquid nitrogen. The cable that connects the hard drives to the CPU weighs more than most PCs.

mapping: Assigning unused drive letters to network drives or unused printer ports to network printers. See also *redirection.*

MB: Megabytes, roughly one million bytes (1,024K, to be precise). See also *K, GB,* and *TB.*

memory: The electronic storage where your computer stores data that's being manipulated and programs that are running. See also *RAM.*

metaphor: A literary construction suitable for Shakespeare and Steinbeck but a bit overused by writers of computer books.

Metro: The original name for Windows 8 UI, a new graphical user interface introduced with Windows 8, optimized for use on touchscreen devices.

MMC: *Microsoft Management Console,* the primary management tool used to configure Windows features.

modem: A device that converts signals the computer understands to signals that can be accurately transmitted over the phone to another modem, which converts the signals back to their original form. Computers use modems to talk to each other. *Modem* is an abbreviation of *modulator–demodulator.*

mouse: The obligatory way to use Windows. When you grab the mouse and move it around, the cursor moves on the screen. After you get the hand–eye coordination down, using it is a snap. *Hint:* Don't pick it up and talk into it like Scotty did in *Star Trek IV.* That's very embarrassing, especially if you've traveled millions of miles to get here.

Mr. McFeeley: The nerdy-looking mailman on *Mister Rogers' Neighborhood.* He'd make a great computer geek. Speedy delivery!

multiboot: A technique that lets you install two or more operating systems on a single computer. When you power up a computer that uses multiboot, you must select which of the installed operating systems you want to boot.

My Network Places: An icon on the Windows XP desktop that enables you to access network servers and resources. (In older versions of Windows, this icon is known as *Network Neighborhood.* In Windows Vista, it's called Network Places, and in Windows 7 and 8, it is simply called *Network.*)

MySQL: An open-source SQL database server for Linux systems.

NAS: *Network Accessible Storage*, a popular form of data storage in which a single storage appliance operates as an independent file server attached to a network.

.NET: A Windows application environment that promises to simplify the task of creating and using applications for Windows and for the web.

NetBIOS: *Network Basic Input/Output System,* a high-level networking standard developed by IBM and used by most peer-to-peer networks. It can be used with NetWare as well.

NetWare: A popular network operating system, the proud child of Novell, Inc.

NetWare Directory Services: A feature of NetWare first introduced with Version 4, in which the resources of the servers are pooled together to form a single entity.

network: What this book is about. For more information, see Books I through IX.

network drive: A drive that resides somewhere out in the network rather than on your own computer.

network interface card: An adapter card that lets the computer attach to a network cable; also known as *NIC*.

Network layer: One of the layers somewhere near the middle of the OSI reference model. It addresses the interconnection of networks.

network manager: Hope that it's someone other than you.

Network Neighborhood: An icon used in older versions of Windows that enables you to access network servers and resources. In newer Windows versions, this icon is known as *My Network Places, Network Places,* or just *Network.*

network operating system: An operating system for networks, such as Linux or Windows Server 2003; also known as *NOS.*

Network Places: An icon on the Windows Vista desktop that enables you to access network servers and resources. (In older versions of Windows, this icon is known as *Network Neighborhood* or *My Network Places.*)

network resource: A disk drive, printer, or other device that's located in a server computer and shared with other users. By contrast, a *local resource* is located in a user's computer.

newsgroup: Internet discussion groups in which people leave messages that can be read and responded to by other Internet users.

NIC: See *network interface card.*

node: A device on the network, typically a computer or printer. A router is also a node.

NOS: See *network operating system.*

Novell: The folks you can thank or blame for NetWare, depending on your mood.

NTFS: A special type of disk format that you can use on Windows Server and Windows XP hard drives for improved performance and security.

obfuscation: A security technique that relies on using obscure names for security objects or particular user accounts. Avoiding obvious user account names can slow would-be intruders.

octet: A group of eight bits. In an IP address, each octet of the address is represented by a decimal number from 0 to 255.

offline: Not available on the network.

online: Available on the network.

operator: A user who has control of operational aspects of the network but doesn't necessarily have the power to grant or revoke access rights, create user accounts, and so on.

organizational unit: A grouping of objects in an Active Directory domain.

OSI: The agency Lee Majors worked for in *The Six Million Dollar Man;* also the *Open System Interconnection* reference model, a seven-layer fruitcake framework upon which networking standards are hung.

Outlook: A mail client from Microsoft, part of the Microsoft Office suite.

package: In Linux, a software component that can be separately installed and configured.

packet filter: A security technique used by firewalls. The firewall examines each packet that passes through it and blocks certain types of packets while allowing others to pass.

packet sniffer: See *protocol analyzer.*

packet: A manageable chunk of data sent over the network. The size and makeup of a packet (also known as a frame) are determined by the protocol being used.

parallel port: An all but obsolete type of data port that was used to connect printers. Parallel ports send data over eight "parallel" wires, one byte at a time. See also *serial port* and *USB.*

partition: A division of a single hard drive into several smaller units that are treated by the operating system as though they were separate drives.

password: The only thing protecting your files from an impostor masquerading as you. Keep your password secret, and you'll have a long and happy life.

patch cable: A short cable used to connect a computer to a wall outlet, or one running from a patch panel to a hub.

PBX: *Private Branch Exchange,* a phone system that manages shared access to one or more phones (called *extensions* or *stations)* to a limited number of external phone lines.

PCI: *Peripheral Component Interconnect,* the high-speed bus design found in modern Pentium computers.

PDC: *Primary Domain Controller,* a server computer that has the main responsibility for managing a domain. See also **BDC.**

peer-to-peer network: A network in which any computer can be a server if it wants to be, kind of like the network version of the Great American Dream. You can easily construct peer-to-peer networks by using Windows.

permissions: Rights that have been granted to a particular user or group of users enabling them to access specific files.

Physical layer: The lowest layer of the OSI reference model (whatever that is). It refers to the parts of the network you can touch: cables, connectors, and so on.

ping: A program that determines whether another computer is reachable. The ping program sends a message to the other computer and waits for a reply. If the reply is received, the other computer is reachable.

plenum cable: Fire-retardant cable that has a special Teflon coating.

pocket protector: A status symbol among computer geeks.

port: A connector on the back of your computer that you can use to connect a device such as a printer, modem, mouse, and so on.

PowerShell: A powerful command-line environment for managing Windows computers.

PPP: *Point-to-Point Protocol,* the most common way of connecting to the Internet for World Wide Web access.

Presentation layer: The sixth layer of the OSI reference model, which handles data conversions, compression, decompression, and other menial tasks.

print job: A report, letter, memo, or other document that has been sent to a network printer but hasn't printed yet. Print jobs wait patiently in the queue until a printer agrees to print them.

Print Manager: In old-style Windows (Windows 3.1 and Windows for Workgroups), the program that handles print spooling.

print queue: The line that print jobs wait in until a printer becomes available.

print server: A computer that handles network printing or a device such as a JetDirect, which enables the printer to attach directly to the network.

PRN: The DOS code name for the first parallel port; also known as *LPT1.*

protocol: (1) The droid C-3PO's specialty. (2) The rules of the network game. Protocols define standardized formats for data packets, techniques for detecting and correcting errors, and so on.

protocol analyzer: A program that monitors packets on a network; also called a *packet sniffer.*

punch-down block: A gadget for quickly connecting a bunch of wires, used in telephone and network wiring closets.

QIC: Quarter-inch cartridge, the most popular and least expensive form of tape backup; now known as a *Travan drive.* See also ***DAT*** and ***Travan.***

queue: A list of items waiting to be processed. The term usually refers to the list of print jobs waiting to be printed, but networks have lots of other types of queues as well.

RAID: *Redundant Array of Independent Disks,* a bunch of hard drives strung together and treated as though they were one drive. The data is spread out over several drives, and one of the drives keeps checking information so that if any one of the other drives fails, the data can be reconstructed.

RAM: *Random access memory,* your computer's memory chips.

redirection: One of the basic concepts of networking, in which a device, such as a disk drive or printer, appears to be a local device but actually resides on the network. The networking software on your computer intercepts I/O requests for the device and redirects them to the network.

Registry: The file where Windows keeps its configuration information.

Remote Desktop Connection: A Windows feature that lets you log on to a Windows server from a remote computer so that you can manage it without physically going to the server.

Remote Installation Service: See *RIS.*

repeater: A device that strengthens a signal so that it can travel on. Repeaters are used to lengthen the cable distance between two nodes. A *multiport repeater* is the same as a *hub.*

Resilient File System (ReFS): A new file system, introduced in Windows Server 2012, that improves on the older NTFS file system.

resource: A hard drive, hard drive directory, printer, modem, CD-ROM, or other device that can be shared on the network.

ring: A type of network topology in which computers are connected to one another in a way that forms a complete circle. Imagine the Waltons standing around the Thanksgiving table holding hands, and you have the idea of a ring topology.

RIS: *Remote Installation Service,* a feature of Windows Server operating systems that lets you install from a remote location without actually being present at the server.

RJ-11: The kind of plug used by phone-system cabling.

RJ-45: The kind of plug used by 10BaseT and 100BaseT networks. It looks kind of like a modular phone plug, but it's bigger.

root: (1) The highest-level directory in a file system. (2) The administrator account in Linux.

root server: One of 13 powerful DNS servers located throughout the world that provide the core of the Internet's DNS service.

router: A device that interfaces two networks and controls how packets are exchanged between them. Routers are typically used to link a local Ethernet network to a broadband Internet connection.

Samba: A program that runs on a Linux server, allowing the Linux computer to work as a file and print server in a Windows network.

SAN: *Storage Area Network*, a type of data storage in which storage devices are networked together, usually with high-speed fiber connections.

SATA: *Serial AT Attachment,* the most common type of hard drive interface in use today, popular because of its low cost and flexibility. For server computers, SCSI is the preferred drive interface. See also *SCSI.*

ScanDisk: A Windows command that examines your hard drive for physical defects.

scheduling software: Software that schedules meetings of network users, which works only if all network users keep their calendars up to date.

scope: In DHCP, a range of IP addresses that a DCHP server manages.

SCSI: *Small Computer System Interface,* a connection used mostly for hard drives but also suitable for CD-ROM drives, tape drives, and just about anything else. SCSI is also the winner of the Acronym Computer Geeks Love to Pronounce Most Award.

segment: A single-run cable, which may connect more than two computers, with a terminator on each end.

Sendmail: An e-mail server used on Unix and Linux systems. By some estimates, 70 percent or more of all mail on the Internet is handled by a version of Sendmail.

serial port: A port normally used to connect a modem or mouse to a DOS-based computer, sometimes called a *communications port.* See also *parallel port.*

server: A computer that's on the network and shares resources with other network users. The server may be *dedicated,* which means that its sole purpose in life is to provide service for network users, or it may be used as a client as well. See also *client.*

Service Pack: A collection of patches that are bundled together to bring an operating system up to a particular service level.

Session layer: A layer somewhere near the middle of the beloved OSI reference model that deals with sessions between network nodes.

SFT: *System Fault Tolerance,* a set of networking features designed to protect the network from faults, such as stepping on the line (known as a *foot fault).*

share name: A name that you assign to a network resource when you share it. Other network users use the share name to access the shared resource.

shared folder: A network server hard drive or a folder on a server hard drive that has been shared so that other computers on the network can access it.

shared resource: A resource, such as a hard drive or printer, that is made available to other network users.

SharePoint: A Microsoft software system that allows users to collaborate via the web.

shielded twisted pair: Twisted-pair cable with shielding, used mostly for Token Ring networks. Also known as *STP.* See also *twisted pair.*

SMB: *Server Message Block,* the protocol that enables file sharing on Windows networks.

smiley: A face made from various keyboard characters; often used in e-mail messages to convey emotion. :-)

SNA: *Systems Network Architecture,* a networking standard developed by IBM that dates from the mid-Mainframerasic Period, approximately 65 million years ago. SNA is used by fine IBM mainframe and AS/400 minicomputers everywhere.

sneakernet: The cheapest form of network, in which users exchange files by copying them to discs and walking them between computers.

SNMP: *Simple Network Management Protocol,* a standard for exchanging network management information between network devices that is anything but simple.

spooling: A printing trick in which data that is intended for a printer is actually written to a temporary hard drive file and later sent to the printer.

SQL: *Structured Query Language,* a popular method of organizing and accessing information in a database.

SQL Server: Microsoft's database manager, which implements SQL databases.

SSID: A name that identifies a wireless network.

star: A type of network topology in which each node is connected to a central wiring hub. This topology gives the network a starlike appearance.

stateful packet inspection: An intelligent type of packet filtering that examines packets in groups rather than individually.

station: In a PBX system, a telephone that can be used for internal or external calls; also known as an *extension.*

subnet mask: A bit pattern used to determine which bits of an IP address represent the subnet.

subnetting: An IP addressing technique that designates the first *n* bits of an IP address as the subnet address and the remaining bits as the host address.

switch: An efficient type of hub that sends packets only to the port that's connected to the packet's recipient rather than sending packets to all the ports, as a simple hub does.

System Fault Tolerance: See *SFT.*

tape drive: The best way to back up a network server. Tape drives have become so inexpensive that even small networks should have one.

task: For a technically accurate description, enroll in a computer science graduate course. For a layperson's understanding of what a task is, picture the guy who used to spin plates on *The Ed Sullivan Show.* Each plate is a task. The poor guy had to move frantically from plate to plate to keep them all spinning. Computers work the same way. Each program task is like one of those spinning plates; the computer must service each one periodically to keep it going.

TB: Terrazzo bytes, imported from Italy; approximately one trillion bytes (1,024GB, to be precise). (Just kidding about terrazzo bytes. Actually, TB stands for terabytes.) See also *GB, K,* and *MB.*

TCP/IP: *Transmission Control Protocol/Internet Protocol,* the protocol used by the Internet.

terminator: (1) The little plug you have to use at each end of a segment of thin coax cable (10BaseT). (2) The former governor of Caleefornia.

thinnet: See *10Base2.*

three-letter acronym: See *TLA.*

time sharing: A technique used on mainframe computers to enable several users to access the computer at the same time.

time-out: How long the print server waits while receiving print output before deciding that the print job has finished.

tip: In phone-system wiring, the wire that's connected to ground. It's called *tip* because in the days of manual switchboards, the ground wire was connected to the tip of the plugs used to manually connect calls to their correct destinations. See also *ring.*

TLA: Three-letter acronym, such as FAT (File Allocation Table), DUM (Dirty Upper Memory), and HPY (Heuristic Private Yodel).

token: The thing that gets passed around the network in a Token Ring topology. See also *Token Ring.*

Token Ring: A network that's cabled in a ring topology in which a special packet called a *token* is passed from computer to computer. A computer must wait until it receives the token before sending data over the network. (*Note:* Do not confuse it with the Tolkien ring, which could mean the ruin of Middle Earth.)

top-level domain: In DNS, a domain that appears immediately beneath the root domain. The common top-level domains include com, net, org, edu, gov, mil, and int.

topology: The shape of the network; how its computers and cables are arranged. See also *bus, star,* and *ring.*

touchscreen monitor: A monitor that responds to a user's touch.

touch-tone dialing: A form of phone dialing that uses a sequence of DTMF tones to indicate the number being dialed.

transceiver: A doohickey that connects a network interface card (NIC) to a network cable. A transceiver is always required to connect a computer to the network, but 10Base2 and 10BaseT NICs have built-in transceivers. Transceivers were originally used with yellow cable. You can also get transceivers that convert an AUI port to 10BaseT.

Transport layer: One of those layers somewhere near the middle of the OSI reference model that addresses the way data is escorted around the network.

Travan: A technology for tape backup that can record up to 800MB on a single tape cartridge. See also *QIC* and *DAT.*

Trojan horse: A program that looks interesting but turns out to be something nasty, like a hard-drive reformatter.

trust: A relationship between domains in which one domain (the *trusting domain)* honors the information in the other domain (the *trusted domain).*

trustee rights: In NetWare, rights that have been granted to a particular user or group of users enabling them to access specific files.

twisted pair: A type of cable consisting of one or more pairs of wires that are twisted in a certain way to improve the cable's electrical characteristics. See also *unshielded twisted pair* and *shielded twisted pair.*

uninterruptible power supply: See *UPS.*

unshielded twisted pair: Twisted-pair cable that doesn't have a heavy metal shield around it. This type of cable (also known as *UTP)* is used for 10BaseT networks. See also *twisted pair.*

UPS: *Uninterruptible power supply,* a gizmo that switches to battery power whenever the power cuts out. The *Enterprise* didn't have one of these, which is why the lights always went out until Spock could switch to auxiliary power.

URL: *Uniform Resource Locator,* a fancy term for an Internet address. URLs are those familiar "dot" addresses, such as www-dot-microsoft-dot-com or www-dot-dummies-dot-com.

USB: A high-speed serial interface that is found on most new computers. USB can be used to connect printers, scanners, mice, keyboards, network adapters, and other devices.

user ID: The name by which you're known to the network.

User Manager for Domains: The program you use on Windows NT to manage user accounts.

user profile: The way Windows keeps track of each user's desktop settings, such as window colors, wallpaper, screen savers, Start-menu options, favorites, and so on.

user rights: Network actions that a particular network user is allowed to perform after he or she has logged on to the network. See also *file rights.*

users' group: A local association of computer users, sometimes with a particular interest, such as networking.

UTP: See *unshielded twisted pair.* See also *10BaseT.*

VBScript: A scripting language that can be used to add fancy features to web pages or create macros for Microsoft Office programs.

VGA: *Video Graphics Array,* an old but still used standard in video monitors.

virtual machine: A simulated computer system running on a host computer, which may support multiple virtual machines.

virtual memory: An operating-system technique in which the system simulates more memory than is physically present in the computer by swapping portions of memory out to disk.

virus: An evil computer program that slips into your computer undetected, tries to spread itself to other computers, and may eventually do something bad like trash your hard drive.

Visio: A program from Microsoft that draws diagrams. It's especially good at drawing network diagrams.

VMWare: The most popular software for implementing virtual machines.

voice mail: A feature of PBX and other types of phone systems in which a caller can record a message for the intended recipient of his or her call.

VoIP: *Voice over IP,* a technique for routing telephone calls over the Internet instead of over traditional phone carriers.

VPN: *Virtual Private Network*, a secure connection between a computer and a remote network or between two remote networks.

wardriving: The act of cruising the streets with special equipment designed to detect open wireless networks and then publicizing their locations.

web browser: A program that enables you to display information retrieved from the Internet's World Wide Web.

WEP: *Wired Equivalent Privacy,* a security standard for wireless networks that makes wireless networking almost (but not quite) as secure as cabled networks.

Wi-Fi: The common name for wireless networking using the 802.11 protocols.

Windows: The world's most popular operating system.

Windows 7: A popular and successful version of Windows that replaced Windows Vista in 2009.

Windows 8: The newest version of Windows, which replaced Windows 7 in late 2012.

Windows 95: A version of Windows that became available in — you guessed it — 1995. Windows 95 was the first version of Windows that didn't require DOS.

Windows 98: The successor to Windows 95, introduced in 1998. Windows 98 included a new user interface that made the Windows desktop resemble the World Wide Web.

Windows 2000 Server: The most popular Windows server operating system, available in three editions: Windows 2000 Server, Windows 2000 Advanced Server, and Windows 2000 Datacenter Server for server computers.

Windows CE: A version of Windows for very small computers, such as those found in phones and other handheld devices. Windows Mobile is based on Windows CE.

Windows for Workgroups: Microsoft's first network-aware version of Windows, now pretty much defunct.

Windows Millennium Edition: The successor to Windows 98, designed especially for home users and featuring a Home Networking Wizard that simplifies the task of setting up a home network.

Windows Mobile: A version of the Windows operating system based on Windows CE and designed for handheld mobile devices, pocket computers, and smartphones.

Windows NT: The predecessor to Windows 2000. Windows NT is available in two versions: Windows NT Client for desktop computers and Windows NT Server for server computers.

Windows Server 2003: The Windows Server operating system version that replaced Windows 2000 Server.

Windows Server 2008: The Windows Server version that replaced Windows Server 2003 in early 2008.

Windows Server 2012: The newest version of Windows Server, which replaced Windows Server 2008 in late 2012.

Windows Vista: The Windows version that replaced Windows XP in early 2007.

Windows XP: A popular and successful version of Windows, designed for home or professional users. It was replaced by Windows Vista in 2007.

wireless: A method of networking that uses radio signals instead of cables to transmit data.

wireless access point: A device that connects wireless devices to a cabled network.

wiring closet: Large networks need a place where cables can congregate. A closet is ideal.

workstation: See *client.*

World Wide Web: A graphical method of accessing information on the Internet.

WPA: *Wi-Fi Protected Access,* a new and improved security standard for wireless networks.

WWW: See *World Wide Web.*

X10: A low-bandwidth protocol for home automation that runs over your home's power lines.

yellow cable: See *10Base5.*

zone: A portion of the DNS namespace that a particular DNS server is responsible for.

Index

G

T

X

Y

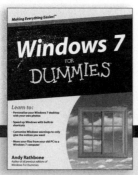

Math & Science

Algebra I For Dummies,
2nd Edition
978-0-470-55964-2

Biology For Dummies,
2nd Edition
978-0-470-59875-7

Chemistry For Dummies,
2nd Edition
978-1-1180-0730-3

Geometry For Dummies,
2nd Edition
978-0-470-08946-0

Pre-Algebra Essentials
For Dummies
978-0-470-61838-7

Microsoft Office

Excel 2010 For Dummies
978-0-470-48953-6

Office 2010 All-in-One
For Dummies
978-0-470-49748-7

Office 2011 for Mac
For Dummies
978-0-470-87869-9

Word 2010
For Dummies
978-0-470-48772-3

Music

Guitar For Dummies,
2nd Edition
978-0-7645-9904-0

Clarinet For Dummies
978-0-470-58477-4

iPod & iTunes
For Dummies,
9th Edition
978-1-118-13060-5

Pets

Cats For Dummies,
2nd Edition
978-0-7645-5275-5

Dogs All-in One
For Dummies
978-0470-52978-2

Saltwater Aquariums
For Dummies
978-0-470-06805-2

Religion & Inspiration

The Bible For Dummies
978-0-7645-5296-0

Catholicism For Dummies,
2nd Edition
978-1-118-07778-8

Spirituality For Dummies,
2nd Edition
978-0-470-19142-2

Self-Help & Relationships

Happiness For Dummies
978-0-470-28171-0

Overcoming Anxiety
For Dummies,
2nd Edition
978-0-470-57441-6

Seniors

Crosswords For Seniors
For Dummies
978-0-470-49157-7

iPad 2 For Seniors
For Dummies, 3rd Edition
978-1-118-17678-8

Laptops & Tablets
For Seniors For Dummies,
2nd Edition
978-1-118-09596-6

Smartphones & Tablets

BlackBerry For Dummies,
5th Edition
978-1-118-10035-6

Droid X2 For Dummies
978-1-118-14864-8

HTC ThunderBolt
For Dummies
978-1-118-07601-9

MOTOROLA XOOM
For Dummies
978-1-118-08835-7

Sports

Basketball For Dummies,
3rd Edition
978-1-118-07374-2

Football For Dummies,
2nd Edition
978-1-118-01261-1

Golf For Dummies,
4th Edition
978-0-470-88279-5

Test Prep

ACT For Dummies,
5th Edition
978-1-118-01259-8

ASVAB For Dummies
3rd Edition
978-0-470-63760-9

The GRE Test For
Dummies, 7th Edition
978-0-470-00919-2

Police Officer Exam
For Dummies
978-0-470-88724-0

Series 7 Exam
For Dummies
978-0-470-09932-2

Web Development

HTML, CSS, & XHTML
For Dummies, 7th Ed
978-0-470-91659-9

Drupal For Dummies
2nd Edition
978-1-118-08348-2

Windows 7

Windows 7
For Dummies
978-0-470-49743-2

Windows 7
For Dummies,
Book + DVD Bundle
978-0-470-52398-8

Windows 7 All-in-On
For Dummies
978-0-470-48763-1

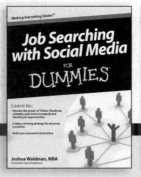

39.99   12/4/12.